The History of Accounting

This is a volume in the Arno Press collection

The History of Accounting

*See last pages of this volume
for a complete list of titles*

CORPORATE DIVIDENDS

By

DONALD KEHL

ARNO PRESS

A New York Times Company

New York — 1976

Editorial Supervision: SHEILA MEHLMAN

————◆————

Reprint Edition 1976 by Arno Press Inc.

Reprinted from a copy in the University
  of Illinois Library

THE HISTORY OF ACCOUNTING
ISBN for complete set: 0-405-07540-5
See last pages of this volume for titles.

Manufactured in the United States of America

————◆————

Library of Congress Cataloging in Publication Data

Kehl, Donald.
    Corporate dividends.

    (The History of accounting)
    Reprint of the ed. published by Ronald Press,
New York.
    Includes bibliographical references.
    1. Corporations—United States—Finance.
2. Corporations—United States—Accounting.
I. Title. II. Series.
KF1439.K43 1976   346'.73'0664   75-18473
ISBN 0-405-07555-3

CORPORATE DIVIDENDS

LEGAL AND ACCOUNTING PROBLEMS
PERTAINING TO CORPORATE DISTRIBUTIONS

By

DONALD KEHL

MEMBER OF THE NEW YORK BAR

THE RONALD PRESS COMPANY ┐ NEW YORK

PRINTED IN THE UNITED STATES OF AMERICA

PREFACE

The declaration of every corporate dividend presents managerial, accounting, and often legal questions. With dividend distributions in the United States totaling from three to ten billion dollars annually, problems of this character have come to occupy not a little time and attention on the part of corporate directors and executives, accountants, and lawyers. This volume has been written to assist those who have the responsibility in making these determinations.

In its treatment the book departs in two respects from the ordinary method employed in the usual legal treatise. First, a careful analysis of the statutory evolution of current dividend statutes in each of the forty-eight states has been given primary emphasis, as distinguished from the practice of giving principal weight to decided cases. This has also served to emphasize that there is no general set of dividend principles applicable in all jurisdictions. Whether or not a dividend meets legal requirements depends, with few exceptions, upon the law of the particular state in which the corporation is organized, as very few states have a dividend statute identical with that of any other state. Second, the statutes in question have been interpreted, not only on the basis of judicial cases, but also in the light of accounting practices and the opinions of accounting writers. A serious effort to harmonize accounting and legal principles has been made. The accountant will find treated many questions of accounting not discussed elsewhere from a legal standpoint.

The general plan has been to present first the earliest statutory provisions of any kind regulating dividends, showing the influence of these provisions on present-day statutory enactments. This is followed by a chapter considering the present dividend statutes in each state. The three basic statutory rules for ascertaining the fund from which dividends may be declared are discussed here: the insolvency test employed by states having the Massachusetts type statute; the balance sheet surplus test as typified by the New York statute; and the modern net profits test used in Delaware. The next two chapters are devoted to the application of accounting principles under these statutes. The treatment of particular asset and liability items which make up the balance sheet and profit and loss statement are discussed both in the light of adjudicated cases and accounting precedents. Particular attention is given to the amount which must be allocated

iii

to capital or stated capital, and the handling of treasury stock is dealt with at length.

Separate chapters are devoted to the liabilities of directors and stockholders in the event an illegal dividend is declared. Included are such problems as the effect of good faith on the liability of a director or stockholder, measure of damages, and parties entitled to enforce liability.

Special consideration is given to the taxation of dividends, the conflicting rights of common and preferred stockholders, and the effect of a merger or consolidation upon future dividends from funds of the constituent corporations previously available for dividends. One division of the preferred stock chapter covers modification of preferred dividend rights through voluntary or quasi-reorganizations. A chapter has been devoted to how a dividend is declared and paid and under what circumstances a declared dividend may be revoked. Attention has also been given to important administrative determinations of the Securities and Exchange Commission concerning dividends, particularly those under the Public Utility Holding Company Act.

The author's special interest in the subject of this volume was aroused during his active practice as a member of the New York and Federal Bars, and the opportunity to do the necessary research work for the completion of the volume was given him through the substantial assistance of grants from the Harvard Law School. In the preparation of the work, advantage was freely taken of the splendid facilities of the Law School Library and of the Baker Library of the Harvard Graduate School of Business Administration. The early accounting precedents relied upon in the discussion of the subject are taken from the large collection of early corporate manuscript records in the possession of the latter.

Grateful acknowledgment is hereby made of the very valuable suggestions and helpful criticisms on the entire manuscript by Professors Ralph J. Baker and E. Merrick Dodd, Jr., of the Harvard Law School. The author is likewise indebted to Professor Erwin N. Griswold also of the Harvard Law School for generously reviewing and making suggestions concerning the chapters on Taxation and Conflict of Laws.

DONALD KEHL

New York City
  January 1941

CONTENTS

CHAPTER 1

PAGE

HISTORICAL BACKGROUND 3

§1. Dividend law a modern development
2. Early English law
3. Charter of the Bank of England
4. Early American bank charters
5. American special charters: profit limitations
6. American special charters: capital impairment limitations
7. New York General Act of 1825
8. Massachusetts insolvency regulation of 1830

CHAPTER 2

DEFINITION OF THE FUND AVAILABLE FOR DIVIDENDS . . . 14

A. PURPOSES OF DIVIDEND REGULATION

§9. Maintenance of a minimum reserve of net assets as a protection
    for creditors
    §9.1. Modern minimization of creditor protection
10. Maintenance of capital in the interest of stockholders
11. Adequate accounting disclosure
12. Public interest in dividend regulation

B. COMMON LAW RESTRICTIONS

§13. Corporate power to pay dividends is implied
14. Restriction to profits
15. Restriction against payment from capital

C. STATUTORY RESTRICTIONS

§16. Three types of modern statutes
17. Growth of the net profits test
18. Comparison of the surplus and net profits tests

D. THE INSOLVENCY TEST

§19. General applicability
20. Meaning of insolvency: equity or bankruptcy test

E. THE BALANCE SHEET SURPLUS TEST

§21. Restriction to excess of assets over liabilities including capital
22. Restriction against division, withdrawal or reduction of capital
    §22.1. Original consideration received less or greater than par
        or stated value of stock
    22.2. Capital impaired at opening of current accounting period

v

PAGE

§23. Restriction against diminishing or impairing capital
24. Effect of stock without par value

F. THE NET PROFITS TEST

§25. Restriction to profits
26. Restriction to net profits or surplus
    §26.1. Meaning of net profits: earned surplus or current net
        earnings
27. Restriction to current net profits or balance sheet surplus:
    Delaware General Corporation Law, Section 34
28. Restriction to net profits or earned surplus

G. PAID-IN AND REDUCTION SURPLUS

§29. Paid-in surplus
30. Reduction surplus

H. RESTRICTIONS OF REGULATORY COMMISSIONS

§31. Public Utility Holding Company Act: Section 12(c)
32. Accounting regulations

I. NON-STATUTORY RESTRICTIONS

§33. Charter and by-laws
34. Trust indenture provisions

CHAPTER 3

COMPUTATION OF THE FUND AVAILABLE UNDER THE BALANCE
SHEET SURPLUS TEST 83

A. BALANCE SHEET ASSETS

§35. The corporate balance sheet
36. Fixed assets generally
    §36.1. Valuation of property sold for securities
    36.2. Realized losses
    36.3. Unrealized losses
    36.4. Realized gains
    36.5. Unrealized gains
37. Cash, accounts receivable and securities
38. Inventory
39. Prepaid expenses
40. Deferred charges
41. Goodwill
42. Hidden reserves

B. BALANCE SHEET LIABILITIES

§43. Funded and current liabilities
44. Reserves generally
    §44.1. Doubtful debts
    44.2. Depreciation and obsolescence

PAGE

§44.3. Depletion: the wasting asset doctrine as to creditors
44.4. Contingent claims
45. Capital stock
§45.1. Stock without par value
45.2. Premium on stock
45.3. Treasury stock
45.4. Resales of treasury stock
46. Surplus
47. Consolidated balance sheets

CHAPTER 4

COMPUTATION OF THE FUND AVAILABLE UNDER NET PROFITS
STATUTES 147
§48. The profit and loss statement
49. Gross sales, cost of goods sold and manufacturing expenses
50. Reserves
51. Fixed charges
52. Capital gains and losses

CHAPTER 5

DECLARATION, PAYMENT, AND REVOCATION 154

A. AUTHORITY AND DISCRETION OF DIRECTORS

§53. Corporate power to declare dividends vested in directors
54. Declaration normally lies in discretion of directors
§54.1. Exercise of equitable authority to compel common dividends
54.2. Preferred dividends
54.3. Discrimination between shareholders of the same class

B. FORM OF THE DIVIDEND

§55. Cash, property and obligations
56. Stock dividends
§56.1. Modern statutes

C. ACTIONS TO RECOVER DECLARED DIVIDENDS

§57. Cash dividends as creating a debt
§57.1. Insolvency of corporation or dividend depositary
58. Stock dividends
59. Effect of revocation

CHAPTER 6

RELATIVE RIGHTS OF PREFERRED AND COMMON STOCKHOLDERS 187

A. CUMULATIVE PREFERRED STOCK

§60. The preferred dividend
61. Cumulative dividend provisions

§62. Participation in dividends beyond preference rate
63. Shift of voting control to preferred on dividend default
64. Dissolution distributions

B. NON-CUMULATIVE PREFERRED STOCK

§65. Unearned dividends
66. Earned dividends

C. MODIFICATION OF DIVIDEND RIGHTS

§67. Stockholder reorganizations
   §67.1. Amendment statutes
   67.2. Merger and consolidation statutes
68. Change in amount of future dividends
69. Change in priority of claims
70. Cancellation of past accrued dividends
   §70.1. Reorganizations under the Public Utility Holding Company Act
   70.2. Adequate disclosure of reorganization plan

D. DIVIDEND RESTRICTIONS IMPOSED TO PROTECT LIQUIDATION PREFERENCES

§71. The wasting asset doctrine as to preferred shareholders
72. Modern statutes
73. Provisions to protect preferred stockholders

CHAPTER 7

REMEDIES AGAINST DIRECTORS WHO DECLARE ILLEGAL DIVIDENDS 235

A. SCOPE OF DIRECTOR LIABILITY

§74. Responsibility of the director
75. Common law liability
76. Statutory liability
   §76.1. Exoneration of directors who are absent or dissent
   76.2. Voting for, or assenting to, an illegal dividend
   76.3. Wilful or negligent violations
   76.4. Exoneration for declaration in good faith
77. Stockholder ratification of illegal dividends
78. Effect of no recourse provisions
79. Time as of which illegality is determined
80. Recovery in states other than corporation's domicil
81. Measure of damages
   §81.1. Amount of illegal dividend
   81.2. Amount of corporate debts and liabilities
   81.3. Amount of loss
82. Criminal liability

B. PARTIES ENTITLED TO ENFORCE LIABILITY   PAGE

§83. The corporation: effect of solvency or insolvency
84. Creditors
     §84.1. Individual or representative suits
      84.2. Prior and subsequent creditors
85. Trustee in bankruptcy
86. Receiver
87. The individual stockholder

CHAPTER 8

REMEDIES AGAINST STOCKHOLDERS WHO RECEIVE ILLEGAL
     DIVIDENDS 269

A. SCOPE OF STOCKHOLDER LIABILITY

§88. Responsibility of the stockholder
89. Insolvency dividends
90. Dividends from capital when corporation is solvent
91. Liability of persons other than stockholders
92. Stockholders liable even though directors also liable
93. Measure of damages
94. Distributions not purporting to be dividends

B. PARTIES ENTITLED TO ENFORCE LIABILITY

§95. The corporation
96. Creditors
97. Trustee in bankruptcy
98. Receiver

CHAPTER 9

RIGHT OF SURVIVING CORPORATION TO PAY DIVIDENDS AFTER SALE
     OF ASSETS, MERGER OR CONSOLIDATION   284

A. CASH ACQUISITIONS

§ 99. Combination method: sale of assets, merger or consolidation
100. Financing method employed

B. PAR VALUE STOCK PLANS

§101. Re-domestication
102. Surplus per share of constituent corporations equal
103. Surplus per share of constituent corporations unequal
104. Effect of financing at other than book value
105. Reduction of new capital below original capital of constituent
      corporations

C. NO-PAR STOCK PLANS

§106. Distinctions between no-par and par stock financing
107. Modern statutes

Chapter 10

PAGE

Choice of Law in Determining Validity of Dividends . . 300

A. WHERE ONLY STATUTE PURPORTING TO REGULATE CORPORATION'S
DIVIDENDS IS THAT OF THE DOMICIL

§108. The choice of law problem
  109. Dividend legality normally determined by law of the corporation's domicil
  110. Obligation of non-domiciliary states to enforce dividend law of the domicil

B. WHERE STATUTE IN STATE IN WHICH FOREIGN CORPORATION
DOES BUSINESS PURPORTS TO REGULATE DIVIDENDS

§111. General statutory provision of non-domiciliary states subjecting foreign corporations doing business in the state to the same duties and liabilities as domestic corporations
  112. New York Stock Corporation Law, Section 114
      §112.1. Corporations doing all or the largest part of their business in New York
      112.2. Corporations doing only a small or minor amount of their business in New York
      112.3. Corporations doing a substantial but not the major part of their business in New York
  113. Dividends violating prohibitions in state of declaration against transfers when insolvent
  114. Multiple incorporation

Chapter 11

The Federal Income Tax on Dividends 319

A. CASH AND PROPERTY DIVIDENDS

§115. Interest of corporation in dividend tax liability of stockholders
  116. Internal Revenue Code Sections 22(a) and 115
  117. A "distribution . . . in money or in other property"
      §117.1. Redemption or cancellation having the effect of a dividend
      117.2. Bargain purchases by stockholders
  118. "Earnings or profits"
      §118.1. "Earnings or profits accumulated after February 28, 1913"
      118.2. "Earnings or profits of the taxable year"
      118.3. "Every distribution is made . . . from the most recently accumulated earnings or profits"
  119. Exemption of dividends out of earnings and profits prior to March 1, 1913
  120. Dividends from paid-in or reduction surplus
  121. Dividends from unrealized appreciation

B. STOCK DIVIDENDS   PAGE

§122. Test of taxability as to stock dividends
  123. Stock dividends from February 28, 1913 to January 1, 1936
  124. Dividends after January 1, 1936
        §124.1. Common stock dividend on common stock
          124.2. Preferred stock dividend on common stock
          124.3. Common stock dividend on preferred stock
          124.4. Preferred stock dividend on preferred stock
          124.5. Dividends in treasury stock
          124.6. Stock dividends under state income tax statutes
  125. Taxability of stock rights
  126. Option dividends in stock, cash or property
  127. Effect of non-taxable stock dividends on subsequent distribu-
        tions

APPENDIX   353
INDEX   357

CORPORATE DIVIDENDS

CHAPTER 1

HISTORICAL BACKGROUND

1. Dividend Law a Modern Development

Individual enterprise, then the partnership, finally joint individual undertakings through guilds and regulated companies had furnished the first methods for investing capital in order to produce income. In the sixteenth and seventeenth centuries, when trade had grown to the point where these limited methods of aggregating capital proved inadequate, the transition to a corporation with one single large capital, in which the individual members held shares, slowly began to take place.[1] These early English joint stock companies all paid dividends. However, the case law of dividends, despite its present-day importance to the corporate lawyer, accountant, and director, is of very modern origin. Prior to 1800 no English or American cases had been decided illustrating the nature of the corporate dividend.[2] Throughout this early period the Anglo-American law of dividends was developed exclusively by special corporate charter provisions and by the large body of actual practice precedents evolved from the everyday business of an increasing number of corporations.[3] From these early non-judicial precedents there developed the first general dividend statutes which in turn constitute the basis of present-day dividend law, both statutory and decisional.

2. Early English Law

The earliest English joint stock companies had no fixed capital of the type common to all present-day corporations. Instead, the practice prevailed of raising new capital for each trading venture and at its close dividing among the proprietors the entire returns, including both the capital and profit, if any.[4] Consequently, the idea of

---

[1] The material in this chapter is taken, with permission of the Harvard Law Review, from Kehl, *The Origin and Early Development of American Dividend Law*, 53 Harv. L. Rev. 36 (1939).

[2] Williston, *History of the Law of Business Corporations Before 1800*, 2 Harv. L. Rev. 149, 160 (1888).

[3] As early as 1695 there were approximately 150 trading companies in existence, two-thirds English and one-third Scotch. 1 Scott, *Joint Stock Companies to 1720* (1912) 327.

[4] *Id.* at 60, 153, 157; see also Warren, *Safeguarding the Creditors of Corporations*, 36 Harv. L. Rev. (1923) 509, 513.

capital as something to be kept intact through dividend restrictions was unknown.[5]

Eventually, however, the single venture joint stocks became impractical. Investments in fixed assets were not easily liquidated except with heavy losses, and confusion resulted from the multiple financial records required for the various ventures. With the general acceptance prior to 1700 of permanent capital by English companies, there came also the genesis of dividend regulation. The necessity for differentiating capital from income had arrived. In the future, enterprises must be managed so as to preserve for stockholders the capital investment from which over the years annual profits were to flow.

During the 1600's charters began including dividend regulations among their provisions. The most common limitation required that dividends be paid from profits. Such was the restriction used in 1620 in the charter of James I to the New River Company.[6] Similar charter provisions became increasingly more common during the eighteenth century.[7]

3. Charter of the Bank of England

The first harbinger of the modern doctrine against impairment of capital through the payment of dividends appeared in an Act of Parliament applicable to the Bank of England. When in 1697, Parliament authorized an increase in the Bank's capital, it expressly provided that recipients of dividends paid from capital should be liable to the Bank's creditors to the extent thereof.[8]

Thus, by 1700, there had already been adopted in England two statutory standards, one or the other of which still controls dividend distributions under present-day statutes in a great many American states. The profit rule, widely enacted in the majority of special charters to early American corporations, fell into disuse during the last century, but has again found favor in the general acts of the liberal corporation states. The capital impairment rule, on the other hand, has long been the backbone of American dividend law.

[5] For examples of very early charters containing no provision for regulating the declaration of dividends, see Russia Company charter of 1555, 2 Hakluyt's *Voyages* (MacLehose Ed. 1903) 304; East India Company charter of 1600, 1 *Indian Constitutional Documents* 1600–1918 (2d Ed.) 1.

[6] Carr, *Select Charters of Trading Companies* (28 Selden Society) 106, 112.

[7] 1720, Bubble Act authorizing charters for two marine insurance companies, 6 Geo. I, c. 18, §6; 1741, Company for Navigation of River Dee, 14 Geo. II, c. 8; 1773, British-cast Plate-Glass Manufacturers, 13 Geo. III, c. 38, §3; 1786, Society for Extending the Fisheries, 26 Geo. III, c. 106, §4; 1789, Northumberland Fishery Society, 29 Geo. III, c. 25, §4; 1791, Sierra Leone Company, 31 Geo. III, c. 55, §4.

[8] 8 and 9 Will. III, c. 20, §49.

More important to students of American dividend law than the Act of 1697 is the original Act of 1694 authorizing the Crown to charter the Bank of England.[9] Although there is no indication that the American colonies modeled their capital impairment provisions after the Act of 1697—the American rule being apparently indigenous—it is clear that Alexander Hamilton, in drafting the important charter of the first Bank of United States, did copy from the original Act of 1694 a provision for liability in the event that debts were created in excess of the Bank's capital. The Act of 1694 made stockholders individually liable for the creation of such excess indebtedness.[10] When Hamilton copied this provision, he made directors of the Bank of United States rather than shareholders liable for the excess, on the ground that they, and not the shareholders, would be responsible for incurring the indebtedness.[11] When in subsequent American charters directors were made liable for the declaration of illegal dividends, it was the Hamiltonian provision in the charter of the Bank of United States which furnished the model.[12] These important influences of the Bank of England Act on early American charters, direct and indirect, make it, from the standpoint of American law, perhaps the most important of all English corporate documents.

4. Early American Bank Charters

The Treaty of Paris ending the American Revolution released economic forces which called for the chartering of many corporations. Whereas scarcely half a dozen business charters were granted in colonial days, there were 11 such incorporations between 1781 and 1785, 22 between 1786 and 1790, and 114 between 1791 and 1795.[13] By the close of the century the roster of American business corporations had reached 335,[14] of which 90 per cent were incorporated after 1789.[15] Of these, Massachusetts had chartered 60, Connecticut 45, New York, Pennsylvania, and New Jersey, respectively, 28, 23, and 13, while Delaware could only account for 3.[16]

[9] 5 and 6 William and Mary, c. 20.

[10] Id. at §26.

[11] Hamilton's Report to the House of Representatives on a National Bank, Dec. 13, 1790, I U. S. Reports on the Finances 1790–1814, 54, 76; Bank of United States Charter, 1 Stat. 191, §7, subs. IX.

[12] See §§6 and 7, infra.

[13] East, Business Enterprise in the American Revolutionary Era (1938) 285; see also Twentieth Century Fund, Big Business, Its Growth and Its Place (1937) 12.

[14] Dodd, First Half Century of Statutory Regulation of Business Corporations in Massachusetts (Harvard Legal Essays 1934) 67.

[15] 2 Davis, Essays in the Earlier History of American Corporations (1917) 8.

[16] Id. at 22.

The development of American dividend law prior to 1825, when New York enacted the first general dividend regulation statute,[17] is the history of *ad hoc* legislation by special charters granted to individual corporations. In that evolution the charters of three banks are of peculiar importance: the Bank of North America, the Bank of United States, and the Bank of New York.

Section VIII of the charter granted to the Bank of North America by the Articles of Confederation Congress in 1781, authorized its board of directors to "make from time to time such dividends, out of the profits, as they may think proper." [18] The exact derivation of the clause is conjectural. A provision for payment of dividends from profits had, of course, been the most common form of limitation in earlier English charters.[19]

When Hamilton prepared the Constitution of the Bank of New York in 1784,[20] under which it operated as an incorporated joint stock company until receipt of a charter in 1791,[21] the dividend Article, in all probability copied from Section VIII of the charter to the Bank of North America, also provided for distributions out of profits.[22] The sequence was completed in 1790 with Hamilton's elaboration of this provision in his draft charter of the Bank of United States,[23] enacted substantially as drafted the following February. As adopted the dividend limitation was an elaboration of the earlier Bank of New York provision. It provided:

> Half yearly dividends shall be made of so much of the profits of the bank, as shall appear to the directors advisable; and once in every three years, the directors shall lay before the stockholders, at a general meeting, for their information, an exact and particular statement of the debts, which shall have remained unpaid after the expiration of the original credit, for a period of treble the term of that credit; and of the surplus profit if any after deducting losses.[24]

This section became the prototype for dividend regulations in the majority of early American special charters.

While the charter of the Bank of United States therefore con-

---

[17] N. Y. Laws 1825, c. 325, §2.
[18] 7 J. of Cong. 1781–82 (Claypoole Ed.) 108–109, 257–258.
[19] See §2, *supra*.
[20] Domett, *History of the Bank of New York* (1884) 11; 2 Davis, *supra* n. 15, at 44.
[21] N. Y. Laws 1791, c. 37; also 2 Laws of N. Y. 1788–92 (Greenleaf's Ed.), p. 360.
[22] Art. 17, 2 Works of Hamilton (John C. Hamilton Ed. 1850) 330, 332.
[23] *Hamilton's Report, supra* n. 11, at 74.
[24] 1 Stat. 191, §7–XIV (1791).

tained no provision forbidding the payment of dividends from capital, such a prohibition, apparently the first American corporate regulation of that character, was included in by-laws adopted at a general meeting of its stockholders eight months after the charter was granted.[25] By-law 10 provided:

> That in case the board of directors shall at any time make a dividend exceeding the profits of the bank, and thereby diminish the capital stock, the members assenting thereto, shall be liable in their several individual capacities for the amount of the surplus so divided.[26]

This provision seems likewise to be of American draftsmanship, adopted without reference to the Bank of England amendment act of 1697.[27] Thus, prior to 1800, both the profit rule and the capital impairment rule had been adopted in America as in England.

5. American Special Charters: Profit Limitations

Early American special charters using the profit rule fall generally into two patterns. The first class, illustrated by the majority of special acts, follows the Bank of United States in limiting dividends simply to profits. Such were the limitations used in charters of many original states,[28] followed in turn by the territories[29] and younger states.[30] These modifications of the simple profit requirement were also used: "profits, rents, premiums and interests,"[31] "clear profits,"[32] "net annual income,"[33] and "net profits."[34]

[25] Dunlap's American Daily Advertiser (Philadelphia), Nov. 14, 1791, p. 2.

[26] *Ibid.*; also in Holdsworth and Dewey, *First and Second Banks of United States* (Nat. Monetary Com. Sen. Doc. 571, 61st Cong. 2d Sess. 1910), p. 134. No similar provision was contained in the by-laws of the Second Bank of United States, *id.* at 282–289.

[27] Cf. 5 and 6 William and Mary, c. 20, §49, n. 9, *supra*.

[28] See Appendix, Note A. References to these and other early special charters are included in the Appendix, as valuable in considering the derivation of the dividend law of any particular state.

[29] See Appendix, Note B.

[30] Allison Turnpike Co. (1825), Ill. Laws 1824, p. 88, §7; Bank of Kentucky, Ky. Acts, Nov. Sess. 1806, p. 11, §13–14; Lexington Manufacturing Co., Ky. Acts 1814, p. 377, §8; Louisiana Planters Bank, La. Acts 1811, c. 22, §7; Clarksville Steam Mill Co. (1833), Mo. Laws 1832–33, c. 15, §10.

[31] Union Bank (1792), Mass. Laws and Resolves 1792–93 (1895 Repr.), 1792–c. 6, p. 14, Rule 15th; Merrimack Bank (1795), Mass. Laws and Resolves 1794–95 (1896 Repr.), 1795–c. 25, pp. 372, 375; Union Bank (1802), 7 N. H. Laws 1801–10, p. 102, §3d–8th.

[32] Washington & Little Rock Turnpike Road (1838), Ark. Acts 1837, p. 92, §21; Baltimore Insurance Co., Md. Laws 1795, c. 59, §9 (but not while capital impaired, §8).

[33] Western & Northern Inland Lock Navigation Companies, N. Y. Laws 1792 (15th Sess.), c. 40, pp. 35, 39, and cf. p. 42.

[34] Eastern Branch Bridge Co., Md. Laws 1795, c. 62, §3; Colorado and Pacific

A simple profit limitation of this first class exists now in only one general corporation act.[35]

The second general category of profit limitations in special charters required the making of certain deductions in computing the profits or net profits available for a dividend. Among deductions required to be made in various charters were repairs and contingent charges,[36] improvements [37] and depreciation.[38] A variation was substitution of clear profits and income as the defined fund from which dividends were to be paid after such specified deductions.[39] Dividend limitations of this second class have not survived the transition to present-day general incorporation acts; but the practice of enumerating mandatory deductions has a counterpart in many of the most recent dividend revisions.[40]

6. American Special Charters: Capital Impairment Limitations

The judicial origin of the doctrine that a corporation cannot pay dividends from capital is usually accredited to Justice Story on Circuit in the case of *Wood v. Dummer*.[41] However, special charter provisions prohibiting payments from capital had preceded such court recognition by a quarter of a century, the first being that in the 1794 charter of the Insurance Company of North America. Its charter provided for the payment of dividends from profits, but in case the capital had been "lessened" by losses, that no subsequent

---

Wagon, Telegraph & Railroad Co., Colo. Terr. Laws, 1st Sess. 1861, p. 457, §15. In some late charters directors were made personally liable for declaring dividends in excess of net profits. Delaware Fire Insurance Co. (1826), Del. Laws 1826, c. 321, §9; Merchants Bank of Newbern (1834), N. C. Acts 1833, p. 10, §20 (liable to creditors when dividends in excess of real profits).

[35] Tex. Civ. Stat. (Vern. 1936), Art. 1329.

[36] See Appendix, Note C.

[37] See Appendix, Note D.

[38] Delaware Bridge Co. at Easton, N. J. Acts, Oct. Sess. 1794, c. 554, p. 1069, §13 ("Such proportion of the said income as may be deemed necessary for a growing fund to provide against the decay, and for the rebuilding and repairing of said bridge" to be deducted; the company's Pennsylvania charter granted five days earlier contained the same provision, 3 Dallas, 1790–95, p. 670, §13).

[39] See Appendix, Note E.

[40] Idaho Code Ann. (1932), §29–129 (sustained depreciation and depletion and all losses); La. Gen. Stat. (Dart. 1939), §1106 (similar provision); Ohio Code Ann. (Baldwin 1938), §8623–38 (depletion, depreciation, losses, and bad debts); Purd. Pa. Stat., Title 15, §2852–701 (sustained depreciation and depletion and losses); Washington Stat. Ann. (Remington), §3803–24 (similar provision).

[41] 3 Mason 308, Fed. Case No. 17,944 (C. C. Me. 1824). The doctrine had in fact been foreshadowed by *dicta* in two earlier Massachusetts decisions, relied upon by Justice Story, *Vose v. Grant*, 15 Mass. 505, 518–520 (1819), and *Spear v. Grant*, 16 Mass. 9, 15 (1819).

dividend should be paid "until a sum equal to such diminution, and arising from profits of the Corporation, shall have been added to the capital." [42] This provision was almost universally copied, verbatim or else with minor modifications, in insurance charters of other states. [43]

The last step in special charter dividend limitations was a section prohibiting in general terms the payment of dividends from capital. The first charter of this type was granted in 1803 by Ohio to the Miami Exporting Company. [44] In 1804 similar charters appeared almost simultaneously in New Jersey [45] and Pennsylvania, [46] neither of which seems to have copied from the other. Within three months Rhode Island copied the Pennsylvania form. [47]

The interesting thing about the New Jersey and Pennsylvania provisions is their apparent derivation of the director liability clause from Hamilton's section in the Bank of United States charter imposing liability upon directors for incurring excessive indebtedness. [48] While the Bank of United States charter did not contain a section imposing liability upon directors for improper dividend declarations, the American director is presently so liable as a direct result of the available pattern offered therein by Hamilton. Under the Act of Parliament authorizing incorporation of the Bank of England, stockholders alone were made liable to creditors for excess indebtedness. [49] When Hamilton came to copy this section, he retained the liability to creditors, but shifted it from stockholders to directors. [50] Finally, when American charters began to make directors liable for declaring dividends out of capital, this Hamiltonian provision was used as the model.

Although New Jersey followed closely the provisions for director liability in the Bank of United States charter, Pennsylvania made modifications. The dividend provisions of the Philadelphia Bank, chartered by Pennsylvania in 1804, were contained in two articles of Section 3.

---

[42] 3 Dallas Laws of Pa. 1790–95, p. 489, §7–8th.
[43] See Appendix, Note F.
[44] 1 Ohio Laws (1803) (1901 Repr.), c. 33, p. 126, §9.
[45] Newark Banking & Insurance Co., N. J. Acts 1803 (Feb. 18, 1804), c. 109, §14–3; Trenton Banking Co., N. J. Acts 1804 (Dec. 3, 1804), c. 154, §13–3rd.
[46] Philadelphia Bank, Pa. Acts 1804 (Mar. 5, 1804), c. 51, §3, Arts. 16, 17.
[47] Rhode Island Union Bank, R. I. Laws, June Sess. 1804, p. 11, §10.
[48] Cf. Newark Banking & Insurance Charter, *supra*, n. 45, §14–3, with 1 Stat. 191, §7–IX.
[49] See n. 9, *supra*.
[50] See Hamilton's Report, *supra* n. 11, at 76.

Art. XVI. Dividends of the profits . . . shall be declared . . . and shall in no case exceed the amount of the net profits actually acquired by the company; so that the capital stock of the company shall never be impaired by dividends; . . .

Art. XVII. If the said directors shall at any time wilfully and knowingly make or declare any dividend, which shall impair the said capital stock, all the directors present at the making or declaring of such dividend and consenting thereto, shall be liable in their individual capacities to the company for the amount or proportion of the said capital stock so divided by the directors; and each director, who shall be present at the making or declaring of such dividend, shall be deemed to have consented thereto, unless he shall immediately enter in writing his dissent, on the minutes of the proceedings of the board, and give public notice to the stockholders that such dividend has been declared.[51]

The New Jersey provisions differed principally (1) in absence of any requirement that the dividend be wilfully and knowingly declared (2) in vesting the right of action in creditors rather than the company and (3) in omission of a clause specifically limiting the extent of liability to the amount of the dividend.[52]

Whether the Pennsylvania limitation was derived not only from the Bank of United States charter but also from its capital impairment by-law is difficult to say. A comparison of the foregoing provisions with the earlier by-law discloses striking similarity in several key phrases.[53] The Bank of United States was still in operation when the Philadelphia Bank was incorporated in 1804. If the by-law, a rule of internal management, was available for modeling the charter of the latter,[54] it is curious that it should not have been resorted to in any of the numerous state bank charters granted during more than ten years previous operation of the Bank of United States.

Both Pennsylvania [55] and New Jersey [56] continued to follow their

---

[51] Pa. Acts 1804, c. 51. Cf. Pa. Laws 1913, p. 336, construed in *Branch v. Kaiser*, 291 Pa. 543, 140 Atl. 498 (1928).

[52] Newark Banking & Insurance Co., *supra* n. 45.

[53] Cf. n. 26, *supra*.

[54] The bank's by-laws had been made public at the time of adoption in 1791. See n. 25, *supra*.

[55] Philadelphia Society for Domestic Manufactures (1807), Pa. Acts 1806–07, c. 50, §8; Farmers & Mechanics Bank (1809), Pa. Acts 1808–09, c. 33, §15; Group of Banks (1814), Pa. Acts 1813–14, c. 98, §7, Art. 13. In rechartering a group of banks in 1824, the clause requiring declarations to be wilfully and knowingly made was omitted. Pa. Acts 1823–24, c. 47, §3, Art. 13.

[56] Cumberland Bank, N. J. Laws 1815, p. 48, §13–3; Salem Steam Mill & Banking Co., N. J. Laws 1822, p. 48, §3, Art. 9; Peoples Bank of Paterson, N. J. Laws 1824, p. 35, §12, Art. 2. In 1812 New Jersey incorporated a group of banks using the Pennsylvania rule, N. J. Acts, Jan. Sess. 1812, p. 3, §§18, 20.

respective capital impairment restrictions. Many states at an early date enacted similar special incorporation statutes modeled as a rule on the Pennsylvania Acts.[57] Others did so somewhat later,[58] followed also by the territories.[59]

Finally, in 1825, New York introduced in a special charter what was, in effect, an improved combination of the Pennsylvania and New Jersey rules.[60] This rule added Pennsylvania provisions, creating liability to the corporation and limiting recovery to extent of the dividend, to the New Jersey and Bank of United States requirement of liability to creditors. It continued exonerations common to both and omitted the express Pennsylvania requirement of wilful declaration.

7. New York General Act of 1825

The practice of copying from earlier enactments, which prevailed with respect to the issuance of special charters, continued when general corporation acts superseded the special act. Federal, Maryland, Pennsylvania, and New Jersey charters had furnished dividend precedents for the majority of special acts.[61] But the leadership in general statutes was taken by New York and Massachusetts. It was 1825 before the adoption of any act generally prohibiting all corporations from declaring dividends out of capital. The New York Act of 1825, entitled "An Act to prevent fraudulent Bankruptcies by Incorporated Companies," included the following dividend provision:

> That it shall not be lawful for the directors or managers of any incorporated company in this state to make dividends, excepting from the surplus profits arising from the business of such corporations; and it shall not be lawful for the directors of any such company to divide, withdraw, or in any way pay to the stockholders, or any of them, any part of the capital stock, without the consent of the legislature; . . . and in case of any violation of the provisions of this section, the directors under whose administration the same may have happened, except those who may have caused their dissent therefrom to be entered at large on the minutes of the said directors at the time, or were not present when the same did happen, shall, in their individual and private capacities, jointly

[57] See Appendix, Note G.
[58] See Appendix, Note H.
[59] See Appendix, Note I.
[60] New York Dry Dock Company, N. Y. Laws 1825, c. 114, §11 (Apr. 12, 1825). Similar provisions: Bank of Albany, N. Y. Laws 1825, c. 117, §8; Utica Insurance Company, N. Y. Laws 1825, c. 123, §4.
[61] See §§4, 5, 6, *supra*.

and severally, be liable to the said corporation, and to the creditors thereof, in the event of its dissolution, to the full amount of the capital stock of the company so divided, withdrawn, paid out or reduced.[62]

This provision has exerted wider influence on the development of American dividend legislation than any other enactment. Slightly more than a week earlier New York had granted a special charter to the New York Dry Dock Company, the dividend section of which was practically identical with the quoted limitation.[63] The contemporaneous usage of similar provisions in both special and general acts apparently suggests application of a consistently developing legislative policy, rather than any copying of the special charter in the general act. In drafting these provisions the New York legislature was quite probably indebted to earlier Pennsylvania, New Jersey, and Bank of United States regulations.[64] Influence of the Bank of United States charter is particularly suggested by juxtaposition to the dividend limitation in the 1825 general act of a section similar to that in the bank's charter imposing liability on directors for excessive indebtedness.[65] The prohibition against "withdrawal" of capital, since it did not appear in either Pennsylvania or New Jersey special charters,[66] may have been suggested by the analogous provision in the New York Limited Partnership Act.[67]

In 1828, the Act of 1825, in its original form, was incorporated as a section of the general corporation provisions of the New York Revised Statutes.[68] It was from this source that it was copied into the early general corporation statutes of many states.[69]

8. Massachusetts Insolvency Regulation of 1830

Of what may be called the three modern statutory dividend rules, two already mentioned, the profits rule and the capital impairment

[62] N. Y. Laws 1825, c. 325, §2. The first intimation of a general capital impairment doctrine came in the New York Limited Partnership Act of 1822. N. Y. Laws 1822, c. 244. The act provided for general and special partners, the latter being exonerated from liability beyond the fund contributed (id. §3), with the proviso: "That no part of the capital, furnished by special partners, shall be withdrawn either in the shape of dividends, profits or otherwise, at any time within the period during which the partnership shall be continued" (§11).

[63] See §6, n. 60, supra.

[64] See §6, supra.

[65] N. Y. Laws 1825, c. 325, §3. Cf. 1 Stat. 191, §7–IX.

[66] See §6, n. 45, 46, 51, supra.

[67] See n. 62, supra. The N. Y. Senate and Assembly journals for 1825 give no clue to the origin of the 1825 act, and there are no printed committee reports.

[68] N. Y. Laws 1828–29 (2d Meeting, 51st and 52d Sess.), c. 20, §17. It became Rev. Stat., Pt. 1, c. 18, Title 4, §2.

[69] See particularly Chapter 2, infra.

rule, were adopted for American corporations at an early date. The third test, which may conveniently be referred to as the insolvency rule, appeared for the first time in the general Massachusetts Manufacturing Regulation Act of 1830.[70] With certain modifications, this act became the basic provision for the following early dividend regulation in the Revised Statutes of 1836:

> If the directors of any such company shall declare and pay any dividend, when the company is insolvent or any dividend, the payment of which would render it insolvent, they shall be jointly and severally liable for all the debts of the company then existing, and for all that shall be thereafter contracted, so long as they shall respectively continue in office; provided, that the amount, for which they shall all be so liable, shall not exceed the amount of such dividend, and that if any of the directors shall be absent, at the time of making the dividend, or shall object thereto, and shall file their objection in writing with the clerk of the company, they shall be exempted from the said liability.[71]

Like the New York Act of 1825, this provision exerted a wide influence on the dividend law of many American states.[72]

Up to 1850 there had been scarcely a score of adjudicated cases dealing with the legality of corporate dividends. Yet by this date, or shortly thereafter, the fundamental concepts of modern dividend law had for the most part already crystallized in the corporate statutes of most states. These early enactments still constitute the crux of our dividend law, both statutory and decisional.

[70] Mass. Laws, Jan. Sess. 1830, c. 53, §9.

[71] Mass. Rev. Stat. 1836, c. 38, §23. The latter differed from the 1830 act in the following respects: (1) directors alone rather than president and directors were made liable; (2) the measure of liability was changed from the amount of the dividend to the extent of the corporation's debts existing, or thereafter contracted but not in excess of the amount of dividend; (3) directors were made jointly and severally liable; (4) and exonerated if absent as well as upon filing protest.

[72] See particularly Chapter 2, *infra*.

CHAPTER 2

DEFINITION OF THE FUND AVAILABLE FOR DIVIDENDS

A. Purposes of Dividend Regulation

9. Maintenance of a Minimum Reserve of Net Assets as a Protection for Creditors

The concept of limited stockholder liability has been firmly established in the law of Anglo-American corporations for many years.[1] Perhaps the most important concomitant of that doctrine was the contemporaneous evolution of an insistence in both statutes and decisions that the stockholder's subscription to capital be dedicated to the risks of the enterprise. An individual merchant may dispose of his capital as he pleases so long as he makes no fraudulent conveyance as to present or future creditors. But his entire assets while he does retain them, and, in the absence of bankruptcy, his future economic expectancy are at the risk of full payment to his creditors. With the liability of corporate stockholders, on the other

---

[1] For early development of limited liability in England see *Salmon v. Hamborough Company,* Cases in Ch. (Pt. 1) 204 (1670); *Naylor v. Brown,* Finch Ch. 83, 84 (1673); 8 Holdsworth, *History of English Law* (2d Ed. 1937) 203; Charter of Sierra Leone Company, 31 Geo. III, c. 55 (1791) (preamble). The principle had for the most part been accepted by the time American corporations were receiving their first special charters. This is indicated by the marked dearth of early cases where attempt was made to hold a stockholder personally liable. In such cases limited liability was generally upheld: *Commonwealth v. Blue Hill Turnpike Corp.,* 5 Mass. 420 (1809); *Spear v. Grant,* 16 Mass. 9 (1819); see also *Myers v. Irwin,* 2 S. & R. 368, 371 (1816); *Tippets v. Walker,* 4 Mass. 595, 597 (1808); *Slee v. Bloom,* 19 John. Rep. 456, 474 (1821) (involving the N. Y. General Manufacturing Incorporation Act of 1811, N. Y. Laws 1811, c. 67); cf. *Adams v. Wiscasset Bank,* 1 Greenl. (Me. 1821) 361, 364; *Merchants Bank v. Cook,* 4 Pick. 405, 414 (1826); *Nichols v. Thomas,* 4 Mass. 232 (1808). In the actual chartering of American corporations, the principle was accepted much earlier. See East, *Business Enterprise in the American Revolutionary Era* (1938) 286; 2 Davis, *Essays in the Earlier History of American Corporations* (1917) 317; 2 Ann. Cong. 1920 (1789-91). So much was limited liability taken for granted that it was felt unnecessary to mention the subject in most charters. However, in Massachusetts and New York stockholders of manufacturing corporations were expressly subjected to personal liability. Dodd, *First Half Century of Statutory Regulation of Business Corporations in America* (Harvard Legal Essays, 1934) 88; Dodd, *American Business Association Law a Hundred Years Ago and Today* (3 Law, A Century of Progress, 1937) 254, 267–268; Charter of Hamilton Manufacturing Society, N. Y. Laws 1797, c. 68, pp. 161, 162.

hand, limited to the amount of capital subscribed, with no possibility of ordinarily compelling additions thereto in case of loss,[2] it soon became apparent that the original capital should be permanently devoted to the needs of the corporation as at least a partial substitute for the unlimited personal liability existing in individual enterprise.

If the creation of a capital fund was not to defeat its purpose, safeguards against its withdrawal by repayment to shareholders in the guise of dividends, or otherwise, were indispensable. Historically, the principal objective of dividend law has therefore been the preservation of a minimum of assets as a safeguard in assuring the payment of creditors' claims.[3] Beginning about 1800, special charters in this country gave to creditors, exclusively or in conjunction with the corporation, a remedy against directors who had declared dividends which impaired the capital of the corporation.[4] This safeguard against withdrawal of capital was the basis of the important New York Act of 1825, later copied into the corporate statutes of many states.[5] This statutory solicitude for creditors soon met the approval of the courts. Whether from familiarity with the statutes of this type or otherwise, Justice Story in 1824 established in *Wood v. Dummer* what has since been known as the trust fund doctrine.[6] "It appears to me very clear upon general principle, as well as the legislative intention, that the capital stock of banks is to be deemed

---

The principal exception, double liability of stockholders in banks and insurance companies, is currently disappearing in many jurisdictions. Effective July 1, 1937, the double liability of stockholders of national banks giving notice by publication six months previously was terminated. 12 U. S. C. A., §64a, as amended 49 Stat. 708 (1935).

[3] On the regulation of dividends generally see: Ballantine and Hills, *Corporate Capital and Restrictions upon Dividends under Modern Corporation Laws*, 23 Cal. L. Rev. 229 (1935); 2 Bonbright, *Valuation of Property* (1937) 912; Briggs, *Dividends and the General Corporation Statutes*, 8 Acc. Rev. 130 (1933); 1 Dodd and Baker, *Cases on Business Associations* (1940), c. VII, §7; Littleton, *Business Profits as a Legal Basis for Dividends*, 16 Harv. Bus. Rev. 51 (1937) (an accountant's analysis of the statutes); Rutledge, *Significant Trends in Modern Incorporation Statutes*, 22 Wash. Univ. L. Q. 305, 333 (1937); Sparger, *Profits, Surplus and the Payment of Dividends*, 8 N. Car. L. Rev. 14 (1929); Weiner, *Theory of Anglo American Dividend Law: American Statutes and Cases*, 29 Col. L. R. 461 (1929); Annotations, "Right or duty of corporation to pay dividends; and liability for wrongful payment," 55 A. L. R. 8, 11; 76 A. L. R. 885, 886; 109 A. L. R. 1381, 1383. For a discussion of questions of business policy in the payment of dividends, see Arsdell, *Problems of Corporate-Surplus Administration*, 13 Acc. Rev. 275 (1938); Dewing, *Financial Policy of Corporations* (3d Rev. Ed. 1934) 615–667; Hoagland, *Corporation Finance* (2d Ed. 1938) 354–369.

[4] See §6, *supra*.

[5] See §7, *supra*.

[6] 3 Mason 308; Fed. Cas. No. 17,944 (C. C. Me. 1824).

a pledge or trust fund for the payment of the debts contracted by the bank." "The individual stockholders are not liable for the debts of the bank in their private capacities. The charter relieves them from personal responsibility and substitutes the capital stock in its stead." The trust fund doctrine *eo nomine* has since met with violent criticism and is now generally rejected.[7] But the principle enunciated in *Wood v. Dummer* that creditors are entitled to protection against the distribution of capital survives with great, if not full vigor, in most American jurisdictions. For example, it is very doubtful that there is any American state in which it would be held that directors of a newly organized corporation, with valid debts outstanding, which had just received from stockholders $100,000 in payment for 1,000 shares of $100 par value common stock, could turn about and legally distribute the $100,000 or any part thereof to shareholders upon a mere dividend resolution unaccompanied by further corporate action toward reduction of capital or liquidation.

Many cases since *Wood v. Dummer,* although they may not subscribe to the trust fund doctrine, and although many of them are decided under statutes which specifically prohibit the payment of dividends by withdrawal of capital, recognize the basis of the capital impairment rule to be protection of creditors.[8] Likewise the object of the Massachusetts type statute against payments which render the corporation insolvent is to protect creditors.[9]

[7] The effect of *Wood v. Dummer* in establishing a common law rule against the payment of dividends from capital is fully discussed in §15, *infra.*

[8] *Martin v. Zellerbach,* 38 Cal. 300, 307 (1869) ; *Spiegel v. Beacon Participations,* 8 N. E. (2d) 895, 912 (Mass. 1937) [comment, 17 B. U. L. Rev. 724 (1937)] (no statute prohibited payment from capital; directors were not held liable for such payments where the corporation was not insolvent and money was not needed to pay creditors) ; *American Steel & Wire Co. v. Eddy,* 130 Mich. 266, 267, 89 N. W. 952 (1902) ; *Coleman v. Booth,* 268 Mo. 64, 86, 186 S. W. 1021 (1916) ; *Rorke v. Thomas,* 56 N. Y. 559, 564 (1874) ; *Small v. Sullivan,* 245 N. Y. 343, 350, 157 N. E. 261 (1927). See *Equitable Life Assurance Society v. Union Pacific Railroad Co.,* 212 N. Y. 360, 366, 106 N. E. 92 (1914) (comment, 27 Harv. L. Rev. 758; 14 Col. L. Rev. 524) ; *Whitfield v. Kern,* 122 N. J. Eq. 332, 344, 192 Atl. 48 (Ct. Err. & App. 1937) ; *Whittaker v. Amwell National Bank,* 52 N. J. Eq. 400, 404, 29 Atl. 203 (Ct. Ch. 1894) ; *Cottrell v. Albany Card & Paper Mfg. Co.,* 142 A. D. 148, 150, 126 N. Y. S. 1070 (3d Dept. 1911) ; *Hochman v. Mortgage Finance Corp.,* 289 Pa. 260, 266–267, 137 Atl. 252 (1927). Cf. *Hazard v. Wight,* 201 N. Y. 399, 402–403, 94 N. E. 855 (1911) (distribution of capital to a single director-stockholder) ; *Goetz v. Williams,* 206 Wis. 561, 564, 240 N. W. 181 (1932) ; 2 Bonbright, *Valuation of Property* (1937) 914; Dewing, *Corporation Securities* (1934) 63–64. For a good discussion of the basis of the rule, see Jessel, M.' R., in *Flitcroft's Case,* L. R. 21 Ch. Div. 519, 533–534 (Ct. App. 1882).

[9] *Pennsylvania Iron Works v. Mackenzie,* 190 Mass. 61, 63, 76 N. E. 228 (1906).

9.1. Modern Minimization of Creditor Protection

The dominant note of dividend legislation and decisions during the nineteenth century was creditor protection. The corporate form of organization was new. Its potentialities unknown, it was looked upon with mixed fear and skepticism. Rapid industrial and frontier expansion produced mushroom corporations frequently of a highly speculative character. Moreover, corporations were small, with the result that insolvency would come quickly by mishandling and dissipation of corporate assets. Under such circumstances, the need for protecting the creditor was strongly felt.

The past quarter of a century has seen a change. While new and difficult corporate problems have come, those of the beginning and frontier period have disappeared. The wildcat mining corporation had largely passed from existence before adoption of the Securities Act. By and large the twentieth century corporation was not viewed as constantly in danger of dissolution; economic responsibility was more certain. Changes in the market level might cause large-scale reorganization, but for causes which dividend regulation could hardly eradicate. Concurrently with these conditions states began to recognize certain advantages to that state most liberal with its general incorporation provisions. Included in that liberalization, quite naturally, was the creditor protection so rigorously guarded by the doctrine against capital impairment.

Although it is probably true that a direct dividend distribution of capital received on the sale of par value stock could not be made in any state, it is far from true that the capital protection afforded a creditor means today what it once did. Under most modern acts the introduction of shares without par value has enabled the corporation to start out with "capital" far less than the consideration actually paid for its shares, the balance being paid-in surplus available for dividends under varying restrictions in most jurisdictions.[10] Thus, at the very outset the protection to creditors from the capital impairment doctrine may be thwarted by small initial capital. Whatever protection there may be from initial capital is further minimized by the liberality of statutes in permitting reduction of capital and distribution to stockholders of the reduction surplus under circumstances somewhat similar to those in which paid-in surplus can be divided.[11] The net result is that the dividend protection to creditors

[10] See §29, infra.

[11] See §30, infra; also 2 Bonbright, Valuation of Property (1937) 914; Dewing, Corporation Securities (1934) 54. The Minnesota Business Corporation Act contains an unusual provision limiting reduction of capital to an amount not less than the par value of all outstanding shares of par value. Minn. Stat. (Mason

from a doctrine against capital impairment is currently much weakened. Add to this a trend toward the Delaware type dividend statute which permits payment of dividends from current profits even though capital is impaired,[12] and it is clear that the creditor has lost much of his historic strength in dividend matters.

10. Maintenance of Capital in the Interest of Stockholders

A second purpose in dividend regulation, sometimes neglected by overemphasis on protection of the creditor, is that of assuring continuous maintenance of capital in order that the enterprise may function for the purposes contemplated by stockholders. In the example suggested of directors attempting to pay back in dividends the $100,000 of capital which stockholders had just contributed, stockholders have as much reason to object as creditors. The purpose of the stockholder is a capital investment, and although he expects dividends, he expects them from profits. When they are paid from capital, it should be an exceptional distribution which he has authorized. Directors have an obligation to keep the corporate capital intact not only to protect creditors but also to insure carrying out for the benefit of stockholders the purposes of incorporation.[13] Permitting a return of capital in the guise of supposed profit distributions is unfair also to subsequent stockholders, who are entitled to expect that past dividends have been paid from profits and not capital.[14]

Liberalization in general corporation laws to permit dividends from funds which are in substance capital affects the stockholder just as it does the creditor. It should not be concluded that merely because a creditor would have no right to object to a capital distribution, a stockholder would be similarly remediless. The distribution may be legal so far as creditors are concerned and at the same time a breach of general management duty on the part of directors toward stockholders of one or more classes.

1938 Supp.) §7492–38. This is practically the only exception to the general tendency permitting reduction of capital as long as there remain sufficient assets to equal the liabilities and capital as reduced.

[12] See §§16(c), 17, *infra.*

[13] *Hutchinson v. Stadler*, 85 App. Div. 424, 436–437, 83 N. Y. S. 509 (1st Dept. 1903) (concurring opinion); see *Salina Mercantile Co. v. Stiefel*, 82 Kans. 7, 9, 107 Pac. 774 (1910); *Martin v. Zellerbach*, 38 Cal. 300, 318 (1869); *Hochman v. Mortgage Finance Corp.*, 289 Pa. 260, 267, 137 Atl. 252 (1927) (the rule applies for the benefit of stockholders of a going concern, but not one which is winding up).

[14] *Appleton v. American Malting Co.*, 65 N. J. Eq. 375, 381, 54 Atl. 454 (1903) (derivative stockholders' suit); *Loan Society v. Eavenson*, 248 Pa. 407, 416, 94 Atl. 121 (1915) (recovery against directors granted to corporation); *MacDougall v. Jersey Imperial Hotel Co.*, 2 Hem. & M. 528, 536 (Ch. 1864).

On the other hand, the principle against impairment of capital from the angle of stockholders is for their benefit, and should stockholders consent to such distributions or accept them, the creditor would be in no position to assert a stockholder objection. This introduces another aspect of the recent tendency to minimize dividend restrictions which favor creditors. To the extent that dividends may be more freely paid as against creditors, there is a correlative increase in the right of stockholders to receive previously restricted corporate assets. Dividend law illustrates at this point an important, though not as yet clearly defined, trend in the law of corporations generally. The line of cleavage which separated the early corporate creditor from the stockholder is slowly disappearing. In modern corporate reorganizations, the creditor is able to stand less and less upon a vested right to insist upon payment of his claim; while, in contrast, the stockholder of a far-flung enterprise comes to resemble more and more an investor with interests resembling those of a creditor.[15] Indicative of this shift in factual emphasis is the statutory tendency toward more liberal treatment of stockholders *contra* creditors when it comes to dividends. As the Maryland Court of Appeals has said recently in refusing to allow recovery of dividends paid from capital when the stockholder-recipients were innocent: "Whatever [the stockholders'] position may be theoretically, practically they are in no better position than creditors to know the condition of the company, and it would be an unfair and unreasonable burden to require them to pay back, years after they have been spent, dividends received in good faith from a solvent corporation in regular course of business."[16]

How far should such assimilation of the stockholder to the creditor go? There is still one fundamental respect in which the stockholder differs from the creditor: if profit is made, he is theoretically the one entitled to it. This right, it must be conceded, is often rendered tenuous by the broad powers allowed corporate management in withholding distribution; even when this is true, however, the stockholder's market equity, where the stock is marketable, will, at least to a degree, reflect the book undistributed profit. Is the innocent stockholder entitled to limited liability, all the profit and his capital too?

---

[15] See Berle and Means, *The Modern Corporation and Private Property* (1932) 279–280; 2 Bonbright, *Valuation of Property* (1937) 915; Dodd, *American Business Association Law a Hundred Years Ago and Today* (3 Law, A Century of Progress) 254, 277–278; Littleton, *The Dividend Base*, 9 Acc. Rev. 140, 144–145 (1934); Note, 49 Yale L. J. 492, 494 (1940).

[16] *Bartlett v. Smith*, 162 Md. 478, 482, 160 Atl. 440 (1932).

With the passing in importance of the sharp distinction between creditor and stockholder, dividend litigation is more frequently taking place over respective rights of conflicting classes of stockholders rather than to enforce claims of creditors.[17] The principle that stockholders are entitled *inter se* to maintenance of their proportionate interests in the capital and earnings of the corporation is one of increasing modern importance.

11. Adequate Accounting Disclosure

A third objective in dividend regulation is the establishment of a system of corporate accounting which will give directors, creditors, and stockholders a fair estimate of the corporation's financial position. Indeed, the declaration of dividends is as much an accounting question as it is a legal problem.[18] Accounting methods, directly or indirectly imposed by dividend statutes, fulfill two functions. The early dividend legislation sought to assure the continued existence of the corporation, the prevention of failure and dissolution. With the present-day economy placing increasingly heavier emphasis on reorganization rather than dissolution, this purpose has in many ways become secondary. Most modern corporations never die; they continue to live in reorganized form. It, therefore, becomes more and more important that corporate accounts should perform another function, that of accurately advising creditors, stockholders, and prospective creditors and stockholders [19] as to the exact current position of the corporation.

12. Public Interest in Dividend Regulation

In addition to the immediate interest of creditors and stockholders in dividend regulations, there is also a broader public interest. Present-day economic activity revolves in very large part around corporations.[20] Almost everyone who is not an owner of stock in

[17] See Chapter 6, *infra*.

[18] Determining the amount of profit available for dividends has been said to constitute the main purpose of corporate accounting. Littleton, *Accounting Evolution to 1900* (1933) 206.

[19] One of the reasons given by the court in *Appleton v. American Malting Co.*, 65 N. J. Eq. 375, 54 Atl. 454, for permitting a solvent corporation to recover dividends from directors for the real benefit of stockholders was the injustice to subsequent stockholders of dividends out of capital. Such dividends, while decreasing the actual value of stock, produce in the eyes of purchasers an increase in its apparent value. Accord: *Siegman v. Electric Vehicle Co.*, 72 N. J. Eq. 403, 408, 65 Atl. 910 (1907). Cf. *Hubbard v. Weare*, 79 Iowa 678, 695–696, 44 N. W. 915 (1890).

[20] All railroads and the majority of public utilities are organized in the corporate form, while nine-tenths of our total manufactured articles are the products of corporations. Dewing, 4 *Encycl. of Soc. Sci.* 423.

some corporation is at least a patron, creditor, or an employee of a corporation, or potentially such. A corporation's dividend declarations go far in establishing its credit and effecting the potential market for bond and stock issues.[21]

Bad dividend policies by corporations as a class may contribute to or aggravate general economic disturbances. The cushion of surplus reserves built up by some large corporations prior to the last depression prevented in many instances complete cessation of operations. All these factors combine to demonstrate the strong interest of the public in the maintenance of sound dividend policies.[22]

B. Common Law Restrictions

13. Corporate Power to Pay Dividends Is Implied

Most corporate statutes, either directly or indirectly, authorize the payment of dividends. Even in the absence of any specific statutory authority, the objective of dividends is implicit in the very act of incorporation. The phrase of Lord Coke, "when a corporation is duly created, all other incidents are *tacitè* annexed," [23] if it has any meaning, certainly applies to the stockholder's right to a dividend. The question of an implied power to pay dividends in the absence of statutory authority arises seldom, but when it does, the power is sustained.[24]

14. Restriction to Profits

While the modern law of dividends has its antecedents in early special charters and general corporation acts, the question naturally arises as to existence of common law dividend restrictions in the absence of any controlling statutory provisions. It is true that in almost every state today general corporation acts regulate the dividend declarations of corporations organized thereunder. This does not, however, render entirely academic common law doctrines. Ascertainment of a common law rule in a particular state will bear

---

[21] Apprising the public as to credit and solvency of corporations was stated as one of the objectives of the corporation provisions of the New York Revised Statutes of 1828. Revisers' Reports and Notes, 3 Rev. Stat. (2d Ed. 1836), pp. 530–531.

[22] *Lockhart v. Van Alstyne*, 31 Mich. 76, 80–81, 84 (1875).

[23] *Sutton's Hospital Case*, 10 Co. 30b (K. B. 1613).

[24] *McKean v. Biddle*, 181 Pa. 361, 37 Atl. 528 (1897) (involving the Philadelphia Contributionship for Insuring Houses from Fire, the charter of which contained no authority to pay dividends, see 1 Dallas, Laws of Pa. 1700–81, p. 492); see *McDonald v. Williams*, 174 U. S. 397, 407 (1899); *Beers v. Bridgeport Spring Co.*, 42 Conn. 17, 27 (1875).

directly upon interpretation of statutory provisions, depending upon whether they restrict or enlarge its limitations. And sometimes the common law rule itself must be invoked, as for example, where the legality of a dividend is drawn in question in a forum other than the corporation's domicile and, through inadvertence, the law of the domicile has not been proved. Under such circumstances, the forum has almost no choice but application of the common law rule, or possibly its own statutes.[25] Indeed, it is surprising how frequently dividend cases are decided without any reference in the opinions to corporation act provisions which would otherwise be controlling. This laxity in judicial procedure makes it likewise important to determine common law restrictions.

The evidence as to a common law rule of dividends is limited. Unlike most fields of the law, there is no body of early English common law precedents.[26] In this country the special charter and early general corporation act furnished the first precedents which would otherwise have been supplied by judicial decisions. Nevertheless, there are a limited number of cases which may be said to establish common law restrictions on the declaration of dividends. These cases have arisen primarily from the judicial construction of charters, by-laws, and subscription provisions authorizing corporations to pay "dividends," without defining the term.[27] In giving judicial content to the term "dividends," the courts have circumscribed it by much the same limitations prescribed by various jurisdictions statutorily.

Many early issues of preferred stock merely stipulated for the payment of "dividends" or guaranteed payment of the same. In all these cases it was uniformly held that a dividend [28] meant a distribu-

[25] For cases of this type see *Bartlett v. Smith*, 162 Md. 478, 160 Atl. 440 (1932); *Cochran v. Shetler*, 286 Pa. 226, 133 Atl. 233 (1926); *Loan Society v. Eavenson*, 248 Pa. 407, 94 Atl. 121 (1915); *Powers v. Heggie*, 268 Mass. 233, 167 N. E. 314 (1929) (applying to a Delaware corporation provisions of the Massachusetts enactment of the Uniform Fraudulent Conveyance Act over objection that the dividends were not illegal in Delaware; Delaware had adopted the same act, but this fact was not referred to); *McGinniss v. Scheebeli*, 28 Pa. D. 368, 370 (1918). For choice of law generally see Chapter 10, *infra*.

[26] The early decisions involving dividends were merely contests by adverse claimants to stock or the dividends thereof, the propriety of the latter not being questioned. *Johnson v. East India Company*, Finch Ch. 430 (1679); *Gardener v. Pullen & Phillips*, 2 Vern. 394 (1700); *Hildyard v. South Sea Company*, 2 P. Wms. 76 (1722); *Monk v. Graham*, 8 Mod. 9 (1722); *Lord Townsend v. Ash*, 3 Atk. 336 (1745); *Ashby v. Blackwell*, 1 Amb. 503 (1765).

[27] Very few of the early special charters simply authorized the declaration of "dividends." Almost without exception the power was defined, limited, or qualified. See §§4, 5, 6, *supra*.

[28] The term "divisione" was used in medieval partnership documents as early as 1384 to signify a division of profits and capital between partners. Edler, *Glossary of Medieval Terms of Business*, Italian Series (1934) 108.

tion of profits.[29] In many other cases where dividend statutes were or might have been applied, courts have also announced the existence of a common law profit limitation.[30]

15. Restriction Against Payment from Capital

The first dividend cases in this country imposed a restriction against the payment of dividends from capital. In *Wood v. Dummer*, the corporation, having ceased to do business and being wound up pursuant to statute, distributed to stockholders assets equal to three-quarters of its capital before paying creditors' claims, thereby rendering the corporation insolvent.[31] The case in holding liable stockholders, fully aware that this was a liquidation, stands on distinguishable ground. Stockholders cannot expect to be paid in priority to creditors on liquidation. Different principles may apply to the dividends of a going corporation. Similarly, cases must be distinguished where the distribution denominated a dividend is openly recognized as a partial liquidation of a corporation which otherwise continues to do business. Quite different considerations apply to payments which purport to be liquidations and payments which purport to be made from profits.[32] It is the latter type of payment which is peculiarly the province of corporate dividend law.

[29] *Lockhart v. Van Alstyne*, 31 Mich. 76, 79, 84 (1875); *Taft v. Hartford, Providence & Fishkill Railroad Co.*, 8 R. I. 310, 333 (1866); *Cratty v. Peoria Law Library Association*, 219 Ill. 516, 76 N. E. 707 (1906) (treated in same manner as a business corporation); *Cring v. Sheller Wood Rim Mfg. Co.*, 98 Ind. App. 310, 183 N. E. 674 (1934); see *Elkins v. Camden & Atlantic Railroad Co.*, 36 N. J. Eq. 233, 236, 237 (Ch. 1882). But cf. *Williams v. Parker*, 136 Mass. 204 (1884), holding that under a guaranteed dividend authorized by statute preferred stockholders were entitled to payment even in the absence of profits since they were creditors to the extent thereof.

[30] *Spiegel v. Beacon Participations*, 8 N. E. (2d) 895, 912 (Mass. 1937) (the Massachusetts statute only prohibits the payment of dividends while the corporation is insolvent or bankrupt or which would render it so, Mass. Laws Ann., c. 156, §37; but recovery was denied where there were sufficient assets to meet creditors' claims); *Nichols v. Olympia Veneer Co.*, 139 Wash. 305, 311, 246 Pac. 941 (1926) (recognizing without reference to Washington statutes a shareholder's right to equality of distribution from profits); *Main v. Mills*, 6 Biss. 98, Fed. Cas. No. 8,974 (C. C. Wis. 1874); see *Wittenberg v. Federal Mining & Smelting Co.*, 15 Del. Ch. 147, 151, 133 Atl. 48 (1926), aff'd 15 Del. Ch. 409, 138 Atl. 347 (1927); *Fernald v. Ridlon Co.*, 246 Mass. 64, 74, 140 N. E. 421 (1923); *Davenport v. Lines*, 72 Conn. 118, 128, 44 Atl. 17 (1899); *Eyster v. Centennial Board of Finance*, 94 U. S. 500, 504 (1876) (statute provided federal government was entitled to reimbursement for an exposition appropriation before any "dividend . . . of profits" to shareholders); see also 1 Dodd and Baker, *Cases on Business Associations* (1940), Note, 1052. The difficult question as to what constitutes "profits" from which dividends may properly be declared is discussed in §§25–28, *infra*.

[31] 3 Mason 308, Fed. Cas. No. 17,944 (C. C. Me. 1824).

[32] See *Mills v. Hendershot*, 70 N. J. Eq. 258, 268, 62 Atl. 542 (1905). In *Kimbrough v. Davies*, 104 Miss. 722, 61 So. 697 (1913), a stockholder was held

The doctrine that the capital of a corporation is a trust fund in the sense that the creditor has something analogous to a specific *res* interest in corporate property is difficult to support,[33] and it is at least doubtful that Story, in promulgating the principle in *Wood v. Dummer,* had any intention of vesting the creditor with an equitable interest in corporate property. The unfortunate reference to a trust fund might have been intended merely to mean, what many special charters had long provided, that the corporation's capital could not be distributed to stockholders against the claim of creditors. In this sense, stripped of equitable charge imputations, *Wood v. Dummer* survives as a common law principle.

Once the rule is accepted that dividends may only be paid from profits, it is an inevitable corollary that dividends cannot be paid from capital itself. Apart from modern statutory modifications, if there are no profits, the only other fund from which dividends could be paid would be capital.[34] The interrelation of these two rules is demonstrated by frequent reference to a common law doctrine that dividends can be paid only from net profits but not out of capital.[35] And there is considerable general support for a common law rule that dividends cannot be paid from capital,[36] and for the fact that this

---

liable for a solvent corporation's liquidating dividend out of capital, irrespective of the trust fund doctrine or the fact the applicable statute only prohibited dividends where the corporation was insolvent or would be rendered insolvent.

[33] *McDonald v. Williams,* 174 U. S. 397 (1899), rejected the doctrine as to innocent stockholders receiving from a solvent corporation dividends out of capital. The doctrine as such has since fallen into disfavor.

[34] Paid-in or reduction surplus, the third source under modern statutes, is discussed in §§29, 30, *infra.* The statement that a dividend cannot be paid from capital itself may have different meanings. (*a*) If the corporation has no current or past earnings and no paid-in surplus, the dividend would necessarily be from capital, irrespective of whether capital was then intact or had been previously impaired. This is the sense referred to in the text. (*b*) If the corporation has current or past earnings it may make a difference whether capital has been previously impaired: (1) If capital stands unimpaired, the profits will normally be distributable. (2) If capital is impaired at the opening of the accounting period, although the dividend can be paid from profits and hence is not a distribution of capital itself in the sense referred to above, yet a distribution of operating profits with a balance sheet impairment of capital would in many jurisdictions be treated as a payment "out of capital." These questions are more fully discussed in §§16, 18, *infra.*

[35] *Spiegel v. Beacon Participations,* 8 N. E. (2d) 895, 912 (Mass. 1937); see *Davenport v. Lines,* 72 Conn. 118, 128, 44 Atl. 17 (1899); *Benas v. Title Guaranty Trust Co.,* 216 Mo. App. 15, 267 S. W. 28, 29 (1924); *Wittenberg v. Federal Mining & Smelting Co.,* 15 Del. Ch. 147, 151, 133 Atl. 48 (1926), aff'd 15 Del. Ch. 409, 138 Atl. 347 (1927).

[36] *Loan Society v. Eavenson,* 248 Pa. 407, 94 Atl. 121 (1915) (directors held liable for paying dividends which they knew or should have known impaired capital); *Cochran v. Shetler,* 286 Pa. 226, 133 Atl. 232 (1926) (directors sim-

doctrine exists even though there may be specific statutes imposing a less stringent liability.[37]

C. Statutory Restrictions

16. Three Types of Modern Statutes

There are two major problems in the law of dividends. The first relates to the fund from which dividends may legally be paid. The second involves the question as to what relief can be obtained from either directors or stockholders if an illegal dividend is paid. These questions, while very closely related, are at the same time quite different. A dividend may be paid from funds not legally available for dividends and yet not be recoverable from either directors or stockholders, or recovery may be possible from one class and not the other.

In considering the fund available for dividends, there are in turn two problems. The first relates to the legal definition, statutory and decisional, of the fund from which payment may be made, demarcation of the limits beyond which dividends cannot go. The legal definition of the fund is, however, only the skeleton upon which the framework of the corporation's accounting is built. Whether or not a dividend can actually be paid depends upon the result of applying the general definition to the complex ledger accounts, balance sheet, and profit and loss statement of the corporation. The question of definition, to be discussed first, is a legal problem. The second ques-

---

ilarly held liable on demurrer for a payment which was wilful and negligent; court said same liability existed under law of Delaware, state of incorporation, which was not in evidence); *Gunkle's Appeal*, 48 Pa. 13, 19 (1864); *Sparling v. General Discount & Mortgage Corp.*, 178 Wash. 663, 35 Pac. (2d) 60 (1934) (although a Washington statute prohibited the payment of dividends from capital it was not referred to); *Johnson v. Nevins*, 87 Misc. 430, 432, 150 N. Y. S. 828 (1914) (for benefit of creditors); see *American Steel & Wire Co. v. Eddy*, 130 Mich. 266, 268, 89 N. W. 952 (1902); §75, n. 11–14, *infra;* Dewing, *Financial Policy of Corporations* (3d Rev. Ed. 1934) 606–607; Douglas and Shanks, *Cases and Materials on Business Units—Losses, Liabilities and Assets* (1932) 173. A corporation cannot distribute its capital to a single shareholder-director, *Hazard v. Wight*, 201 N. Y. 399, 94 N. E. 855 (1911) (statute and common law both relied upon). In *Russell v. Bristol*, 49 Conn. 251 (1881), stockholders of an insolvent corporation contributed a $75,000 "guarantee capital" to be used only if the resources of the company were exhausted and to be returned to the stockholders at the end of three years. It was held that dividends could not be paid therefrom by a successor corporation: "to neither corporation could it ever be anything but a debt" (273).

[37] *Spiegel v. Beacon Participations*, 8 N. E. (2d) 895, 912 (Mass. 1937); *Kimbrough v. Davies*, 104 Miss. 722, 61 So. 697 (1913) (a liquidating dividend). Restriction against dividend payments by insolvent corporations on the theory of a common law fraudulent conveyance is discussed in §19, *infra*.

tion of applying the definition is a mixed legal and accounting problem.

With the exception of such limited common law concepts as have been discussed, there is no general body of American dividend law. The rules for determining the fund from which dividends may be paid depend upon the particular statutes of the state of incorporation which must be consulted every time a dividend problem is considered. The law of no two states is exactly the same. The several dividend statutes may, however, be grouped into three general classes.[38] The first prohibits dividends when the corporation is insolvent or would be rendered insolvent thereby. The second prohibits distributions except from a surplus as normally computed on a corporate balance sheet. The third prohibits payments except from current or past net profits most frequently determined by a corporate profit and loss statement. Every state has statutes enacting in substance at least one of these rules. Many states have the insolvency rule in addition to either the balance sheet surplus or net profits restriction. In some states all three restrictions will be found applicable in one way or another.

(a) Massachusetts, where the insolvency test for dividends originated,[39] is still the leading exponent of this rule. The statute provides that directors shall be jointly and severally liable for the debts of the corporation when they declare or assent to a dividend "if the corporation is, or thereby is, rendered, bankrupt or insolvent." [40] In the present act, the provision has been extended to impose liability on directors not only when the corporation is insolvent, as provided in the original act, but also when the corporation is bankrupt, thereby

---

[38] Some corporation acts, particularly those more recently revised, expressly apply their dividend restrictions to the corporation. See e.g. Cal. Civ. Code (1937), §§346, 346a; Del. Rev. Code (1935), c. 65, §35; Idaho Code Ann., §29–129; 32 Ill. Ann. Stat. (Smith-Hurd), §157.41; N. Y. Stock Corp. Law, §58, as amended N. Y. Laws 1939, c. 364; 15 Purd. Pa. Stat. Ann., §2852–701; Wash. Rev. Stat. Ann. (Rem.), §3803–24. In a great many states the only limitations on a corporation's power to declare dividends are found in sections imposing civil or criminal liability upon corporate directors who participate or who hold office at the time. In *Baldwin v. Miller & Lux*, 152 Cal. 454, 92 Pac. 1030 (1907), it was held that a provision prohibiting directors from withdrawing capital in the form of dividends did not render such a payment illegal as to stockholders of a corporation formed expressly for liquidating assets. It was said the statute merely made directors liable for the payment. Generally, see 1 Dodd and Baker, *Cases on Business Associations* (1940), Note on Statutes Relating to Funds Available for Dividends, 1153; Ballantine and Lattin, *Cases and Materials on the Law of Corporations,* Note on Statutory Definitions of Legal Capital, 434 (1939) ; Graham and Katz, *Accounting in Law Practice* (2d Ed. 1938) 148–151.

[39] See §8, *supra.*

[40] Mass. Laws Ann., c. 156, §37.

pointing the principal issue under most statutes of this type which still retain the original prohibition against payment when insolvent. Which of the two tests of insolvency is to be applied? Under the so-called equity rule, the corporation is insolvent when it is unable to meet its obligations as they mature. Under the bankruptcy test, it is insolvent when its liabilities, exclusive of capital, exceed its assets.

Under the equity test, a corporation with ample assets to pay all claims on liquidation, so it is not bankrupt, may have an inverse current ratio under which it is unable to meet current liabilities. With the equity rule applicable, it is prohibited from paying dividends. On the other hand, it may have sufficient current assets to meet all current claims but have insufficient gross assets to pay all creditors, so it is insolvent in the bankruptcy sense. Yet under the equity rule, without any further dividend restrictions, a dividend could be paid. The converse result would follow in each of these cases if the bankruptcy test were applied.

(*b*) Typical of balance sheet surplus jurisdictions is New York which has had a capital impairment statute of some form applicable to some or all of its corporations continuously since enactment of the original general act of 1825. The present New York statute provides that,

> No stock corporation shall declare or pay any dividend which shall impair its capital, nor while its capital is impaired, nor shall any such corporation declare or pay any dividend or make any distribution of assets to any of its stockholders . . . unless the value of its assets remaining after the payment of such dividend . . . shall be at least equal to the aggregate amount of its debts and liabilities, including capital.[41]

It is the theory of statutes in this class that the surplus of corporate assets over and above corporate capital and liabilities is available for dividends.

The important question under this type of statute is the meaning of capital. The accountant clearly recognizes that when it is said that dividends cannot be paid from capital, no reference is made to any specific assets or fund of the corporation from which dividends are prohibited. It is simply meant that as a result of the system of double entry bookkeeping, there is an accounting restriction called capital on the liability side of the balance sheet which operates to prevent reduction of the total assets on the asset side of the balance

[41] N. Y. Stock Corp. Law, §58, as amended N. Y. Laws 1939, c. 364; see §7, *supra*.

sheet to a sum less than the amount entered as capital.[42] The capital
stock liability then is the technical accounting method for preserving
an amount of assets—whether they be fixed assets or current assets—
equivalent to some dollar value assigned to capital upon the sale of
the corporation's stock.

To the lawyer unfamiliar with accounting, the following illustration may serve to demonstrate what the technical system of double
entry bookkeeping does in an accounting way to restrict capital withdrawal. Assume that corporate assets of every kind, after having
first paid or provided for all corporate obligations, are dumped into
a huge bin. If the corporation's capital is $100,000, a mark will be
placed on the side of the bin at the level required to hold $100,000
of the mixture of assets. The directors and stockholders are now
free to draw out of the bin assets for dividend purposes until they
reach the line marking the $100,000 level. This latter amount is
always restricted against withdrawal, both as a guarantee to creditors
that they will have a cushion of protection in substitution for the
personal liability of stockholders, and also as an assurance to stockholders that their principal investment will be preserved to carry on
the future business of the corporation.

For dividend purposes capital may mean one of several things,
the dollar value of the consideration received on the issuance of
stock, the par or stated value at issuance, or the actual capital at the
opening of the current accounting period. Three balance sheets will
illustrate these respective possibilities. Assume that on January 1,
1939 the corporation issues 1,000 shares of $100 par value stock for
property reasonably worth to the knowledge of directors not over
$75,000; that during the year 1939 the corporation suffers a net
operating loss of $10,000; that during the year 1940 its net profits
from operations are $15,000 and that there are no outstanding debts.
Under the first alternative of treating the capital as the dollar value

[42] Although some courts have had considerable difficulty, there is ample judicial
recognition for this fundamental accounting concept: *Equitable Life Assurance
Society v. Union Pacific Railroad Co.*, 212 N. Y. 360, 366, 106 N. E. 92 (1914);
Peters v. U. S. Mortgage Co., 13 Del. Ch. 11, 18, 114 Atl. 598 (1921); *Williams v.
Western Union Telegraph Co.*, 93 N. Y. 162, 187–188 (1883); *Cox v. Leahy*, 209
App. Div. 313, 315, 204 N. Y. S. 741 (3d Dept. 1924); *Cannon v. Wiscassett
Mills Co.*, 195 N. C. 119, 141 S. E. 344 (1928); *Lubbock v. British Bank of South
America*, (1892) 2 Ch. 198, 202; see Ballantine and Hills, *Corporate Capital and
Restrictions upon Dividends under Modern Corporation Laws*, 23 Cal. L. Rev.
229, 231 (1935); 2 Bonbright, *Valuation of Property* (1937) 916; 1 Dodd and
Baker, *Cases on Business Associations* (1940), Note, 1049–1050; Deinzer, *Capital
Stock and Surplus: Legal and Accounting Relations*, 10 Acc. Rev. 333 (1935);
Isaacs, *Principal—Quantum or Res*, 46 Harv. L. Rev. 776 (1933) (an excellent dis-
cussion of the theory underlying the concept of capital).

of consideration received, a balance sheet at December 31, 1940 would show:

ASSETS		LIABILITIES	
Plant, inventory, etc.	$ 75,000	Capital	$ 75,000
Cash	5,000	Surplus	5,000
	$ 80,000		$ 80,000

Under the second alternative of treating capital as the par value of stock, the balance sheet under the same circumstances would show:

ASSETS		LIABILITIES	
Plant, inventory, etc.	$ 75,000	Capital	$100,000
Cash	5,000		
Deficit	(20,000)		
	$100,000		$100,000

Under the third alternative of treating capital as the actual capital at the opening of the current accounting period (January 1, 1940) the balance sheet would show:

ASSETS			LIABILITIES	
Plant, inven-			Capital	$ 65,000
tory, etc., as			Surplus	15,000
of Jan. 1, 1940	$ 65,000			
Replacement of				
depleted in-				
ventory	10,000	$ 75,000		
Cash		5,000		
		$ 80,000		$ 80,000

This third theory reduces the liability item for capital where in prior accounting periods capital has been impaired. Under this view capital would either be the consideration received or, if prior losses had impaired this amount, then the capital as impaired at the opening of the accounting period.

With surplus as the fund available for dividends, the corporation could distribute under the first theory $5,000, under the second nothing and under the third $15,000. Which of these theories is selected in the particular case will depend very largely on the statute in question. In many jurisdictions the third would not be acceptable. In many others the second alone is available. In some the first is permissible.

(c) Typical states accepting the current or past net profits test are Delaware and New Jersey. They permit as an alternative fund for paying dividends net profits generally or net profits of certain current years.[43] Thus, the Delaware statute provides that, in the absence of a balance sheet surplus, dividends may nevertheless be declared out of "net profits for the fiscal year then current and/or the preceding fiscal year." Assuming the same corporation transactions in (b) above, there are at least five possible alternatives for the meaning of net profits.

Net profits may mean, first of all, the earnings of the corporation from the beginning of its existence. Under this theory past operating profits and losses would be taken into consideration in determining the availability for distribution of current earnings. Thus, the loss of $10,000 suffered in 1939 would be deducted from the $15,000 of earnings in 1940, leaving available for dividends $5,000 on December 31, 1940.

Secondly, net profits may mean the profit for the current accounting period as shown by the profit and loss statement without any regard for prior operating losses. Under this theory the $15,000 which would appear on the profit and loss statement of the corporation as of December 31, 1940 would be available in its entirety for dividends.

There is a third possibility. It is to be observed that the same result is reached under the second profit and loss statement test as under the third alternative balance sheet test. This is merely coincidental. If a building were destroyed by fire in 1940 with insurance coverage short $15,000 so as to reduce the gross assets in the third balance sheet to $65,000, no dividends could be paid under the surplus theory. This loss would not necessarily be charged either completely or even in part against current operations as reflected by the profit and loss statement. The profit and loss statement for December 31, 1940 might still show $15,000 of current net earnings, or at least some portion thereof. It, therefore, becomes material to determine whether under the particular statute net profits for the current year means the balance shown by a profit and loss statement or the profit disclosed by a comparison of the balance sheet position at the opening of the accounting period with that at the close of the period.

Two additional but less probable interpretations may be given to net profits. It may mean the earned surplus as shown by a balance

---

[43] Del. Rev. Code (1935), c. 65, §34; N. J. Stat. (1937), §14:8-19.

sheet — that is, profits arising from operations tested by the balance sheet. Since the third alternative balance sheet test has already been considered as a test of net profits, that leaves only the first two balance sheet methods still available. As in balance sheet jurisdictions, if these tests are also adopted for net profits, the amount thereof is contingent on what theory of capital is accepted. As the discussion of this alternative method seems to demonstrate, it has very little relation to net profits and is substantially a balance sheet surplus test. Indeed, it is more restrictive than the balance sheet surplus test, because even though there is a surplus dividends cannot be paid unless it is an earned surplus.

A final possibility of considering net profits as meaning a straight balance sheet surplus (earned or unearned) seems to be excluded by a statutory dichotomy in the net profit states which necessitates making some differentiation between surplus and net profits.

17. Growth of the Net Profits Test

The principal statutory conflict centers between the balance sheet surplus rule and the net profits rule. The enacted dividend test in most jurisdictions is still the balance sheet surplus, modified sometimes by additional limitations with respect to payments from certain kinds of surplus. The question of permitting dividends from current or accumulated net profits first became acute following the great industrial combinations at the end of the last century. The assets of 183 such combines, while representing capital of 3 billion dollars, were actually worth less than $1\frac{1}{2}$ billion dollars, the balance being accounted for principally by goodwill.[44] On the part of directors, there was obviously involved a heavy personal risk in declaring dividends on such balance sheets, particularly in view of the strong possibility that courts might adopt the par theory of capital as illustrated in the second balance sheet above. Under this theory no dividends could be paid until earnings had absorbed the water portion of the goodwill or the capital had first been reduced. In 1904, New Jersey opened the movement toward profits as an alternative test to surplus by amending its law so as to remove any doubt as to the existence of these two alternatives.[45] The Delaware law, which continued for some years the older New Jersey form, was clarified in

---

[44] Larcom, *The Delaware Corporation* (1937) 82–83.
[45] N. J. Laws 1904, c. 143. That there should have been no doubt that the prior law provided the same alternatives, see §26, *infra*.

1927 so as to make both surplus and profits of the current or preceding year unequivocal alternatives.[46]

The profits rule was the earliest dividend rule in both England and America;[47] it is still the basis of the English law,[48] and has the support of accountants today.[49] The right to pay dividends from current profits can be had in most surplus jurisdictions by going through the formality of reducing capital. Since that method is available, the question arises whether corporations ought not to be authorized to make such payments without the necessity for periodic expenditures and trouble incident to reduction. In the corporation act revisions of the last decade, however, the tendency to accept the profits test in imitation of Delaware has for the most part stopped, and the surplus test as embodied in the Ohio and Uniform Acts has furnished the model.[50]

18. Comparison of the Surplus and Net Profits Tests

In two situations the same result is reached whether the balance sheet surplus test or the net profits test is applied: where the corporation has no impairment of capital and has current earnings, the same may be distributed; where the corporation has no balance sheet surplus and no current earnings, no dividend can be paid. Likewise, each rule permits payment of dividends in one situation where the other does not. Dividends may be paid under the plain surplus test if there is a past accumulated surplus, even though there may be no net earnings for the current periods specified in the profits rule. More important, where there is a balance sheet deficit preventing payment under the surplus test, dividends may nevertheless be paid out of net earnings under the profits theory.

---

[46] 35 Del. Laws, c. 85, §16. From the Act of 1899 through 1936 Delaware chartered 108,122 corporations. Of the industrials listed on the New York Stock Exchange in 1932, 34 per cent were Delaware corporations, its closest competitors being New York with 16 per cent and New Jersey with 14 per cent. Larcom, n. 44, *supra*, at 156, 175. It has been said that adoption of the profits rule in Delaware was obviously designed primarily to please directors and bankers. 2 Bonbright, *Valuation of Property* (1937) 970.

[47] See §§2, 4, 5, *supra*.

[48] For a good statement of the English rule, see *Verner v. General & Commercial Investment Trust*, (1894) 2 Ch. 239, 264–265, and generally §25, n. 179, *infra*.

[49] See Littleton, *Tests for Principles*, 13 Acc. Rev. 16, 23 (1938); Littleton, *The Dividend Base*, 9 Acc. Rev. 140 (1934). The income statement is recognized as more important than the balance sheet. Dohr, *Income Divorced from Reality*, 66 J. of Accountancy 361 (1938); Kaplan and Reaugh, *Accounting, Reports to Stockholders and the S. E. C.*, 48 Yale L. J. 935, 939 (1939).

[50] Ohio Code Ann. (Baldwin 1938), §8623-38; Uniform Business Corp. Act, §24.

D. The Insolvency Test

19. General Applicability

In a considerable number of states, statutes expressly provide that insolvency dividends shall not be paid. The basic statutory provision of some modern enactments, that a corporation shall not pay dividends while insolvent, or which would render it insolvent, appeared for the first time in the manufacturing corporation regulation act adopted by Massachusetts in 1830,[51] from which it was carried over into the Massachusetts Revised Statutes of 1836.[52] The restriction has since been amended to render directors liable for paying a dividend when the corporation is either insolvent or bankrupt, or through the dividend becomes such.[53] The Connecticut insolvency provision is directly descended from that in the Massachusetts Revised Statutes of 1836.[54] New Hampshire, having originally copied the Revised Statutes of 1836, has since amended its dividend section to provide that no dividend shall be paid from and no part of the capital stock withdrawn when the corporate property is insufficient or will be rendered insufficient for the payment of all its debts.[55]

In a larger number of states, the insolvency restriction is descended from the original Massachusetts enactment through the New York Manufacturing Act of 1848. The latter act, while it followed the general scheme of the Massachusetts manufacturing provisions in the Revised Statutes of 1836,[56] contained a curious change in the dividend section. In addition to omitting the clause in the Massachusetts Act limiting director's liability to the amount of the dividend, New York interpolated a provision making directors liable for dividends which "would diminish the amount of its capital stock."

[51] Mass. Laws (Jan. Laws 1830), c. 53, §9. For a detailed study of the earliest statutory dividend regulations by special and general enactments in Massachusetts, see Dodd, *First Half Century of Statutory Regulation of Business Corporations in Massachusetts* (Harvard Legal Essays, 1934) 64.

[52] Mass. Rev. Stat. (1836), c. 38, §23. For the text of this provision, see §8, *supra*. For important subsequent amendments see Mass. Acts and Resolves 1862, c. 218, §1; Mass. Acts and Resolves 1870, c. 224, §38; Mass. Acts and Resolves 1877, c. 230, §1; Mass. Acts and Resolves 1903, c. 437, §35.

[53] Mass. Laws Ann., c. 156, §37. *Source of amendment:* Mass. Acts and Resolves 1903, c. 437, §35.

[54] Conn. Gen. Stat. (1930), §3386. *Source:* Conn. Pub. Laws 1836–37, c. 63, §20; Conn. Pub. Acts 1901, c. 157, §33; Conn. Acts 1903, c. 194, §5.

[55] N. H. Pub. Laws (1926), c. 225, §79. The earliest predecessor of the present provision is N. H. Laws, June Sess. 1837, c. 322, §21 [see also N. H. Laws, June Sess. 1846, c. 321, §2 (4)], taken from Mass. Rev. Stat. (1836), c. 38, §23. For amendments to modern form see N. H. Gen. Stat. 1867, c. 135, §§3, 5, 6, 7.

[56] 2 N. Y. Sen. Doc. No. 53 (1847) 14–15.

As amended the clause read:

> If the trustees of any such company shall declare and pay any dividend when the company is insolvent, or any dividend the payment of which would render it insolvent, or which would diminish the amount of its capital stock, they shall be jointly and severally liable for all the debts of the company . . .[57]

The result was an anomalous hybrid of the Massachusetts insolvency rule and the New York capital impairment doctrine.[58] This provision was widely copied and is still in force in several states, minor changes being made in some cases.[59] The Iowa law has the double insolvency —capital impairment restriction of the New York Act of 1848, but also a peculiar separate clause making stockholders liable to persons sustaining damage from dividends which leave insufficient assets to meet corporate liabilities.[60] By construction this is treated as imposing liability when the corporation is insolvent in the bankruptcy sense.[61]

Several modern corporation act revisions include insolvency provisions in new language substantially similar to that employed in the earlier New York and Massachusetts enactments. Thus, the Illinois Business Corporation Act provides that no dividends shall be paid when the corporation is insolvent or its net assets are less than its stated capital, or when payment of the dividend would produce that effect.[62] The new California Act prohibits dividends when the corporation is insolvent in either the equity or bankruptcy sense.[63] In the

---

[57] N. Y. Laws 1848, c. 40, §13. A similar section was made applicable to gaslight companies, c. 37, §13. The General Business Incorporation Act of 1875 continued this provision in force as to other than monied and railroad corporations. N. Y. Laws 1875, c. 611, §19. The provision was repealed by the Stock Corporation Law of 1890. N. Y. Laws 1890, c. 564, §§23, 70.

[58] The capital impairment clause was added by amendment from the floor, since the conference report on the act included only the Massachusetts form of regulation. 8 N. Y. Ass. Doc. No. 240 (1847) 12.

[59] Colo. Stat. Ann. (1935), c. 41, §34. *Source:* Colo. Terr. Laws, 3d Sess. 1864, p. 53, §16; Md. Ann. Code (1935 Supp.), Art. 23, §87. *Source:* Md. Laws 1852, c. 338, §11; Md. Laws 1908, c. 240, §50; Miss. Code Ann. (1930), §4149. *Source:* Miss. Rev. Code 1857, c. 35, Art. 33; Miss. Ann. Code (Thompson 1892), §852 (although having the double insolvency and capital impairment provision dating back to 1857, it is not entirely clear that the New York statute was followed); Ore. Code Ann. (1930), §25-219 (no dividends which render corporation insolvent or other than out of net profits or surplus). *Source:* Ore. Gen. Laws (Deady 1866), Act of Oct. 14, 1862, p. 658, §15; Ore. Laws 1925, c. 291, §1; Wyo. Rev. Stat. (1931), §28-131. *Source:* Wyo. Terr. Laws, 1st Terr. Sess. 1869, p. 239, §15. Cf. Ind. Stat. Ann. (Burns 1933), §§25-211, 251.

[60] Iowa Code (1939), §§8377, 8378. *Source:* Iowa Code (1851), §§686, 687; Iowa Code (1897), §1621.

[61] *Miller v. Bradish*, 69 Iowa 278, 28 N. W. 594 (1886).

[62] 32 Ill. Ann. Stat. (Smith-Hurd 1935), §157.41.

[63] Cal. Civ. Code (Deering 1937), §346.

subsection of the Minnesota Business Corporation Act providing alternative authority for payment of dividends out of net earnings when capital is impaired, an exception is provided in the case where the assets of the corporation are less than the aggregate of its liabilities.[64] Ohio does not permit dividends when there is reasonable ground for believing that the corporation is unable to satisfy its obligations and liabilities.[65] A rather vague provision in Nebraska also makes it illegal to pay dividends when the corporation has insufficient funds to meet its liabilities.[66] Under Section 15 of the New York Stock Corporation Law, no corporation which has refused to pay its obligations when due may transfer any of its property to any of its directors or stockholders without full consideration. Every such transfer is void.

In the majority of states it is still true, however, that no specific corporation act provision prohibits a corporation from paying dividends when insolvent. It is important to inquire in these states as to the existence of either general statutory provisions or a common law doctrine which might render such dividends illegal.

Many states have general fraudulent conveyance statutes prohibiting the transfer of property by insolvent debtors. In several of the leading corporation states, the Uniform Fraudulent Conveyance Act has been adopted.[67] Under Section 4 of this act, every conveyance without consideration by a person who is or thereby will be rendered insolvent is fraudulent. Does this apply in states which have no insolvency provision in their corporation acts? As an additional restriction in states which do have such a provision?

The term person in Section 4 of the Uniform Act is not defined, but Section 1 concerning definitions speaks of assets of "a debtor" as meaning property not exempt from liability for his debts, and other terms defined in that section are general enough to apply to a corporation. Authority on whether in the absence of a specific provision in a corporation act, the Uniform Act applies to render insolvency dividends illegal is meager. In *Powers v. Heggie,* where the court allowed recovery by a trustee in bankruptcy of a Delaware corporation of dividends paid when the corporation was insolvent,

---

[64] Minn. Stat. (Mason 1938 Supp.), §7492–21.

[65] Ohio Code Ann. (Baldwin 1938), §8623–38.

[66] Neb. Comp. Stat. (1929), §24–218.

[67] Del. Rev. Code (1935), §§6059–6070; Md. Ann. Code (Bagby 1924), Art. 39B; Mass. Laws Ann., c. 109A, §§1–13; Mich. Stat. Ann., §§26.881–26.894; Minn. Stat. (Mason 1927), §§8475–8489; N. J. Rev. Stat. 1937, §§25:2–7, 25:2–19; N. Y. Debtor and Creditor Law, Art. 10; 39 Purd. Pa. Stat. Ann., §§351–363. Many of the provisions of the Uniform Act have been largely incorporated in §67 of the Bankruptcy Act (12 U. S. C. A., §107).

it was stated that any doubt as to the right to recover dividends paid by an insolvent corporation had been removed by the enactment in Massachusetts of the Uniform Act.[68] It had been urged there was nothing to show the dividends were illegal under the law of Delaware, but the Delaware corporation law was not in evidence. Though not referred to, the Uniform Act was likewise in force in Delaware. The decision is further weakened on this point by the court's principal reliance on a common law rule against payment of dividends by a corporation when insolvent.

Although the problem seems never to have been squarely presented as to whether or not a general statutory prohibition against transfers when insolvent would apply where the controlling corporation act contains no such prohibition, the question is extremely important. It would seem fairly clear that a corporation, like an individual or any unincorporated group, is subject to general restrictions against fraudulent conveyances. It is reasonable to presume that the provisions specifically regulating dividends in general corporation acts are intended to be additional safeguards and not regulations limiting liability so as to exclude restrictions which exist as to all other persons.[69] Where the corporation act, however, contains a provision dealing specifically with the question of insolvency dividends, it would seem that the mere fact more stringent regulations existed in some general act ought not to affect the corporation. The legislature having dealt expressly with the corporate insolvency situation, general provisions in other statutes ought not to be given effect.

Finally, there is the question as to existence in the absence of statute of a common law doctrine making illegal the payment of dividends when a corporation is insolvent. Such a rule may be supported either on the theory of a common law fraudulent conveyance, or that it violates an alleged principle that assets of an insolvent corporation are a trust fund for creditors.[70] In *Powers v. Heggie,* the court permitted recovery of an insolvency dividend from a stockholder principally on the common law right of creditors to recover money fraudulently paid without receipt of any consideration, the right of recovery being considered not one "peculiar to corporation

[68] 268 Mass. 233, 167 N. E. 314 (1929).

[69] Where the creditor bases his action on the theory that a dividend violates a corporation law provision against payment from capital, it has been held that recovery would not be allowed on a shift to the theory of the Uniform Fraudulent Conveyance Act. *Island Paper Co. v. Carthage Timber Corp.,* 128 Misc. 246, 218 N. Y. S. 346 (1926).

[70] See 1 Dodd and Baker, *Cases on Business Associations* (1940), Note, 1053.

law, but merely an instance of payment from an insolvent estate." [71]
The Maryland court in *Bartlett v. Smith* has, on the other hand,
based the right of recovery on the ground that money paid after
insolvency is taken from a fund held in trust for creditors.[72]

20. Meaning of Insolvency: Equity or Bankruptcy Test

With the exception of general corporation acts of the last decade,
the dividend insolvency provisions of almost all existing statutes are
derived from either the Massachusetts Revised Statutes of 1836 or
the New York Manufacturing Act of 1848. It becomes important,
therefore, to determine the meaning of the word "insolvency" at the
time these statutes were enacted. At the time of enactment of the
Massachusetts Manufacturing Act of 1830, which contained the basis
for the insolvency provision in the Revised Statutes of 1836,[73] it was
well established by English decisions that insolvency meant inability
to pay one's debts in ordinary course,[74] the rule generally applied in
equity cases. This was likewise the construction given to other than
dividend insolvency statutes by the earliest Massachusetts cases,[75] and
that which prevailed under the National Bankruptcy Act of 1867.[76]
It was not until the National Bankruptcy Act of 1898 that we get on

---

[71] 268 Mass. 233, 167 N. E. 314 (1929), *supra;* see *Wood v. National City Bank,* 24 F. (2d) 661, 663 (C. C. A. 2d, 1928); *Whitfield v. Kern,* 122 N. J. Eq. 332, 338, 344–345, 192 Atl. 48 (Ct. Err. & App. 1939).

[72] 162 Md. 478, 160 Atl. 440 (1932); compare *McDonald v. Williams,* 174 U. S. 397, 403 (1899), where the court, in refusing recovery from innocent stockholders of dividends paid when the corporation was solvent, distinguished the situation of transfers made by an insolvent corporation.

[73] See §19, n. 51, *supra.*

[74] *Bayly v. Schofield,* 1 M. & S. 338, 350 (1813) (per Lord Ellenborough, C. J.); *Shone v. Lucas,* 3 Dow & R. 218 (1823); *Cutten v. Sanger,* 2 Younge & Jerv. 459 (Exch. Chamber 1828).

[75] *Lee v. Kilburn,* 3 Gray 594 (1854) (construing "insolvent or in contemplation of insolvency" in statute applicable to transfers by insolvent debtors, Mass. Laws, Jan. Sess. 1841, c. 124, §3; the court cited the *Bayly* and *Shone* cases); *Hazelton v. Allen,* 3 Allen 114 (1861); *Thompson v. Thompson,* 4 Cush. 127 (1849) (construing Mass. Laws, Jan. Sess. 1838, c. 163, giving benefit of insolvency statutes to any debtor "setting forth his inability to pay all his debts"). For a modern Massachusetts case stating this to have been the common law rule, see *Calnan v. Guaranty Security Corp.,* 271 Mass. 533, 542, 171 N. E. 830 (1930). In *Brouwer v. Harbeck,* 9 N. Y. 589, 594 (1854), the court stated that at the time of enactment of a provision in the N. Y. Rev. Stat. of 1828 prohibiting preferences by a bank "when insolvent, or in contemplation of insolvency," insolvency had a well-known signification of inability to meet in the course of business liabilities existing and capable of being enforced.

[76] *Webb v. Sachs,* Fed. Cas. No. 17,325 (D. Ore. 1877) (Bankruptcy Act of 1867, §35; 14 Stat. 517, 534); see *Toof v. Martin,* 13 Wall. 40, 47 (1871); *Hussey v. Richardson-Roberts Dry Goods Co.,* 148 Fed. 598, 600 (C. C. A. 8th, 1906); 11 Ann. Cas. 452 (1909).

a general scale an insolvency test based on insufficiency of total assets to meet total liabilities.[77] That the Massachusetts dividend provision of 1830 intended to connote insolvency in the equity rather than the bankruptcy sense is further demonstrated by the subsequent history of that provision in Massachusetts. Until the enactment of the Bankruptcy Act of 1898, the Massachusetts provision on dividends continued merely to prohibit the payment of dividends while insolvent. In 1903, however, the act was amended to prohibit dividends "if the corporation is, or thereby is, rendered, bankrupt or insolvent." [78] The addition of the bankruptcy limitation was surplusage unless insolvency meant only the inability to meet debts as they matured.

In those jurisdictions which have the double insolvency-capital impairment form of the New York Manufacturing Act of 1848, and they are a majority of those states having insolvency provisions,[79] it is even clearer that the equity test of insolvency should be applied. By adding the additional capital impairment clause to the earlier Massachusetts insolvency provision, New York rendered the insolvency limitations redundant unless it was intended to proscribe dividends when a corporation was insolvent in the equity sense, even though its capital was not impaired under analogy to the bankruptcy rule.[80] It is unlikely that the New York legislature adverted to the effect its capital impairment amendment might have in making the equity test of insolvency clearly applicable, since the amendment seems to have been merely the result of superimposing a familiar New York principle upon a completely integrated Massachusetts regulation.[81] Yet the amendment was made, and, under the principle of construction which endeavors to give effect to all language of a statute, may properly be construed as an effective demonstration that it is the equity and not the bankruptcy test of insolvency that is to apply.

In no case dealing with the question whether the equity or the bankruptcy rule should be applied to a dividend matter has the court considered either the derivation of the statute under construction or

---

[77] 30 Stat. 544, §1, subs. 15. For the present provision, see 52 Stat. 840, §1, subs. 19 (1938).

[78] Mass. Acts and Resolves 1903, c. 437, §35.

[79] See §19, n. 59, *supra*.

[80] Assuming the bankruptcy test to be insufficiency of assets to pay liabilities excluding capital (see this section, n. 84, *infra*), the provision of the New York Manufacturing Act of 1848 that no dividends should be paid "which would diminish the amount of its capital stock" would make entirely unnecessary resorting to the bankruptcy test, since the capital would be impaired long before bankruptcy insolvency was reached.

[81] See §19, n. 58, *supra*.

the important question as to the meaning of insolvency at the time the statute was enacted.[82] Not only is it clear that these older American statutes were enacted with the equity test in mind, but it is also clear as a matter of principle that this is the sound interpretation for dividend purposes. It is in many ways much more important, from the standpoint of both stockholders and creditors, that the corporation keep itself in a position to meet its current obligations than that it maintain a theoretical liquidation position which will satisfy all creditors, but which when resorted to seldom does. Moreover, it is only the equity test which will mean anything in most jurisdictions, since other dividend provisions in almost all cases are more stringent than the bankruptcy test.

In a few states the question is expressly handled by statute. In Massachusetts and California the problem is covered by making the dividend illegal if the corporation is insolvent in either the equity or bankruptcy sense.[83] Bankruptcy insolvency means insufficient assets to meet all liabilities excluding capital.[84] In Illinois much the same situation prevails as under the New York Manufacturing Act of 1848. There is a double prohibition against payment when the dividend will render the corporation insolvent or impair its capital, or

---

[82] *Hofkin v. U. S. Smelting Co.,* 266 Fed. 679 (C. C. A. 3d, 1920), dealing with an older Pennsylvania statute of the Massachusetts type, is inconclusive as to which test applies. The court mentions accounting facts to support either view and then concludes generally that the corporation was not insolvent. Cf. *Childs v. Adams,* 43 Pa. Super. 239, 244 (1910) (similar statute; mere impairment of capital not enough to constitute insolvency; whether the bankruptcy or the equity test applicable not indicated); *Tradesman Publishing Co. v. Car Wheel Co.,* 95 Tenn. 634, 665, 32 S. W. 1097 (1895) (charter prohibited dividends when insolvent or which would diminish capital; the bankruptcy test of insolvency was adopted); *Wood v. National City Bank,* 24 F. (2d) 661, 662 (C. C. A. 2d, 1928) (where in the absence of an applicable statutory provision the bankruptcy test of insolvency was selected for common law purposes. See *Whitfield v. Kern,* 122 N. J. Eq. 332, 338, 344–345, 192 Atl. 48 (Ct. Err. & App. 1939) (suggesting possible liability in addition to statute for dividends paid when insolvent under the equity test).

[83] Mass. Laws Ann., c. 156, §37, for source see §19, n. 51, 52, 53, *supra;* Cal. Civ. Code (1937), §346.

[84] National Bankruptcy Act, §1, subs. 19; *Curtis v. Dade County Security Co.,* 30 F. (2d) 325 (C. C. A. 5th, 1929). See *Tepel v. Coleman,* 229 Fed. 300, 303 (D. Pa. 1914), aff'd 230 Fed. 63 (C. C. A. 3d, 1916); Weiner, *Theory of Anglo American Dividend Law: American Statutes and Cases,* 29 Col. L. Rev. 461, 466 (1929). Cf. *Miller v. Bradish,* 69 Iowa 278, 28 N. W. 594 (1886) (statute making stockholders liable for dividends leaving "insufficient funds to meet the liabilities of the corporation" construed to mean insufficient assets to meet liabilities excluding capital). Occasionally the mistake is made of including capital among the liabilities. See Levin, *Blind Spots in the Present Wisconsin General Corporation Statutes,* 1939 Wis. L. Rev. 173, 204; cf. 2 Bonbright, *Valuation of Property* (1937) 916.

when either of those situations already prevails.[85] Since there is no ambiguity, such as that in the early New York provision, with respect to the Illinois Act unequivocally providing a straight balance sheet surplus test, insolvency is necessarily used in the equity sense.[86] In the subsection of the Minnesota Business Corporation Act providing alternative authority for payment out of net earnings when there is no surplus, an exception is made in the case where assets of the corporation are less than the aggregate of its liabilities.[87] This section seems to contemplate the bankruptcy test in the situation where the capital is completely impaired and it is proposed to pay dividends out of current earnings. The Ohio Act simply provides that dividends shall not be paid when there is reasonable ground to believe the corporation will be unable to satisfy its obligations and liabilities (nothing being said as to their maturing).[88] Since Ohio has the balance sheet surplus rule as its general restriction, it seems reasonably clear that it was intended to enact the equity insolvency rule. New Hampshire has a provision different from that in any other state, and whether it amounts to an absolute prohibition against payment from capital, or merely a prohibition against payment from capital when the assets will be insufficient to meet corporate debts as they mature, is not entirely clear.[89] From the fact that the provision was originally derived from the insolvency clause in the Massachusetts Revised Statutes of 1836, it seems reasonable to suppose that the statute has the latter effect.[90]

Under Section 2 of the Uniform Fraudulent Conveyance Act, in force in almost all leading corporation states,[91] "a person" is insolvent when the present fair salable value of his assets is less than the amount required to pay his probable liability on existing debts as they become absolute and mature.

[85] 32 Ill. Ann. Stat. (Smith-Hurd 1935), §157.41.

[86] See Chicago Bar Assoc., *Illinois Business Corporation Act Ann.* (1934) 151; Spaeth, Book Review, 29 Ill. L. Rev. 821, 822 (1935). It does not seem that use of the bankruptcy rule could produce any legal effect. But see Ballantine, *A Critical Survey of the Illinois Business Corporation Act*, 1 Univ. of Chic. L. Rev. 357, 371 (1934).

[87] Minn. Stat. (Mason 1938 Supp.), §7492–21.

[88] Ohio Code Ann. (Baldwin 1938), §8623–38c.

[89] N. H. Pub. Laws (1926), c. 225, §79, provides that no dividend shall be paid out and no part of the capital stock withdrawn when the corporate property is insufficient or will thereby be rendered insufficient for the payment of all its debts. See also §§80, 81, 82.

[90] The earliest predecessor of the present provision is N. H. Laws, June Sess. 1837, c. 322, §21 [see also N. H. Laws, June Sess. 1846, c. 321, §2(4)], taken from Mass. Rev. Stat. (1836), c. 38, §23. For amendments to modern form see N. H. Gen. Stat. 1867, c. 135, §§3, 5, 6, 7.

[91] As to application thereof, see §19, *supra*.

Where the insolvency rule is applicable, it will make no difference whether the corporation has par or no-par stock, the result will be the same. If the ability to meet obligations as they mature is taken as the test of insolvency, the share structure of the corporation is wholly immaterial. If the bankruptcy rule of excess of assets over liabilities is the test, again the existence of no-par rather than par shares will be immaterial because the corporation's capital is excluded from liabilities considered.

Assuming that by statute or by force of a common law doctrine dividends cannot be declared when the corporation is insolvent, what is the effect on other general provisions regulating the declaration of dividends? If the insolvency test is the bankruptcy test and the state has a general capital impairment statute, the net effect of the insolvency provision will be to create no greater duty than existed without it, since observance of the capital impairment restriction automatically means compliance with the bankruptcy rule. If the bankruptcy test is applied in a net profits jurisdiction, it will prevent payment of dividends from current earnings in the extreme situation where assets are less than liabilities. But the corporation is not very apt to be either continuing its operations or showing net profits with such an asset position. On the other hand, if, as should be true in most jurisdictions, the test of insolvency is inability to meet obligations as they mature, the corporation may be prevented from paying dividends under either the balance sheet surplus test or the net profits test, even though it has met the general requirement as to existence of surplus or net profits. It is important to keep this in mind in considering the declaration of every dividend.

E. The Balance Sheet Surplus Test

21. Restriction to Excess of Assets over Liabilities Including Capital

In addition to limitations against payment of insolvency dividends based essentially on the doctrine against fraudulent conveyances, American corporation statutes from their inception have imposed restrictions peculiarly applicable to the corporation. The basic American statutory limitation has long been that against capital impairment, the rule that a corporation should not pay dividends from its capital. There are at least three possible interpretations of what is meant by a dividend which is paid from capital. It may mean a dividend leaving less net assets than the corporation originally received when it sold its stock, less net assets than the par or stated capital value of its stock, or less net assets than the corporation had at the opening of the accounting period in question.[92]

The oldest general dividend regulation statute in this country, the "Act to prevent fraudulent Bankruptcies by Incorporated Companies," adopted by New York in 1825, contained a provision prohibiting the division, withdrawal, or reduction of a corporation's capital stock.[93] This act is the forerunner of modern statutory provisions. The broadest and most unambiguous rule against the payment of dividends from capital is that recently adopted by modern statutes providing in so many words that dividends may not be paid when the corporation's assets are, or after payment will be, less than its liabilities including capital stock. In provisions of this type it is absolutely clear that a balance sheet surplus is the test of the fund available for dividends. This means that no dividends can be paid which would either be directly out of capital or at a time when capital is impaired, removing a serious question which arises under the earlier New York type provision merely providing against division and reduction of capital, without at the same time prohibiting dividends when capital is impaired by prior losses.

Among states which have enacted the general rule (frequently with varying additional restrictions) that dividends cannot be paid when corporate assets are less than corporate liabilities including capital, are: New York,[94] Ohio,[95] Pennsylvania,[96] Idaho,[97] Louisi-

---

[92] See §16(b), *supra*.

[93] N. Y. Laws 1825, c. 325, §2.

[94] N. Y. Stock Corp. Law, §58; N. Y. Laws 1939, c. 364. *Origin and principal amendments:* Laws 1825, c. 325, §2, see §7, *supra* (for early special charter precedents, see §6, n. 60); Rev. Stat. (1828), Pt. I, c. 18, Title 4, §2, see §7, n. 68, *supra;* Laws 1848, c. 40, §13; Laws 1890, c. 564, §23; Laws 1892, c. 688, §23; Laws 1901, c. 354, §23 (Consol. Laws of 1909, c. 59, §28); Laws 1923, c. 787, §58; Laws 1938, c. 685, §5. The present New York provision, in addition to prescribing the balance sheet surplus test, specifically provides that no corporation shall declare or pay a dividend which will impair its capital or while its capital is impaired.

[95] Ohio Code Ann. (Baldwin 1938), §8623-38; see Wright, *The New Ohio General Corporation Act,* 75 U. of Pa. L. R. 753 (1927). Under the Ohio Act the guiding principle is to prevent payment out of capital as specifically defined therein. Report of Committee on Revision of Ohio General Corporation Act (Dec. 1926) 33.

[96] 15 Purd. Pa. Stat. Ann., §2852-701 (but not out of paid-in surplus except on preferred, §2852-704). For Reviser's annotations, see Shockley, *Pennsylvania Corporation Laws 1933 Ann.* (1933) 84-88.

[97] Idaho Code Ann. §29-129 (taken like the Louisiana and Washington provisions from Uniform Business Corporation Act, §24 with revisions). For the entirely different form in early drafts of the Uniform Act authorizing dividends from "the surplus or net profits arising from the business," see *Handbook of National Conference of Commissioners on Uniform State Laws* (1924), p. 594.

ana,[98] Washington,[99] and Vermont.[100] The same result is reached in Illinois by a provision that no dividends shall be paid when the net assets are less than stated capital.[101]

Many other states which provide for dividends from the double alternative of balance sheet surplus or current net profits state the former alternative in terms of net assets in excess of capital, or excess of assets over liabilities including capital. Among these states are: Delaware,[102] Georgia,[103] Arkansas,[104] Kansas,[105] Virginia,[106] Tennessee,[107] and Florida.[108]

[98] La. Gen. Stat. (Dart. 1939), §1106.
[99] Wash. Rev. Stat. Ann. (Rem.), §3803–24. See Greenough and Ayer, *Funds Available for Corporate Dividends in Washington,* 9 Wash. L. Rev. 123 (1934).
[100] Vt. Pub. Laws (1933), §5850. *Source:* Vt. Laws 1853, No. 71, §§20, 21, taken from Conn. Laws 1836–37, c. 63, §§19, 20; Vt. Laws 1915, No. 141, §24.
[101] 32 Ill. Ann. Stat. (Smith-Hurd 1935), §157.41 (but not out of paid-in or reduction surplus except to preferred). Committee comment: that no dividend should be paid "when the net assets of the corporation are less than the stated capital, or which will reduce the net assets below the stated capital." See Ballantine, *A Critical Survey of the Illinois Business Act,* 1 Univ. of Chic. L. Rev. 357, 369 (1934). See also Katz, *The Illinois Business Corporation Act,* 12 Wis. L. Rev. 473, 475 (1937); Frese, *Property Rights of Stockholders under the 1933 Illinois Business Corporation Act,* 10 Acc. Rev. 136, 145–148 (1935). For criticism of the section, see Little, *Illinois Business Corporation Law,* 28 Ill. L. Rev. 997, 1014 (1934).
[102] Del. Rev. Code, c. 65, §34 (net assets in excess of capital). *Source:* 15 Del. Laws, c. 119, §10 (1875); 17 Del. Laws, c. 147, §7 (1883) (from N. J. Revision of Apr. 7, 1875, N. J. Rev. 1709–1877, p. 178, §7); 21 Del. Laws, c. 273, §18 (1899) (following N. J. Laws 1896, c. 185, §30); 22 Del. Laws, c. 167, §§34, 35 (1901); 35 Del. Laws, c. 85, §16 (1927) (first appearance of modern form); 36 Del. Laws, c. 135, §16 (1929) (additional amendments not bearing on this clause are considered elsewhere). For entry of the surplus and net profit alternatives into the N. J. Revision of Apr. 7, 1875, see §26, n. 194, 195, *infra.* In the absence of current net profits, the balance sheet surplus test was applied in *Vogtman v. Merchants Mtg. & Credit Co.,* 20 Del. Ch. 364, 178 Atl. 99 (1935).
[103] Ga. Code Ann. (1936), §§22–1835. *Source:* Ga. Laws 1937–38, p. 214, §16, as a modification of §34 of the Del. Gen. Corp. Law.
[104] Ark. Stat. (1937), §2183. *Source:* from Delaware with substantial changes, Ark. Acts 1927, c. 250, §22; Ark. Acts 1931, c. 255, §25. In 1931 present §2184 was also added (Ark. Acts 1931, c. 255, §26) introducing the further limitation that directors shall not pay out any part of the corporate capital.
[105] Kans. Laws 1939, c. 152, §80 (net assets in excess of capital), a modification of Del. Gen. Corp. Law, §34. For comment on these provisions by a member of the revision committee, see Lee, *Memorandum Explaining Differences Between Corporation Code and Existing Statutes,* 7 J. of Bar Assoc. of Kans. 260, 265 (1939).
[106] Va. Code (1936), §3840 (net assets in excess of capital). *Source:* Va. Acts 1836–37, c. 82, §6; c. 84, §13; c. 118, §26; Va. Code (1849), c. 57, §§30, 31; Va. Code (1860), c. 57, §§30, 31; Va. Acts 1932, c. 122.
[107] Tenn. Code Ann. (1934), §3737 (§3759 contains an older form of prohibition against payment from capital). *Source:* Tenn. Acts 1929, c. 90, §26.
[108] Fla. Comp. Gen. Laws (1927), §6549. *Source:* Fla. Acts 1925, c. 10,096, §23; substantially copied from Delaware. Connecticut has a provision prohibiting pay-

The important thing in conjunction with statutes of this class is the specific definition which is generally given to capital. This is either par value as to shares having par value, or the stated value, provided in various ways for shares having no-par value.[109] Thus, there is a definite figure to place on the balance sheet as the capital which may not be impaired and which determines the surplus from which alone dividends may be paid.

22. Restriction Against Division, Withdrawal, or Reduction of Capital

The dividend statutes in many states are still substantially in the form of the New York Act of 1825. Under these statutes it is by no means clear which of the three balance sheet tests should be held to apply. The Act of 1825 prohibited the payment of dividends except from the surplus profits arising from the business of the corporation, and also prohibited the division, withdrawal, or reduction of capital stock.[110] This provision was copied by California in 1849 and became the ultimate basis of Section 309 of the California Civil Code of 1872.[111] While the recent revision of the California General Corporation Law has resulted in abandonment of this test in California,[112] other western states which copied Section 309 of the Code of 1872 still retain, with minor modifications, the basic provisions of the New York Act of 1825. These states are: Oklahoma,[113] Montana,[114] North Dakota,[115] South Dakota,[116] Utah,[117] and

---

ment except from net profits or actual surplus unless in accordance with provisions allowing reduction of capital stock. Conn. Gen. Stat. (1930), §3386. The previous history of the section tends to indicate that the surplus alternative is based on the capital impairment theory. *Source:* Conn. Pub. Laws 1836–37, c. 63, §§19, 20 (taken from Mass. Rev. Stat. 1836, c. 38, §§21, 23) ; Conn. Pub. Acts 1867, c. 120, §1 ; Conn. Gen. Stat. (1875), p. 280, §16; Conn. Pub. Acts 1901, c. 157, §§32, 33 (first introduction of the net profit and actual surplus limitations; apparently patterned after N. J. Laws 1896, c. 185, §30) ; Conn. Pub. Acts 1903, c. 194, §5.

[109] See §§45, 45.1, *infra.*

[110] See §7, n. 62, *supra.*

[111] Cal. Stat., 1st Sess. 1849, c. 128, §13; Cal. Stat. 1853, c. 65, §13; Cal. Civ. Code (1872), §309.

[112] Cal. Civ. Code (1937) §§346, 346a.

[113] Okla. Stat. Ann. (Perm. Ed.), §18–106. *Source:* Okla. Stat. (1890), §983; Dak. Terr. Rev. Civ. Code (1877), §409, taken from Cal. Civ. Code (1872), §309.

[114] Mont. Rev. Code (1935), §5939. Originally enacted, Mont. Civ. Code (1895), §438. See *Continental Oil Co. v. Montana Concrete Co.,* 63 Mont. 223, 228, 207 Pac. 116 (1922).

[115] N. D. Comp. Laws (Supp. 1913–25), §§4543–44. Originally Dak. Terr. Rev. Civ. Code (1877), §409, and continued in N. D. Code (1895), §§2891–92, as amended N. D. Laws 1919, c. 100.

[116] S. D. Code 1939, §11.0706. Originally Dak. Terr. Rev. Civ. Code (1877), §409.

[117] Utah Rev. Stat. (1933), §18–2–17. North Carolina authorizes dividends from

New Mexico.[118] The National Banking Act regulations for dividends should probably also be included with this type statute. No dividend out of capital is permitted, and no dividend greater than the net profits then on hand deducting losses and bad debts.[119] The difficulty sometimes encountered by engrafting provisions from the corporation laws of other states is illustrated by the present dividend sections in the Nevada General Corporation Law. The oldest dividend provision, Section 1674, prohibiting the payment of dividends from capital,[120] was permitted to remain in the law substantially unchanged when the modern Delaware alternative sources of net earnings or balance sheet surplus were recently added by Section 1625.[121]

From the statutory language and dividend history antedating adoption of the New York Act of 1825, it is extremely difficult to determine whether the provision for payment of dividends out of "surplus profits arising from the business" [122] means anything different from the provision prohibiting the division or withdrawal of "capital stock." In other words, do statutes of this character fall within a double alternative rule such as that clearly authorized by the modern acts, or do they fall in the category of capital impairment statutes which allow only one fund for the payment of dividends?

Considering the question first from the standpoint of statutory language, these enactments as a rule do not phrase the balance sheet

---

surplus or net profits arising from business but not when debts exceed two-thirds of its assets, nor may capital be reduced, divided, or withdrawn. N. C. Code (1939), §1179. In Oregon the test is net profits or surplus. Ore. Code Ann. (1930), §25–219. *Source:* Ore. Gen. Laws (Deady 1866), Act of Oct. 14, 1862, p. 658, §15; Ore. Laws 1925, c. 291, §1.

[118] N. Mex. Stat. (1929), §32–135 (also surplus or net profits alternative). *Source:* N. Mex. Terr. Laws 1905, c. 79, §34, taken from N. J. Laws 1896, c. 185, §30.

[119] 12 U. S. C. A., §56. *Source:* 12 Stat. 665, §44 (1863); 13 Stat. 110, §38 (1864); R. S. 5204.

[120] Nev. Comp. Laws (Hillyer 1929), §1674. *Source:* Nev. Stat. 1864–65, c. 111, §13 (copied from Cal. Stat. 1853, c. 65, §13), as amended Nev. Stat. 1866, c. 91, p. 188. Nev. Acts 1903, c. 88, §§66, 68; Nev. Stat. 1925, c. 177, §75; Nev. Stat. 1931, c. 224, §9.

[121] Nev. Comp. Laws (Hillyer 1929), §1625. *Source:* Nev. Stat. 1925, c. 177, §26; Nev. Stat. 1931, c. 224, §8. With §1623 specifically defining the amount which shall be assigned to capital, there seems to be a direct conflict between §§1625 and 1674 and doubt whether the latter prevents payment from current net profits when there is a capital impairment. Missouri has a special section prohibiting corporations having no par stock from paying dividends out of capital or anything except net profits or surplus earnings. 3 Mo. Stat. Ann. (Perm. Ed.), §5107.

[122] The prohibition against declaring dividends "except from the surplus profits" has always been assumed to be the equivalent of an express grant to pay out of surplus profits.

surplus provision in the alternative as is done in the modern revisions, but it exists as a mandatory additional limitation. The dividend cannot in any event impair capital. No construction can, therefore, be given to surplus profits which would permit a dividend resulting in a direct payment from capital. The surplus profits provision cannot exceed the power given by the balance sheet surplus limitation, because the restriction against impairing capital exists as an additional limitation on dividends from surplus profits.

The really important question is the date as of which the statute speaks when it says that there shall be no division of capital. Does it mean the value of property received at the beginning of the enterprise (or whenever subsequently increased by sale of additional stock), or does it mean the par value of the shares, or only the actual capital at the beginning of the particular accounting period?

Unlike present statutes, such as the New York Stock Corporation Law, which make perfectly clear that capital means a fixed amount equal to the par or stated value of the shares at issuance,[123] the statutes considered in this section leave this difficult question completely open.

22.1. Original Consideration Received Less or Greater Than Par or Stated Value of Stock.

When the issue as to the undefined meaning of capital in dividend statutes has been a conflict between par value or stated value and dollar value of consideration received for shares, it is held that capital means the value of the consideration received, and not the par value of the shares, where the consideration received is less than par, and possibly also if it is more than par.

One of the most important cases in the law of dividends is *Goodnow v. American Writing Paper Company.*[124] There the corporation purchased property at a grossly excessive valuation in exchange for its stock. When it was later proposed to declare a dividend, the present value of its assets was less than the aggregate of its debts and the par value of its stock, but there was an excess of gross earnings over operating expenses of the current year larger than the dividend, and the present value of assets exceeded the *actual* value of assets with which the corporation began business by an amount at least equal to the proposed dividend. The applicable New Jersey statute provided that directors of the corporation should not pay dividends except from its surplus, or from the net profits arising

---

[123] See §21, *supra.*
[124] 73 N. J. Eq. 692, 69 Atl. 1014 (Ct. Err. & App. 1908).

from the business, nor should they divide, withdraw, or in any way pay to the stockholders any part of the capital stock or reduce its capital stock.[125]

In denying a stockholder an injunction, it was held the dividend could be paid. First, the statute provided two funds from which dividends might be paid—surplus and net profits. There were net profits, whether net profits be considered the difference between current gross earnings and current operating expenses, or as the difference between the present value of the assets and the value of assets at the commencement of business. Second, the clause against division and withdrawal of capital was not being violated. Capital stock means the property invested and not par value, because only actual assets can be divided. Hence, not the par value at time of issuance, but actual value, is the capital which cannot be divided. So if the stock issued is watered, it is not necessary to squeeze the water.

Under somewhat different statutory provisions the same result was reached in two other leading cases—*Peters v. U. S. Mortgage Company*[126] and *Guaranty Trust Company v. Grand Rapids, Grand Haven and Muskegon Railway Co.*[127] In the former case the Delaware statute in addition to a provision for payment of dividends out of surplus or net profits, provided capital was not divided or paid to stockholders,[128] contained another section authorizing dividends out of the whole of its accumulated profits in excess of an amount reserved over the capital stock paid in.[129] The court relied upon the provision in excess of capital stock paid in, construing it to mean the consideration actually received on the sale of stock and not the par value. Furthermore, the Delaware law had been amended in 1917 to strike out provisions previously a part thereof prohibiting the withdrawal or reduction of capital stock.[130] The court, therefore, had a basis for treating the clause that capital stock should not be

---

[125] N. J. Laws 1904, c. 143.

[126] 13 Del. Ch. 11, 114 Atl. 598 (1921); see also *Merchants & Insurers' Reporting Co. v. Schroeder*, 39 Cal. App. 226, 229, 178 Pac. 540 (1918).

[127] 7 F. Supp. 511 (W. D. Mich. 1931), modified on other grounds and as modified affirmed *sub nom. United Light & Power Co. v. Grand Rapids Trust Co.*, 85 F. (2d) 331 (C. C. A. 6th, 1936); *cert. gr.* on petition of receiver, 299 U. S. 534 (1936); *dism.* per stipulation, 299 U. S. 618 (1936); *cert. den.* on petition of United Light & Power Co., 299 U. S. 591 (1936) [comment, 31 Ill. L. Rev. 670 (1937)]. In jurisdictions like New York providing for payment of dividends out of a balance sheet surplus and specifically providing that capital shall be a given amount, the actual value of the consideration received would seem to be immaterial in determining what constitutes capital. See §21, *supra*.

[128] 29 Del. Laws, c. 113, §14 (1917).

[129] 22 Del. Laws, c. 167, §34.

[130] See n. 128, *supra*.

divided or paid to stockholders except in accordance with the provisions of the act as meaning stock dividends should not be paid
except out of surplus or net profits as previously defined. The statute
in *Guaranty Trust Company v. Grand Rapids, Grand Haven and
Muskegon Railway Company* followed the New York Manufacturing Act of 1848, prohibiting dividends while insolvent "or which
would diminish the amount of its capital stock." Under this type of
capital impairment provision, a much stronger case can be made for
the position that it does not preclude dividends from profits while
capital is impaired, but merely prohibits dividends when there are no
profits, thereby necessarily requiring capital to be diminished.[131]

Is it significant that the statutes in the *Goodnow* and *Peters* cases
contained alternative sources for dividend payments, surplus, and
net profits, in addition to the clause against capital reduction, whereas
the statutes patterned on the New York Act of 1825 merely have the
single source of surplus profits or net profits? It would seem that
this should make no difference, since the courts were concerned with
construing the prohibition against reduction of capital stock which
is the same in both types of statutes. The question as to kind of profits
from which dividends may be paid, assuming capital stock to mean
the actual value of property received, is entirely separate. Capital
could hardly be taken to mean one thing for the clause against division and reduction and another thing for determining surplus profits,
if surplus profits be taken only to mean a balance sheet surplus.[132]

Ordinarily the meaning of capital is raised in cases where the
corporation has received less dollar value of property than the par
value of stock issued, and it is sought to pay dividends out of profits
in spite of the impairment of capital computed on the basis of par.
The converse situation may also take place. Stock may be sold at a
premium, when it becomes material to determine whether the capital
is the entire consideration received rather than the par value. In
Merchants and Insurers' Reporting Co. v. Schroeder, with a statute
of the type here considered applicable, the court held that the entire
consideration received was capital and unavailable for a dividend.[133]

---

[131] See §23, *infra.* But *Shields v. Hobart,* 172 Mo. 491, 517–518, 72 S. W. 669
(1902), holds that capital under this type statute means the par value of stock and
not the consideration received.

[132] "Surplus profits" may have a meaning more nearly equivalent to earned surplus, see §25, *infra.*

[133] 39 Cal. App. 226, 178 Pac. 540 (1918). The case was decided under Cal.
Civ. Code, §309 (Deering 1909). The court seemed to rely both on the clause
against distribution of capital and the clause against paying dividends except from
"the surplus profits arising from the business." There is a current movement among
some accountants in favor of always treating the consideration on the sale of stock

The case is of questionable authority, and it is doubtful that it would be followed.

22.2. Capital Impaired at Opening of Current Accounting Period

Statutes patterned on the New York Act of 1825 do not specifically provide that dividends shall not be paid when capital has been previously impaired; they merely prohibit the division, withdrawal, or reduction of capital stock. There is a difference between paying a dividend directly out of capital when there are no profits and paying a dividend out of profits even though capital may have been impaired in prior accounting periods. Modern statutes for the most part recognize this distinction and are either so phrased as to expressly prohibit the payment of dividends from current earnings when there is a capital impairment, through provisions requiring payment out of balance sheet surplus,[134] or else expressly permitting the payment.[135] This precise distinction was appreciated and used in the special charters which antedated the New York Act of 1825. When it was desired to prohibit the payment of dividends from profits, where there had been a preceding capital impairment, it was expressly stipulated that dividends might be paid from profits, but that in case of losses diminishing the capital stock no dividends should be paid until a sum equal to such diminution, and arising from the profits of the corporation, should have been added to the capital.[136] Provisions of this character were common in special charters to New York insurance companies.[137] Yet the Act of 1825 made no attempt to provide that dividends should not be made while capital was impaired. On the contrary it provided no dividend should impair capital. Some light may be gleaned as to the meaning of this clause from earlier charters which must have been used as precedents in drafting the Act of 1825. What is apparently the first corporate provision against impairment of capital, the 1791 by-law of the Bank of United States, provided that if the directors should make "a dividend exceeding the profits of the bank and thereby diminish the capital stock," they should be liable.[138] One of the very first of the special charters containing a general capital impairment provision

as capital in its entirety. See e.g. Broad, *Some Comments on Surplus,* 66 J. of Accountancy, 215 (1938); but see, Kester, *Principles of Accounting* (3d Rev. Ed. 1930) 421.

[134] See §21, *supra.*

[135] See §§26–28, *infra.*

[136] Charter of Insurance Company of North America, 3 Dallas Laws of Pa. 1790–95 (1795) 489, §7(8); see §6, n. 42, *supra.*

[137] See Appendix, Note F.

[138] See §4, n. 26, *supra.*

provided that directors should not "make any dividend of any part of the capital stock of the said company, but only the net profits thereof." [139] Contemporaneous Pennsylvania charters provided for dividends out of profits which should "in no case exceed the amount of the net profit actually acquired by the company; so that the capital stock shall never be impaired by dividends." [140] From these provisions [141] it seems reasonably clear that when the New York legislature in 1825 authorized the payment of dividends from surplus profits but not out of capital, it meant that the dividend must be from profits so as not to be directly from capital, rather than that no dividend should be paid if the balance sheet should show an impairment over the entire history of the company despite contemporaneous earnings. [142]

With the question still open in many states which derive their law from the New York Act of 1825, the antecedent background of that act may be relied on to authorize the payment of dividends from net profits even though capital is impaired. This seems reasonably to have been the original intention, is clearly made the law in modern acts, and from the economic standpoint is the sound approach. [143]

The case law bearing directly on this question is meager. It is quite clear that a payment which impairs capital directly cannot be made. [144] Whether that means capital as of the time of stock issuance,

[139] Newark Banking & Insurance Company Charter, N. J. Acts 1803, c. 109, §14-3. See §6, n. 45, *supra*.

[140] Philadelphia Bank Charter, see §6, n. 51, *supra*.

[141] For the probable influence of these provisions on the New York Act of 1825, see §7, *supra*.

[142] Some indication of the meaning of surplus profits may be derived from considering the provisions in the Revised Statutes of 1828 with respect to Monied Corporations. They were also authorized to pay dividends from "surplus profits arising from the business of the corporation" but prohibited from dividing or withdrawing any part of the capital stock. The act further significantly provided that "in order to ascertain the surplus profits, from which alone a dividend can be made, there shall be charged in the account of profit and loss and deducted from the actual profits" certain enumerated items. N. Y. Rev. Stat. (1828), Pt. 1, c. 18, Title 2, Art. 1, §§1, 3. Thus surplus profits meant at the time of the adoption of the Revised Statutes profit as shown by the profit and loss account and not by the balance sheet. Furthermore, it was specifically provided that in cases of losses impairing the capital, no dividends should be paid until the deficit should be made good either out of recoveries or subsequent profits. §4. No similar provision was made in the general corporation dividend section which was copied directly from the Act of 1825.

[143] In strict balance sheet surplus jurisdictions, the stockholder not only stakes his capital, but guarantees the maintenance of assets equal to capital when the general market level falls, a cause for which he is no more responsible than the creditor. See §9.1, *supra*.

[144] *Small v. Sullivan*, 245 N. Y. 343, 157 N. E. 261 (1927); *Wesp v. Muckle*, 136 App. Div. 241, 120 N. Y. S. 976 (4th Dept. 1910), aff'd 201 N. Y. 527, 94 N. E.

or as of the beginning of the current accounting period, is seldom
stated. There is authority that under a statute of the type providing
that dividends shall not exceed net profits, so that the capital shall
not be impaired by dividends, capital deficits of prior operating
periods must be made up out of earnings before further dividends
are paid.[145] On the other hand, in *Titus v. Piggly Wiggly Corporation*, the corporation had a capital impairment together with current
earnings, but the earnings were insufficient to dispose of the deficit.[146]
It also had an unrealized appreciation gain on intangibles which, if
available for wiping out the deficit, would free the current earnings.
Creditors and certain stockholders contended that the deficit had to
be eliminated under the applicable Delaware law [147] out of earnings.
The court held, however, that the losses might be charged against
the capital surplus created from intangibles, thereby freeing the
earned surplus for dividends. In pursuance of the reasoning in
Goodnow v. American Writing Paper Company, that there can be
no division of capital which the corporation did not receive in the
first instance,[148] it would seem there can be no division of capital
dissipated by losses in a prior accounting period and the proposed
payment is made from surplus profits arising from the corporation's
business.[149] This result has been reached in England where there is

110 (1911) ; *Berryman v. Bankers Life Ins. Co.,* 117 App. Div. 730, 102 N. Y. S.
695 (1st Dept. 1907); *Ulness v. Dunnell,* 61 N. D. 95, 237 N. W. 208 (1931)
(corporation insolvent in bankruptcy sense after the dividend) ; *Siegman v. Electric
Vehicle Co., 72* N. J. Eq. 403, 65 Atl. 910 (1907) (Ct. Err. & App.). For the English
common law doctrine in accord see *Ammonia Soda Co., Ltd. v. Chamberlain,*
(1918) 1 Ch. 266, 273, and §25, n. 179, *infra.* But a corporation formed solely for
the purpose of liquidating assets may pay dividends from capital irrespective of
the statutory prohibition, at least where no rights of creditors are involved. *Baldwin
v. Miller & Lux,* 152 Cal. 454, 92 Pac. 1030 (1907) (construing former Cal. Civ.
Code, §309). The rule against payment from capital in this type of statute applies
to preferred stockholders although they are not expressly referred to therein.
Cartwright v. Albuquerque Hotel Co., 36 N. Mex. 189, 11 P. (2d) 261 (1932).

[145] *Branch v. Kaiser,* 291 Pa. 543, 140 Atl. 498 (1928). In *Small v. Sullivan,*
245 N. Y. 343, 350, 157 N. E. 261 (1927), where there was no evidence of current
profits from which the dividend might be paid, the court said the object of the provision against capital distributions was to prevent a reduction of "the value of its
assets below the sum limited for its capital in its charter." For the view of an
accountant that a capital impairment restriction is more than a prohibition against
a direct impairment of capital, and includes also a prohibition against payment
from current earnings while capital is impaired, see Littleton, *Business Profits as a
Legal Basis for Dividends,* 16 Harv. Bus. Rev. 51, 53 (1938).

[146] *Titus v. Piggly Wiggly Corp.,* 2 Tenn. App. 184 (1925).

[147] 22 Del. Laws, c. 167, §§34, 35, authorized payment out of "accumulated profits"
(§34) and out of "surplus or net profits" but otherwise a division or payment of
capital stock was prohibited (§35).

[148] See §22.1, n. 124, *supra.*

[149] As to whether the restriction to payments from surplus profits in this type
of statute means an earned surplus or current net profits, see §25, *infra.*

no statutory prohibition against payment from capital, but where the court recognizes such a common law restriction.[150]

Even if capital is taken to mean the amount of capital as it stands at the opening of the accounting period, it is to be observed that the test of current profits must be a balance sheet test by comparison of balance sheets at the opening and close of the period, rather than a profit and loss statement test, since the statutory prohibition against division of capital at least requires that the capital be kept intact during the accounting period.[151] This is an important difference between statutes of this type and statutes of the Delaware type which may possibly permit dividends from a current profit and loss statement profit without taking into account either in whole or in part capital losses during the accounting period.

23. Restriction Against Diminishing or Impairing Capital

The argument in favor of permitting dividends on the basis of capital computed at the opening of the accounting period is, if anything, stronger in those jurisdictions functioning under the New York Manufacturing Act provision of 1848 which only prohibits a corporation from declaring dividends "which would diminish the amount of its capital stock." [152] Here, as a matter of statutory history it is quite clear that "diminish" means a withdrawal when there are no profits so that there is necessarily a reduction of capital.[153]

Section 13 of the New York Manufacturing Act of 1848 was copied by many states and still survives in Maryland,[154] Colorado,[155] Kentucky,[156] and Wyoming.[157] The statutes in some other states,

[150] *Ammonia Soda Co., Ltd. v. Chamberlain,* (1918) 1 Ch. 266, 296. The English statutory rule merely limits dividends to "profits" (see §25, n. 178, *infra*). For this reason English dividend authorities are often inapposite precedents, but there are certain points such as accounting treatment of certain assets not dependent on statute, or points of general agreement, where English decisions may be relied on. For the English rule against direct payment from capital, see §25, n. 179, *infra*.

[151] The principle has been recognized in England. *Foster v. New Trinidad Lake Asphalt Co.,* (1901) 1 Ch. 208.

[152] N. Y. Laws 1848, c. 40, §13, see §19, n. 57, *supra*.

[153] See §22.2, n. 136–140, *supra*.

[154] Md. Ann. Code (1935 Supp.), c. 23, §87, as enacted Laws Maryland 1931, c. 480. *Source:* Md. Laws 1852, c. 338, §11 (prior to this act Maryland had its own independent general act making directors liable for dividends out of capital, Md. Laws 1838–39, c. 267, §13); Md. Laws 1908, c. 240, §50.

[155] Colo. Stat. Ann. (1935), c. 41, §34. Original enactment, Colo. Terr. Laws, 3d Sess. 1864, p. 49, §16. The section has since been amended to cover officers and agents as well as directors participating in the declaration.

[156] Ky. Stat. Ann. (Carroll 1936), §548. The provision was originally enacted in 1 Ky. Acts, 1853–54, p. 179, §16 (an earlier manufacturing corporation regulation act had adopted the Massachusetts rule of 1836, Ky. Acts 1840, p. 49, §17) and adopted in its present form, Ky. Laws 1891–93, c. 171, §11.

[157] Wyo. Rev. Stat. (1931), §28–131. *Source:* Wyo. Terr. Laws, 1st Terr. Sess.

while not in the form of the Act of 1848, have substantially the same effect. Among the latter are the provisions in West Virginia [158] and Wisconsin.[159] The Maine dividend statute, authorizing the payment of dividends out of profit, but not so as to impair capital,[160] is particularly interesting, because it is descended directly from the decision in *Wood v. Dummer*.[161]

The state of the statutory dividend law in Missouri is extremely unsatisfactory and badly in need of modern revision. In 1845 Missouri copied the basic insolvency dividend provision of Chapter 38 of the Massachusetts Revised Statutes of 1836,[162] applicable to corporations generally. In 1849 it copied the insolvency-capital impairment provisions of the New York Manufacturing Act of 1848, making the latter applicable to manufacturing, mining, and chemical corporations.[163] Both still exist in the present law, the New York type of provision being made specifically applicable to mining, manufacturing, chemical, smelting, and petroleum corporations among others.[164]

Again there are few decisions construing statutory provisions of this general character. If there are no net earnings so that the pay-

---

1869, p. 239, §15. Cf. Miss. Code Ann. (1930), §4149, which resembles in some respects the New York Act of 1848. For derivation of this provision, see Miss. Rev. Code (1857), c. 35, Art. 33, and Miss. Ann. Code (Thompson 1892), §852.

[158] W. Va. Code (1937), §§3082, 3090. *Source:* W. Va. Acts, 1st Sess. 1863, c. 83, §§38, 39, taken from Va. Code (1860), c. 57, §§30, 31; W. Va. Code (1932), §3090; W. Va. Acts 1935, c. 24.

[159] Wis. Stat. (1937), §182.19. *Source:* Wis. Laws 1850, c. 232, §19 (insurance corporations); Wis. Laws 1852, c. 479, §40 (banks); Wis. Laws 1853, c. 68, §§21, 22; Wis. Laws 1872, c. 144, §20; Wis. Rev. Stat. (1878), §1765; Wis. Laws 1893, c. 57; Wis. Laws 1925, c. 398. The Wisconsin statute contains the unusual provision that no dividend shall be paid until at least 50 per cent of the authorized capital has been paid in. In *Goetz v. Williams*, 206 Wis. 561, 240 N. W. 181 (1932), it was held that stockholders receiving dividends when 50 per cent of the capital had not as yet been paid in were liable to the trustee in bankruptcy under this section and §180.06. Generally see Levin, *Blind Spots in the Present Wisconsin General Corporation Statutes*, 1939 Wis. L. Rev. 173, 203; Notes, Limitations on Dividends, 8 Wis. L. Rev. 338, 10 Wis. L. Rev. 269, taking the view that under this section of the law dividends cannot be paid from current profits when capital is impaired.

[160] Me. Rev. Stat. (1930), c. 56, §§37, 102, as amended by Me. Laws 1933, c. 53.

[161] Me. Acts (1828), c. 385, §3, incorporated with modifications in Me. Rev. Stat. (1840), c. 78, §§15, 16; Me. Laws 1848, c. 64, §1; Me. Rev. Stat. (1857), c. 48, §10; Me. Acts and Resolves 1871, c. 205, §2.

[162] Mo. Rev. Stat. (1845), c. 34, Art. 1, §19, as amended Mo. Laws 1865, p. 20, §16.

[163] Mo. Laws 1849, p. 18, §13, as amended Mo. Laws 1865, p. 64, §5.

[164] 3 Mo. Stat. Ann., §§4569, 4942. For a case treating both provisions as prohibiting the payment of dividends from capital, see *Hodde v. Nobbe*, 204 Mo. App. 109, 122, 221 S. W. 130 (1920).

ment is directly from capital, it violates the prohibition against diminution.[165] On the other hand, if there exists a balance sheet surplus even though it may not arise from earnings, a dividend may be paid.[166] No case seems ever to have passed upon the right to pay dividends from current net profits even though the capital is impaired.[167]

24. Effect of Stock Without Par Value

The fact that a corporation is capitalized on a non-par stock basis [168] does not remove the necessity for considering restrictions against payment of dividends from capital. In most jurisdictions no-par stock will be represented on the balance sheet by a capital entry of some amount. Some portion of the consideration received on the sale of such stock must, under many statutes, be allocated to stated capital.[169] This item of stated capital occupies the same position on the balance sheet, and is subject to the same restrictions so far as dividends are concerned, as the entry for capital where the corporation's stock has a par value.

Stock without par value complicates the declaration of dividends in balance sheet surplus jurisdictions because of the new item of paid-in surplus which it introduces. Although paid-in surplus appears on the balance sheet as an item entirely distinct from capital, it is in fact part of the stockholder's capital contribution and its availability for dividend purposes must be colored by this fact. Where, as in New York, the test is a plain and simple excess of assets over liabilities including capital, paid-in surplus falls within the excess and is available. In other jurisdictions which construe their statutes as permitting dividends from a balance sheet surplus, the premium paid on par value stock has been considered available for dividends, and presumably the same result would follow as to paid-in surplus on no-par stock. Many states in the adoption of recent statutes have, however, limited the use of paid-in surplus for dividends. The availability of various types of unearned surplus,

---

[165] *Rorke v. Thomas,* 56 N. Y. 559 (1874); *Hamblock v. Clipper Lawn Mower Co.,* 148 Ill. App. 618 (1909).

[166] *Haggard v. Lexington Utilities Co.,* 260 Ky. 261, 84 S. W. (2d) 84 (1935) (reduction surplus composed of earnings after impairment but before reduction).

[167] For an opinion that such dividends might be paid under an earlier Illinois statute of this type, see Revisers' comment on the new Illinois Business Corporation Law, Chicago Bar Association, Ill. Business Corporation Act (1934) 152, 164.

[168] One survey shows that 85 per cent of the large modern industrial and public utility companies have one or more classes of no-par stock. Dewing, *Corporation Securities,* 66 (1934).

[169] The various statutes are discussed in §45.1, *infra.*

including paid-in surplus, is a difficult question and must be given separate consideration, since it affects generally statutes of both the balance sheet surplus type and the net profits type.[170]

F. The Net Profits Test

25. Restriction to Profits

A provision for the payment of dividends from profits, without other alternatives, is the oldest form of dividend limitation in both England and this country, and was the most common provision used in early special charters.[171] One of the most troublesome questions in dividend history is the meaning of such a provision limiting dividends merely to profits. Only in Texas today is the dividend regulation in this form.[172] In jurisdictions which still retain the provision of the New York Act of 1825, the fund available is "surplus profits arising from the business of the corporation." [173] In many other states, some form of profits appears as an alternative fund to a balance sheet surplus. The necessary comparison implied between profits and surplus in statutes of this latter character gives content to the meaning of profits which it may not have standing alone.

At least several accounting methods may be used when the test is only profits or surplus profits. First, profits may mean the ordinary balance sheet excess of assets over liabilities including capital—in short, the same test employed for determining the fund available under the capital impairment rule. Secondly, it may mean the current net earnings of the corporation. This in turn may permit of varied interpretations. Does profits mean gross receipts less current expenses? Or are the net earnings to be determined by the difference between balance sheet net assets at the opening of the accounting period and balance sheet net assets at the close, disregarding capital impairments occurring prior to the opening of the period? Thus, the simple provision for distribution from profits might conceivably call for application of any one of the accounting methods applied under the varying statutes already reviewed.

Historically, it was the practice of corporations operating under charters providing for payment out of profits to use either the simple receipts and disbursements method [174] or the balance sheet surplus

---

[170] See §§29, 30, infra.

[171] See §2, 4, and 5, supra.

[172] Tex. Stat. (Vern. 1936), Art. 1329.

[173] For statutes of this character, see §22, supra.

[174] There is evidence that the receipts and disbursements method was in general use at least up to 1650, and probably much later. The records of the Mines Royal

test,[175] with a tendency to favor the former. The charter of the Hallowell and Augusta Bank, involved in *Wood v. Dummer,* contained a provision of the profits type.[176] But the court, in holding the capital impairment rule applicable to its affairs, made no mention anywhere in its opinion of this provision.

One thing is clear judicially, that a provision for payment from profits requires the existence of earnings and prevents a payment

---

for 1576 show that against gross sales two debits were set off, "the whole charges of the work this year" and "sundry other debts owing by the mines in divers ways." 2 Scott, *Joint Stock Companies to 1720* (1912) 392–393. Under the 1620 charter of the New River Company, the treasurer was to distribute as dividends the "clear gain and profit thereby arising, all necessary charges and expenses and the officers' fees and allowances first deducted," one moiety to the king and the other to the shareholders. Carr, *Select Charters of Trading Companies* (28 Selden Society, 1913) 106, 112. There was early application of this method in America. The charter of the Massachusetts Bank contained no dividend section, but the bank's by-laws limited payments to profits. Mass. Laws and Resolves 1782–83 (1890 Repr.), 1783–c. 25, p. 558; Gras, *Massachusetts First National Bank of Boston* (1934) 222–223, 228. Although using a double-entry ledger in 1784, no record of a balance sheet appears until thirteen years later, during which time the bank paid dividends based on profit and loss statements. MSS 781 (1784–1904), M. 414, v. 31; Gras, *supra* at pp. 29–30, 82 n. 58. The payments were charged by a debit to profit and loss. MSS 781 (1784–1906), M 414, v. 31, p. 135; v. 34, p. 9. Beginning in 1841 income statements, but no balance sheets, were set forth in directors' minutes as dividends were declared. MSS 781 (1784–1904), M. 414, v. 9, Meeting of Directors, Sept. 23, 1841. In many other cases, where charters contained no dividend section or limited payment to profits, the receipts and disbursements method was exclusively used. Boston & Providence Railroad, Rep. of June 6, 1849, p. 11 (charter, 7 Mass. Spec. Laws 1830–37, p. 134); Boston & Worcester Railroad, Rep. of June 6, 1842, p. 14 (charter, 7 Mass. Spec. Laws, *supra* at 152); Conn. River Railroad, Second Ann. Rep. (1847), p. 4 (charter, N. H. Laws, June Sess. 1848, c. 661, incorporating by reference, N. H. Rev. Stat. 1842, c. 142); Western Railroad Corporation, Tenth Ann. Rep. (1845), pp. 13, 31 (charter, 7 Mass. Spec. Laws, *supra* at p. 344); Suffolk Bank, MSS 781 (1818–1904), S46, v. 5, Directors' Meetings of Feb. 19, 1831 and Sept. 14, 1831 (charter, 5 Mass. Spec. Laws 1814–22, p. 214, incorporating 4 Mass. Spec. Laws 1806–14, p. 370, §3–10th); Union Canal Co., Ann. Reps., Feb. 4, 1851, p. 13, Feb. 7, 1854, p. 11 (charter, Pa. Acts 1810–11, p. 226, §21); Southwestern Railroad Bank, Proceedings of Stockholders of S. C. Railroad Co. and Southwestern Railroad Bank (Feb. 11–13, 1845), p. 11 (charter, S. C. Acts 1836, c. 2, §16). (All manuscript references are to materials in the Baker Library of the Harvard Business School.)

[175] Bank of United States, 19 Ann. Cong. 456–461 [charter, 1 Stat. 191, §7 (14)]; Bunker Hill Bank, MSS Directors' Records Mar. 21, 1826 (charter, Mass. Laws, May Sess. 1825, c. 53, incorporating 4 Mass. Spec. Laws 1806–14, p. 370, §3–10th); Boston Manufacturing Co., MSS Directors' Rec. Oct. 20, 1813 to Oct. 4, 1825, Meetings of Sept. 21, 1818 and Sept. 29, 1819 (no dividend provision in charter, 4 Mass. Spec. Laws 1806–14, p. 466, incorporating Mass. Laws, Jan. Sess. 1809, c. 65; by-laws authorized directors to "declare dividends," MSS Stockholders' Minutes, Meeting of Oct. 18, 1813); Morris Canal & Banking Co., Rep. of Apr. 5, 1858, p. 12 (charter, N. J. Laws 1824, p. 158, §9); American Life Insurance & Trust Company, Rep. of Committee of Trustees Previous to Declaration of a Dividend (Nov. 1837), p. 4 (charter, Md. Laws 1833, c. 256, §7).

[176] Mass. Laws and Resolves 1802–03 (1898 Repr.), 1803–c. 110, p. 684, §3–10th.

from capital if there are no profits.[177] Decisions to this effect under the English statutes which prescribe the profits tests [178] may be relied upon.[179] Beyond this the authorities as to plain profit provisions are too few to be conclusive. In *Eyster v. Centennial Board of Finance,* the Board was incorporated under a statute which provided that at the close of the proposed exposition, the property, after payment of liabilities, should be divided among the stockholders.[180] After incorporation the federal government made an appropriation for use of the Board under a statute requiring repayment before "any dividend or percentage of profits" should be paid to stockholders. At the close of the exposition there was an impairment of capital but operating profits. The stockholders contended they were entitled to repayment of their "capital" before payment of the government appropriation, apparently on the theory that the only restriction on repayment to stockholders was against payment of profits before payment of the government appropriation, and that to repay stockholders the amount of their capital was not a distribution of profits. The court pointed out, however, that the capital had really been impaired, and the only way stockholders could be paid their capital in full was by a restoration out of operating profits, a thing

---

[177] *Mente v. Groff,* 10 Ohio N. P. (N. S.) 148 (1910); (statute prohibited dividends "except from the surplus profits arising from the business of the corporation," contained no express capital impairment provision, but required deduction from profit and loss of all losses sustained); see Littleton, *A Substitute for Stated Capital,* 17 Harv. Bus. Rev. 75 (1938). Counsel in *Vose v. Grant,* 15 Mass. 505, 512 (1819), argued: "Why should they be specially authorized to divide the *profits* semi-annually if, without permission, they could divide, not the profits only, but the whole capital?"

[178] Under the Companies Act of 1929, dividends are limited to profits. 19 and 20 Geo. 5, c. 23, First Schedule, Table A, Reg. 91. This has been the statutory rule since the Companies Act of 1862. The Companies Clauses Consolidation Act of 1845, 8 and 9 Vict. c. 16, §121, providing that companies could not declare dividends which would reduce their capital stock, is an exception to the English scheme of statutory control.

[179] *Flitcroft's Case,* L. R. 21 Ch. Div. 519 (Ct. App. 1882) (under Companies Act of 1862); *Moxham v. Grant,* (1900) 1 Q. B. 88 (Ct. App.) (directors paying dividends from capital when held liable on liquidation were permitted to recover from stockholders); *MacDougall v. Jersey Imperial Hotel Co., Ltd.,* 2 Hem. & M. 528 (Ct. Ch. 1864); see Lindley, L. J. in *Verner v. General and Commercial Investment Co.,* (1894) 2 Ch. 239, 264, 266: "The law is much more accurately expressed by saying that dividends cannot be paid out of capital, than by saying that they can only be paid out of profits." See also Cooke, *Legal Content of the Profit Concept,* 46 Yale L. J. 436, 440 (1937). For general discussion of the English cases see Weiner, *Theory of Anglo-American Dividend Law: The English Cases,* 28 Col. L. Rev. 1046 (1928); *Theory of Anglo-American Dividend Law,* 30 Col. L. Rev. 330; Ballantine and Hills, *Corporate Capital and Restrictions upon Dividends under Modern Corporation Laws,* 23 Cal. L. Rev. 229, 252 (1935).

[180] 94 U. S. 500 (1876).

prohibited by the statute if "profits" meant, as the court held it did, "the receipts of the exhibition, over and above its current expenses." Here in a dividend case is a clear holding that profits alone means current receipts less current expenditures and not a balance sheet surplus.[181] From the historical and accounting [182] standpoints, this interpretation should be favored.[183] By contrast two Georgia decisions under statutes providing for dividends out of "net earnings" use the balance sheet surplus method to determine the earnings available, with little indication that the court appreciated the difference between the balance sheet and profit and loss tests.[184]

Under provisions following the New York Act of 1825 for payment out of surplus profits arising from the business, an interesting question arises as to whether surplus profits means accumulated earned surplus or merely current net profits. The fact that the clause

181 Where preferred stockholders are entitled to dividends from "net earnings," it is held that the rule applicable is gross receipts less expenses of operation. *St. John v. Erie Railway Co.,* 10 Blatchf. 271, 279 (S. D. N. Y. 1872), aff'd 22 Wall. 136 (1874); *Belfast & Moosehead Lake Railroad Co. v. Belfast,* 77 Me. 445, 452 (1885). See also *Mobile & Ohio Railroad Co. v. Tennessee,* 153 U. S. 486, 497 (1894) (taxation case). Under English cases, which would not be authority where there is also an express statutory prohibition against payment from capital such as that in the New York Act of 1825, but which might be relied on when the statute is drawn in terms of profits, dividends may be paid from current operating profits regardless of prior capital impairments or operating losses. *Ammonia Soda Co., Ltd. v. Chamberlain,* (1918) 1 Ch. 266, 283; *Bolton v. Natal Land & Colonization Co.,* (1892) 2 Ch. Div. 124 (articles provided for dividends out of "net profits"). See Cooke, *Legal Content of the Profit Concept,* 46 Yale L. J. 436, 442 (1937). The House of Lords, however, has reserved judgment on the distinction of lower English courts between fixed and floating capital and the question whether a dividend can be paid when capital is impaired. See Earl of Halsbury in *Dovey v. Cory,* (1901) A. C. 477, 487, also Lord Davey at 493–494.

182 For the accountant's case in favor of profits as the test for dividends, see Littleton, *Business Profits as a Legal Basis for Dividends,* 16 Harv. Bus. Rev. 51 (1938), and *A Substitute for Stated Capital,* 17 Harv. Bus. Rev. 75 (1938). A tentative report of the American Institute of Accountants defines net profits and net income as profits from the disposition of any corporate asset other than the corporation's stock. Tentative Report, *Year Book of American Institute of Accountants* (1930) 173, 174.

183 But in Ballantine and Hills, *Corporate Capital and Restrictions upon Dividends under Modern Corporation Acts,* 23 Cal. L. Rev. 229, 242, 246–247 (1935), it is stated: "In most, if not all, of the statutes in which the terms 'net profits' or 'earnings' are employed without specifying some particular period for their determination" balance sheet surplus is meant.

184 *Mangham v. State,* 11 Ga. App. 440, 75 S. E. 508 (1912); see *Bank of Morgan v. Reid,* 27 Ga. App. 123, 107 S. E. 555 (1921). That it means surplus over and above capital and debts. See *Barry v. Merchants Exchange Co.,* 1 Sandf. Ch. 280, 307 (1844) (charter, N. Y. Laws 1823, c. 15, §1); cf. *Park v. Grant Locomotive Works,* 40 N. J. Eq. 114, 121, 3 Atl. 162 (1885), aff'd on opinion below 45 N. J. Eq. 244, 19 Atl. 621 (1888) ("net profits" payable on assignment of stock to creditors as security determined by balance sheet surplus).

authorizes not merely payment from profits but from surplus profits gives strong support to the view that a showing of earnings over the entire history of the business is required. It has been said that such a provision imports an excess of receipts over expenditures; [185] also that even when capital is impaired, dividends may be paid from profits whether earned during the current year or carried over from any former year.[186]

26. Restriction to Net Profits or Surplus

In many states the dividend statute is so phrased as to permit the payment of dividends from the alternatives of either balance sheet surplus or net profits. Under Section 30 of the New Jersey General Corporation Law, dividends may be paid from surplus or from net profits arising from the business of the corporation, but the capital stock may not be divided, withdrawn or reduced.[187] In *Goodnow v. American Writing Paper Company,* a predecessor section containing substantially this provision was held to create alternative dividend funds, surplus, or net profits.[188] From 1875 to 1904 the New Jersey statute had prohibited dividends "except from the surplus or net profits arising from its business." [189] In 1904 the

[185] *People v. San Francisco Savings Union,* 72 Cal. 199, 13 Pac. 498 (1887) (state entitled to prevent declaration of dividends out of accrued but unreceived interest on United States government bonds and interest on real estate loans).

[186] See *Mente v. Groff,* 10 Ohio N. P. (N. S.) 148, 157 (1910). In *Roberts v. Roberts-Wick Co.,* 184 N. Y. 257, 266, 77 N. E. 13 (1906), the certificate of incorporation provided for preferred dividends "out of the surplus profits arising from the business of the corporation." The court used the balance sheet surplus test.

[187] N. J. Stat. (1937), §14:8–19. *Source:* N. J. Acts 1846, p. 16, §7, taken from N. Y. Rev. Stat. (1828), Pt. 1, c. 18, Title 4, §2 (the insolvency provisions in N. J. Acts 1846, p. 64, §26, and N. J. Acts 1849, p. 300, §25, have not survived); N. J. Rev. Stat. (1709–1877), p. 178, §7 (Revision of Apr. 7, 1875); N. J. Laws 1896, c. 185, §30; N. J. Laws 1904, c. 143, §30; N. J. Laws 1930, c. 120, §1. For history of the basic provision in the N. Y. Rev. Stat. (1828), see §7, *supra.*

[188] *Goodnow v. American Writing Paper Co.,* 73 N. J. Eq. 692, 69 Atl. 1014 (Ct. Err. & App. 1908), see §22.1, n. 124, *supra;* see also L. Hand, J. in *Borg v. International Silver Co.,* 11 F. (2d) 147, 151 (C. C. A. 2d, 1925). The holding in the *Goodnow* case is questioned in Ballantine and Lattin, *Cases and Materials on the Law of Corporations* (1939) 467. In *Edwards v. Douglas,* 269 U. S. 204, 214 (1925), holding stockholders taxable for dividends distributed out of the most recent current earnings under a provision of the Revenue Act of 1916 that dividends should be deemed to be "from the most recently accumulated undivided profits or surplus," Justice Brandeis said: "The surplus account represents the net assets of a corporation in excess of all liabilities including its capital stock. This surplus may be paid-in surplus, as where the stock is issued at a price above par. It may be earned surplus, as where it was derived wholly from undistributed profits. Or it may, among other things, represent the increase in valuation of land or other assets made upon a revaluation of the company's fixed property."

[189] N. J. Rev. Stat. (1709–1877), p. 178, §7 (Revision of Apr. 7, 1875); N. J. Laws 1896, c. 185, §30.

statute was amended to read, close to its present form, "except from its surplus, or from the net profits arising from the business." [190] The *Goodnow* case was decided under the 1904 amendment. The court held that the amendment definitely contemplated alternative funds, and that it was, therefore, unnecessary to decide whether the law prior to 1904 had also legalized alternative sources. It does become necessary, however, to decide this latter question, since some states have statutes today which were copied from New Jersey before the 1904 amendment, still retaining the earlier provision of payment from "the surplus or net profits." The New Mexico dividend provisions are based on Section 30 of the New Jersey General Corporation Act of 1896,[191] as are those of North Carolina.[192] Quite similar provisions in Rhode Island provide that dividends shall not be paid except from surplus or net profits, nor shall the capital be divided or withdrawn.[193]

The statutory dividend history in New Jersey demonstrates, with apparent conclusiveness, that the earlier provision for payment from "the surplus or net profits" was not merely a redundant definition of a single fund, namely profits, but that it was definitely intended to prescribe two alternative funds, surplus and net profits. The original Act of 1846, which was copied from the New York Revised Statutes of 1828, simply contained the provision that dividends might be paid out of "surplus profits arising from the business." [194] In the Revision of 1875, however, it was changed to read out of "surplus or net profits arising from the business." [195] Unless it was intended to create a fund other than surplus from which dividends might be paid, the amendment of the words "or net" was obviously superfluous.

In *Peters v. U.S. Mortgage Company,* decided under the un-

---

[190] N. J. Laws 1904, c. 143.

[191] N. Mex. Stat. (1929), §32–135, as enacted N. Mex. Terr. Laws 1905, c. 79, §34. See *Cartwright v. Albuquerque Hotel Co.,* 36 N. Mex. 189, 191, 11 P. (2d) 261 (1932).

[192] N. C. Code (1939), §1179, as enacted N. C. Laws 1901, c. 2, §33. There is the additional limitation that dividends shall not be paid when debts exceed two-thirds of the assets.

[193] R. I. Gen. Laws (1938), c. 116, §§38, 41. *Source:* R. I. Acts and Resolves, June Sess. 1847, p. 30, §§5, 6; R. I. Acts and Resolves, Jan. Sess. 1920, c. 1925, §§38, 41. In Oregon dividends cannot be paid out of assets other than net profits or surplus. Ore. Code Ann. (1930), §25–219. *Source:* Ore. Gen. Laws (Deady 1866), Act of Oct. 14, 1862, p. 658, §15; Ore. Laws 1925, c. 291, §1. Similarly, the Connecticut General Corporation Law prohibits dividends except from net profits or actual surplus unless in accordance with provisions for reduction of stock or dissolution. For source see §21, n. 108, *supra.*

[194] N. J. Acts 1846, p. 16, §7; N. Y. Rev. Stat. (1828), Pt. I, c. 18, Title 4, §2.

[195] N. J. Rev. Stat. (1709–1877), p. 178, §7.

amended form of the New Jersey provision, it was held that although the capital to be considered material was the amount of
consideration received, "to ascertain whether there is a surplus, or
there are net profits, we must balance assets against liabilities and
list capital stock among the liabilities." [196] Thus the court treated
surplus and net profits as meaning the same thing. In *Wittenberg v.
Federal Mining and Smelting Company,* the Chancellor held, where
capital was impaired, that the "surplus or net profits" clause was
insufficient to permit payment out of current earnings, distinguishing the Delaware statute on the ground that it had not been amended
as in New Jersey.[197] It was stated that the New Jersey amendment
was evidently regarded as necessary in order to make it clear that
two funds were created.[198] In neither the *Goodnow* case nor these
two Delaware cases did the courts consider the statutory history
which makes it clear that no such amendment was necessary and that
two sources were clearly contemplated by the legislature.

26.1. Meaning of Net Profits: Earned Surplus or Current Net Earnings

Granting that dividends may be paid from the alternative fund of
net profits under statutes of the New Jersey type even though
capital is impaired, what is the meaning of net profits? [199]

The narrowest possible construction of the term would treat
net profits as earnings over and above capital as shown in a balance
sheet surplus, in short a rule more strict than that in the straight
balance sheet surplus jurisdictions such as New York which do not

[196] 13 Del. Ch. 11, 18, 114 Atl. 598 (1921).

[197] 15 Del. Ch. 147, 162-3, 133 Atl. 48 (1926), aff'd 15 Del. Ch. 409, 138 Atl.
347 (1927).

[198] The possibility for a difference between net profits and surplus in the case
where there is a general balance sheet surplus was suggested (*id.,* 163-164). See
§26.1, n. 200, *infra.* Arkansas, while it copied its dividend provisions from earlier Delaware acts, made substantial changes. The present act provides for payment from net
earnings or from the surplus of assets over liabilities including capital. Ark. Stat.
(1937), §2183 (Ark. Acts 1927, c. 250, §22; Ark. Acts 1931, c. 255, §25). In 1931
present §2184 was also added (Ark. Acts, 1931, c. 255, §26) introducing the further
limitation that directors should not pay out any part of the corporate capital. As a
subsequent amendment it should not be construed to limit the double alternatives
provided before its enactment. In this view dividends may be paid out of current
net earnings under §2183 regardless of a capital deficit, but not in the absence of
such earnings, which would constitute a payment from capital under §2184.
Tennessee and Virginia also have clear alternative provisions for payment from
net earnings or a balance sheet surplus. Tenn. Code Ann. (1934), §§3737, 3759.
Source: Tenn. Acts 1929, c. 90, §26; Virginia Code (1936), §3840. *Source:* Va.
Acts 1836-37, c. 82, §6; c. 84, §13; c. 118, §26; Va. Code (1849), c. 57, §§30, 31;
Va. Code (1860), c. 57, §§30, 31; Va. Acts 1932, c. 122.

[199] For possible constructions see the discussion in §§16(c) and 25, *supra.*

restrict dividends to surplus arising solely from earnings. This restricted meaning of net profits was suggested, but not passed upon,
by the lower court opinion of the Chancellor in *Wittenberg v. Federal Mining and Smelting Company*.[200]

The more likely constructions attribute to net profits some
meaning disassociated entirely from the corporation's original capital.
In *Goodnow v. American Writing Paper Company*, it was not
necessary to decide this question, because there were both current
annual net profits and net profits upon the whole of the company's
business from its organization.[201] The New Jersey Chancery Court
has recently had occasion to treat the issue in *National Newark and
Essex Banking Company v. Durant Motor Company*.[202] In that case
a corporation was formed to purchase from a trustee the property
of an insolvent corporation, the bid providing that the new corporation would issue to bondholders of the old corporation preferred
stock which should be entitled to dividends, only to the extent
"earned in any fiscal year." The new corporation filed a petition for
approval by the court of a form of preferred stock certificate to be
issued in compliance with the bid. The form submitted and approved
by the court provided that whether a dividend had been earned
should be determined by deducting from gross income in any year
the net operating loss, if any, accumulated since the new corporation
had taken over the business. In the first five years of its operation,
the new corporation had an accumulated loss of $230,000. It was
argued by the bondholders who were to receive the preferred stock
that should the corporation have in the sixth year an annual net
profit of $50,000, this would constitute earnings for dividend pur-
poses, even though distribution might have to await more favorable
general financial conditions. Relying on the clause of the New
Jersey statute above referred to permitting dividends from "net
profits," the court held that there could be no dividends out of net
profits until there was a balance of assets over liabilities, arising
from the business of the company. Therefore, current net earnings
in any one year would necessarily have to be applied in wiping out
deficits of prior years before dividends could be paid. The case deals
with the construction of provisions to be included in a prospective
preferred stock issue, yet the court gave as its reason for requiring
prior operating losses to be made up the fact that any other provision

---

[200] 15 Del. Ch. 147, 163–4; n. 197, *supra*.
[201] See §26, n. 188, *supra*.
[202] 124 N. J. Eq. 213, 1 Atl. (2d) 316 (1938), aff'd 125 N. J. Eq. 435, 5 Atl. (2d)
315 (1939).

would violate the net profits alternative of the New Jersey statute. Aside from the decision being a lower court opinion, it is not likely, unless its basic reasoning is wholly rejected, that a different construction would be given to the same provision were the question directly raised as to validity of a dividend payment.

It is not easy to support this decision either as a matter of theory or on authority. From the standpoint of accounting, surplus standing alone has always carried the connotation of taking into account past corporate history through the balance sheet; in antithesis, profit, particularly net profit, carries the meaning of current earnings.[203] The older cases give support to the view that net profits signifies receipts less expenses of operation.[204] These authorities, assuming net profits should properly be determined on the basis of the current accounting period, tend to support use of the profit and loss statement, which may eliminate from profit certain capital gains and losses, rather than a comparison of balance sheets at the opening and close of the accounting period which would necessarily take into account all capital gains and losses.

Even taking *National Newark and Essex Banking Company v.*

[203] In early American corporate records funds described as "net earnings," or "net income," and determined on the basis of receipts less expenditures or on an income statement, were often treated as available for dividend purposes: Vermont Central Railroad Co., Third Ann. Rep. (1848) 10 (income statement) ; Housatonic Railroad Company, Ann. Rep. Jan. 1850 (being difference between total interest on debt and dividends) ; Cumberland Railroad, Treasurer's Rep. to Stockholders, July 1, 1851, MSS 724 (1845–1867), v. 527, p. 2, folder, Stockholders' Meetings, etc. (receipts less expenditures) ; Pittsfield & N. Adams Railroad Co. (1853), MSS 724 (1829–1880), W. 527, v. 8, folder Western Railroad Corp. Finances 1842–1853; Bunker Hill Bank, MSS Bunker Hill Bank Directors' Records (balance sheets 1826 through 1864). For a modern accounting view that net income may, but need not necessarily, be computed by comparing opening and closing balance sheets for the period in question, see Porter and Fiske, *Accounting* (1935) 330.

[204] *Belfast & Moosehead Lake Railroad Co. v. Belfast*, 77 Me. 445, 452 (1885) (by-law provided for preferred dividends from "net earnings") ; *St. John v. Erie Railway Co.*, 10 Blatchf. 271, 279 (S. D. N. Y. 1872), aff'd 22 Wall. 136 (1874) (preferred entitled to "net earnings") ; *Union Pacific Railroad Co. v. United States*, 99 U. S. 402, 419–20 (1878) (under statute entitling government to percentage of "net earnings" of road) ; cf. *Cotting v. New York & New England R. R. Co.*, 54 Conn. 156, 168 (1886) (a special statute authorizing the payment of preferred dividends out of "net earnings" was held to permit dividends out of earnings of the current year irrespective of prior earning deficits, where the preferred was issued at a time of financial difficulty; the court distinguished net earnings from surplus or profits saying that as to the latter prior deficits would have to be considered). In *Kingston v. Home Life Insurance Co.*, 11 Del. Ch. 258, 272–273, 101 Atl. 898, aff'd 11 Del. Ch. 428, 104 Atl. 25 (1918), the court, while Delaware still had the unamended New Jersey form of "surplus or net profits," declared a dividend illegal by way of dictum—"the income was less than disbursements." But cf. *Hutchinson v. Curtiss*, 45 Misc. 484, 489, 92 N. Y. S. 70 (1904), for the view that under the old New Jersey act net profits means a balance sheet surplus.

Durant Motor Company, to indicate, at least until the New Jersey Court of Error and Appeals passes on the question, that net profits under the New Jersey statute does not mean current net profits as disclosed by a profit and loss statement, still the decision leaves uncertainties. It leaves in doubt what was meant to be indicated as the applicable rule for making sure losses are absorbed. This doubt remains in the language of Vice-Chancellor Bigelow, referring to the net profits clause as meaning "no dividends out of net profits are earned until there is a balance of assets over liabilities, arising from the business of the corporation." To speak of "assets and liabilities" is to use balance sheet language as distinguished from "receipts and expenses" generally used when speaking of a profit and loss statement. On the other hand, qualifying the limitation by the clause "arising from the business" must inevitably exclude certain types of capital losses which would only appear on a balance sheet. It obviously makes a great deal of difference in some cases which rule is applied. Under the first or balance sheet theory, all capital losses arising after the original acquisition of property must first be made up before dividends can be paid. Under the second, or earned surplus theory, such losses need not be made up and dividends may be declared in spite of their existence, taking into account only all prior annual operating profits and losses.

27. Restriction to Current Net Profits or Balance Sheet Surplus: Delaware General Corporation Law, Section 34

The double difficulty under the New Jersey type statute as to the existence of alternative funds for dividends and the meaning of net profits was met in Delaware in 1927 by an amendment giving the right to pay dividends either out of annual net profits or out of net assets in excess of capital.[205] In 1929 this clause was amended to its present form which permits declaration out of net assets in excess of capital, or, in case there is no such excess, out of net profits for the current or preceding fiscal year.[206]

Under this statute, it is very clear that net profits means profits for the current or preceding accounting period. Not only this, but the introductory clause specifying that, in the absence of an excess of net assets over capital, dividends may be paid from current profits seems to indicate that profits are to be determined on the

[205] 35 Del. Laws, c. 85, §16. For earlier history see §21, n. 102, *supra.*
[206] Del. Rev. Code (1935), c. 65, §34; 36 Del. Laws, c. 135, §16. But if capital is impaired to an amount less than that allocable to all classes of preferred stock entitled to preference on distribution of assets, the directors are enjoined from paying dividends "out of such net profits" until the deficiency is repaired.

basis of the profit and loss statement rather than by comparative balance sheets as of the opening and close of the period.[207] If there should be capital losses during the current year impairing capital of a character which accounting practice would not recognize as proper charges to current income, the section appears to provide expressly that dividends may still be paid out of the current net profit.

Two problems of construction arise from the wording of the Delaware clause. Dividends may be paid out of net profits for the current fiscal year. Does this mean the year still in progress? If so, how could net profits ever be determined for the current fiscal year until it had ended, except through an estimate of what profit and losses would be for the balance of the period? This would be unsound practice from either a legal or managerial standpoint. The clause must therefore mean the last fiscal year currently completed and the preceding fiscal year. It would have been much better, and probably nearer to the intention of the draftsman, if the statute had read "dividends may be paid out of net profits earned during either of the two years next preceding the last quarterly accounting period of the corporation." This would assure profits computed on the annual basis, which is the important principle to be retained, while at the same time removing the ambiguity inherent in the present provision. A second question relates to whether losses during the two-year period must be offset against any gains during the period. The statute in permitting dividends from net profits "for the fiscal year then current and/or the preceding fiscal year" seems (1) to allow dividends from net profits of a single year if there are profits in either of the two periods, irrespective of what the losses may be in the other, and (2) to permit dividends from the combined profits of the two years, in which case, of course, losses normally chargeable to either year would have to be taken into account.[208]

Under Section 34, a Delaware corporation may find itself in one of three positions: (1) it may have a balance sheet surplus; (2) it may have a capital impairment as shown by its balance sheet but current net profits as shown by profit and loss statements of the current or preceding year; or (3) its balance sheet may show a capital impairment and profit and loss statements for both of the

[207] This construction is supported by most authorities construing net profits and similar terms for dividend purposes. See §§25, 26.1, *supra*.

[208] While following the general scheme of the Delaware Act, Kansas permits the payment of dividends not merely from net profits of the preceding two years but out of net profits for all preceding years when there is a capital impairment. Kans. Laws 1939, c. 152, §80 (but not if there is an impairment of capital required to liquidate preferred stock, §81). Thus, dividends may be paid either out of current net profits of the year or out of accumulated earned surplus.

last two years a loss. In both of the first two cases dividends may be paid, while in the last no dividends may be paid. Thus, even in one of the most liberal states today a dividend cannot be paid where there are no favorable balances under one theory of accounting or another. To put it somewhat differently, a distribution cannot be made which would constitute not merely a payment while the balance sheet shows prior impairments of capital, but actual present division of capital.

28. Restriction to Net Profits or Earned Surplus

Section 346 of the California General Corporation Law, providing for payment of cash or property dividends to common stock out of earned surplus, or if there is an impairment of capital, out of net profits earned during the preceding accounting period, raises some question as to whether anything like the Delaware balance sheet-profit and loss account alternatives is given.[209] It seems the second alternative that dividends may be paid from current net profits despite a capital impairment was intended to indicate that, if there is an impairment, dividends can only be paid from current profits. But this is not entirely obvious when one considers the first alternative of earned surplus, which is definitely recognized as a separate source for dividends. Under the phrasing of the section, it is arguable that there may be an earned surplus at the same time that capital asset losses have produced a balance sheet deficit, just as there may be current net earnings while such a condition exists. The latter possibility is expressly recognized in the other alternative of the statute. In Delaware it is perfectly clear that the alternatives are a balance sheet surplus or a current profit and loss statement profit. That earned surplus in the California Act is not synonymous with a balance sheet surplus is demonstrated by the third subdivision of Section 346 which mentions paid-in and reduction surpluses which would, of course, also appear as a part of surplus on the balance sheet. Earned surplus in the accounting sense does not mean a balance sheet surplus, but rather the accumulated account of net earnings from the beginning of the corporation's existence.[210]

As the California Act now stands, it seems to have been quite

209 Cal. Civ. Code (1937), §346(1), (2) (but not out of net profits if capital required to pay liquidation preferences on preferred stock is impaired, except to the preferred stock). See Ballantine, *Questions of Policy in Drafting a Modern Corporation Act,* 19 Cal. L. Rev. 465, 477 (1931); Ballantine, *Changes in the California Corporation Laws,* 17 Cal. L. Rev. 529, 532 (1929); Sterling, *Modernizing California's Corporation Laws,* 12 Wis. L. Rev. 453, 467 (1937).

210 See Paton and Littleton, *Introduction to Corporate Accounting Standards* (1940) 105; Tentative Statement of American Institute of Accountants, *Year*

clearly intended to restrict corporations with impaired capital to the payment of dividends out of current earnings,[211] because if dividends may be paid from an accumulated earned surplus arising from prior current earnings under the first alternative, the second is rendered nugatory. In order to remove any doubt on this score, the alternatives provided should have been (1) out of earned surplus to the extent that the net assets of the corporation exceed its stated capital, (2) despite the fact that the net assets of the corporation are less than the stated capital, out of net earnings during the preceding accounting period.

Section 346 of the California Act removes the difficulty as to meaning of current fiscal period in the Delaware law by a provision for declaration of dividends out of net profits for the preceding accounting period. But it creates another difficulty by permitting this period to be of only six months' duration. A corporation engaged in a seasonal industry may show a large net profit during the first six months of the year, but a larger deficit in the final six months, with a resulting net deficit for the year. Under the California law, the entire net profits for the first six months could be distributed. If net profits is to be an alternative test for dividends, it should in fairness be upon a yearly basis in order to reflect all the earnings and losses of the annual business cycle. Indeed, in some industries a fair cycle is longer than a year.

At least one modern statute phrasing its common stock dividend alternatives in the form of earned surplus and current earnings does not offer the ambiguity as to earned surplus found in Section 346 of the California Act. The Minnesota Business Corporation Act authorizes cash or property dividends on common stock out of earned surplus or net earnings for the current or preceding fiscal year whether or not it then has a paid-in or earned surplus.[212] It is

---

Book of Am. Inst. of Accountants (1930) 173, 174; 1 Dodd and Baker, *Cases on Business Associations* (1940) 737; cf. 2 Bonbright, *Valuation of Property* (1937) 918. Thus for the purpose of taxing dividends "earned surplus" is surplus "derived wholly from undistributed profits." *See Edwards v. Douglas,* 269 U. S. 204, 214 (1925).

[211] See Ballantine and Sterling, *California Corporation Laws* (1938 Ed.) 195.

[212] Minn. Stat. (Mason 1938 Supp.), §7492-21, II [(1) no dividends may be paid out of net earnings except to preferred stockholders if the capital required to satisfy liquidation preferences of preferred stock is impaired; (2) no dividends may be declared out of net earnings if the corporation is insolvent; (3) dividends on common may be declared from paid-in surplus if there are no preferred shares outstanding]. See generally, Hoshour, 17 Minn. L. Rev. 689, 698 (1933); Colman and Finn, *Comparison of Business Corporation Law of Minnesota and Delaware,* 22 Minn. L. Rev. 661, 670 (1938); Solether and Jennings, *Minnesota Business Corporation Act,* 12 Wis. L. Rev. 419 (1937).

made clear in this act, however, that earned surplus requires the existence of both accumulated profits from earnings and an unimpaired general balance sheet surplus.[213] The shorter provision in the Michigan General Corporation Act for payment of common dividends from earned surplus or from net earnings leaves some of the difficulties inherent in the California provision.[214] Again the act does not make it clear whether earned surplus means merely the accumulated earnings over the history of the corporation or whether there must be in addition to such earnings an unimpaired balance sheet. It is significant that the net earnings alternative is not limited to the situation where capital is impaired, as in California. It would, therefore, seem that in Michigan the only requirement for payment of common dividends is profits, past or present, with no regard to the balance sheet position of the corporation.

The Indiana General Corporation Law presents an instance among modern revisions of almost unintelligible dividend regulation. It involves the same difficulties inherent in the California law by offering at the outset the alternatives of surplus earnings and net profits, adding also cash paid-in surplus.[215] Whatever enlarging effect the surplus or net profit provisions may have had seems to be counteracted by an express provision in the same section that no dividend shall be paid if the corporation's capital is, or thereby becomes, impaired.[216]

G. Paid-In and Reduction Surplus

29. Paid-In Surplus

It cannot be broadly stated that a separate rule applies to the payment of dividends from paid-in and reduction surplus. In some jurisdictions the general definition of the dividend fund is broad enough to permit payment of dividends from these types of surplus; in others it is so restrictive as to exclude availability; while in still

[213] §7492–21, I.

[214] Mich. Stat. Ann. (Henderson 1937), §21.22. See generally, Payne, *Net Worth under the Delaware and Michigan Corporation Laws*, 8 Acc. Rev. 1 (1933); Lewis, *Some Legal and Accounting Questions Presented by the Michigan General Corporation Act*, 8 Acc. Rev. 145, 149 (1933).

[215] Ind. Stat. Ann. (Burns 1933), §25–211.

[216] Section 25–251 also makes directors liable for knowingly and wilfully declaring or assenting to a dividend if the corporation's capital is thereby impaired. Special problems connected with the fund from which dividends may be declared when the corporation has preferred stock in addition to common are considered in Chapter 6, *infra;* those in conjunction with the payment of dividends by so-called wasting asset corporations in Chapters 3 and 6, *infra;* and stock dividends generally in Chapter 5, *infra.*

others specific provision is made as to the circumstances in which either may be resorted to.[217]

Paid-in surplus is primarily a concomitant of no-par stock. While there was always the possibility of paid-in surplus as to the excess over par on the sale of par value stock, there is almost inevitably a paid-in surplus for the difference between the stated value and the purchase price of no-par stock.[218] The problems in conjunction with dividends from paid-in surplus arise from the peculiar nature of this type of surplus. Prior to adoption of no-par stock, a share of $100 par value stock sold for $100 would appear on the balance sheet as a cash asset of $100, and as a capital liability of $100. With a similar sale of a share of stock without par value, the balance sheet will show the same cash asset of $100, but the treatment on the liability side may be entirely different. The corporation may continue to treat the entire $100 as stated capital, in which case there will be no difference. But under authority of most statutory provisions, it will be permissible to allocate only a portion of the consideration to capital, crediting the balance to paid-in surplus. This possibility for dividing the consideration is one of the chief objectives of issuing stock without par value. The corporation may, therefore, have on the liability side of its balance sheet two entries: stated capital $50; paid-in surplus $50. The fact that this paid-in surplus is really a part of the stockholders' original capital contribution has led to a feeling that it should be treated as capital and its availability for dividends correspondingly restricted.[219] Not all statutes meet the problem directly.

[217] See generally, 1 Dodd and Baker, *Cases on Business Associations* (1940), Note on Paid-in Surplus, p. 1142; Berle, *Cases on Corporation Finance* (1930), Note on Paid-in Surplus, 394; Berle, *Corporate Devices for Diluting Stock Participations,* 31 Col. L. Rev. 1239, 1246 (1931); Note, "Declaration of Dividends from Paid-in Surplus," 31 Col. L. Rev. 844 (1931); Note, 49 Yale L. J. 492, 496–497 (1940). Distinctions between capital surplus and earned surplus are currently presenting many accounting questions in the work of the S. E. C. See Werntz, *Some Current Problems in Accounting,* 14 Acc. Rev. 117 (1939).

[218] Cf. *Edwards v. Douglas,* 269 U. S. 204, 214 (1925), where, in construing the provisions in the Federal Revenue Act of 1916 imposing a tax on dividends "from the most recently accumulated profits or surplus," the court said: "The surplus account represents the net assets of a corporation in excess of all liabilities including its capital stock. This surplus may be 'paid-in surplus' as where the stock is issued at a price above par." For the accounting problem as to what constitutes stated capital and what paid-in surplus, see §§45, 45.1, *infra.*

[219] Illustrative of the flagrant abuse to which paid-in surplus may be subjected is the *Associated Gas & Electric Company* case. There the company used the proceeds of debenture financing to purchase stock of a subholding corporation in the amount of $671,000,000. Of this amount $663,000,000 was credited by the subholding company to paid-in surplus, available for dividends to the parent company. This capital surplus to the extent of $300,000,000 was then used by the subholding

Where the test for dividends is, without further qualifications, the existence of a balance sheet surplus, dividends may be distributed from paid-in surplus. These jurisdictions include those such as New York where the single test of balance sheet surplus prevails, and those such as Delaware where this is an alternative to net profits.[220] Even in these jurisdictions, however, stockholders may have, in the absence of statute, an equitable right to prevent the use of paid-in surplus derived from one class of stock in order to pay dividends to another class. Probably the most legitimate use of paid-in surplus for dividends is in the payment of cumulative preferred dividends immediately after the corporation's organization and before there are any earnings. These dividends would otherwise accrue, depressing the value of both preferred and common stock. A court of equity might well hesitate to enjoin at the suit of a common stockholder the declaration of such dividends out of paid-in surplus contributed by the common, or even where after organization there were no earnings to meet the preferred requirements. Sometimes it is advisable to issue preferred stock rather than a funded obligation in raising new money. This is hard money preferred and in no way like the differential classification stocks issued on a reorganization. The stockholders expect, and have a right to expect, that their dividends will be paid in much the same fashion that interest would be paid. If the corporation had bonds outstanding, interest would have to be paid even though it came out of capital. Paid-in surplus, whether from preferred or common, will make it possible to pay preferred dividends during a period when the corporation may

---

company to pay debenture dividends to the parent out of which the parent could effectuate a recapitalization plan for its original debentures. Report of S. E. C. on Protective and Reorganization Committees, Pt. VII, pp. 28–32. For the accounting view in support of dividends only from earned surplus and not from paid-in surplus, see Berle and Means, *Modern Corporation and Private Property* (1932) 163; Paton, *Essentials of Accounting* (1938) 667, 694; Securities & Exchange Commission, Holding Company Act Release No. 2282 (1940), pp. 3–4. Special considerations possibly lead to different conclusions where the new shares of a going corporation with an earned surplus available for dividends are issued, see §45.2, *infra*.

[220] See Graham and Katz, *Accounting in Law Practice* (2d Ed. 1938) 152. Statutes of this general class are collected in §21, *supra*. For the availability of paid-in surplus under §34 of the Delaware Act, see Sanders, Hatfield, and Moore, *A Statement of Accounting Principles* (1938) 51; Corporation Trust Company, *Analysis of the Delaware Amendments of 1929*, p. 36; under Ohio Code Ann. (Baldwin 1938), §8623–38, see Draft of Committee on Revision of Ohio General Corporation Act (Dec. 1926) 92. In *Matter of Associated Gas & Electric Corporation*, the S. E. C. held that a Delaware public utility had no right, even prior to the effective date of the Public Utility Holding Company Act, to pay dividends from paid-in surplus until it had first exhausted its earned surplus. Holding Company Act Release No. 1873 (1940).

be developing its earning capacity. But this use of paid-in surplus contributed by common to pay dividends to preferred should not equitably be extended farther than the necessity of meeting these minimum preference requirements. For example, paid-in surplus allocated to common should not be used to pay dividends to preferred when there are available earnings, or under clauses for sharing of dividends between the two classes after both have received a certain percentage. In such situations an injunction should be granted at the suit of common stockholders.[221] In this connection it should be borne in mind that the dividend will actually be out of paid-in surplus allocable to common whenever the preferred, regardless of what amount of its contribution is devoted to paid-in surplus, has a liquidation preference in an amount equal to or approximating both its stated capital and paid-in surplus.

The situation may also be such that preferred stockholders would be in a position to enjoin payment of dividends from paid-in surplus contributed either by themselves or by common stockholders. Common stockholders, finding only enough earnings to pay the preferred dividend, but at the same time also sufficient paid-in surplus contributed by either preferred shareholders or themselves to pay the preferred, might through their control of directors have the preferred dividend paid out of the paid-in surplus, thus freeing the earnings for distribution to themselves. If paid-in surplus of the preferred is used to pay preferred dividends, the result is quite similar to distributing preferred capital to common stockholders. The preferential right to dividends is normally one against earnings. Should earnings be used to pay the preferred, it would seem that the preferred should have a right to enjoin the payment of common dividends out of preferred's own paid-in surplus.

Where the payment to preferred is out of the paid-in surplus of common at a time when there are earnings, it is not so clear that an injunction would lie. The argument in this situation would have to rest on the contention of preferred shareholders that they are entitled to maintenance not only of a cushion of capital contributed by the common but also a cushion of paid-in surplus contributed by the latter.

---

[221] Compare *Roberts v. Roberts-Wicks*, 184 N. Y. 257, 77 N. E. 13 (1906), §30, n. 250, *infra* [capital reduced, but preferred, having no liquidation preference right, held not entitled to be paid out of reduction surplus where certificate gave preferred right to 6 per cent out of the surplus profits arising out of the business of the corporation; (1) the surplus was not surplus profits arising from the business, (2) the reduction surplus really constituted capital and as such preferred had no prior claim as it belonged to all stockholders ratably].

In the second class of balance sheet surplus jurisdictions where the right to pay dividends is further circumscribed by a restriction to payment from "surplus profits arising from the business" (acts patterned on the New York Act of 1825), it seems that paid-in surplus is not a profit arising from the business and is not available for dividends.[222]

Under the type of statute following the New York Manufacturing Act of 1848 with a provision against dividends "which would diminish the amount of its capital stock," it seems there is no restriction against payment of dividends from paid-in surplus.[223]

In Indiana [224] and Maine [225] there are specific general provisions which seem to permit dividends out of paid-in surplus on all classes of stock.

In the recent revisions there is evident an effort to restrict paid-in surplus dividends to preferred shareholders. Thus, under the Illinois Business Corporation Act such surplus is available for dividends to such shareholders only.[226] Similar provisions are made in Pennsylvania,[227] Michigan,[228] and in California,[229] except that in the latter

[222] *Merchants & Insurers' Reporting Co. v. Schroeder*, 39 Cal. App. 226, 178 Pac. 540 (1918) (alternative ground), 22.1, n. 133, *supra;* cf. *Dominguez Land Corp. v. Daugherty*, 196 Cal. 468, 238 Pac. 703 (1925) ; *People v. Knight*, 96 A. D. 120, 89 N. Y. S. 72 (3d Dept. 1904) (a payment to stockholders from paid-in surplus is not "dividends" for tax purposes under this type statute). For statutes of this general type, see §22, *supra*.

[223] In *Haggard v. Lexington Utilities Co.*, 260 Ky. 261, 84 S. W. (2d) 84 (1935), §23, n. 166, *supra,* a dividend from reduction surplus was sustained under this type statute. The same result would seem to apply to paid-in surplus. In *Metropolitan Trust Co. v. Becklenberg*, 300 Ill. App. 453, 21 N. E. (2d) 152 (1939), recovery by creditors from a stockholder of a dividend paid either from profits or paid-in surplus was denied. There was no reference to the statute, but apparently part of the dividends were paid at a time when the old Illinois Act prohibiting a dividend "if its capital is thereby impaired" was in force. Callaghan's Ill. Stat. Ann. (1924), c. 32, §23. For statutes in this third general class, see §23, *supra*.

[224] Ind. Stat. Ann. (Burns 1933), §25–211.

[225] Me. Rev. Stat. (1930), c. 56, §19, as amended by Me. Laws 1931, c. 150, p. 121. But compare §37 (as amended Me. Laws 1933, c. 53) which provides that "Dividends of profit may be made by the directors, but the capital shall not thereby be reduced."

[226] 32 Ill. Stat. Ann. (Smith-Hurd), §157.41. But compare §157.60 which apparently contemplates the distribution of paid-in surplus to common stockholders under certain enumerated conditions. Provision for payment of dividends on preferred stock out of paid-in surplus was primarily intended to enable newly organized corporations to pay dividends during the initial period of development. See Chicago Bar Assoc., Ill. Bus. Corp. Act Ann. (1934), p. 156.

[227] 15 Purd. Pa. Stat. Ann., §2852–704.

[228] Mich. Stat. Ann. (Henderson 1937), §21.22 (dividends generally are authorized only from earned surplus or net earnings, but dividends on preferred stock may be paid from any surplus).

[229] Cal. Civ. Code (1937), §346, 346a.

the restriction is to cash and property dividends, stock dividends from paid-in surplus being permitted. In all cases the source of the dividend must be disclosed to stockholders. This is an effort to notify shareholders that the "dividend" is actually a return of capital and not a distribution of profits. In Minnesota cash or property dividends may be paid from paid-in surplus on common stock if the corporation has no preferred stock, otherwise only on preferred stock. Share dividends may be paid without such restriction.[230]

30. Reduction Surplus

Much the same considerations apply to both paid-in and reduction surplus.[231] The former is a capital surplus created upon the original issuance of stock, the latter a similar surplus created by subsequent reduction of capital or canceling of shares. In the case of the latter, however, the position of the prior creditor who extended credit at a time when the capital of the corporation was larger introduces new considerations.[232]

Even in the absence of a statute specifically providing that a reduction surplus is available for dividends, it has been held that distribution from this type surplus may be made.[233] In fact, where the reduction surplus is no longer needed in the business, directors may be compelled to make distribution—one of the exceptional cases where a court of equity will interfere with the discretion of directors in declaring dividends.[234] Creditors have no constitutional ground for

[230] Minn. Stat. (Mason 1938 Supp.), §7492-21.

[231] The suggestion has been made that capital write-downs should only be used to wipe out losses, but not to create a surplus. See Werntz, *Some Current Problems in Accounting*, 14 Acc. Rev. 117, 119 (1939); Broad, *Some Comments on Surplus Account*, 66 J. of Accountancy 215, 223 (1938). For discussion of this use of reduction surplus, see §36.3, *infra*.

[232] In general, see Note, *Capital Stock Reduction as Affecting the Rights of Creditors*, 47 Harv. L. Rev. 693 (1934); S. E. C. Report on Protective and Reorganization Committees, Pt. VII, 483–493; Annotation, "Reduction of capital stock and distribution of capital assets upon reduction," 44 A. L. R. 11, 40.

[233] *Strong v. Brooklyn Cross-Town R. R. Co.*, 93 N. Y. 426 (1883); *Dominguez Land Corp. v. Daugherty*, 196 Cal. 453, 238 Pac. 697 (1925); *Continental Securities Co. v. Northern Securities Co.*, 66 N. J. Eq. 274, 57 Atl. 876 (1904); *Haggard v. Lexington Utilities Co.*, 260 Ky. 261, 268, 84 S. W. (2d) 84, (1935) (corporation having a deficit but current earnings reduced its capital; held the reduction made the earnings available for dividends); see *Irvine v. Old Kentucky Distillery*, 208 Ky. 414, 418, 271 S. W. 577 (1924); see also Note, 13 Corn. L. Q. 276, 281.

[234] *Seeley v. New York National Bank*, 8 Daly 400 (1878), aff'd on opinion below, 78 N. Y. 608 (1879); see *Continental Securities Co. v. Northern Securities Co.*, 66 N. J. Eq. 274, 282, 57 Atl. 876 (1904), and §54.1, *infra*. But cf. *McCann v. First National Bank*, 112 Ind. 354, 14 N. E. 251 (1887).

objecting to the reduction of capital,[235] but a dividend cannot be paid which would impair even the capital as reduced.[236]

As in the case of paid-in surplus, the availability of reduction surplus for dividends is specifically covered by statute in a number of states. In many jurisdictions the only limitation is that indicated in the absence of statute, namely, the payment shall not impair the capital as reduced.[237] This type of provision offers little or no protection to creditors against indiscriminate reduction and distribution of capital. A corporation with a very large capital, which undoubtedly must have entered into its credit rating, may reduce it to the few hundred dollar minimum required by most statutes as long as it retains assets barely sufficient to meet creditors' claims. More protection is given by the statutes of some states which provide that the capital as reduced must exceed the liabilities.[238] This means there will be at least a two to one ratio of assets against liabilities to creditors. The Minnesota Business Corporation Act contains an exceptional provision limiting reduction of capital to an amount not less than the par value of all outstanding shares having par value.[239]

In some jurisdictions, particularly those which use the insolvency test for dividends, distributions from reduction surplus cannot be paid when the corporation is insolvent or would be rendered insolvent thereby.[240] Under the New Jersey type statute, in default of publication of a certificate stating the reduction, directors are made liable

[235] *Dominguez Land Corp. v. Daugherty*, 196 Cal. 453, 238 Pac. 697 (1925); *Dominguez Land Corp. v. Daugherty*, 196 Cal. 468, 238 Pac. 703 (1925) (reduction surplus had previously been a paid-in surplus).

[236] *Benas v. Title Guaranty Trust Co.*, 216 Mo. App. 53, 267 S. W. 28 (1924); *Kassler v. Kyle*, 28 Colo. 374, 65 Pac. 34 (1901). Where there are losses, the surplus arising from reduction cannot be used for dividends but must be used to wipe out the losses. *State v. Bank of Ogalalla*, 65 Neb. 20, 90 N. W. 961 (1902); *McCann v. First Nat. Bank*, 131 Ind. 95, 30 N. E. 893 (1891); see *Jerome v. Cogswell*, 204 U. S. 1, 7 (1907).

[237] Idaho Code Ann., §29-148; La. Gen. Stat. (Dart. 1939), §1125; Md. Ann. Code (1935 Supp.), Art. 23, §32 (6); Minn. Stat. (Mason 1938 Supp.), §7492-38; N. Y. Stock Corp. Law, §38 (4); R. I. Gen. Laws (1938), c. 116, §53; Tenn. Code Ann. (1934), §3736; Wash. Rev. Stat. Ann. (Rem.), §3803-40.

[238] 3 Mo. Stat. Ann., §4948; Mont. Rev. Code (1935), §5927; Utah Rev. Stat. (1933), §18-2-44 (no reduction of capital to an amount less than 50 per cent in excess of corporate indebtedness).

[239] Minn. Stat. (Mason 1938 Supp.), §7492-38.

[240] Conn. Gen. Stat. (1930), §3420; 32 Ill. Ann. Stat. (Smith-Hurd), §60; Ind. Stat. Ann. (Burns 1933), 25-229 (insolvent or bankrupt); Mass. Laws Ann., c. 156, §45 (insolvent or bankrupt); N. H. Public Laws (1926), c. 225, §47 (insolvent or bankrupt); Ohio Code Ann. (Baldwin 1938), §8623-40, as amended Ohio Laws 1939, S. B. 47; R. I. Laws (1938), c. 116, §53. As to whether the equity or bankruptcy rule of insolvency applies under these statutes, see §20, *supra*.

for all debts contracted before filing and stockholders for such sums as they respectively receive.[241] In Delaware and Maine, reduction is prohibited unless the assets remaining are sufficient to pay any debts the payment of which is not otherwise provided for.[242] The Wisconsin provision is apparently intended to preclude any possibility of reducing capital without stockholders assuming the same risk as though the reduction had not been made. Under its terms they are rendered liable to existing creditors to the amount refunded to them, and stockholders voting in favor of the reduction are liable to the full amount refunded to all stockholders.[243]

Elaborate regulations for handling reduction surplus are found in Illinois and California. In Illinois there can be no reduction below the amount of capital required to satisfy liquidation preferences on preferred stock; reduction surplus is to be treated as paid-in surplus; [244] it cannot be distributed if the corporation is or would be rendered insolvent, and must first be used in meeting past preferred dividends.[245] In California, if there are outstanding preferred shares, cash and property dividends can be paid only out of reduction surplus on such shares, otherwise to common stockholders *pro rata*.[246] No similar restriction exists as to stock dividends.[247] But no dividend can be paid which would render the corporation insolvent or if the remaining assets are not equal to one and one-quarter times its debts and liabilities.[248]

In still a few other states there is merely a general provision that the rights of creditors shall not be affected by the reduction.[249] What this means is conjectural. Stockholders might conceivably be held

---

[241] N. J. Stat. (1937), §14:11–5; N. Mex. Stat. (1929), §32–134; N. C. Code (1939), §1161.

[242] Del. Rev. Code (1935), c. 65, §28; Me. Rev. Stat. (1930), c. 56, §51, as amended Me. Laws 1931, c. 183.

[243] Wis. Stat. (1937), §182.08.

[244] Under 32 Ill. Ann. Stat. (Smith-Hurd), §157.41, it is provided that paid-in surplus may only be used to pay dividends to preferred stockholders. Section 157.60 clearly provides for cases in which reduction surplus may not be so restricted.

[245] 32 Ill. Ann. Stat., *supra* §157.60. Reduction surplus, since it does not fall within the general classes of earned surplus or net profits, is probably available only for preferred dividends in Michigan. Mich. Stat. Ann. (Henderson 1937), §21.22. Likewise in Pennsylvania, reduction surplus apparently becomes paid-in surplus available only for dividends to preferred. 15 Purd. Pa. Stat. Ann. §2852–706B(4), 704.

[246] Cal. Civ. Code (1937), §§346, 348b.

[247] §346a.

[248] §348b.

[249] Neb. Comp. Stat. (1929), §24–103; Mich. Stat. Ann. (Henderson 1937), §21.59; Va. Pub. Laws (1933), §3781; Tex. Stat. (Vern. 1936), §1332.

liable to prior creditors for all reduction surplus received, on the theory credit had been extended in reliance on such capital.

Problems similar to those referred to in connection with dividends out of paid-in surplus also arise when there are conflicting claims of different classes of shareholders to a reduction surplus. Reduction surplus is actually capital and its distribution as between preferred and common stockholders must be treated as such. Therefore, where the preferred stock is not entitled to a capital preference on dissolution, it cannot claim that a reduction surplus should be exclusively paid to it.[250] Being in the nature of capital, common shareholders are entitled to share in it, even though as to operating profits the preferred stock has a preference. Conversely, if the preferred is entitled to a preference upon any distribution or liquidation of capital, it would seem that it is entitled to priority payment from a reduction surplus before anything is paid to the common stock.[251]

H. Restrictions of Regulatory Commissions

31. Public Utility Holding Company Act: Section 12(c)

Increasingly more important in the determination of funds available for dividends are the regulations of federal and state governmental agencies. The liberal provisions of a state corporation act do not necessarily guarantee the availability of dividends, particularly in the case of public utilities and corporations affected with a public interest. Most important of the governmental regulations affecting dividends are those of the Securities and Exchange Commission under Section 12(c) of the Public Utility Holding Company Act.[252]

---

[250] *Roberts v. Roberts-Wicks Co.,* 184 N. Y. 257, 77 N. E. 13 (1906).

[251] Cf. *Page v. Whittendon Mfg. Co.,* 211 Mass. 424, 97 N. E. 1006 (1912), where it was held that the common in such circumstances had to bear the entire brunt of a reduction; no distribution was, however, involved; S. E. C. Report on Protective and Reorganization Committees, Pt. VII, 487 (1938). But compare *Shanak v. White Sewing Machine Corp.,* 15 A (2d) 169 (Del. Ch. 1940); also *Matter of Kinney,* 279 N. Y. 423 (1939), where it seems to be assumed that payment could be made to common out of the reduction surplus, but that this results in an alteration of preferred preferences within the appraisal statute. In *Rochester Gas & Electric Corp. v. Maltbie,* 18 N. Y. S. (2d) 630 (3d Dept. 1940), an order of the public service commission refusing a certificate for the reduction of common capital where a utility had preferred stock outstanding was approved. The corporation proposed to use the reduction surplus solely for the purpose of adjusting its depreciation reserve. The right to reduce the common capital was denied, however, on the ground that the reduction surplus might be used by some later board of directors for dividends, thereby adversely affecting the interest of bondholders and preferred stockholders in the assets of the corporation.

[252] 15 U. S. C. A., §79 (*l*) (c). Generally see 1 Dodd and Baker, *Cases on Business Associations* (1940), Note on Control of Dividends by Securities and Ex-

Some parent corporations, and this was a practice sometimes condemned with respect to public utility holding companies, compel their subsidiaries to distribute dividends which may be unfair to other classes of shareholders or which may even be from funds not legally available. Under Section 12(c), the Commission is authorized to regulate dividends of both the parent.and the subsidiary by its rules and regulations in order to "protect the financial integrity of companies in holding-company systems, to safeguard the working capital of public utility companies, to prevent the payment of dividends out of capital or unearned surplus . . ." or circumvention of Commission regulations.

Two regulations affecting the declaration of dividends have been promulgated under this section. Rule U-12C-2 provides that except upon application to, and approval by the Commission, no registered holding company or subsidiary shall declare or pay any dividend out of capital or unearned surplus, other than a dividend in liquidation of a wholly owned subsidiary.[253] Rule U-12C-3 prohibits such corporations from paying the principal or interest on obligations issued as, or based on, dividends from capital or unearned surplus without the consent of the Commission, whether such dividends were declared before or after the act took effect.[254]

The early operation of the act is illustrated by applications of the Columbia Gas and Electric Corporation, organized under the laws of Delaware, for permission to declare preferred and common dividends from a composite surplus account of $13,000,000 designated, "Surplus at December 31, 1937." [255] The account was composed of surpluses of subsidiary companies previously consolidated, earnings and unrealized appreciation. The Commission found it impossible on the facts presented to determine what was earned surplus and what portion, if any, was capital surplus. It also found that in past years the corporation paid dividends largely in excess of current earnings; that some preferred stockholders had liquidation preference rights which should be protected; and that pending litigation claims and general business conditions were such as to require retention of assets. On these facts the application to pay dividends on preferred stock by a charge against this composite sur-

change Commission under Public Utility Holding Company Act, 1158; Note, 49 Yale L. J. 492 (1940).

[253] Holding Company Act Release No. 460, Dec. 7, 1936.

[254] Holding Company Act Release No. 1781, Nov. 8, 1939.

[255] *Matter of Columbia Gas & Electric Corp.*, Holding Company Act Release No. 1055 (1938); Annual Report of Columbia Gas & Electric Corporation (1938) 6–11. The proceeding is noted in 33 Ill. L. Rev. 220 (1938).

plus account was approved on condition that the corporation restore
to this account an equivalent amount out of the first net earnings
accumulated after December 31, 1937; the application to pay common dividends was denied completely; and the Commission reserved
jurisdiction over payment of the next two quarterly installments on
preferred.[256] Under the law of Delaware it was probably doubtful
that a dividend could have been paid. Appraising assets at present
values (Columbia's principal assets being securities in subsidiaries),
the Commission was of the opinion there would be an impairment
of capital and estimated current earnings were barely sufficient to
pay the proposed dividends.

In order to remove the necessity for obtaining the Commission's
approval for each preferred dividend and to make possible payment
of common dividends, Columbia, in 1939, with the approval of the
Commission, carried out a plan of recapitalization by which it reduced its capital from $194,000,000 to $12,000,000, using the reduction surplus in part to write off its investment in subsidiaries.[257] The
Commission conditioned its approval, however, on a requirement
that no dividends should be paid on common shares unless after the
declaration there should remain, after making provision for all existing dividend requirements of preferred, sufficient surplus earned
after December 31, 1937, to pay six quarterly dividend installments
on all classes of preferred stock outstanding. The Commission,
furthermore, reserved jurisdiction to enter such orders as might be
necessary to effectuate this requirement.[258]

Under the laws of Delaware and other states there can be no
doubt that dividends may be paid from current earnings even though
capital is impaired. Rule U-12C-2 only provides that dividends may
not be paid without approval of the Commission if "out of capital or
unearned surplus." Yet the opinion approving the Columbia recapitalization states that this rule requires the Commission's approval
not merely when the dividend is out of capital but when it is being

---

[256] For similar approval for payment of the next three quarterly dividends on
the preferred stock, see Holding Company Act Releases No. 1152, July 5, 1938;
No. 1265, Oct. 6, 1938; No. 1413, Jan. 25, 1939. In *Matter of Securities Corporation
General,* Holding Company Act Release No. 1704, Aug. 29, 1939, approval was
given for payment of preferred dividends from capital surplus on the similar condition that restoration be made from the first earned surplus.

[257] Holding Company Act Release No. 1417, Jan. 26, 1939; Annual Report of
Columbia Gas & Electric Corporation for year 1938; N. Y. Times, Jan. 27, 1939,
pp. 27, 35.

[258] For shareholders' acceptance of the plan as approved by the Commission,
see N. Y. Times, Mar. 8, 1939, p. 31. The first dividend to common stockholders
was not declared until Apr. 4, 1940. N. Y. Times, Apr. 5, 1940, p. 33.

made from current earnings at a time when capital is impaired.[259] To date the Commission has made no direct effort to restrict public utility dividends paid from earned surplus in the absence of an impairment on the theory of protecting the "financial integrity" of the corporation. The language is broad and may be construed to give such authority.[260]

Particularly interesting is the Commission's treatment of the application of International Utilities Corporation for permission to pay preferred dividends out of capital surplus.[261] Permission was granted a Maryland corporation to pay dividends from capital surplus on two issues of preferred stock where the balance sheet showed that, while the corporation's legal capital was not impaired, the capital required to satisfy liquidation and dissolution preferences of a third class of preferred stock was impaired. The Commission noted the opinion of counsel that under Maryland law it was unnecessary to set up a capital reserve in addition to legal capital in order to assure payment of the liquidation preferences on this third class. By permitting the distribution, the Commission did not itself require such a reservation. In approving the second application, the need of a capital reorganization was emphasized with the comment that approval of this practice would not be given indefinitely.[262] This raises one of the more recent problems in dividend law—whether there is any necessity, where preferred stock has a liquidation preference in excess of its par or stated capital value, to treat an amount equal to such preference either as capital or a reserve restricted against dividends.[263]

One of the most important decisions of the Securities and Exchange Commission under the Public Utility Holding Company Act

[259] See Release No. 1417, n. 257, *supra*.

[260] This possibility was suggested on the original Columbia Gas application, see Holding Company Act Release No. 1055, p. 6; see also *Matter of Associated Gas and Electric Corporation*, Holding Company Act Release No. 1873, p. 18 (1940); Note, 49 Yale L. J. 492, 505, 509 (1940).

[261] *Matter of International Utilities Corporation*, Holding Company Act Releases No. 1643, July 20, 1939, and No. 1753, Oct. 18, 1939.

[262] For a discussion of state statutes affecting dividends of public utilities, see Note, *Extending Control Over Public Utility-Affiliate Financial Transactions*, 46 Harv. L. Rev. 508, 513–515 (1933). In *N. Y., Pa., N. J. Utilities Co. v. Public Service Comm. of N. Y.*, 23 F. Supp. 313 (S. D. N. Y. 1938), the court refused a declaratory judgment making void a condition in a state utility commission order, consented to by the complainant, authorizing refunding of preferred stock if the corporation agreed to pay no dividends on its common stock until the termination of a pending rate proceeding.

[263] The rights of preferred stockholders to protection against distribution of assets required to meet their preferential liquidation claims are discussed in Chapter 6, *infra*.

is that in the case of the Associated Gas and Electric Corporation where the Commission refused to permit the latter to pay dividends, or interest on debentures issued as a dividend to its parent Associated Gas and Electric Company, on the ground that such interest payments would constitute a dividend to the parent out of capital or unearned surplus in violation of Rules U-12C-2 and U-12C-3.[264] The subsidiary, having a paid-in surplus amounting to 99 per cent of the consideration received on the shares of its stock, had prior to the Public Utility Holding Company Act, as part of a plan of adjustment of debentures of its parent, declared a dividend in debentures out of this paid-in surplus. After the effective date of the act, it proposed to pay the interest on these debentures and also to pay dividends to the parent corporation out of a book earned surplus.

On examining the subsidiary's accounts, the Commission concluded no earned surplus existed and that payment of either the interest or dividends would violate its rules under Section 12(c). (1) Losses on the sales of investments on stocks and bonds charged to paid-in surplus over a period from 1922 to 1937 were held to be improper; that the charge should have been to earned surplus; and that as a result the book earned surplus was inflated, actually constituting a deficit. (2) Similar charges to paid-in surplus upon the cancellation of debts owed by subsidiaries and affiliated companies, it was likewise held, should have been made to earned surplus. (3) Although Associated was a Delaware corporation authorized under Section 34 of the Delaware General Corporation Act to pay dividends from surplus, it was held improper to pay dividends from paid-in surplus at a time when the corporation had an unexhausted earned surplus. (4) That an "accounting reorganization" designed to eliminate prior earnings deficits was ineffective because not "sufficiently thoroughgoing," having failed to provide for a write-down of assets which was found to be necessary two years later.

In view of recent interest in the federal licensing of corporations, the decisions of the Securities and Exchange Commission under Section 12(c) may become of important significance in the interpretation of dividend provisions contained in any such legislation. The Commission's rulings and decisions concerning this matter have evolved a pattern which is quite different from that contained in state statutes.

[264] *Matter of Associated Gas & Electric Corporation,* Holding Company Act Release No. 1873 (1940) (comment, 49 Yale L. J. 1319).

32. Accounting Regulations

Although decisions of the various regulatory commissions directly affecting dividends are as yet relatively few, a vital influence upon the fund available for dividends is being exerted through the uniform accounting systems promulgated by almost all of these agencies. These accounting systems, while they do not directly or indirectly prescribe the fund from which dividends may be paid, have much the same practical effect. A corporation cannot readily have one set of books for computing its dividends and another for meeting the accounting requirements of the Interstate Commerce Commission. Included among the more important federal regulatory statutes authorizing administrative promulgation of accounting requirements are the Interstate Commerce Act,[265] Motor Carrier Act of 1935,[266] Federal Water Power Act,[267] and Federal Communications Act.[268] These regulations bear directly upon the treatment of specific assets and liabilities appearing in the financial statements of a corporation. Most important in this field are, of course, the detailed accounting rules and regulations of the Securities and Exchange Commission in Regulation S-X prescribing the form and content of financial statements in registration statements filed under the Securities Act and the Securities Exchange Act.[269]

I. Non-Statutory Restrictions

33. Charter and By-Laws

Additional restrictions upon the dividend fund not found in statutes, state or federal, may arise from the charter, articles of incorporation, or by-laws. A dividend may be illegal because of a restriction of the latter character.[270] Although such provisions may

---

[265] 49 U. S. C. A., §20(5) (authority to prescribe forms of accounts and classes of property for which depreciation charges may be included under operating expenses with amount thereof).

[266] 49 U. S. C. A., §320.

[267] 16 U. S. C. A., §§797(f), 825(h) (elaborate provisions as to details of accounting which may be regulated).

[268] 47 U. S. C. A., §220(a). See 1 Dodd and Baker, *Cases on Business Associations* (1940) 1115.

[269] Securities Act, 15 U. S. C. A., §77aa, Schedule A(25) (26) ; Securities and Exchange Act, 15 U. S. C. A., §78 (1) (m) ; Accounting Series Releases No. 12, 14; Securities Act Release No. 2179; Securities Exchange Act Release No. 2414. For various rulings of the Commission, see Chapter 3, *infra*.

[270] *Wagstaff v. Holly Sugar Corp.*, 253 App. Div. 616, 3 N. Y. S. (2d) 552 (1st Dept. 1938), aff'd 279 N. Y. 625 (1938); see *Stringer's Case*, L. R. 4 Ch. App. 475, 490 (1869) ; *Gallagher v. New York Dock Co.*, 19 N. Y. S. (2d) 789 (1940) (provision in certificate of incorporation limiting preferred noncumulative

curtail a corporation's power to make distribution to shareholders, they cannot enlarge it beyond the statutory limitations.

34. Trust Indenture Provisions

Outstanding trust indentures must always be consulted before the declaration of any dividend. They frequently contain clauses requiring the establishment of a sinking fund out of net income or the maintenance of a certain ratio between current assets and current liabilities. A corporation paying dividends from earnings without careful consideration of such provisions may very easily find itself in default on its bonds and mortgages.

In *Hoyt v. du Pont de Nemours,* it was held that bondholders, relying on the provisions of the trust indenture, might enjoin the reduction of a corporation's capital and distribution of the reduction surplus, apparently on the theory that while ordinary surplus could be distributed in dividends under a clause in the indenture providing that the corporation might dispose of all of its profits and income in the shape of dividends, this did not apply to a reduction surplus "from the fund created and pledged to secure the debt," even though after the proposed reduction there would be a book surplus of $1,500,000 and assets in the ratio of $5 for every dollar of indebtedness.[271] The indenture contained the usual charge upon property of all kinds belonging to the corporation, present and after acquired. The case raises serious questions for every corporation with bonds and mortgages outstanding if it proposes to reduce its capital. Unless limited to the terms of the trust indenture there involved, the case is open to the construction that bondholders have a general right to enjoin the reduction of capital and distribution of reduction surplus to stockholders, on the ground that it impairs the mortgage lien, even though there may be an undistributed surplus after the reduction.

Since the provisions of trust indentures are for the protection of bondholders, corporate stockholders have no standing to contest distributions in violation thereof.[272]

---

dividends to surplus net earnings of each fiscal year held to prevent declaration from surplus accumulated in other years even though N. Y. Stock Corporation Law, §58, would have permitted such dividends).

[271] 88 N. J. Eq. 196, 102 Atl. 666 (Ct. Ch. 1917).

[272] *Gallagher v. New York Dock Co.,* 19 N. Y. S. (2d) 789 (N. Y. Spec. Term, Kings County, 1940).

CHAPTER 3

COMPUTATION OF THE FUND AVAILABLE UNDER THE BALANCE SHEET SURPLUS TEST

A. Balance Sheet Assets

35. The Corporate Balance Sheet

The principal statutory restriction on the payment of dividends defines the fund available as the excess of assets over liabilities including in the latter capital.[1] The application of this rule in practice necessitates the use of a corporate balance sheet. Specifically, the problem becomes one of determining what particular assets and what particular liabilities must or may be included in a balance sheet in order to meet the broad statutory definition. It is at this point that services of the corporate accountant become necessary.[2] Having to comply with the requirements of the statute, his determination is necessarily both a legal and an accounting function. Accountants do not consider it the purpose of financial statements to show merely the surplus available for dividends, but rather to present all the pertinent information to a general consideration of the corporation's financial position.[3] Financial statements meet a

[1] See §§16, 21–23, *supra*.

[2] Generally, see Paton and Littleton, *An Introduction to Corporate Accounting Standards* (1940); Ballantine and Lattin, *Cases and Materials on the Law of Corporations* (1939), Note on Accounting and Legal Capital, 437; Berle and Fisher, *Elements of the Law of Business Accounting*, 32 Col. L. Rev. 573 (1932); 2 Bonbright, *Valuation of Property* (1937) 920–972; Deinzer, *Capital Stock and Surplus: Legal and Accounting Relations*, 10 Acc. Rev. 333 (1935); 1 Dodd and Baker, *Cases on Business Associations* (1940), c. VII, §7; Douglas and Shanks, *Cases and Materials on Business Units—Losses, Liabilities and Assets* (1932), Note, 192–195; Douglas and Shanks, *Management Volume* (1931) 602–606; Hills, *Accounting in Corporation Law*, 12 Wis. L. Rev. 494 (1937); Graham and Katz, *Accounting in Law Practice* (2d Ed. 1938); Kaplan and Reaugh, *Accounting, Reports to Stockholders and the SEC*, 48 Yale L. J. 935 (1939); Littleton, *Evolution of Accounting to 1900* (1933) (a valuable historical study on the development of the dividend concept in accounting); Marple, *Capital, Surplus and Corporate Net Worth* (1936); Note, *Nature of Corporate Dividends*, 3 Brooklyn L. Rev. 91 (1934); Reiter, *Profits, Dividends and the Law* (1926); Weiner and Bonbright, *Theory of Anglo-American Dividend Law: Surplus and Profits*, 30 Col. L. Rev. 330, 954 (1930); Annotations, "Right or duty of corporation to pay dividends; and liability for wrongful payment," 55 A. L. R. 8, 23; 76 A. L. R. 885, 887; 109 A. L. R. 1381, 1383. For an excellent legal analysis of the accounting problems in this chapter, see 1 Dodd and Baker, *Cases on Business Associations* (1940), Note on Capital and Surplus, 730–772.

variety of new demands which require that they be confined to presenting facts rather than drawing conclusions which might be applicable to one legal demand but not another. Principal among these new demands is use of financial records as a basis for the income tax and work of the various regulatory commissions, including especially the Securities and Exchange Commission, Interstate Commerce Commission, Federal Power Commission and allied stated commissions. For this reason, the corporate lawyer and director when examining a balance sheet or a profit and loss statement for the purpose of declaring dividends cannot stop with the line earned surplus in the one case, or net profits in the other. Careful consideration must be given each asset and liability fact recorded to ascertain whether a fund larger or smaller than that *prima facie* appearing will in fact be available for dividends.

Accounting practice in large measure does, however, represent legal doctrines common to the law of dividends. At many points the interplay of law and accounting synchronize. Principal attention must be directed to points where they do not or to points where there is doubt. How far general accounting practices can be followed in dividend matters may best be determined by a consideration of the individual asset and liability items of a corporate balance sheet.

December 31, 1940

ASSETS		LIABILITIES	
Fixed assets:		Funded debt:	
Land	$ 20,000	Bond issue	$ 10,000
Buildings	50,000	Current liabilities:	
Machinery and equipment	30,000	Accounts payable	6,000
Current assets:		Accrued accounts for interest, wages, and taxes	4,000
Cash and bank deposits	25,000	Reserves:	
Notes and accounts receivable	20,000	Doubtful debts	2,000
Inventory	15,000	Depreciation	8,000
Deferred charges:		Depletion	2,000
Discount on funded debt	1,000	Contingent claims	1,000
Prepaid interest, insurance, and rent	500	Capital stock:	
Development expense	1,000	1,000 shares, $100 par	100,000
Organization expense	1,500	Surplus:	
Goodwill	5,000	At Dec. 31, 1939 $30,000	
		Earnings 1940 6,000	36,000
	$169,000		$169,000

[3] See Broad, *Some Comments on Surplus Account,* 66 J. of Accountancy 215 (1938); Littleton, *Concepts of Income Underlying Accounting,* 12 Acc. Rev. 13, 16 (1937).

In addition to ascertaining what specific assets or liabilities may or must be included in the balance sheet, there is always the equally important question of determining what valuation should be assigned to each item.

36. Fixed Assets Generally

Broadly speaking, the assets of a corporation are divided into three groups—fixed assets, current assets, and deferred charges. Fixed assets are those of relatively permanent retention as media for the production and conversion of current assets, or inventory items, which the corporation sells and from which it normally makes its profits for dividend purposes.[4] Included in fixed assets are such principal items as land, buildings, machinery, tools, and equipment. Only assets acquired by purchase or through initial investment are ordinarily included in the balance sheet.[5]

The important problem in connection with fixed assets is that of valuation. The precedents for carrying fixed assets at cost go back to early days of the corporation.[6] Subsequent events may make permissible deviation either up or down, but the first accounting entry is the original cost of the asset. This is the only objective figure that appears on a balance sheet. Where the property is purchased for cash, the problem is relatively simple, as cost will be measured by the cash outlay.[7]

In order that cost may be taken as the proper valuation, it is

---

[4] Division into fixed assets and current assets is old in the history of corporate accounting. In a 1678 balance sheet of the East India Company, assets were divided into "Dead stock—fortifications &c." and "Quick stock—ships and goods." 2 Scott, *Joint Stock Companies to 1720* (1912) 138.

[5] Porter and Fiske, *Accounting* (1935) 245.

[6] In 1682, the fixed assets of the East India Company were valued, not at their worth to the trade, but at the total outlay upon them. 2 Scott, *supra* n. 4, at 145. In 1704, the banking office of the Bank of Scotland was listed as an asset at "first coast" plus all "reparations." 3 Scott, 263. For early American precedents see Massachusetts Bank (1784), MSS 781 (1784-1906), M 414, v. 31, p. 4; Delaware Canal Co., Thirty-second Ann. Rep. (1851) 13; Schuylkill Navigation Co., Rep. of Jan. 5, 1829, p. 9; Boston Manufacturing Co., MSS Boston Manufacturing Co., Directors' Records Oct. 20, 1813 to Oct. 4, 1825, Meeting of Jan. 27, 1815.

[7] American Accounting Association, *Tentative Statement of Accounting Principles,* 11 Acc. Rev. 187, 188 (1936); 2 Bonbright, *Valuation of Property* (1937) 920; Paton and Littleton, *An Introduction to Corporate Accounting Standards* (1940) 27. Valuation placed on assets in good faith at time of purchase will not be upset. *Davenport v. Lines,* 77 Conn. 473, 59 Atl. 603 (1905) (statute providing that directors must have knowledge dividend is from capital). Because current assets, particularly inventory, are usually valued on a basis of cost or market whichever is lower (§38, *infra*), it is important to determine whether a particular asset is a fixed asset or a current asset.

necessary, however, that the purchase be a fair, arm's length transaction. Many situations can be supposed where cost is apt to be a fictitious rather than a real indicator of actual value. Sales to the corporation by promoters or officers and directors suggest themselves as susceptible to this practice. Another situation to be scrutinized is the transfer of property from subsidiary to parent or *vice versa*. As is common in manufacturing enterprises, subsidiaries are often employed in the production of basic inventory materials for use at a later stage by the parent. When the transfer is made to the parent, there is an obvious opportunity for a sale which would produce a cost to the parent amounting to merely an inventory write-up. To illustrate, suppose a wholly owned subsidiary corporation supplies castings to its parent. Assume the balance sheets of the corporations before sale of the castings to be as follows:

PARENT

ASSETS		LIABILITIES	
Stock of subsidiary	$ 500,000	Capital	$1,000,000
Cash	1,500,000	Surplus	1,000,000
	$2,000,000		$2,000,000

SUBSIDIARY

ASSETS		LIABILITIES	
Iron castings	$1,000,000	Capital	$ 500,000
Other assets	500,000	Surplus	1,000,000
	$1,500,000		$1,500,000

Assume the subsidiary then sells $500,000 of its castings to the parent for $1,000,000, with the resulting balance sheets as follows:

PARENT

ASSETS		LIABILITIES	
Stock of subsidiary	$ 500,000	Capital	$1,000,000
Iron castings	1,000,000	Surplus	1,000,000
Cash	500,000		
	$2,000,000		$2,000,000

SUBSIDIARY

ASSETS		LIABILITIES	
Iron castings	$ 500,000	Capital	$ 500,000
Cash	1,000,000	Surplus	1,500,000
Other assets	500,000		
	$2,000,000		$2,000,000

It may be very unfair to permit the parent corporation to declare dividends on the assumption that cost of $1,000,000 for the castings represents a proper valuation. When inflations take place through dealings between parent and subsidiary or between affiliated companies, the real value of the assets rather than their fictitious book value applies for purposes of dividend accounting.[8] For quite similar reasons, stock in subsidiary or affiliated companies is not valued at cost but on the basis of the intrinsic worth or net asset value supporting the stock.[9]

The expense of moving and putting in place items of plant and machinery is properly included in their asset valuation.[10] This expense is properly an asset, since it enters into the cost of a complete production unit just as much as the amount paid the vendor for the machinery. Put somewhat differently, any other corporation which sought to establish the same type of production unit would have similar initial placement expenses. Comparable expenditures which add values to the corporation's property which could be realized on a resale should likewise be recognized as assets.

36.1. Valuation of Property Sold for Securities

The problem of valuation inherent in every purchase of property in exchange for corporate securities cuts across subsequent dividend determinations. Accountants normally favor using fair market value of property acquired in exchange for securities.[11] In those jurisdictions which use the "true value" test in determining the liability of stockholders for watered stock, it would seem that excessively valued property should be carried as an asset only at its real value, and that dividends should not be paid until assets equivalent to the difference between the real value and the inflated value have been accumulated out of earnings. Under such a rule, stockholders would be satisfying their liability with respect to watered

[8] *Irving Trust Co. v. Gunder,* 152 Misc. 83, 271 N. Y. S. 795 (1934). See Graham and Katz, *Accounting in Law Practice* (2d Ed. 1938) 397; Paton and Littleton, *An Introduction to Corporate Accounting Standards* (1940) 27; Sanders, Hatfield, and Moore, *Statement of Accounting Principles,* 30; Kracke, *Consolidated Financial Statements,* 66 J. of Accountancy 372, 380–381 (1938); Littleton, *Business Profits as a Legal Basis for Dividends,* 16 Harv. Bus. Rev. 51, 59 (1938).

[9] *Irving Trust Co. v. Gunder,* n. 8, *supra.*

[10] *Hubbard v. Weare,* 79 Iowa 678, 692–693, 44 N. W. 915 (1890); 2 Bonbright, *Valuation of Property* (1937) 926; Paton and Littleton, *An Introduction to Corporate Accounting Standards* (1940) 31.

[11] See American Accounting Association, *Tentative Statement of Accounting Principles,* 11 Acc. Rev. 187, 188 (1936); 2 Bonbright, *Property Valuation* (1937) 927.

stock out of current earnings. On the other hand, in those jurisdictions, many expressly by statute,[12] where the valuation of directors is conclusive for watered stock purposes in the absence of fraud, it would seem that such valuation should likewise be conclusive for dividend purposes. Otherwise stockholders are, in fact, liable for watered stock to the extent of corporate earnings which should have been used to eliminate the deficiency.

The dividend cases dealing with overvaluation of property do not as a rule rely upon analogies to the watered stock situation. In *Goodnow v. American Writing Paper Company* and *Peters v. U. S. Mortgage Company,* the problem was handled by treating capital as equal to the reduced value of the property received, thereby recognizing the right to pay dividends out of assets in excess of this adjusted capital but at the same time apparently accepting the principle that actual value and not watered stock value should be assigned to corporate assets for dividend purposes.[13] Thus, there are two theories under which dividends may be paid even though stock has been issued in excess of the value of property received. The capital may be treated as reduced to the value of the property, or the property may be carried at the par or stated value of the capital, on the theory that the directors' valuation is conclusive for dividend as well as stock watering purposes.

As a result of tax requirements[14] and the provisions of the Securities Act,[15] corporations have been forced to segregate from their tangible book valuations of fixed assets those amounts which substantially represent the intangible item of goodwill or purchase price in excess of actual asset value.[16] Although the income tax merely

---

[12] See e.g. Del. Rev. Code (1935), c. 65, §14; N. Y. Stock Corp. Law, §69; Cal. Civ. Code (1937), §300a; 32 Ill. Ann. Stat. (Smith-Hurd 1935), §157.18.

[13] For discussion of these cases see §22.1, *supra.* For agreement by two leading accountants, see Paton and Littleton, *An Introduction to Corporate Accounting Standards* (1940) 27–28, 37, 40. In *Pardee v. Harwood Electric Co.,* 262 Pa. 68, 105 Atl. 48 (1918), property was taken at an overvaluation on a merger. Thereafter reserves were set up out of earnings to write off the overvaluation. This was held proper as against a claim of preferred stockholders under certificates entitling them to cumulative dividends out of "net earnings . . . after payment of all operating expenses," the court indicating it could not be said that this was not a proper operating expense. Cf. *Washburn v. National Wall Paper Co.,* 81 Fed. 17 (C. C. A. 2d, 1897).

[14] Depreciation is allowed for income tax purposes only upon intangibles used in the business which have a definitely limited duration, such as patents, copyrights, and licenses. Depreciation is not allowed on the intangible values resulting from the acquisition of property in excess of its value. Reg. 103, §19.23(1)–3.

[15] The intangible items of cost must be segregated for the purpose of registration statements filed with the S. E. C. [Securities Act, Schedule A (25)].

[16] See e.g. Report of United States Steel Corporation (1938), p. 14; Plan of

prohibits the deduction of depreciation on such items, the effect has been more far-reaching from the dividend standpoint. Once these intangible items, usually substantial, are segregated, the corporation may not like to keep assets of this character on its balance sheet. As a result, they are often charged off against some form of surplus.

A distinction has been suggested in overvaluation cases where at the time the rights of creditors are not involved, but only the conflicting rights of common and preferred stockholders. Under these circumstances, it was held in *Star Publishing Company v. Ball,* that a valuation placed upon assets at acquisition for the purpose of allocating common and preferred stock was later binding upon the common in determining rights of preferred to dividends.[17] It was, therefore, unnecessary to make up out of earnings the overvaluation deficit before the preferred would be entitled to dividends. In this case only a small portion of the corporation's bonded indebtedness remained still unpaid, and the court called attention to the absence of any controversy between a creditor and the corporation. It may be seriously questioned as to whether a present jeopardy of creditors should be prerequisite to a rule that water must be eliminated from the balance sheet for dividend purposes. The theory of capital maintenance is that an accounting reserve of assets equivalent to capital should at all times be maintained before dividends are declared. In this regard, it is wholly immaterial whether creditors are presently pressing the corporation. These or other creditors having a presumed right to rely on the corporation's capital may do so later.

Assuming that stock is issued for excessively valued property, will subsequent undistributed earnings be held in any event to satisfy the deficiency to the extent the stock is watered? In *Hyams v. Old Dominion Copper Mining and Smelting Company,* the corporation proposed to declare a dividend from the proceeds of a judgment against promoters for damages.[18] The payment was contested by a shareholder on the ground that the amount of the judgment constituted capital. This contention was substantially correct as the recovery represented payment for shares which had not been paid for in the first instance. However, in the interim following illegal is-

---

American Smelting & Refining Company (Apr. 3, 1935). See also 1 Dodd and Baker, *Cases on Business Associations* (1940), Note on Unrealized Diminution in Value of Fixed Assets; Intangibles, 1105.

[17] 192 Ind. 158, 134 N. E. 285 (1922).

[18] 82 N. J. Eq. 507, 89 Atl. 37 (1913), aff'd on opinion below 91 Atl. 1069 (1914).

suance of the shares, the corporation had prospered, earning sufficient current net profits to make good the original balance sheet impairment, and at the time of the proposed dividend the balance sheet showed, including the amount of the judgment, a surplus of assets over liabilities, including capital stock. The court, therefore, held that under the New Jersey Act of 1904 (substantially similar to the present provision), the first alternative—a corporate surplus—was clearly met.[19]

36.2. Realized Losses

There is implicit in the balance sheet net asset test an assumption that there may be changes from historic cost of assets to some lesser figure which might create an impairment of capital and a restriction upon dividends. Quite different from the problem of whether or not unrealized market gains and losses are to be taken into consideration is the question whether the balance sheet must reflect actual losses. Where it is a problem of unrealized market gain or loss, subsequent events may entirely change the situation. What was an unrealized gain may turn out to be a sustained loss when a sale actually takes place, and conversely, an unrealized loss may prove to be an actual profit. However, if property has been stolen, destroyed by fire, or its value permanently impaired or obliterated, there is a sustained loss which time cannot remove. Such losses must obviously be taken into consideration for dividend purposes.[20] Many of the more recent corporation acts expressly make this requirement.[21] In several other states, if the capital of the corporation, due to losses, falls to an amount below the liquidation preferences of preferred stock, dividends cannot be paid.[22]

---

[19] In *Cole v. Adams,* 19 Tex. Civ. App. 507, 49 S. W. 1052 (1898), aff'd 92 Tex. 171, 46 S. W. 790 (1898), it was held that earnings which had not been distributed in dividends had the effect of paying the balance due on watered stock. Cf. *Kenton Furnace Railroad & Mfg. Co. v. McAlpin,* 5 Fed. 737 (S. D. Ohio 1880) (accumulated profits and increase in value of real estate held available to discharge 50 per cent balance remaining due on original stock subscription).

[20] See *Jennery v. Olmstead,* 36 Hun (N. Y.) 536, 539–540 (3d Dept. 1885) (dictum as to construction of provision for payment out of "net profits" under an employment contract); cf. 2 Bonbright, *Valuation of Property* (1937) 957; Sanders, Hatfield, and Moore, *Statement of Accounting Principles* (1938) 40.

[21] Idaho Code Ann., §29–129; La. Gen. Stat. (Dart. 1939), §1106; Minn. Stat. (Mason 1938 Supp.), §7492–21; Ohio Code Ann. (Baldwin 1938), §8623–38; 15 Purd. Pa. Stat. Ann., §2852–701; Vt. Pub. Laws (1933), §5850; Wash. Rev. Stat. Ann. (Rem.), §3803–24.

[22] Del. Rev. Code (1935), c. 65, §34 (not out of net profits); Kans. Laws 1939, c. 152, §81 (similar provision); Cal. Civ. Code (1937), §346 (no dividends to shares other than those having liquidation preferences).

36.3. Unrealized Losses

Whether a corporation should be required by statute or decision to reduce asset valuations in conformity to declines in the price level is a question fundamental in the theory of dividend regulation. The investment of capital in a corporation may be viewed two ways, either as a fixed dollar investment or as the purchase of a unit of economic wealth fluctuating in value with the change in purchasing power of the dollar. The adoption of one or the other of these theories is closely allied to the operation of the double entry system of bookkeeping. Assume that upon organization on January 1, 1937 stockholders contribute property reasonably worth $100,000 in return for 1,000 shares of $100 par value stock. The journal entries will show a debit to property account of $100,000 and a credit to capital stock account of $100,000. A balance sheet at this point would show:

ASSETS		LIABILITIES	
Property	$100,000	Capital Stock	$100,000

If the corporation transacts no business subsequent to its organization until after the break in the market in the fall of 1937, the question arises as to how a drop in the market value of the original property to $75,000 is to be treated on the balance sheet. On December 31, 1937, it would require only $75,000 of capital to purchase the same property. If the capital investment is considered as a unit of economic wealth which fluctuates with the price level, then the asset side of the balance sheet should be written down to $75,000. This is the procedure followed when a corporation takes account of an unrealized market loss. The balance sheet adjustment stops here (in the absence of further steps to reduce capital), producing this one-sided result:

ASSETS		LIABILITIES	
Property	$75,000	Capital Stock	$100,000
		Deficit	(25,000)

There is no objection to accepting the economic unit interpretation providing the basic theory underlying double entry bookkeeping is applied not only on the asset side of the balance sheet but also on the liability side. Under the economic unit theory, the corporation no longer has capital of $100,000 but only of $75,000, since only $75,-000 is required to purchase the property which the corporation possesses. Assets should not be valued on the economic unit theory and liabilities on the conflicting fixed dollar investment theory. Consistency requires that both sides of the balance sheet should be written down or neither. Since it is the usual practice in the absence of a formal stock reduction to treat capital stock as though it were still equal to the original consideration received, the property should be carried also as an asset at cost.

The practical effect of adopting the economic unit theory only as to the asset side of the balance sheet is to compel the stockholder to carry the entire risk of market declines. He in effect is compelled to assure the creditor against losses from fluctuations in the market to the extent that there are subsequent earnings which would otherwise have been available for dividends. Thus, in the case suggested, where the assets are written down to $75,000 but the capital left at $100,000, stockholders must allow earnings of $25,000 to accumulate to discharge the deficit before being entitled to further dividends. In short, the stockholder will have made a contribution to capital in the amount of $125,000 rather than $100,000. There is no reason why stockholders rather than creditors should bear the risk of market declines. The stockholder has contributed his original capital, and that stands dedicated as a safeguard against just such market fluctuations, but to require him to make further contributions is inconsistent with the theory of limited liability and the modern tendency to treat stockholders and creditors of large corporations as more nearly on a parity.[23]

It is the general practice among accountants to carry fixed assets at original cost, certainly in the absence of a very sharp market decline.[24] To do this, however, may prove dangerous in many jurisdictions. Even in the absence of any statute giving express indication that present value must be used, the language in many dividend cases indicates a possible requirement that valuation of fixed assets must be on the basis of present value rather than book value.[25] Direct

---

[23] See §9.1, *supra*. On this problem generally, see Briggs, *Asset Valuation in Dividend Decisions*, 9 Acc. Rev. 220 (1934); 1 Dodd and Baker, *Cases on Business Associations* (1940), Note on Unrealized Diminution in Value of Fixed Assets, 1105.

[24] There is some tendency recently, however, to take account of all diminutions or expirations of cost even when the amounts thereof are not subject to precise measurement and must be estimated. *American Accounting Principles*, 11 Acc. Rev. 187, 188 (1936). See Dewing, *Financial Policy of Corporations* (3d Rev. Ed. 1934) 593; Rorem, *Accounting Theory: A Critique of the Tentative Statement of Accounting Principles*, 12 Acc. Rev. 133, 134 (1937); but cf. Paton and Littleton, *An Introduction to Corporate Accounting Standards* (1940) 28.

[25] See *Cannon v. Wiscassett Mills Co.*, 195 N. C. 119, 125, 141 S. E. 344 (1928) (in holding depreciation must be taken into account the court stated, "Manifestly, for the purposes of determining the amount to be declared and paid as a dividend,

authority that a decline in the market level must be reflected by a write-down of book asset values is, however, meager. In *Southern California Home Builders v. Young,* directors were held liable where the balance sheet and books on which they relied in declaring dividends showed "assets" of the corporation "to be of a value very largely in excess of their actual value." [26]

It would seem that, in the absence of statute, a distinction should at least be made where the decline in the price level is merely a normal market fluctuation as distinguished from a broad cyclical collapse. In the case of normal market changes, to require a revaluation of assets would necessitate the expense of annual appraisals, produce a fluctuating balance sheet, and render the corporation's accounting a system of conjectural valuations. Historical cost, in the absence of pronounced changes in the price level, should therefore be adhered to. [27]

In many jurisdictions the question of market losses is the subject of statutory regulation. Statutes, with the broad provision that "losses of every character" must be taken into account before dividends are declared, would seem to encompass declines in the price level. [28] Delaware corporations with outstanding preferred stock

---

it is necessary that the true value of the assets, in cash, and not the mere book value, should be ascertained, for no dividend can be lawfully declared and paid except from the surplus or net profits of the business"); *Siegman v. Electric Vehicle Co.,* 140 Fed. 117, 121 (D. N. J. 1905) (the directors "must value its assets at no higher figures than reasonably prudent men would do"); *Hyams v. Old Dominion Copper Mining & Smelting Co.,* 82 N. J. Eq. 507, 514, 89 Atl. 37 (1913), aff'd 91 Atl. 1069 (1914) (in sustaining valuation placed on mining claim assets, court said their "real value" exceeded the sum at which they were carried on the books); *Whittaker v. Amwell National Bank,* 52 N. J. Eq. 400, 406, 29 Atl. 203 (Ct. Ch. 1894) (in requiring depreciation for wear and tear to be taken into account, the court stated the test as to whether or not there is a surplus to be "what was the fair value" of the assets). Cf. *Vogtman v. Merchants Mortgage & Credit Co.,* 20 Del. Ch. 364, 178 Atl. 99 (1935) (loss in market value of assets of a loan and investment corporation not held for permanent investment must be deducted); *Washburn v. National Paper Co.,* 81 Fed. 17, 21 (C. C. A. 2d, 1897), but see 2 Bonbright, *Valuation of Property* (1937) 925.

[26] 45 Cal. App. 679, 689, 188 Pac. 586 (1920). *In re Commonwealth Telephone Co.,* P. U. R. 1932 D. 299 (P. S. C. Wis. 1932), payment of dividends was enjoined pending further hearing because of a possible decline in value of fixed assets as well as possible inadequacy of depreciation reserves.

[27] American Accounting Assoc., *Tentative Statement of Accounting Principles,* 11 Acc. Rev. 187, 189 (1936); 1 Dodd and Baker, *Cases on Business Associations* (1940) 1107; *Gallagher v. New York Dock Co.,* 19 N. Y. S. (2d) 789, 798–800 (1940); cf. *Kahle v. Mount Vernon Trust Co.,* N. Y. L. J., Sept. 9, 1940, p. 569.

[28] Idaho Code Ann., §29–129; La. Gen. Stat. (Dart. 1939), §1106; Minn. Stat. (Mason 1938 Supp.), §7492–21 ["losses of every character whether or not realized"; it has been suggested that since only sound accounting practice was intended by the act, only declines in the market value of current assets need be

entitled to preferential payment on a distribution of assets must consider the provision in Section 34 of the Delaware General Corporation Law prohibiting the payment of dividends where there has been a "depreciation in the value of its property, or by losses, or otherwise" to an amount less than that required to meet the distribution preferences. The clause is extremely broad. If merely accounting depreciation had been meant, no further provision than depreciation would have been necessary; but the section prohibits payment when there is depreciation in the "value" of its property. Since there is no limitation to current assets, the section presumably covers declines in the market value of the corporation's fixed assets.[29] The possibility that the section may receive this construction is strengthened by the balance of the clause requiring diminution of preference capital "by losses, or otherwise" to be taken into account. In the absence of a broad cyclical swing affecting the soundness of cost values on fixed assets, the section should not be construed as requiring recognition of depreciation in value of property or a loss. Particularly should this result be reached where, as will be the usual case, the corporation's accounting officers continue to carry these assets at cost and directors rely on good faith on their valuation. The last part of Section 34 of the Delaware Act protects directors relying in good faith upon the value and amount of assets as shown by books and statements prepared by the corporation's officers.[30]

Section 41 of the Illinois Business Corporation Act provides that dividends shall not be paid unless net assets exceed stated capital.[31] In dealing with the conditions under which directors may be exonerated from liability, it is provided in Section 42 that a director shall not be liable if he relies in good faith on accounting statements

---

taken, but not declines in fixed assets where there are adequate reserves, Solether and Jennings, *Minnesota Business Corporation Act,* 12 Wis. L. Rev. 419, 433 (1937); the language of the statute seems too broad to permit of this construction]; 15 Purd. Pa. Stat. Ann., §2852–701; Wash. Rev. Stat. Ann. (Rem.), §3802–24. In Ohio and Vermont "losses" must be deducted. Ohio Code Ann. (Baldwin 1938), §8623–38; Vt. Pub. Laws (1933), §5850.

[29] For the view that the Delaware law by clear implication requires a valuation of assets to determine whether a dividend fund exists, see Colman and Finn, *Comparison of Business Corporation Law of Minnesota and Delaware,* 22 Minn. L. Rev. 661, 671 (1938).

[30] Similar problems are presented by the recent amendments in Kansas. Kans. Laws 1939, c. 152, §§81, 86.

[31] Section 41, by prohibiting dividends when "net assets" are less than capital, was intended to leave open the question of what effect was to be given to initial overvaluations, shrinkages in market value, and similar accounting questions. It was felt these practices had not sufficiently crystallized to warrant the formulation of statutory rules. See Chicago Bar Assoc., *Illinois Business Corporation Act Ann.* (1934) 152.

"nor . . . if in good faith . . . he considered the assets to be of their book value." Certainly where the director has knowledge that the assets are not of their book value, there is no protection against personal liability. If he is only negligent, but acts in good faith, it would seem, on the other hand, that he is not liable.

In California dividends are prohibited on all stock except shares having a liquidation preference where the capital required to meet such preference has been impaired by losses or otherwise.[32]

Certain special problems arise where there is a requirement that market declines be taken into consideration before declaring a dividend. First, how is the new valuation to be determined? Obviously, the determination is a question of opinion upon which final responsibility will usually rest with directors. There is some indication that, as in other management matters, valuation must be left to their honest, non-fraudulent judgment.[33]

Secondly, how should reductions in market value be handled—by direct write-offs or reserves? The method adopted makes a great deal of difference. If the valuation of the asset is directly charged down, any subsequent appreciation presumably cannot be recredited until a sale has taken place.[34] If a reserve is created, while maintaining the asset at its original cost, it may be abolished when the need for it has disappeared leaving the original asset value intact in whole or in part. The right to pay subsequent dividends may depend very largely on which method has been used.

There is a further question as to whether unrealized appreciation may be used to offset losses. In *Titus v. Piggly Wiggly Corporation,* the corporation increased on its books the value of patents, trade name, goodwill, and licensee contracts from $810,000, original cost, to $4,000,000.[35] The court overruled an objection of creditors and

[32] Cal. Civ. Code (1937), §346. The obligation to take account of market declines is implied from the provision in §346c that paid-in and reduction surplus may be used to write off diminution in value of assets.

[33] *Hyams v. Old Dominion Copper Mining & Smelting Co.,* 82 N. J. Eq. 507, 515, 89 Atl. 37 (1913), aff'd 91 Atl. 1069 (1914). The presumption is that directors acted in good faith. *Guaranty Trust Co. v. Grand Rapids, G. H. & M. Ry. Co.,* 7 F. Supp. 511 (W. D. Mich. 1931), modified on other grounds and as modified affirmed, 85 F. (2d) 331 (C. C. A. 6th, 1936), *cert. gr.* on petition of receiver 299 U. S. 534 (1936); dismissed per stipulation 299 U. S. 618 (1936); *cert. den.* on petition of *United Light & Power Co.,* 299 U. S. 591 (1936). In the latter case the court indicated that earning capacity of a public utility was one of the principal indices of the value of its property.

[34] Michigan provides, however, that readjustments of previous reductions of value to correctly reflect the accounts of the corporation may be made. Mich. Ann. Stat. (Henderson 1937), §21.22.

[35] 2 Tenn. App. 184 (1925) [comment, Dewing, *Financial Policy of Corporations* (3d Rev. Ed. 1934) 599].

stockholders that this procedure was illegal and unavailable for wiping out a prior capital deficit, so as to permit dividends from subsequent earnings.[36]

Finally, there is the important question of eliminating unrealized market losses in fixed assets in order that the corporation may be restored to a dividend basis. A corporation with a capital impairment resulting from earnings deficits or market declines is confronted with complete termination of dividend distributions or some voluntary readjustment of capital structure. What is in effect a quasi-reorganization becomes necessary, in which the asset side of the balance sheet is written down from cost to present values and the write-down met on the liability side of the balance sheet either out of paid-in surplus or surplus created by the reduction of capital.[37] Where the decrease in value of assets is due to a collapse in the market level, this practice is sound in theory. A capital loss has actually been sustained. Writing off paid-in surplus or reducing capital simply recognizes an accomplished fact. The same decline in the price level which has reduced the value of corporate assets has likewise reduced the value of the capital invested.[38] The view toward

[36] See also *Ammonia Soda Co., Ltd. v. Chamberlain*, (1918) 1 Ch. 266, 275, criticized in 2 Bonbright, *Valuation of Property* (1937) 938–939. Write-ups for the purpose of writing off other assets have met the censure of the S. E. C. Kaplan and Reaugh, *Accounting, Reports to Stockholders and the S. E. C.*, 48 Yale L. J. 935, 963 (1939). See also, Healy, *The Next Step in Accounting*, 13 Acc. Rev. 1, 2–3 (1938) ; MacChesney, *The Security and Exchange Commission's Development of Accounting Standards*, 26 Cal. L. Rev. 349 (1938).

[37] Paton and Littleton, *An Introduction to Corporate Accounting Standards* (1940) 112. For current examples of such readjustments see Pullman, Inc., N. Y. Times Financial Section, Mar. 22, 1939; American Radiator & Standard Sanitary Corp., N. Y. Times Financial Section, Apr. 13, 1939; United Cigar-Whelan Stores Corp., N. Y. Times Financial Section, Aug. 12, 1939. The S. E. C. in its Accounting Releases has adopted the term "quasi reorganization" as meaning the corporate procedure whereby "a company, without the creation of a new corporate entity, is enabled to eliminate a deficit and establish a new earned surplus account for the accumulation of earnings subsequent to the date selected." Accounting Series Release No. 15, C. C. H. Stock Exchange Reg. Serv., §8625 (Mar. 16, 1940). Where a corporation eliminates a prior deficit by a charge to capital surplus, the S. E. C. requires the corporation's subsequent reports to set forth clearly, that this has been done. Accounting Series Releases No. 15, 16. Generally see Note, *Revaluation of Assets under Quasi-Reorganizations*, 49 Yale L. J. 1319 (1940).

[38] The American Institute of Accountants and the American Accounting Association have each taken a position in the main opposed to the use of any form of capital surplus to reduce asset values in a manner which would relieve the income account of current or future years of a portion of the charges which would otherwise fall against it. An exception is recognized where the write-off is to effect an informal reorganization, but a restricted interpretation of reorganization is taken. See 65 J. of Accountancy 89, 90 (1938) ; Broad, *Some Comments on Surplus Account*, 66 J. of Accountancy 215, 223 (1938) ; American Accounting Assoc.,

which many accountants seem to be turning—that deficits, particularly earned deficits, cannot be eliminated by charges to reduction or paid-in surplus—if rigorously extended, will cause serious freezing of corporate financial structures. A corporation which has a deficit but is still short of bankruptcy should not be forced to wait until it is *in extremis* for reorganization relief. Its capital is impaired; the fact should be recognized and the usual remedy of reorganization sanctioned before the situation becomes worse. Any other course will place corporate enterprise in a position where it cannot get back onto a dividend-paying basis until it has met the bankruptcy wringer. Forestalling reorganization until corporations throughout the nation reach insolvency might well entail strains on the financial economy too great to bear.

Considerable interest attaches to the case where the corporation has both an earned surplus and a paid-in surplus and wishes to write off losses arising from market declines. Can such write-offs be made against the paid-in surplus, thereby retaining the past earned surplus for dividend purposes? In jurisdictions where dividends are legally distributable from paid-in surplus, it will make no difference whether the charge is made against one or the other, because whichever is left will still be available for dividends. But a quite different problem is presented in those jurisdictions where paid-in surplus is never available for dividends or only for limited purposes. In such states the write-down should be against paid-in surplus. The argument that it should be against earned surplus fails to analyze the nature of the loss. Corporate assets are at a lower figure because of a fall in the price level, a shift in the purchasing power of the dollar. The same assets which it took capital of $100,000 to buy on January 1, 1937, could be bought with capital of $75,000 at the end of the year. The

---

Tentative Statement of Accounting Principles, 11 Acc. Rev. 187, 191; Werntz, *Some Current Problems in Accounting,* 14 Acc. Rev. 117, 118 (1939); Paton and Littleton, *An Introduction to Corporate Accounting Standards* (1940) 100–102. But a large majority of accounting writers recognize the writing off of even operating deficits out of paid-in surplus, thus making possible dividends out of earnings of succeeding years. Hatfield, *Operating Deficit and Paid-in Surplus,* 9 Acc. Rev. 237 (1934); see also Littleton, *A Substitute for Stated Capital,* 17 Harv. Bus. Rev. 75, 76 (1938). The Securities and Exchange Commission, in its accounting releases, has taken the position that capital surplus created by reduction of capital (and presumably its view would be the same as to paid-in surplus) should not be used to write off losses, which had they been currently recognized, would have been chargeable against income, but that the charge should be to earned surplus. In the case presented the write-down was to offset loss from obsolescence, lessened utility value, and difference between book value and replacement cost. S. E. C. Accounting Series Release No. 1, Apr. 1, 1937; Werntz, *Some Current Problems in Accounting,* 14 Acc. Rev. 117, 120 (1939).

loss is a capital loss having nothing to do with past earnings.[39] If it is held that earnings must be used to accomplish the write-off, stockholders, as heretofore pointed out, are made to assume the complete risk of cyclical market changes, and in effect to contribute additional capital where capital is impaired from such causes.

A ruling of the Attorney General of Illinois construes the provision of the Illinois Act that paid-in surplus may be applied to elimination of deficits arising from losses or diminution in value of its assets as permitting the use of paid-in surplus even though there is an existing earned surplus.[40] In Ohio, paid-in or reduction surplus is available to write off any particular loss or a deficit in the earned surplus account, making available for dividend purposes any resulting or remaining excess of assets.[41] Michigan permits use of reduction surplus to charge off losses from operations, revaluations, or otherwise.[42]

An extra-judicial reorganization by charges to paid-in surplus must, however, be "sufficiently thoroughgoing" to eliminate all questionable items in the balance sheet, presenting a restatement of assets in the light of conditions at the time of the reorganization, so that the corporation will be put "on substantially the same accounting basis as a new enterprise."[43]

36.4. Realized Gains

If with the balance sheet given in Section 35, the corporation had during the year 1940 sold one-half of its land, buildings, machinery,

[39] The S. E. C. has taken the opposite view under the Public Utility Holding Company Act in the important decision in *Matter of Associated Gas & Electric Corp.*, Holding Company Act Release No. 1873 (1940). In that case the Commission refused to recognize write-offs to paid-in surplus of realized losses on the sale of stocks and bonds during a period from 1922 to 1937. It took the position that the charges should have been to earned surplus; that since they had not been so made, the earned surplus account was inflated; and that in fact a deficit existed preventing the declaration of dividends under §12(c) of the act. See also Werntz, *Some Current Problems in Accounting*, 14 Acc. Rev. 117, 120–121 (1939); Paton and Littleton, *Introduction to Corporate Accounting Standards* (1940) 96.

[40] 32 Ill. Ann. Stat. (Smith-Hurd 1935), §157.60a; 1934 Op. Att. Gen. No. 682, criticized in Katz, *The Illinois Business Corporation Act*, 12 Wis. L. Rev. 473, 476–477 (1937). Where the deficit arises from current operations, and the corporation has a prior earned surplus, the deficit ought to be charged against the latter rather than against the paid-in surplus. Graham and Katz, *Accounting in Law Practice* (2d Ed. 1938) 152. The deficit relates to earnings and should be met out of the earned surplus account as long as it has a credit balance available.

[41] Ohio Code Ann. (Baldwin 1938), §8623–38.

[42] Mich. Stat. Ann. (Henderson 1937), §21.20; for further reference to statutes governing the use of paid-in and reduction surplus, see §§29, 30, *supra*.

[43] *Matter of Associated Gas & Electric Corp.*, Holding Company Act Release No. 1873 (1940).

and equipment costing $50,000 for $100,000 cash, the corporation's journal entries would show, apart from adjustments for reserves, a debit to cash of $100,000, balanced first by a credit to property accounts of $50,000, the cost of the property sold, plus a credit of $50,000 to surplus account. The corporation having changed physical assets of $50,000 for cash assets of $100,000, has $50,000 more in net assets. Is this $50,000, tentatively credited to surplus, available for dividends in the ordinary balance sheet surplus jurisdiction? If the economic unit theory were applied, a sale of capital assets would produce merely an increment in capital unavailable for dividend purposes. It is well established, however, that this theory does not apply and that a sale of capital assets at a price in excess of cost produces a balance sheet increase in assets which may be distributed as dividends.[44]

36.5. Unrealized Gains

Corollary to the problem of unrealized fixed asset losses [45] is that of unrealized gains.[46] A corporation organized in a low market receives property reasonably worth $100,000 in exchange for its capital stock of $100,000. The balance sheet reads:

ASSETS		LIABILITIES	
Property	$100,000	Capital Stock	$100,000

[44] *Equitable Life Assurance Society v. Union Pacific Railroad Co.*, 212 N. Y. 360, 106 N. E. 92 (1914) (gain on the sale of stocks of other corporations); *National Newark and Essex Banking Co. v. Durant Motor Co.*, 124 N. J. Eq. 213, 1 Atl. (2d) 316 (1938), aff'd 125 N. J. Eq. 435, 5 Atl. (2d) 315 (1939) (construing provision in proposed preferred stock certificate providing for distributions from earnings); see 2 Bonbright, *Valuation of Property* (1937) 922–923; Douglas and Shanks, *Cases and Materials on Business Units—Management* (1931), Note, 621–622; Frey, *Cases and Statutes on Business Associations* (1935), Note, 776; Montgomery, *Dealings in Treasury Stock*, 65 J. of Accountancy 466, 470 (1938); cf. *Mackintosh v. Flint, etc. R. R. Co.*, 34 Fed. 582, 601 (E. D. Mich. 1888) (charter provided for payment of preferred dividends from "earnings" less specified deductions); *People ex rel. Queens County Water Co. v. Travis*, 171 A. D. 521, 157 N. Y. S. 943 (3d Dept. 1916), aff'd 219 N. Y. 571, 114 N. E. 1079 (1916) (dividend tax case); *Lapham v. Tax Commissioner*, 244 Mass. 40, 138 N. E. 708 (1923) (dividend tax case). For an early example of profit on sale of investment assets being considered available for dividend purposes, see 2 Davis, *Essays in the Earlier History of American Corporations* (1917) 68.

[45] See §36.3, *supra*.

[46] Generally see 1 Dodd and Baker, *Cases on Business Associations* (1940) 1118; Hills, *Dividends from Unrealized Capital Appreciation*, 6 N. Y. L. Rev. 155, 193 (1928); Note, *Significance of Appreciation and Changing Price Levels in Corporate Dividend Policies*, 35 Mich. L. Rev. 286 (1936); Note, *Effect of Depreciation, Depletion and Appreciation of Assets on the Payment of Dividends*, 28 Col. L. Rev. 231 (1928); "Accretions in value of corporate assets as basis of dividends," L. R. A. 1915 D. 1052.

Before any business is transacted, the general market level appreciates so that the property is now reasonably worth $125,000. Is there a surplus of $25,000 available for dividends? If the property were actually sold and the profit realized, there would be a recognized increment which could be distributed. But a corporation does not normally hold its fixed assets for sale, and to permit a distribution of dividends on the basis of unrealized gains may place the corporation in a position of bad capital impairment should the market level again subsequently decline. The gain is merely a factor of the change in price level and, since fixed assets are not ordinarily held for disposition, should not be taken into account. Furthermore, the uncertainty which arises from the necessity that revaluations be merely an estimate discourages treating such gains as accounting values.[47] In the absence of controlling statutory provisions, the majority of cases refuse to recognize the right to treat unrealized fixed asset gains as available for ordinary dividends.[48] Where by the inherent nature of the asset there is accretion in value by growth or productivity, the problem is not that of recognizing a mere unrealized increase in market value. The asset or its product is more valuable even when

[47] See Draft of Committee on Revision of Ohio General Corporation Act (Dec. 1926) 92. In *La Belle Iron Works v. U. S.*, 256 U. S. 377, 393–394 (1921), sustaining valuations at cost in a tax case, the court said: "There is a logical incongruity in entering upon the books of a corporation as the capital value of property acquired for permanent employment in its business and still retained for that purpose, a sum corresponding not to its cost but to what probably might be realized by sale in the market. It is not merely that the market value has not been realized or tested by sale made, but that sale cannot be made without abandoning the very purpose for which the property is held."

[48] *Southern California Home Builders v. Young*, 45 Cal. App. 679, 695, 188 Pac. 586 (1920) (under statute restricting dividends to "surplus profits arising from the business"); *Kingston v. Home Life Insurance Co.*, 11 Del. Ch. 258, 272, 101 Atl. 898 (Ct. Ch. 1917) (dictum under statute limiting dividends to "surplus or net profits arising from the business"); see also *Titus v. Piggly Wiggly Corporation*, 2 Tenn. App. 184, 196–197 (1925); *Vogtman v. Merchants Mfg. & Credit Co.*, 20 Del. Ch. 364, 178 Atl. 99, 102 (1935); Ballantine and Lattin, *Cases and Materials on the Law of Corporations* (1939), Note on Unrealized Appreciation and Depreciation, 459; 2 Bonbright, *Valuation of Property* (1937) 922–923, 968; Kester, *Principles of Accounting* (3d Rev. Ed. 1930) 424; 1 Dodd and Baker, *Cases on Business Associations* (1940), Note on Unrealized Appreciation in Assets, 1118; Sanders, Hatfield and Moore, *A Statement of Accounting Principles* (1938) 40; *contra: Randall v. Bailey*, N. Y. L. J., Oct. 29, 1940, p. 1309 (comment, 50 Yale L. J. 306); and see *Wittenberg v. Federal Mining & Smelting Co.*, 15 Del. Ch. 351, 354, 138 Atl. 352 (1927); Dewing, *Financial Policy of Corporations* (3d Rev. Ed. 1934) 604. *In Jennery v. Olmstead*, 36 Hun (N. Y.) 536 (3d Dept. 1885), aff'd 105 N. Y. 654 (1887), unrealized appreciation of bonds held for investment purposes by a savings bank was held not to constitute "net profits" under an employment contract. Cf. *Dealers Granite Corp. v. Faubion*, 18 S. W. (2d) 737 (Tex. Civ. App. 1929) (unrealized appreciation of quarries not "net profits" under corporate notes).

the market remains stationary. The profit is still unrealized, but this should not militate against its recognition if there is a reasonably accurate method of estimating the value. In the case of inventory the value of which has been increased by processing, unrealized gain is uniformly recognized in the balance sheet.[49]

There is a further exception recognized where the unrealized increase is used as the basis for a stock dividend. In such cases the dividend is generally sustained.[50] The theory permitting stock dividends from unrealized appreciation while condemning cash dividends from the same source is that with a stock dividend there is no distribution of assets based upon a valuation which may subsequently prove to be unrealized.[51] So far as past creditors are concerned, it is true there can be no harm from a stock dividend; assets in the possession of the corporation remain what they were before. This analysis disregards, however, the situation of the subsequent creditor and

[49] There is a dictum in *Hill v. International Products Co.*, 129 Misc. 25, 45–46, 220 N. Y. S. 711 (1925), aff'd 226 App. Div. 730, 233 N. Y. S. 784 (1929), that an alleged increase in the book value of cattle from fattening and breeding would not be a proper addition to surplus for dividend purposes; but the cattle had not actually been weighed, it being assumed they were heavier because older.

[50] *State v. Bray*, 323 Mo. 562, 20 S. W. (2d) 56 (1929) (*quo warranto*); *Northern Bank & Trust Co. v. Day*, 83 Wash. 296, 145 Pac. 182 (1915) (holding proper an increase in value of a boat originally carried on books below cost; but new valuation did not exceed original cost); *McGinnis v. O'Connor*, 72 Atl. 614 (Md. 1909) (increase in value of plant, goodwill, and whiskey on hand from $15,000 to $25,000 treated as a sufficient basis for a stock dividend of $10,000; only relative rights of stockholders at issue); *Knapp v. Publishers, George Knapp & Co.*, 127 Mo. 53, 29 S. W. 885 (1895); cf. *Kenton Furnace Railroad & Mfg. Co. v. McAlpin*, 5 Fed. 737, 743 (S. D. Ohio 1880) (increase in value of real estate held available to meet balance unpaid on original stock in order to constitute the latter fully paid); 2 Bonbright, *Valuation of Property* (1937) 968; Douglas and Shanks, *Cases and Materials on Business Units—Losses, Liabilities and Assets* (1932), Note, 192; but cf. *Fitzpatrick v. Despatch Publishing Co.*, 83 Ala. 604, 2 So. 727 (1887) (the right to issue a stock dividend on the basis of unrealized appreciation was denied on the ground it violated a constitutional provision against issuance of stock except for money, labor, or property actually received; the court said the corporation always had the surplus and therefore was not receiving the new consideration required by the Constitution). For criticism of the rule permitting declaration of stock dividends out of unrealized appreciation, see Kerrigan, *Limitations on Stock Dividends*, 12 Acc. Rev. 238, 245–247. In *Pontiac Packing Co. v. Hancock*, 257 Mich. 45, 241 N. W. 268 (1932), it was held that a stock dividend on the basis of a fraudulent write-up of a leasehold without evidence of increased value could be cancelled. In *E. L. Moore & Co. v. Murchison*, 226 Fed. 679 (C. C. A. 4th, 1915), assets of a former bankrupt corporation inventoried at $15,000 were purchased for $7,500 and delivered by the purchaser to a new corporation in exchange for stock of the par value of $7,500. These assets were listed on the books of the new company at $15,000. Accounts receivable were carried at their face value when they were worth much less. Upon this record recovery was allowed against directors for negligence in declaring dividends.

[51] See Reviser's comment in Chic. Bar Assoc., *Ill. Bus. Corp. Act Ann.* (1934) 158.

condones a species of stock watering. It is as objectionable to increase a corporation's capitalization upon the basis of uncertain asset values as it is to pay dividends out of such illusory funds.

People ex rel. Queens County Water Company v. Travis, a dividend tax case, presents an interesting factual situation.[52] A corporation owning land which cost $200,000, organized a subsidiary, transferring the land to the latter in exchange for a purchase money mortgage of $200,000 and $700,000 in par value shares of the subsidiary. The mortgage was retained by the parent corporation but the stock was distributed to its shareholders. This was held to be a dividend by the first corporation for tax purposes.

Is this a property dividend out of unrealized appreciation and illegal, or is it in substance a stock dividend and permissible?

(*a*) If the corporation had revalued the property on its books at $900,000, the revaluation surplus of $700,000 would be available only for stock dividends. Declaration of a stock dividend would capitalize the surplus, preventing its subsequent distribution.[53]

(*b*) By distributing stock of the subsidiary, the parent does not capitalize any part of the unrealized appreciation. Since it now has only a secured but limited interest in the land, the stock dividend is analogous to a property distribution of the unrealized increase in value. The transaction, therefore, seems doubtful, particularly under statutes expressly prohibiting the payment of dividends from unrealized appreciation.

In many states the availability of unrealized appreciation for cash, property, or stock dividends is expressly covered by statute. The majority of such provisions specifically prohibit the declaration of cash or property dividends from this source.[54] In all of these states,

---

[52] 171 App. Div. 521, 157 N. Y. S. 943 (1916), aff'd without opinion 219 N. Y. 571, 114 N. E. 1079 (1916).

[53] A question arises as to the right immediately thereafter to reduce capital, creating a reduction surplus subject to cash distribution under limitations provided for reduction surplus. See §30, *supra*. This must depend upon whether the write-up, capitalization of surplus, payment of share dividend, reduction of capital, and payment of cash dividend were all part of one plan to pay a cash dividend out of unrealized appreciation. If so, technical compliance with the statute where the net result achieved is a distribution expressly prohibited by other legal restrictions will not serve as a protection. Cf. *Small v. Sullivan,* 245 N. Y. 343, 157 N. E. 261 (1927). To countenance the device suggested would afford a simple method of nullifying the rule against cash dividends from unrealized appreciation. But see Ballantine, *A Critical Survey of the Illinois Business Corporation Act,* 1 Chic. L. Rev. 357, 371 (1934). Should the reduction be unrelated to the original write-up and capitalization, it would seem the surplus is a valid reduction surplus subject to distribution like any similar surplus.

[54] Idaho Code Ann., §29-129 (no cash or property dividends to be paid from unrealized appreciation of fixed assets; no cash dividends from unrealized ap-

with the exception of Minnesota, stock dividends from unrealized appreciation are either authorized directly or by implication.[55] Wisconsin has an unusual provision which authorizes either cash or stock dividends based on an increase in the value of corporate property.[56]

An interesting question is presented as to the meaning of a prohibition, such as that in Section 41(c) of the Illinois Act, against the payment of cash dividends "out of" surplus arising from unrealized appreciation. Suppose that the corporation has current net earnings of an amount sufficient to pay the dividend in question, but that taking assets at cost there is a balance sheet deficit which would be converted into a balance sheet surplus in excess of the amount of the current net earnings if assets were carried at their current fair value. There is some opinion that the dividend could be paid and would not be out of unrealized appreciation.[57] It seems difficult to sustain this view. Where the test of dividend availability is phrased (as in Illinois) in terms of a balance sheet surplus, the dividend paid is from that surplus generally, and it is difficult to see how it can be said that it is either from the earned surplus or from surplus created by revaluation of assets. In the absence of satisfactory proof that it is not the result of revaluation, declaration of a dividend in these circumstances involves serious risks.

37. Cash, Accounts Receivable, and Securities

The second principal asset category of the corporate balance sheet is that denominated current assets. Included first in this category are

---

preciation in inventories); 32 Ill. Ann. Stat. (Smith-Hurd 1935), §157.41c; Ind. Stat. Ann. (Burns 1933), §25–211; La. Gen. Stat. (Dart. 1939), §1106 (cash or property dividends based on unrealized appreciation in fixed assets or inventories prohibited); Mich. Stat. Ann. (Henderson 1937), §21.22 (but prohibition against declaration from unrealized appreciation does not include "increases which result from readjustment of previous reductions of value to correctly reflect the accounts of the corporation"); Minn. Stat. (Mason 1938 Supp.), §7492–21 (but securities having a readily ascertainable market value, other than securities issued by the corporation, may be valued at not more than such market value); Ohio Code Ann. (Baldwin 1938), §8623–38; 15 Purd. Pa. Stat. Ann., §§2852–701, 702 (covering unrealized increase in value of fixed assets and inventories); Wash. Rev. Stat. Ann. (Rem.), §3803–24 (no cash or property dividends to be paid from unrealized appreciation in fixed assets; no cash dividends from unrealized appreciation in inventories).

[55] In states such as Idaho, Louisiana, Pennsylvania, and Washington, where statutes follow the Uniform Business Corporation Act, authority to pay stock dividends was intended to be given by provisions denying the right to pay cash or property dividends. See Draft of Uniform Business Corporation Act with Explanatory Notes (July 1928) 51; Shockley, Pa. Corp. Law Ann. (1933) 85.

[56] Wis. Stat. (1937), §182.19. *Source:* Wis. Laws 1893, c. 59.

[57] See Revisers' opinion to this effect under the Illinois provision, Chicago Bar Assoc., *Illinois Business Corporation Act Ann.* (1934) 158.

cash and bank deposits. Cash includes not only legal tender but checks and money orders. Ordinarily cash and bank deposits create no peculiar dividend accounting problems. Where cash or bank deposits are in foreign currency, however, there may be fluctuations in value of which account should be taken in the balance sheet. There is early precedent for treating gain derived from fluctuation in exchange as an asset.[58] The problem is of considerable importance to corporations having bank deposits abroad, particularly at the present time when such deposits are subject to war risks. Where there would be any substantial loss by conversion into American exchange, foreign cash and bank deposits should either be proportionally written down or adequate reserves created.[59]

Accounts receivable present more difficult problems. There is initially the question at what point obligations received upon the sale of corporate property become available as dividend assets.[60] The difference between the cost of producing the goods sold and the sale price as reflected in the buyer's bill or note will in many cases constitute the profit upon which the dividend, if any, may be based. The sale must be complete; the corporation must be entitled to the account receivable. The usual rule-of-thumb test for accrual of the profit is passage of title attending a bona fide sale.[61] Partially executed or future contracts, because of fluctuations in the market and uncertainty as to their completion, may produce a condition where estimated profits will prove in fact to be losses. They are treated, therefore, as not available for dividend purposes.[62]

---

[58] Massachusetts Bank (1784), Gras, *Massachusetts First National Bank of Boston*, 654. The bank's profit and loss account also carries a debit "Short on Gold" (*id.*), and a later debit for "Loss on Dollars" [MSS 781 (1784–1904), M 414, v. 33, p. 9].

[59] The Procter & Gamble Company for the duration of the war has adopted the practice of excluding from consolidated earnings all profits of English and Canadian subsidiaries except those which may be available in this country in United States funds. President's Report, Oct. 11, 1939. The Socony-Vacuum Oil Company increased its reserve this past year for loss on foreign exchange in countries with exchange restrictions from $1,000,000 to $6,000,000. Report for 1938, p. 5. See also Graham and Katz, *Accounting in Law Practice* (2d Ed. 1938) 200.

[60] It is well established that book accounts concerning which there is no question may be included in the assets of a corporation in determining whether or not there has been a net profit. *Quinn v. Quinn Mfg. Co.*, 201 Mich. 664, 167 N. W. 898 (1918); *Spencer v. Lowe*, 198 Fed. 961 (C. C. A. 8th, 1912); see *Slayden v. Seip Coal Co.*, 25 Mo. App. 439, 445 (1887).

[61] Littleton, *Suggestions for the Revision of the Tentative Statement of Accounting Principles*, 14 Acc. Rev. 57, 58 (1939); cf. Berle and Fisher, *Elements of the Law of Business Accounting*, 32 Col. L. Rev. 573, 582 (1932); Graham and Katz, *Accounting in Law Practice* (2d Ed. 1938) 203, 208.

[62] *Hutchinson v. Curtiss*, 45 Misc. 484, 489–490, 92 N. Y. S. 70 (1904) (con-

The value of accounts receivable depends, of course, upon the contingency of future payment. They are assets dependent upon the uncertainties attendant to credit transactions. Presumably most accounts will be paid in full, but there will always be some which are bad in whole or part. Normal business experience will disclose that some percentage of others which cannot be currently classified as bad will ultimately prove to be uncollectible. As to this latter group, it will be necessary to establish reserves.[63] Until such accounts are determined to be bad, their full face amount should be reflected on the balance sheet, relying upon reserves to prevent use of doubtful portions of their value for dividend purposes.

Where the debt is definitely determined to be bad, it should be directly charged off in whole or in part. The practice of deducting bad debts before payment of dividends dates back to early days of the corporation.[64] When debts were completely bad, a direct charge off was made.[65] Doubtful debts were handled either by a separate asset item in the balance sheet so designated,[66] or by reserves.[67] Bad

tracts for future delivery of malt from materials not yet purchased; statute provided for dividends "from the surplus or net profits arising from the business"); *Southern California Home Builders v. Young*, 45 Cal. App. 679, 694, 188 Pac. 586 (1920) ; see *Davis v. Flagstaff Silver Mining Co.*, 2 Utah 74, 89 (cash paid in advance on future ore contracts not available under English Companies Act provision for dividends "out of profits arising from the business") ; cf. *Park v. Grant Locomotive Works*, 40 N. J. Eq. 114, 3 Atl. 162 (1885), aff'd on opinion below 45 N. J. Eq. 244, 19 Atl. 621 (1888) (holding corporation would not be compelled to distribute to creditors "net profits" on stock assigned to them under contract where balance sheet assets included accounts maturing from a few months to five years but having no market value and being unsalable; net profits meant "net gains which had been actually realized or which could be quickly realized without loss by a sale of the assets representing the profits") ; *Lexington L. F. & M. Insurance Co. v. Page*, 17 B. Mon. 412 (Ky. 1856) (unearned premiums are not available to an insurance company as an asset for dividends). On treating sales to a subsidiary as profit, see *People ex rel. Queens County Water Co. v. Travis*, §36.5, n. 52, *supra*.

[63] Reserves for doubtful debts are discussed under liabilities in §44.1, *infra*.

[64] A separate entry for "desperate debts" was set up by the East India Company in 1671. 2 Scott, *Joint Stock Companies to 1720* (1912) 134.

[65] Bank of United States (1822), Rep. of Condition (1822) 6 (deduction on inside column of asset side of balance sheet for interest on bad debts) ; Boston & Maine Railroad, Rep. of Sept. 13, 1848, p. 10 (charged to accumulated income) ; Great Falls Manufacturing Co., MSS 44 (1823–1933), G 786, v. 4, Meeting of July 31, 1844 (charged off before carrying accounts receivable to balance sheet) ; Delaware & Hudson Canal, Rep. of Mar. 6, 1832; Buck Mountain Coal Co. (1877) (deduction in income statement) ; South Carolina Railroad Co. and Southwestern Railroad Bank, Proceedings of Stockholders (Feb. 11–13, 1845).

[66] Suffolk Bank, MSS 781 (1818–1904), S 46, v. 7, Balance Sheet of Mar. 27, 1852; Great Falls Manufacturing Co., MSS, *supra* n. 65; Balance Sheets for 1860, 1861 (separate items for "suspended debts" and "doubtful debts"; "guarantee" item carried as an offset on liability side) ; Del. & Hud. Canal, Rep., Mar. 6, 1832.

[67] Mass. Bank (1793–1795), MSS 781 (1784–1904), M 414, v. 33, p. 6, v. 34,

debts charged off but subsequently liquidated were recredited to income.[68]

This accounting practice of long standing is supported by cases which require the exclusion of bad debts in computation of the fund available for dividends.[69] In many jurisdictions which require by statute that losses of every character be deducted, all debts which have been ascertained to be bad will necessarily be included.[70]

Securities in the portfolio of a corporation may be difficult to classify as either current or fixed assets. Some investments may be of a permanent character, thereby more nearly resembling fixed assets; others may be of a temporary nature more like current assets. In problems of valuation where the market has declined, standards at least as strict as those applicable to fixed assets should be observed, with the more conservative practice, particularly in the case of securities with a ready market value, being to follow the market down.[71] Likewise with respect to unrealized appreciation of securities, particularly where held for permanent investment, it is probable that the same difference between cash and stock dividends observed as to

---

pp. 4, 7 (Dec. 31, 1794 the bank owned unpaid bills discounted in the amount of $639,629.62, with a reserve of $2,214.18—v. 3, pp. 314, 6); see also Boston Manufacturing Co., MSS Directors' Records, Oct. 20, 1813 to Oct. 4, 1825, Committee to Examine Treasurer's Report of Sept. 29, 1819; Great Falls Manufacturing Co., *supra* n. 65, v. 4, Balance Sheet of June 30, 1843.

[68] Morris Canal & Banking Co., Rep. of Apr. 6, 1868, p. 10.

[69] *American Steel & Wire Co. v. Eddy,* 130 Mich. 266, 89 N. W. 952 (1902); *Penzel v. Townsend,* 128 Ark. 620, 195 S. W. 25 (1917); *Sparling v. General Discount & Mtg. Co.,* 178 Wash. 663, 35 P. (2d) 60 (1934); *Main v. Mills,* 6 Biss. 98, Fed. Cas. No. 8,974 (C. C. Wis. 1874); *Cabaniss v. State,* 8 Ga. App. 129, 68 S. E. 849 (1910) (criminal indictment of director); see *Vogtman v. Merchants Mtg. & Credit Co.,* 20 Del. Ch. 364, 178 Atl. 99, 102 (1935); S. E. C. Regulation S-X, Rule 5.02(3, 4); 1 Dodd and Baker, *Cases on Business Associations* (1940), Note on Other Necessary Deductions, 1133; Porter and Fiske, *Accounting* (1935) 145; Berle and Fisher, *Elements of the Law of Business Accounting,* 32 Col. L. Rev. 573, 580 (1932); 2 Bonbright, *Property Valuation* (1937) 964–965; Graham and Katz, *Accounting in Law Practice* (2d Ed. 1938) 201. The mere fact some accounts receivable are in the hands of attorneys for collection does not require their deduction as bad where directors have not been so informed. *Davenport v. Lines,* 77 Conn. 473, 59 Atl. 603, 605 (1905).

[70] See §36.3, n. 28, *supra.* The Ohio Act and the National Banking Act require deductions for bad debts in computing dividends. Ohio Code Ann. (Baldwin 1938), §8623–38; 12 U. S. C. A., §56.

[71] See §36.3, *supra;* Graham and Katz, *Accounting in Law Practice* (2d Ed. 1938) 211; cf. 2 Bonbright, *Valuation of Property* (1937) 952, 961. For the alternative method of setting up reserves to cover the shrinkage in market value, see e.g. Diamond Match Company Report, Dec. 31, 1932. Where the corporation deals in marketable securities, it is prudent to inventory them at the lower of cost or market. 1 Dodd and Baker, *Cases on Business Associations* (1940) 1106.

fixed assets would be followed.[72] In a few states it is provided that the unaccrued or unearned portion of unrealized profits on securities is not available for cash or property dividends, but as to marketable securities purchased at a discount permission to value at the market is given.[73] Minnesota provides an exception to its rule against dividends from unrealized appreciation in the case of securities having a readily ascertainable market value.[74]

In the case of accounts receivable, and securities generally, the problem arises as to whether accrued interest which will become payable only after the close of the accounting period may be treated as an asset available for dividend purposes. The problem differs considerably from that of unrealized appreciation of assets. In the case of interest, the amount is definitely fixed as contrasted with the estimate value for unrealized appreciation; the receipt of payment may be relatively certain or uncertain, but it is deferred, so that at the time it is proposed to treat the amount as a dividend asset the corporation does not have its equivalent in cash. It is the general accounting practice to accrue interest. But in *People v. San Francisco Savings Union,* a case probably inapplicable under most present statutes or modern views, the practice was condemned.[75] The bank in this case proposed to declare a dividend out of two months' accrued interest on United States government bonds and six months' interest on secured real estate, the mortgage more than adequately covering both principal and interest. The statute was similar to the New York Act of 1825 prohibiting dividends "except from surplus profits arising from the business of the corporation." The court, however, did not place its decision on the ground the profits did not arise from the business, but rather on the ground the statute required "an excess of *receipts* over expenditures" and that the interest had not been received.[76]

---

[72] See §36.5, *supra;* Graham and Katz, *Accounting in Law Practice* (2d Ed. 1938) 211. In *Glover v. Thompson Connellsville Coke Co.,* 66 Pitts. L. J. 525 (C. P. Allegheny County, Pa., 1918), it was held that bonds purchased at $80 and resold at $100 produced a profit of $20 available for dividends.

[73] Idaho Code Ann., §29-129 (cash dividends); La. Gen. Stat. (Dart. 1939), §1106; 15 Purd. Pa. Stat. Ann., §2852-704 (but prohibiting dividends from the accrued portion of unrealized profits on securities purchased at a discount); Wash. Rev. Stat. Ann. (Rem.), §3803-24 (cash dividends).

[74] Minn. Stat. (Mason Supp. 1938), §7492-21.

[75] 72 Cal. 199, 13 Pac. 498 (1887).

[76] For criticism of the case, see Graham and Katz, *Accounting in Law Practice* (2d Ed. 1938) 202-203. In *Vogtman v. Merchants Mtg. & Credit Co.,* 20 Del. Ch. 364, 178 Atl. 99 (1935), accrued interest due from a subsidiary to a parent was held unavailable where there was no showing that interest was ever paid or that the subsidiary could pay it.

Installment sales contracts present a special problem for dividend purposes. Under the federal income tax, profit on installment sales may be returned either on the ordinary accrual or cash receipts basis, or on the basis of that proportion of installment payments received in the year which the total profit to be realized when the property is paid for bears to the total contract price.[77] From the standpoint of dividends, the latter method seems more in accord with the purpose of balance sheet surplus statutes. Indeed, the most conservative view would refuse to recognize availability until all installments were paid, on the theory that only then could it be determined whether there was in fact any gain.[78] With respect to ordinary accounts receivable, postponement of payment to the future is of relatively short duration, frequently less than six months, and the collection risk is normally much smaller. Treatment of such accounts as completely available dividend assets should not necessitate the same result in the installment sale case where the credit is of longer duration and the risk much greater. If the entire sale price is credited as an asset immediately, substantial reserves indicated by experience in the particular business should be set up to prevent dividend payments which might otherwise ultimately prove to be out of capital. Only the accrued and earned portion of unrealized profit on installment contracts is available for cash or property dividends under a few statutes.[79] Similar general treatment should be given to long-term contracts.[80]

38. Inventory

With respect to fixed assets, in the absence of statute the prevailing legal and accounting practice is valuation at cost. It is also the prevailing accounting practice to value current inventory, on the

[77] I. R. C., §44; Reg. 103, §19.44–1.

[78] Cf. *Marks v. Monroe County Permanent Savings & Loan Assoc.,* 52 N. Y. State Rep. 451, 22 N. Y. S. 589 (1889) (corporation made a loan deducting the premium in advance; a stockholder was held not entitled to compel a dividend distribution out of the premium under a statute providing for dividends from earnings, because there was no certainty of profit until the loan should be repaid); *Sparling v. General Discount & Mtg. Corp.,* 178 Wash. 663, 35 P. (2d) 60 (1934) (held improper in computing dividends to set up open accounts purchased at a discount as though the discount had been actually earned and paid).

[79] Idaho Code Ann., §29–129 (cash dividends); La. Gen. Stat. (Dart. 1939), §1106; 15 Purd. Pa. Stat. Ann., §2852–702; Wash. Rev. Stat. Ann. (Rem.), §3803–24 (cash dividends).

[80] It is acceptable accounting practice to recognize revenue from installment sales in proportion to collections, and to recognize revenue from long-term contracts on the basis of the amount completed. See Littleton, *Suggestions for Revision of the Tentative Statement of Accounting Principles,* 14 Acc. Rev. 57, 58 (1939).

other hand, at cost or market whichever is lower.[81] Two principal reasons may be given for this differentiation in valuing the major classes of corporate assets. A corporation's fixed assets are normally to be retained as the working materials of the business; they are not ordinarily for sale, consequently market fluctuations in their value will not materially affect the earnings position of the corporation. The inventory of current assets, on the other hand, is the corporation's stock in trade, the source from which its profit must be made. Any fluctuation in the value of this class of assets immediately affects the earnings of the corporation. A second reason for using the lower of cost or market valuations with respect to current inventory is the general statutory authorization of these alternatives over a period of many years for purposes of the federal income tax.[82] The corporation gladly takes the market price when it is lower than cost, because it thereby, at least temporarily, reduces its taxable net income. The lower the valuation on inventory remaining at the end of the accounting period, the larger will be the balance for cost of goods sold; the higher the cost of goods sold, the lower will be the net income.[83] But obviously a method which holds income down for tax purposes also holds it down for dividend purposes.[84]

By amendment in the Revenue Act of 1939, taxpayers with the consent of the Commissioner of Internal Revenue may now adopt a method under which inventory is steadily carried at cost.[85] In order to use this alternative, the taxpayer is also required to use the last-in first-out method of determining the inventory remaining on hand at

[81] See Committee Report of American Institute of Accountants on Valuation of Inventory, 65 J. of Accountancy 29 (1938); Briggs, *Asset Valuations in Dividend Decisions,* 9 Acc. Rev. 220, 236 (1934); 1 Dodd and Baker, *Cases on Business Associations* (1940) 1106; Douglas and Shanks, *Cases and Materials on Business Units—Management* (1931), Note, 606; Montgomery, *Auditing Theory and Practice* (5th Ed. 1934) 207–208; Draft of Committee on Revision of Ohio Gen. Corp. Act (Dec. 1926), p. 91. The suggestion has been made that instead of carrying current assets directly at market when that is lower than cost, they continue to be carried at cost, but that a reserve be set up to await objective determination by sales that cost is not sound. See Littleton, *Suggestions for Revision of the Tentative Statement of Accounting Principles,* 14 Acc. Rev. 57, 61.

[82] I. R. C. 22 (c); Reg. 103, §19.22 (c)–2.

[83] That the alternatives of the lower of cost or market originally found favor in accounting practice as a convenient method for reducing taxable income, see Paton, *Comments on "A Statement of Accounting Principles,"* 65 J. of Accountancy 196, 202 (1938).

[84] This is a conspicuous instance of where the adoption of a rule of accounting for some other legal purpose has had the practical effect of establishing a similar rule for dividends.

[85] I. R. C. 22(d), as amended by Revenue Act of 1939, §219. See Note, *Base Stock Inventories and Federal Income Taxation,* 51 Harv. L. Rev. 1430, 1434 (1938).

the end of the year, whereas under the lower of cost or market alternative he is required to use the first-in first-out method. The lower of cost or market results in showing larger profits in a period of rising prices when the corporation is in a better position to distribute profits, and lower profits in a declining market when the corporation's dividend distribution policy should be more conservative. The cost method, on the other hand, results in showing larger profits in a declining market. From the dividend standpoint, the lower of cost or market would seem to be preferable, particularly in declining markets, when making available large amounts for dividends may be hazardous policy. The effect of the two methods sanctioned for income tax purposes may be illustrated in the case where a corporation starts with an inventory of 50,000 units costing $50,000, during the year purchases 50,000 units at $75,000, sells 50,000 units for $100,000, and closes the year with a balance of 50,000 units, the market being unchanged.

LOWER OF COST OR MARKET (first-in first-out)			COST (last-in first-out)		
Sales		$100,000	Sales		$100,000
Cost of goods sold:			Cost of goods sold:		
Opening inventory	$ 50,000		Opening inventory	$ 50,000	
Purchased	75,000		Purchased	75,000	
	125,000			125,000	
Closing inventory	75,000	50,000	Closing inventory	50,000	75,000
Gross Profit		$ 50,000	Gross Profit		$ 25,000

In boom times the corporation will be able, therefore, to distribute twice as much in dividends under the lower of cost or market rule as it would under the plain cost method. The converse situation may be illustrated in a declining market.

LOWER OF COST OR MARKET			COST		
Sales		$ 75,000	Sales		$ 75,000
Cost of goods sold:			Cost of goods sold:		
Opening inventory	$ 50,000		Opening inventory	$ 50,000	
Purchased	25,000		Purchased	25,000	
	75,000			75,000	
Closing inventory	25,000	50,000	Closing inventory	50,000	25,000
		$ 25,000			$ 50,000

Over a period of years the cost method combined with the last-in first-out rule produces a more uniform yearly income, leveling the peaks and valleys. It is a serious question, however, whether from a dividend standpoint a loss on inventory valuation during a declining market should be deferred in the hope of a leveling equalization in later years. Dividends should be based on the present position and ability of the corporation to pay them.[86] In the case last put, under the cost method the corporation will carry on its balance sheet as inventory an item of $50,000, when a sale on the market would realize only $25,000.

How far do dividend precedents support one or the other of these methods? The leading case is *Branch v. Kaiser*.[87] In that case, as a result of a post-war condition in the commodities market, with respect to which the directors were in no way negligent or responsible, sugar held by a wholesale grocery company declined from 26 or 28 cents a pound, the purchase price, to 5½ cents a pound. The resulting loss on sugar and other food products amounted to $1,000,000, wiping out the surplus and capital of the corporation, and apparently rendering it insolvent. However, these inventory losses were not taken on the books of the corporation. Inventory continued to be carried at cost and in some instances was inflated. In years subsequent to that in which the inventory losses were sustained, current operating profits were realized which were distributed in dividends. The directors were held liable for the dividends paid. The court pointed out that the decline of the inventory below its cost price had impaired the corporation's capital, and that under the Pennsylvania statute permitting dividends only from "the net profits acquired by the company so that the capital stock shall never be impaired thereby," these losses had to be made up from subsequent profits before a dividend could be paid. It is to be noted that the value of the inventory, as the court put it, had "enormously decreased." The decline was not the routine market fluctuation that accompanies inventory items. Quite clearly, a collapse in the price level cannot be disregarded when valuing inventories for dividend purposes. It would not seem that a corporation is obliged to follow day-to-day fluctuations in valuing its inventory. Inventory valued at cost should be upheld for dividend purposes, in the absence of proof of a recognizable lowering of the price level.[88]

[86] The accounting argument in favor of the first-in first-out rule is ably presented in Paton and Littleton, *An Introduction to Corporate Accounting Standards* (1940) 78–79.

[87] 291 Pa. 543, 140 Atl. 498 (1928).

[88] See Paton and Littleton, *An Introduction to Corporate Accounting Standards* (1940) 80–81.

As in the case of fixed assets, an obligation to follow the market down may be imposed by the provisions of general corporation acts in many states. Certainly general requirements for taking recognition of losses, if construed to apply to fixed assets, would *a fortiori* necessitate the writing down of current inventory.[89]

The normal rule for valuing work in progress, like that for raw materials, is cost, including labor and similar expenses,[90] or, in the case where market is definitely lower than cost, then at market. There is an important exception in the case where the corporation is under a firm commitment to deliver at a set price. In that situation, if the cost at any stage of the production of unfinished goods should exceed the sale price, the goods cannot be carried as an asset at cost. The loss should be taken anticipatorily, carrying the goods at a maximum not exceeding the sale price.[91]

There is very little authority on the availability of unrealized appreciation of current assets for dividends. The generally accepted rule of valuing at the lower of cost or market excludes such increment. In the few cases construing the meaning of profits under corporate contracts, it has been held that unrealized appreciation in current assets is not distributable.[92] Idaho, Louisiana, Pennsylvania, and Washington expressly prohibit cash or property dividends from unrealized appreciation in inventory.[93]

39. Prepaid Expenses

There is hardly a corporate balance sheet today which does not list among its assets certain prepaid expenses.[94] These items, such as prepaid interest, rent, insurance, and taxes, are not in any normal

[89] These provisions are discussed in §36.3, *supra;* see particularly n. 28–32.

[90] *Davenport v. Lines,* 77 Conn. 473, 59 Atl. 603, 605 (1905); see MSS Boston 1, Stockholders' Minutes, Aug. 31, 1819. In *Hutchinson v. Curtiss,* 45 Misc. 484, 491, 92 N. Y. S. (1904), included among assets held properly available for dividends was malt which in the process of manufacture from barley increased 15% per bushel. There was a custom in the industry to take into account the increased value.

[91] *Cornell v. Seddinger,* 237 Pa. 389, 85 Atl. 446 (1912); see Report of Committee on Stock List of New York Stock Exchange, 65 J. of Accountancy 99 (1938); Graham and Katz, *Accounting in Law Practice* (2d Ed. 1938) 208; cf. MSS Boston 1, Stockholders' Minutes, Aug. 31, 1819 (balance sheet entry carrying cloth on hand "at prices previously settled, or sold by the company"); Anaconda Copper Mining Co., Rep. Dec. 31, 1932 (inventory—"Metals and manufactured products—sold at sales price; unsold at market").

[92] See 1 Dodd and Baker, *Cases on Business Associations* (1940), 1132, n. 6; Graham and Katz, *Accounting in Law Practice* (2d Ed. 1938) 206; but cf. *Hutchinson v. Curtiss,* n. 90, *supra.*

[93] See §36.5, n. 54, *supra.*

[94] Generally see 1 Dodd and Baker, *Cases on Business Associations* (1940), Note on Deferred Charges and Prepaid Expenses, 1122.

sense assets, and it is open to question whether they should ever be available from the dividend viewpoint. Take the following example which exaggerates a possible dividend situation:

ASSETS			LIABILITIES	
Cash, etc.		$100,000	Capital	$100,000
Deferred charges:			Surplus	5,000
Prepaid rent..	$ 2,000			
Prepaid taxes	3,000	5,000		
		$105,000		$105,000

Almost all accountants will show a book surplus of $5,000 in this situation. Yet could a New York corporation under Section 58 safely pay dividends out of this surplus without impairing the corporation's capital? These advance payments represent actual withdrawal of assets from the corporation's treasury. Whether or not they have actual *present* value should be the test of availability as balance sheet assets for dividend purposes.[95] The fact that they are amounts paid for the benefit of some future accounting period and will be duly taken up when that period occurs, does not presently justify using them as assets for the basis of dividends in this accounting period. From the standpoint of long-range accounting, the practice of treating deferred charges as assets may be justified. From the standpoint of a corporation's present position, it is like capitalizing expenses and calling them assets. In the average case, however, the amount of assets resulting from prepayments and deferred charges will be small, and if the declaration of a dividend depends on such a small margin, it doubtless will not in any event be paid. But if the legality of the dividend is a close question, it is well to exclude doubtful prepaid items.

40. Deferred Charges

From some expenses a corporation derives benefit for a considerable period of time. With respect to such items, it is the practice to

---

[95] Cf. Montgomery, *Auditing Theory and Practice* (5th Ed. 1934) 300–301. In *Cox v. Leahy*, 209 A. D. 313, 317, 204 N. Y. S. 741 (1924), the court held that prepaid insurance to the extent of the unearned premium might be treated as an asset for dividend purposes, but not prepaid taxes since "they are in no wise available for a refund and are paid for past expenses of government as well as future." In *Majestic Co. v. Orpheum Circuit*, 21 F. (2d) 720 (C. C. A. 8th, 1927), prepaid rent was deemed an available dividend asset; see Porter and Fiske, *Accounting* (1935) 252. Accounting practice shows instances as early as the sixteenth century of advance payments being considered corporate assets. 2 Scott, *Joint Stock Companies to 1720* (1912) 388–389.

capitalize the expenditure as an asset, amortizing a portion thereof
each year of its use value. Original organization expenses are of this
character.[96] Considerable justification exists for such treatment.
Organization is, realistically, an asset. Any group of businessmen
desiring to enter into corporate competition with an existing corporation would have the same expense. Any sale of the corporation as a
going concern would take that item into consideration.

Almost every business also has what may be generally denominated development expenses. The typical example is the automotive
industry. With each season's new models, there is a large preproduc-
tion expense for plans, new tools, dies, machinery, and factory
rearrangements before the new cars can actually be produced. This
is at the time simply expenditure. However, it is clear that, when
the valuation of the finished new cars is made (cost), these initial
expense items should be included. In the case of the automotive industry, development expenses are rather easily absorbed in the
current year through the cost of goods sold item. A somewhat more
difficult problem arises when the development redounds to the benefit of future production for a good many years. It then takes on
the nature of an intangible asset which may be carried on the balance
sheet to be subsequently amortized or charged off as the value of the
development to the enterprise decreases.[97] There are limitations, however, to capitalizing development expenses. It would be improper,
from the dividend standpoint, for an infant enterprise to capitalize

[96] 2 Bonbright, *Valuation of Property* (1937) 945; Paton and Littleton, *An
Introduction to Corporate Accounting Standards* (1940) 32, 73, 93; Berle and
Fisher, *Elements of the Law of Business Accounting*, 32 Col. L. Rev. 573, 585
(1932). The practice is to amortize the item in three to five years after organization. Graham and Katz, *Accounting in Law Practice* (2d Ed. 1938) 276; Porter
and Fiske, *Accounting* (1936) 256; 1 Dodd and Baker, *Cases on Business Associations* (1940) 1122. Ohio provides that the cost of organization to the extent not
charged off shall be stated on the corporate books and balance sheet. Ohio Code
Ann. (Baldwin 1938), §8623–29.

[97] *Excelsior Water & Mining Co. v. Pierce*, 90 Cal. 131, 27 Pac. 44 (1891);
see 2 Bonbright, *Valuation of Property* (1937) 949, n. 93; Paton and Littleton,
An Introduction to Corporate Accounting Standards (1940) 72–74; but cf. *Hill v.
International Products Co.*, 129 Misc. 25, 49–50, 220 N. Y. S. 711 (1925), aff'd
226 App. Div. 730, 233 N. Y. S. 784 (1920). Accountants frequently take a position
that development expenses may not be capitalized. See 2 Bonbright, *Valuation of
Property* (1937) 946–947; Berle and Fisher, *Elements of the Law of Business
Accounting*, 32 Col. L. Rev. 573, 585 (1932). In *Haebler v. Crawford*, 258 N. Y.
130, 134, 179 N. E. 319 (1932), it was held that a stockholder might rescind a
purchase of stock on the ground the corporation had misrepresented that it had
profits from which dividends were paid. The corporation had capitalized, as
engineering and development expenses, 80 per cent of the expenses incurred during
the preceding year without any showing that any real increase in the value of
corporate property resulted.

its expense in experimenting on a new machine, until there was assurance that it would be a sales success.[98]

In all cases where deferred charges are of a character properly evaluated as assets, they should be written off annually in proportion as the use value diminishes. Some statutes make this specific requirement.[99]

When a corporation issues its bonds at a discount, it is customary to carry the full amount of the obligation at maturity as a liability. This means that the system of double entry requires a "balancing asset" entry in addition to the sale price for the difference between net sale price and par amount of the obligation.[100] Like prepaid expenses, this balancing entry is treated as though it were an asset of present value. It obviously is not that, but on the contrary indicates a complete absence of assets in the amount of the discount. It should not be taken into consideration in computing assets for dividends. Here again, the tax practice which permits annual deduction as a business expense of a *pro rata* portion of the unamortized amount of the discount [101] cannot be relied upon in the dividend field. Under tax practice the balance of the unamortized discount continues on the balance sheet as a "balancing asset." From the dividend standpoint, this indicates an actual absence of assets just as much as a loss would. The language in dividend statutes should be observed closely for indications that surplus must be determined upon a present value of assets, thus excluding such balancing assets as bond discount and prepaid assets which are nothing more than capitalized expenses.

Among the deferred charges sometimes appearing on a balance sheet are losses not currently or completely charged to earnings or surplus. This practice of paying dividends out of "loss assets" cannot be sanctioned—the deduction should be made from surplus. A loss is a loss and must appear as such.

[98] *Hubbard v. Weare,* 79 Iowa 678, 694, 44 N. W. 915 (1890).

[99] Idaho Code Ann., §29–129; La. Gen. Stat. (Dart. 1939), §1106; 15 Purd. Pa. Stat. Ann., §2852–701; Wash. Rev. Stat. Ann. (Rem.), §3803–24.

[100] The American Accounting Association has tentatively promulgated a rule requiring the amount of the discount to be deducted directly from the face value of the indebtedness on the ground that it represents interest payable at maturity. American Accounting Association, *Tentative Statement of Accounting Principles,* 11 Acc. Rev. 187, 188–189 (1936); see also Paton and Littleton, *An Introduction to Corporate Accounting Standards* (1940) 39; Porter and Fiske, *Accounting* (1935) 255. This practice misrepresents the extent of the corporation's obligation. Whatever the nature of the obligation, it is of the face amount and not the face amount less the discount, and it must appear on the balance sheet as the former when dividends are declared.

[101] Reg. 103, §19.22(a)–18 (3) (a). This likewise is the accounting practice generally approved. Graham and Katz, *Accounting in Law Practice* (2d Ed. 1938) 280–281.

41. Goodwill

One of the most troublesome accounting problems with respect to dividend declaration is the matter of goodwill.[102] Two questions are involved. Should goodwill ever be classed as an asset available for dividend purposes? Assuming it is, how is the valuation to be determined? The answer to the first question may depend in part upon the manner in which the alleged goodwill is acquired. This may be either through purchase by the corporation of property in which part of the purchase price represents goodwill, or through the building up of the corporation's own reputation in the business community.

It is common practice when a corporation buys the assets of a partnership or of another corporation to pay something in addition to the actual value of the tangible assets purchased. This is similarly true in mergers and consolidations. That this practice does prevail vouches for the fact that in these situations the intangible business reputation of the absorbed enterprise is recognized by the commercial community as an item of worth. To deny legality to this type of goodwill would, or might, prevent the declaration of dividends by many of our largest and ostensibly strongest corporations. It is not surprising, therefore, to find accountants and the courts sanctioning the consideration of goodwill acquired by purchase, merger, or consolidation.[103] The important question pertains to valuation. Safeguards against stock watering must be observed. The value of the goodwill [104] will be the difference between the fair appraised value of

[102] A recent survey of 50 large corporations shows that while goodwill, patents, and other intangibles were carried at $1.00 by the majority, 20 corporations carried them at substantial figures, one as high as $54,000,000. Walker, *Goodwill on Financial Statements*, 13 Acc. Rev. 174, 175–176 (1938).

[103] *Randall v. Bailey,* New York Law J., October 29, 1940, p. 1309; *Davenport v. Lines,* 77 Conn. 473, 59 Atl. 603 (1905) [goodwill of prior piano partnership allowed to be included in pattern and scales account; for earlier case indicating that in absence of showing such value continued after purchase, it should have been reduced, see 72 Conn. 118, 127, 44 Atl. 17 (1899)]; see *Washburn v. National Wall Paper Co.,* 81 Fed. 17, 20 (C. C. A. 2d, 1897); Berle and Fisher, *Elements of the Law of Business Accounting,* 32 Col. L. Rev. 573, 588 (1932); 2 Bonbright, *Valuation of Property* (1937) 939–943; Paton and Littleton, *Introduction to Corporate Accounting Standards* (1940) 92; Walker, *Nonpurchased Goodwill,* 13 Acc. Rev. 253 (1938). Profits may be used to write off formulas, trademarks, and goodwill which constitute the principal assets of a proprietary medicine corporation against objection of a stockholder that he is entitled to dividends. See *Robertson v. Bucklen & Co.,* 107 Ill. App. 369, 372–373 (1903). But in Alabama there is a statutory provision that no dividend shall ever be based upon the valuation of other than tangible assets. Alabama Code (1928), §6991.

[104] Cf. *Washburn v. National Wall Paper Co.,* 81 Fed. 17, 18, 20 (C. C. A. 2d, 1897).

tangible assets purchased and the purchase price. Attention must be given to whether this difference is a fair and reasonable valuation. The party having the burden of proof on this issue, and it is usually held that one seeking to upset the valuation bears this burden, has an almost insuperable task.[105]

One other point must be observed in examining the balance sheet of a corporation which has acquired assets by purchase. In many cases the item of goodwill, if present, will be concealed by silent absorption in the valuation placed on fixed assets. This only masks the problem. But it does make it more difficult for anyone seeking to establish an improper valuation of goodwill at some later date. No figure having been placed upon tangible assets apart from goodwill, the complainant has the added burden of establishing in the first instance a value for tangible assets.

If a going enterprise has a goodwill asset which is salable for cash should it choose to dispose of its property, it must likewise have such an asset when it does not sell its property. But conservatism among accountants has generally disapproved of goodwill asset entries based on the reputation of a continuing business.[106] It is sometimes said that if the corporation is prospering, it will have sufficient assets for dividends without considering goodwill; that if the corporation is failing, goodwill must be largely fictitious and, therefore, not really available for dividends. But it should be pointed out that the difficulty from the legal and accounting standpoint is not in the absence of any such asset—it does exist, in the case of most

[105] *Id.* at 21, 23.

[106] *Coleman v. Booth*, 268 Mo. 64, 79, 186 S. W. 1021 (1916) (goodwill created on organization when no reputation of value could as yet have been established); *Davenport v. Lines*, 72 Conn. 118, 128, 44 Atl. 17 (1899) (advertising expenses where not shown to have a present value at time of dividend; but upon showing of benefit to corporation over a period of years, it was held proper to carry as an asset, charging off a proper proportion thereof annually, 77 Conn. 473, 59 Atl. 603 (1905)); see 2 Bonbright, *Valuation of Property* (1937) 939; Douglas and Shanks, *Cases and Materials on Business Units—Management* (1931), Note, 606; Graham and Katz, *Accounting in Law Practice* (2d Ed. 1938) 279; *Porter v. Fiske*, Accounting (1935) 245; Walker, *Nonpurchased Goodwill*, 13 Acc. Rev. 253 (1938); cf. *State v. Bray*, 323 Mo. 562, 20 S. W. (2d) 56 (1929) (goodwill available to pay stock increase); *Stapley v. Read Bros.*, Ltd., §42, *infra*. Sometimes goodwill may be reflected by added valuation of other assets. In *Hubbard v. Weare*, 79 Iowa 678, 693, 44 N. W. 915 (1890), advertising expenses were added to the valuation of general assets. But this practice must be disapproved, since it tends definitely to mislead. Intangible values accruing by way of advertising and other items of general goodwill, if recognized at all, should be clearly disclosed on the balance sheet as such. Capitalizing advertising expenses as goodwill is usually disapproved, see Walker, *Nonpurchased Goodwill*, 13 Acc. Rev. 253, 256 (1938).

going corporations—but rather in the valuation thereof. The valuation problem is even more difficult than in the case where property of another corporation has been purchased. In that situation there is at least one arm's length figure to work from, namely, the purchase price, and if the tangible assets have been appraised there will be complete objectivity in the valuation of the goodwill item. Whereas in the case in which the corporation values its own goodwill, it must be purely an estimate. If through reasonably objective methods a sound estimate can be placed on goodwill, doing so should not be condemned on the ground that goodwill of a going concern can never be an asset for dividend purposes.[107]

42. Hidden Reserves

An important problem is that of hidden reserves. When property depreciates, the estimated amount thereof may be handled by debiting the surplus or profit and loss account and crediting a reserve account for depreciation. This will appear on the balance sheet as a liability under caption of Depreciation Reserve or on the asset side of the balance sheet as an inner column deduction from the particular assets as against which the reserve has been established. Similar practice may be adopted with respect to reserves for bad and doubtful debts and other purposes. These reserves are not hidden; they are clearly disclosed on the face of the balance sheet. But this accurate disclosure of reserves does not always take place. Frequently corporations, particularly in prosperous years, write off certain of their assets out of current profits. When this is done, surplus or profit and loss is debited and the asset in question directly credited without taking the intermediate step of setting up any reserve. The net result on the balance sheet is very different than where the liability reserve is set up. The asset appears at the written-off value (or not at all if entirely charged off) and to that extent reduces the total of assets in the asset column. Similarly, on the liability side there is a complete absence of any entry for the amount of the write-off, eliminating what would otherwise have been the Depreciation or other Reserve entry. Obviously, if the write-off is greater than the depreciation in value of the asset, there is a latent asset value which in no way appears by reserve or otherwise on the balance sheet. In time of eco-

---

[107] Cf. Paton and Littleton, *An Introduction to Corporate Accounting Standards* (1940) 92–93. For an extreme case of padding a balance sheet for dividend purposes through the use of fictitious goodwill, see *Coleman v. Booth*, 268 Mo. 64, 186 S. W. 1021 (1916).

nomic difficulty such latent assets—most commonly referred to as hidden reserves—may constitute a source for the legal declaration of dividends.

The leading case on the retrievability of hidden reserves is the English decision in *Stapley v. Read Brothers, Ltd.*[108] There a goodwill item of £140,000 was completely written off over a period of eleven years by charges against profits and a reserve account. Several years later the corporation had a net operating loss, followed the succeeding year by a small net profit. The corporation proposed to pay accrued dividends on preferred shares out of this profit, after having first wiped out the prior deficit by restoring goodwill as an asset in the amount of £40,000, which in the light of the history of the corporation the directors determined was a conservative value. The Court of Chancery Division refused an injunction to halt such action, pointing out that the corporation still owned the asset, in spite of having treated it for accounting purposes as of no value, that the direct charge off instead of using a reserve did not indicate an intention to permanently capitalize the profits required in making the write-off, and that the corporation was now entitled to take back into its profit account so much of the write-off as proved to have been in excess of proper requirements.[109] Where excessive reserves have been taken in prior years, there is no objection to restating the accounts to reflect their true condition. However, a court will probably scrutinize carefully any contention that amounts previously set aside for reserves were not properly computed. The case where a corporation seeks to readjust prior accounting methods is generally viewed with certain suspicion.

---

[108] (1924) 2 Ch. 1 [comment, Douglas and Shanks, *Cases and Materials on Business Units—Management* (1931) 624].

[109] Cf. *Hiscock v. Lacy*, 9 Misc. 578, 30 N. Y. S. 860 (1894) (corporation compelled to declare dividend at suit of minority stockholder upon showing that good assets, otherwise available for dividend purposes, had been charged off for the purpose of making a poor financial record) ; *Dykman v. Keeney*, 10 A. D. 610, 42 N. Y. S. 488; second trial 16 A. D. 131, 45 N. Y. S. 137, aff'd on opinion below 160 N. Y. 677, 54 N. E. 1090 (1899) (notes given by stockholders and directors to bank because of its weak position were not included in assets at time dividend was declared; if they had been included there would have been no impairment; held, in suit to recover against directors, they should be treated as assets) ; *Northern Bank & Trust Co. v. Day*, 83 Wash. 296, 298, 145 Pac. 182 (1915) (holding proper an increase in valuation of fixed assets, where resulting valuation did not exceed original cost) ; see Graham and Katz, *Accounting in Law Practice* (2d Ed. (1938) 152–153, 221–222. In some states statutes expressly provide that reserves which have been set up out of funds available for dividends may later be abolished. Ark. Stat. (1937), §2183; Del. Rev. Code (1935), c. 65, §34; Kans. Laws 1939, c. 152, §83; Mich. Stat. Ann. (Henderson, 1937), §21.22; Ohio Code Ann. (Baldwin 1938), §8623–38.

B. Balance Sheet Liabilities

43. Funded and Current Liabilities

Counterbalancing the assets of a corporate balance sheet are the various claims and interests which must be met out of corporate property. The liability side of the balance sheet is divided principally into the claims of creditors, reserves, and the interest of shareholders.

Corporate funded obligations issued at par appear at their face amount as liabilities. These obligations, however, may be issued at a discount [110] or a premium. If a corporation issues its ten-year $1,000 par bond for $1,050, the balance sheet will show an excess of assets over liabilities of $50, as a result of the transaction. May this $50 or any part thereof be treated as a dividend asset at the end of the first year of issuance? The question is raised as to whether the premium should be considered a reduction of the interest rate on the bonds or as a profit. If it is the former it is not available for dividends, but will go annually in *pro rata* amounts to reduce the charge in the operating statement for interest. Under this interpretation a reserve would be set up on issuance of the bonds in the amount of $50, reduced each year in proportion to use of the premium. For federal income tax purposes, the premium constitutes income rather than a reduction of interest.[111] There appears to be no reason why the same rule should not be adopted for dividend purposes, provided bonds are not issued under circumstances indicating a device to create a profit at the expense of assuming heavy fixed charges. The income tax practice of amortizing the gain over the life of the bonds seems also desirable from the dividend standpoint, rather than permitting complete distribution in the year that the bonds are issued.[112] The gain is one accruing over the full life of the bonds. To assure this type of treatment, a reserve of the character mentioned above should be set up, releasing each year only the accrued portion of the premium.[113]

A corporation may after issuance retire its bonds at a discount. The problem is quite different from originally issuing bonds at a discount. In the case of bonds issued at a discount, the corporation assumes a larger obligation than the consideration it receives. In the

---

[110] For the accounting treatment of discount see §40, *supra*.

[111] Reg. 103, §19.22(a)–18(2)(a).

[112] Cf. 2 Bonbright, *Valuation of Property* (1937) 967.

[113] Cf. *Irving Trust Co. v. Gunder*, 152 Misc. 83, 271 N. Y. S. 795 (1934) (under long-term service contracts payment was received in full in advance for services to be rendered over a period of years; it was held improper to treat the entire amount as surplus for dividends in the year received and that the same should have been prorated over the entire period by setting up a "deferred as future earnings" charge against surplus).

case of bonds retired at a discount, the corporation pays less consideration than the obligation which it discharges. For example, suppose a corporation has a balance sheet showing assets of $500,000, and on the liability side, capital $150,000, bonds outstanding $100,-000, surplus $250,000. If the bond issue is retired by payment of $90,000 in cash, the balance sheet will show assets of $410,000, and on the liability side capital $150,000, surplus $260,000. Thus, a reduction of liabilities increases surplus just as much as would a *pro tanto* increase in the amount of assets. The surplus which arises from the discount of a corporation's liabilities is available for dividend purposes just as much as other types of surplus where the balance sheet is the controlling test for dividends.[114] In this situation the transaction is completely closed in the accounting period in which the retirement is made and the full amount of the gain is immediately distributable.

All current obligations to creditors are also included in liabilities.[115] Where at the end of the accounting period there are accrued obligations for wages, taxes, rent, and interest which do not become actually payable until later, they must also be listed as liabilities.[116] But purely future and unaccrued liabilities may be excluded.[117]

44. Reserves Generally

General recognition that proper accounting practice requires the setting up of reserves for assumed or sustained losses arising from depreciation, obsolescence, bad debts, and similar diminutions in asset value demonstrates that factors other than the historic cost of assets must be taken into account for dividend purposes. Reserves are a conspicuous instance of the type of accounting situation which is almost entirely a matter of judgment. In the absence of a showing

[114] Cf. *Equitable Life Assurance Society v. Union Pacific R. R. Co.*, 212 N. Y. 360, 106 N. E. 92 (1914) (comment, 27 Harv. L. Rev. 758; 14 Col. L. Rev. 524). The federal income tax practice is the same. *U. S. v. Kirby Lumber Co.*, 284 U. S. 1 (1931); Reg. 103, §19.22(a)–18.

[115] Obligations which creditors are estopped to assert are excluded. Where officers of the corporation had been voted a certain salary, but always drew less, it was held in *Cox v. Leahy*, 209 App. Div. 313, 318, 204 N. Y. S. 741 (3d Dept. 1924), that the claim to additional compensation had been waived and need not be considered among liabilities.

[116] *Hubbard v. Weare*, 79 Iowa 678, 693–694, 44 N. W. 915 (1890) (accrued interest on bills payable; accrued interest on bills receivable had been included among assets); *Glover v. Thompson Connellsville Coke Co.*, 66 Pitts. L. J. 525 (C. P. Alleghany County, Pa., 1918) (accrued income taxes).

[117] *Majestic Co. v. Orpheum Circuit*, 21 F. (2d) 720 (C. C. A. 8th, 1927) (future installments of rent and taxes under a lease); *Hofkin v. U. S. Smelting Co.*, 266 Fed. 679 (C. C. A. 3d, 1920). It is customary, however, to set up reserves for contingent liabilities. 2 Bonbright, *Valuation of Property* (1937) 967.

that reserves taken are quite clearly inadequate, it is hardly the field of the lawyer or the court to condemn what prudently selected independent engineers or auditors have determined to be a fair reserve allowance.

Two methods of handling reserves may be used. They may be set up as direct deductions from assets. Many accountants do this. The other method is that of carrying a reserve on the liability side rather than charging down the asset. This method is employed on the theory that the amount is an estimate and has not as yet become a realized charge justifying a complete write-down. This is aptly illustrated in the case of reserves for bad debts. If a direct charge-off is made and the debt is subsequently paid in full, it may be said that a profit is now realized, when in fact a receivable which always should have been carried as an asset has merely been paid and a cash asset substituted for it.[118]

44.1. Doubtful Debts

If a debt is definitely ascertained to be bad in whole or part, it should to that extent be entirely excluded from the assets of the balance sheet.[119] In the majority of cases, however, the worthless character of notes and accounts receivable cannot be precisely determined. There is, nevertheless, in the experience of almost every business a certain percentage of debts which ultimately proves uncollectible. Though this amount cannot be determined with exactness, a reserve must be set up for what experience reasonably indicates to be the expectable loss.[120] There is some doubt as to whether such reserves are required by statutes making mandatory the deduction of losses of every character,[121] since a reserve is created on the theory

---

[118] Cf. §42, *supra*. The Southern Pacific Company for the year 1939 set up a reserve of $150,000,000 out of accumulated surplus to provide for decline in value of various securities, principally of affiliates, carried at cost. "This procedure was adopted rather than a direct write-down of individual investments because it is impossible to estimate at this time the ultimate loss that might be suffered with respect to any particular investment." N. Y. Times, Mar. 22, 1940, p. 31. Regulation S–X, Rule 3.11, of the S. E. C., governing financial statements in registrations under the Securities Act and the Securities and Exchange Act, provides that ordinarily valuation and qualifying reserves shall be shown "as deductions from the specific assets to which they apply."

[119] See §37, n. 64–70, *supra*.

[120] *Hubbard v. Weare*, 79 Iowa 678, 693, 44 N. W. 915 (1890); 2 Bonbright, *Valuation of Property* (1937) 961, 964; Douglas and Shanks, *Cases and Materials on Business Units—Losses, Liabilities and Assets* (1932), Note, 192; Graham and Katz, *Accounting in Law Practice* (2d Ed. 1938) 201. The amount of reserves depends on the locality and economic conditions. 1 Dodd and Baker, *Cases on Business Associations* (1940), Note on Other Deductions, 1134.

[121] See §36.3, n. 28, *supra*.

that a loss has not as yet been sustained. Those statutes requiring diminutions arising from losses "or otherwise" to be taken into consideration presumably apply to reserves for doubtful debts.[122]

44.2. Depreciation and Obsolescence

In addition to diminutions in value suffered from ordinary wear and tear, which are normally taken care of through repairs, there takes place a general decline in the value of a corporation's buildings, machinery, and equipment below the original cost. This loss in value, even though there may be no corresponding loss in utility, is met by reserves for depreciation.[123] From the dividend standpoint distributions to stockholders without first keeping the capital with which the corporation operates intact would constitute payments from capital as distinguished from profits. While the stockholder may be under no obligation to protect creditors against declines in the market value of the corporation's plant and equipment, he cannot claim a right to distributions of the enterprise until diminutions arising from the use of these assets in producing income have first been provided for through depreciation reserves.[124] Many statutes expressly require

[122] Del. Rev. Code (1935), c. 65, §34 (when diminution is of preference capital required to satisfy liquidation preferences) ; Kans. Laws 1939, c. 152, §81 (similar provision) ; Cal. Civ. Code (1937), §346 (if preferred preference capital is impaired, dividends out of net profits may not be paid except to preferred shareholders) ; cf. Minn. Stat. (Mason 1938 Supp.), §7492-21.

[123] Generally see Berle and Fisher, *Elements of the Law of Business Accounting*, 32 Col. L. Rev. 573, 596 (1932) ; Paton and Littleton, *An Introduction to Corporate Accounting Standards* (1940) 81; Dewing, *Financial Policy of Corporations* (3d Rev. Ed. 1934) 505–546; Fitzhugh, *Accounting for Depreciation and Depletion*, 45 W. Va. L. Q. R. 134 (1939) ; Sanders, Hatfield, and Moore, *Statement of Accounting Principles* (1938) 31. For a discussion of depreciation principally from the rate making standpoint, see Wis. Public Service Comm., *Depreciation: A Review of Legal and Accounting Problems.*

[124] *Cannon v. Wiscassett Mills*, 195 N. C. 119, 141 S. E. 344 (1928) (statute prohibiting dividends except from the surplus or net profits arising from its business and the reduction, division or withdrawal of any part of the capital stock) ; *Whittaker v. Amwell Nat. Bank*, 52 N. J. Eq. 400, 29 Atl. 203 (Ct. Ch. 1894) ; see *People ex rel. Jamaica Water Supply Co. v. State Board of Tax Commissioners*, 128 App. Div. 13, 17–18, 112 N. Y. S. 392 (3d Dept. 1908) ; dictum approved 196 N. Y. 39, 57–58 (1909) (tax case) ; Graham and Katz, *Accounting in Law Practice* (2d Ed. 1938) 219; cf. *Dealers Granite Corp. v. Faubion*, 18 S. W. (2d) 737 (Tex. Civ. App. 1929) (holding depreciation must be taken in determining liability on corporate note payable from "net profits", which the court determined by a balance sheet surplus test). Compare also an early Supreme court case stating that in computing profits depreciation is not taken into account, *Eyster v. Centennial Board of Finance*, 94 U. S. 500, 503 (1876) ; but compare a statement to the opposite effect in a more recent tax case, *Von Baumbach v. Sargent Land Co.*, 242 U. S. 503, 524 (1916). Deductions for depreciation are allowed in computing the federal income tax. I. R. C., §23(1), and Reg. 103, §19.23(1) 1–10.

deductions for depreciation.[125] Where large amounts are spent on repairs and maintenance, the requirement for depreciation reserves is not as great.[126] Thus, it is the practice of many utilities, for example, to spend large sums on maintenance while setting aside relatively small amounts for depreciation.

There are two important problems in conjunction with depreciation, the base upon which it is to be taken and the method of computation. These problems are principally of an accounting nature and, so long as reasonable solutions are adopted, should not be objected to on legal grounds.[127]

The normal base is cost, and not the amount which it would take at the end of the asset's useful life to affect a replacement. The question becomes particularly acute in times of economic stress when revenues are curtailed. Asset values will have fallen materially. If the corporation continues to figure its depreciation on cost as of boom levels, exceedingly large portions of its curtailed revenue will be going into reserves, often precluding the declaration of dividends. One of the results of depression financing was writing down assets with the purpose of obtaining a lower depreciation base, and in turn a larger portion of current revenues for dividends.[128] Some account-

[125] Cal. Civ. Code (1937), §346 (in paying dividends out of net profits if capital required to satisfy liquidation preferences on preferred stock is thereby impaired) ; Del. Rev. Code (1935), c. 65, §34 (if capital required to meet preferred liquidation preferences is impaired by "depreciation in the value of its property," no dividends are permitted out of net profits) ; Kans. Laws 1939, c. 152, §81 (similar provision) ; Idaho Code Ann., §29-129 ("depreciation and depletion sustained") ; La. Gen. Stat. (Dart. 1939), §1106 (similar provision) ; Minn. Stat. (Mason 1938 Supp.), §7492-21 ; Ohio Code Ann. (Baldwin 1938), §8623-38 ; 15 Purd. Pa. Stat. Ann., §2852-701 ("depreciation and depletion sustained") ; Wash. Rev. Stat. Ann. (Rem.), §3803-24 (similar provision) ; Vt. Pub. Laws (1933), §5850.

[126] *Cox v. Leahy*, 209 App. Div. 313, 316–317, 204 N. Y. S. 741 (3d Dept. 1924) (where depreciation had been offset by maintenance and improvements, reserves not required) ; *Guaranty Trust Co. v. Grand Rapids, G. H. & M. Ry. Co.*, §22.1, n. 127, *supra; Dewing, Financial Policy of Corporations* (3d Rev. Ed. 1934) 510; cf. *Park v. Grant Locomotive Works*, 40 N. J. Eq. 114, 119–120, 3 Atl. 162 (1885), aff'd on opinion below, 45 N. J. Eq. 244, 19 Atl. 621 (1888) (depreciation disallowed as deduction under contract providing for payment of corporate "net profits" where maintenance expenditures were large).

[127] For discussion of the several methods of computing depreciation see *Guaranty Trust Co. v. Grand Rapids, G. H. & M. Ry. Co.*, §22.1, n. 127, *supra;* 2 Bonbright, *Valuation of Property* (1937) 934–936; Dewing, *Financial Policy of Corporations* (3d Rev. Ed. 1934) 525–531; Graham and Katz, *Accounting in Law Practice* (2d Ed. 1938) 217–221, 246–274; Paton and Littleton, *An Introduction to Corporate Accounting Standards* (1940) 82–88; Note, *Depreciation and Net Profits for Dividend Purposes*, 33 Mich. L. Rev. 783 (1935).

[128] See Note, *Writing Down Fixed Assets and Stated Capital*, 44 Yale L. J. 1025 (1935) ; May, *Twenty-Five Years of Accounting Responsibility* (1936) 95–96.

ants look upon such procedure with disfavor.[129] Assuming, however, a sustained market decline, asset values and capital should both be reduced and the new asset base used. To use the fictitious valuation of original cost for computing depreciation results in postponing dividends in order to build up a capital asset value no longer existent.

In *Guaranty Trust Company v. Grand Rapids, Grand Haven and Muskegan Railway Company,* it was held that in computing dividends, external obsolescence, arising not from any physical deterioration or ordinary depreciation, but from decline in the value of an interurban railway due to automobile competition, must be taken into account.[130] The determinative criterion of this type of obsolescence was taken to be the sharp decline in earnings.[131] Thus, even though depreciation is taken for the ordinary physical exhaustion of corporate property, it is necessary to provide in addition reserves for decline in the functional utility of depreciable assets, arising either from improved production methods or a shift of interest to other types of economic demand.

44.3. Depletion: The Wasting Asset Doctrine as to Creditors

Few dividend problems are more difficult than the question whether so-called wasting asset corporations, with principal property consisting of mines, patents, copyrights, leaseholds, and other assets having a limited life or value, may declare dividends without deductions for depletion of their capital assets.[132] For example, under the wasting asset doctrine, a coal mining corporation need not deduct from gross sales any amount for the coal removed from its shafts, even though the piecemeal sale of a capital asset is taking place.

[129] See e.g. Littleton, *Business Profits as a Legal Basis for Dividends,* 16 Harv. Bus. Rev. 51, 59 (1938).

[130] See §22.1, n. 127, *supra;* 2 Bonbright, *Valuation of Property* (1937) 934; Dewing, *Financial Policy of Corporations* (3d Rev. Ed. 1934) 519; Paton and Littleton, *Introduction to Corporate Accounting Standards* (1940) 83. I. R. C. 23(1), and Reg. 103, §19.23(1)–6, permit reasonable allowances for obsolescence from economic conditions that will result in abandonment of physical property prior to the end of its normal useful life.

[131] Total passengers carried had declined 38 per cent in 4 years; total passengers per thousand of population had declined over 50 per cent in 11 years.

[132] Generally see Ballantine and Hills, *Corporate Capital and Restrictions upon Dividends under Modern Corporation Laws,* 23 Cal. L. Rev. 229, 248 (1935); 2 Bonbright, *Valuation of Property* (1937) 936; Paton and Littleton, *An Introduction to Corporate Accounting Standards* (1940) 90–91; 1 Dodd and Baker, *Cases on Business Associations* (1940), Note on Statutes Relating to Wasting Assets and Depletion, 1102; Weiner, *Theory of Anglo-American Dividend Law: American Statutes and Cases,* 29 Col. L. Rev. 461, 477 (1929); Note, *Dividends from Wasting Asset Corporations,* 43 W. Va. L. Q. 53 (1936).

The English case of *Lee v. Neuchatel Asphalte Company* is said to establish the general principle that wasting asset corporations need not set up reserves for depletion.[133] Aside from the fact that no rights of creditors were there involved, the contest being confined to the conflicting interests of common and preferred shareholders,[134] the case can be of little persuasive authority in the many American jurisdictions confined by statute to the balance sheet surplus rule,[135] since the English companies acts have consistently permitted dividends from profits, generally construed by the English courts to mean earnings of the current accounting period.[136] Where there is an express prohibition against payment from capital in the statute, and no specific exception for wasting asset corporations, it is extremely hazardous to rely upon the *Neuchatel* case. In *Wittenberg v. Federal Mining and Smelting Company,* which also was a proceeding by preferred shareholders to enjoin payment of dividends to common shareholders without making depletion deductions, and therefore not controlling as to the situation in which creditors are involved, the Delaware courts held the Neuchatel doctrine would not be followed, particularly in view of the difference between English companies acts and American statutes.[137] The Delaware courts, having to deal with a situation arising before amendment of the Delaware statute authorizing the payment of wasting asset dividends, held that failure to deduct depletion, where the balance sheet disclosed a capital impairment, would constitute a payment of dividends directly from capital as to which preferred shareholders had a dissolution preference. While the case is a stockholder decision, its rationale of a dividend payment without depletion constituting a payment from capital applies equally to the situation where a creditor is making the protest.[138]

---

[133] L. R. 41 Ch. Div. 1 (1889) [the company's articles of association expressly provided that such deduction need not be made, but the court (Cotton, L. J.) was of opinion the same result would follow without reference thereto] ; see Kester, *Principles of Accounting* (3d Rev. Ed. 1936) 428.

[134] Questions concerning relative rights of common and preferred stockholders of wasting asset corporations are discussed in §§71, 72, *infra.*

[135] For these statutes, see §§21, 22, 23, *supra.*

[136] See §25, n. 178, 179, *supra.*

[137] 15 Del. Ch. 147, 133 Atl. 48 (1926), aff'd 15 Del. Ch. 409, 138 Atl. 347 (1927).

[138] The lower court said "All that has hereinbefore been said should of course be understood as being confined solely to controversies *intra* the corporation. If creditors' rights are involved, an entirely different situation would be presented for consideration." 15 Del. Ch. 147, 166, 133 Atl. 48 (1926). In at least one lower court case in Pennsylvania, it has been held that a capital impairment statute, whatever else the rule might be in its absence, prevented the payment of dividends by a coal mining corporation unless depletion reserves were set up. *Glover v. Thompson Connellsville Coke Co.,* 66 Pitts. L. J. 525 (C. P. Alleghany County,

It is sometimes contended that the wasting asset doctrine of the *Neuchatel* case was a common law exception to the requirement that no dividends be paid from capital, and that statutes regulating dividends must be deemed to have been enacted subject to such exception.[139] The fallacy in this contention is that by 1880, when the wasting asset doctrine was first advanced or suggested,[140] the basic American statutory concepts of dividend regulation had already been established for three-quarters of a century;[141] these statutes could not have been enacted subject to a common law exception which at the time was non-existent. Even assuming the existence of such a common law doctrine, the express provision of statutes prohibiting the declaration of dividends from capital, without providing a wasting asset exception, should prevail.[142]

As a result of the *Wittenberg* case, Delaware in 1927 adopted the first American statutory provision permitting wasting asset corporations to pay dividends without deduction for depletion.[143]

1918) (bill by stockholder to restrain declaration); cf. *Commonwealth v. Central Transportation Co.*, 145 Pa. 89 (1891) (a reserve set up for loss in value of expiring patents and contracts is a capital reserve, and a subsequent reduction of capital and distribution of this reserve constitutes a distribution of capital for tax purposes); *De Brabant v. Commercial Trust Co.*, 113 N. J. Eq. 215, 218, 166 Atl. 533 (Ct. of Ch., 1933) (holding dividends of a copper mining company paid from earnings without any deduction for depletion to be "income" payable to life tenant under trust deed; the court said: "That such corporations, as between their stockholders and themselves, may, in the absence of a contract to the contrary, legally pay dividends out of revenue without first creating or providing for a depletion reserve for recoupment for its wasting assets, was long ago decided in a number of cases . . ."); but cf. *Excelsior Water & Mining Co. v. Pierce*, 90 Cal. 131, 27 Pac. 44 (1891) (action by corporation but no evidence creditors harmed; statute permitted dividends from surplus profits arising from the business but prohibited reduction of capital; no depletion allowance was held necessary); *Dealers Granite Corp. v. Faubion*, 18 S. W. (2d) 737 (Tex. Civ. App. 1929) (in determining amount due creditor on corporate note payable out of "net profits," which court computed by balance sheet surplus test, it was held that a depletion allowance for capital consumed in working granite quarries need not be made). The wasting asset doctrine has been sustained by American courts in many situations not directly involving the authority of a corporation to declare dividends. Such instances include for example contracts based on corporate "profits," dividend controversies between life tenant and remainderman and tax cases. See 1 Dodd and Baker, *Cases on Business Associations* (1940) 1101, n. 4.

[139] See *Federal Mining & Smelting Co. v. Wittenberg*, 15 Del. Ch. 409, 417–418, 138 Atl. 347 (1927).

[140] The first suggestion seems to have been made in 1 Morawetz, *Private Corporations* (1886), §442. The *Neuchatel* case was decided in 1889.

[141] See Chapter 1, *supra*.

[142] *Federal Mining & Smelting Co. v. Wittenberg*, 15 Del. Ch. 409, 418, 138 Atl. 347 (1927).

[143] 35 Del. Laws, c. 85, §16 (with a provision, however, protecting the capital required to pay preferred stockholders on liquidation, see §72, *infra*). See Corporation Trust Company, *Analysis of the Recent Delaware Amendments* (1927) 26.

Similar provisions have been included in almost all recent corporate revisions.[144] With the exception of the Delaware type statute, these provisions as a rule specify the types of corporations which shall be considered as doing a wasting asset business.

Keeping in mind rejection of the wasting asset doctrine in the first *Wittenberg* cases, an important question arises with respect to how far that result has been changed by the 1927 amendment to Section 34 in Delaware. The 1927 amendment enacted in their present form the two alternative sources for dividends—balance sheet surplus and current net profits—and by the wasting asset amendment authorized directors to determine "net profits" without taking into consideration depletion.[145]

(*a*) If the dividend is being paid in reliance on the net profits alternative of the statute, quite clearly depletion deductions, aside from questions as to preferred stockholders, need not be made.

(*b*) On the other hand, if there are no current net profits and it is desired to pay a dividend from surplus, a much more difficult question is presented. The wasting asset clause authorizes directors only to disregard depletion in determining net profits; it says nothing

---

[144] Cal. Civ. Code, §346 (but "adequate provision for meeting debts and liabilities must be made," and if assets fall below capital required to meet preferences of preferred stock on liquidation as a result of depletion, no dividends are to be paid under the net profits alternative except upon preferred shares); Idaho Code Ann., §29–129 (as to non-wasting asset corporations, depletion sustained must be taken into consideration); Kans. Laws 1939, c. 152, §82 (similar to Delaware provision); La. Gen. Stat. (Dart. 1939), §1106 (no depreciation or depletion need be taken if articles so provide, subject, however, to rights of shareholders of different classes; as to non-wasting asset corporations, sustained depletion must be taken); Mich. Stat. Ann. (Henderson 1937), §21.22; Minn. Stat. (Mason 1938 Supp.), §7492–21 (provided adequate provision is made for meeting liabilities and fixed preferences on liquidation of preferred stock); Ohio Code Ann. (Baldwin 1938), §8623–38; 15 Purd. Pa. Stat., §2852–701 (subject to the rights of shareholders of different classes; as to non-wasting asset corporations, depletion sustained must be taken); Wash. Rev. Stat. Ann. (Rem.), §3803–24 (similar provision); W. Va. Code (1937), §3082. A very limited provision has been included in the recent Georgia revision. The non-depletion right is given only to corporations organized substantially for the liquidation or exploitation of specific assets. Ga. Code Ann. (1936), §22–1835 as amended. Enacted Ga. Laws 1937–38, p. 229, §16; apparently taken from Hills, *Model Corporation Act*, 48 Harv. L. Rev. 1334, 1365 (1935). The wasting asset exemption in the Indiana General Corporation Law is rendered practically meaningless by the proviso that it shall be subject both to the rights of shareholders of different classes and also the rights of creditors. Ind. Stat. Ann. (Burns 1933), §25–211. It is common to reserve the rights of different classes of stock, but to add creditors takes away the remaining effect of the granted authority. Creditors are the only other parties in addition to the corporation or the state in a position to object and against whom the provision could give protection.

[145] See n. 143, *supra*.

about determination of surplus. In view of the fact that the alternative provisions were amended contemporaneously with the insertion of the wasting asset clause, it is fair to assume that the limitation of the wasting asset clause to profits was considered in the draftsmanship. Delaware corporations should proceed cautiously in declaring dividends from a balance sheet surplus which, were adequate depletion reserves to be considered, would produce a capital impairment or raise a question of that character. Caution is particularly in order in view of the decision in *Petroleum Rights Corporation v. Midland Royalty Corporation,* where the Delaware Chancery Court, in determining what was "surplus" to pay preferred dividends, held that no balance sheet surplus existed unless adequate depletion reserves were set up.[146]

Even in jurisdictions where the wasting asset doctrine applies, some protection to creditors is possible. Trust indentures of coal mining corporations, for example, generally provide for the creation of sinking funds out of all receipts from the sale of coal whereby there is assurance that the principal amount of the bonds will ultimately be paid.[147] While this does not fully protect general creditors, clearing away the fixed obligations does help to make possible more ready payment of unfunded claims.

44.4. Contingent Claims

The general possibility that a corporation is subject to the contingency of future losses is not enough to deprive it of the right to pay dividends. It is not necessary that it retain all its surplus as a reserve against such possibilities.[148] Any other rule would mean many corporations would be permanently deprived of the power to declare dividends. However, where judgments have resulted, or are likely to result, or where the only dispute is as to the amount of a judg-

---

[146] 167 Atl. 835 (1933). The case is discussed at length in connection with the effect which preferred liquidation rights have on the power to declare wasting asset dividends. See §72, *infra.* This is a striking illustration of a situation in which accounting for income tax purposes cannot be relied upon as to dividends. The income tax provisions of revenue acts have for some time allowed taking, in certain businesses, a fixed percentage of gross income as a depletion charge. I. R. C. §114b(3) (4), §23(m); Reg. 103, §19.23(m)–4–5. In the instant case it was held that taking a 27½ per cent depletion deduction for oil well properties in accordance with such provisions was an arbitrary and inadequate allowance so far as determination of funds available for dividends was concerned.

[147] See 1 Dodd and Baker, *Cases on Business Associations* (1940), Note on Statutes Relating to Wasting Assets and Depletion, 1103.

[148] *McKean v. Biddle,* 181 Pa. 361, 37 Atl. 528 (1897); *Carpenter v. New York & N. H. Railroad Co.,* 5 Abb. Pr. 277 (N. Y. 1857) (claims on excess stock issued fraudulently by transfer agent).

ment, the balance sheet should reflect the amount of the probable liability.

45. Capital Stock

The third division in balance sheet liabilities is the section for capital stock. This liability entry determines what portion of the corporation's total assets are to be restricted from use for dividend purposes in jurisdictions where the balance sheet surplus is the test employed.[149]

From the earliest use of the balance sheet in American corporate accounting, capital or capital stock has appeared as a liability item.[150] The par value share was originally the exclusive method of issuing stock in American corporations. Two of the first American corporations, the Bank of North America[151] and the Bank of United States,[152] had shares of the par value of $400. However, by 1800 the normal share unit was $100.[153] Until the adoption of the first no-par value stock statute by New York in 1912,[154] shares of fixed par value

---

[149] See §16(b), *supra.* The basis of the rule is well stated in *Equitable Life Assurance Society v. Union Pacific Railroad Co.,* 212 N. Y. 360, 366, 106 N. E. 92 (1914): ". . . Capital stock is carried as a liability and universally, so far as I am aware, at its par amount. It is thus carried as a liability because this is the proper bookkeeping entry. But aside from this, such entry also serves to emphasize the duty of the corporation to keep its capital stock unimpaired for the protection of those dealing with it." And by Judge Lurton in *Hamlin v. Toledo, St. Louis & Kansas City R. Co.,* 78 Fed. 664, 671 (C. C. A. 6th, 1897): "There is a sense in which every shareholder is a creditor of the corporation to the extent of his contribution to the capital stock. In that sense every corporation includes its capital stock among its liabilities. But the creditor relation is one which exists between the corporation and its shareholders. It is a liability which is postponed to every other liability, and no part of the capital can be lawfully returned to the stockholders until all debts are paid or provided for."

[150] First Bank of United States, 19 Ann. Cong. 458 (1809), also Clarke and Hall, *Legislative and Documentary History of the Bank of United States* (1832) 117–118; Second Bank of United States, Report of Condition (1822), 5–6; Boston Manufacturing Co., MSS Boston 3 (1830); Delaware & Hudson Canal Co., Report for year 1831 (1832); Morris Canal & Banking Co., Report of June 1836; Bank of Pennsylvania, 2 Hazard's *U. S. Commercial and Statistical Register* (1840) 112; Great Falls Manufacturing Co., Balance Sheet of July 30, 1841, MSS 44 (1823–1933), G. 786, v. 4; *Winnisimmet Company* (Mass. 1833), Annual Report June 1843, pp. 24–26.

[151] 7 J. of Cong. (1781–82) (Claypoole Ed.), p. 108, §1.

[152] 1 Stat. 191, §1 (1791).

[153] See e.g. Society for Establishing Useful Manufactures, N. J. Acts, Oct. Sess. 1791, c. 346, p. 730, §6; *Bank of Columbia,* Md. Laws 1793, c. 30, §2; Merrimack Bank (1795), Mass. Laws and Resolves 1794–95 (1896 Reprint), 1795–c. 25, pp. 372, 373; Massachusetts Fire Insurance Co. (1795), Mass. Laws and Resolves 1794–95 (1896 Reprint), 1795–c. 22, pp. 362–363; Norwich Bank (1796), 1 Conn. Priv. Laws (1837), p. 131, §2–1.

[154] N. Y. Laws 1912, c. 351.

were unqualifiedly the rule. The older statutes prohibiting the declaration of dividends from capital do not define what shall be meant by capital or capital stock, whether it is to mean par or some amount above or below par.[155] By construction it has been held under such statutes that capital constitutes the actual consideration received rather than the par value of the stock.[156] Thus, if a corporation issues stock of the par value of $100 for property worth $50, the capital under these statutes which cannot be distributed in dividends is $50. In some of these jurisdictions, the amount of capital is ascertained as of the opening of the particular accounting period rather than the time of issuance of the stock.[157] Most modern revisions adopting the balance sheet surplus test, either exclusively or as an alternative, solve these difficult questions by making an express provision that the entry for capital or stated capital shall constitute the amount of the par value of shares having a par value.[158]

45.1. Stock Without Par Value

The chief manner in which stock without par value affects the fund available for dividends under balance sheet surplus statutes is in determination of what, if any, amount must be entered as capital and what amount as paid-in surplus.[159] Strict application of the principle of no-par stock would result in entering no part of the con-

---

[155] For statutes of this type see §§22, 23, *supra*.

[156] See §22.1, *supra*.

[157] See §22.2, *supra*.

[158] Cal. Civ. Code (1937), §300b (but if par value shares are issued as fully paid up for a consideration less than par, only the agreed consideration constitutes capital; if issued for consideration in excess of par, the excess is to be credited to paid-in surplus); Del. Rev. Code (1935), c. 65, §34; Idaho Code Ann. §29–101; 32 Ill. Ann. Stat. (Smith-Hurd 1935), §157.2(k), 157.19 (a); Kans. Laws 1939, c. 152, §43; La. Gen. Stat. (Dart. 1939), §1080 (x); Mich. Stat. Ann. (Henderson 1937), §21.20; Minn. Stat. (Mason 1938 Supp.), §7492–1(x); N. J. Stat. (1937), §14:8–1; N. Y. Stock Corp. Law, §§12, 13; Ohio Code Ann. (Baldwin 1938), §8623–37 (for conditions under which par shares may be sold at less than par, see §8623–16); 15 Purd. Pa. Stat., §2852–614; Tenn. Code Ann. (1934), §3735; Wash. Rev. Stat. Ann. (Rem.), §3803–1. Virginia provides that the capital shall be the consideration received for its shares, whether par or no-par, but shall not include contributed surplus when it is provided under terms of the subscription agreement that the same shall be paid in addition to the consideration. Va. Code (1936), §3840.

[159] Generally see Berle, *Studies in the Law of Corporation Finance* (1928) 64; Ballantine and Lattin, *Cases and Materials on the Law of Corporations* (1939), Note, 436–437; 1 Dodd and Baker, *Cases on Business Associations* (1940), Note on Consideration for Issue of No-Par Shares, 1001; Masterson, *Consideration for Non-Par Shares and Liability of Subscribers and Stockholders*, 17 Tex. L. Rev. 247 (1939); Weiner, *The Amount Available for Dividends Where No-Par Shares Have Been Issued*, 29 Col. L. Rev. 906 (1929); Robbins, *No-Par Stock* (1927) 15.

sideration received for such stock as capital. When any portion of the consideration is treated as capital, what is created is not true stock without par value, but rather par value stock of lower denomination.[160] Yet in most jurisdictions statutes provide for allocating some part of the consideration received on the sale of no-par shares to capital or stated capital.

Statutes dealing with this subject may be divided into four general classes. A few merely require statement of the number of no-par shares issued and seem broad enough not to require any entry for capital.[161] Some require that the entire consideration received be treated as capital;[162] New Jersey that it shall be the amount fixed by the board of directors;[163] while the majority of states provide it shall be the amount of consideration received unless some part thereof is allocated by the board to paid-in surplus.[164]

What is the effect of a change from par to no-par stock? Suppose a corporation has assets $150,000, capital 100,000 (divided into 1,000 shares of the par value of $100), and surplus of $50,000. If

---

[160] It has been said, however, that good accounting practice requires the total money or property received for no-par shares to be credited entirely to the capital account. Sparger, *Profits, Surplus, and the Payment of Dividends*, 8 N. Car. L. Rev. 14, 27 (1929).

[161] Ga. Ann. Code, §22–809; Ky. Stat. Ann. (Carroll 1936), §564–2; Mass. Laws Ann., c. 156, §14. Generally see 1 Dodd and Baker, *Cases on Business Associations* (1940), Note on Statutes: Par and No-Par Shares, 1030.

[162] La. Gen. Stat. (Dart. 1939), §1080; Mich. Stat. Ann. (Henderson 1937), §21.20 (at least 50 per cent of the consideration received must be allocated to capital); Va. Code (1936), §3840 (unless the terms of the subscription agreement provide for contributed surplus); Wash. Rev. Stat. Ann. (Rem.), §3803–1(x); Wis. Stat. (1937), §182.14 (with exceptions for stock issued when there is an existing surplus or when shares are issued in exchange for shares of an existing corporation having a surplus). By §12 of the New York Stock Corporation Law, a corporation's capital in the event that no-par shares are issued is determined by one of two alternative provisions which must appear in its certificate of incorporation. Under alternative A, the capital is the par value of the aggregate par value shares plus at least one dollar per share of no-par value stock. Under alternative B, the capital is the par value of the aggregate par value shares plus the consideration received for no-par value shares.

[163] N. J. Stat. (1937), §14:8–6.

[164] Cal. Civ. Code (1937), §300b (but in the case of no-par shares with liquidation preference, the entire agreed consideration must be credited to stated capital); Del. Rev. Code (1935), c. 65, §14; Idaho Code Ann., §29–101; 32 Ill. Ann. Stat. (Smith-Hurd 1935), §157.2(k), 157.19 (if all shares are without par value and if all have preferential right in assets on involuntary liquidation, then stated capital shall not be less than the preferential amount); Kans. Laws 1939, c. 152, §43; Minn. Stat. (Mason 1938 Supp.), §7492–1(x), 20(III) (but as to shares having a preference on liquidation, the amount of such preference must be treated as capital); Ohio Code Ann. (Baldwin 1938), §8623–17, 37; 15 Purd. Pa. Stat. Ann., §2852–614 (stated capital as to shares with preferential right in assets on involuntary liquidation to be the amount of agreed consideration received); Tenn. Code Ann. (1934), §3735.

the 1,000 par shares are now exchanged for 2,000 no-par shares, is the surplus a part of the consideration received for the new no-par shares and as such a part of the corporation's new capital? In *Public Service Commission v. Consolidated Gas, Electric Light and Power Company,* it was held in the absence of affirmative evidence to show it was intended to capitalize the surplus, it would be presumed that this had not been done.[165] Merely an exchange of shares and not a stock dividend is the normal intention. The financial structure should, therefore, remain unchanged.

45.2. Premium on Stock

The only direct authority on availability for dividends of a premium paid upon stock issued at organization is *Merchants and Insurers' Reporting Company v. Schroeder,* which denied use for that purpose on the ground it constituted capital.[166] The case was decided, however, under a type statute no longer existing in most balance sheet surplus jurisdictions.[167] Under modern statutes of this class which provide that the par value of par stock shall constitute capital, the premium on stock issued at organization will be available for dividends.[168]

Quite a different problem is the question whether in the absence of statute the premium on par value stock of a corporation already doing business is capital or a surplus equalizer. If a corporation in business for some time accumulates a surplus, must stock issued at a premium be capitalized in the entire amount of the consideration received? In *Equitable Life Assurance Society v. Union Pacific Railroad Company,* it was held that the corporation need only

---

[165] 148 Md. 90, 129 Atl. 22 (1925). See also cases cited in 1 Dodd and Baker, *Cases on Business Associations* (1940) 1143, n. 2.

[166] 39 Cal. App. 226, 178 Pac. 540 (1918). Apparently the shares were part of the original issue because no business profits had been made subsequent to their sale. There is a dictum in accord in a dividend tax case. See *People ex rel. Queens County Water Co. v. Travis,* 171 A. D. 521, 524, 157 N. Y. S. 943 (3d Dept. 1916), aff'd 219 N. Y. 571, 114 N. E. 1079 (1916); cf. Kester, *Principles of Accounting* (3d Rev. Ed. 1936) 423.

[167] Former Cal. Civ. Code, §309, providing directors should not declare dividends "except from the surplus profits arising from the business thereof . . . nor must they withdraw or pay to the stockholders, or any of them any part of the capital stock. . . ."

[168] See §§21, 45, n. 158, *supra.* California, Illinois, and Minnesota provide, however, that the consideration received in excess of par shall be paid-in surplus, subject to the restrictions applicable thereto. Cal. Civ. Code (1937), §300b; 32 Ill. Ann. Stat. (Smith-Hurd. 1935), §157.2(1); Minn. Stat. (Mason 1938 Supp.), §7492–20, 21; Ballantine and Lattin, *Cases and Materials on the Law of Corporations* (1939), Note, 436. Cf. *Edwards v. Douglas,* 269 U. S. 204, 214 (1925), §29, n. 218, *supra.*

capitalize an amount equal to par, treating the premium as an equalizing credit to surplus, in order that the interests of old and new stockholders in the surplus might be kept on a parity.[169] Take, for example, a corporation with assets of $175,000, capital of $100,000, and surplus of $75,000. If 1,000 additional shares of stock were issued for $175,000 and the entire amount capitalized, the balance sheet would show assets of $350,000, capital of $275,000, and surplus still $75,000, but now distributable among 2,000 shareholders instead of 1,000. Obviously, this is unfair to the old stockholders who potentially had the right to distribution of $75,000, among 1,000 stockholders.[170] The old and new stockholders are, therefore, equalized by capitalizing only $100,000 of the sale price of the new shares and crediting the balance to surplus.[171]

The contention is sometimes made that the entire consideration paid for new shares should be treated as capital, because as to a purchaser, for example a trustee, the entire amount is a capital investment.[172] This does not mean, however, that as between respective

[169] 212 N. Y. 360, 106 N. E. 92 (1914); cf. *Smith v. Cotting*, 231 Mass. 42, 120 N. E. 177 (1918) (holding a life tenant entitled to dividends paid out of the premium on the sale of stock on the ground that the same constituted income); *Miller v. Payne*, 150 Wis. 354, 136 N. W. 811 (1912); see, 1 Dodd and Baker, *Cases on Business Associations* (1940) 1143; 2 Bonbright, *Valuation of Property* (1937) 918; Dewing, *Financial Policy of Corporations* (3d Rev. Ed. 1934) 608n.; Paton and Littleton, *An Introduction to Corporate Accounting Standards* (1940) 42; Marple, *The Sources of Capital Surplus*, 9 Acc. Rev. 75, 76 (1934); cf. Berle, *Cases on Corporation Finance* (1930), Note, 395; but see Ballantine and Lattin, *Cases and Materials on the Law of Corporations* (1939) 452, n. 56. For an English case in accord on its facts but failing to analyze the reason for the rule, see *Drown v. Gaumont-British Picture Corp. Ltd.*, (1937) Ch. 402 [comment, 54 L. Q. Rev. 11 (1938)].

[170] Note that any unfairness in distribution would be compensated for were the corporation to dissolve without intermediate loss in value of its assets. Upon dissolution there would be $75,000 of additional capital supplied by the new stockholders but in which the old stockholders would share ratably under the rule that all shares are treated the same. It is hardly fair, however, to defer old stockholders until a voluntary or involuntary dissolution for equal treatment.

[171] There is a current tendency among accountants, how strong is not clear, to treat all consideration on the sale of stock including premium received as capital. See e.g. American Assoc. of Accountants, *Tentative Statement of Accounting Principles*, 11 Acc. Rev. 187, 191 (1936); Broad and Paton, *Various Kinds of Surplus*, 65 J. of Accountancy 281, 282, 287 (1938); Paton, *Essentials of Accounting* (1938) 666; Montgomery, *Dealings in Treasury Stock*, 65 J. of Accountancy 466, 472 (1938) (as to stock retired and reissued); and §45.3, *infra*. There is no indication in these discussions that the inequity of such a rule is appreciated or the legal obstacles to its use in view of the *Equitable Life* case.

[172] However, in *Smith v. Cotting*, 231 Mass. 42, 47, 120 N. E. 177 (1918), a case in which dividends were declared out of the premium on the sale of prior issues of stock, a life tenant was held entitled to the same as income, the court saying: "Whatever might be said as to premiums paid on shares originally issued,

shareholders of the corporation a portion of the consideration may not still have to be treated as surplus for dividend purposes, leaving the trustee to allocate his dividends, as he does in other situations, between capital and income. If a trustee were to purchase in the open market at a premium a share issued upon organization as to which a surplus had accumulated, it could not be contended that the surplus should not be distributed in dividends, because he had made a capital investment. Yet so far as a trustee or other purchaser is concerned, the investment is as much capital in the one case as the other. In both cases the distribution problem is properly approached as one of internal corporate relations between old and new stockholders, rather than from the standpoint of the type investment being made by the purchasing stockholder.

The rule applied in the *Equitable Life* case may offer difficulties in particular situations. The premium paid on stock is not necessarily the equivalent of an amount necessary to equalize the interest of old and new stockholders in book surplus. Indeed, the premium is much more apt to represent market value above par rather than book surplus. In this situation to credit surplus with the entire amount of the premium as was done in the *Equitable Life* case would work an injustice. Assume, for example, a corporation with assets of $150,000, capital $50,000, surplus $100,000. If 500 shares of stock are now sold at $300, the book value of each share, the balance sheet will show assets of $300,000, capital $100,000, and surplus $200,000, maintaining intact the previous ratio. There may, however, be situations in which it is not possible or desirable to sell stock at $300. It may be expedient to sell stock to employees at $150 a share. If 500 employees are now brought in at $150 a share, they obviously have not contributed sufficiently to equalize their equity interest in the sur-

---

it is obvious that the very large premiums received by the corporation on some subsequent issues were paid not as capital, but for the right to share in the profits, surplus and other earnings which had been accumulated and remained undistributed." In *U. S. v. Phellis,* 257 U. S. 156 (1921), a similar result was reached in holding taxable as income dividend shares distributed on a reorganization, the contention having been made that they constituted a return of capital. ". . . if an investor happened to buy stock shortly before the dividend, paying a price enhanced by an estimate of the capital plus the surplus of the company, and after distribution of the surplus, with corresponding reduction in the intrinsic and market value of the shares, he were called upon to pay a tax upon the dividend received, it might look in this case like a tax upon his capital. But it is only apparently so. In buying at a price that reflected the accumulated profits, he of course acquired as a part of the valuable rights purchased the prospect of a dividend from the accumulations bought 'dividend on'—as the phrase goes—and necessarily took subject to the burden of the income tax proper to be assessed against him by reason of the dividend if and when made."

plus with that of the old stockholders. A balance sheet at this point would read: assets $225,000, capital $100,000, surplus $125,000. Each share, including the old shares, would be worth only $225, or a loss to the old shares of $75. In order to remedy this, a prior dividend to old shareholders should be paid which will bring the interest of all the stockholders in the surplus into a parity.[178] In the example suggested, a cash dividend of $75,000 to old shareholders would leave the relative interests on a parity. Such a dividend would reduce the book value of the old stock prior to issuance of new stock to $150 a share. Bringing in the new stock at $150 would now result in equitable allocation of surplus and capital.

The situation more likely to occur is the sale of stock above its book value. Taking again the example of book value stock of $300, the market price may, in fact, be $400. Suppose 500 shares are sold at $400; this will produce a balance sheet of assets $350,000, capital $100,000, and surplus $250,000. It is at once apparent that the book value of the old stock has increased $50 a share and as to book value the new stock has lost an equivalent amount. Presumably the assets prior to issuance of the new stock had a value in excess of their $300 book value, so that were the corporation to liquidate immediately, both classes of stockholders would receive theoretically $400 a share. But liquidation normally is not contemplated, and the immediate question is, How does this type of financial operation affect the relative dividend interests of the two sets of shareholders? Prior to the issuance of the new stock, the old stock had a surplus of $200 per share. After the issuance of the new stock, the surplus allocable to all shares is $250 per share. The old stock thereby obtains a $50 dividend surplus it did not have before. As has been stated, this might be offset on liquidation by realization of extra asset values which would then go toward equal distribution with the new stock, but the new stock should not be compelled to carry this risk. A portion of the surplus arising from the $400 purchase price of new shares ought, therefore, to be earmarked as possibly a capital surplus, but in any event segregated so as not to be treated as surplus available for ordinary dividends payable alike to both classes of common stockholders. This suggestion would result in the following balance sheet: assets $350,000, capital $100,000, dividend surplus $200,000, special surplus $50,000. This would result in no prejudice to the old common since the dividend surplus is $200 per share under the new arrangement just as it was previously. The

---

[178] Semble: Bowers v. Post, 209 Fed. 660 (D. Ill. 1913), aff'd 220 Fed. 1006 (1915).

special surplus is held in abeyance as more nearly resembling a capital surplus than an earned surplus.

Statutes which expressly provide that capital shall be par value as to par shares permit application of the *Equitable Life* doctrine and its variations in order to assure fair distribution between old and new stockholders.[174] However, statutes such as those in California, Illinois, and Minnesota which require the premium to be credited to paid-in surplus will produce inequities through the restrictions which attach to paid-in surplus.[175] Where the corporation has no-par stock with stated capital, essentially the same problem of equitably allocating proper proportions of consideration on new issues between stated capital and both earned and paid-in surplus will arise. With the exception of states requiring the entire consideration to be entered as capital, or the difference between capital and the consideration to be specifically earmarked as paid-in surplus, no-par stock provisions are flexible enough to permit such allocation.[176]

45.3. Treasury Stock

Treatment of treasury stock is one of the most uncertain matters in corporate accounting.[177] A corporation may acquire its own shares for purposes of speculation; but often the acquisition is for legitimate purposes, as for example, the purchase of stock from an estate upon death of a stockholder, purchases from dissentient stockholders, and accumulation of shares for an employee stock plan.

Accounting problems are presented in two situations, first as to treatment upon the purchase of treasury shares, and secondly as to the method of handling a resale thereof. With respect to the first problem, if a corporation having assets of $200,000, capital of $100,000 (par value shares of $100), and surplus of $100,000, purchases 250 shares of its stock at $200, the book value, there are three ways of presenting the effect of the purchase in a balance sheet.

---

[174] See §45, n. 158, *supra.*

[175] See this section, n. 168, *supra.*

[176] See §45.1, n. 162–164, *supra.* Under Wis. Stat. (1937), §182.14, if no-par shares are sold by a corporation having an accumulated surplus, such proportion of the price as bears the same proportion to the total price as the surplus bears to the total of capital and surplus may be treated as available for dividends, provided a resolution of directors adopted prior to the sale so specifies.

[177] Leading accountants currently differ on justification for treating treasury stock as an asset available for dividends and also on considering the profit realized on a resale as available for that purpose. See Report of Committee on Accounting Procedure of the American Institute of Accountants, 65 J. of Accountancy 417 (1938); Montgomery, *Dealings in Treasury Stock, id.,* at 466; May, *Recent Opinions on Dealings in Treasury Stock,* 66 J. of Accountancy 17 (1938).

First, the purchased treasury shares may be treated as assets similar to any other assets purchased for a like amount. The balance sheet would read:

ASSETS		LIABILITIES	
Assets generally	$150,000	Capital	$100,000
Treasury stock	50,000	Surplus	100,000
	$200,000		$200,000

Under this method no change is effected in the surplus, and dividends can still be paid to the extent of $100,000 in spite of the fact that tangible assets have been reduced $50,000 in return for a treasury stock asset which on liquidation is worthless to creditors. Indeed, this method permits continued treasury purchases out of the maintained surplus and continued distribution of dividends until all the real assets are exhausted. It is quite generally agreed, therefore, that it is improper accounting practice to treat treasury stock as an asset.[178] A few statutes expressly provide that treasury shares shall not be considered an asset for dividend purposes.[179]

Second, the shares may be omitted entirely from the asset side of the balance sheet and the purchase met on the liability side by charging capital for the par value of the shares and surplus for the premium paid:

ASSETS		LIABILITIES		
Assets generally	$150,000	Capital:		
		1,000 shares,		
		$100 par	$100,000	
		Less treasury		
		250 shares	25,000	$ 75,000
		Surplus		75,000
	$150,000			$150,000

[178] *Haebler v. Crawford,* 258 N. Y. 130, 179 N. E. 319 (1932) (action to rescind stock purchase on ground of misrepresentation that dividend had been earned); cf. *Borg v. International Silver Co.,* 11 F. (2d) 147, 150 (C. C. A. 2d, 1925) (suit by common stockholders to prevent the sale of stock at public auction on ground of preemptive right) ; see Graham and Katz, *Accounting in Law Practice* (2d. Ed. 1938) 164–165; Robbins, *No-Par Stock* (1927) 154–155; May, *Twenty-Five Years of Accounting Responsibility* (1936) 93; Porter and Fiske, *Accounting* (1935) 255; Berle and Fisher, *Elements of the Law of Business Accounting,* 32 Col. L. Rev. 573, 582–583 (1932); Hills, *Model Corporation Act,* 48 Harv. L. Rev. 1334, 1367, n. 53 (1935).

[179] Cal. Civ. Code, §342b; Idaho Code Ann., §29–129 (cash dividends are prohibited from profit on treasury shares before resale) ; 32 Ill. Ann. Stat., §157.2(m) ; La. Gen. Stat. (Dart. 1939), §1106 (cash and property dividends from profit on treasury shares before resale prohibited); 15 Purd. Pa. Stat. Ann., §2852–702 (similar provision); Wash. Rev. Stat. Ann. (Rem.), §3803–24 (similar provision as to cash dividends).

This method is subject to two objections. It effects a reduction of capital without formally meeting the statutory requirements for reduction,[180] and reduces surplus account only $25,000, whereas actual assets were reduced $50,000 by the purchase. The indirect effect is much the same as though treasury shares were considered an asset to this extent.[181]

Third, in the majority of jurisdictions where purchase of treasury stock is only allowed from surplus, the stock is not carried as an asset and the charge is completely made to surplus account:

ASSETS		LIABILITIES		
Assets generally	$150,000	Capital:		
		Outstanding	$ 75,000	
		In treasury ..	25,000	$100,000
		Surplus		50,000
	$150,000			$150,000

or

ASSETS		LIABILITIES		
Assets generally	$150,000	Capital:		
		Issued	$100,000	
		Less treasury	25,000	
			75,000	
		Surplus reserved as capital	25,000	
				$100,000
		Surplus:		
		Earned surplus ...	100,000	
		Less surplus reserved on purchase of treasury stock:		
		As capital $25,000		
		As premium 25,000	50,000	50,000
	$150,000			$150,000

[180] For approval of such action, see Kester, *Principles of Accounting* (3d Ed.) 369–370; Paton, *Essentials of Accounting* (1938) 683–684; but cf. Graham and Katz, *Accounting in Law Practice* (2d Ed. 138) 165; Robbins, *No-Par Stock* (1927) 155. The statement made in *Borg v. International Silver Co.*, 11 F. (2d) 147, 150 (C. C. A. 2d, 1925), that treasury shares would not be considered a liability on dissolution, because obligor and obligee are one, disregards creditors as to whom capital exists until it is reduced. The California Civil Code, §342b, provides that treasury shares may be retired and restored to the status of authorized and unissued shares without reduction of stated capital.

[181] The American Accounting Association has tentatively adopted the principle that the cost of treasury shares should be considered an unallocated reduction of capital and surplus. American Accounting Assoc., *Tentative Statement of Accounting Principles*, 11 Acc. Rev. 187, 190 (1936). This is no solution to

The second of the last two alternatives seems in some respects prefer-able,[182] not only because it discloses more fully the real nature of the transaction, but also because it lays the basis for a restoration to earned surplus of $25,000 should the shares ultimately be retired. Suppose that instead of first purchasing the shares and then reducing capital, an arrangement for immediate reduction were made upon payment to the 250 shareholders of the purchase price of $50,000. The balance sheet would then show:

ASSETS		LIABILITIES	
Assets generally	$150,000	Capital	$ 75,000
		Surplus	75,000
	$150,000		$150,000

The same result should also follow where the reduction takes place in two steps instead of one. Upon the actual reduction or retirement in the two step method, the $25,000 surplus appropriated for capital, as indicated in the second of the last alternative balance sheets, is released and made free for the usual purposes of surplus.[183]

A distinction must be drawn between treasury stock which has been purchased at a discount below par and a corporate bond which has been purchased at a similar discount. In the case of a bond for $1,000 which is purchased for $900, the effect upon the balance sheet is to reduce the asset side $900 and the liability side $1,000, resulting in a net increase to surplus of $100:

BEFORE PURCHASE

ASSETS		LIABILITIES	
Assets generally	$10,000	Capital	$ 5,000
		Bond debt	2,000
		Surplus	3,000
	$10,000		$10,000

the problem, as the question is to which of the two should the charge be made, or if to both, in what proportions.

[182] Some accountants recognize that when treasury stock is purchased the capital account cannot be reduced, but the complete charge should be to surplus. Graham and Katz, *Accounting in Law Practice* (2d Ed. 1938) 164–167; Payne, *Net Worth under the Delaware and Michigan Corporation Laws,* 8 Acc. Rev. 1, 8 (1933); Marple, *The Sources of Capital Surplus,* 9 Acc. Rev. 75, 78 (1934). Michigan provides that upon purchase of treasury shares the effect must be shown on its books by a deduction from surplus, or by classifying surplus accounts in such a manner as to show the amount of surplus applied to such purchases which shall not be available for dividends. Mich. Stat. Ann. (Henderson 1937), §21.10(h). The S. E. C. in Regulation S–X, Rule 3.16, governing registration statements, authorizes deduction of the cost of the shares from surplus as one of several alternative methods of accounting.

[183] Cf. 1 Dodd and Baker, *Cases on Business Associations* (1940) 757.

AFTER PURCHASE

ASSETS   LIABILITIES

Assets generally .... $ 9,100   Capital .... $ 5,000
                                     Bond debt   1,000
                                     Surplus   3,100

                          $ 9,100 $ 9,100

The same situation, however, does not follow with respect to ten shares of $100 par stock purchased for $900. The asset side is similarly reduced, but without retirement of the shares, the capital cannot be touched in the majority of jurisdictions. The purchase must be debited to surplus, and the potential increase in surplus must await final reduction or retirement of the stock. In the example put, the balance sheet after purchase would read:

ASSETS   LIABILITIES

Assets generally ....$ 9,100   Capital:
                                       Issued .... $ 5,000
                                       Less treasury..   1,000

                                                         4,000
                                     Surplus re-
                                       served as
                                       capital   900
                                     Capital surplus
                                       from acquisi-
                                       tion of treas-
                                       ury shares ..   100 $ 5,000

                                     Debt   2,000
                                     Surplus:
                                       Earned surplus   3,000
                                       Less surplus re-
                                       served as
                                       capital   900   2,100

                          $ 9,100 $9,100

45.4. Resales of Treasury Stock

The second accounting question in conjunction with treasury stock is the availability for dividend purposes of profit on a resale. Some leading accountants currently take the position that no part of the resale price of treasury shares may be credited to earned surplus.[184] If any surplus created is treated as a paid-in or capital sur-

[184] See S. E. C. Accounting Series Release No. 6 (1938); May, *Twenty-Five Years of Accounting* (1936) 93–95; American Accounting Assoc., *Tentative Statement of Accounting Principles*, 11 Acc. Rev. 187, 190 (1936); Report of Com-

plus, it will be available for dividends only in restricted circumstances in many jurisdictions.[185] Suppose a corporation, with $500,-000 earned surplus and capital of $500,000, purchases 1,000 shares of its $100 par value common stock at $200,000. Assuming the purchase does not automatically reduce the capital, surplus must be reduced to $300,000.[186] Since there are now only 4,000 shares outstanding, these shares are entitled, from the dividend standpoint, to this surplus.[187] Assume further that the corporation thereafter increases its surplus through earnings to $1,000,000. The 4,000 shares are now entitled to dividends of $250 each from this surplus, either currently or in addition to capital on liquidation.[188] At this point the balance sheet would show:

ASSETS		LIABILITIES		
Assets generally	$1,500,000	Capital:		
		Issued	$ 500,000	
		Less treasury	100,000	
			400,000	
		Surplus reserved as capital	100,000	$ 500,000
		Surplus:		
		Earned	1,200,000	
		Less surplus reserved on purchase of treasury stock:		
		As capital $100,000		
		As premium 100,000	200,000	1,000,000
	$1,500,000			$1,500,000

Suppose the corporation now sells its 1,000 treasury shares for $375,000, their book value. In order to restore the *status quo,* the $200,000 charged to earned surplus upon the corporation's purchase of the shares is now recredited to that account.[189] Is it not also true

mittee on Accounting Procedure of American Institute of Accountants, 65 J. of Accountancy 417 (1938); May, *Recent Opinions on Dealings in Treasury Stock,* 66 J. of Accountancy (1938) 17. For a partial criticism of the Institute's position, see Montgomery, *Dealings in Surplus Stock,* 65 J. of Accountancy 466.

[185] See §29, *supra.*

[186] See §45.3, *supra.*

[187] Section 342b of the California Civil Code expressly provides that treasury shares shall not carry dividend rights or be counted outstanding for any purpose.

[188] On liquidation if creditors are paid there would also become available for distribution the additional $100,000 retained in capital account for the treasury shares, making total divisible surplus $1,100,000, and per share net worth $375.

[189] It is possible some accountants would not even restore this amount to surplus, treating the entire consideration received as capital, or that they would allow a credit only to the extent of the $100 charged to surplus in respect of capital on the corporation's original purchase. Cf. accounting methods in §45.3, *supra.*

that the additional $175,000 should be credited as an equalizer to earned surplus and not to paid-in surplus where its use would be restricted by statute in many states? What result would otherwise follow? If the $175,000 is credited to paid-in surplus, there will be an earned surplus available for general dividends of only $1,200,-000 (original surplus plus $200,000 of sale price of treasury shares) which must be divided among the holders of 5,000 shares. The amount the old and new shareholders could receive currently in dividends would, therefore, be $240 a share as against the right of the old shareholders to $250 a share prior to the resale. If the additional $175,000 is credited as an equalizer to earned surplus, the old and new stock are now entitled to current dividends out of surplus of $1,375,000, or $275. The old stock is entitled to a larger dividend after the sale than before as a result of restoring to surplus the $100,000 of capital which had been charged against it on purchase of the treasury shares. This may be illustrated by comparing balance sheets using the different methods:

CREDITING TO PAID-IN SURPLUS

ASSETS		LIABILITIES		
Asset generally	$1,875,000	Capital		$ 500,000
		Surplus:		
		Earned, avail-able for general dividends	$1,200,000	
		Paid-in	175,000	1,375,000
	$1,875,000			$1,875,000

EQUALIZING EARNED SURPLUS

ASSETS		LIABILITIES		
Asset generally	$1,875,000	Capital		$ 500,000
		Surplus:		
		Earned	$1,200,000	
		Premium on sale of treasury stock to equalize earned surplus [190]	175,000	
		(Available for general dividends)		1,375,000
	$1,875,000			$1,875,000

[190] By thus indicating that the entry is for purposes of equalizing earned surplus, any objection of misrepresentation which would arise from simply calling the amount earned surplus is avoided.

In this case the purchaser of treasury stock for $375 a share buys an interest representing a capital investment of $100 and an accrued profit investment of $275. Fair legal treatment to old stockholders cannot sanction accounting which does not recognize this situation, entering the consideration received on the books in a manner protecting all stockholders. The reasoning of the New York Court of Appeals, in *Equitable Life Assurance Society v. Union Pacific Railroad Company,* compels this result: "the payment of this premium was not for permanent capital but for the purpose of equalizing as between new and old stockholders their respective rights in accumulated profits which so far as we know were current and distributable in dividends. When paid in, this premium became part of such accumulation of profits and surplus and distributable as such." [191]

In most jurisdictions there are no applicable statutory provisions dealing with this problem, and the statutes in those states which take legislative cognizance of treasury stock are unsatisfactory. In states adopting the Uniform Business Corporation Act or modifications thereof, the provision prohibiting dividends based on profit from treasury stock before resale suggests at least the availability upon resale of the difference between sale price and purchase price.[192] In California the entire consideration received on the sale of treasury shares must be added to paid-in surplus, except so far as needed to write off a deficit of net assets below the amount of stated capital.[193]

The Attorney General of Illinois has expressed the opinion that under the new Illinois Business Corporation Act, the "profit" on the resale of treasury shares constitutes earned rather than paid-in surplus.[194]

46. Surplus

The residuum after deducting from assets all liabilities and corporate capital constitutes surplus from which dividends are payable in balance sheet surplus jurisdictions. Unless some statutory

---

[191] 212 N. Y. 360, 368, 106 N. E. 92 (1914), §45.3, n. 169, *supra;* see *Commonwealth v. Boston & Albany Railroad Co.,* 142 Mass. 146, 153, 7 N. E. 716 (1886). In holding shareholders had no preemptive right to treasury shares, the court in *Borg v. International Silver Co.,* 11 F. (2d) 147, 151 (C. C. A. 2d, 1925), said: "All he can demand is that they bring to the corporate treasury their existing value. If they do, his proportion in any surplus is not affected."

[192] Idaho Code Ann., §29-129; La. Gen. Stat. (Dart. 1939), §1106; 15 Purd. Pa. Stat. Ann., §2852-702; Wash. Rev. Stat. Ann. (Rem.), §3803-24.

[193] Cal. Civ. Code (1937), §342b.

[194] Op. Att. Gen. of Ill. (1933), p. 715.

provision limits payments from paid-in or reduction surplus,[195] distribution may be made irrespective of whether the surplus is earned or not. Nor is it material in these jurisdictions whether there is any profit shown on the year's profit and loss statement. The balance sheet is the sole test.

The fact a corporation does not completely distribute its surplus as earned, or invests it in additions to plant or equipment, does not capitalize the surplus or prevent its subsequent distribution.[196] There is one condition, however. At the time when it is sought to pay the dividend, the corporation must have a current surplus. For example, where an insurance company is rendered insolvent by a widespread city fire, stockholders are not entitled to the surplus which could have been legally distributed in dividends if paid the day before the fire occurred. All corporate assets, including both capital and prior surplus, then belong to creditors.[197]

47. Consolidated Balance Sheets

It is the usual accounting practice in the case of a parent and subsidiary, or affiliated companies, to consolidate into a single statement all the assets and all the liabilities of the related companies, eliminating intercompany assets and liabilities.[198] Care must be observed in declaring dividends on these consolidated statements. The original investment of a parent in a subsidiary may be much less as shown by cost on its own individual balance sheet than would be the equity in the surplus of the subsidiary if a consolidated balance sheet is used. The question becomes acute, for example, if the individual balance sheet of the parent shows a capital impairment, but the consolidated balance sheet, due to a large surplus of the subsidiary, discloses a balance sheet surplus. For the parent legally to declare dividends to its stockholders would require a determination of surplus by disregarding the separate corporate identity

---

[195] See §§29, 30, *supra.*

[196] *Beers v. Bridgeport Spring Co.,* 42 Conn. 17 (1875) ; *Colorado v. Great Western Sugar Co.,* 29 F. (2d) 810 (C. C. A. 8th, 1928) (preferred claiming right to distribution ahead of common from accumulated surplus under clause giving preferred a right to par on "liquidation or distribution of assets"). *National Lock Co. v. Hogland,* 101 F. (2d) 576 (C. C. A. 7th, 1938) (even earmarking of a surplus reserve with a provision that it shall not be used for dividend purposes does not prevent the board of directors from revoking its earlier determination) ; see *Maryland v. Baltimore & Ohio Railroad Co.,* 6 Gill 363, 384–385 (1847).

[197] *Scott v. Eagle Fire Company,* 7 Paige 198 (1838) (charter, N. Y. Laws 1806, c. 152).

[198] Generally see Graham and Katz, *Accounting in Law Practice* (2d Ed. 1938) 384–403; Kracke, *Consolidated Financial Statements,* 66 J. of Accountancy 372 (1938).

of the subsidiary. Questions analogous to those of unrealized appreciation are involved. As to the parent which purchased its interest in the subsidiary at an amount less than the present book value of the subsidiary, the increment resembles unrealized appreciation and might fall within decisions and statutes relating to that problem.[199]

An interesting question also arises where the parent on an unconsolidated statement has a surplus, which, due to losses of the subsidiary, would be turned into a deficit on consolidation. Again, analogy to the decisions and statutes dealing with unrealized loss may indicate a duty to recognize this loss in declaring dividends of the parent even though gains of the subsidiary might not be similarly treated.[200] As in the case of unrealized losses generally, a distinction might conceivably be drawn with respect to fixed and current assets of the subsidiary.[201]

---

[199] See §36.5, *supra*. In support of the view that the parent under the facts stated would not be authorized to declare a dividend, see Ballantine and Lattin, *Cases and Materials on the Law of Corporations* (1939), Note, 472–473.

[200] See Graham and Katz, *Accounting in Law Practice* (2d Ed. 1938) 385–386.

[201] See §36.3, *supra*.

CHAPTER 4

COMPUTATION OF THE FUND AVAILABLE UNDER NET PROFITS STATUTES

48. The Profit and Loss Statement

In the jurisdictions where net profit is an alternative or exclusive source of dividends, the usual accounting method for determining net profit will be the profit and loss statement of the current year or current accounting period.[1] Balance sheet surplus jurisdictions, unless using the test of comparative balance sheets at the opening and close of the particular accounting period,[2] reflect the corporation's position as based on its entire financial history. Net profit jurisdictions, as a rule, base their dividends solely on the recent financial operations of the current period. In determining the net amount available for dividends in these jurisdictions, the items in a typical profit and loss statement most often giving rise to questions may be considered:

PROFIT AND LOSS STATEMENT

For Year Ending December 31, 1940

Gross sales		$1,200,000
Less: Returns and allowances		50,000
Net sales		1,150,000
Cost of goods sold, including manufacturing expenses		710,000
Gross profit		440,000
Selling, administrative, and general expenses		80,000
		360,000
Reserves:		
Doubtful debts	$ 60,000	
Depreciation	50,000	
Depletion	10,000	120,000
Net operating profit		240,000
Add: Non-operating profit		25,000
		265,000
Income deductions:		
Interest	20,000	
Taxes	120,000	
Other deductions	5,000	145,000
Net profit		$ 120,000

[1] See §§25–28, *supra;* also Graham and Katz, *Accounting in Law Practice* (2d Ed. 1938) 149.

[2] See §§22.2, 23, *supra.*

In balance sheet surplus jurisdictions, all asset increases and all liability increases during any part of the corporation's history are reflected. Under net profit statutes, the corporation may currently suffer a loss attributable to prior operations which will not decrease its current income but be a charge to surplus of past years earned or unearned. Again, it may receive income for services to be performed or goods to be delivered in a future year. This is not current income available for dividends. The principal questions in analyzing profit and loss statements concern, therefore, the proper allocation in time of various receipts and expenditures.

49. Gross Sales, Cost of Goods Sold, and Manufacturing Expenses

Gross receipts will ordinarily be the total billings of goods sold or services rendered during the period.[3] As in the case of availability of profit on sales for balance sheet purposes, there must be a valid and enforceable sale, usually accompanied by passage of title.[4] It is perhaps more important than in balance sheet jurisdictions, that only that portion of the profit on installment sales and long-term contracts which accrues to the current accounting period be taken into consideration in determining current net profit.[5]

From gross receipts must be deducted the cost of goods sold, including the expenses incident to production.[6] The problems of inventory are similar to those discussed under capital impairment statutes.[7] Under *Branch v. Kaiser,* inventory must be valued at the lower of cost or market.[8] As to opening inventory, this means that the loss suffered in the decline from cost will have been taken in previous accounting periods, or charged to capital. On the theory of the current period being independent of prior periods, it properly should not bear this loss. Market declines from cost suffered during

[3] Sanders, Hatfield, and Moore, *A Statement of Accounting Principles* (1938) 28; Berle and Fisher, *Elements of the Law of Business Accounting,* 32 Col. L. Rev. 573, 590 (1932).

[4] See §37, *supra;* also Kaplan and Reaugh, *Accounting, Reports to Stockholders and the S. E. C.,* 48 Yale L. J. 935, 945 (1939); Sanders, Hatfield, and Moore, *A Statement of Accounting Principles* (1938) 28–29.

[5] See §37, *supra.*

[6] See *Verner v. General & Commercial Investment Trust,* (1894) 2 Ch. 239, 266; *Ammonia Soda Co. v. Chamberlain,* (1918) 1 Ch. 266, 297. Because the profits rule is accepted in England (see §25, n. 178, 179, *supra*), English precedents are apposite where they frequently would not be in balance sheet surplus jurisdictions.

[7] See §38, *supra.*

[8] 291 Pa. 543, 140 Atl. 498 (1928), §38, n. 87, *supra.* See Hosmer, *Effect of Direct Charges to Surplus on the Measurement of Income,* 13 Acc. Rev. 31, 44 (1938).

the current period, however, will appropriately be borne by the income of that period as the result of valuing closing inventory at the market. For example:

Sales		$ 75,000
Cost of goods sold:		
Opening inventory, 50,000 units	$ 50,000	
Purchased, 50,000 units	50,000	
	100,000	
Closing inventory, 50,000 units (at market)	40,000	60,000
Profit		$ 15,000

By valuing inventory at the declined market of $40,000, the cost of goods sold is increased from $50,000 to $60,000 and profit consequently reduced from $25,000 to $15,000.

The line between maintenance and repairs on the one hand and improvements on the other must be carefully drawn. The former are properly charges in determining dividend profit of the current period; the latter as capital expense items are not, because they redound to the benefit of future accounting periods as well.[9]

50. Reserves

The reserves for depreciation, depletion, and doubtful debts appearing on the balance sheet are built up through annual charges to profit and loss. Expiration in plant value is one of the current costs of production which it is conceded must be provided for by a deduction from profit of a fixed amount for depreciation.[10] Statutes frequently permit the payment of dividends from net profits without deduction for depletion in the case of wasting asset corporations.[11] Indeed, some states which use the balance sheet surplus test for

[9] Cf. *Burk v. Ottawa Glass Co.*, 87 Kans. 6, 123 Pac. 857 (1912) (public utility extensions held normally not to be a proper deduction to determine "net profits" from which preferred dividends were payable); *Inscho v. Mid-Continent Development Co.*, 94 Kans. 370, 146 Pac. 1014 (1915) (expense of a pipe line extension and drilling of new wells to keep a gas field active held proper deductions as against claim of preferred to dividends out of net earnings); *Mackintosh v. Flint etc. R. R. Co.*, 34 Fed. 582, 606–609 (E. D. Mich. 1882).

[10] *National Newark & Essex Bank v. Durant Motor Co.*, 124 N. J. Eq. 213, 1 Atl. (2d) 316 (1938), aff'd 125 N. J. Eq. 435, 5 Atl. (2d) 315 (1939) (construing provision of prospective preferred stock certificate); see May, *Twenty-Five Years of Accounting Responsibility* (1936) 114–115; Porter and Fiske, *Accounting* (1935) 145–146; Sanders, Hatfield, and Moore, *A Statement of Accounting Principles* (1938) 33; but cf. *Eyster v. Centennial Board of Finance*, 94 U. S. 500, 503 (1876). For general discussion of accounting problems in conjunction with depreciation, see §44.2, *supra*.

[11] See §44.3, n. 143, 144, *supra*.

general dividend purposes provide that corporations engaged in wasting asset enterprises may determine annual net profits without taking into consideration depletion.[12] In several net profit jurisdictions, the right to pay dividends out of net profits is conditioned on a showing that assets required to meet liquidation preferences on preferred stock have not been impaired through depletion.[13] Determination of net profit also requires deduction of a reserve for doubtful debts consonant with experience in the particular business.[14]

51. Fixed Charges

The drain of fixed charges more than anything else may place the corporation in financial difficulties. In the payment of dividends, scrupulous charges against income for interest on indebtedness are, therefore, necessary.[15] But the complete funded indebtedness of the corporation need not be deducted, since it is in no way a current expense.[16] If this requirement existed very few corporations could pay dividends, and the larger the corporation the more remote dividends would probably be.

A more difficult question is this, assuming that fixed principal obligations do not need to be completely liquidated out of the earnings of any one year, must there be a deduction from earnings in order to amortize such obligations over a period of years? If there

[12] Idaho Code Ann., §29–129; La. Gen. Stat. (Dart. 1939), §1106 (from the net profits arising from such assets without deduction for depreciation or depletion); 15 Purd. Pa. Stat. Ann., §2852–701 (from the net profits arising from its business without deduction for depletion); Wash. Rev. Stat. Ann. (Rem.), §3803–24 (similar provision).

[13] Cal. Civ. Code, §346 (if capital is so impaired as a result of depletion, dividends out of net profits may only be paid on preferred shares); Del. Rev. Code (1935), c. 65, §34 (if diminution results from depreciation in value of property, losses or otherwise); Kans. Laws 1939, c. 152, §82 (similar provision); Minn. Stat. (Mason 1938 Supp.), §7492–21.

[14] See §41.1, *supra*.

[15] *Gratz v. Redd*, 4 B. Mon. 178, 188–189 (Ky. 1843) (charter provided for dividends from net profits after deducting necessary, current and probable contingent expenses, Ky. Acts 1829, c. 293, §22); *Taft v. Hartford, Providence & Fishkill R. R. Co.*, 8 R. I. 310 (1866); *St. John v. Erie Railway Co.*, 10 Blatchf. 271 (S. D. N. Y. 1872), aff'd 22 Wall. 136) (1874) (as to preferred stock entitled to dividends from "net earnings"); see *Belfast & Moosehead Lake Railroad Company v. Belfast*, 77 Me. 445, 452 (1885) (under by-law providing for preferred dividends out of "net earnings"); cf. *Mobile & Ohio Railroad Co. v. Tennessee*, 153 U. S. 486, 498 (1894) (a tax case).

[16] *Hazeltine v. Belfast & Moosehead Lake R. R. Co.*, 79 Me. 411, 10 Atl. 328 (1887) (preferred stock entitled to dividends out of net earnings); *Excelsior Water & Mining Co. v. Pierce*, 90 Cal. 131, 27 Pac. 44 (1891); *O'Shields v. Union Iron Foundry*, 93 S. C. 393, 76 S. E. 1098 (1912); *Corry v. Londonderry & Enniskillen Ry. Co.*, 29 Beav. 263, 272 (1860); see *Belfast & Moosehead Lake R. R. Co. v. Belfast*, 77 Me. 445, 456 (1885).

is no obligation to pay the whole debt, is there an obligation to pay part of it? In *Hazeltine v. Belfast and Moosehead Lake Railroad Company,* the railroad had a bonded debt of $150,000 which fell due in four years.[17] It had current net income of $27,000 a year which was not likely to increase or decrease during this period, and un-distributed cash assets of $22,000. The by-laws of the road pro-vided for payment of preferred dividends semi-annually from net earnings. The amount of the preferred dividend annually was $16,000. The court sustained a bill in equity to compel payment of this dividend to preferred stockholders. The contention that the bonded debt should be wholly provided for before payment of pre-ferred dividends was rejected. A suggestion by the complainants that provision for amortizing the debt over the period of a lease the railroad had made of its lines was also rejected, and full payment decreed. It is clear that if dividends continued to be paid during the four years remaining before maturity of the bond issue, as provided by the court, the railroad could not have cash assets sufficient to dis-charge its debt of $150,000, and some kind of an extension would have to be sought. The theory of net income statutes being that current earnings are distributable, there is no obligation to deduct from these earnings sums for retirement of capital obligations of the corporation.[18] Fixed obligations will normally represent an in-vestment in building, plant, and similar fixed assets, against which they will be a charge. It is the assumption that under net profit statutes, these fixed assets have all been kept in repair, and allow-ance provided for depreciation. These are the only charges which it can legitimately be contended should be borne by gross receipts. The capital involved in the fixed obligation is represented pre-sumably by at least its equivalent in fixed assets, and, if ultimate payment should be necessary, would be made out of these assets.

52. Capital Gains and Losses

Perhaps the most difficult accounting problem in computing divi-dends on the basis of a profit and loss statement is treatment of capital gains and losses. Fixed assets are not, in normal contempla-tion, property to be sold for profit. On the contrary, they are re-tained to produce continuously the current inventory upon which

[17] 79 Me. 411, 10 Atl. 328 (1887).

[18] Cf. *Excelsior Water & Mining Co. v. Pierce,* 90 Cal. 131, 27 Pac. 44 (1891) (all of fixed obligations paid during period need not be deducted where a share satisfactory to creditors and reasonably proportioned to the amount of the in-debtedness is allowed); but see *Gratz v. Redd,* 4 B. Mon. 178, 188 (1843); *Belfast & Moosehead Lake R. R. Co. v. Belfast,* 77 Me. 445, 456 (1885).

profits are to be based. As in balance sheet surplus jurisdictions,[19] unrealized gains on fixed assets are likewise unavailable when net profits is the test.[20] The same treatment should apply to unrealized capital losses. These losses should not be a deterrent to dividends in the absence of express statutory provision, even in balance sheet surplus jurisdictions,[21] and, being based on general market declines, clearly are not of a character which can be assigned with certainty to a particular accounting period, as must be done under the net profits rule. The general practice, therefore, is to charge plant write-downs to surplus.[22] There is some authority, however, for the view that the income statement should reflect all costs written off during the period, regardless of whether or not they are the results of operations in the period.[23] If this rule were accepted, the distinction for dividend purposes between profit and loss current net income and balance sheet earned surplus would be, in large part, broken down. If all capital gains and losses are to increase and reduce current income, there is a radical departure from the concept that there is a difference between profit of a given period and shifts in the capital account. The current income statement becomes a vehicle for making good capital impairments, in direct conflict with the accounting premise on which the Delaware type of statute is drawn: that even though capital is impaired there shall be something called net income arising out of the receipts, expenditures, and charges properly assignable to the current period from which dividends may be paid.

Nor can much be said for the operation in practice of a system of carrying capital items through the income account. If there were no major cyclical changes, capital gains might offset on the whole capital losses and the income statement would not be materially affected. But the test of applying this theory comes in major market movements. To treat capital gains in a rising market as income will inflate the income account in any year in which there

---

[19] See §36.5, *supra.*

[20] See Sanders, Hatfield, and Moore, *Statement of Accounting Principles* (1938) 40; Editorial, 65 J. of Accountancy 89, 90 (1938).

[21] See §36.3, *supra.*

[22] Hosmer, *The Effect of Direct Charges to Surplus on the Measurement of Income,* 13 Acc. Rev. 31, 45 (1938); 1 Dodd and Baker, *Cases on Business Associations* (1940) 767–770.

[23] American Association of Accountants, *Tentative Statement of Accounting Principles,* 11 Acc. Rev. 187, 189–190 (1936). For criticism of this position as lacking in accounting flexibility and inadequate to many situations, see Hosmer, *The Effect of Direct Charges to Surplus on the Measurement of Income,* 13 Acc. Rev. 31, 49–50 (1938); Sanders, *Comments on the Statement of Accounting Principles,* 12 Acc. Rev. 76 (1937); Scott, *Tentative Statement of Principles,* 12 Acc. Rev. 296, 299 (1936).

are material capital gains out of all proportion to the actual business done. Worse, however, in time of depression when operating income is already low, carrying capital losses through the income account would result in putting the income statements of many corporations into red figures.[24]

The treatment of an actual gain or loss realized through sale or otherwise is even more difficult. There is some tendency to treat profits on the sale of capital assets as income in the current period and losses as charges to surplus account. This duality of treatment, of course, produces distorted income. At least uniformity for both gains and losses must be insisted upon. Ordinarily capital gains and losses are disassociated with the income of the current accounting period and should not, therefore, reduce or increase the amount available for dividends.[25]

[24] See Hosmer, *The Effect of Direct Charges to Surplus on the Measurement of Income*, 13 Acc. Rev. 31 (1938).

[25] Cf. Dewing, *Financial Policy of Corporations* (3d Rev. Ed. 1934) 594-595. In no event should gains on the sales of capital assets be considered as profits where such gains are offset by capital asset losses during the same period. In *Foster v. New Trinidad Lake Asphalt Co., Ltd.,* (1901) 1 Ch. 208 (see 1 Brit. Ruling Cases 965), notes included in the corporation's capital assets were paid off resulting in a profit, the entire amount of which the corporation proposed to distribute in a dividend without reference to the other assets or business of the company. The Court of Chancery, recognizing that dividends might be paid out of earned profits although there was an impairment of capital, nevertheless enjoined a payment which would not take into consideration the whole accounts for the year, capital as well as profit and loss.

CHAPTER 5

DECLARATION, PAYMENT, AND REVOCATION

A. Authority and Discretion of Directors

53. Corporate Power to Declare Dividends Vested in Directors

The declaration of dividends by corporate directors is a contribution of American jurisprudence. In England the distribution of corporate profits rested for many years with the general court of stockholders,[1] and a scattered number of early American special charters made similar provision.[2] But the important early charters to the Bank of North America[3] and Bank of United States,[4] which were widely copied in the formative period of the American corporation,[5] vested the power to declare dividends in the directors. Although statutory provisions expressly giving directors authority to declare dividends were abandoned in the earliest general corporate legislation, the practice of having directors function for the corporation in declaring dividends, impliedly sanctioned by statutory provisions rendering them liable for illegal distributions, continued and became the basis of the case law on the subject.

The earnings of a corporation do not *ipso facto* become the property of its stockholders. Even though a fund legally available for dividends is earned, stockholders are not entitled to distribution thereof until a dividend has been declared by the corporation, acting as a rule through its directors.[6] Most modern statutes either directly

[1] 1 Scott, *Joint Stock Companies to 1720* (1912) 157; Charter and By-Laws of Bank of England, Lawson, *History of Banking* (2d Ed. 1855), Appendix 460, 470; DuBois, *The English Business Company After the Bubble Act* (1938) 291. The Hudson Bay Company was one of the few early exceptions, a committee of the management declaring dividends.

[2] Durham Aqueduct Co. (1798), 1 Conn. Priv. Laws (1837 Ed.), pp. 42, 43; Newbury Port Woolen Manufactury, Mass. Laws and Resolves 1792–93 (1895 Repr.), 1793–c. 27, pp. 427, 431; Greenwich Turnpike, R. I. Laws, Feb. Sess. 1803, p. 20, §13.

[3] 7 J. of Cong. 1781–82 (Claypoole Ed.) 108–109, §8.

[4] 1 Stat. 191, §7–XIV (1791).

[5] See §§4, 5, *supra*.

[6] *Knight v. Alamo Mfg. Co.*, 190 Mich. 223, 157 N. W. 24 (1916) (dividend in provision for semi-annual "cumulative dividend" does not mean profits earned but such part as the directors order distributed); *Corgan v. George F. Lee Coal Co.*, 218 Pa. 386, 67 Atl. 655 (1907); *Central of Ga. Railway Co. v. Central Trust Co.*, 135 Ga. 472, 69 S. E. 708 (1910); *Bank of Morgan v. Reid*, 27 Ga.

or indirectly authorize directors to declare dividends.[7] When it
has been determined through examination of the corporate books by
its accountants and lawyers that a fund is legally available to pay
a dividend, a formal resolution declaring all or some portion thereof
as a dividend is adopted by the directors. The resolution normally
provides the time and amount of the dividend, the class of stockholders to whom it shall be paid, and the record date as of which
stockholders entitled to payment shall be determined.

There may, however, be a division of available profits among
stockholders without the formality of a dividend if the distribution
is by their consent.[8] Particularly is this true of distributions by
closely held corporations, where dividends are frequently paid on
the basis of informal agreement.[9] Likewise, if the governing board
of a controlled subsidiary turns over its profits to the parent, it is
the equivalent of a valid dividend.[10] Nor can a creditor attack an
informal distribution of profits from an available dividend surplus,

---

App. 123, 107 S. E. 555 (1921). A distribution from corporate property not
called a dividend which may be unauthorized for its designated purpose, such as
an excessive salary, may, nevertheless, be treated as a dividend, and will be valid
as such if statutory limitations upon dividends are complied with. *Whitfield v.
Kern*, 122 N. J. Eq. 332, 192 Atl. 48 (Ct. Err. & App. 1937).

[7] This power may even be found on the ground that general corporation act
provisions clothe directors with the power of general management which includes
distribution of profits. *McNab v. McNab & Harlin Mfg. Co.*, 62 Hun 18 (N. Y.
App. Div., 1st Dept. 1891), aff'd on opinion below, 133 N. Y. 687 (1892).

[8] *Berryman v. Bankers Life Ins. Co.*, 117 App. Div. 730, 102 N. Y. S. 695
(1907); *Barnes v. Spencer & Barnes Co.*, 162 Mich. 509, 127 N. W. 752 (1910);
Childs v. Adams, 43 Pa. Super. 239 (1910) (dividend distributed at direction of
president was acquiesced in by stockholders and directors); *Kearneysville Creamery Co. v. American Creamery Co.*, 103 W. Va. 259, 137 S. E. 217 (1927) (all stockholders and directors except one agreed informally to distribution); *Quinn v.
Quinn Mfg. Co.*, 201 Mich. 664, 167 N. W. 898 (1918) (directors attended stockholders' meeting approving dividend); *Spencer v. Lowe*, 198 Fed. 961 (C. C. A.
8th, 1912) (similar facts); *Ratcliff v. Clendenin*, 232 Fed. 61 (C. C. A. 8th,
1916).

[9] *Brown v. Luce Mfg. Co.*, 231 Mo. App. 259, 96 S. W. (2d) 1098 (1936);
Breslin v. Fries-Breslin Co., 70 N. J. L. 274, 58 Atl. 313 (1903); *Fidelity &
Columbia Trust Co. v. Louisville Ry. Co.*, 265 Ky. 820, 97 S. W. (2d) 825 (1936);
Metropolitan Trust Co. v. Becklenberg, 300 Ill. App. 453, 21 N. E. (2d) 152
(1939) [comment, 18 Chic.-Kent L. Rev. 93 (1939)] (defendant sole beneficial
owner of stock, made irregular withdrawals); *Atherton v. Beaman*, 264 Fed. 878
(C. C. A. 1st, 1920); *O'Shields v. Union Iron Foundry*, 93 S. C. 393, 76 S. E.
1098 (1912). Sometimes in closely held corporations which have been capitalized
below their real value, earnings are distributed in salaries rather than in what
would amount to excessive dividends.

[10] *Central of Georgia Railway Co. v. Central Trust Co.*, 135 Ga. 472, 491–492,
69 S. E. 708 (1910); *Fidelity & Columbia Trust Co. v. Louisville Ry. Co.*, 265 Ky.
820, 97 S. W. (2d) 825 (1936) (earnings entered on books of subsidiary as debt
of parent, under resolution providing net earnings might be paid to parent in
advance of formal dividend declaration, created an enforceable debt).

where all the stockholders and directors consent to the distribution, merely because directors have not officially declared a dividend.[11]

Can stockholders, however, declare a dividend over the negative vote of directors on the theory that the ultimate management of the corporation is vested in the stockholders? The question is particularly important in most jurisdictions which impose liability on directors for declaration of illegal dividends. In some cases these statutes are so phrased as to impose possible liability on directors holding office at the time an illegal dividend is declared.[12] Stockholders under such statutes should not have the power to force a dividend, since the risk of liability, should the payment prove illegal, would fall on directors.[13]

54. Declaration Normally Lies in Discretion of Directors

The question whether or not a dividend should be paid generally arises in suits by stockholders seeking to compel a distribution of accumulated surplus profits. It cannot arise where the corporation has no fund legally available for distribution. It usually does not arise where the amount distributable is small or where the period of accumulation has been relatively short.

It became the general rule at an early date not only to give directors the power to declare dividends, but also broad discretion to determine its exercise. The evolution of the latter is illustrated in by-laws of the Massachusetts Bank. The original by-laws, providing directors "shall" declare dividends, were amended after two years to provide for such dividend "as the Directors shall think proper . . . and in the manner which they shall prescribe." [14] Discretionary power in dividend matters was given to directors in the charters to the Bank of North America [15] and Bank of United States [16]

---

[11] *Griffin v. Brody, Adler & Koch Co.*, 167 N. Y. S. 725 (N. Y. Spec. Term, 1917).

[12] See Chapter 7, *infra*.

[13] See *Hamblock v. Clipper Lawn Mower Co.*, 148 Ill. App. 618, 622 (1909) ("If stockholders by such action can compel the payment of dividends, and directors are bound thereby, then the stockholders can force the directors to do illegal acts and assume a personal liability against their will"). In *Thiry v. Banner Window Glass Co.*, 81 W. Va. 39, 93 S. E. 958 (1917), the power to declare dividends was given by statute to directors. A dividend declared by stockholders at a meeting in which directors participated was held valid, it being assumed directors gave approval. See also *Atwood v. Huff*, 130 Va. 624, 629, 108 S. E. 562 (1921); Annotation, "Declaration of dividends by stockholders," L. R. A. 1918B, 1051.

[14] Gras, *Massachusetts First National Bank of Boston* (1934) 222–223, 228.

[15] 7 J. of Cong. 1781–82 (Claypoole Ed.) 108–109.

[16] 1 Stat. 191 (1791).

which were copied in other early special charters. Early precedents of this character doubtless influenced adoption of the common law rule that in the absence of "fraud," [17] "bad faith," [18] or other extenuating circumstances, [19] courts will not interfere with the discretion of directors in refusing to declare a dividend. The discretion rule extends to payment of stock as well as cash dividends. [20] Illustrating the strength of the doctrine, a pre-incorporation contract between copartners that the profits of a corporation shall be annually distributed to stockholders cannot be enforced so as to deprive directors of their discretion not to declare dividends. [21] But where, contrary to a charter provision, a corporation fails to distribute its earnings, a suit will lie to compel distribution. [22]

In the usual case, the stockholder is insisting that the corporation should be compelled to pay a dividend. The opposite situation, where the stockholder claims that a surplus available to pay divi-

[17] *Hunter v. Roberts, Throp & Co.*, 83 Mich. 63, 47 N. W. 131 (1890); *Raynolds v. Diamond Mills Paper Co.*, 69 N. J. Eq. 299, 306–307, 60 Atl. 941 (1905). Generally see Dewing, *Corporation Securities* (1934) 118; Wormser, *May the Courts Compel the Declaration of a Corporate Dividend*, 3 So. L. Q. 281 (1918); Note, *Shareholder's Right to Compel the Declaration of a Dividend*, 10 Rocky Mountain L. Rev. 201 (1938); Annotations, "Right or duty of corporation to pay dividends and liability for wrongful payment," 55 A. L. R. 8, 44; 76 A. L. R. 885, 888; 109 A. L. R. 1381, 1386.

[18] *Raynolds v. Diamond Mills Paper Co.*, 69 N. J. Eq. 299, 306–307, 60 Atl. 941 (1905); *Murray v. Beattie Mfg. Co.*, 79 N. J. Eq. 604, 82 Atl. 1038 (Ct. Err. & App. 1912); *Williams v. Western Union Telegraph Co.*, 93 N. Y. 162, 192 (1883); *Burden v. Burden*, 159 N. Y. 287, 54 N. E. 17 (1899); *Kranich v. Bach*, 209 A. D. 52, 204 N. Y. S. 320 (1st Dept. 1924); *Barrows v. Fauver Co.*, 280 Mich. 553, 274 N. W. 325 (1937); *Hopkins v. Union Canvas Goods Co.*, 104 Pa. Super. 264, 158 Atl. 301 (1932).

[19] *Stevens v. U. S. Steel Corp.*, 68 N. J. Eq. 373, 59 Atl. 905 (Ct. Ch. 1906) (court would interfere only if directors improperly refused to make a division of unused profits); *Marks v. American Brewing Co.*, 126 La. 666, 52 So. 983 (1910) (capricious, arbitrary, or discriminatory management); *Hopkins v. Union Canvas Co.*, 104 Pa. Super. 264, 158 Atl. 301 (1932) (arbitrary or manifestly erroneous); *Bickel v. Bickel Co.*, 184 Ky. 582, 212 S. W. 602 (1919) (oppressive withholding).

[20] *Schmitt v. Eagle Roller Mill Co.*, 199 Minn. 382, 272 N. W. 277 (1937) [comment, 21 Minn. L. Rev. 849 (1937)]. In *Strout v. Cross, Austin & Ireland Lumber Co.*, 283 N. Y. 406, 414 (1940), it was held that a provision for a preferred "cumulative annual dividend" entitled preferred stockholders to payment in cash and that payment in long term income notes of subsidiaries could be refused.

[21] *Dejonge v. Zengraf*, 182 App. Div. 43, 169 N. Y. S. 377 (2d Dept. 1918).

[22] See *Southworth v. Louisiana Levee Co.*, Man. Unrep. Cas. (La.) 166. The same result may be achieved by a corporate by-law providing that surplus shall not be accumulated in excess of a maximum amount. *Pinkham Medicine Co. v. Gove*, 20 N. E. (2d) 482 (Mass. 1939). Where a charter provision authorizes such dividends as are deemed expedient and proper, directors have very broad powers of discretion as to time of payment. See *Barry v. Merchants Exchange Co.*, 1 Sandf. Ch. 280, 304 (1844).

dends should not be so appropriated, is rare. Again, however, whether or not a dividend should be paid rests in the good faith discretion of directors, and in the absence of a showing of bad faith minority stockholders are in no position to enjoin the declaration.[23]

The reasons generally assigned for judicial non-interference in the declaration of corporate dividends bear on the desirability of business management by corporate directors rather than the courts. Very often corporate surplus is needed as working capital by which inventory can be purchased, maturing current obligations met, and protection afforded against exceptional needs.[24] A very significant factor influencing courts against compelling dividend declarations is the fact that frequently the claim to a dividend will be based, not on current earnings, but largely on the existence of a surplus which is generally invested in plant, equipment, and property in such a way as not to be readily available for cash distribution.[25]

Even though a court differs in its view as to a proper corporate dividend policy, it cannot be expected in the ordinary case to interfere with the discretion of directors. Doing so would place the propriety of all dividend declarations in court hands, a heavy burden at the very least.[26] Moreover, statutes in most jurisdictions impose upon directors severe liabilities for declaring improper dividends. If courts take from directors their discretion in this matter, it cannot very well be held later that a dividend which a court order

[23] *Liebman v. Auto Strop Co.*, 241 N. Y. 427, 150 N. E. 505 (1926); *Hyams v. Old Dominion Copper Mining & Smelting Co.*, 82 N. J. Eq. 507, 89 Atl. 37 (1913), aff'd on opinion below 91 Atl. 1069 (1914); *Browne v. Monmouthshire Railway & Canal Co.*, 13 Beav. 32 (1851).

[24] *Blancard v. Blancard & Co., Inc.*, 96 N. J. Eq. 264, 125 Atl. 337 (Ct. Ch. 1924) (no dividend would be compelled out of current earnings where there were substantial fixed or contingent obligations which might absorb them; none out of surplus because expansion of business required investment in capital assets); *McNab v. McNab & Harlin Mfg. Co.*, 62 Hun 18 (1st Dept. 1891), aff'd 133 N. Y. 687 (1892); *Jones v. Motor Sales Co.*, 322 Pa. 492, 185 Atl. 809 (1936) (large surplus needed for extending sales credit); *Wilson v. American Ice Co.*, 206 Fed. 736 (D. N. J. 1913); *Raynolds v. Diamond Mills Paper Co.*, 69 N. J. Eq. 299, 60 Atl. 941 (1905); *Kranich v. Bach*, 209 A. D. 52, 204 N. Y. S. 320 (1st Dept. 1924); *Schmitt v. Eagle Roller Mill Co.*, 199 Minn. 382, 272 N. W. 277 (1937); *Hofeller v. General Candy Corp.*, 275 Ill. App. 89 (1934).

[25] *Hunter v. Roberts, Throp & Co.*, 83 Mich. 63, 47 N. W. 131 (1890) (accounts receivable could only be liquidated at 30 to 50 per cent discount); *Ochs v. Maypole Hammer Co.*, 138 Misc. 665, 246 N. Y. S. 539 (1930) (comment, 5 St. John's L. Rev. 271); *Blancard v. Blancard & Co., Inc.*, 96 N. J. Eq. 264, 125 Atl. 337 (Ct. of Ch., 1924); Berle, *Cases on Corporation Finance* (1930) 355–356.

[26] Cf. *Hopkins v. Union Canvas Goods Co.*, 104 Pa. Super. 264, 158 Atl. 301 (1932); *McNab v. McNab & Harlin Mfg. Co.*, 62 Hun 18 (1st Dept. 1891), aff'd, 133 N. Y. 687 (1892). For a case in which the court made provision for supervising a dividend it had ordered paid, see *Laurel Springs Land Co. v. Fougeray*, 50 N. J. Eq. 756, 760, 26 Atl. 886 (1893).

directed to be paid is recoverable from directors should the corporation fail as a result of its payment.[27]

The injustice resulting to the common stockholder from non-distribution of corporate profits may be more apparent than real. The undistributed profit increment is not lost to him. Although not realized in the form of dividends, his stock appreciates on the market, often nearly in proportion to the increase in assets and surplus. If he is in need of cash, even that may be met by a sale of some of his stock. To this there is only the objection that he is forced *pro tanto* to give up valuable voting rights. In cases where the stock is closely held, this may well be true, and in such situations it would seem more rigid court scrutiny of refusals to declare dividends is justified.[28] Likewise, where the corporation is small, shares are not as a rule readily salable, so it is not possible in many cases to realize an increment arising from non-distribution of profits. As the size of the corporation increases, the availability of these arguments diminishes. Practically, there is very little basis for the contention that the stockholder in the million share corporation has any very vital interest in maintaining his vote at 100 shares rather than 80. He does have a vital interest, however, in the protection of his equity. But that should be reflected by the increment in value of stock when dividends are not paid. On the other hand, it may be argued that such increase in market value is subject to dissipation by the vicissitudes of general market conditions or economic difficulties in the particular industry or corporation. If profits are plowed back into the business instead of being distributed in dividends, a depression may reduce the surplus or destroy it entirely, with the result that stockholders who have retained their stock, rather than selling it during the period of prosperity, will have obtained no advantage from the corporation's earnings. Had dividends been paid, stockholders would have received the direct benefit of the corporation's profits.

A few jurisdictions provide by statute that directors shall have discretion in making dividend payments.[29] North Carolina[30] and

---

[27] See *Hunter v. Roberts, Throp & Co.*, 83 Mich. 63, 71, 47 N. W. 131 (1890). See also §53, n. 13, *supra*.

[28] See *Raynolds v. Diamond Mills Paper Co.*, 69 N. J. Eq. 299, 309–310, 60 Atl. 941 (1905).

[29] N. J. Stat. (1937), §14:8–20; 15 Purd. Pa. Stat. Ann., §2852–701; Texas Stat. (Vern. 1936), Art. 1329; Utah Rev. Stat. (1933), §18–2–16(4); W. Va. Code (1937), §3082; 12 U. S. C. A., §60 [cf. similar provisions in charters to the Bank of United States: 1 Stat. 191, §7–14 (1791); 3 Stat. 266, §11–13 (1816)].

[30] N. C. Code (1939), §1178. *Source:* N. C. Laws 1901, c. 2, §52. Cf. S. C. Code (1932), §7725 [upon petition of one-fifth of the stockholders, showing that

New Mexico [31] both have an earlier form of the New Jersey statute [32] providing that after a sum for working capital has been reserved over and above the capital stock, directors shall declare a dividend of the accumulated profits exceeding the amount reserved. It is held under this type of statute that directors have no discretion with respect to the declaration of dividends out of the accumulated profits in excess of the reserve. Stockholders may compel distribution of the excess. [33]

54.1. Exercise of Equitable Authority to Compel Common Dividends

It is frequently stated that the discretion of directors in declaring dividends is not absolute, and that a court of equity reserves the right to compel a declaration if the directors act in bad faith, or improperly, or abuse their discretion. While such exceptions to the general rule are reiterated in almost all instances in which the question has arisen, still there is a marked paucity of cases where a court has actually granted a decree compelling a corporation to distribute profits. That there are, however, limitations to the discretion conceded directors in declaring dividends follows from the well-established corporate doctrine that directors in the management of corporate affairs act in the capacity of fiduciaries.

One of the strongest cases denying a stockholder equitable relief is *City Bank Farmers Trust Company v. Hewitt Realty Company.* [34] Plaintiffs, widow and daughter of the testator, were beneficiaries

---

for three years the net earnings of the corporation have not been sufficient to pay a dividend, the court may order dissolution; the discretion to do so rests in the sound judgment of the court which has the power to deny the petition, *Towles v. South Carolina Produce Assoc.,* 187 S. C. 290, 197 S. E. 305 (1938)].

[31] N. Mex. Stat. (1929), §32–156. *Source:* N. Mex. Terr. Laws 1905, c. 79, §53.

[32] For prior history of these provisions in New Jersey see N. J. Laws 1866, p. 1034; N. J. Rev. Stat. (1709–1877), p. 186, §52 (Revision of Apr. 7, 1875); N. J. Laws 1891, p. 176; N. J. Laws 1896, c. 185, §47; N. J. Laws 1901, c. 110, §2.

[33] *Cannon v. Wiscasset Mills Co.,* 195 N. C. 119, 141 S. E. 344 (1928); *Griffing v. Griffing Iron Co.,* 61 N. J. Eq. 269, 48 Atl. 910 (1901); see *Raynolds v. Diamond Mills Paper Co.,* 69 N. J. Eq. 299, 304, 50 Atl. 941 (1905). Such a provision may be waived by stockholders adopting a by-law giving directors discretion in dividend matters. *Raynolds v. Diamond Mills Paper Co.,* 69 N. J. Eq. 299, 60 Atl. 941 (1905); *Murray v. Beattie Mfg. Co.,* 79 N. J. Eq. 604, 82 Atl. 1038 (1912). For other cases discussing the early New Jersey provisions, see *Stevens v. U. S. Steel Corp.,* 68 N. J. Eq. 373, 59 Atl. 905 (Ct. Ch. 1906); *Lillard v. Oil, Paint & Drug Co.,* 70 N. J. Eq. 197, 56 Atl. 254 (1905) (Ct. Ch. 1905); *Wilson v. American Ice Co.,* 206 Fed. 736 (D. N. J. 1913). A statutory provision for the compulsory payment of dividends in excess of the amount required for conduct of the business is constitutional. *Merchant v. Western Land Assoc.,* 56 Minn. 327, 57 N. W. 931 (1894).

[34] 257 N. Y. 62, 177 N. E. 309 (1931).

under a trust, entitled only to the income from shares of stock in a closely held family real estate development corporation. If no dividends were paid, they received nothing from the trust. From an original capital of $6,000 and paid-in surplus of $249,000, there had accumulated a substantial book excess of assets over liabilities, and current profits ran from $60,000 to $100,000 a year. There was evidence that the earnings did not exceed the reasonable requirements of the corporation for paying off indebtedness and providing reserves for contingencies; that there was personal hostility of the management to the plaintiffs; and that no dividends had been paid for seven years. Relief was denied. Granting that a real estate corporation is something different from an industrial enterprise,[35] nevertheless the case stands as an extreme instance of judicial refusal to interfere in the declaration of corporate dividends.

By way of contrast is the decision in *Dodge v. Ford Motor Company*.[36] The Ford Company had capital of $2,000,000, surplus of $112,000,000 and prospects of profits for the year of $60,000,000. No dividends had been declared during the past year and Henry Ford, who controlled the board of directors, had stated that no special dividends would be declared and the greater part of the profits would be put back into the business. "Considering only these facts, a refusal to declare and pay further dividends appears to be not an exercise of discretion on the part of the directors but an arbitrary refusal to do what the circumstances required to be done." It was also shown to be the purpose of the corporation to reduce the sale price of cars in order to make it possible for more people to enjoy the benefits of automotive transportation, thereby sharing the corporation's profits with the public. "It is not within the lawful powers of a board of directors to shape and conduct the affairs of a corporation for the merely incidental benefit of shareholders and for the primary purpose of benefiting others, and no one will contend that if the avowed purpose of the defendant directors was to sacrifice the interests of shareholders it would not be the duty of the courts

---

[35] A real estate development company, in contradistinction to a manufacturing or mercantile enterprise, has the purpose frequently of holding and expanding its interests. For this reason a court will be even more reluctant than otherwise to compel the declaration of dividends. *Gesell v. Tomahawk Land Co.*, 184 Wis. 537, 200 N. W. 550 (1924) (distinguishing *Dodge v. Ford Motor Co.*, 204 Mich. 459, 170 N. W. 668, on this ground).

[36] 204 Mich. 459, 170 N. W. 668 (1919) [comment, 28 Yale L. J. 710 (1919); 17 Mich. L. Rev. 502 (1919)]. For the decree in this case, see *Kales v. Woodsworth*, 20 F. (2d) 395, 398 (E. D. Mich. 1927). For discussion of the basis of the holding, see Dodd, *For Whom Are Corporate Managers Trustees?* 45 Harv. L. Rev. 1145, 1146–1148 (1932).

to interfere." A judgment ordering the corporation to pay a dividend of $19,000,000 was affirmed.

At what point in the ground between these two cases a court of equity can be moved to act will depend largely on the circumstances of the particular situation. The general assertion of the cases is that a court of equity will interfere if the directors act "fraudulently" [37] or in "bad faith." [38] There is some little authority that relief will follow even if there is only an abuse of discretion. [39] In a great many of these cases, the actual holding is that directors have so exercised their discretion that the court will not interfere.

What courts call the breach of duty by directors, whether it be fraud or mere abuse of discretion, affords little assistance in forming a concrete determination as to whether in any specific case a court may reasonably be expected to act favorably upon a petition seeking to compel a dividend distribution. Fraud, when used with respect to the action of directors in declaring a dividend, can mean no more than an exercise of power which the court disapproves. Fraud as here used has none of the objectivity of a false statement

[37] *Laurel Springs Land Co. v. Fougeray,* 50 N. J. Eq. 756, 26 Atl. 886 (1893); see *Jones v. Motor Sales Co.,* 322 Pa. 492, 185 Atl. 809 (1936) (fraud or abuse of discretion stated as alternative tests; court found neither); §54, n. 17, *supra.*

[38] *W. Q. O'Neall Co. v. O'Neall,* 25 N. E. (2d) 656 (Ind. App. 1940) (preferred dividend); *Morey v. Fish Bros. Wagon Co.,* 108 Wis. 520, 84 N. W. 862 (1901); *Hiscock v. Lacy,* 9 Misc. 578, 30 N. Y. S. 860 (1894) (bad faith and without reasonable cause alternative grounds); *Jones v. Van Heusen Charles Co.,* 230 App. Div. 694, 246 N. Y. S. 204 (3d Dept. 1930); *Ritchie v. People's Telephone Co.,* 22 S. D. 598, 119 N. W. 990 (1909) (dividend ordered paid out of excessive salaries and other payments restored to corporation by majority stockholders); see *Wilson v. American Ice Co.,* 206 Fed. 736, 742 (D. N. J. 1913); *Smith v. Prattville Mfg. Co.,* 29 Ala. 503, 508 (1857); §54, n. 18, *supra;* cf. *Eaton v. Robinson,* 19 R. I. 146 (1895) (minority stockholders entitled to recover directly excessive salaries, which would otherwise have to be restored to the corporation and then paid out in dividends).

[39] *Hiscock v. Lacy,* 9 Misc. 578, 30 N. Y. S. 860 (1894) (alternative ground with bad faith); *Brown v. Buffalo, N. Y. & Erie R. R. Co.,* 27 Hun 342 (4th Dept. 1882) (complaint alleging refusal to declare proper dividends sufficient); see *Jones v. Motor Sales Co.,* 322 Pa. 492, 185 Atl. 809 (1936) (fraud and abuse of discretion alternative grounds; neither found to exist); *Pratt v. Pratt, Read & Co.,* 33 Conn. 446, 456–457 (1866) (can be ordered to declare a dividend "needlessly and improperly withheld," test being "whether there is a reasonable cause for withholding it"); *Field & Lamson v. Goodnow Mfg. Co.,* 162 Mass. 388, 395, 38 N. E. 1126 (1894); *Raynolds v. Diamond Mills Paper Co.,* 69 N. J. Eq. 299, 306–308, 60 Atl. 941 (1905); *Stevens v. U. S. Steel Corp.,* 68 N. J. Eq. 373, 378, 59 Atl. 905 (Ct. Ch. 1906); *Wolfe v. Underwood,* 96 Ala. 329, 333, 11 So. 344 (1891) (profits cannot be arbitrarily withheld from stockholders); *McLean v. Pittsburgh Plate Glass Co.,* 159 Pa. 112, 117, 28 Atl. 211 (1893) (similar statement); *Daniels v. Briggs,* 279 Mass. 87, 95, 180 N. E. 717 (1932) (court will not interfere except in extraordinary circumstances); 1 Dodd and Baker, *Cases on Business Associations* (1940) 1199.

found in the law of deceit. The court interferes to compel a dividend when it feels the refusal of directors is clearly unwarranted. It may be helpful to observe some of the factors which have led to the court's intervention, or, as is more frequent, its non-intervention. The chances for moving a court of equity to action are probably best where minority stockholders of closely held corporations complain because of oppressive action of the majority in failing to distribute dividends.[40] In fact, the owners of all the stock in such a corporation may agree to distribute dividends out of the earnings in proportion to their interests, and declaration of dividends in accordance with the agreement will be compelled.[41] The minority stockholder in a closely held corporation is at the mercy of a majority which unscrupulously withholds dividends, explaining the willingness of courts to interfere when loath to do so otherwise. For similar reasons a declaration of dividends by the majority control for its own benefit and at the expense of the minority may be enjoined.[42]

No very definite indication as to whether or not a court will direct

---

[40] *Ritchie v. People's Telephone Co.,* 22 S. D. 598, 119 N. W. 990 (1909); *Laurel Springs Land Co. v. Fourgeray,* 50 N. J. Eq. 756, 26 Atl. 886 (1893); *Lawton v. Bedell,* 71 Atl. 490 (N. J. Ch. Ct. 1908); *Anderson v. Dyer & Brothers,* 94 Minn. 30, 101 N. W. 1061 (1904); *Channon v. Channon Co.,* 218 Ill. App. 397 (1920); *Keough v. St. Paul Milk Co.,* 285 N. W. 809 (Minn. 1939); *W. Q. O'Neall Co. v. O'Neall,* 25 N. E. (2d) 656 (Ind. App. 1940). In *Miner v. Belle Isle Ice Co.,* 93 Mich. 97, 53 N. W. 218 (1892), the court took the unusual step of appointing a receiver and dissolving the corporation, where as a result of frauds of a majority stockholder in managing corporate affairs, no dividends had been paid to a minority stockholder for seven years. In the following cases of closely held corporations the court refused to order the declaration of a dividend: *Tefft v. Schaefer,* 136 Wash. 302, 239 Pac. 837 (1925) (surplus needed for necessary plant improvement); *Leviton v. North Jersey Holding Co.,* 106 N. J. Eq. 517, 151 Atl. 389 (1930); *Gehrt v. Collins Plow Co.,* 156 Ill. App. 98 (1910) (capital $75,000, surplus $161,000; no dividend had been declared for 18 years); *Gesell v. Tomahawk Land Co.,* 184 Wis. 537, 200 N. W. 550 (1924); *Blancard v. Blancard & Co., Inc.,* 96 N. J. Eq. 264, 125 Atl. 337 (Ct. Ch. 1924) (capital $113,000, surplus $195,000, current annual profit $25,000; preceding ten years' dividends averaged 8½ per cent; current dividend was 5 per cent); *Ochs v. Maypole Hammer Co.,* 138 Misc. 665, 246 N. Y. S. 539 (1930) (capital $80,000, surplus $263,000 but latter had decreased from surplus of $459,000 eight years previously; over a period of 22 years 82 per cent of the profits had been distributed); *Hopkins v. Union Canvas Goods Co.,* 104 Pa. Super. 264, 158 Atl. 301 (1932) (capital $5,200, surplus $21,780, cash balance $8,139; surplus proposed to be used for new building and machinery; 56 per cent in dividends paid over preceding two years).

[41] *Kassel v. Empire Tinware Co.,* 178 App. Div. 176, 164 N. Y. S. 1033 (2d Dept. 1917).

[42] See *Liebman v. Auto Strop Co.,* 241 N. Y. 427, 434, 150 N. E. 505 (1926) (holding that minority cannot object to declaration by a holding company of a dividend in stock of another corporation where there is no evidence the majority is acting dishonestly or for its own benefit).

the declaration of a dividend can be gleaned from the amount of available surplus either in cases where relief has been granted [43] or where it has been refused.[44] The mere fact a corporation has a large surplus is not in itself sufficient. Accompanying factors are usually determinative.[45] Pursuant to the general judicial policy against interference in the business affairs of a corporation, principal stress is placed on any uses the corporation may have for surplus in expansion, purchasing inventory, meeting debts, and similar needs.[46] In *Seeley v. New York National Exchange Bank,* it was held that stockholders were entitled to distribution of the entire surplus created by the reduction of capital stock, there being nothing to indicate it was necessary in the business.[47] Other factors, such as the desirability of protecting the interest of a life tenant under a trust of corporate stock, should be considered. Since the life tenant is only entitled to income, action of a board of directors composed of remaindermen, for example, should be subject to careful scrutiny.

54.2. Preferred Dividends

The rule that declaration of dividends normally lies in the discretion of directors may be limited in the case of preferred stock. The right of common stockholders to dividends is, for the most part, uniform as to corporations generally and depends on general statutes and court decisions. This is not true of preferred stock. Rights

[43] *Seitz v. Union Brass & Metal Mfg. Co.,* 152 Minn. 460, 189 N. W. 586 (1922) (capital $189,100, available surplus $107,000; dividend directed to be paid $18,910). *Hiscock v. Lacy,* 9 Misc. 578, 30 N. Y. S. 860 (1894) (capital $400,000, surplus $200,000; dividend of 12 per cent ordered paid); *Jones v. Van Heusen Charles Co.,* 230 App. Div. 694, 246 N. Y. S. 204 (3d Dept. 1930) (capital $770,000, surplus $800,000; only one small dividend had been declared in over 30 years); *Dodge v. Ford Motor Co.,* §54.1, n. 36, *supra.*

[44] *Gesell v. Tomahawk Land Co.,* 184 Wis. 537, 200 N. W. 550 (1924) (capital of real estate development corporation $600,000, surplus approximately $1,000,000; only $85,000 in dividends had been declared over a period of over 20 years); *Murray v. Beattie Mfg. Co.,* 79 N. J. Eq. 604, 82 Atl. 1038 (Ct. Err. & App. 1912) (dividends of 10 per cent had been declared annually for past six years; current earnings varied from 10 to 25 per cent of capital); *Schmitt v. Eagle Roller Mill Co.,* 199 Minn. 382, 272 N. W. 277 (1937) (15 per cent dividends declared annually over period of years); *Stevens v. U. S. Steel Corp.,* 68 N. J. Eq. 373, 59 Atl. 905 (Ct. Ch. 1906) (surplus of $66,000,000 in fact constituted only 6 per cent of outstanding capital); *City Bank Farmers Trust Co. v. Hewitt Realty Co.,* §54.1, n. 34, *supra,* and cases in n. 40, *supra.*

[45] *Wilson v. American Ice Co.,* 206 Fed. 736 (D. N. J. 1913).

[46] See §54, n. 24, *supra.*

[47] 8 Daly 400 (1878), aff'd on opinion below, 78 N. Y. 608 (1879). Where a corporation fraudulently withholds declaration of dividends in order to prevent creditors of a stockholder from reaching them, a trustee in bankruptcy is entitled to an order to determine the profits of the company reasonably available for dividends. *In re Brantman,* 244 Fed. 101 (C. C. A. 2d, 1917).

possessed by shareholders of the latter class are, as a rule, defined by specific provisions in articles of incorporation, by-laws, and stock certificates. Nevertheless, the discretion rule as to common stock, established long before the general use of preferred stock, has often been applied to the preferred stockholder.

The right to compel declaration of a preferred dividend may vary, depending upon whether the stock is guaranteed, cumulative, or non-cumulative, and upon whether or not there is a preferential right as to dividends on liquidation. Where the dividend is guaranteed, it is established that the right of the preferred stockholder still continues as a dividend right. There is no fixed obligation to pay in the absence of a fund otherwise legally available for dividends, as in the case of interest on a bond.[48] Where there are funds available, the cases are about equally divided on the question whether the guarantee provision takes away the discretion of directors not to declare a dividend if they deem that course proper.[49] In those cases where it is recognized that directors still have the discretion to refuse payment, it is stated that the guarantee merely relates to the rights of the preferred and common stockholders *inter se,* that if a dividend is declared it must be paid to preferred shareholders first.[50]

With respect to cumulative preferred stock having no guarantee of dividends, the majority of cases hold directors have discretion to refuse payment.[51] It might at first seem that cumulative preferred

[48] *Taft v. Hartford, Providence & Fishkill R. R. Co.,* 8 R. I. 310 (1866) ("preferred and guaranteed stock") ; *Chaffee v. Rutland Railroad Co.,* 55 Vt. 110 (1882) (special charter provided for "dividends from the earnings and income of said company") ; see *McGregor v. Home Insurance Co.,* 33 N. J. Eq. 181, 184 (Ct. Ch. 1880) ; *Fidelity Trust Co. v. Lehigh Valley R. R. Co.,* 215 Pa. 610, 615, 64 Atl. 829 (1906) ; *Field v. Lamson & Goodnow Mfg. Co.,* 162 Mass. 388, 392, 38 N. E. 1126 (1894) ; Donaldson, *Business Organization and Procedure* (1938) 223; cf. *Lindgrove v. Schluter & Co.,* 256 N. Y. 439, 444, 176 N. E. 832 (1931).

[49] In the following cases the right to recover an earned preferred dividend was sustained: *Cratty v. Peoria Law Library Assoc.,* 219 Ill. 516, 76 N. E. 707 (1906) (on ground guarantee in by-laws created a contractual obligation to pay) ; *Boardman v. Lake Shore & Mich. So. Ry. Co.,* 84 N. Y. 157 (1881) ; cf. *Storrow v. Texas Consolidated Compress & Mfg. Assoc.,* 87 Fed. 612 (C. C. A. 8th, 1898), *cert. den.* 174 U. S. 800 (1899) (certificate provided directors should annually determine net profits "and shall then and there declare such guaranteed dividend"; court would compel dividend where directors did not exercise a reasonable discretion).

[50] *Field v. Lamson & Goodnow Mfg. Co.,* 162 Mass. 388, 38 N. E. 1126 (1894) ; *Williston v. Michigan So. & Northern Indiana R. R. Co.,* 13 Allen 400 (1866) ; cf. *Lindgrove v. Schluter & Co.,* 256 N. Y. 439, 444, 176 N. E. 832 (1931).

[51] *Hastings v. International Paper Co.,* 187 App. Div. 404, 176 N. Y. S. 815 (1st Dept. 1919) (surplus was double amount of accrued dividends of 33½ per cent; heavy bond maturities were falling due) ; *Fernald v. Frank Ridlon Co.,* 246 Mass. 64, 140 N. E. 421 (1923) ; *Hofeller v. General Candy Corp.* 275 Ill. App. 89 (1934) ; *Wilson v. American Ice Co.,* 206 Fed. 736 (D. N. J. 1913) ; *Knight v.*

shareholders have little cause for complaint if directors pass a current earned dividend, because this dividend will have to be paid before distributions are made to the common shareholders, or at liquidation if the certificate provides for a preference as to dividends as well as capital. Actually there is the possibility of serious damage to the preferred. Non-distribution subjects this accumulated surplus to the risks of the business. Bad times for the particular corporation or a general depression may destroy it entirely, preventing dividend payments in the future. If not actually lost by business reverses, the accumulation of large preferred arrearages will frequently result in pressure from management and common stockholders for a "funding" operation, sometimes on unfair terms. Even the dissolution dividend clause may be of little protection. In the usual dissolution, if there is anything at all left for stockholders, there will normally be no surplus, and in some states without a surplus preferred stockholders may not be able to claim a liquidation preference as to accumulated dividends which would have to be paid out of common capital.[52]

Alamo Mfg. Co., 190 Mich. 223, 157 N. W. 24 (1916) (provision for "preferred dividend semi-annually"; alternative ground if no earnings could not compel dividend); cf. Dewing, *Corporation Securities* (1934) 146; but cf. *Warburton v. John Wanamaker Philadelphia,* 329 Pa. 5, 196 Atl. 506 (1938) (court ordered declaration of dividend on special type "preferred" issued through desire of owner of practically all the common to provide income for beneficiaries of a trust); *W. Q. O'Neall Co. v. O'Neall,* 25 N. E. (2d) 656 (Ind. App. 1940) (close corporation controlled by common stockholder ordered to pay earned accrued preferred dividends); and see the statement in *Titus v. Piggly Wiggly Corp.,* 2 Tenn. App. 184, 204 (1925): "The Directors of the corporation have less discretion in the matter of declaring and paying dividends on preferred stock than on common stock. If the corporation shows earnings and profits out of which dividends on the preferred stock may be lawfully paid, the holders of preferred stock have the contractual right to demand and receive dividends as stipulated in the certificate of stock, provided there is no impairment of the capital stock, and other legal obligations of the corporation are met."

[52] *Michael v. Cayey-Caguas Tobacco Co.,* 190 App. Div. 618, 180 N. Y. S. 532 (1st Dept. 1920) [certificate provided for cumulative preferred dividends "from the surplus or net profits of the company. . . . In case of liquidation or dissolution of the company (assets to be applied to pay principal on preferred) and all accrued and unpaid dividends thereon"]. *Contra: Drewry-Hughes Co. v. Throckmorton,* 120 Va. 859, 92 S. E. 818 (1917) (dividends to be cumulative out of net earnings of the corporation and on liquidation or dissolution preferred to be entitled to "any arrears of dividend due and unpaid"); *Johnson v. Johnson-Briggs,* 138 Va. 487, 122 S. E. 100 (1924); *Willson v. Laconia Car Co.,* 275 Mass. 435, 176 N. E. 182 (1931) (dividends to be from "surplus or net profits" and on liquidation or dissolution "unpaid dividends accrued" were to be paid); *Penington v. Commonwealth Hotel Construction Co.,* 17 Del. Ch. 394, 155 Atl. 514 (1931); *Pennsylvania Co. v. Cox,* 199 Atl. 671 (Del. 1938); *Fawkes v. Farm Lands Inv. Co.,* 112 Cal. App. 374, 297 Pac. 47 (1931); *Levin v. Pittsburgh United Corp.,* 330 Pa. 457, 199 Atl. 332 (1938) (on partial liquidation).

Normally, of course, the common stockholder cannot compel a declaration of dividends against the discretion of directors. An interesting question arises whether this situation is modified where there are in addition to common stockholders cumulative preferred stockholders who have been paid their current dividends, and the issue is as to whether or not any remaining current earnings should be distributed to common stockholders. The argument of the common in this situation is that if the balance is not distributed to them, it will in effect build up a reserve guarantee fund which would go to pay preferred dividends in years when no dividends were earned, thus depriving the common of ever getting the benefit, as was intended, of earnings in excess of the preference rate. The contention that the existence of such conflicting common and preferred rights varied the normal discretion rule was rejected in *Stevens v. U. S. Steel Corporation,* where there was no charge that the accumulation was being made for the benefit of the preferred to the prejudice of common.[53] The court did not indicate what the rule might be if actual intent to build up a reserve for future preferred dividends were established. It might be argued that the principle protecting conflicting interests of shareholders should apply to invalidate such action.[54] On the other hand, this type of protection for preferred shareholders may not be unfair to common shareholders if not carried to extremes.

Even when the preferred dividend right is non-cumulative, it is held that directors have much the usual discretion in refusing to declare dividends from earnings.[55] In jurisdictions following *Wa-*

[53] 68 N. J. Eq. 373, 59 Atl. 905 (Ct. Ch. 1906).

[54] See Chapter 6, *infra*.

[55] *McLean v. Pittsburgh Plate Glass Co.,* 159 Pa. 112, 28 Atl. 211 (1893) (certificate provided for non-cumulative "dividends out of the net earnings for each year, when declared by the board of directors"; earnings were used to pay debts and make extensions) ; *N. Y., Lake Erie & Western R. R. v. Nickals,* 119 U. S. 296 (1886) (provision for payment of non-cumulative dividends, "but dependent on the profits of each particular year, as declared by the board of directors"; earnings used for betterments) ; *Morse v. Boston & Me. R. R. Co.,* 263 Mass. 308, 160 N. E. 894 (1928) ; *Belfast & Moosehead Lake R. R. Co. v. Belfast,* 77 Me. 445, 1 Atl. 362 (1885) (income used to pay principal of outstanding note) ; see *Wabash Railway Co. v. Barclay,* 280 U. S. 197, 203 (1930) ; *Continental Insurance Co. v. U. S.,* 259 U. S. 156, 179 (1922) (but provision was for payment "when and as determined by the Board of Directors, and only if and when the Board shall declare dividends therefrom") ; *Joslin v. Boston & Maine R. R. Co.,* 274 Mass. 551, 555, 175 N. E. 156 (1931) ; Stevens, *The Discretion of Directors in the Distribution of Non-Cumulative Preferred Dividends,* 24 Geo. L. J. 371 (1936). In *Star Publishing Co. v. Ball,* 192 Ind. 158, 134 N. E. 285 (1922), a dividend to a non-cumulative preferred stockholder was compelled where a single common stockholder was paying dividends to himself; see *Wood v. Lary,* 47 Hun 550, 557 (N. Y. App. Div., 1st Dept. 1888) ; cf. *Burk v. Ottawa Glass Co.,* 87 Kans. 6, 123 Pac. 857 (1912)

bash Railway Company v. Barclay,[56] if directors are given the same type of discretion as with respect to common stock, serious injustice to non-cumulative preferred shareholders may result. Under broad application of the Wabash doctrine, the non-cumulative dividend, though earned, is lost forever if not paid. In such jurisdictions a considerably closer scrutiny of director discretion is certainly necessary. Often, however, non-cumulative preferred stock will be issued upon a reorganization, when it definitely is not the purpose thereby to impose anything resembling a compulsory charge upon the corporation. During the period of rehabilitation, sufficient latitudes should be accorded the directorate in declining to declare dividends.

There can be no doubt that in the lay mind incidents of favor, preference, and priority are ordinarily associated with preferred stocks generally. The history of preferred stock in the courts makes it clear, however, that such incidents are, for the most part, recognized with reluctance. With respect to payment of dividends on preferred stock when earned, much is to be said for a rule which would place the burden on the corporation of showing why the dividend should not be paid, instead of according directors the same free discretion they have in declaring dividends on common stock. The respective claims to dividends in the two situations are hardly on a parity. The whole history of common stock is the history of primary risk, with the distribution of profits dependent upon business expediency as directors see it, whereas the purpose underlying preferred stock, so far as dividends are concerned, is the desire for greater regularity in time and certainty in amount of dividends than would be true with common stock. The stipulation upon issuance of preferred stock to pay dividends out of earnings resembles very much a fixed charge; it is like common stock in that no payment can be made until creditors are cared for—that is, the distribution must be out of profits; but it is like a bond in fixing precisely the amount to be paid. Like common, the right of preferred to dividends should be subject to the discretion of directors to retain the earnings in the business where there is real need. Unlike common, and in contradistinction to what most of the cases now hold, the presumption should be in favor of the preferred shareholder when

---

(normally directors have no discretion to refuse payment of dividends on non-cumulative preferred, but if needed for expansion of a public utility may); *Hazeltine v. Belfast & Moosehead Lake R. R. Co.,* 79 Me. 411, 10 Atl. 328 (1887); Dewing, *Corporation Securities* (1934) 175.

[56] 280 U. S. 197 (1930), §66, n. 35, *infra.*

he shows that the corporation has earnings sufficient to pay a dividend. The burden of proof should properly fall on the corporation and its directors to show that a dividend should not be paid.

54.3. Discrimination Between Shareholders of the Same Class

If stock is divided into different classes, provision is usually made for disparity in treatment as to dividends. This inequality follows the original agreement of the stockholders. Members of the same class, however, rank *pari passu* under elementary principles of corporation law against discrimination between stockholders of the same class. Each stockholder of a particular class is entitled to the same amount of dividend paid in the same manner as every other member of the class.[57] Dividends declared must be paid to all stockholders at the same time. Payment cannot be postponed as to some.[58] A dividend payable to stockholders owning less than a certain number of shares in cash and to the others partly in cash and partly in bonds is illegal.[59] Nevertheless, the stockholders discriminated against cannot maintain an action of assumpsit for payment in cash, since that would be forcing a type of dividend directors had no intention to pay and which the corporation may not be in a position to pay.[60]

Indirect methods of discrimination are also sometimes resorted to. A payment of wages to stockholder-employees at a rate twice

[57] *Railway Company v. Martin*, 57 Ark. 355, 21 S. W. 465 (1893); *Redbank v. Iowa National Bank*, 127 Iowa 572, 103 N. W. 796 (1905); *Adams v. Protective Union Co.*, 210 Mass. 172, 96 N. E. 74 (1911); *Segerstrom v. Holland Piano Co.*, 160 Minn. 95, 199 N. W. 897 (1924); *Hill v. Atoka Coal & Mining Co.*, 21 S. W. 508 (Mo. 1893); *Jackson's Admin. v. Newark Plankroad Co.*, 31 N. J. L. 277 (1865); *Billingham v. Gleason Mfg. Co.*, 101 App. Div. 476, 91 N. Y. S. 1046 (1905), aff'd 185 N. Y. 571, 78 N. E. 1099 (1906) (scrip dividend); *Dousman v. Wis. & Lake Superior Mining & Smelting Co.*, 40 Wis. 418 (1876) (stock dividend); *Chaffee v. Rutland Railroad Co.*, 55 Vt. 110 (1882) (preferred stock); *Cratty v. Peoria Law Library Assoc.*, 219 Ill. 516, 76 N. E. 707 (1906) (guaranteed preferred stock); *Coon v. Schlimme Dairy Co.*, 294 Mich. 51, 292 N. W. 560 (1940) (cash payment to some stockholders and stock to others which would shift voting control held improper); see *Ryder v. Alton & Sangamon Railroad Co.*, 13 Ill. 516, 520–521 (1851). A plaintiff who fails to show there is enough to pay all stockholders the dividend in question cannot recover. *Barnard v. Vermont & Mass. Railroad Co.*, 7 Allen 512 (1863).

[58] *Tichenor v. Dr. G. H. Tichenor Co.*, 164 So. 275 (La. 1935). A dividend declared as of an earlier date cannot exclude from participation stockholders becoming such between that date and the date of actual declaration. *Jones v. Terre Haute & Richmond R. R. Co.*, 57 N. Y. 196 (1874).

[59] *Maryland v. Baltimore & Ohio R. R. Co.*, 6 Gill 363 (Md. 1847). In *McGahan v. United Engineering Corp., Inc.*, 118 N. J. Eq. 410, 180 Atl. 195 (Ct. Ch. 1935), the payment of twice as large a dividend on non-voting par stock of $10 was required as on voting par stock of $5.

[60] But cf. *Johnson v. Bradley Knitting Co.*, 288 Wis. 566, 280 N. W. 688 (1938).

as high as the prevailing wage scale for similar labor is tantamount to a distribution of profits, and a stockholder not an employee is entitled to recover from the corporation the difference between the approximate value of the services rendered by stockholder-employees and the amount actually paid to them.[61] But there is no objection to stockholders owning a majority of stock sanctioning payment of a dividend to the minority without any payment being made to themselves;[62] and stockholders of a closely held corporation may, by unanimous agreement among themselves, distribute profits in some manner other than according to their *pro rata* holdings.[63] It has also been recognized, particularly with respect to railroad and similar companies requiring a considerable period of construction before operations can commence, that original shareholders may be paid dividends (usually equivalent to and often called interest) upon their stock during the period of construction in priority to later purchasers of stock, to the extent that there are sufficient subsequent earnings. This preferential treatment is accorded in order to assure initial investment and prompt payment of stock calls. Any other system would permit those waiting until the construction was completed to enjoy the same rights as shareholders who took the original risk and made the enterprise possible. These so-called interest dividends are contingent upon the subsequent earning thereof when operations have commenced.[64]

B. Form of the Dividend

55. Cash, Property, and Obligations

The accepted method for dividend distribution is, of course, cash. Frequently, a dividend is declared in a certain sum without mention of the mode of payment. Unless some other medium is indicated, it is a cash dividend. Although it will not, as a rule, be considered good business policy to borrow money in order to pay dividends, there may be occasions when a corporation's liquid assets can be most advantageously put to use by investment in necessary corporate developments or improvements. In such circumstances, where the corporation otherwise has an available dividend surplus, it is per-

---

[61] *Nichols v. Olympia Veneer Co.,* 139 Wash. 305, 246 Pac. 941 (1926); for early report see 135 Wash. 8, 236 Pac. 794 (1925). *Accord: De Martini v. Scavenger's Protective Assoc.,* 3 Cal. App. 691, 40 P. (2d) 317 (1935).

[62] *Brown v. Luce Mfg. Co.,* 231 Mo. App. 259, 96 S. W. (2d) 1098 (1936).

[63] *Breslin v. Fries-Breslin Co.,* 70 N. J. L. 274, 58 Atl. 313 (1913).

[64] *Richardson v. Vermont & Mass. Railroad Co.,* 44 Vt. 613 (1872).

fectly permissible to borrow money in order to pay current dividends.[65]

In the early years of trading companies, dividends were frequently paid in commodities.[66] The practice of paying dividends in property suitable for distribution, although not nearly as common as the cash distribution, is sanctioned even in the absence of statute.[67] In the case of property dividends, it is important that stockholders be treated equally. Some types of property, however, readily lend themselves to *pro rata* distribution among shareholders.

A bargain purchase offered to stockholders by the corporation may be tantamount to a partial property dividend. In *Venner v. Southern Pacific Company,* the Southern Pacific, in order to meet the Commodities Clause of the Hepburn Act, formed a subsidiary corporation to which were transferred oil properties indirectly held by the Southern Pacific.[68] As a result the Southern Pacific acquired the stock of the oil company which it offered to stockholders at $15 per share. The court refused to set aside this action on the complaint of a stockholder that he was entitled to the stock as a dividend without further payment. Since the organization of the subsidiary had cost the Southern Pacific $52,500,000, it is likely that a distribution of oil company stock without receiving anything from stockholders might have constituted an illegal dividend, because impairing capital. Similar cases are likely to arise where a corporation under legislation such as the Public Utility Holding Company Act, or for reasons of business policy, finds it desirable to distribute a large block of assets to shareholders, but only if it is able partially to recoup its asset position by requiring stockholders to make a partial payment for the assets. In such bargain purchases, the difference between the price paid and the value of the assets received constitutes, of course, a

---

[65] *Gilbert Paper Co. v. Prankard,* 204 App. Div. 83, 198 N. Y. S. 25 (3d Dept. 1923) ; *Excelsior Water & Mining Co. v. Pierce,* 90 Cal. 131, 27 Pac. 44 (1891) ; *Stringer's Case,* L. R. 4 Ch. App. 475 (1869) ; Douglas and Shanks, *Cases and Materials on Business Units—Losses, Liabilities and Assets* (1932), Note, 192.

[66] For example, the East India Company in the 1640's declared dividends in silk, calico, and cloves. *Court Minutes of the East India Company 1640-1643,* V, vii, xxiii; see also 2 Scott, *Joint Stock Companies to 1720* (1912) 139.

[67] *Williams v. Western Union Telegraph Co.,* 93 N. Y. 162 (1883) ; *Equitable Life Assurance Society v. Union Pacific Railroad Co.,* 212 N. Y. 360, 106 N. E. 92 (1914) ; *Grant's Pass Hardware Co. v. Calvert,* 71 Ore. 103, 142 Pac. 569 (1914) ; Graham and Katz, *Accounting in Law Practice* (2d Ed. 1938) 174; cf. *City Bank Farmers Trust Co. v. Ernst,* 263 N. Y. 342, 346, 189 N. E. 241 (1934) (construing provision for disposition of "stock dividends" under a trust deed, the court said: "a dividend of the stock of other corporations is not a stock dividend but is the same as a dividend of cash").

[68] 279 Fed. 832 (C. C. A. 2d, 1922), *cert. den.* 258 U. S. 628 (1922).

dividend to stockholders,[69] which must meet the ordinary rules as to existence of a surplus or profits from which to make the distribution.

The older type dividend statute makes no reference to the medium in which dividends are to be paid.[70] Modern enactments for the most part specifically provide for the payment of dividends from cash and property.[71]

Many times a corporation finds it desirable to invest its earnings in expansion of its business, while at the same time wishing to distribute to stockholders a dividend. In these circumstances, it is not an uncommon practice to issue, in lieu of cash dividends, certificates of indebtedness or scrip payable at some future date when the corporation expects to be better able to raise cash. Such obligations of the corporation, when it otherwise has net profits or surplus available for dividends, are a valid means of stockholder distribution.[72] But the issuance of obligations which if treated as valid would create a capital impairment constitutes a violation of statutes prohibiting payment of dividends from capital. Indeed, it has been held that such a dividend is invalid if at the time of subsequent enforcement payment would cause an impairment.[73] In a few cases

[69] *Continental Insurance Co. v. U. S.*, 259 U. S. 156 (1922) (distribution by Reading Company of stock rights in a new coal company for $2 per share when rights were selling for between $11 and $20).

[70] See particularly statutes in §§22, 23, *supra*.

[71] Cal. Civ. Code, §346; Del. Rev. Code (1935), c. 65, §35; Ga. Code Ann. (1936), §22-1835; Idaho Code Ann., §29-129; Ind. Stat. Ann. (Burns 1933), §25-211; 32 Ill. Ann. Stat. (Smith-Hurd 1935), §157.41; Kans. Laws 1939, c. 152, §85; La. Gen. Stat. (Dart. 1939), §1106; Minn. Stat. (Mason 1938 Supp.), §7492-21; Ohio Code Ann. (Baldwin 1938), §8623-38; 15 Purd. Pa. Stat. Ann., §2852-701; Wash. Rev. Stat. Ann. (Rem.), §3803-24. For the prohibition in most of these jurisdictions against payment of cash or property dividends from unrealized appreciation, see §36.5, n. 54, *supra*.

[72] *Bankers Trust Co. v. Dietz Co.*, 157 App. Div. 594, 142 N. J. S. 847 (1st Dept. 1913); *Wood v. Lary*, 47 Hun 550 (N. Y., 1st Dept. 1888), *app. dism.* 124 N. Y. 83 (1891) (bonds); *Billingham v. Gleason Mfg. Co.*, 101 App. Div. 476, 91 N. Y. S. 1046 (1905), aff'd 185 N. Y. 571, 78 N. E. 1099 (1906); *Chafee v. Rutland Railroad Co.*, 55 Vt. 110 (1882); *Richardson v. Vermont & Mass. Railroad Co.*, 44 Vt. 613 (1872); but cf. *Merz v. Interior Conduit & Insulation Co.*, 87 Hun 430 (1st Dept. 1895), *app. dism.* 151 N. Y. 638 (1896) (holding that bonds distributed in satisfaction of a scrip dividend are not issued for money, labor, or property as required by statute; view of dissent that discharge of an outstanding obligation on the scrip constitutes a thing of value sufficient to be classified as property seems sound); *Strout v. Cross, Austin & Ireland Lumber Co.*, 283 N. Y. 406, 414 (1940) (provision for preferred "cumulative annual dividend" entitles preferred stockholders to payment in cash and a payment in long term income notes of subsidiaries may be refused).

[73] *In re Bay Ridge*, 98 F. (2d) 85 (C. C. A. 2d, 1938) (N. Y. Stock Corporation Law, §58); *Guaranty Trust Co. v. Grand Rapids, G. H. & M. Ry. Co.*, §22.1, n. 127,

interesting devices have been used with the purpose of circumventing the normal rule against payment of dividends from capital. Certificates of indebtedness and bonds covering the amount of future expected dividends are issued to stockholders, thus attempting to insure payment whether dividends are earned or not. The arrangement when contested has generally been branded as an effort to evade the rule and statutes against capital impairment.[74]

56. Stock Dividends

The stock dividend performs valuable functions in corporate finance.[75] It permits the actual retention of assets for use in the business, while at the same time enabling a distribution to the stockholder which may be retained or disposed of by the latter.[76] Furthermore, it enables a corporation to pass to old stockholders a surplus before doing new financing. Frequently, it is desirable upon issuing new stock, as in the case of merger or consolidation, to keep available existing surpluses for future dividends. On the other hand, there are situations where it is sometimes equally desirable to get this surplus into the hands of old stockholders before new stock is issued, thereby assuring the prior equity owners that such surplus will not have to be divided with incoming shareholders.[77] Par-

---

supra (notes executed by subsidiary to parent, though not paid, make the parent liable if the dividend for which the notes were issued is illegal).

[74] *Jorguson v. Apex Gold Mines Co.,* 74 Wash. 243, 133 Pac. 465 (1913); *Strickland v. National Salt Co.,* 79 N. J. Eq. 182, 81 Atl. 828 (Ct. Err. & App. 1911); *National Salt Co. v. Ingraham,* 122 Fed. 40 (C. C. A. 2d, 1903), *cert. den.* 201 U. S. 644 (1906).

[75] Generally see Ballantine and Hills, *Corporate Capital and Restrictions upon Dividends under Modern Corporation Laws,* 23 Cal. L. Rev. 229, 255 (1935); Kerrigan, *Limitations on Stock Dividends,* 12 Acc. Rev. 238 (1937). Legislation has been suggested providing that share dividends should only be paid upon the authorization of two-thirds of all stockholders and two-thirds of the class in which the shares are to be issued. Hills, *Model Corporation Act.* 48 Harv. L. Rev. 1334, 1368 (1935).

[76] Stock dividends were being declared before the end of the seventeenth century. Hudson Bay Company (1690), 2 Scott, *Joint Stock Companies to 1720, 232, 235* (sufficient surplus); African Company (1691), 1 Scott, at 317–318; see also South Sea Company (1725 *circa*), MSS 13, Harvard Law Library, Cases submitted to Sergeant Pengelly, unnumbered p. 47.

[77] For an example of such corporate action see *McGinnis v. O'Connor,* 72 Atl. 614 (Md. 1909); cf. *Atwood v. Huff,* 130 Va. 624, 108 S. E. 562 (1921) (at the time of issuance of new stock, old shares had a surplus of $10 per share; before authorizing the new stock a resolution was adopted providing that old shareholders should be paid $10 out of the last installment of purchase price); *Bowers v. Post,* §45.2, n. 173 and the discussion in that section. For early English and American examples of use of the stock dividend to protect the equity interest of existing shareholders of a corporation contemplating the issue of new stock, see 1 Scott, *Joint Stock Companies to 1720* (1912) 304; Boston Manufacturing Co. (1819–20),

ticularly is this true where the surplus is large so as to make it difficult to sell new shares at a price which would bring in from the latter a ratable contribution to surplus of the recapitalized corporation.

Both by decision [78] and statute [79] it is now well established that a corporation may pay dividends in the shares of its own stock. In the absence of some contrary provision in the statute or charter, directors may declare a dividend payable in shares of stock of a subsidiary [80] or some other corporation [81] which it holds. Distributions of this type are practically property dividends and raise none of the problems connected with dividends in the shares of a corporation's own stock.

MSS Boston 1, Stockholders' Meetings, Apr. 7, 1819, Oct. 3, 1820; Committee Report, Jan. 25, 1820. The preemptive right doctrine, in addition to assuring the stockholder his proportionate voting control upon the issuance of new stock, also serves to maintain his proportionate interest in the corporate assets. This was recognized in *Gray v. Portland,* 3 Mass. 364, 384 (1807), the first preemptive right case.

[78] *Williams v. Western Union Telegraph Co.,* 93 N. Y. 162 (1883); *Howell v. Chicago & N. W. Ry. Co.,* 51 Barb. 378 (1868); *Grant's Pass Hardware Co. v. Calvert,* 71 Ore. 103, 142 Pac. 569 (1914); *Stamford Trust Co. v. Yale & Towne Mfg. Co.,* 83 Conn. 43, 75 Atl. 90 (1910); *Whitlock v. Alexander,* 160 N. C. 465, 76 S. E. 538 (1912); *Bowers v. Post,* 209 Fed. 660 (D. Ill. 1913), aff'd 220 Fed. 1006 (1915); but cf. *United Hosiery Mills Corp. v. Stevens,* 146 Tenn. 531, 243 S. W. 656 (1921) (holding a stock dividend out of surplus illegal under statutory provisions that stock must be paid for in cash, land, or patent rights where there was nothing to show the surplus out of which the dividend was to be declared consisted of such property; the statute is now probably obsolete in Tennessee).

[79] Ark. Stat. (1937), §2183; Cal. Civ. Code (1937), §346a; Del. Rev. Code (1935), c. 65, §35—*source:* 22 Del. L., c. 167, §35 (1901); 29 Del. Laws, c. 113, c. 14 (1917); 35 Del. Laws, c. 85, §17 (1927); Fla. Comp. Gen. Laws (1927), §6549; Ga. Code Ann. (1936), §22–1836; Idaho Code Ann., §29–129; 32 Ill. Ann. Stat. (Smith–Hurd 1935), §157.41; Ind. Stat. Ann. (Burns 1933), §25–211; Kans. Laws 1939, c. 152, §85; Mich. Ann. Stat. (Henderson 1937), §21.22; Minn. Stat. (Mason 1938 Supp.), §7492–21; Nev. Comp. Laws (Hillyer 1929), §1625; N. J. Stat. (1937), §14:8–20; Ohio Code Ann. (Baldwin 1938), §8623–38; 15 Purd. Pa. Stat. Ann., §2852–701; Tenn. Code Ann. (1934), §3737; Wash. Rev. Stat. Ann. (Rem.), §3803–24; W. Va. Code (1937), §3042. For derivation of these provisions, see §§21–23, *supra.* Massachusetts by statute prohibits the declaration of any stock or scrip dividend by its public utility companies. Mass. Laws Ann., c. 160, §56, 57 (railroads); c. 161, §§36, 37 (street railroads); c. 164, §§11, 12 (gas and electric companies). For statutes authorizing payment of stock dividends out of unrealized appreciation, see §36.5, n. 54, *supra.*

[80] *Continental Securities Co. v. Northern Securities Co.,* 66 N. J. Eq. 274, 57 Atl. 876 (1904); *Venner v. Southern Pacific Co.,* 279 Fed. 832 (C. C. A. 2d, 1922), *cert. den.* 258 U. S. 628 (1922); *Fraser v. Great Western Sugar Co.,* 14 N. J. Misc. 610, 185 Atl. 60 (1935), aff'd on ground of complainant's laches 120 N. J. Eq. 288, 185 Atl. 64 (1936).

[81] *Liebman v. Auto Strop Co.,* 241 N. Y. 427, 150 N. E. 505 (1926); *Continental Insurance Co. v. U. S.,* 259 U. S. 156 (1922) (certificates of stock interest in corporation organized to meet requirements of anti-trust decree).

The essential problem upon declaration of a dividend in a corporation's own shares concerns the consideration for issuance of the stock. Met most frequently upon the sale of stock, questions as to an adequate *quid pro quo* also arise on declaration of a stock dividend. Similar principles to those giving rise to liability for stock which has been sold for a consideration less than the stated or par value, prevail in the analogous dividend situation. If there is surplus available and it is capitalized, the stock is wholly supported by consideration and the stockholder legally entitled to receive the dividend.[82] If, on the other hand, there is insufficient surplus, the stock of the corporation is watered to that extent. This results from the accounting standpoint in a situation where liabilities, considering the increased capital, exceed assets, producing a balance sheet impairment of capital. Such a dividend is illegal.[83] It is to be observed, however, that any liability should be predicated on principles of watered stock and not on dividend law so far as creditors existing at the time of the declaration are concerned. A stock dividend, unlike a cash or property dividend, takes nothing from the assets of a corporation available at the time of the declaration to pay creditors' claims. For that reason, this type dividend does not fall within the ban of statutes such as the basic New York Act of 1825 prohibiting the division or withdrawal of capital.[84] Indeed, so far as existing creditors are concerned, a stock dividend is highly advantageous, since to the extent that surplus is capitalized, funds which were previously available for cash distribution are now restricted against withdrawal

[82] *Williams v. Western Union Telegraph Co.*, 93 N. Y. 162 (1883); *Grant's Pass Hardware Co. v. Calvert*, 71 Ore. 103, 142 Pac. 569 (1914); *Stamford Trust Co. v. Yale & Towne Mfg. Co.*, 83 Conn. 43, 75 Atl. 90 (1910); *Lantz v. Moeller*, 76 Wash. 429, 136 Pac. 687 (1913); *Bowers v. Post*, 209 Fed. 660 (D. Ill. 1913), aff'd 220 Fed. 1006 (1915); *Whitlock v. Alexander*, 160 N. C. 465, 76 S. E. 538 (1912). A transfer from surplus meets the requirement common in many corporate statutes that stock be paid for in money, labor, or property. *Matter of Watertown Gas Light Co.*, 127 App. Div. 462, 111 N. Y. S. 486 (3d Dept. 1908); but cf. *United Hosiery Mills Corp. v. Stevens*, this section, n. 78, *supra*.

[83] *Brown Seed Co. v. Brown*, 240 Mich. 569, 215 N. W. 772 (1927); *Christienson v. Eno*, 106 N. Y. 97, 12 N. E. 648 (1887) (distribution resembling dividend); *Hollingshead v. Woodward*, 35 Hun 410 (1st Dept. 1885), reversed as to separate aspect of case 107 N. Y. 96, 13 N. E. 621 (1887) (a revocation where there is no surplus voids a stock dividend and terminates any liability of the stockholder in respect thereto); *Joyce v. Congdon*, 114 Wash. 239, 195 Pac. 29 (1921); *Pontiac Packing Co. v. Hancock*, 257 Mich. 45, 241 N. W. 268 (1932) (write-up of a leasehold was without evidence of increased value and fraudulent); *Cockrill v. Abeles*, 86 Fed. 505 (C. C. A. 8th, 1898) (directors participating in stock dividend based on fictitiously written-up assets liable); Graham and Katz, *Accounting in Law Practice* (2d Ed. 1938) 155.

[84] See *Williams v. Western Union Telegraph Co.*, 93 N. Y. 162, 189 (1883) (the corporation had a surplus from which to pay the dividend).

from the corporation in cash dividends.[85] As is frequently done in stock watering cases, a distinction is often made between prior and subsequent creditors. A stock dividend based on insufficient surplus, not having reduced the actual assets of the corporation existing at the time prior creditor's claims were incurred, is not subject to attack in their behalf.[86] As to subsequent creditors, the corporation, by having capitalized insufficient surplus, or none at all, may be said to misrepresent its paid-in capital. These creditors do have cause to complain.[87] However, as to subsequent creditors, the question is whether a stockholder receiving a stock dividend supposedly based on a surplus adequate to pay it should be held to the same degree of liability that might be imposed on the ordinary recipient of watered stock who turns over to the corporation insufficient property for his stock. The situations are sufficiently different to permit different results. The dividend recipient relies on the action and judgment of directors in declaring the dividend, and is not himself a direct participant in the wrongful declaration. If he receives the dividend in good faith under circumstances which do not charge him with knowledge that there is no sufficient surplus from which to pay the dividend, there should be no liability even to subsequent creditors.[88]

56.1. Modern Statutes

The capitalizing of surplus upon the declaration of stock dividends is the subject of statutory regulation in many states. In most states treating the question, a transfer to capital or stated capital of the par value of shares having a par value is required.[89] As to

---

[85] See *Whitlock v. Alexander,* 160 N. C. 465, 472–473, 76 S. E. 538 (1912); *Williams v. Western Union Telegraph Co.,* 93 N. Y. 162, 191 (1883); Graham and Katz, *Accounting in Law Practice* (2d Ed. 1938) 154.

[86] *Anglo-American Land, Mortgage & Agency Co. v. Lombard,* 132 Fed. 721 (C. C. A. 8th, 1904; Van Devanter, C. J.), *cert. den.* 196 U. S. 638 (1904); *Whitlock v. Alexander,* 160 N. C. 465, 76 S. E. 538 (1912); see *Grant's Pass Hardware Co. v. Calvert,* 71 Ore. 103, 123, 142 Pac. 569 (1914).

[87] See the cases in n. 86.

[88] Compare the general tendency holding innocent stockholder-recipients of illegal cash and property dividends free from liability. Chapter 8, *infra.*

[89] Cal. Civ. Code (1937), §346a; Del. Rev. Code (1935), c. 65, §35; Idaho Code Ann., §29–129; 32 Ill. Ann. Stat. (Smith-Hurd 1935), §157–41e; Ind. Stat. Ann. (Burns 1933), §25–211; Kans. Laws 1939, c. 152, §85; La. Gen. Stat. (Dart. 1939), §1106; Minn. Stat. (Mason 1938 Supp.), §7492–21; Ohio Code Ann. (Baldwin 1938), §8623–24, 37; 15 Purd. Pa. Stat. Ann., §2852–703; Tenn. Code Ann. (1934), §3737 (surplus must be reduced to an amount equal to the value of the stock issued); Wash. Rev. Stat. Ann. (Rem.), §3803–24; cf. the provision in W. Va. Code (1937), §3042, that consideration for the dividend shall be "the capitalization thereby of the surplus or net profits of the corporation."

shares without par value, California and Minnesota provide that if there is a preference on liquidation, the amount of the preference shall be capitalized, but otherwise only the "estimated fair value" of all other shares, as determined by the directors.[90] These provisions are very unsatisfactory. Directors may choose market value, book value, liquidation value, or some entirely independent value. Apart from this uncertainty, it seems reasonably clear that "estimated fair value" does not mean the stated capital of shares already issued; it probably also reflects the interest the new shares will have in any remaining surplus.[91] If that is true, the same inequities that result in capitalizing the premium on the sale of new issues or treasury shares will follow.[92] The part of the earned surplus which should be kept free for dividends on the new shares in order to maintain a dividend surplus parity between old and new shares is instead capitalized. It may be urged that, since a stock dividend is paid to existing shareholders, it is immaterial that earned surplus is capitalized. This is not true, however. If more of the earned surplus is capitalized than is equal to capital on the old shares, the fund for paying future cash dividends on all shares is proportionally reduced. Moreover, if the shareholder sells either the dividend share or his original share, there will be a smaller earned surplus from which dividends can be paid to both shareholders. The Michigan provision for capitalizing the average original consideration of all shares without par value outstanding at the time of the dividend declaration is far more equitable.[93] Some states leave the question open by providing that shares without par value may be capitalized at such amount as the board of directors shall fix.[94] Under these statutes stock dividends of no-par shares could not be issued gratuitously,[95] but capitalization of very small amounts may be pos-

---

[90] Cal. Civ. Code (1937), §346a; Minn. Stat. (Mason 1938 Supp.), §7492–21.

[91] But see Solether and Jennings, *Minnesota Business Corporation Act,* 12 Wis. L. Rev. 419, 437–438 (1937).

[92] See §§45.2, 45.3, and 45.4, *supra;* cf. Berle, *Studies in the Law of Corporation Finance* (1928) 84–86.

[93] Mich. Stat. Ann. (Henderson 1937), §21.22.

[94] Del. Rev. Code (1935), c. 65, §35; Ind. Stat. Ann. (Burns 1933), §25–211; 32 Ill. Ann. Stat. (Smith-Hurd 1935), §157–41f; Kans. Laws 1939, c. 152, §85; 15 Purd. Pa. Stat. Ann., §2852–703.

[95] Generally on the necessity of consideration for no-par share dividends, see Robbins, *No-Par Stock* (1927) 167; Masterson, *Consideration for Non-Par Shares and Liability of Subscribers and Stockholders,* 17 Tex. L. Rev. 247, 293 (1939); Masterson, *Consideration for Corporate Shares with Special Reference to Shares Without Par Value,* 2 Idaho L. J. 75, 107 (1932); cf. *Stone v. Young,* 210 App. Div. 303, 206 N. Y. S. 95 (4th Dept. 1924); 1 Dodd and Baker, *Cases on Business Associations* (1940) 1015, n. 5.

sible. There is a serious possibility that stockholders will be misled where only small amounts are transferred from surplus to stated capital. The result is a form of no-par stock watering.

Two additional questions concerning no-par stock are not treated in the statutes. Where the corporation has shares without par value outstanding, there will normally be, in addition to stated capital, a paid-in surplus as well as whatever earned surplus the corporation will have accumulated. On the issuance of a stock dividend in no-par shares, a part of the "consideration" assigned to the shares, as stated, should be retained in earned surplus, in order not to cut down the dividend equity in the surplus of old shares. Should not some effort also be made, in the absence of statutory provisions requiring otherwise, to allocate a portion of the "consideration" to paid-in surplus, as well as to stated capital?[96] The same considerations which suggest making an allocation to earned surplus in order to maintain parity interests of old and new stock, also require that the proportionate paid-in surplus be maintained, since paid-in surplus, though restricted, is still available for certain dividend purposes, whereas stated capital would not be.[97]

Secondly, under some statutes there would seem to be no restriction against declaring no-par share dividends by transferring paid-in surplus to capital. This amounts to paying dividends out of what was in substance originally capital. Such procedure is objectionable in the highest degree, because the fair implication of any dividend is that it comes from profits. Merely subdividing further the original capital under the guise of a dividend misleads stockholders, unless they are expressly informed of the method used, into believing that the corporation is earning money and prospering.

In states having the net profits alternative for dividends,[98] the question may arise as to the right to pay stock dividends in either par or no-par shares based solely on current earnings when the balance sheet is impaired. Assuming these provisions broad enough to permit stock as well as cash dividends from net profits, difficult questions as to the amount assignable to stated capital will be met, especially when no-par shares are issued. The accounting treatment will depend on the facts of the particular case.

The recent revision of the Georgia General Corporation Act has introduced a provision that stock dividends need not be paid out

---

[96] There seems to be no obstacle to this procedure under the Delaware type of statute. See statutes in n. 94; 1 Dodd and Baker, *Cases on Business Associations* (1940), Note on Capital and Surplus, 743.

[97] See §29, *supra*.

[98] See particularly §27, *supra*.

of surplus or earnings of the corporation, but a deficit may not be created or increased thereby.[99] The meaning is far from clear. If it is not necessary to allocate anything to capital or stated capital upon issuance of share dividends, no deficit can be created or increased thereby. Yet the clause concerning the creation or increase of a deficit seems to assume issuance of a stock dividend can in some way have that effect. The only manner in which it can is to assign to the new stock some capital value in the balance sheet. If, as seems to be the case, the provision was intended to abrogate the need for capitalizing any surplus upon the issuance of stock dividends,[100] it is open to serious objection. Such dividends permit fictitious stock issues based on no consideration. It is no answer to say that a stock split-up and a stock dividend amount to the same thing, and that since it is not necessary to make any transfer from surplus to capital on a stock split-up, it should not be necessary to do so on a stock dividend. The two are recognized in the business community as entirely different financial operations.[101] A stock split-up does not mean the corporation is declaring a dividend; it may take place when the corporation has no surplus at all—for example, for purposes of reducing the par value of its shares. A stock dividend definitely connotes that it is a distribution based on funds which might have been distributed in cash, but for reasons considered expedient by directors are instead retained in the business and the stock substituted. If this differentiation between stock split-up and stock dividend were assumed to have insufficient merit as an original question, it cannot be said to work injustices great enough to warrant a late attempt to reform the entire thinking and practice of the business community on the subject.

If a corporation holds treasury shares purchased from surplus under the majority rule, such shares should be available for dis-

---

[99] Ga. Code Ann., §22–1836 as amended. The provision apparently follows Hills, *Model Corporation Act,* 48 Harv. L. Rev. 1334, 1360, 1363 n. 46 (1935). Ohio provides that a dividend in shares without par value may be declared upon the transfer to stated capital of any amount that may be ordered by the board of directors, or without any change of stated capital, as the board may determine. Ohio Code Ann. (Baldwin 1938), §8623–38.

[100] Cf. Hills, *Model Corporation Act,* 48 Harv. L. Rev. 1334, 1360, 1363 n. 46.

[101] See e.g. May, *Twenty-Five Years of Accounting Responsibility* (1936) 385. Listing agreements filed by corporations listed on the New York Stock Exchange provide that the corporation will not take up, nor will it permit any of its subsidiaries to take up, as income stock dividends received to an amount greater than that charged against earnings, earned surplus or both, of the corporation paying the dividend. N. Y. Stock Exchange Listing Agreement Application, form 22, II(6).

tribution as a dividend. Surplus has already borne the complete cost of their acquisition, and the capital they represent has been maintained.[102]

A corollary to the rule that the declaration of dividends normally lies in the discretion of directors is the principle that directors may decide whether a dividend is to be paid in cash, property, or stock.[103]

C. Actions to Recover Declared Dividends

57. Cash Dividends as Creating a Debt

If a corporation has declared a dividend [104] when in fact it has no funds legally available for that purpose, it is under no obligation to make an illegal distribution. The rule against payment of dividends except from specifically prescribed sources would be thwarted, if such dividends became collectible upon action of the corporation overtly violating the prohibition. Stockholders seeking to collect such dividends in actions against the corporation fail.[105]

On the other hand, if a fund is properly available for dividends, at what point does the corporation come under a binding obligation to pay the same to the stockholder? At least three points might conceivably be taken as marking the line of severance. The determina-

---

[102] Cf. *Dock v. Schlichter Jute Cordage Co.*, 167 Pa. 370, 31 Atl. 656 (1895). In *Joyce v. Congdon*, 114 Wash. 239, 195 Pac. 29 (1929), a dividend of treasury shares was held illegal, because no showing was made as to the financial condition of the corporation. The court thought it necessary to disclose the existence of a surplus.

[103] *Williams v. Western Union Telegraph Co.*, 93 N. Y. 162 (1883); *Howell v. Chicago & Northwestern Railway Co.*, 51 Barb. 378 (1868); *Schell v. Alston Mfg. Co.*, 149 Fed. 439 (E. D. Pa. 1906).

[104] A resolution declaring something called a "dividend" to be credited with the corporation to a trustee for expenditure in the interest of the corporation in such manner and at such time as the board of directors may determine is not a dividend. *State v. Nebraska State Bank*, 123 Neb. 289, 242 N. W. 613 (1932). Generally see Note, *Declaration of Dividends—Stockholders as Creditors*, 28 Mich. L. Rev. 914 (1930).

[105] *Lockhart v. Van Alstyne*, 31 Mich. 76 (1875); *Berryman v. Bankers Life Ins. Co.*, 117 App. Div. 730, 102 N. Y. S. 695 (1st Dept. 1907); and Chapter 2, generally. Mere proof of discrimination in paying dividends to other stockholders is insufficient to establish a cause of action in behalf of the stockholder discriminated against. All the funds available for dividends as against creditors may have been paid out to other stockholders. The plaintiff has the burden of showing in addition to the discrimination that there are available funds from which an equalizing dividend can be paid. *Mobile Towing & Wrecking Co. v. Hartwell*, 208 Ala. 420, 95 So. 191 (1922); *Hamblock v. Clipper Lawn Mower Co.*, 148 Ill. App. 618 (1909) (preferred stock); *contra: Stoddard v. Shetucket Foundry Co.*, 34 Conn. 542 (1868); *Thiry v. Banner Glass Co.*, 81 W. Va. 39, 93 S. E. 958 (1917).

tion at the end of an accounting period that the corporation has available profits legally distributable might be taken *ipso facto* to create a right in the stockholder. This simplest dividing line is at odds with the entire theory that profits do not become dividends until appropriate action to that end is taken by the corporation.[106] A second point is the actual declaration of the dividend by appropriate corporate action, usually a resolution of the directors. The majority of the authorities choose this as the point of definitive separation. The mere declaration of the dividend without more is held to create a debt from the corporation to the stockholder, thereafter enforceable by the latter in an action against the former.[107] The third alternative is to require some act by the corporation in addition to mere declaration such as an entry on the corporate books debiting surplus and crediting an account for dividends, or going even further, the actual earmarking of a specific fund for the purpose.[108] Obviously, the real corporate action occurs when the resolution declaring the dividend is adopted. The bookkeeping entries are routine steps to recognize the action taken, and hardly significant enough to be chosen as determinative of the point at which the stockholder's right accrues. Since the normal obligation created by a dividend declaration is at most a debt, it likewise cannot be granted that any earmarking of specific funds is necessary. The essence of debt is a general obligation. Once a fund is specifically earmarked, another step has been taken. The stockholder may then be in the position of a *cestui que trust*, with the usual rights recognized with respect to specific property in such cases.

[106] See §§53, 54, *supra*.

[107] *King v. Paterson & Hudson River R. R. Co.*, 29 N. J. L. 504 (Ct. Err. & App. 1861); *McLaran v. Planing Mill Co.*, 117 Mo. App. 40, 93 S. W. 819 (1905); *Ellis v. Proprietors of Essex Merrimack Bridge*, 2 Pick. (Mass.) 243 (1824); Ballantine and Lattin, *Cases and Materials on the Law of Corporations* (1939) 480; Donaldson, *Corporation Organization and Procedure* (1938) 223, 326; Dewing, *Corporation Securities* (1934) 200. A dividend declared and credited on the books of the corporation to stockholders, but payable "at such time as may be directed by the board," creates at once a debt to the stockholder which the corporation is bound to pay in a reasonable time. Directors cannot postpone payment indefinitely. But the payment need not be made until it can be done without serious injury to the corporation. *Beers v. Bridgeport Spring Co.*, 42 Conn. 17 (1875); *Northwestern Marble & Tile Co. v. Carlson*, 116 Minn. 438, 133 N. W. 1014 (1912); *Billingham v. Gleason Mfg. Co.*, 101 App. Div. 476, 91 N. Y. S. 1046 (1905), aff'd 185 N. Y. 571, 78 N. E. 1099 (1906) (scrip dividend "payable at the pleasure of the Company," and which had in fact been paid to some stockholders, merely meant payable in a reasonable time).

[108] In sustaining revocation of a dividend in *Ford v. Easthampton Rubber Co.*, 158 Mass. 84, 88, 32 N. E. 1036 (1893), the court emphasized the fact no fund had been set aside.

57.1. Insolvency of Corporation or Dividend Depositary

The question as to the nature of a dividend—whether it creates a debt or an interest in a specific fund—becomes important where either the corporation or a depositary with whom the dividend has been placed fails. Where a corporation has legally declared a dividend, but becomes insolvent before its payment, a stockholder, unless facts appear to show the setting apart of a fund to create a trust, is only entitled to prove as a general creditor.[109] The situation is expressly provided for in the Illinois Business Corporation Act. Not only the declaration of the dividend, but also the payment must be made so as not to impair stated capital and at a time when the corporation is not insolvent.[110]

There is always the possibility for a contest when a corporation having a special dividend account with a depositary from which stockholders have not been paid fails, or the depositary fails. When the corporation fails, the stockholders will be claiming that the depositary holds as their debtor or trustee; on the other hand, if the depositary fails, the stockholders will be insisting that the corporation still remains its debtor, that the depositary was merely the corporation's agent for payment and the risk of loss the corporation's. Illustrative of the situation where the corporation fails is *In re Interborough Consolidated Corporation*.[111] By resolution of the directors checks were drawn on the corporation's general account with the depositary and credited to a separate dividend account against which corporate officers were authorized to draw checks for the purpose of paying stockholders. The stockholders were held entitled to priority out of

---

[109] *Hunt v. O'Shea*, 69 N. H. 600, 45 Atl. 480 (1899); see *Lowene v. American Fire Ins. Co.*, 6 Paige Ch. (N. Y.) 482, 484–485 (1837); *Ford v. Easthampton Rubber Co.*, 158 Mass. 84, 87, 32 N. E. 1036 (1893); Donaldson, *Business Organization and Procedure* (1938) 326. It was held in *Le Roy v. Globe Insurance Co.*, 2 Edw. Ch. 657 (1836), that where the corporation had declared a dividend, debited its profit and loss, and issued signed checks to its secretary for indorsement and delivery to stockholders as they called for them, all before a fire rendering the corporation insolvent, a stockholder calling for payment after the fire was entitled to priority, the amount being considered a trust fund.

[110] 32 Ill. Ann. Stat. (Smith-Hurd 1935), §157.41; Chicago Bar Assoc., *Illinois Business Corporation Act Ann.* (1934) 155; cf. Ind. Stat. Ann. (Burns 1933), §25–211 (no dividend to be paid if the corporation is, or is thereby rendered, insolvent). Ballantine and Lattin argue that the Illinois provision does not necessarily mean that a dividend becomes uncollectible if, at the time the claim is asserted, the corporation is insolvent. They say the provision may be construed as merely forbidding either declaration or payment without a formal declaration. See Ballantine and Lattin, *Cases and Materials on the Law of Corporations* (1939), Note, 480.

[111] 267 Fed. 914 (S. D. N. Y. 1920).

the latter account after insolvency,[112] the court stating that the corporation's deposit created a trust fund of which the corporation became trustee for the stockholders.[113] The imposition of a trust would not have been necessary to sustain the result. The depositary was solvent, and it would have been sufficient to hold that, at most, the special deposit earmarked the account for the benefit of stockholders, taking it out of further control of the corporation, the depositary thereby becoming the debtor of the stockholders. This approach leads to difficulties, however, when neither the corporation nor the depositary fails, but stockholders for one reason or another do not collect their dividends. To hold that the depositary has a direct obligation to the stockholders will usually result in the depositary receiving a windfall. If the deposit is treated as principally for the benefit of the corporation on the doctrine of agency, or trust for the benefit of the stockholders, then the corporation will be entitled to the unclaimed dividends.[114]

When the depositary rather than the corporation fails, it has been held in New Jersey that the stockholder may still have recourse against the corporation on the theory that the corporation becomes a debtor upon declaration of the dividend, and has no power, in the absence of consent of the stockholder, to discharge its obligation unilaterally by depositing the dividend with an escrowee.[115] The result reached in this case is extremely doubtful. There is no reason why the corporation should bear the risk of having a dividend depositary fail. If the dividend were large, having to appropriate for it a second time might seriously embarrass the corporation. A by-law or stock certificate clause, similar to that used on call provisions for bonds or preferred stock, relieving the corporation of further liability as to dividends deposited with prudently selected distributing agents,

[112] The opposite result was reached in *In re Interborough Consolidated Corp.*, 288 Fed. 334 (C. C. A. 2d, 1923), where a similar deposit by the same corporation to pay interest on bonds was held not to create a trust for bondholders.

[113] In *Matter of Le Blanc*, 14 Hun 8 (1878), aff'd 75 N. Y. 598 (1878), a dividend deposited by the corporation for payment with a banking company was not collected by the plaintiff stockholder due to his absence. Upon insolvency the corporation's receiver withdrew the balance from the bank. It was held the plaintiff had a lien on the fund and was entitled to payment in full.

[114] In *Hupp Motor Car Corp. v. Guaranty Trust Co.*, 171 Misc. 21, 11 N. Y. S. (2d) 855 (1939), the plaintiff corporation deposited with the defendant trust company funds to pay holders of certain scrip dividends. Thereafter the plaintiff revoked its offer to pay the scrip in cash and demanded return of the money remaining on deposit. The defendant refused, claiming it was trustee for the scrip holders. Recovery was granted the plaintiff: the relationship between plaintiff and defendant was that of creditor and debtor; the defendant was not a trustee but an agent to carry out plaintiff's offer which was revocable.

[115] *King v. Paterson & Hudson River Railroad Co.*, 29 N. J. L. 504 (1861).

should be sufficient to remove the common risk the corporation is otherwise possibly subject to.

58. Stock Dividends

One claiming a right to a stock dividend must assert it promptly. Failure to do so misleads others who purchase outstanding shares of the corporation in reliance on a surplus against which stock dividends have not been charged. Issuing stock to the tardy complainant would require capitalizing a portion of this surplus. Interim purchasers would thus lose a substantial part of their bargain. Estoppel of stock dividend claimants, therefore, arises rapidly.[116] It is also clear that where the dividend is declared in stock, a stockholder cannot obtain recovery in cash.[117] The stock dividend would in no way deplete cash resources; a cash dividend would, perhaps jeopardizing the current position of the corporation. It is frequently with this in mind that a directorate selects a stock dividend. In such circumstances if it were a question of a cash dividend or none, the directors would usually pass the dividend entirely.

59. Effect of Revocation

It follows that, once the declaration of a cash dividend is treated as creating a debt from the corporation to the stockholder, as is done in the cases,[118] the corporation cannot relieve itself of its obligation by unilaterally revoking, recalling, or rescinding the debt.[119] This illustrates the difficulty of superimposing upon dividend law concepts already having preconceived boundaries in other fields of the

---

[116] *Terry v. Eagle Lock Co.,* 47 Conn. 141 (1879) (suit brought one year after dividend) ; *Branch & Co. v. Riverside & Dan River Cotton Mills, Inc.,* 139 Va. 291, 123 S. E. 542 (1924) (preferred stockholders entitled to participate in an offering of common stock below its value, held barred from equitable relief where the bill was not filed until after the stock had already been issued to common stockholders).

[117] *Staats v. Biograph,* 236 Fed. 454 (C. C. A. 2d, 1916) ; see *Terry v. Eagle Lock Co.,* 47 Conn. 141, 163–164 (1879) ; cf. *Maryland v. Baltimore & Ohio R. R. Co.,* 6 Gill 363 (Md. 1847) (dividend of cash to those owning less than 50 shares, to those owning 50 shares or more one-third in cash and two-thirds in bonds; held, latter could not recover entire amount of dividend in cash) ; *St. Lawrence Furniture Co. v. Binet,* 25 Dom. L. R. 316 (1915) (where the declaration of stock dividends is prohibited by statute, but the corporation nevertheless declares a dividend partly in cash and partly in stock, the corporation cannot be compelled to pay the equivalent of both in cash).

[118] See §57, *supra.*

[119] Generally see Note, *Declaration and Rescission of Cash and Stock Dividends,* 16 Col. L. Rev. 599 (1916) ; Annotation, "Power of corporation to rescind declaration of dividend," L. R. A. 1917B 736. For an excellent summary of the law applicable to revocation of different types of dividends, see *Staats v. Biograph Co.,* 236 Fed. 454, 458–459 (C. C. A. 2d, 1916).

law. It seems that courts in the early cases, when faced with the question of the nature of a dividend obligation, took the familiar debt analogy without analysis as to its appositeness. A dividend does not actually create a debt arising, as that term is generally thought of in contracts, in return for a consideration or upon an obligation equitably imposed.[120] Since directors have the discretion to declare or not to declare a dividend in the first instance, a more realistic approach would recognize that they may likewise decide in good faith that the necessities of the business require the retention of a dividend already declared but not as yet paid. The authorities, though few in number, do not support this position. A cash dividend cannot generally be revoked.[121] To this rule there are two recognized exceptions. A dividend which impairs capital may be revoked.[122] And apparently a revocation before stockholders learn of the declaration and before any funds have been set aside to pay the dividend is good.[123] However, if there is any substance to the rule that declaration of a dividend creates a debt, consent of stockholders hardly seems necessary or appropriate.

Even in those jurisdictions adhering to the doctrine that a cash dividend creates an irrevocable debt, it is held that stock dividends are not governed by the same rule.[124] The distinction drawn is this: a cash dividend requires nothing but the declaration to create the debt obligation; but a stock dividend entails further corporate action,

[120] See *Ford v. Easthampton Rubber Thread Co.*, 158 Mass. 84, 87–88, 32 N. E. 1036 (1893).

[121] *McLaran v. Planing Mill Co.*, 117 Mo. App. 40, 93 S. W. 819 (1905); *Brown v. Luce Mfg. Co.*, 231 Mo. App. 259, 96 S. W. (2d) 1098 (1936); n. 122, 123, *infra*.

[122] *Benas v. Title Guaranty Trust Co.*, 216 Mo. App. 53, 267 S. W. 28 (1924); see also §57, n. 105, *supra*. But where the dividend has been credited to the stockholder at a time when there are funds available, it cannot be revoked in order to wipe out losses of subsequent years. *Brown v. Luce Mfg. Co.*, 231 Mo. App. 259, 96 S. W. (2d) 1098 (1936).

[123] *Ford v. Easthampton Rubber Thread Co.*, 158 Mass. 84, 32 N. E. 1036 (1893).

[124] *Terry v. Eagle Lock Co.*, 47 Conn. 141 (1879) (where a stock dividend is voted to be used by stockholders for a specific purpose in furthering the business, it may be revoked when that purpose fails before issuance); *Staats v. Biograph Co.*, 236 Fed. 454 (C. C. A. 2d, 1916) [comment, 15 Mich. L. Rev. 432 (1917); 26 Yale L. J. 598 (1917)] (scrip payable by corporation in cash, stock, or evidence of indebtedness; recovery of cash denied); cf. *Cohn v. Cities Service Co.* (unreported case S. D. N. Y. 1930), 39 Yale L. J. 1163 (it was held that stockholders could not enjoin the revocation of an offer of stock rights, the market collapse of 1929 having taken place before the date for exercising the rights); *Hupp Motor Car Corp. v. Guaranty Trust Co.*, 171 Misc. 21, 11 N. Y. S. (2d) 855 (1939), §57, n. 114; but cf. *Dock v. Schlicter Jute Cordage Co.*, 167 Pa. 370, 31 Atl. 656 (1895) (holding irrevocable dividend in treasury shares issued as part of a plan of stockholders to sell to another corporation which ultimately failed).

usually in the way of certificates filed with proper state authorities, and then actual issuance of new shares; moreover, it is said a stock dividend does not change the interest of the shareholder or give him anything of value, since it merely represents by paper what is now capital but was previously surplus.[125]

[125] See *Terry v. Eagle Lock Co.*, 47 Conn. 141, 164–165 (1879); *Staats v. Biograph Co.*, 236 Fed. 454, 457, 462 (C. C. A. 2d, 1916).

CHAPTER 6

RELATIVE RIGHTS OF PREFERRED AND COMMON STOCKHOLDERS

A. Cumulative Preferred Stock

60. The Preferred Dividend

From the standpoint of dividends, the term "preferred stock" is generally understood to mean stock which is entitled to receive corporate distributions, either cumulatively or non-cumulatively, before any dividends are paid on the common. The preferred stockholder is a late participant in corporate profits. There are examples of English preferred stockholders during the seventeenth century,[1] but the first provisions for preferred stock do not appear in American charters until well into the 1800's. In 1836, the Baltimore and Ohio Railroad Company and the Chesapeake and Ohio Canal Company received statutory authority to issue preferred stock.[2] It was not until the middle of the last century, however, that preferred shares came into quite general use in the organization of railroads. The law governing preferential dividend rights has consequently had a relatively short period of development.

Calling stock preferred stock does not of itself determine the rights of the holders, for the extent of the preference is to be governed by the certificate of incorporation, by-laws,[3] stock certificate and applicable statutory provisions. All leading states of incorporation have statutes which in broad general language authorize corporations to issue preferred stocks designating, usually in the certificate of incorporation, the dividend preferences and priorities which such stocks shall have over other classes of stock.[4] These

---

[1] See 1 Scott, *Joint Stock Companies to 1720* (1912) 364–365.

[2] Md. Laws 1835, c. 395, §§7, 9; see Evans, *Early Industrial Preferred Stocks in the United States,* 40 J. of Pol. Ec. 227 (1932).

[3] Where the only definition of preferred rights is set forth in a corporate by-law, preferred stockholders thereafter subscribing for stock are governed by its terms. *Belfast & Moosehead Lake Railroad Co. v. Belfast,* 77 Me. 445, 1 Atl. 362 (1885); see also *Hazeltine v. Belfast & Moosehead Lake R. R. Co.,* 79 Me. 411, 10 Atl. 328 (1887). For limitations on the power of a Delaware corporation to extend preference provisions through by-laws in excess of those provided by the certificate of incorporation, see *Gaskill v. Gladys Belle Oil Co.,* 16 Del. Ch. 289, 146 Atl. 337 (1929).

[4] Cal. Civ. Code (1937), §294; Del. Rev. Code (1935), c. 65, §13; 32 Ill.

provisions and corporate action taken pursuant thereto not only create rights as between the corporation and the preferred stockholder, but they also determine the relative dividend rights of preferred and common stockholders *inter se*.[5] Whatever rights preferred shareholders have in addition to those incident to common stock derive directly from these priority provisions or arise as a necessary corollary to their protection.

61. Cumulative Dividend Provisions

Where a dividend of a fixed amount per year is to be paid preferred stockholders, an express provision for an annual cumulative dividend of the amount in question in the certificate of incorporation, or other duly authorized corporate instrument, achieves this purpose.[6] Even under such provisions, earnings or funds otherwise legally available for dividends are a prerequisite to payment.[7] Strong reasons of public policy militate against permitting the payment of dividends to preferred stockholders out of capital where there is no fund legally available. The interests of preferred and common stockholders when the corporation is not prospering become diametrically opposed, and may result in a management deadlock or even insolvency. A preferred stockholder entitled to dividends irrespective of earnings is interested in keeping a failing concern in existence until his dividends wholly exhaust its common capital. On the other hand, a common stockholder is interested in forcing a dissolution, because then the capital assets will be divided, giving him an opportunity to share therein. Consequently, the affairs of the corporation would be placed at the mercy of internecine conflict between the preferred and common stockholders.

Ann. Stat. (Smith-Hurd 1935), §§157.14, 15; Md. Code Ann. (Bagby 1924), c. 23, §38, as amended Md. Laws 1937, c. 504, §7; Mass. Laws Ann., c. 156, §14; Mich. Ann. Stat. (Henderson 1937), §21.17; Minn. Stat. (Mason 1938 Supp.), §7492-13; N. J. Stat. (1937), §14:8-1; N. Y. Stock Corp. Law, §5 (4); Ohio Code Ann. (Baldwin 1938), §8623-4; 15 Purd. Pa. Stat. Ann., §2852-701.

[5] See *Morris v. American Public Utilities Co.*, 14 Del. Ch. 136, 144, 122 Atl. 696 (1923); *Pronick v. Spirits Distributing Co.*, 58 N. J. Eq. 97, 100, 42 Atl. 586 (1899), *Roberts v. Roberts-Wicks Co.*, 184 N. Y. 257, 77 N. E. 13, 15 (1906).

[6] Generally see Berle and Means, *The Modern Corporation and Private Property* (1932) 153, 189; Harno, *Rights of Common and Preferred Stockholders to Share in Surplus*, 20 Ill. L. Rev. 288 (1925); Christ, *Rights of Holders of Preferred Stock to Participate in the Distribution of Profits*, 27 Mich. L. Rev. 731 (1929); Note, *Cumulative Dividends*, 11 Corn. L. Q. 230 (1926); Note, *Cumulative and Non-Cumulative Preferred Shares, Participation in Dividends and Assets*, 22 Minn. L. Rev. 676 (1937); Annotations: "Right of holders of preferred stock in respect of dividends," 6 A. L. R. 802; 67 A. L. R. 765; 98 A. L. R. 1526.

[7] See Chapter 2, and §54.2, n. 48, *supra*.

Preferred stocks currently issued normally provide whether they are to be cumulative or non-cumulative. When this is not done, as is quite often the case with earlier issues, the question arises whether a provision for "preferred dividends" will be treated as one or the other. If in addition to the preference provision there is also a guarantee of the dividend, this is deemed sufficient to make it cumulative.[8] If even this is lacking, and there is no specific provision in the articles of incorporation, stock certificate, or by-laws as to cumulation, the stock is, nevertheless, as a general rule treated as cumulative.[9] In most cases no attention is given to whether the past dividends in question were earned in the year of accrual or not. Certainly to the extent that dividends are earned, they should be held to be cumulative. A plain provision that dividends shall be preferred in a certain percentage each year at least means that if there are sufficient earnings in any given year, a claim to payment of the accrued dividend for that year becomes fixed, even though actual payment may be postponed to some other date. To hold otherwise would make the dividend specifically non-cumulative in the questionable *Wabash* sense of being lost if not paid in the very year earned.[10] On the other hand, if the dividend is not earned, any language which

[8] *Boardman v. Lake Shore & Mich. So. Ry. Co.,* 84 N. Y. 157 (1881) (arrearages not earned in any year must be made up out of earnings in subsequent years); *Storrow v. Texas Compress & Mfg. Assoc.,* 87 Fed. 612 (C. C. A. 5th, 1898), cert. den. 174 U. S. 800 (1899); see *Taft v. Hartford, Providence & Fishkill R. R. Co.,* 8 R. I. 310, 335 (1866); *Prouty v. Michigan S. & N. Indiana R. R. Co.,* 1 Hun 655, 663–665 (N. Y. App. Div., 1st Dept. 1874); *Lockhart v. Van Alstyne,* 31 Mich. 76, 84 (1875); *Austin v. Wright,* 156 Wash. 24, 286 Pac. 48, 50 (1930).

[9] *Fidelity Trust Co. v. Lehigh Valley R. R. Co.,* 215 Pa. 610, 64 Atl. 829 (1906); *West Chester & Philadelphia R. R. Co. v. Jackson,* 77 Pa. 321 (1875) (act authorizing issuance of preferred provided for a dividend "of 8 per cent per annum on its par value . . . from the time of payment therefore, before any interest or dividend should be paid to the holders of unpreferred stock"; a redemption clause was also conditioned on payment of "8 per centum from the time of the original payment to the company therefor"); *Inscho v. Mid-Continent Development Co.,* 94 Kans. 370, 146 Pac. 1014 (1915); *Hazel Atlas Glass Co. v. Van Dyk & Reeves,* 8 F. (2d) 716, 720 (C. C. A. 2d, 1925); *Elkins v. Camden & Atlantic R. R. Co.,* 36 N. J. Eq. 233, 236 (1882) (but since statute provided for dividends "not to exceed seven per centum per annum, before any dividend shall be set apart or paid on the other and ordinary stock," the dividend must be earned in the year or it is lost); cf. *Warburton v. John Wanamaker Philadelphia,* 329 Pa. 5, 196 Atl. 506 (1938) (special type preferred issued, income to take care of beneficiaries of a trust). In *Hazeltine v. Belfast & Moosehead Lake R. R. Co.,* 79 Me. 411, 10 Atl. 328 (1887), it was held a by-law, providing that, after both preferred and common had received dividends equal to the preferred preference, the surplus net earnings "in any one year . . . shall be divided pro rata on all the stock," negatived any intent to make the preferred dividend cumulative. Complete distribution was contemplated each year.

[10] *Wabash Railway Co. v. Barclay,* 280 U. S. 197 (1930), is discussed in §66, *infra.*

might be construed to indicate the preference was to be from earnings of the particular year may be relied upon to indicate that there was no intention to make the preference cumulative in the broad sense of being payable out of earnings in future years.[11] To hold otherwise attributes to a weak provision all the strength of a specific clause for cumulation, when it is questionable whether that should be done in view of the difficulties recently experienced with strict cumulative dividends. The compromise suggested avoids the temptation to pass earned dividends inherent in the Wabash result, and at the same time prevents burdening the corporation with the equivalent of unearned fixed charges. It should be noted that there is a decided tendency in recent issues of cumulative preferred stock to provide expressly that dividends shall be cumulative only to the extent of earnings.

In dealing with preferred stock having no express provision as to cumulation, careful attention should be given the date of issue. It has been the established custom, certainly since as early as the end of the last century, to make express provision for accumulation where that is desired. When that is not done in any recently issued preferred stock, the presumption should be against treating it as strictly cumulative.[12]

62. Participation in Dividends Beyond Preference Rate

Is the preferred clause for a preference on dividends also a restriction to the dividend specified? Like other provisions respecting preferred stock, this can and should be handled by an express stipulation as to what, if any, participation rights with common the pre-

---

[11] In *Murphy v. Richardson Dry Goods Co.*, 326 Mo. 1, 31 S. W. (2d) 72 (1930), the articles of incorporation specified preferred stock should be entitled to a dividend of 6 per cent per annum out of the net yearly income earned in any one current year. It was held, the dividend was not cumulative where no income had been earned in the years in question. See *Belfast & Moosehead Lake R. R. Co. v. Belfast*, 77 Me. 445, 452, 1 Atl. 362 (1885). But in *West Chester & Philadelphia R. R. Co. v. Jackson*, 77 Pa. 321 (1875), under a similar provision it was held the dividend should be paid out of earnings of later years (for statute see n. 9, *supra*).

[12] Surveys of a substantial number of corporations have indicated that prior to 1900 provisions for non-cumulative preferred dividends were relatively common, but that in the first quarter of the century most issues carried cumulative clauses. Of 301 issues of preferred stock from 1925 to 1930, 95 per cent carried definite cumulative dividend provisions. Dewing, *Corporation Securities* (1934) 169, 171. Even when the dividend is expressly, or by implication, held to be cumulative, whether actual distribution shall be made immediately or deferred while the funds are retained for corporate purposes, is a matter in which directors are given wide discretion. See §54.2, *supra*.

ferred stock shall have after the preference dividend has been paid.[13] More often than not such a provision is omitted.[14] Most courts in such cases, relying upon the principle that preferred stock is limited to rights provided in the articles of incorporation, by-laws, or stock certificate, hold that when the percentage of preferred dividend has been paid, preferred stock which has a preference as to dividends can participate no further in surplus. Common stockholders are held entitled to the balance.[15] The extent to which this protection for common stockholders goes is demonstrated by *Tennant v. Epstein.*[16] Preferred stock entitled to 7 per cent cumulative dividends "and no more," and par value plus accrued dividends on liquidation, had received its regular dividend of 7 per cent. Thereafter a dividend in common stock out of surplus was declared payable to each share of common and preferred stock outstanding. It was held a common stockholder could maintain a bill to cancel the dividend

[13] Generally see Berle, *Studies in the Law of Corporation Finance* (1928) 111; Donaldson, *Business Organization and Procedure* (1938) 224, 226; Rowell, *Right of Preferred Shareholders in Excess of Preference,* 19 Minn. L. Rev. 406 (1935); Thompson, *Respective Rights of Preferred and Common Shareholders,* 19 Mich. L. Rev. 463 (1921); Note, *Right of Preferred Shareholders to Participate in Distribution of Cash Surplus after Receipt of Their Stipulated Dividends,* 11 Corn. L. Q. 234 (1926); Note, *Right of Preferred Stockholders to Participate in Dividends beyond the Specified Amount,* 33 Mich. L. Rev. 968 (1935).

[14] The problem of draftsmanship was met in an early special charter provision for preferred stock in this country by a stipulation for sharing between preferred and common of dividends beyond the preference payment and an equal payment to common stockholders. Md. Laws 1835, c. 395, §§7, 9.

[15] *James F. Powers Foundry Co. v. Miller,* 166 Md. 590, 171 Atl. 842 (1934) [comment, 33 Mich. L. Rev. 968] (charter provided the corporation should "be bound to pay an annual dividend of not less than six per cent, before any dividend shall be paid to the holders of the common stock"); *Will v. United Lankat Plantations Co.* (1914) A. C. 11; and cases in n. 16. 17, *infra.* Cf. *Lyman v. Southern Ry. Co.,* 149 Va. 274, 141 S. E. 240 (1928) (non-cumulative preferred not entitled to participate in excess of its preference rate where directors were authorized to distribute remaining surplus profits to any other stock); *Colorado v. Great Western Sugar Co.,* 29 F. (2d) 810 (C. C. A. 8th, 1928) (articles provided preferred not entitled to dividends from "surplus or net profits" beyond 7 per cent, but that in case of "liquidation or distribution of assets" to be paid par value in full; preferred having been paid 7 per cent, current earnings and a portion of accumulated surplus were held properly distributable to common); Donaldson, *Business Organization and Procedure* (1938) 227. But in Pennsylvania the presumption is that preferred shareholders participate with common where the common has received dividends equal to those of the preferred for the year in question. *Sternbergh v. Brock,* 225 Pa. 279, 74 Atl. 166 (1909); *Englander v. Osborne,* 261 Pa. 366, 104 Atl. 614 (1918); *Fidelity Trust Co. v. Lehigh Valley R. R. Co.,* 215 Pa. 610, 64 Atl. 829 (1906). See also *Coggeshall v. Georgia Land & Investment Co.,* 14 Ga. App. 637, 639, 82 S. E. 156 (1914).

[16] 356 Ill. 26, 189 N. E. 864 (1934) (comment, 2 Univ. of Chic. L. Rev. 133; 83 U. of Pa. L. Rev. 91).

to the preferred shareholders, in the face of the contention of preferred that they were entitled to participate in order to prevent a change in the voting control. The court indicated a dividend to the common would not shift the voting control, and that, more important in its view, a dividend in common to the preferred would pass a right in present surplus and the privilege of sharing in future cash dividends on common shares, in derogation of the right of existing common stockholders.[17]

The cases denying further participation to preferred stock seem fair. Preferred stock has the benefit of a steady preference in dividends, and will normally be fully protected on distribution as to capital. Common stock bears the risk and should not be compelled to share equally with preferred when the corporation prospers.

The situation changes considerably where the preference of the preferred stock is given only as to dividends. Without a preference as to capital, a dividend to common shareholders alone might mean that on liquidation the preferred shares could not recover their entire *pro rata* share of capital. Problems of this character were involved in *Branch and Company v. Riverside and Dan River Cotton Mills*.[18] The charter provided the preferred stock should receive only 6 per cent cumulative dividends and be preferred only as to dividends. The corporation proposed to issue new shares only to common stockholders at par when their actual value was far in excess of that. The court stated that, since the preferred had no preference in capital on liquidation, it would be entitled to participate in the dividend in order to maintain its proportionate interest in

---

[17] Under quite similar facts, the court in *Stone v. U. S. Envelope Co.*, 119 Me. 394, 111 Atl. 536 (1920), granted an injunction to a common stockholder against the issuance of common shares to both common and preferred shareholders at a price substantially less than their value. The court did not discuss whether, despite the fact that preferred stockholders had equal voting rights with the common, it would be permissible to issue the new shares exclusively to common stockholders. Cf. *Niles v. Ludlow Mfg. Co.*, 202 Fed. 141 (C. C. A. 2d, 1913), *cert. den.* 231 U. S. 748 (1913) (a preferred stockholder's effort to enjoin declaration of a dividend in common shares payable only to common stockholders failed; no mention was made that a shift in voting control from preferred to common stockholders would take place) ; *Russell v. American Gas & Electric Co.*, 152 App. Div. 136, 136 N. Y. S. 602 (1st Dept. 1912) (preference provision entitled preferred to cumulative 6 per cent dividends and to par and accumulated dividends on distribution and "to no further dividend or distribution"; an order of the lower court denying an injunction against sale of common stock exclusively to common stockholders, but conditioning it on grant of permission to preferred stockholders to subscribe to an equivalent amount of preferred stock, was affirmed). See Donaldson, *Business Organization and Procedure* (1938) 233–236; Hills, *Pre-emptive Right of Preferred Stockholders to Subscribe to New Stock*, 5 N. Y. L. Rev. 207 (1927).

[18] 139 Va. 291, 123 S. E. 542 (1924).

the assets, even though had a cash dividend been paid it would have no claim to any portion thereof;[19] but the bill was dismissed as lacking in equity, since the stock had already been issued to common stockholders when suit was brought; leave was granted, however, to amend the pleadings to state a cause of action at law. Application of the doctrine in this case may cause difficulties. There can be no objection to protecting the ratable interest of the preferred shareholders in their original capital contributions. But the basic premise of the case is that on liquidation preferred stockholders are also entitled to share ratably in the entire assets of the corporation, including the dividend surplus in which, under the terms of the charter, they could not have participated if distribution had been made immediately prior to liquidation. Cash distribution would defeat the preferred stockholders. Should the corporation be forced to deplete its assets in order to give common stockholders the dividend to which they are entitled? A possible solution might be to declare a stock dividend in favor of common stockholders but payable on liquidation only out of surplus. This would be in effect a special stock and objectionable from the standpoint of requiring special listing. The corporation seems confronted, therefore, where the preferred has no liquidation preference, with the alternatives of either declaring extra cash dividends exclusively to common stockholders or declaring extra common stock dividends equally between common and preferred.

The problem is affected by statutes in some jurisdictions. In several states no stock dividend may be paid to shareholders of any other class unless the articles so provide or the payment is authorized by a majority, or greater percentage, of the holders of the class in which the dividend is to be paid.[20] Ohio provides generally that no dividend shall be paid to the holders of any class of stock in violation of the rights of the holders of any other class.[21] This provision leaves the subject to the preferred contract or the same equitable regulation indicated in the cases. Illinois prohibits the payment of dividends in shares having a preference over the shares on which the dividend is paid, unless provision is otherwise made in the articles.[22] In other words, a preferred dividend cannot be paid on

---

[19] See *Jones v. Concord & Montreal R. R. Co.*, 67 N. H. 119, 137–140, 38 Atl. 120 (1891).

[20] Idaho Code Ann., §29–129; Ind. Stat. Ann. (Burns 1933), §25–211; La. Gen. Stat. (Dart. 1939), §1106; Minn. Stat. (Mason 1938 Supp.), §7492–21; 15 Purd. Pa. Stat. Ann., §2852–703; Wash. Rev. Stat. Ann. (Rem.), §3803–24.

[21] Ohio Code Ann. (Baldwin 1938), §8623–38.

[22] 32 Ill. Ann. Stat. (Smith-Hurd 1935), §157.41(d).

common stock, so as to subordinate or affect a prior issue of preferred. In Georgia, any dividend paid in stock of a special class must be approved by the vote or written consent of two-thirds of the shareholders of that class and, if it affects adversely any right or preferences of the holders of any other class of stock, the consent of two-thirds of those shareholders adversely affected must be obtained.[23]

Occasionally, the question arises as to precedence of common stockholders claiming they are entitled to dividends equal to the preferred dividends of prior years before there is any necessity of sharing excess surplus with the preferred. It is held they are not entitled to equalize for past preferred dividends, as that would be tantamount to creation of a partial preference right.[24]

63. Shift of Voting Control to Preferred on Dividend Default

It is common, particularly in corporations not recently organized, to vest the sole voting power in common stockholders with a provision shifting the exclusive vote to preferred stockholders upon the passing of a certain number of preferred dividends. These provisions may bring the preferred into management control too late to save the corporation from reorganization, and they tempt directors elected by the common stockholders to declare doubtful dividends in order to maintain their control. If a dividend is in fact declared from funds which are not legally available, it does not prevent the voting control from passing to the preferred stockholders.[25] The voting powers accruing to the preferred on a default under such a clause are broad. In *Krell v. Krell Piano Company*, they were held inclusive enough to permit the preferred to approve a statutory sale of assets without consent of common stock.[26] In actual practice, however, a provision for shift in voting control is of dubious value to the preferred shareholders. The common stock management is usually able to perpetuate itself in control by the proxy solicitation mechanism at its disposal. The preferred shareholders do the voting,

---

[23] Ga. Code Ann., §22–1836.

[24] *Lockwood v. General Abrasive Co.*, 210 App. Div. 141, 205 N. Y. S. 511, aff'd 240 N. Y. 592, 148 N. E. 719 (1925); *Englander v. Osborne*, 261 Pa. 366, 104 Atl. 614 (1918); see Donaldson, *Business Organization and Procedure* (1938) 236–238.

[25] *Vogtman v. Merchants Mtg. & Credit Co.*, 20 Del. Ch. 364, 178 Atl. 99 (1933); *Petroleum Rights Corp. v. Midland Realty Corp.*, 167 Atl. 835 (Del. Ch. 1933).

[26] 14 Ohio App. 74 (1921). The Chandler Act, in Chapter X, requires that a plan of reorganization shall provide for inclusion in the charter of the debtor of adequate provisions whereby preferred stockholders may elect directors in the event of a default in the payment of preferred dividends, 11 U. S. C. A., §616(12)(a).

but they select the same proxies that would be presented to common stockholders.

64. Dissolution Distributions

Where the preferred stock only has a preference as to dividends, it is not entitled to preference in the distribution of capital on liquidation.[27] But on the other hand, it is entitled to share ratably with common stockholders in a surplus accumulated prior to dissolution which, had the directorate chosen to do so, might have been previously distributed completely to common stockholders.[28] Where, however, there is a provision for preference as to capital on dissolution, it defines the full extent of the preference and precludes the preferred from sharing in the surplus available after payment of par on the preferred and common.[29]

If in addition to a provision for payment of capital on liquidation or dissolution there is also a clause for priority payment of dividends, the majority of cases permit preferred shareholders to recover in the absence of an earned surplus, in addition to their capital, the equivalent of what would have been the amount of dividends had there been earnings.[30] As a result, on liquidation the capital of common stockholders is used to pay unearned preferred dividends. The normal purpose of the rule against payment of dividends from capital, that of protecting creditors, no longer exists, since on dissolution creditors' claims must all be satisfied before there is any problem of distribution between preferred and common stockholders. More doubtful is the question whether the fair understanding between preferred and common contemplates the use of common capital to pay accrued but unearned dividends on the preferred. When common capital is used for this purpose, the claim of the

[27] *Lloyd v. Pennsylvania Electric Vehicle Co.*, 75 N. J. Eq. 263, 72 Atl. 16 (Ct. Err. & App. 1909) (statute required statement of preferences in certificate of incorporation and only provision so included was for preference as to dividends) ; *In re London India Rubber Co.*, L. R. 5 Eq. 519 (1868).

[28] *Continental Insurance Co. v. U. S.*, 259 U. S. 156 (1922) (involuntary distribution of assets under an anti-trust decree; stock was non-cumulative) ; see *Branch & Co. v. Riverside and Dan River Cotton Mills*, 139 Va. 291, 303–304, 123 S. E. 542 (1924).

[29] *Williams v. Renshaw*, 220 App. Div. 39, 220 N. Y. S. 532 (3d Dept. 1927) ; *Murphy v. Richardson Dry Goods Co.*, 326 Mo. 1, 31 S. W. (2d) 72 (1930) (provision that on distribution of assets non-cumulative preferred should "be first paid in full") ; but cf. *In re William Metcalfe & Sons, Ltd.*, (1933) Ch. 142 (cumulative preferred shareholders having a preference as to dividends and on winding-up as to capital were held entitled to share in surplus profits available for distribution after preferred and common had been paid par).

[30] See §54.2, n. 52, *supra*.

preferred shareholder resembles closely the fixed charge of the creditor, rather than, as the entire concept of dividends imports,[81] a distribution of profits.

B. Non-Cumulative Preferred Stock

65. Unearned Dividends

Cumulative dividends must be paid, regardless of the year in which they are earned, while non-cumulative dividends depend upon the earnings of the particular year.[32] If in any year the latter are not earned, stockholders are not entitled to dividends for that year, and the earnings of subsequent years are not used to make up the deficiency.[33] This much at least is the natural result of a provision for non-cumulation. If such dividends were payable irrespective of earnings, there would be no distinction between cumulative and non-cumulative stock.

66. Earned Dividends

Difficulties concerning non-cumulative dividends arise principally in the case where dividends for the year in question are earned but not paid, and it is sought to treat the right to payment in subsequent years as lost. The problem arises because under the majority rule payment of earned non-cumulative dividends in the year in which they accrue cannot be compelled, payment being a question of business judgment in which the discretion of directors is generally upheld by the courts.[34] When in subsequent years the corporation seeks to pay dividends on common stock, it will then be met by a claim of the non-cumulative holders that they are entitled to payment of back dividends before any distribution can be made to

---

[81] See §§14, 15, *supra*.

[32] Generally on both earned and unearned non-cumulative dividends see Berle, *Non-cumulative Preferred Stock*, 23 Col. L. Rev. 357 (1923); Lattin, *Is Non-Cumulative Preferred Stock in Fact Preferred?* 25 Ill. L. Rev. 148 (1930); Stevens, *Rights of Non-cumulative Preferred Stockholders*, 34 Col. L. Rev. 1439 (1934); Note, *Claim of Non-cumulative Preferred Shareholders to Payment of "Passed" Dividends before Current Dividends Are Paid to Common Stockholders*, 27 Col. L. Rev. 53 (1927); Note, *Cumulation of Dividends on Non-Cumulative Preferred Stock*, 42 Harv. L. Rev. 805 (1929); Note, *Right of Non-Cumulative Preferred Stockholders to Back Dividends Earned but Unpaid*, 74 U. of Pa. L. Rev. 605 (1926); Note, *Rights of Non-Cumulative Preferred Stockholders in Undivided Profits*, 34 Yale L. J. 657 (1925).

[33] *Murphy v. Richardson Dry Goods Co.*, 326 Mo. 1, 31 S. W. (2d) 72 (1930); see *Barclay v. Wabash Railway Co.*, 30 F. (2d) 260, 262 (C. C. A. 2d, 1929), §66, n. 35, *infra*.

[34] See §54.2, n. 55, *supra*.

common stockholders. The leading case is *Wabash Railway Company v. Barclay*.[35] The corporation, having earned the dividend on its non-cumulative first preferred stock over a period of seven years, failed to distribute the same to such shareholders, instead using these sums in the amount of $16,000,000 for working capital or betterments. The surplus account was duly credited with the amount retained. At the end of this period, the first preferred having been paid its annual dividend, the corporation proposed to distribute dividends, not out of surplus but out of current earnings, to its second preferred and common shareholders without having paid to the first preferred the earned, but unpaid, dividends of past years. A first preferred stockholder sought to enjoin payment to other stockholders out of current earnings, and also payment of any dividends, until the corporation had first paid the undistributed dividends of prior years on the first preferred. The majority of the Circuit Court of Appeals was of the opinion that no dividend even out of current earnings could be paid on the subordinate stocks until the prior preferred had been paid in full the earned, but unpaid, dividends. The Supreme Court took the contrary view, Mr. Justice Holmes stating that it is the common understanding of lawyers and business men that if directors justifiably apply the earnings on non-cumulative preferred stock for any one year to improvements in the business rather than paying a dividend, the right to claim the dividend is gone and cannot be asserted later.[36]

Several considerations are of importance in discussing this problem. The *Wabash* case itself presented a considerably restricted factual issue. The first preferred had been paid the regular annual dividend to which it was under the terms of the certificate of incorporation entitled. It was not proposed to pay the dividend to other stockholders out of surplus accumulated from having failed in the

---

[35] 280 U. S. 197 (1930) (comment, 30 Col. L. Rev. 260; 43 Harv. L. Rev. 829; 39 Yale L. J. 581). For a more complete statement of the facts and discussion of the law, see the Circuit Court of Appeals decision which was reversed, 30 F. (2d) 260 (C. C. A. 2d, 1929). See Hicks, *The Rights of Non-cumulative Preferred Stock—a Doubtful Decision of the U. S. Supreme Court*, 5 Temple L. Q. 538 (1931).

[36] In *Joslin v. Boston & Maine R. R.*, 274 Mass. 551, 175 N. E. 156 (1931), an injunction, restraining the declaration of a dividend to common (whether current earnings were sufficient does not appear) unless earned arrearages on non-cumulative stock should be paid, was refused. The court stated it would follow the decision in the *Wabash* case in order to make uniform a question of general commercial law in both state and federal courts. In view of the overruling of *Swift v. Tyson*, 16 Pet. 1 (1842), by *Erie Railroad Co. v. Tompkins*, 304 U. S. 64 (1938), it would seem a different result could now be reached on the merits in Massachusetts.

past to pay dividends on the first preferred; the dividend to other stockholders was being paid from current earnings. The first preferred having been paid all that was provided for out of these earnings, it would have been difficult to sustain a claim to further distribution therefrom.[37]

The troublesome question arises where it is sought to distribute to common stockholders the surplus accumulated from passing dividends on the non-cumulative preferred. A consideration of importance in most of these cases is the fact that non-cumulative preferred is a common method of financing in reorganizations.[38] It is issued in order to keep down anything resembling fixed charges. The achievement of this purpose is of great importance during periods when the corporation has no earnings available to meet the dividend. And there is no dispute that the provision for non-accumulation bars any claims for years in which there are no earnings.[39] But as to years where there are admitted earnings, the situation is considerably different. It may still be held that the directorate has no obligation to distribute non-cumulative earned dividends where in its discretion such funds are necessary to the business, and at the same time be held that if any distribution out of such funds is made in subsequent years, it must be to those shareholders originally entitled thereto rather than to common stockholders. It is relatively easy to sustain a case for permitting the corporation to retain the earnings in the business in the first instance, even though doing so results in strengthening the corporation for common as well as preferred shareholders. It is very difficult, however, to justify a case to show the common stock is entitled to the dividend should the corporation ultimately decide it can make a distribution. When the corporation has earnings in any one year adequate to meet non-

[37] In accord with the *Wabash* case on this point is *Norwich Water Co. v. Southern Railway Co.,* 11 Va. L. Reg. 203 (Richmond City Ct. 1925). But in *Day v. U. S. Cast Iron Pipe & Foundry Co.,* 95 N. J. Eq. 389, 123 Atl. 546, aff'd by an equally divided court 96 N. J. Eq. 736, 126 Atl. 302 (1924) (comment, 38 Harv. 686), the court enjoined payment to common stockholders of a dividend out of current earnings, where the preferred had been paid the full amount of its preference for the year but had only been paid in part for dividends earned and unpaid in prior years. The court relied largely on the New Jersey statute providing for preferred dividends not exceeding 8 per cent annually "before any dividend shall be set apart or paid on the common" as requiring payment of the full earned dividends of the preferred for all past years before any current distribution to common.

[38] This was true in the *Wabash* case. See Bonbright and Bergerman, *Two Rival Theories of Priority Rights of Security Holders in a Corporate Reorganization,* 28 Col. L. Rev. 127, 140, table 4 (1928).

[39] See §65, *supra.*

cumulative dividends, but decides to pass the same, the non-cumulative holders should be recognized as having an equity in the surplus thus retained, entitling them to payment of such dividends ahead of common when dividends are proposed to be paid out of accumulated surplus in later years.[40]

The fact that voting control will often be vested in the common offers opportunity for wide abuse if the doctrine of the *Wabash* case is extended to permit payment to common out of past accumulated surplus. Close scrutiny should especially be given a situation where non-cumulative dividends are passed for a short period of a year or two and then an effort made to distribute the surplus to common stock.

With the passing of *Swift v. Tyson,* the influence of the *Wabash* case may in the future be much curtailed, since state law will be the source of substantive rules for both state and federal courts. Of course, the *Wabash* result may be reached by specific provisions in the articles or stock certificates that non-cumulative preferred shareholders shall only be entitled to dividends actually declared by the directors, irrespective of the amount of net profits which the corporation may have earned prior to the date of any dividend declarations.

---

[40] In *Moran v. U. S. Cast Iron Pipe & Foundry Co.,* 95 N. J. Eq. 389, 123 Atl. 546, aff'd on opinion below 96 N. J. Eq. 698, 126 Atl. 329 (1924), it was held that a common stockholder could not enjoin the payment of past dividends to non-cumulative preferred shareholders out of undistributed earnings allocable to prior years. *Accord: Bassett v. U. S. Cast Iron Pipe & Foundry Co.,* 75 N. J. Eq. 539, 73 Atl. 514 (Ct. Err. & App. 1909) ; *Star Publishing Co. v. Ball,* 192 Ind. 158, 134 N. E. 285 (1922) (the preferred had no voting rights; the common was held by one shareholder seeking to get rid of the preferred; payment of a dividend to the preferred was compelled) ; *Wood v. Lary,* 47 Hun 550 (N. Y., 1st Dept. 1888), *app. dism.* 124 N. Y. 83 (1891) (non-cumulative preferred was "entitled to dividends . . . whenever in any year the net earnings, after payment of all interest charges, shall suffice for the payment thereof"; amounts otherwise payable in dividends were expended over a period of four years on betterments at the end of which a dividend to the preferred was declared for the four years; it was held a common stockholder could not enjoin the declaration). The theory that non-cumulative preferred stock has an inchoate claim against earned but undistributed dividend surplus was strongly advanced by Professor Berle before the decision in the *Wabash* case. Berle, *Non-Cumulative Preferred Stock,* 23 Col. L. Rev. 358 (1923) [reprinted in Berle, *Studies in the Law of Corporation Finance* (1928) 92] ; but cf. Dewing, *Corporation Securities* (1934) 173. It is difficult, however, to support the view of W. H. S. Stevens, that whether or not preferred dividends which have been previously passed shall be subsequently paid rests in the discretion of directors. Stevens, *Discretion of Directors in the Distribution of Non-Cumulative Preferred Dividends,* 24 Geo. L. J. 371, 377–379 (1936). If the preferred stockholders have any legal claim to payment of earned but undistributed dividends, that claim cannot be one which the caprice or discretion of directors is allowed to defeat by a decision to distribute the fund to common stock after all.

C. Modification of Dividend Rights

67. Stockholder Reorganizations

Creditors, when claims and interest are not paid, can force a corporation into reorganization or liquidation. A preferred stockholder, when the corporation fails either to pay or to earn dividends, has no similar recourse. At the same time, the common stockholder sees the corporation continue with the burden of arrearages on preferred stock preventing the prospect of any declaration of common dividends. In these circumstances, in what way and to what extent may a "stockholder reorganization" subordinate or entirely abolish the claims of preferred shareholders? With respect to future dividends? With respect to past dividends, (a) unearned, (b) earned but undistributed? [41]

If it is merely a question of inability to pay current dividends because of an impairment in value of assets, relief may be quite readily obtained by writing off the loss through use of paid-in or reduction surplus, or these sources may in some jurisdictions even be utilized for paying preferred dividends, so as to place the corporation in a position to pay common dividends from current earnings.[42] Frequently, however, there will not only be a capital impairment but a large arrearage of dividends which the reduction of capital does not eliminate.[43] Or the accumulation of unpaid earned dividends may be so large that to pay them would seriously jeopardize the working capital position of the corporation. Or payment of accumulated earned dividends to preferred shareholders may leave nothing for the common stock.

In cases of this character, where the corporation is still short of insolvency, if the corporate structure is to be reorganized at all it must be through an adjustment between the conflicting claims of preferred and common shareholders. Although preferred shareholders may attempt to stand upon the strict letter of their right to

[41] See generally *Report of S. E. C. on Protective and Reorganization Committees,* Pt. VII, pp. 109–197, 496–525 (1938); Berle and Means, *The Modern Corporation and Private Property* (1932) 207; Dodd, *Dissenting Stockholders and Amendments to Corporate Charters,* 75 Univ. of Pa. L. Rev. 585, 723 (1927); Curran, *Minority Stockholders and the Amendment of Corporate Charters,* 32 Mich. L. Rev. 743 (1934); Funiak, *Reducing Rate of Dividend on Preferred Stock,* 14 Notre D. L. Rev. 23 (1938); Note, *Corporate Recapitalization by Charter Amendment,* 46 Yale L. J. 985 (1937).

[42] See §§29, 30, *supra.*

[43] *Roberts v. Roberts-Wicks Co.,* 184 N. Y. 257, 77 N. E. 13 (1906) (even though the accrued dividends were unearned at the time of reduction); *Kennedy v. Carolina Public Service Co.,* 262 Fed. 803 (D. Ga. 1920).

payment of accrued dividends in full, as a practical matter the majority may be expected to take a somewhat less adamant position. The common, usually in voting control, will have considerable latitude under the discretion rule in declining to pay earned dividends, and, where there are no earnings, but an actual impairment, in refusing to go along with a plan for reduction of capital. Preferred stockholders are to that extent dependent upon cooperation from the common stock control. How far this *de facto* power of common stockholders to hold up preferred dividends should be given legal sanction is an important and debatable question. While arrearages remain, the common stock is deprived of dividends. Should the ability of the common stock control to keep the preferred stock also from getting earned dividends be recognized as an effective consideration for surrender of priority rights by the preferred shareholders?

There are available in most jurisdictions two methods of effecting, by majority action, certain adjustments between various classes of stockholders. The first is through amendment of the articles of incorporation or by-laws. The second is by utilizing the merger, consolidation, or sale of assets statute to create issues of stock modifying prior interests. Under both arrangements there is present the problem of the dissenting shareholder who insists he has a vested contract right which cannot be abrogated or modified without his consent.

67.1. Amendment Statutes

Probably the simplest method for effecting changes in the dividend rights of stockholders is by charter amendment. Most state corporation acts contain provisions whereby certain charter amendments may be effected by consent of less than all stockholders. The statutory evolution of amendment provisions is enlightening. Although many of the earliest general corporation acts contained sections reserving the power of the state to amend the same, they made no direct provision for amending charters through a vote of stockholders.[44] The earliest statutes in effect authorizing charter

---

[44] The early Pennsylvania Act of 1836 for incorporating iron manufacturing companies was an exception. It contained a provision for "improving, amending or altering" the articles of incorporation in the manner provided for original adoption. Pa. Laws 1835–36, P. L. 800, §4. The Delaware Act of 1875 provided that amendments or alterations might be submitted by petition to the legislature, which reserved the right to approve or reject the same. 15 Del. Laws, c. 119, §3 (1875).

amendments were general acts permitting the increase or decrease of capital stock.[45] Many statutes of this character required the consent of stockholders,[46] when it was usually provided that the change might be made on the consent of some fixed percentage, usually two-thirds or three-fourths, or on a majority vote.[47] The first statutes specifically authorizing charter amendments were either of this character,[48] granted permission to amend so as to change the purpose or place of business of the corporation,[49] or authorized common stockholders by a vote less than the majority to approve issuance of preferred stock.[50] As a rule there were no provisions permitting amendments generally. A few later statutes did include such authority. The Delaware General Corporation Act of 1883 provided that amendments and alterations of the original certificate of incorporation might be made by a supplemental certificate approved and recorded in the same manner.[51]

These early amendment provisions made no reference to changing or modifying the relative rights of preferred and common stockholders. The most comprehensive of the nineteenth century amendment provisions was that in the New Jersey Act of 1896. It specifically authorized charter amendments changing many charter provisions, including the creation of one or more classes of preferred stock, and the making of "such other amendment, change or alteration as may be desired."[52] Significant as indicating advertence to

[45] Mass. Laws, Jan. Sess. 1830, c. 53, §10, incorporated in Mass. Rev. Stat. (1836), c. 38, §20; 17 Del. Laws, c. 147, §18 (1883); N. Y. Laws 1848, c. 40, §20; N. Y. Laws 1866, c. 73; N. J. Acts 1846, p. 68, §23; Pa. Laws 1874, pp. 82–83.
[46] Mass. Laws Jan. Sess. 1830, c. 53, §10, incorporated in Mass. Rev. Stat. (1836), c. 38, §20; N. J. Acts 1846, c. 68, §23; Pa. Laws 1864, p. 1104, §14.
[47] N. Y. Laws 1848, c. 40, §21; N. Y. Laws 1866, c. 73, §2; 17 Del. Laws, c. 147, §18 (1883); Pa. Laws 1864, p. 1104, §14.
[48] N. J. Acts 1849, pp. 303, 305, §§14, 22; N. J. Laws 1878, c. 91 (change in par value of shares); Md. Pub. Gen. Laws (1860), Art. 26, §§60–67.
[49] N. Y. Laws 1848, c. 40, §20; N. Y. Laws 1864, c. 517, §1; N. Y. Laws 1892, c. 688, §32; N. Y. Laws 1896, c. 929; Mass. Acts and Resolves 1852, c. 195; Md. Pub. Gen. Laws (1860), Art. 26, §§60–67.
[50] Mass. Acts and Resolves 1855, c. 290.
[51] 17 Del. Laws, c. 147, §11. A similar provision was incorporated in the Delaware General Corporation Act of 1899. 21 Del. Laws, c. 273, §10. The New York Banking Act of 1838 contained a clause providing that no change should be made in the articles to weaken rights and remedies of existing creditors. N. Y. Laws 1838, c. 260, §19. A New York act for incorporation of railroads operating in foreign countries adopted in 1881 provided two-thirds of the stockholders might reduce or increase the capital "or may otherwise alter and amend its articles of association." N. Y. Laws 1881, c. 468, §11. See also Md. Laws 1868, c. 470, §42.
[52] N. J. Laws 1896, c. 185, §27. See also N. J. Laws 1892, c. 2.

possible conflicting rights of preferred and common stockholders in the approval of such amendments, this act required the consent of "two-thirds in interest of each class of the stockholders having voting powers." For the most part, however, the amendment statutes of the types presently in force are the product of the twentieth century.

Among the leading corporation states, present corporation acts of several provide generally for changing the preferences, participation, or other special rights of stockholders.[53] Some provide specifically for classifying or reclassifying shares,[54] canceling all or part of an issue,[55] changing issued shares of one class into a different number of the same or different classes,[56] creating new classes of shares having rights and preferences superior to any class already issued,[57] and funding or satisfying rights in respect to dividend arrearages by issuance of stock or otherwise.[58] In some states the amendment section, following the form in very early statutes, merely provides in general terms for amendments containing any provisions which might have been contained in the original articles.[59] In almost all these statutes provision is made that preferred shareholders affected by the amendment are entitled to vote as a class.[60] It is important to note that in most states dissenting stockholders have no remedy by appraisal in the case of an amendment,[61] whereas

[53] Cal. Civ. Code (1937), §362(7); Del. Rev. Code (1935), c. 65, §26; 32 Ill. Ann. Stat. (Smith-Hurd), §157; Ohio Code Ann. (Baldwin), §8623–14 (3i); 15 Purd Pa. Stat., §2852–801.

[54] Cal. Civ. Code (1937), §362(7); Del. Rev. Code (1935), c. 65, §26; 32 Ill. Ann. Stat. (Smith-Hurd), §157.52; Md. Ann. Code, Art. 23, §28; N. J. Rev. Stat. (1937), §14:11–1(p); N. Y. Stock Corp. Law, §36(E); 15 Purd. Pa. Stat., §2852–801(4).

[55] 32 Ill. Ann. Stat. (Smith-Hurd), §157.52; N. Y. Stock Corp. Law, §36C.

[56] 32 Ill. Ann. Stat. (Smith-Hurd), §157.52; N. J. Rev. Stat. (1937), §14: 11–1(j); N. Y. Stock Corp. Law, §36D; Ohio Code Ann. (Baldwin), §8623–14(3f).

[57] 32 Ill. Ann. Stat. (Smith-Hurd), §157.52; N. J. Rev. Stat. (1937), §14:11–1(i).

[58] N. J. Rev. Stat. (1937), §14:11–1(n); Ohio Code Ann. (Baldwin), §8623–14(3i).

[59] Mich. Stat. Ann. (Henderson 1937), §21.43; Minn. Stat. (Mason 1938 Supp.), §7492–36 (provision which would be lawful to include in original articles if adopted at the time of the amendment may be added); cf. Mass. Gen. Laws, c. 156, §42.

[60] Cal. Civ. Code (1937), §362a (3); Del. Rev. Code (1935), c. 65, §26; 32 Ill. Ann. Stat. (Smith-Hurd), §157.52; Mich. Stat. Ann. (Henderson 1937), §21.43; Minn. Stat. (Mason 1938 Supp.), §7492–36; N. J. Rev. Stat. (1937), §14:11–3; N. Y. Stock Corp. Law, §37(3c); Ohio Code Ann. (Baldwin), §8623–15(4); 15 Purd. Pa. Stat., §2852–804.

[61] Among important exceptions are New York and Ohio. N. Y. Stock Corp. Law, §38(9); Ohio Code Ann. (Baldwin), §8623–14, 72.

in a considerable number of jurisdictions such a remedy is accorded dissenters on a merger or consolidation.[62]

67.2. Merger and Consolidation Statutes

Merger and consolidation statutes made their appearance at a somewhat more advanced stage of corporate statutory regulation than charter amendment provisions. This, and the fact that mergers and consolidations necessarily involved consideration of the capital structure of the new corporation, doubtless account for broader provisions for modification of the rights of stockholders of the constituent corporations. Early corporation acts either provided that corporations might be merged or consolidated on such terms as the stockholders or directors might agree upon,[63] or more specifically that the manner of converting the shares of stock of the constituent corporations into shares of the new corporation might be specified.[64] In almost all cases, a clause required approval of the merger or consolidation by some percentage less than all of the stockholders. Unlike early amendment statutes, a great number of merger and consolidation statutes contained clauses for appraisal and payment to dissenting stockholders.[65]

Among present merger and consolidation statutes, almost all important incorporating states provide, as did the early acts, that the plan shall be approved by a certain percentage of stockholders and shall specify the manner and basis of converting shares of the constituent corporations into shares of the new corporation.[66] The

[62] See §67.2, infra.

[63] N. Y. Laws 1849, c. 250, §8 (plankroad and turnpike companies); Md. Laws 1868, c. 471, §36; 21 Del. Laws, c. 273, §54 (General Corp. Law of 1899).

[64] N. Y. Laws 1867, c. 960, §1; N. Y. Laws 1869, c. 917, §2 (railroads); N. Y. Laws 1877, c. 374, §2; N. Y. Laws 1882, c. 409, §49; N. Y. Laws 1884, c. 367 (applicable to all corporations previously or subsequently organized); N. J. Laws 1883, c. 198, §1 (dock and shipyard corporations); N. J. Laws 1888, c. 294, §2; N. J. Laws 1896, c. 185, §104 (General Corporation Act of 1896); Conn. Pub. Acts 1901, c. 157, §38. In 1874 New York enacted a statute providing for the reorganization of railroads sold under mortgage deeds of trust so as to authorize, at the time of sale, plans for representation of the interests of creditors and stockholders in the new corporation. Under these plans the corporation was authorized to establish preferences in respect to payment of dividends "in favor of any portion of its said capital stock, and to divide such stock into classes." N. Y. Laws 1874, c. 430, §§1, 2.

[65] N. Y. Laws 1867, c. 409, §56 (banks); N. Y. Laws 1884, c. 367, §2 (all corporations); N. J. Laws 1883, c. 198, §2; N. J. Laws 1888, c. 294, §4; N. J. Laws 1896, c. 185, §108; 21 Del. Laws, c. 273, §56 (1899).

[66] Cal. Civ. Code (1937), §361; Del. Rev. Code (1935), c. 65, §59; 32 Ill. Ann. Stat. (Smith-Hurd), §§157.61, 62; Mich. Stat. Ann. (Henderson 1937), §21.52; Minn. Stat. (Mason 1938 Supp.), §7492-41 (specifically authorizing the plan to state whether the same or a different number of shares of the consolidated

Ohio General Corporation Act contains probably the most comprehensive section with respect to affecting the rights of shareholders of the constituents. It authorizes terms of the plan to provide for distribution to shareholders of the constituents, in extinguishment or substitution of the old shares, of shares of any class or classes of the new corporation or property other than shares or both.[67] Thus under merger and consolidation provisions, the basis for modifying stockholders' rights may be somewhat broader than under many amendment statutes. Moreover, in all of the modern provisions cited, arrangement is made for appraisal and payment of interests of dissenting shareholders.[68]

68. Change in Amount of Future Dividends

There are three principal ways in which preferred dividend claims may be modified. The future rate of the dividend may, in the first place, be reduced. This is the simplest form of modification. Second, a new issue of preferred with priority over the old preferred may be issued, the old preferred being given a right to exchange for the new stock. Those failing to do so thus have their claims subordinated to the new preferred. Finally, an outright plan of funding accrued arrearages may be resorted to. By amendment of the charter or a merger, the terms and dividend rights of the preferred stock are changed. The result of this last type of change is usually to substitute new stock for the preferred stock, or even for all classes of stock outstanding, under a new plan of capitalization. The accrued preferred dividends under this method are abolished so far as all old preferred stockholders are concerned.

The objection advanced to varying the dividend participation rights as between preferred and common stockholders may be twofold: the dissenting stockholders have vested contract rights which

---

or surviving corporation are to be issued) ; N. J. Rev. Stat. (1937), §§14:12–1, 8 (§14:12–8 authorizes the consolidated corporation to issue common or preferred stock to the holders of the constituent corporations "in the manner and on the terms specified in the agreement of merger or consolidation") ; N. Y. Stock Corporation Law, §86(9) ; 15 Purd. Pa. Stat., §2852–902.

[67] Ohio Code Ann. (Baldwin), §8623–67(IA6).

[68] Cal. Civ. Code (1937), §369(17), provides that "The rights and remedies of any shareholder at law or in equity to object to or litigate as to any such merger or consolidation shall be and are hereby limited to the right to receive the fair market value of his shares" except actions to test formal compliance with the statute. For the view that under this section an injunction may, nevertheless, be brought on the ground of fraud before the approval by shareholders of the merger or consolidation, see Ballantine and Sterling, *Upsetting Mergers and Consolidations: Alternative Remedies of Dissenting Shareholders in California*, 27 Cal. L. Rev. 644 (1939).

can in no event be impaired under state and federal constitutions; assuming a change can constitutionally be made, the statute does not authorize the modification in question.

Constitutionally there is no objection to modifying the relative rights of stockholders to have future dividends continue at the same rate if statutes make provision for such change.[69] The same liberality is evidenced in construing amendment statutes so as to permit a change in future dividends.[70] It is likewise possible to terminate the right of preferred stockholders to future dividends by a merger or consolidation plan.[71] However, in *Pronick v. Spirits*

[69] *Johnson v. Bradley Knitting Co.*, 288 Wis. 566, 280 N. W. 688 (1938) (amendment of certificate); *Harbine v. Dayton Malleable Iron Co.*, 61 Ohio App. 1, 22 N. E. (2d) 281 (1939) (amendment plan changing existing preferred into stock with lower dividend rate sustained under statute passed after organization of corporation); *Williams v. National Pump Corp.*, 46 Ohio App. 427, 188 N. E. 756 (1933), err. dism. 126 Ohio St. 457, 186 N. E. 403 (1933) (appraisal statute only remedy where amendment changes preferred stock under statute authorizing change of shares of one class into shares of another); *Davis v. Louisville Gas & Electric Co.*, 16 Del. Ch. 157, 142 Atl. 654 (1928) (prior to amendment Class A was only entitled to share with Class B, in the ratio of 1 to 4, surplus remaining above preference dividends; amendment increased preference rate slightly and provided for sharing of surplus equally; statute authorizing amendment, passed under reserve power, after corporation's organization; corporation's original certificate of incorporation included a provision that the corporation should have the right to amend, alter, or repeal in the manner "now or hereafter" prescribed by statute). On the constitutionality of amendments affecting preferred dividend rights, see *S. E. C. Report on Protective and Reorganization Committees*, Pt. VII, 514 (1938).

[70] *Williams v. National Pump Corp.*, 46 Ohio App. 427, 188 N. E. 756 (1933), err. dism. 126 Ohio St. 457, 186 N. E. 403, n. 69, supra; *Johnson v. Bradley Knitting Co.*, 228 Wis. 566, 280 N. W. 688 (1938); *Peters v. U. S. Mortgage Co.*, 13 Del. Ch. 11, 114 Atl. 598 (1921) (amendment abolished right to share with common after preferred had been paid 7 per cent and common an equal amount; statute gave right to alter or change "preferences" by amendment); *Yoakam v. Providence Biltmore Hotel Co.*, 34 F. (2d) 533 (D. R. I. 1929); see *Morris v. American Public Utilities Co.*, 14 Del. Ch. 136, 151, 122 Atl. 696 (1923); *Keller v. Wilson*, 190 Atl. 115, 119 (Del. 1936). In *Wagstaff v. Holly Sugar Corp.*, 253 App. Div. 616, 3 N. Y. S. (2d) 552 (1st Dept. 1938), aff'd 279 N. Y. 625 (1938), the charter provided that dividends should not be paid to the common stock in excess of $10 per share in any one year and that amendments to the article containing this provision should require the consent of 95 per cent of the preferred shareholders. By majority vote of stockholders, the common stock was split five for one. It was held preferred stockholders were not entitled to enjoin payment of dividends in excess of $10 per share on the number of common shares previously outstanding. Common dividends to the extent of $50 rather than $10 thus received the court's sanction. The case indicates strict limitation of the rights of preferred stockholders.

[71] *Colgate v. U. S. Leather Co.*, 73 N. J. Eq. 72, 90, 67 Atl. 657 (1907) reversed on other grounds 75 N. J. Eq. 229, 72 Atl. 126 (1909). Cf. *Outwater v. Public Service Corp. of N. J.*, 103 N. J. Eq. 461, 143 Atl. 729, aff'd on opinion below 104 N. J. Eq. 490, 146 Atl. 916 (1929) [under long-term leases partly owned subsidiaries were guaranteed rentals assuring dividends to their shareholders (ap-

Distributing Company, where there was no provision dealing specifically with alteration or amendment of the preferred stock in the certificate of incorporation, a general statutory power to "amend" the certificate was held not broad enough to permit a reduction of the interest rate on two classes of cumulative and non-cumulative preferred stock.[72]

A lowering of future interest rates is an important feature of almost every plan to scale down preferred claims.[73] It probably affects the interests of preferred stockholders the least of any alteration contemplated by the plan, and it is certainly the type change within the purview of statutes authorizing amendments.

69. Change in Priority of Claims

Freedom to subordinate the profit claims of common or preferred stockholders is desirable in two situations, first, where the corporation wishes to raise new money through a prior stock issue, and secondly, as an almost indispensable adjunct to any plan of voluntary reorganization.

If corporations are not to be seriously restricted in their stock financing, the power to amend articles of incorporation to create issues of stock with preferential rights over existing shares is necessary.[74] If bonds are issued to raise new money, the interest of shareholders is subordinated to the prior payment of both principal and interest. In such case shareholders are without ground for complaint. Creation of a prior preferred issue has much the same effect as a bond in subordinating existing shareholders to the prior payment of dividends on the new stock.[75] But there is this difference. In

---

parently on preferred stock) of 8, 5, and 4 per cent; a merger with the parent which would give to the outstanding shareholders of the subsidiaries 6 per cent preferred stock at an exchange rate yielding slightly more than the prior dividends from rentals, but subject to redemption in three years was held to be unfair and enjoined].

[72] 58 N. J. Eq. 97 (1899). In *Morris v. American Public Utilities Co.,* 14 Del. Ch. 136, 122 Atl. 696 (1923), it was held that a statute generally permitting amendment of articles was not sufficient to cover the specific case of abolishing accrued dividends.

[73] Out of 51 proxy solicitations filed during the period of a year under the Securities Exchange Act in connection with recapitalization plans, 38 carried proposals for lowering preferred dividends or eliminating them entirely. Report of S. E. C. on Protective and Reorganization Committees, Pt. VII, p. 125 (1938).

[74] *Salt Lake Automobile Co. v. Keith-O'Brien Co.,* 45 Utah 218, 143 Pac. 1015 (1914); *In re Sharood Shoe Corp.,* 192 Fed. 945 (D. Minn. 1912); see Dodd, *Amendments to Corporate Charters,* 75 U. of Pa. L. Rev. 723, 732 (1927).

[75] *General Hide & Leather Co. v. American Hide & Leather Co.,* 98 N. J. Eq. 326, 129 Atl. 244 (Ct. Err. & App. 1925); *Rutland & Burlington R. R. Co., v. Thrall,* 35 Vt. 536 (1863); *In re Sharood Shoe Corporation,* 192 Fed. 445 (D. Minn. 1912).

the case where bonds are issued, the existing preferred or common can get rid of the priority claim when the bonds are paid. If a new issue of preferred is given priority, this cannot be done unless the latter is made redeemable. The new preferred has an interest, which, depending upon its terms, may permit a sharing in general assets on dissolution. Nevertheless, the need of the corporation for new money will usually outweigh added subordinations caused by a preferred issue that might not accompany bond financing.

It has been held when it is sought to create an issue of preferred stock ahead of common where no provision in the articles of incorporation or statute authorizes such action, the existing common stock need not submit to the subordination.[76] But a statute passed under the reserve power subsequent to original issuance of a corporation's common stock may authorize a fixed majority of stockholders to approve an issue of preferred stock subordinating the rights of existing stockholders, although at the time of the statute's enactment consent of all stockholders to the issuing of preferred stock was necessary.[77]

The only effective way of assuring practical success to a voluntary reorganization plan where there are outstanding accrued dividends is to sustain a provision, giving prior preferred shares to those preferred shareholders coming in, which will rank preferentially as to dividends over the accrued claims of the existing preferred. If non-assenting preferred shareholders are not subordinated as to accrued claims, there is no advantage to any preferred shareholders in joining the plan. The majority of cases do recognize that a plan which

[76] *Campbell v. American Zylonite Co.*, 122 N. Y. 455, 25 N. E. 853 (1890). In *Kent v. Quicksilver Mining Co.*, 78 N. Y. 159 (1879), it was held a violation of the vested constitutional right of holders of common stock to create by amendment of the by-laws an issue of preferred stock ranking in priority to common as to dividends, even though the charter and original by-laws granted the power to alter, amend, or repeal by-laws; but the rights of the common stockholders were held to have been lost through laches. On the other hand, in *Covington v. Covington & Cincinnati Bridge Co.*, 10 Bush. 69 (Ky. 1873), a railroad originally organized with common stock was subsequently authorized by special statute to issue, with the consent of the majority of existing shareholders, new stock having priority as to dividends over the common. The statute was held constitutional; there was no impairment where it was necessary to amend to carry out the purposes of incorporation and in fact save the corporation itself. Common was given preemptive rights. The contrary result was reached as to preferred shares issued with priority over existing preferred shares in *West Chester & Philadelphia R. R. Co. v. Jackson*, 77 Pa. 321 (1875).

[77] *Hinckley v. Schwarzchild & Co.*, 107 App. Div. 470, 95 N. Y. S. 357 (1st Dept. 1905), *app. dism.* on procedural grounds, 193 N. Y. 599 (1908). Where the charter makes provision for increasing the amount of stock, a common stockholder cannot object to the creation of a preferred issue with guarantee of dividends. *Rutland & Burlington R. R. Co. v. Thrall*, 35 Vt. 536 (1863).

provides for new preferred ranking in priority as to dividends over existing non-assenting preferred is valid.[78] Sometimes it is possible to reach this result by construction of a provision merely giving the existing preferred a preference over common stock or existing stocks.[79] The use of this method of subordinating accrued preferred dividends should be restricted to legitimate reorganization purposes. In some cases where new preferred issues have been permitted priority over existing accrued dividend claims, the accrued dividends had actually been earned and funds were legally available for distribution.[80] Priority preferred issues should be held invalid if they are merely a device for getting rid of earned accumulated arrearages which the corporation could pay without embarrassment.

An interesting consequence of plans under which existing preferred shareholders exchange their stock for new prior preferred is

[78] *Shanak v. White Sewing Machine Corp.*, 15 A. (2d) 169 (Del. Ch. 1940); *Thomas v. Laconia Car Co.*, 251 Mass. 529, 146 N. E. 775 (1925) (statute authorized two-thirds of stock to change classes of stock subsequently to be issued or make any other lawful amendment or alteration, Mass. Acts and Resolves 1903, c. 437, §40; the plan provided that on liquidation non-assenting preferred should be paid in full, principal and unpaid accrued dividends; it was held that, therefore, payment to non-assenting preferred was merely deferred); *Matter of Kinney*, 279 N. Y. 423 (1939) (issuance of prior preferred stock not an alteration of preferences entitling dissenters to relief under appraisal statute); *Morris v. American Public Utilities Co.*, 14 Del. Ch. 136, 122 Atl. 696 (1923) (creating two new issues of preferred entitled to prior dividends and on dissolution to par plus accumulated dividends valid under amendment statute authorizing change in "preferences"); *Ainsworth v. Southwestern Drug Corp.*, 95 F. (2d) 172 (C. C. A. 5th, 1938) (charter provision authorized creation of new preferred with consent of majority of existing preferred shareholders; notes for the accrued dividends also part of the plan); *General Investment Co. v. American Hide & Leather Co.*, 98 N. J. Eq. 326, 129 Atl. 244 (Ct. Err. & App. 1925) (statute authorized corporation to "create one or more classes of preferred stock" with the consent of two-thirds in interest of each class of stock outstanding); see *Johnson v. Lamprecht*, 133 Ohio St. 567, 15 N. E. (2d) 127, 129 (1938); *Keller v. Wilson & Co.*, 190 Atl. 115, 119 (Del. 1936); Dewing, *Corporation Securities* (1934) 172; cf. *Matter of Duer*, 270 N. Y. 343, 1 N. E. (2d) 457 (1936) (new prior preferred entitled to preferences on dissolution over non-consenting existing preferred); *Davis v. Louisville Gas & Electric Co.*, 16 Del. Ch. 157, 142 Atl. 654 (1928) (amendment increased extent of preferred participation with common after preferential rate had been paid and an equal amount to common; a question was raised as to the soundness of this decision in *Keller v. Wilson & Co.*, 190 Atl. 115, 121 (1936)); *Yoakam v. Providence Biltmore Hotel Co.*, 34 F. (2d) 533 (D. R. I. 1912) (charter provided prior preferred might be issued with consent of three-fourths of outstanding preferred; the court noted that the plan provided for payment of priority dividends to new stock only out of future earnings). Some states provide by statute for amendments creating prior preference stock. Ark. Stat. (1937), §2133(g); 32 Ill. Ann. Stat. (Smith-Hurd), §157.52; N. J. Rev. Stat. (1937), §14:11-1(i)(j); Ohio Code Ann. (Baldwin), §8623-14(f)(g).

[79] *Morris v. American Public Utilities Co.*, 14 Del. Ch. 136, 122 Atl. 696 (1923).

[80] See e.g. *Thomas v. Laconia Car Co.*, 251 Mass. 529, 146 N. E. 775 (1925).

the effect on liquidation. Non-assenting stockholders, where their liquidation provisions cover accrued dividends, are entitled to recover dividends in full; but assenting stockholders, who have given up their claims to accrued dividends existing prior to adoption of the plan in exchange for the right to current priorities, are limited on liquidation to dividends accrued since adoption of the plan.[81]

Sometimes an attempt is made by amendment to condition stockholder participation in profits on the amount of business done with the corporation. However, such amendments have been held invalid.[82]

70. Cancellation of Past Accrued Dividends

The principal problem in stockholder reorganizations is cancellation or modification of the claim to accrued dividends. Here the constitutional argument of a vested right not subject to impairment has been made with more than average success. It has been held in Delaware that accumulated preferred dividends cannot be canceled by amendment whether the corporation was organized and the stock issued before or after the basic 1927 Act authorizing Delaware corporations in broad terms to amend their articles so as to reclassify stocks by changing designations, preferences, relative, participating or other special rights.[83] In *Keller v. Wilson and Company,* where the 1927 Act was adopted after organization of the corporation and issuance of the preferred stock, the abrogation of accrued cumulative dividends by amendment to the articles was held invalid, both on the ground that the accrual created a "vested right of property" not constitutionally subject to abrogation, and on the ground that the statute operated prospectively only, so as not to authorize annulment of a dividend obligation once it had matured.[84]

---

[81] *Willson v. Laconia Car Co.,* 275 Mass. 435, 176 N. E. 182 (1931).
[82] *Allen v. White,* 103 Neb. 256, 171 N. W. 52 (1919); *Farrier v. Ritzville Warehouse Co.,* 116 Wash. 522, 199 Pac. 984 (1921) (conditions unreasonable).
[83] 35 Del. Laws, c. 85, §10 (1927). The present provision is Del. Rev. Code (1935), c. 65, §26. *Source:* 21 Del. Laws, c. 273, §10 (1899); 22 Del. Laws, c. 167, §26 (1901); 22 Del. Laws, c. 392, §11 (1903); 25 Del. Laws, c. 155 (1909); 29 Del. Laws, c. 113, §12 (1917); 34 Del. Laws, c. 112, §7 (1925); 35 Del. Laws, c. 85, §10 (1927); 37 Del. Laws, c. 129, §8 (1931); 38 Del. Laws, c. 91, §3 (1933); 40 Del. Laws, c. 148, §4. Generally on the cancellation of accrued preferred dividends, see Becht, *The Power to Remove Accrued Dividends by Charter Amendment,* 40 Col. L. Rev. 633 (1940); S. E. C. Report on Protective and Reorganization Committees, Pt. VII, 506–514 (1938); Note, 4 Newark L. Rev. 323 (1939); Note, 25 Corn. L. Q. 431 (1940).
[84] 190 Atl. 115 (Del. 1936).

On the constitutional question the case has been followed as to earned accrued dividends in North Carolina,[85] but not elsewhere. In *Consolidated Film Industries v. Johnson,* the Delaware Supreme Court likewise held that a corporation organized after the 1927 amendment could not destroy the right of preferred shareholders to accrued cumulative dividends, this time on the second ground of the *Keller* case, that the Delaware amendment statute, although it is in almost the broadest conceivable language, does not authorize canceling the dividend once it has accrued.[86] There is a possibility that as to accrued but unearned dividends of Delaware corporations organized after 1927, there may be a basis for cancellation through charter amendment. In the *Consolidated Film* case, the dividend had actually been earned.[87] There is a distinction of substance between the two cases. To permit the abolition by amendment of accrued earned cumulative dividends would raise much the same type of problem presented by the *Wabash* case. If directors could pass cumulative dividends which were earned and later put through a plan of reorganization permanently depriving the preferred shareholders of the right to this earned surplus, and in substance turn it over for dividend purposes to common stockholders, cumulative preferred stock could be effectively changed into non-cumulative stock subject to the added vicissitudes of the *Wabash* case.

Whether the rigid rule against amendment modification of accrued dividends enunciated in the *Keller* and *Consolidated* cases still prevails is at least doubtful. In *Federal United Corporation v. Havender,* the Delaware Supreme Court upheld a merger of a parent with its wholly owned subsidiary, both Delaware corporations, which canceled and funded accrued dividends on the preferred stock of the parent in exchange for new shares of the surviving corporation.[88] Prior to the merger, the parent, while it did

---

[85] *Patterson v. Durham Hosiery Mills,* 214 N. C. 806, 200 S. E. 906 (1939) (charter gave right to three-fourths of preferred stock to issue stock having a priority or preference over it); *Patterson v. Henrietta Mills,* 216 N. C. 728 (1940).

[86] 197 Atl. 489 (Del. 1937). Even in Delaware, however, if a preferred stockholder delays in objecting to an amendment canceling arrearages, he is barred by laches. The amendment is not void. *Romer v. Porcelain Products, Inc.,* 2 A. (2d) 75 (1938).

[87] See the opinion of the Court of Chancery, *Johnson v. Consolidated Film Industries,* 194 Atl. 844, 845 (1937). In *Keller v. Wilson,* the corporation had a surplus but it was insufficient to meet the accrued dividends on both the first and second preferred stocks. The court did not consider it material, however, on the question of vested rights whether the dividend was earned or not.

[88] 11A (2d) 331 (1940) (comment, 53 Harv. L. Rev. 877; 88 U. of Pa. L. Rev. 624; 26 Va. L. Rev. 822).

not have earned surplus sufficient to pay accrued dividends of $29 per share, did have a sufficient balance sheet surplus available to pay such dividends under Delaware law. Under the plan, substantially all of this surplus was capitalized by new preferred and common shares issued to the old preferred shareholders. It was conceded that the terms of the merger were in all respects fair and equitable. The issue was whether the merger was effective to terminate claims of dissenting preferred shareholders to accrued unpaid dividends, claimed to be vested rights under the doctrine of *Keller v. Wilson.* In sustaining the recapitalization plan in the *Havender* case, the court distinguished *Keller v. Wilson* on the ground that the amendment statute had been enacted subsequent to the organization of the corporation. This distinction might have meant something had the court not already decided in the *Consolidated* case that accrued preferred dividends could not be funded even when the corporation was organized after enactment of the amendment statute. The court's failure to mention the important *Consolidated* decision in the *Havender* opinion until reargument seems significant as indicating a possible doubt as to the soundness of its vested right theory propounded in the *Keller* and *Consolidated* cases. It may well be, however, that the *Keller* and *Consolidated* cases will be adhered to, and funding of accumulated arrearages permitted in Delaware only by the merger method. There is no Delaware appraisal provision allowing dissenters to have their stock valued in the case of amendment, whereas appraisal is provided by Section 61 of the Delaware General Corporation Law for stockholders dissenting to mergers and consolidations. At any rate, the decision in the *Havender* case is at odds with the position in the earlier cases that a preferred shareholder has a vested right as to accumulated dividends which cannot be modified.

In the *Havender* case, the merger was that of parent and wholly owned subsidiary. Will a different result be reached when the merger technique is used to fund accrued preferred dividends of independent corporations? A different result is not likely. Nothing in the court's opinion turned on the fact that the merged corporation was a subsidiary. In fact, it was argued the merger statute encompassed only combinations of independent corporations and was inapplicable to a parent-subsidiary combine. Where the subsidiary is wholly owned, as in the *Havender* case, utilization of the merger technique solely as a device for funding preferred dividends is easily possible. Therefore, in mergers of independent corporations, where other considerations will normally be present, the funding involved as part of the plan, if fair, should be sustained.[89]

As to earned dividends there is, on the whole, a decided reluctance on the part of courts to approve plans for cancellation.[90] In *Johnson v. Lamprecht,* the court recognized that preferred stockholders could not be compelled to give up their right to accrued earned dividends, but sustained a plan for an amendment which gave the non-redeemable preferred stockholders the option of accepting prior redeemable preferred which would yield the same rate of dividends previously payable, plus three-fourths of a share of common stock worth $6, in cancellation of $20 in arrearages, or in the alternative of retaining their preferred shares, subject, however,

---

[89] The merger technique bids fair to be the method used in recapitalization, under the Public Utility Holding Corporation Act of Delaware utility holding corporations since the *Havender* decision. See *Matter of Federal Water Service Corp.,* Holding Company Act Releases Nos. 1999, 2021 (1940).

[90] *Patterson v. Durham Hosiery Mills,* 214 N. C. 806, 200 S. E. 906 (1939) (charter gave right to three-fourths of preferred stock to issue stock having a priority or preference over it) ; *Frank v. Wilson & Co.,* 9 A. (2d) 82 (Del. Ch. 1939) ; *Yoakam v. Providence Biltmore Hotel Co.,* 34 F. (2d) 533, 542 (D. R. I. 1912) ; and see merger cases n. 96, *infra;* cf. *General Investment Co. v. American Hide & Leather Co.,* 98 N. J. Eq. 326, 129 Atl. 244 (Ct. Err. & App. 1925) (preferred stockholders entitled to enjoin use of earned surplus available to pay accrued dividends for purchase and retirement of part of preferred stock) ; see Becht, *The Power to Remove Accrued Dividends by Charter Amendment,* 40 Col. L. Rev. 633, 634–635 (1940) ; Note, 53 Harv. L. Rev. 877, 879 (1940) ; Note, 25 Corn. L. Q. 431, 433 (1940) ; *contra: Thomas v. Laconia Car Co.,* 251 Mass. 529, 146 N. E. 775 (1925). In *Hastings v. International Paper Co.,* 187 App. Div. 404, 175 N. Y. S. 815 (1st Dept. 1919), a voluntary plan provided for funding arrearages on cumulative preferred dividends by a small payment in cash and the balance in preferred and common stock. At the time of adoption of the plan, the corporation had twice as much surplus as was necessary to liquidate the accumulations. A dividend in cash and stock was declared to those consenting to the plan. A minority preferred stockholder was held not entitled to recover in an action to compel payment of the accrued arrearages, on the ground directors had discretion not to declare such dividends. In some cases where it does not appear whether there was surplus to pay the accruals or not, it has been held illegal to cancel the same by amendment. *Harbine v. Dayton Malleable Iron Co.,* 61 Ohio App. 1, 22 N. E. (2d) 281 (1939) (under amendment statute adopted after organization of corporation; the Ohio law was amended following this decision to authorize elimination or modification of rights to accrued undeclared cumulative dividends, Ohio Code Ann. (Baldwin), §8623–14(i)) ; *Johnson v. Bradley Knitting Co.,* 228 Wis. 566, 280 N. W. 688 (1938) (plan provided for discharging $35 in accumulated dividends by issuance of a $20 convertible dividend warrant; held a minority preferred stockholder was entitled to $20 cash on his shares). But in *McQuillen v. National Cash Register Co.,* 27 F. Supp. 639 (D. Md. 1939), under a Maryland statute authorizing amendments changing terms (defined as "contract rights") of outstanding stock by classification, reclassification, or otherwise, a plan, giving non-cumulative stockholders a new class of stock with the same dividend rights as the existing cumulative preferred stock, was sustained.

to the payment of the prior preferred dividends.[91] If the old shares were retained, they would be entitled to dividends in priority to the common. There was evidence that if the corporation paid the back dividends, working capital would be dangerously impaired. There may be such situations where payment of large accruals, even though surplus is available, could not be made without impairing the corporation's working capital, or endangering its ability to meet obligations. In such cases there may be times when the legitimate interests of the corporation should favor a construction of the amendment power to cover modifying even earned accruals, but ordinarily the purpose of the amending section is not to enable interests of shareholders resembling property rights to be swept away.[92]

On the other hand, where the corporation's need to get rid of accrued cumulative arrearages is most acute—namely, where the corporation has no earnings to meet the dividend—it should be permitted to annul the accrual under some equitable plan. To speak of a right to accrued unearned preferred dividends as a vested right constitutionally protected from change under the reserve power, is extremely unrealistic. It is a right which no stockholder could enforce in a court action. In the absence of express statute, a corporation which has no earnings cannot be compelled to pay dividends to preferred shareholders out of capital even when the dividend is guaranteed.[93] The passing of a preferred dividend creates no debt due from the corporation to the stockholder. The payment of such dividends depends on the future contingency of earnings. And, since the abrogation of future dividends has been found per-

---

[91] 133 Ohio St. 567, 15 N. E. (2d) 127 (1938) (the original articles of incorporation authorized creation of shares in priority to existing preferred with a two-thirds consent). Cf. *Ainsworth v. Southwestern Drug Corp.*, 95 F. (2d) 172 (C. C. A. 5th, 1938) (option provision where dividends unearned); *Gedwitz v. Armour & Co.*, 299 Ill. App. 618, 20 N. E. (2d) 175 (1939) (relief denied where stockholder had exercised the option).

[92] Cf. Dodd, *Amendments to Corporate Charters*, 75 U. of Pa. L. Rev. 723, 746 (1927).

[93] See §54.2, n. 48, *supra*. The uncertainty of dividends being paid even on the highest grade preferred stock is illustrated by the experience of preferred shareholders of the United States Steel Corporation. From 1901 to 1930 the corporation had strengthened its balance sheet position by reducing bonded indebtedness, creating a depreciation reserve of $700,000,000 and a surplus of $600,000,000. Presumably the position of the preferred stock was strong. In 1932 the corporation experienced the first operating loss in its history—a loss of $18,000,000. The February 1933 quarterly preferred dividend was immediately cut to one-third of the amount due. The $600,000,000 of surplus proved to be of no practical benefit to preferred shareholders. See Dewing, *Corporation Securities* (1934) 180–181.

missible in other circumstances, the same result should follow as to collection in the future of past unearned dividends.[94] With stockholder reorganization needs what they are, judicial recognition of the urgent necessity for scaling down unearned accumulations should be given.[95] In the meantime, corporations are left, in states such as Delaware and New Jersey, with the merger as a possibility for getting rid of unearned arrearages;[96] in Delaware, a prior issue of pre-

[94] Prior to *Erie Railroad Co. v. Tompkins,* 304 U. S. 64 (1938), this result was reached in the Circuit Court of Appeals for the Second Circuit under the 1927 amendment to the Delaware law. *Harr v. Pioneer Mechanical Corporation,* 65 F. (2d) 332 (C. C. A. 2d, 1933), *cert. den.* 290 U. S. 673 (1933), sustained a plan canceling accrued cumulative dividends where the corporation at the time had a deficit; the plan also provided for issuance of prior preference stock; cf. *Haggard v. Lexington Utilities Co.,* 260 Ky. 261, 84 S. W. (2d) 84 (1935) (amendment plan reducing preferred capital and providing for dividends not in excess of 50 per cent of earnings to be paid common until capital should be restored approved); *Matter of Duer,* 270 N. Y. 343, 1 N. E. (2d) 457 (1936) (corporation had accrued unearned dividends; plan provided for prior preferred entitled to preferences on dissolution; held, these preferences would be recognized on dissolution against non-consenting preferred); *contra: Lonsdale Securities Corp. v. International Mercantile Marine Co.,* 101 N. J. Eq. 554, 139 Atl. 50 (1927); *Morris v. American Public Utilities Co.,* 14 Del. Ch. 136, 122 Atl. 696 (1923) (statute authorizing changes or alterations in "preferences" by amendment not broad enough, since this is a "vested right"). In *Roberts v. Roberts-Wicks Co.,* 184 N. Y. 257, 77 N. E. 13 (1906), the corporation having suffered an impairment of capital through losses, the outstanding preferred and common stock were duly reduced. After the reduction, the corporation voted to pay preferred dividends on the amount of cumulative preferred stock as reduced and also a dividend to common out of earnings since the reduction. An old preferred shareholder was held entitled to recover out of the current earnings the amount of all accrued but unearned dividends due before reduction on the total amount of unreduced preferred stock. *Accord: Kennedy v. Carolina Public Service Co.,* 262 Fed. 803 (D. Ga. 1920); but cf. *Wiedersum v. Atlantic Products, Inc.,* N. Y. L. J., May 6, 1940, p. 2069, col. 6.

[95] At the end of 1938 there were arrearages of $372,000,000 in dividends on $1,500,000,000 out of a total of $3,500,000,000 invested in preferred stocks of public utility companies alone. New York Times, Nov. 22, 1939, p. 31; see also issue of June 17, 1939, p. 28. These arrearages have been no small factor in perpetuating the depressed condition in this major industry.

[96] *Federal United Corp. v. Havender,* 11 A. (2d) 331 (Del. 1940). In *Windhurst v. Central Leather Co.,* 101 N. J. Eq. 543, 138 Atl. 772 (Ct. Ch. 1927), dividends of 43 per cent on 7 per cent cumulative preferred stock were in default; the common capital had been completely lost and half of the preferred capital. To relieve this situation, a plan of merger was proposed under which the old preferred was to give up its claims, including that for dividend arrearages, in return for new stocks and $5 in cash. Dissenting preferred stockholders sought an injunction against a payment of dividends by the new company. The court refused relief, holding the plan to be fair, and the complainant barred because of laches. Even though the assured dividends for any one year amounted to only $6.50 as compared to $7.00 on the old stock, this was considered a small price if the corporate organization itself could be saved. Thereupon, the complainants amended their bills in order to compel payment at law of the accrued dividends. The court held the merger did not effect a dissolution vesting consequent rights in the

ferred can probably be provided by amendment, subordinating the old preferred;[97] or resort must be made to purely voluntary plans of recapitalization.

In stockholder reorganizations, a blanket rule against modifying the rights of preferred stockholders seems highly undesirable. Treating preferred dividend rights as immutable, accords to preferred stockholders a protection not even given creditors who must submit (under insolvency reorganization proceedings) to a scaling down of their claims. The question should rather be one of fairness of terms of the plan, whether the stockholder reorganization be by amendment,[98] merger,[99] or voluntary agreement. If the plan comports with standards of equity and fairness, it should be sustained even though provision is made for modifying or eliminating preferred dividend claims.

At the time when the Delaware Supreme Court in the *Havender* case was doing an about face, by sanctioning the destruction of dividend priority rights of preferred stockholders, the United States Supreme Court decided *Case v. Los Angeles Lumber Products Company,*[100] with implications of an opposite character. In the latter case it was held that a plan of reorganization under Section 77B of the Bankruptcy Act, which permitted stockholders to share in the reorganization of a corporation insolvent in both the equity

---

preferred, but did not pass upon the question of damages otherwise, preferring first to permit the new corporation to admit the old stockholders on terms originally granted to others. 105 N. J. Eq. 621, 148 Atl. 36 (1930), aff'd 107 N. J. Eq. 528, 153 Atl. 402 (1931). In *Colgate v. U. S. Leather Co.,* 73 N. J. Eq. 72, 67 Atl. 657 (1907), reversed on grounds in no way affecting determination of this point, 75 N. J. Eq. 229, 72 Atl. 126 (1909), it was held preferred shareholders could not be compelled on consolidation to take less than accrued dividends; it was suggested an option should be given to accept the plan or retain previous rights. There was an available surplus. By statute New Jersey corporations are also authorized to fund or satisfy dividend arrearages by charter amendment. Two-thirds of the preferred stockholders must vote in favor of the change unless the certificate of incorporation provides otherwise. N. J. Rev. Stat. (1937), §14:11-1 (n), 3.

[97] See §69, n. 78, *supra.* For a refunding plan carried out by a sale of assets to a new corporation, see *United Milk Products Corp. v. Lovell,* 75 F. (2d) 923 (C. C. A. 6th, 1935), *cert. den.* 295 U. S. 751 (1935).

[98] *Haggard v. Lexington Utilities Co.,* 260 Ky. 261, 267, 84 S. W. (2d) 84 (1935); cf. *Davis v. Louisville Gas & Electric Co.,* 16 Del. Ch. 157, 142 Atl. 654 (1928); see *Patterson v. Durham Hosiery Mills,* 214 N. C. 806, 200 S. E. 906, 909 (1939); *Report of S. E. C. on Protective and Reorganization Committees,* Pt. VII, 519 (1938).

[99] *Federal United Corporation v. Havender,* 11 A. (2d) 331 (Del. 1940); cf. *Colgate v. U. S. Leather Co.,* 73 N. J. Eq. 72, 67 Atl. 657 (1907), n. 96, *supra.*

[100] 308 U. S. 106 (1939), discussed in Dodd, *The Los Angeles Lumber Products Company Case and Its Implications,* 53 Harv. L. Rev. 713 (1940).

and the bankruptcy sense, was not "fair and equitable," and that, since the capital of the stockholders had been lost, they were entitled to no participation in the reorganized corporation. As a result, creditors may exclude stockholders from sharing in plans for reorganization under 77B or Chapter X of the Chandler Act, if the corporation is insolvent and no new cash contribution is made by the stockholders. This rule of "absolute priority" as between creditors and stockholders will doubtless be extended as between preferred and common stockholders in bankruptcy proceedings. But capital readjustments as to dividends are effectuated in amendment and merger plans prior to bankruptcy. The only part played by a court occurs when a dissenter seeks an injunction. While the issue is different, any amendment or merger plan must at least pass the test of fairness and equity just as was true by statute in the *Los Angeles* case.

Ordinarily, when a plan to cancel or modify dividends is advanced, there will be a burdensome arrearage of dividends, but the common stock will still have some equity in corporate capital. Whatever principle of absolute priority the *Los Angeles* case may offer by analogy in stockholder reorganizations, it does not in this situation require exclusion of the common stock from the recapitalization. However, should the corporation's capital be impaired to an extent where the common capital is destroyed, it may well be argued that strict application of the theory of the *Los Angeles* case renders a plan giving common stockholders a participation unfair and inequitable. On the other hand, distinguishing differences exist. The right of the creditor to payment *vis à vis* stockholders is quite different from the claim of preferred stockholders to dividends and participation in corporate assets *vis à vis* common stockholders. As between creditor and stockholder, there is an obligation that the creditor be paid on maturity. As between preferred and common stockholder, there is no maturity date short of dissolution; both are venturers in the hope of future profit. The mere fact that presently the common capital may be impaired is not a conclusive demonstration that the common stock has no equity in any future recovery the corporation may make. There is nothing in the relation of preferred and common stockholder, such as that between creditor and corporation, to require a final reckoning of rights prior to a dissolution. To permit the common some interest in the amendment or merger recapitalization may not be in any way unfair. This will depend, it would seem, on the circumstances of the particular case. For example, if the current earnings of the corporation are largely in excess of the annual dividend requirements on the preferred, it would indicate that the common stock still has an equity even though its capital has been completely impaired. The Securities and Exchange Commission, in approving a public utility holding company simplification plan in the *Community Power and Light* case, allowed the common a continued participation where the facts were of this nature.[101]

70.1. Reorganizations under the Public Utility Holding Company Act

Section 6 of the Public Utility Holding Company Act of 1935 provides that no registered holding company or subsidiary shall exercise "any privilege or right to alter the priorities, preferences, voting power or other rights of the holders of an outstanding security of such company," unless after a declaration filed with the Securities and Exchange Commission has become effective.[102] By Section 7(e), the Commission is directed to permit a declaration affecting such priorities, preferences, and other rights to become effective, unless the Commission finds the plan "will result in an unfair or inequitable distribution of voting power among the holders of the securities of the declarant or is otherwise detrimental to the public interest or the interest of investors or consumers." [103] And Section 11(e) provides that the Commission shall not approve any

---

[101] Holding Company Act Releases Nos. 1803, 1804. However, in *In re Utilities Power & Light Corp.*, 29 F. Supp. 763 (D. Ill. 1939), it was held that a reorganization plan under 77B of a public utility, solvent in the bankruptcy sense, but having the capital of junior issues of stock entirely impaired, might exclude from participation all issues junior to the preferred stock. In this case, however, the preferred capital had itself been seriously impaired and there were preferred dividend arrearages equal to half the par value of the preferred. It would have been difficult in these circumstances to hold that the common had an equity entitled to representation in the plan. The court recognized this distinction: "If the corporation is solvent, but without a present equity for common stock, though with an equity for the preferred, and there is a reasonable probability of an appreciation of the value of the assets, the common stock should be given an interest properly subordinated. But where, as here, it appears certain that the holders of the A, B, and common stock have not the slightest equity in the assets of the debtor, nor will the earnings ever be sufficient to permit participation therein by the holders of the common stock, the plan need make no provision for such classes of stockholders" (p. 769). See comment on this case, Dodd, *The Los Angeles Lumber Products Case and Its Implications*, 53 Harv. L. Rev. 713, 744 (1940). Cf. *In re Chicago, G. W. R. Co.*, 29 F. Supp. 149 (D. Ill. 1939); *In re National Food Products Corp.*, 23 F. Supp. 979 (D. Md. 1938). See also §70.1, *infra*.

[102] 15 U. S. C. A., §79f(a). Generally on recapitalizations under the Public Utility Holding Company Act, see Meck and Cary, *Regulation of Corporate Finance and Management Under the Public Utility Holding Company Act*, 52 Harv. L. Rev. 216 (1938); Note, 52 Harv. L. Rev. 1331 (1939); Note, 49 Yale L. J. 1297 (1940).

[103] 15 U. S. C. A., §79g(e).

simplification plan submitted by a registered public utility holding company or subsidiary which is not "fair and equitable to the persons affected." [104]

Under these provisions the Securities and Exchange Commission is given broad power to adjust equitably the rights of respective classes of shareholders either on an ordinary plan of recapitalization or in cases of simplification. In authorizing the Columbia Gas and Electric Corporation to reduce its capital from $194,000,000 to $12,000,000, upon a declaration filed pursuant to Sections 7 and 6(a) of the act, the Commission conditioned its approval with a requirement that no dividends should thereafter be paid on common shares unless subsequent to the declaration there should remain, after making provision for all the existing dividend requirements of the preferred, sufficient earned surplus to pay six quarterly dividend installments on all classes of preferred stock outstanding.[105] The Commission, furthermore, reserved jurisdiction to enter such orders as might be necessary to effectuate this requirement.

In the early reorganization plan of International Paper and Power Company, an applicant for exemption from the provisions of the Holding Company Act, it appeared that the corporation had a deficit of $19,000,000, arrearages of $36,000,000 which at the rate of current earnings could not be eliminated so as to pay common dividends for almost twenty years, and the capital was impaired to such an extent that there was no liquidation equity for the last two classes of common stock.[106] The plan provided for eliminating accrued preferred dividends of $40 per share, in exchange for new preferred stock reduced in dividends from 7 per cent to 5 per cent plus one share of new common stock. The Commission, not having as yet passed upon the question of the corporation's exemption, permitted submission of the plan to stockholders, pointing out it was a "bargain" between common stockholders who were to receive some concessions and preferred stockholders, but not for that reason neces-

---

[104] 15 U. S. C. A., §79k(e). The plan must also be "necessary to effectuate the provisions of subsection (b)" of §11. Subsection (b) (2) makes it the duty of the Commission to require public utility holding companies and their subsidiaries to "take such steps as the Commission shall find necessary to ensure that the corporate structure or continued existence of any company in the holding company system does not unduly or unnecessarily complicate the structure . . . of such holding-company system . . ."

[105] Holding Company Act Release No. 1417 (1939). The recapitalization of public utility holding companies is a major financial problem. In 1939 there were at least 20 holding companies with consolidated assets aggregating $6,500,000,000 which required recapitalization. See Holding Company Act Release No. 1798, p. 1 (1939).

[106] Holding Company Act Release No. 671 (1937).

sarily unfair. Commissioner Healy dissented on the ground the Commission had no jurisdiction, and that, if it did, the plan was unfair to preferred stockholders.

The *International Paper and Power Company* case was one of the early decisions of the Commission and it probably would not take the same position on similar facts today. Two later cases are of considerable importance and furnish an interesting contrast to the *International* case. In *Utilities Power and Light Corporation,* the Commission, under Section 11(f) of the Public Utility Holding Company Act, passed upon the plan of reorganization of a holding company in 77B.[107] The assets of the corporation were less than its liabilities and preferred stock, so that two-thirds of the preferred capital and all the capital of junior issues of stock was impaired. The corporation was not able to meet its fixed charges, of which there were accumulated arrearages; there were likewise arrearages on the preferred stock equal to half the par value of the stock in that class. The reorganization plan approved by the Commission excluded the junior shareholders from any participation, on the theory that these interests had no equity. It was argued for the junior interests that, where a corporation is solvent in the bankruptcy sense, recognition should be given to all classes of securities even though the capital of such classes might on the basis of the corporation's balance sheet be impaired. In answer the Commission relied in large part on the provision in Section 77B, and continued in Chapter X, that acceptance of the plan need not be obtained from classes where adequate protection is given for realization of the "value of their equity, if any,"[108] arguing that where no equity exists no provision need be made for the class. Thus, prior to the Supreme Court's decision in the *Los Angeles* case, the Commission had already taken the position that in a bankruptcy reorganization junior stock interests might be eliminated under the rule of "absolute priority." The Commission was careful to indicate that it was excluding the junior stockholders because it was "certain" that they fell far short of having any kind of right.[109] The position of the

---

[107] Holding Company Act Release No. 1655 (1939); see comment on case, Dodd, *The Los Angeles Lumber Products Case and Its Implications,* 53 Harv. L. Rev. 713, 744 (1940). Section 11(f) provides: ". . . a reorganization plan for a registered holding company or any subsidiary company thereof shall not become effective unless such plan shall have been approved by the Commission after opportunity for hearing prior to its submission to the court."

[108] Holding Company Act Release No. 1655, p. 24.

[109] *Ibid.,* p. 26. In *Matter of Inland Power & Light Corp.,* Holding Company Act Release No. 2042 (1940), the Commission approved a plan under §11(f) excluding stockholders where assets were insufficient to meet claims of creditors.

Commission and the plan were approved by the District Court for submission to interested classes of security holders.[110]

The *Utilities Power and Light* case was a bankruptcy reorganization. However, if a solvent public utility holding company should propose a plan for funding arrearages by amendment or merger under Sections 6 and 7 of the Holding Company Act, the basic principle of the case would doubtless be followed. If the junior securities clearly and unmistakably are without equity, they will be excluded from the plan.[111]

An interesting contrast is furnished by the Commission's decision in *Community Power and Light Company,* where a plan of corporate simplification under Section 11(e) was passed upon.[112] Community, a Delaware corporation, filed with the Commission a plan for simplification alleging that its corporate structure was unduly and unnecessarily complicated. Accumulated arrears on its preferred stock amounted to $46 per share. Under the plan which, after approval by the Commission and a federal court, was to be consummated by amending the charter or by organization of a new corporation to take over the assets and assume the liabilities of the old corporation, the outstanding preferred and common stocks were to be exchanged for new common stock. Prior to the proposed recapitalization, the preferred capital was $6,900,000, that of the common $2,500,000. Under the plan the old preferred in exchange for its stock and dividend accruals would receive 95 per cent of the new common, and the old common the remaining 5 per cent. The plan was approved by the Commission.

As already stated under Section 11(e), it was necessary for the Commission in giving its approval to find (1) that under Section 11(b) the corporate structure of Community was of such a nature as to require steps (the language of the act is somewhat redundant) to insure that such structure did not unduly or unnecessarily complicate the corporate structure of the holding company, and (2) that the plan was "fair and equitable to the persons affected." [113] The Commission found that when certain asset revaluations and other questionable assets were removed from the

---

[110] *In re Utilities Power & Light Corp.,* 29 F. Supp. 763 (D. Ill. 1939).

[111] It is interesting in this regard to note that the *Amicus Curiae Brief* filed on behalf of the United States in the *Los Angeles* case took the position that the "absolute priority" rule should be sustained and was signed by General Counsel and assisting attorneys of the S. E. C.

[112] Holding Company Act Releases Nos. 1803, 1804 (1939); comment, 49 Yale L. J. 1297 (1940). The plan was confirmed, 33 F. Supp. 901 (S. D. N. Y. 1940).

[113] See n. 104, *supra.*

balance sheet, Community had $3,350,000 less in assets than the prior claims of preferred stockholders in liquidation preferences and accruals. It also found, however, that apart from the preferred accruals it had current earnings of $150,000 available for common ($400,000 if earnings of a subsidiary were consolidated) over and above $400,000 required to pay preferred dividends. The excess over the annual preferred requirements was, nevertheless, grossly inadequate to enable contemplating satisfaction of the accrued arrearages in any reasonable period of time. In these circumstances the Commission held Community's corporate structure to be unduly and unnecessarily complicated within the meaning of Section 11(b). On the issue of fairness and equity of the plan, it was held that the common stock was entitled to participate even though on a proper balance sheet it had no capital equity. The Commission relied largely on evidence of an interest in the common stock, as disclosed by earnings in excess of preferred requirements, which, after a period of years, would have discharged the accruals and placed the common stock on a dividend basis. Since the participation given to common stock was slight, it was held unnecessary to appraise its value with exactitude, the small 5 per cent allocation being reasonable under the circumstances. The Commission, therefore, allowed submission of the plan to stockholders for their approval.

The *Community Power and Light* case breaks important new ground: (1) It indicates the willingness of the Commission to approve a plan which, as one of its alternatives, would eliminate by charter amendments dividend arrearages that under the decisions in the *Keller* and *Consolidated* cases are "vested rights" not subject to modification pursuant to state law. It would seem that where the provisions of the Public Utility Holding Company Act require a simplification within the power of the Commission to prescribe, the question is one clearly of federal law and that the position of the Commission on this point is sound. (2) There may exist a difference as to the right of participation of common stock having no balance sheet equity between the case where the recapitalization is a plan of simplification under Section 11(e), and where it is merely a capital readjustment under Sections 6 and 7, or in a bankruptcy proceeding.[114] Thus, where it is shown in the case of simplification that there are earnings available for the common (apart from considering arrearages) over and above annual preferred dividend requirements, it is proper to give the common at least a small participating inter-

---

[114] See Dodd, *The Los Angeles Lumber Products Company Case and Its Implications,* 53 Harv. L. Rev. 713, 746–447, n. 81.

est.[115] (3) There is a tendency, in recapitalizations under the Public Utility Holding Company Act, to produce a simple stock structure composed entirely of common stock in substitution for previously outstanding preferred and common.[116]

70.2. Adequate Disclosure of Reorganization Plan

A subsidiary question, entitled to more careful consideration than is ordinarily given, relates to the information furnished to stockholders. The extra-judicial recapitalization is usually handled by charter amendments or mergers. For these changes stockholders' consent is normally necessary. This consent comes via the familiar proxy method. Since the common stock management is seeking a plan of recapitalization presumably for the greater benefit of the common stockholders, it is in a peculiarly delicate position in soliciting management proxy consents [117] for a plan which it has promulgated. If the plan leans in favor of the common stockholder through the aegis of management draftsmanship, the preferred stockholder should at least be told what it is that he is asked to approve. The situation under the old capitalization and under the new plan ought to be fairly presented.[118] An interesting case on the question of disclosure, because of different approaches made by the Securities and Exchange Commission and the Delaware Chancery Court, is the recapitalization plan of *Consolidated Film Industries, Inc.* The corporation proposed to amend its charter to eliminate arrearages of $5 per share on its cumulative preferred stock. The Commission took the

[115] ". . . for reorganization purposes earning power rather than the book value of assets is the best test of value." *Matter of Community Power & Light Co.*, Holding Company Act Release No. 1803, p. 10 (1939). There is evidence that other plans similar to that of Community are being promulgated where the 95–5 ratio of allotting the new common between old preferred and common stockholders is followed. See *Matter of Federal Water Service Corp.*, Holding Company Act Releases Nos. 1999, 2021 (1940).

[116] *Matter of Community Power & Light Co.*, Holding Company Act Release No. 1803, p. 11, n. 4; see also Public Utility Holding Company Act, §7c(1); *Matter of Federal Water Service Corp.*, Holding Company Act Releases Nos. 1999, 2021 (1940); Meck and Cary, *Regulation of Corporate Finance and Management under the Public Utility Holding Company Act of 1935*, 52 Harv. L. Rev. 216, 219 (1938).

[117] In each of 44 cases of recapitalization plans solicited under provisions of the Securities Exchange Act over a period of a year, proxies were asked on behalf of managements. Report of S. E. C. on Protective and Reorganization Committees, Pt. VII, p. 126 (1938).

[118] One of the conditions in extra-judicial reorganizations chiefly objected to in the survey of the Securities and Exchange Commission was the frequent failure of the management to make adequate disclosure either of the terms of the plan or its interest in junior securities. Report of S. E. C. on Protective and Reorganization Committees, Pt. VII, pp. 12–13, 135–148, 414–415 (1938).

position that there had been an inadequate disclosure in the notice of meeting, letter explaining the plan, and proxy.[119] When the corporation declined to furnish further information, the Commission proceeded to publish available data which it deemed would bear on the adequacy of the corporation's disclosures: (1) The president of the corporation, in his letter accompanying solicitation of proxies in support of the plan, had stated that the corporation had not been able to pay the quarterly dividends for a period of three years, whereas the Commission found that earnings in each year had been in excess of the dividend requirements and that the corporation had a sufficient earned surplus. The corporation stated to the Commission that business reasons had necessitated the use of earnings to provide working capital for current operations, but the Commission was of the opinion that if such were the case it should have been so indicated. (2) The corporation's analysis of the existing rights of the preferred as compared with rights under the plan was misleading in that it did not indicate advantages in distribution which the existing preferred possessed. The same questions as to inadequate disclosure were raised in the Delaware Chancery Court in a minority stockholder's suit to enjoin consummation of the plan.[120] The court took a position at variance with that of the Commission, being of the opinion that the facts had been truthfully stated and that there was no duty to state "the obvious consequences of those facts." [121] The Supreme Court of Delaware, in affirming a judgment of the Chancery Court invalidating the plan, made no reference to the question of disclosure.[122]

The most effective requirements for disclosure of reorganization plan details are those of the S. E. C. under Section 14(a) of the Securities Exchange Act of 1934. This section prohibits solicitation of proxies in respect of securities registered on national exchanges in contravention of rules and regulations of the Commission. Regulations promulgated under this section require that the proxy solicitation state the purpose and general effect of any amendment to the charter or by-laws and detailed information concerning any merger, consolidation, or plan involving the modification of any class of

---

[119] S. E. C. Release No. 903, Securities Exchange Act of 1934.

[120] *Johnson v. Consolidated Film Industries*, 194 Atl. 844 (1937).

[121] See also *Johnson v. Consolidated Film Industries, Inc.*, N. Y. Law J., Oct. 24, 1936, p. 1347; cf. *Cooper v. Central Alloy Steel Corp.*, 43 Ohio App. 455, 183 N. E. 439, 444 (1931) ; *United Milk Products Corp. v. Lovell*, 75 F. (2d) 923 (C. C. A. 6th, 1935), cert. den. 295 U. S. 751 (1935) (holding that failure to disclose to preferred stockholders the amount of common stock held by the directors promulgating the plan did not constitute fraud).

[122] *Consolidated Film Industries, Inc. v. Johnson*, 197 Atl. 489 (Del. 1937).

securities.[123] They require that any modification plan shall be described so as to show any material differences between the outstanding securities and the new securities, and the dividends in arrears, together with the effect of the plan thereon.[124] Similar statements as to dividend arrearages and treatment under plans of merger, consolidations, or sale of assets are required.[125]

D. Dividend Restrictions Imposed to Protect Liquidation Preferences

71. The Wasting Asset Doctrine as to Preferred Shareholders

As a rule, preferred stock is given a preference not only as to current dividends, but also upon liquidation or dissolution as to capital, and often accrued dividends. The normal rule that dividends cannot be paid directly from capital will serve to preserve the amount of capital necessary to satisfy the preferred priority claim to par or other fixed amount on liquidation,[126] with the possible exception of jurisdictions recognizing the wasting asset doctrine.[127] If in the case of mining, oil, and similar wasting asset corporations, dividends may be paid from receipts less the usual deductions, but without making any allowance for depletion from capital exhaustion, it is obvious that the corporation may distribute its capital by driblets in current dividends until a point may be reached where, if liquidation were to take place, there would be little or no capital out of which to pay the claim of preferred stockholders to a preference in capital.[128]

---

[123] Reg. X–14, Schedule A, Items 8, 10–11. See Note on these regulations, 53 Harv. L. Rev. 1165 (1940).

[124] *Id.*, Item 10(c)(d).

[125] *Id.*, Item 11(c)(3). Section 12(e) of the Public Utility Holding Company Act gives the Commission power to regulate proxies of companies subject to that act. Under this section the Commission has issued elaborate regulations governing proxy solicitations in reorganizations. See Rules U–12E–1 through U–12E–6. For a comprehensive statement by the S. E. C. as to the effect of a recapitalization plan subject to the Public Utilities Holding Company Act, see *Matter of Community Power & Light Co.*, Holding Company Act Release No. 1804 (1939).

[126] See Chapter 2, and particularly §15, *supra*. While the right of the preferred stockholder not to have dividends paid from capital may be legally clear, as a practical matter, the management, elected by the common stockholders, will often be in a position to adopt methods which indirectly violate this limitation to the prejudice of the preferred shareholders.

[127] For the doctrine as to creditors, see §44.3, *supra*.

[128] Generally see 1 Dodd and Baker, *Cases on Business Associations* (1940) 1102; Note, *Rights of Preferred Stockholders in Wasting Asset Corporations*, 12 Corn. L. Q. 79 (1926); Note, *Rights of Stockholders Preferred as to Capital to Safeguard Their Interests in a Corporation*, 75 U. of Pa. L. Rev. 350 (1927).

In *Wittenberg v. Federal Mining and Smelting Company,* the plaintiff was the holder of 7 per cent cumulative preferred par value stock entitled to payment of par upon dissolution plus unpaid dividends before payment of anything to the common stock.[129] The defendant corporation owned mines with a probable life of a few months to six years. Preferred dividends to date being paid, the corporation voted to pay a dividend of $10 a share to common stock out of the earnings of the current year, excluding, however, from deductions against these earnings any charge for depletion resulting from exhaustion of the mines. The balance sheet showed the assets to be so depleted that they were insufficient to pay preferred stock upon liquidation the par value thereof. The relief prayed was an injunction against payment of the proposed dividend to common, and against the payment of any other common dividends until the corporation should have completely made good the balance sheet deficit out of earnings, or, in the alternative, until a reserve had been set up equal to the difference between the value of the present assets and the par value of all outstanding preferred stock. The corporation's demurrer to the bill was overruled. The court held that a payment out of profits without deduction for ore depleted was a direct payment from capital, and therefore unauthorized by the Delaware statute and also at common law. Preferred stockholders had a right to maintenance of sufficient capital assets to pay their liquidation preferences. Answering the argument in favor of permitting the dividend, it said, under such a rule "all that a preferred stockholder, who has a senior charge on capital as well as dividends, is assured of from the corporation is a right to a series of dividends while the assets last and that the common stockholders may be paid all remaining proceeds from the sale of the transformed capital without any deduction of its value in the raw state. If this be true, such preferred stock of a wasting asset corporation as we are concerned with in the instant case is grossly misnamed. The common stock is the real preferred, for in the end it may receive not only so much of the capital as equals its par, but all there is in excess of its par, leaving possibly not so much as a crumb for its supposedly more favored companion." [180]

For the part of the S. E. C. in protecting the rights of preferred stockholders, see §§31, 70.1, *supra.*

[129] 15 Del. Ch. 147, 133 Atl. 48 (1926), aff'd 15 Del. Ch. 409, 138 Atl. 347 (1927).

[180] In *Mellon v. Mississippi Wire Glass Co.,* 77 N. J. Eq. 498, 78 Atl. 710 (Ct. Ch. 1910), a preferred stockholder's bill for a mandatory injunction, compelling a corporation whose principal assets were patents to establish a "deficiency fund"

In the *Wittenberg* cases as originally presented, the situation was such that the payment of the dividend would have impaired not merely the corporation's aggregate capital but the very amount of capital necessary to liquidate the preferences on the preferred stock.[131] This the court could hardly have been expected to permit. It was unnecessary, however, to determine what right preferred stockholders might have to object if only the capital of the common stock had been impaired. The two situations may be illustrated.

PREFERRED CAPITAL IMPAIRED

ASSETS		LIABILITIES	
Cash, etc.	$ 75,000	Capital:	
Deficit	(75,000)	Preferred stock	$100,000
		Common stock	50,000
	$150,000		$150,000

COMMON CAPITAL IMPAIRED

ASSETS		LIABILITIES	
Cash, etc.	$125,000	Capital:	
Deficit	(25,000)	Preferred stock	$100,000
		Common stock	50,000
	$150,000		$150,000

Assuming that, in the absence of applicable statutory provisions, the wasting asset doctrine is rejected where the rights of conflicting classes of stockholders are concerned, does the right of the preferred to prevent a reduction of capital by dividend payments without depletion extend to the cushion of common capital? Under the preferred stock provisions of most corporations, stipulating that upon dissolution or liquidation of assets preferred stockholders are entitled to prior payment, a strong case is made for enjoining a distribution of capital to common stockholders by the payment of wasting asset dividends. To permit such dividends means that the common

---

to redeem the preferred stock at par on dissolution, was dismissed on authority of *Lee v. Neuchatel Asphalte Co.*, L. R. 41 Ch. Div. 1 (1889). For the doubtful character of the *Lee* case as a precedent in American jurisdictions, see §44.3, *supra*.

[131] Prior to final hearing the Delaware law was amended to permit payment of wasting asset dividends, with a provision, however, that no dividends should be paid from net profits if capital required to satisfy liquidation preferences should be impaired by depletion. 35 Del. Laws, c. 85, §16. It appearing at the time of the final hearing that payment of the dividend would leave assets greater than the amount required to meet the liquidation preference on the preferred stock, the bill was dismissed. 15 Del. Ch. 351, 138 Atl. 352 (1927).

stockholders receive priority in distribution of capital assets in the face of an express provision that the preferred shall be paid first. This might result, with a market decline, in the preferred never receiving its full capital investment.[132]

The first *Wittenberg* cases raise another question. Assuming that preference stockholders having liquidation preferences may enjoin dividends when there are no current profits and the payment would directly impair either common or preferred capital, may they in the right of liquidation-preference-stockholders, as distinct from any statutory provisions, also prevent the payment of dividends from current profits when either common or preferred capital is impaired? In short, must the common stockholders make up out of subsequent earnings prior capital losses? This question vitally affects not only wasting asset corporations but corporations generally, since it would require the restoration of capital out of subsequent earnings whenever there was an impairment. While it may well be held that, as between preferred and common stockholders, dividends cannot be paid to the latter directly from the capital of the former, or even from common capital, it can hardly be urged that common stockholders, in the absence of statutes compelling maintenance of original balance sheet capital unimpaired,[133] should also act as replenishers of preferred capital lost in the business. Or go further and restore both preferred and common capital when both are impaired. But if, as in the first *Wittenberg* cases, the current net profits are computed under the wasting asset doctrine, they do directly impair capital to the extent of depleted capital which they include, and the preferred stockholder is in a position to object.

Finally, in the *Wittenberg* cases the stock had a dissolution preference, and the court distinguished *Lee v. Neuchatel Asphalte Company* on the ground that the preferred stock there involved had no such preference. The question remains, therefore, whether even as to such stock preferred stockholders can insist upon depletion reserves. The argument of the court in the *Wittenberg* cases for prohibiting the complete distribution of capital in dividends to common stockholders when there is a preferred dissolution preference, applies only in lesser degree where there is no such preference. With the preference, the preferred is entitled to be paid in full on dissolution before anything goes to common; without the preference, the preferred and common share equally on dissolution. If while the

---

[132] For the effect of the 1927 amendment on this question in Delaware, see §72, *infra.*

[133] See Chapter 2, *supra.*

corporation is a going concern its capital assets are distributed exclusively to the common stock by wasting asset dividends, there will be a proportionately smaller amount of capital in which the preferred can ultimately share.[134]

72. Modern Statutes

Protecting the preferred dissolution capital is the subject of legislation in some states. A few provide that the general wasting asset exception granted shall be subject to the "rights" of the shareholders of different classes.[135] Such a provision is obviously very general, but apparently it was intended in the draft of the Uniform Business Corporation Act, from which the proviso was taken by most of these states, to insure the retention of a sufficient amount of net profits to repay preferred shareholders as to principal.[136] In California,[137] Georgia,[138] and Minnesota,[139] if capital is impaired below the amount necessary to satisfy liquidation preferences, no dividends out of net profits may be paid on shares other than those having the liquidation preference until the impairment is made good. In Illinois, where shares of no par value have a preferential right as to capital on liquidation, the stated capital must be not less than the preferential right; and dividends may only be paid when there is an excess of net assets over stated capital.[140]

The Delaware provision in Section 34, added by amendment in 1927 as a result of the *Wittenberg* case, is particularly interesting.[141] The clause against impairment of capital necessary for liquidation preferences is entirely separate from the sentence which, without limitation, authorizes the payment of wasting asset dividends regardless of depletion. Both, however, came into the law at the same time, and the former must be considered in *pari materia* with the latter and a limitation thereon.

The language of these amendatory provisions is important. The

---

[134] For the possible restrictions against using paid-in surplus of one class of shareholders to pay dividends to another class, see §29.

[135] La. Gen. Stat. (Dart. 1939), §1106; Ohio Code Ann. (Baldwin 1938), §8623-38; 15 Purd. Pa. Stat. Ann., §2852-701; Wash. Rev. Stat. Ann. (Rem.), §3803-24.

[136] Draft of Uniform Business Corp. Act with Explanatory Notes (July 1928), p. 51.

[137] Cal. Civ. Code (1937), §346.

[138] Ga. Code Ann., §22-1835.

[139] Minn. Stat. (Mason 1938 Supp.), §7492-21.

[140] 32 Ill. Ann. Stat. (Smith-Hurd 1935), §§157.19, 41. The stated capital of par value shares is par, §157.19.

[141] Del. Rev. Code (1935), c. 65, §34; 35 Del. Laws, c. 85, §16. Kansas has a similar provision, Kans. Laws 1939, c. 152, §81.

general wasting asset clause authorizes directors to determine the corporation's "net profits" without considering depletion; the preferred stock clause prohibits the payment of dividends "out of such net profits" if preference capital is or will be impaired. The reference of both provisions to net profits is extremely significant in view of the double alternative provision in the same section for payment out of balance sheet surplus or net profits. This double provision in its present form was also a part of the 1927 amendment, so that again close correlation of the provisions is in order.

(a) How broad is the power in Delaware to declare wasting asset dividends where there are current net profits (not taking into account current depletion) but the *common* capital is impaired? The answer seems to be that such dividends may be paid. The general clause authorizes such payment; the preferred stock protection clause does not apply because there is still sufficient capital to meet the preferred liquidation requirements. This would seem to be the effect of the *Wittenberg* case decided after the Delaware amendments.[142] There the corporation had current earnings for the past year and apparently the current year, and there was a showing, not made in the first case because limited to the pleadings, that there would remain sufficient capital to pay liquidation requirements on the preferred. The dividend was sustained.

(b) How broad is the power to declare wasting asset dividends without taking into account depletion where there are current net profits but the *preferred* capital is impaired? This situation seems to be that explicitly covered by the statute. Although there are net profits to satisfy the general wasting asset clause, the preferred protection clause operates to make illegal the payment of dividends because of impairment of preferred capital.

(c) How broad is the power to declare wasting asset dividends where there are no net profits but, nevertheless, a balance sheet surplus if depletion reserves are not considered, but an impairment of *common* capital if such reserves are considered? The first *Wittenberg* cases did not have to consider the right to pay dividends out of profits of current years if only common capital was impaired. They did, however, reject the wasting asset doctrine in principle. The Delaware statute authorizes a dividend when there are no net profits only from a balance sheet surplus. The first *Wittenberg* cases seem to indicate, that in computing surplus, depletion cannot be disregarded. This third type of dividend is, therefore, prohibited not only on the peculiar ground of inter-stockholder rights, but also by

142 15 Del. Ch. 351, 138 Atl. 352 (Ct. Ch. 1927).

the general limitation against all dividends not out of surplus. This result seems to be supported by *Petroleum Rights Corporation v. Midland Royalty Corporation.*[143] That case turned on the right of preferred stockholders to elect a majority of the board of directors upon default in six quarterly dividend installments whenever "the surplus of the corporation applicable to the payment of dividends shall be insufficient to pay all accrued dividends." There is no reference in the opinion to presence or absence of current earnings. The court considered only the effect of depletion allowances upon the "surplus" available for dividends. After taking deductions for depletion of 27½ per cent in the amount of $172,000, as alternatively allowed for federal income taxes, the balance sheet did show a surplus of $230,000. This method of computing depletion the court denominated an arbitrary formula allowed by the Internal Revenue Bureau, but inapplicable for dividend purposes. It held, if properly computed, depletion should be taken in the amount of $758,000, converting the book surplus of $230,000 into an actual deficit. The right of the preferred shareholders to elect a majority of directors was, therefore, sustained. Surprisingly, the depletion question is treated by the court entirely on principle with no reference to any decisions or the clearly relevant provisions of Section 34. The "surplus" with which the court did deal, however, was a balance sheet surplus, and presumably is the legal balance sheet surplus referred to in Section 34.[144]

(*d*) How broad is the power to declare wasting asset dividends where there are no net profits, and a balance sheet surplus if depletion reserves are not considered, but an impairment of *preferred* capital if such reserves are considered? This situation seems only a projection of that last considered. If in the absence of current profits dividends cannot be paid without taking into account depletion when the result would be to impair common capital, such prohibition likewise obtains when the effect would be a further impairment, this time of preferred capital.

Assuming a rule which protects capital required to meet liquidation preferences of preferred stock, important questions arise with

[143] 167 Atl. 835 (Del. Ch. 1933).

[144] Although the facts of the *Petroleum Rights* case do not so disclose, it appears from financial information of the Midland Royalty Corporation that taking into account the amount of depletion held by the court to be necessary would have wiped out the common capital and impaired preferred capital. Moody's *Industrials* (1933) 1658–1659. The court in omitting mention of this fact apparently computed required surplus in the ordinary way as including both common and preferred capital. An impairment of common capital resulting from failure to take depletion reserves would therefore prevent existence of the necessary surplus.

respect to issuance of no-par value shares. Suppose a corporation issues its no-par shares having a liquidation preference right of $100 for an agreed consideration of $100. May the corporation treat some amount less than $100, say $20, as its stated capital and carry the balance of $80 to paid-in surplus? If this procedure is adopted, what so far as interrelation of preferred and common stockholders is concerned, is the "liquidation capital" which cannot be paid out in dividends, at least to common stockholders?[145] In some modern statutes, the problem is handled by requiring the corporation to treat as stated capital the amount of any liquidation preference which the preferred stock may have,[146] thereby preventing possible use of a portion of this amount for dividends. In most jurisdictions, however, no such provision is made. The amount required to pay liquidation preferences ought not to be distributed in common dividends, irrespective of its nominal designation on the balance sheet. Where there is a liquidation preference, even stronger reasons exist for prohibiting the use of preferred paid-in surplus for dividends to common than where the preferred has no such clause.[147]

73. Provisions to Protect Preferred Stockholders

A covenant by the corporation in its preferred stock issues (a) to maintain regular depletion reserves, or (b) to pay no dividends to common shareholders unless it shall have left after the dividend net assets equal to its preferred or common capital, or both, will give protection in the absence of insolvency.[148] Upon insolvency, of course, any reserves and the capital would first toward payment of corporate debts.

If it is felt advisable to preclude any question as to the right of preferred stockholders of wasting asset corporations to a fund for liquidating the par amount of their stock, a clause should be inserted in the articles or stock similar to a sinking fund provision in an indenture, requiring that a certain percentage of receipts be set

---

[145] For possible restrictions against the use of paid-in surplus, contributed by preferred shareholders not having liquidation preferences, to pay dividends on common, see §29, *supra*.

[146] See §45.1, n. 164.

[147] See §29, *supra*. The question will often have to be met even though no such dividend is in contemplation because the S. E. C. requires that, in the case of preferred stock with an involuntary liquidation preference significantly in excess of capital, an opinion of counsel must be furnished as to whether there are any restrictions on surplus with respect to the liquidation excess. S. E. C. Accounting Series Release No. 9, Dec. 23, 1938; see MacChesney, *The Security and Exchange Commission's Development of Accounting Standards*, 26 Cal. L. Rev. 349, 351–352 (1938).

[148] 1 Dodd and Baker, *Cases on Business Associations* (1940) 1104.

aside for the express purpose of meeting the liquidation requirements.[149] This provision will be good under any circumstances
against the common stockholders. As against creditors it will be
good in so far as the sinking fund is actually set up out of amounts
which would have been available for dividends. In the absence of
wasting asset statutes or a common law wasting asset doctrine,[150]
it will be subject to creditor attack, if on insolvency corporate assets
prove inadequate, and it is shown that the preferred stock sinking
fund was, in fact, established out of capital or at a time when the
corporation was insolvent. In *Ellsworth v. Lyons,* the attempt was
made to create a fund for redemption and retirement of preferred
stock by taking out an insurance policy on the life of a corporate
officer in face amount equal to that required to accomplish the redemption, and specified by the by-laws to be for that purpose only.[151]
The policy was made payable to the corporation. Premiums were
paid by the corporation at a time when it was not insolvent. After
insolvency the trustee in bankruptcy collected the cash surrender
value. The claim of the preferred stockholders to these proceeds
was denied, the court taking note that the title to the policy at the
time of bankruptcy was in the trustee. But it took the principal
position that preferred stockholders could not, in effect, be made
creditors with a right to priority payment; that they remained
stockholders and, therefore, must rank subordinately to creditors.
The case can be sustained on its facts, because the policy was an
asset of the corporation at the time of bankruptcy; it is difficult to
see how a lien on the fund could be created in favor of the preferred
shareholders so long as the corporation was the beneficiary. It is
the familiar problem of getting the security sufficiently out of the
control of the debtor (in this case the corporation is, of course, not
technically a debtor) to make it hold as against the claim of creditors
that the transfer is merely colorable and a fraud. In order to avoid
this aspect of the *Ellsworth* case in setting up a sinking fund for
preferred stockholders of wasting asset corporations, it is necessary
that the sinking fund be trusteed.[152]

[149] Some states handle this question by a provision that a corporation may create
a sinking fund out of net profits for the purchase, retirement or redemption of preferred stock. See e.g. N. J. Stat. (1937), §14:8–20.

[150] See §44.3, *supra.*

[151] 181 Fed. 55 (C. C. A. 6th, 1910).

[152] In *Tweedie Footwear Corp. v. Fonville,* 115 S. W. (2d) 421 (Tex. Civ. App.
1938), an insurance policy was taken out on the life of a corporate officer payable
to a trustee for the purpose of retiring preferred stock. Premiums were paid by
the corporation out of surplus while solvent. Over objection of a subsequent creditor
the proceeds were held to belong to the preferred stockholders after death of the
officer and insolvency of the corporation.

More difficult to dispose of is the second ground of the court's decision. The premiums were not paid at a time when the corporation was insolvent. The court condemned the entire proceeding as an effort to make a stockholder a creditor, without reference to controlling dividend statutes. If the security for meeting the preferred dissolution preference is set up out of funds which might have been legally distributed in dividends, it should not be subject to attack after insolvency. This would seem to permit the creation of sinking funds for preferred stock from wasting asset dividends without deduction of depletion in those jurisdictions accepting the wasting asset doctrine. In other jurisdictions permitting redemption of preferred stock out of capital, such a sinking fund, if properly created, would also seem good against creditor attack.

CHAPTER 7

REMEDIES AGAINST DIRECTORS WHO DECLARE ILLEGAL DIVIDENDS

A. Scope of Director Liability

74. Responsibility of the Director

When dividends have been declared from funds not legally available, under either common law doctrines [1] or statutory restrictions,[2] questions of liability for the violation are presented. There are two groups upon whom the liability may fall—the directors who hold office when the dividend is declared, or the stockholder recipients. It is a generally accepted principle of American corporate law today, for the most part under statutory sanction, that directors are liable for the illegal declaration of dividends. This was not always true. The circumstances attending introduction of the rule that directors shall be responsible are important. The 1697 Amendment Act to the charter of the Bank of England, one of the very first statutory provisions imposing liability for illegal dividends, made recipient stockholders rather than directors liable to the Bank's creditors.[3] The explanation for American statutes and cases which now make directors rather than stockholders principally liable is in large part historical. The first American special charters to impose liability on directors [4] copied their provisions from an analogous clause in the charter of the Bank of United States making directors responsible for incurring corporate debts in excess of the Bank's capital.[5] The latter clause had itself been taken from the 1694 Act authorizing the Crown to charter the Bank of England,[6] but in the copying, Alexander Hamilton substituted directors' liability for that of stockholders as originally provided in the Act of Parliament.[7]

Since the present-day doctrine of directors' liability is a substitute for what was originally the liability of stockholders, and

---

[1] See §§14, 15, *supra*.
[2] See §§16–30, 33–34, *supra*.
[3] 8 and 9 Will. III, c. 20, §49.
[4] See §6, notes 45, 46, 47, *supra*.
[5] 1 Stat. 191, §7–IX.
[6] 5 and 6 William and Mary, c. 20, §26.
[7] See §6, *supra*.

developed more or less fortuitously from excess liability provisions, it becomes important to re-examine its fundamental basis.

75. Common Law Liability

It is one question whether funds are legally available for dividend declaration in the first instance; it is quite another matter whether either directors or stockholders should be held liable where illegal distribution is actually made.[8] The arguments in favor of placing the primary responsibility as a matter of principle on the stockholder who receives all the material benefit of the dividend are readily apparent. The historical shift of that responsibility to directors, which first found expression in statutes, was accepted by the courts on broad principles of director responsibility for general corporate management. The general doctrine that directors owe certain duties of care in the supervision and management of corporate funds and property offered a ready basis for imposing liability on directors who, as part of their managerial duties, transgressed rules against distribution of corporate funds and property by payment of dividends.

Common law decisions and statutes have established a rule in many jurisdictions that dividends may not be paid when the corporation is insolvent, or when through the payment it is rendered insolvent.[9] In analogy to cases holding directors responsible for general management of corporate assets, it is not surprising to find some indication that, even in the absence of a statute imposing personal liability, directors may be held liable for dividends declared when the corporation is insolvent.[10] The majority of cases, however, deal with common law liability for payment out of capital. Again consistent with principles concerning the general duty of care in management of corporate affairs, directors, in the absence of statu-

---

[8] Generally see 1 Dodd and Baker, *Cases on Business Organizations* (1940), Note, 1164; Annotations, *Right or Duty of Corporation to Pay Dividends; and Liability for Wrongful Payment,* 55 A. L. R. 8, 73; 76 A. L. R. 885, 892; 109 A. L. R. 1381, 1388.

[9] See §§19–20, *supra.*

[10] *Branch v. Kaiser,* 291 Pa. 543, 140 Atl. 498 (1928) (comment, 28 Col. L. Rev. 662) (statute prohibited payment of dividends from anything except net profits "so that the capital stock shall never be impaired thereby," but contained no provision with respect to liability of directors, Pa. Laws 1913, p. 336) ; *Jesson v. Noyes,* 245 Fed. 46 (C. C. A. 9th, 1917), *cert. den.* 245 U. S. 667 (statute relied upon in alternative) ; *Montgomery v. Whitehead,* 40 Colo. 320, 90 Pac. 509 (1907). In *Hutchinson v. Stadler,* 85 App. Div. 424, 83 N. Y. S. 509 (1st Dept. 1903), it was held that in the absence of statute a director is not liable to the corporation for a distribution out of capital, so long as the payment of the dividend does not impair the power of the corporation to discharge its indebtedness.

tory provisions, are not held liable if in declaring the dividend they have acted in good faith and with due care.[11] Of course, if a dividend is wilfully and intentionally paid from capital, the director is liable.[12] And likewise if the payment is negligently made.[13] In *Cornell v. Seddinger*, directors declared a dividend at a time when the corporation's capital was badly impaired and when it had no profits.[14] In so doing they relied upon the face of the treasurer's reports showing profits without making further investigation. In-

[11] *Excelsior Petroleum Co. v. Lacey*, 63 N. Y. 422 (1875) (directors had acted in good faith; negligence had not been put in issue); *Chick v. Fuller*, 114 Fed. 22 (C. C. A. 7th, 1902), *cert. den.* 187 U. S. 640 (1902) (directors not liable at common law or under statute for negligence when they had no sufficient means to put them on notice that affairs of the company were not being properly managed); *Blythe v. Enslen*, 209 Ala. 96, 95 So. 479 (1923); *Dovey v. Cory*, (1901) A. C. 477 (branch offices sent in reports containing bad debts which it was the duty of the general manager to examine, making a report to directors; the reports, which would have taken a couple of days to examine, were submitted to the board with the general manager's statement upon which defendant relied in approving the dividend; defendant not negligent in failing to examine all reports); *Stringer's Case*, L. R. 4 Ch. App. 475 (1869) (managing director not liable for dividend received where in valuation of assets there was "absence of any fraudulent intent as against the shareholders, or as against the creditors or the public"); see *E. L. Moore & Co. v. Murchison*, 226 Fed. 679, 681 (C. C. A. 4th, 1915); *Quintal v. Greenstein*, 142 Misc. 854, 859, 256 N. Y. S. 462 (1932), aff'd 236 A. D. 719, 257 N. Y. S. 1034 (1st Dept. 1932). If the statute makes illegal certain types of dividends, but imposes no specific liability on directors, the latter are not liable for its violation if they act with due care and in good faith. *Williams v. Spensley*, 251 Fed. 58 (C. C. A. 7th, 1917) (under National Banking Act); *Witters v. Sowles*, 31 Fed. 1 (D. Vt. 1887) (same; directors had no knowledge of illegality); cf. Dewing, *Corporation Securities* (1934) 73.

[12] *Cochran v. Shetler*, 286 Pa. 226, 133 Atl. 232 (1926) (complaint alleged directors of a Delaware corporation had "wilfully and negligently" paid dividend from capital; court said if dividend is result of "an honest error or mistake of judgment no responsibility attaches" but this is a question of fact); *E. L. Moore & Co. v. Murchison*, 226 Fed. 679 (C. C. A. 4th, 1915) (where directors know or ought to know dividends have not been earned they are liable; directors who were officers and agents having entire management and control of operations held liable where accounts carried at face value turned out to be worth only a quarter of that amount); *Johnson v. Nevins*, 87 Misc. 430, 432, 150 N. Y. S. 828 (1914) (but liability is only for benefit of creditors); see Lord Halsbury in *Dovey v. Cory*, (1901) A. C. 477, 482; 1 Dodd and Baker, *Cases on Business Associations* (1940), Note, 1052–1053.

[13] *Fell v. Pitts*, 263 Pa. 314, 106 Atl. 574 (1919) (no discussion of the Pennsylvania statute; the report states the corporation's "liabilities greatly exceeded its assets"); *Loan Society v. Eavenson*, 248 Pa. 407, 94 Atl. 121 (1915) (Delaware corporation, but no reference to Delaware or Pennsylvania statutes); see *Spiegel v. Beacon Participations*, 8 N. E. (2d) 895, 912 (Mass. 1937) (but no recovery allowed where corporation not insolvent or unable to pay creditors); *City Investing Co. v. Gerken*, 121 Misc. 763, 764, 202 N. Y. S. 41 (1923); *Stratton v. Bertles*, 238 App. Div. 87, 90, 263 N. Y. S. 466 (1st Dept. 1933); *Southern California Home Builders v. Young*, 45 Cal. App. 679, 691, 188 Pac. 586 (1920); *Lexington & Ohio R. R. Co. v. Bridges*, 7 B. Mon. 556, 557–558 (1847); Douglas and Shanks, *Cases and Materials on Business Units—Losses, Liabilities and Assets* (1932), Note, 207.

[14] 237 Pa. 389, 85 Atl. 446 (1912).

quiry into the make-up of the items would have disclosed a capital impairment. The corporation was organized under the Pennsylvania Act of 1874 in which the only provision imposing personal liability upon directors did so as to dividends declared "when the company is insolvent or the payment of which would render it insolvent." [15] The court mentioned the corporation's organization under the Act of 1874, but made no mention of this dividend provision. The directors were held liable for negligently declaring the dividend in reliance on the reports, apparently on the theory of a common law liability for paying dividends directly from capital. "Directors can hardly be regarded as discharging their duty, and protecting the trust imposed upon them, when they accept a report which upon its face calls for explanation and analysis, and after a glance at it, to see that it purports to show profits, proceed without further investigation to declare dividends." "It is admitted that two of the directors had personal knowledge of the real condition of the company, and after a careful examination of the evidence, we cannot avoid the conclusion that the other directors might, by the exercise of common prudence, have readily ascertained the worthless character of much that was carried upon the reports of the treasurer as assets." It is significant that the dividend was one directly from capital, not merely a dividend paid at a time when the balance sheet showed a capital impairment. Stated somewhat differently, the case is not authority for the proposition that a corporation having current profits may not distribute the same in dividends if its balance sheet shows an impaired capital. The case merely imposes liability upon directors, in accordance with the established common law rule as to funds available,[16] when the distribution is necessarily a distribution of capital.

Under Section 60 of the New York General Corporation Law, an action may be brought against one or more directors to compel them to account for their official conduct, including any neglect or failure to perform their duties in the management and disposition of funds and property of the corporation.[17] Apparently under this provision, liability is not limited to payment out of capital, but in-

---

[15] Pa. Laws 1874, p. 73, §39(5). This provision applied to manufacturing corporations. Whether the corporation was organized as a manufacturing corporation, or as a shipping or commerce corporation under other provisions of the chapter, is not stated in the opinion.

[16] See §15, *supra*.

[17] *Source:* N. Y. Rev. Stat. (1828), Pt. 3, c. 8, Title 4, Art. 2, §33; Code of Civ. Proc., §1781; N. Y. Laws 1907, c. 157; N. Y. Consol. Laws (1909), c. 28, §90; N. Y. Laws 1929, c. 650, §1(60).

cludes waste of any and all assets even out of surplus. But to show that there is liability for payment out of surplus, it is necessary to allege that creditors were in existence at the time of the unlawful act and that they are still creditors, or that under the provisions applicable to fraudulent transfers the depletion was fraudulent as against subsequent creditors.[18]

76. Statutory Liability

Statutes expressly imposing personal liability on directors for illegal dividend declarations are the principal source of such liability.[19] These statutes in the main fall into four general categories. The older type imposes liability on the directors holding office at the time of the declaration, with provisions exonerating directors who are absent or dissent. The second class makes directors voting for or assenting to the dividend liable. The third class imposes liability on directors who wilfully or negligently participate in the declaration. The last class exonerates directors who act in good faith.

76.1. Exoneration of Directors Who Are Absent or Dissent

The New York Act of 1825, patterning its director liability clause after the Hamiltonian excess liability provision in the first Bank of United States charter, provided that directors under whose administration illegal dividends were declared, except those absent or dissenting, should be jointly and severally liable to the corporation and to its creditors in event of dissolution for full amount of capital paid out.[20] This was substantially the provision of Section 58 of the New York Stock Corporation Law until the amendment of 1939.[21] It is still the effective rule in a number of states.[22]

[18] Cf. *New Credit Men's Assoc. v. Harris*, 170 Misc. 988 (1939) (purchase of stock out of surplus).

[19] It has been said that the remedy against directors for illegal dividends provided by statute is exclusive. *Childs v. Adams*, 43 Pa. Super. 239 (1910).

[20] See §7, n. 62, *supra*. Generally see Note, *Statutory Responsibility of Directors for Payment of Dividends out of Capital*, 35 Yale L. J. 870 (1926).

[21] N. Y. Laws 1939, c. 364. For the earlier form see §21, n. 94, *supra*.

[22] Mont. Rev. Code (1935), §5939 (that the exceptions are to be exclusive may be emphasized by their parenthetical placement after the provision for liability of directors in whose administration the dividend is declared) ; N. Mex. Stat. (1929), §32–135 (if absent dissent must be entered on minutes of directors after director receives notice and such dissent must be published) ; N. C. Code (1939), §1179 (similar provision except publication not required) ; N. Dak. Comp. L. 1913 (Supp. 1913–25), §4544; Okla. Stat. Ann., §18–106; S. Dak. Code (1939), §11.0706. Cf. W. Va. Code (1937), §3090 (members present liable unless they dissent and enter on books). For source of these provisions, see §§22, 23, *supra*. Although dividends paid from improper funds may subject directors to a criminal penalty, they are only held civilly liable in Connecticut where the declaration renders the corporation in-

Some modern statutes, such as the recent revision in Pennsylvania, still follow the basic provision for liability of directors in whose administration the illegal dividend is paid.[23]

Balance sheets and income statements upon which directors declare dividends, it is quite generally recognized, are in large part the result of individual judgment. Whose function and responsibility is it to exercise this judgment? Is it the function of the corporation's accounting officers, its controller, and the independent accountants who audit the books, or is it the function of the directors? Can it be said that it is the exclusive function of one group or the other? The directors are the corporation's representatives empowered by law with the declaration of its dividends. Certain penalties for illegal declaration fall on them. They have a responsibility in the matter. But how far does that responsibility extend? Apart from absence or dissent, are directors who act prudently and in good faith absolutely liable for dividends which in fact turn out to be illegal? The majority of cases construing statutes which mention only absence or dissent as grounds of exoneration hold these exoneration exceptions to be exclusive, barring the director from showing the dividend was declared without negligence and in good faith.[24] Of

---

solvent. Conn. Gen. Stat. (1930), §3386. Alabama, while prescribing limitations upon the funds from which dividends may be paid, fails to provide any statutory liability on the part of either directors or stockholders. Ala. Code (1928), §6991. Even under a provision exonerating directors "not present when such action was taken," attendance at a subsequent directors' meeting at which directors are advised of the declaration and payment and approve the same makes a director liable. *City Investing Co. v. Gerken,* 121 Misc. 763, 202 N. Y. S. 41 (1923); *Walker v. Man,* 142 Misc. 277, 253 N. Y. S. 458 (1931) (not clear director was absent at time of declaration; court said it was immaterial if he later ratified action or accepted dividends); but cf. *Hutchinson v. Curtiss,* 45 Misc. 484, 491, 92 N. Y. S. 70 (1904).

[23] 15 Purd. Pa. Stat. Ann., §2852–707 (if absent written objection must be filed with secretary upon learning of the dividend).

[24] *Quintal v. Greenstein,* 142 Misc. 854, 256 N. Y. S. 462 (1932), aff'd without opinion 236 App. Div. 719, 257 N. Y. S. 1034 (1932) (comment, 32 Col. L. Rev. 905) (neither good faith nor due care a defense); *Irving Trust Co. v. Allen,* 244 App. Div. 788, 280 N. Y. S. 965 (1st Dept. 1935) (affirming memorandum opinion of the Special Term under New York Stock Corporation Law, §114, holding that a Delaware corporation doing business in New York must comply with §58); *Wesp v. Muckle,* 136 App. Div. 241, 120 N. Y. S. 976 (4th Dept. 1910), aff'd 201 N. Y. 527, 94 N. E. 1100 (1911) (mere lack of knowledge of corporate condition no defense; director has a duty to ascertain whether there are earnings sufficient for the dividend; see dictum to this same effect as to a bank organized under the monied corporation provisions of the Revised Statutes, *Gaffney v. Colvill,* 6 Hill 567, 576 (1844)); *Southern California Home Builders v. Young,* 45 Cal. App. 679, 188 Pac. 586 (1920); see *Siegman v. Electric Vehicle Co.,* 72 N. J. Eq. 403, 408, 65 Atl. 910 (Ct. Err. & App. 1907); but cf. *Siegman v. Electric Vehicle Co.,* 140 Fed. 117, 121 (D. N. J. 1905); *Gallagher v. New York Dock Co.,* 19 N. Y. S. (2d) 789, 801 (1940) (necessary to show that directors through negligence or mistake failed to

course, directors who fraudulently declare a dividend, when they know that there actually are no funds available for that purpose, are liable.[25] And there is something to be said historically for the argument that statutes of this general class were intended to exclude at least the defense of mere good faith. The earliest Pennsylvania charters imposing liability upon directors for declaring dividends illegally, did so upon the condition that the declaration be wilfully and knowingly made. Later Pennsylvania special charters and the general New York Act of 1825 omitted this provision.[26]

But when it comes to imposing an absolute liability upon directors, making them liable even though they act within the standards of care imposed upon the "ordinary prudent man" of the law, serious objection must be raised. The legal categories in which one is held liable without fault are very limited. It serves no useful purpose to require directors to declare dividends at their peril. It cannot make them more careful, because such a rule operates without reference to the attention, deliberation, or care of the director. The director who, with care and fidelity, uses his best judgment in declaring a dividend, is held liable to the same extent as the dishonest director who knowingly dissipates the corporate capital. The effect of the absolute liability rule is to mulct innocent directors. Making a director a guarantor is peculiarly harsh when his determinations must necessarily be based almost wholly on the work of other people, the corporation's accountants.

The last and principal stronghold of absolute director liability fell with the recent amendment of Section 58 of the New York Stock Corporation Law, giving a defense to directors who sustain the burden of proof that they had reasonable grounds to believe, and did believe, that the dividend would not impair the corporation's capital.[27] The statutory history in Connecticut unfortunately points

make deductions in value of assets carried at cost) ; *Kahle v. Mount Vernon Trust Co.*, N. Y. L. J., Sept. 9, 1940, p. 569.

[25] *Union Discount Co. v. MacRobert*, 134 Misc. 107, 234 N. Y. S. 529 (1929).

[26] See §§6, 7, n. 51, 55, 60, 62, *supra*. In *Southern California Home Builders v. Young*, 45 Cal. App. 679, 695, 188 Pac. 586 (1920), the court said: "If that defense (good faith) could ever be considered, it would be where the pleadings clearly and in detail show the facts of fraud and dishonesty practiced upon the directors, and further show facts from which the conclusion would follow irresistibly that the directors could not have guarded against such fraud." Cf. *Scott's Executor v. Young*, 231 Ky. 577, 21 S. W. (2d) 994 (1929), and action by a stockholder under a statute imposing liability for debts upon directors who "declare and pay" an illegal dividend.

[27] N. Y. Laws 1939, c. 364. The act does not affect accrued causes of action. While Pennsylvania in its recent enactment adopts absence and dissent provisions (n. 23, *supra*), it would seem that the general provision in §2852–408 that directors

toward absolute liability. In predecessor provisions to the present dividend section, directors were only rendered liable for knowingly or negligently making declarations in violation of the statute.[28] By amendment in 1901, the prerequisite of knowledge or negligence was dropped from the statute and has remained absent since.[29] The basis for arguing absolute liability is strengthened in New Hampshire by the technical alignment of the statute. One section provides generally, if any corporation declares an illegal dividend, the directors shall be liable for corporate debts to the extent of the dividend.[30] Provisions exempting directors who are absent or dissent are left to a separate and succeeding section.[31]

76.2. Voting for, or Assenting to, an Illegal Dividend

The original Massachusetts provisions prohibiting dividends when insolvent imposed liability upon directors who "shall declare and pay" such dividends.[32] Kentucky and Oregon still have a provision of this character imposing liability for declaration and payment.[33] In other states directors who "assent" to the declaration of an illegal dividend are liable.[34] The present Massachusetts section contains a peculiar provision with respect to director liability. It is first provided that directors shall be liable for declaring and assenting to an illegal dividend, seeming to indicate participation, or at least subsequent assent, is a prerequisite to liability. There then follows a clause providing that directors who vote against declaring the dividend shall not be liable, seeming to indicate that a director who is absent and therefore does not vote against the dividend might be liable.[35] The Massachusetts statutory history shows, however, that the first part of the section is older, and that the subsequent clause must have been added to give more protection to directors rather than to extend their liability.[36]

Under statutes such as these making directors who assent liable,

---

should discharge their positions in good faith and with due care might make available these additional defenses.

[28] Conn. Pub. Laws 1836–37, c. 63, §20; Conn. Pub. Acts 1867, c. 120, §1.

[29] Conn. Pub. Acts 1901, c. 157, §33.

[30] N. H. Public Laws (1926), c. 225, §80.

[31] §81.

[32] See §8, n. 71, *supra*.

[33] Carroll's Ky. Stat. Ann. (1936), §548; Ore. Code Ann. (1930), §25–219.

[34] Colo. Stat. Ann. (1935), c. 41, §34; Iowa Code (1935), §8378 (all directors or agents knowingly consenting thereto); Miss. Code Ann. (1930), §4190 (directors who assent or declare).

[35] Mass. Laws Ann., c. 156, §37.

[36] The modern form of requiring declaration or consent was added by Mass. Acts and Resolves 1862, c. 218, §1; the clause exonerating those voting against the dividend by Mass. Acts and Resolves 1903, c. 437, §35.

and possibly also where the liability is imposed on directors declaring the dividend, no liability attaches for an illegal declaration if the directors act in good faith and without negligence.[37]

76.3. Wilful or Negligent Violations

The majority of states only impose liability upon directors wilfully or negligently participating in illegal dividend declarations.[38] Directors who do not have reason to believe there are sufficient net profits are made liable by the Wisconsin statute.[39] Michigan has a provision commendable for its precision. In determining what is earned surplus, the judgment of the board of directors shall be conclusive, unless it shall be shown that the directors acted in bad faith or were grossly negligent.[40]

When, within the meaning of these statutes, can a dividend be

[37] *Chick v. Fuller,* 114 Fed. 22 (C. C. A. 7th, 1902), *cert. den.* 187 U. S. 640 (1902) (under Illinois statute, now superseded); *White-Wilson-Drew Co. v. Lyon-Ratcliff Co.,* 268 Fed. 525 (C. C. A. 7th, 1920) ("assenting thereto means a conscious approval of facts actually known"); *Childs v. Adams,* 43 Pa. Super. 239 (1910) (good faith a defense even though directors are inefficient and careless); *Lippitt v. Ashley,* 89 Conn. 451, 94 Atl. 995 (1915) (assent requires actual knowledge or negligence); but cf. *Rorke v. Thomas,* 56 N. Y. 559 (1874) (acting in good faith no defense under New York Manufacturing Act of 1848 making directors who "declare and pay" illegal dividends liable, N. Y. Laws 1848, c. 40, §13). In *Cunningham v. Shellman,* 164 Ky. 584, 175 S. W. 1045 (1915), a director was held liable under a statute allowing recovery from directors who shall "declare and pay" illegal dividends, even though he was not present, because he accepted the dividend declared, thereby approving it. *Accord: Calkins v. Wire Hardware Co.,* 267 Mass. 52, 165 N. E. 889 (1929) (under statute creating liability "for declaring or assenting").

[38] Ark. Stat. (1937), §2184 (in case of wilful or negligent payment from capital directors in whose administration the same takes place, except absentees and dissenters who record their dissent); Cal. Civ. Code (1937), §363 (similar provision, except dissent need not be entered where absent); Del. Rev. Code (1935), c. 65, §35 (this provision was added by amendment in 1911, 26 Del. Laws, c. 188, §1); Idaho Code Ann., §29-130 (directors who knowingly or without reasonable inquiry vote in favor); Kans. Laws 1939, c. 152, §85 (similar to Arkansas provision); La. Gen. Stat. (Dart. 1939), §1107 (directors who knowingly or without exercising the care of ordinary prudent men in like positions vote in favor); Md. Ann. Code (1935 Supp.), c. 23, §87 (voting for or assenting to knowingly or without making reasonable inquiry; but a dividend in accordance with good accounting practice is not deemed to be out of capital); Minn. Stat. (Mason 1938 Supp.), §7492-22; Nev. Comp. L. (Hillyer 1929), §1674; N. J. Stat. (1937), §14:8-19; Ohio Code Ann. (Baldwin 1938), §8623-123b; R. I. Gen. Stat. (1938), c. 116, §41; Tenn. Code Ann. (1934), §3759; Vt. Pub. Laws (1933), §§5850, 5853 (no liability for dividends in good faith and with such care as might reasonably be expected of a person in his office); Wash. Rev. Stat. Ann. (Rem.), §3803-25; Wyo. Rev. Stat. (1931), §28-131. For the source of these provisions, see §§21, 22, 23, *supra.* For the New York amendment of 1939, see §76.1, n. 27, *supra.*

[39] Wis. Stat. (1937), §182.19. *Source:* Wis. Rev. (1878), §1765.

[40] Mich. Stat. Ann. (Henderson 1937), §21.22. It is not clear why the judgment of directors should not be accorded the same effect where the payment is made from net earnings, the other alternative specified in the statute.

called wilfully in violation of the statutory prohibition? Will anything less than actual knowledge that the dividend is illegal suffice? If the circumstances present are such that the director should have known of the illegality, proof of actual knowledge is not necessary.[41]

Of more importance is the question, What constitutes negligence? The director who casually attends meetings is not given preferred consideration. Thus, in *Fell v. Pitts,* a director of six years' standing, who chanced to attend during this period only the meeting at which the illegal dividend was declared, was held liable.[42] He had no knowledge of, and did not investigate, the corporation's ability to pay the dividend. In *Cornell v. Seddinger,* the Pennsylvania Supreme Court likewise refused to treat more leniently the purely business directors of the board of a ship building corporation who were not personally familiar with the processes of construction in the industry.[43] The negligence, however, was failure to note that a treasurer's report carried at the amount expended in production certain vessels which the corporation was obligated to deliver to the purchaser at a price $180,000 less than the cost of construction. The question of negligence did not, therefore, rest upon any technical knowledge of the corporation's business. It would be surprising if for purposes of dividends all directors of a corporation were held to the same standard of knowledge concerning its technical processes.

Most frequently questions of negligence in dividend declaration will concern the right of directors to rely on the work, advice, or reports of others. In modern enterprise, the fund available as an accounting matter is determined entirely by the corporation's accountants and lawyers.[44] The director, unless he is himself an accountant or lawyer, is left to rely upon their determination as to whether the corporation has funds legally available; his independent determination is actually made only on the business question whether

[41] *Hodde v. Nobbe,* 204 Mo. App. 109, 221 S. W. 130 (1920) (under Missouri statute creating liability for "knowingly" violating the act); *Franklin v. Caldwell,* 123 Ky. 528, 96 S. W. 605 (1906) (statute created liability for "knowingly" violating act; "that which they ought, by proper diligence, to have known, they will be presumed to have known").

[42] 263 Pa. 314, 106 Atl. 574 (1919) (question determined in absence of statute).

[43] 237 Pa. 389, 85 Atl. 446 (1912) (no reliance on statute).

[44] In *Stratton v. Anderson,* 278 Mich. 499, 270 N. W. 764 (1936), directors of a Delaware corporation who declared dividends in reliance on the statement of counsel that a sale of franchises would result in a profit legally available for dividends were held not to have violated the prohibition against wilful and negligent dividends contained in §35. Reliance on the advice was said to show both good faith and lack of negligence. But where good faith and due care are not generally recognized as defenses, relying on advice of counsel is not a defense. *Southern California Home Builders v. Young,* 45 Cal. App. 679, 188 Pac. 586 (1920).

the corporation should make a distribution from the fund he has been told is legally available. To be sure, the ultimate responsibility for distribution rests under the statute with the director. But, if without negligence directors delegate to proper officials the duty of drawing up the accounts and rely on properly authorized audits of the same in making their distribution, there can be very little room for calling such reliance on purely accounting questions negligence.[45] But the standard of supervision set down in the cases, particularly with respect to banks and moneyed corporations, is on the whole strict. The tendency toward a high standard of care for banking directors is demonstrated by *Lippitt v. Ashley*.[46] Over a period of 39 years directors declared dividends, relying on falsified books of the treasurer which the directors failed to examine, nor did they require trial balances as was the banking custom; but the books were audited throughout this period and examined by the bank examiner who failed to apprehend the falsifications. The audit apparently did not purport to be a finding as to whether the books were correctly kept. The reliance of the directors on the books of the treasurer, and the reports of the auditors and bank examiner, without further investigation, was held to constitute negligence.[47] In *Guaranty Trust*

---

[45] In *Chick v. Fuller*, 114 Fed. 22 (C. C. A. 7th, 1902), cert. den. 187 U. S. 640 (1902), there was held to be no negligence by directors in failing to go back of what appeared on the books where (1) the president and his co-conspirators failed to enter all purchases, so liabilities were understated; (2) the president brought in fictitious accounts receivable for goods sold of which directors had no knowledge; and (3) there was gross overvaluation of assets purchased from promoters which the directors could not have reasonably discovered. Similarly, in *Gallagher v. New York Dock Co.*, 19 N. Y. S. (2d) 789 (1940), it was held that directors who in good faith relied upon the judgment and advice of accountants as to valuation of assets and correctness of income were not liable for dividends which exceeded annual net earnings. See *Dovey v. Cory*, (1901) A. C. 477, §75, n. 11, *supra*. But in *Fell v. Pitts*, 263 Pa. 314, 106 Atl. 574 (1919), a director was held negligent in declaring a dividend on the perfunctory statement of the president indicating net income, when the corporation's liabilities in fact exceeded assets and the dividend impaired capital. Directors at the same meeting authorized the borrowing of $5,000 to meet current expenses. Where due care is not recognized as a defense, reliance upon books of account is, of course, not a defense either. *Quintal v. Greenstein*, 142 Misc. 854, 256 N. Y. S. 462 (1932), aff'd 236 A. D. 719, 257 N. Y. S. 1034 (1st Dept. 1932); *Southern California Home Builders v. Young*, 45 Cal. App. 679, 188 Pac. 586 (1920).

[46] 89 Conn. 451, 94 Atl. 995 (1915).

[47] In *Cunningham v. Shellman*, 164 Ky. 584, 175 S. W. 1045 (1915), directors relied entirely on the bank's cashier, checking neither the assets nor accounts. There were no false entries in the books which fully disclosed the bank's condition, and the slightest inspection would have shown the cashier to be overdrawn and that loans were being made to insolvent people. The directors were held liable. Cf. *Cabaniss v. State*, 8 Ga. App. 129, 68 S. E. 849 (1910) (director who controlled bank and was cashier and president many years could not rely on books of subordinates showing insolvent debts).

Company v. Grand Rapids, Grand Haven and Muskegan Railway Company, an interurban railway company's books failed to show any allowance for external obsolescence which had taken place. In holding the dividend illegal and recoverable from stockholders, the decision of the District Court, which was affirmed by opinion on appeal, stated, "If theoretical accounting fails to record obvious facts, the duty of the board of directors in considering declaration of dividends is not performed unless such facts are given due weight and consideration." [48]

The problem of relying on books and audits is so important that it is handled in some states by a special statutory provision. In 1929, Section 34 of the Delaware General Corporation Law was amended to provide that directors relying in good faith on the books of account or statements of the corporation prepared by any of its officials as to the value and amount of assets, liabilities, and net profits available for dividends should be fully protected. [49] Similar provisions have been adopted by other states. [50] Protection is given in Illinois and Tennessee if the statements are represented by corporate officers to be correct. [51] Presentation to a meeting of directors by the corporate officer in question should be deemed a compliance with this requirement. Maryland in 1931 enacted a provision that surplus or net profits determined in accordance with good accounting practice should not be deemed to diminish the capital stock in violation of the statute. [52] There is considerable to be said in favor of such a provision. It is very difficult to enact specific accounting rules to be followed in all cases for determination of the fund available for dividends. What may be highly improper for most corporations in most situations may be the only rule to apply to other corporations in certain specific situations. Since the actual computation of the fund is a specialized accounting question as to which the lawyer and

---

[48] 7 F. Supp. 511, 523 (W. D. Mich. 1931), §22.1, n. 127, *supra.*

[49] 36 Del. Laws, c. 135, §16.

[50] Ark. Stat. (1937), §2183; Cal. Civ. Code (1937), §363 (protection given also if balance sheet or profit and loss statement is certified to be correct by accountants selected with reasonable care); Ga. Code Ann., §22–1835; Kans. Laws 1939, c. 152, §86; Minn. Stat. (Mason 1938 Supp.), §7492–22 (similar to California provision); Nev. Comp. L. (Hillyer 1929), §1625.

[51] 32 Ill. Ann. Stat. (Smith-Hurd 1935), §157.42; Tenn. Code Ann. (1934), §3759.

[52] Md. Ann. Code (1935 Supp.), c. 23, §87; Md. Laws 1931, c. 480. The section also makes directors liable for payment of dividends while insolvent. The failure to make good accounting practice conclusive as to insolvency, as well, was apparently an oversight. Ohio provides a director shall not be negligent if he considered assets at their book value, nor if in any case he followed what he believed in good faith to be sound accounting and business practice. Ohio Code Ann. (Baldwin 1938), §8623–123b.

the director are almost wholly dependent upon the expert work of qualified accountants, it is doubtful that more should be done in the way of statutory legal regulation than blocking out general boundaries of the fund from which a dividend is to be permitted.

Statutes of the Delaware type fully protecting directors who rely in good faith upon the books of account as to the amount of assets and liabilities and funds generally available for dividends, raise the question as to whether good faith has become practically the sole criterion of liability in spite of other provisions in the statute creating liability for negligence.[53] Almost every negligent director will be negligent with respect to some item of assets, liabilities, or fund available for dividends appearing on a corporate financial statement. Yet his mere negligence in examining these statements does not suffice to impose liability. If he acts on these statements in good faith, he is, on the contrary, immune. It should be noted that the duty incumbent on a director, who is excused merely upon showing good faith, is considerably less stringent than that applied in most jurisdictions to directors' management of other corporate affairs. In most jurisdictions, general liability results from failure to exercise due care of one standard or another. Because of the necessity that corporate officials rely almost entirely on assurance of accountants and corporate bookkeeping officials, this seeming liberality toward directors is not only justified, but quite clearly the most workable rule. The director is being called upon to pass judgment upon the highly specialized conclusions of accounting experts. Relying upon accounting conclusions should not constitute negligence in the absence of a reasonably clear showing of facts tantamount to stigmatizing the reliance as bad faith.[54]

76.4. Exoneration for Declaration in Good Faith

In a few jurisdictions, the good faith rule applied as to reliance on corporate accounts is extended to declaration of dividends generally. These statutes provide that directors who knowingly declare a dividend in violation of their provisions are to be liable.[55]

[53] Many states imposing liability on directors who wilfully or negligently declare dividends, also provide a defense for relying on financial statements in good faith. See this section, n. 38, 49, 50, 52, *supra*.

[54] In *Stratton v. Anderson*, 278 Mich. 499, 270 N. W. 764 (1936), the executive committee voted to adjust the books and on this basis the president reported affairs to be in satisfactory condition when in fact there was a loss. A director who had no knowledge of the adjustment was held to have acted in good faith under §34 of the Delaware Act.

[55] Ind. Stat. Ann. (Burns 1933), §25–251 (knowingly and wilfully declaring or assenting to payment); Iowa Code (1935), §8378; Mo. Stat. Ann., §§4569, 2942; Va. Code (1936), §3840.

77. Stockholder Ratification of Illegal Dividends

On the theory that dividends paid in express violation of statute are completely *ultra vires*, and not merely an irregularity in the exercise by directors of a granted power, it is held that ratification by stockholders is wholly ineffective to validate the dividend.[56] It requires no extended argument to justify this result where the statute gives a remedy to creditors which is being enforced for their benefit. The remedy would be meaningless if all that were necessary to protect directors in illegally dissipating corporate capital were the approval of those receiving the spoils.[57]

78. Effect of No Recourse Provisions

Corporate bonds and mortgages frequently contain clauses purporting to exculpate directors, and sometimes stockholders, from liability to bondholders in respect of the corporate indebtedness. In *Small v. Sullivan,* such a clause provided that no recourse under any bond should be had against any director by enforcement of any assessment or by any legal or equitable proceeding or otherwise.[58] The complaint of a bondholder against directors alleged a fraudulent scheme of consolidation in order to reduce the corporation's capital, and make it available for dividends, in violation of the New York statute. A defense of good faith action under the no-recourse clause was held bad, since it added nothing to a denial of the allegation of fraud in the complaint. The no-recourse clause "did not and could not cover future fraudulent acts of the directors." [59]

79. Time as of Which Illegality Is Determined

Where a statute prohibits the declaration of dividends when the corporation is insolvent, or out of capital, the question as to whether

---

[56] *Siegman v. Electric Vehicle Co.,* 72 N. J. Eq. 403, 65 Atl. 910 (1907) (prior dividend from capital ratified in good faith by over 99 per cent of the stockholders and a new board of directors); *Siegman v. Electric Vehicle Co.,* 140 Fed. 117 (D. N. J. 1905); *Grant v. Ross,* 100 Ky. 44, 37 S. W. 263 (1896); *Flitcroft's Case,* L. R. 21 Ch. Div. 519 (Ct. App. 1882); see *Whitfield v. Kern,* 122 N. J. Eq. 332, 344, 192 Atl. 48 (Ct. Err. & App. 1937).

[57] A quite different problem is presented where the recovery is for the benefit of a solvent corporation whose shareholders will then in effect receive the benefit of a double dividend, the first from the property of the corporation, the second from the pockets of directors. This problem is an aspect of the general right of a solvent corporation to recover illegal dividends from directors, discussed *infra* §83.

[58] 245 N. Y. 343, 157 N. E. 261 (1927).

[59] A no-recourse clause cannot be asserted by a stockholder having knowledge the dividend is bad. *Abercrombie v. United Light & Power Co.,* 7 F. Supp. 530 (D. Md. 1934).

or not the corporation is insolvent, or its capital impaired, is deter-mined as of the time of the dividend, and the subsequent failure of the corporation in no way affects this issue.[60] No liability results under an insolvency provision, if at the time of declaration the corpo-ration was solvent, even though but for the payment insolvency might not subsequently have occurred.[61] But a large shrinkage in net assets from supposed book value in a relatively short period is evidence that funds were not legally available when the dividend was declared.[62] Under the Illinois Act, the time liability becomes fixed is the time of payment of the dividend and not declaration. If the cor-poration is insolvent then or its assets are insufficient, the directors are liable.[63]

A question of present importance is determination of funds avail-able for dividends by corporations subject to the hazards of war. Shipping companies may lose their ships, shippers may lose their cargoes, the solvency of credits extended to belligerent nations or their nationals may be entirely contingent on the outcome of the war. In such and similar circumstances, may assets subject to war con-tingencies be the basis for war-time dividends, or must the corpo-ration, knowing the inherent dangers, defer payment of dividends until its termination? The question was directly passed upon in *Stringer's Case.*[64] There a blockade running company, incorporated

---

[60] *Miller v. Bradish,* 69 Iowa 278, 28 N. W. 594 (1886) ; *Hofkin v. U. S. Smelting Co.,* 266 Fed. 679 (C. C. A. 3d, 1920) ; *Vogtman v. Merchants Mtg. & Credit Co.,* 20 Del. Ch. 364, 178 Atl. 99 (1935) (bill to establish default in payment of preferred dividends) ; *Gallagher v. New York Dock Co.,* 19 N. Y. S. (2d) 789 (1940). In *Brown Seed Co. v. Brown,* 240 Mich. 569, 215 N. W. 772 (1927), an action against a director-stockholder of a seed company doing a seasonal business, seeds were sold and profits made showing a surplus on June 30, but the last half-year there were losses. The court said the deficit which was certain to come in succeeding months must be considered. Cf. *In re Bay Ridge Inn,* 98 F. (2d) 85 (C. C. A. 2d, 1938) (a chattel mortgage issued without consideration to stock-holders was treated as a secretive dividend; at execution, if considered valid, it con-stituted an impairment of capital under New York Stock Corporation Law, §58; after bankruptcy if sought to be enforced it had the same effect; court said, if not bad as to stockholders initially, the subsequent payment sought would violate §58).

[61] *Miller v. Bradish,* 69 Iowa 278, 28 N. W. 594 (1886) ; *Ellis v. French Canadian Cooperative Assoc.,* 189 Mass. 566, 76 N. E. 207 (1905) ; *Hofkin v. U. S. Smelting Co.,* 266 Fed. 679 (C. C. A. 3d, 1920) ; cf. *Greene v. Boardman,* 143 Misc. 201, 203–204, 256 N. Y. S. 340 (1932), aff'd 240 App. Div. 745, 265 N. Y. S. 965 (1933) (dictum that under N. Y. Stock Corp. Law, §58, imposing liability for "any loss sustained by such corporation or by its creditors," loss does not mean conse-quential loss, such as insolvency resulting from a dividend which impairs capital).

[62] *Wesp v. Muckle,* 136 App. Div. 241, 120 N. Y. S. 976 (4th Dept. 1910), aff'd 201 N. Y. 527, 94 N. E. 1100 (1911) (shrinkage of net assets from $70,000 to $9,000 in six months rendering corporation insolvent).

[63] 32 Ill. Stat. Ann. (Smith-Hurd 1935), §157.42(a, b).

[64] L. R. 4 Ch. App. 475 (1869).

for purposes of trade with the Confederate States, was authorized by the Companies Act of 1862[65] and its articles to pay dividends only from "profits." Among assets included in a balance sheet, on the basis of which dividends were declared in 1864, were cotton in the Confederate States and obligations of the Confederate government to the company, all of which became total losses at the close of the war. The Vice-Chancellor took the view that since the war was such that it must reasonably end within one to three years, the company could not determine whether or not profits had been earned until that time. The Court of Appeal held that, since the company had non-fraudulently placed a fair valuation on these assets as of the time the dividend was declared, the balance shown as profits was legally available for distribution, and not subject to recovery from a recipient after the company's failure. It must be observed that the court was undoubtedly influenced by the fact that the balance sheet, disclosing all the facts, had, prior to the declaration of the dividend, been submitted to the principal creditor, a bank, which in fact advanced the money necessary to pay the dividend. It is to be noted also that the case was decided in the absence of any statutory or charter provision against paying dividends from capital. The balance sheet, however, was the actual test applied in determining profits available, just as would be true under a capital impairment statute, and the court assumed this to be the proper test.

What is the effect of a recoupment of assets which removes a capital impairment existing at the time the dividend was declared? In *Dykman v. Keeney,* a receiver, seeking to hold a director liable for illegal dividends, contended a large amount in notes should have been classed as a loss and, as such, not available for dividends.[66] The defendant argued that many of the notes which the receiver classed as losses had been paid to the bank shortly after the dividend was declared. The evidence was held relevant on the ground that directors were only obligated to make good losses actually sustained, and not to account for merely having violated the statute.[67]

---

[65] 25 and 26 Vict., c. 89, Table A, Rule 73.

[66] 10 App. Div. 610, 42 N. Y. S. 488 (2d Dept. 1896); second trial 16 App. Div. 131, 45 N. Y. S. 137, aff'd on opinion below 160 N. Y. 677, 54 N. E. 1090 (1899).

[67] But where a director has declared illegal dividends, accrued profits made under a new management cannot be credited in his favor. *Hutchinson v. Curtiss,* 45 Misc. 484, 492, 92 N. Y. S. 70 (1904). Col. Stat. Ann. (1935), c. 41, §34, makes directors liable for declaring and paying dividends when insolvent or out of capital to the extent of "all debts of such corporation then existing, and for all that shall thereafter be contracted while the capital remains so diminished." Cf. 32 Ill. Stat. Ann. (Smith-Hurd 1935), §157.42, n. 63, *supra.*

80. Recovery in States Other than Corporation's Domicil

It is generally recognized that courts will not exercise visitorial power over corporations chartered by another state; nor will they interfere with the management by directors and officers of corporations organized under the laws of a foreign jurisdiction. However, it is not an interference with internal management, as the latter is interpreted, to compel directors of a foreign corporation to account for losses sustained from their action as directors.[68] An action against directors in the foreign jurisdiction necessitates an investigation of acts of prior management, but it in no way regulates the present conduct of corporate affairs. Considerations of policy abundantly support this result. If jurisdiction were denied in foreign states, redress would be lost against directors residing outside the state of the corporation's domicil, unless, by chance, they should enter the state of incorporation. With present-day corporations organized very largely in states other than those in which they do business, to refuse jurisdiction in such other states, particularly the state in which the corporation is doing its business, would be quite untenable.[69] Of course, whether or not directors have been guilty of declaring an illegal dividend will normally be governed by the law of the corporation's domicil.[70]

81. Measure of Damages

In the absence of an amount fixed by statute, it is doubtful that directors are liable for dividends violating common law or statutory rules beyond the amount of the illegal distribution.[71] Almost all statutes imposing liability on directors for illegal declaration specify

[68] *Loan Society v. Eavenson,* 241 Pa. 65, 88 Atl. 295 (1913) [for fact dividend problems were involved, see 248 Pa. 407, 94 Atl. 121 (1915)]; *Stratton v. Bertles,* 238 App. Div. 87, 263 N. Y. S. 466 (1st Dept. 1933); *Hutchinson v. Curtiss,* 45 Misc. 484, 92 N. Y. S. 70 (1904); cf. *Edwards v. Schillinger,* 245 Ill. 231, 91 N. E. 1048 (1910) (jurisdiction sustained against stockholders of foreign corporation).

[69] Statutes imposing liability on directors for illegal dividends are not penal. *Stratton v. Bertles,* 238 App. Div. 87, 263 N. Y. S. 466 (1st Dept. 1933) (Delaware Gen. Corp. Law, §35 creating liability "to the full amount of the dividend"); *Greene v. Boardman,* 143 Misc. 201, 256 N. Y. S. 340 (1932), aff'd 240 App. Div. 745, 265 N. Y. S. 965 (1933) (N. Y. Stock Corporation Law, §58); but cf. *Rorke v. Thomas,* 56 N. Y. 559 (1874) (calling "highly penal" the New York Manufacturing Act of 1848, c. 40, §13, making directors liable for "all the debts of the company then existing, and for all that shall thereafter be contracted, while they shall respectively continue in office"). It has been said that statutory provisions making directors liable even if not considered to be penal, do impose a liability like that of a surety, and must be strictly construed. *White-Wilson-Drew Co. v. Lyon-Ratcliff Co.,* 268 Fed. 525 (C. C. A. 7th, 1920).

[70] See Chapter 10, *infra.*

[71] See *Lexington & Ohio R. R. Co. v. Bridges,* 7 B. Mon. 556, 562 (Ky. 1847).

the extent of recovery. Such statutes are of three types. The first creates liability for the amount distributed in violation of the statute; the second for debts and liabilities of the corporation; and the third for the amount of loss to either the corporation, creditors, or stockholders.

81.1. Amount of Illegal Dividend

The oldest statutory rule of damages in actions against directors for declaration of illegal dividends goes back to the New York act of 1825. The latter made directors liable for the amount of the illegal dividend, specifically, "to the full amount of the capital stock of the company so divided, withdrawn, paid out or reduced." [72] In many modern statutes the damages clause limits recovery to the amount of the illegal dividend; most provisions of this character survive in practically the form of the earlier New York act.[73] Under statutes of this character, courts accept the amount of the dividend as the measure of liability.[74] Illinois draws a distinction as to whether or not the corporation is insolvent or its capital impaired.[75] If either condition exists at the time of the dividend, directors are liable for the full amount. If either condition is produced by the dividend, then directors are only liable to the extent the corporation is rendered insolvent or capital is impaired.

81.2. Amount of Corporate Debts and Liabilities

The Massachusetts Revised Statutes of 1836 made directors liable for all corporate debts, but with the proviso that such liability should not exceed the amount of the dividend.[76] When New York used the

[72] N. Y. Laws 1825, c. 325, §2. See §7, n. 62, *supra.* For derivation of the provision in the Act of 1825 from earlier special charters, see §6, *supra.*

[73] Conn. Gen. Stat. (1930), §3386 (if dividend renders corporation insolvent directors are liable for "the amount so paid or distributed"); Del. Rev. Code (1935), c. 65, §35 (full amount of dividend unlawfully paid with interest); Idaho Code Ann., §29–130; Ind. Stat. Ann. (Burns 1933), §25–211; Kans. Laws 1939. c. 152, §85 (similar to Delaware); La. Gen. Stat. (Dart. 1939), §1107; Mich. Stat. Ann. (Henderson 1937), §21.48; Minn. Stat. (Mason 1938 Supp.), §7492–22; Miss. Code Ann. (1930), §4149; Mont. Rev. Code (1935), §5939; N. Mex. Stat. (1929), §32–135 (also interest); N. C. Code (1939), §1179; N. D. Comp. L. 1913 (Supp. 1913–25), §4544; Ohio Code Ann. (Baldwin 1938), §8623–123b (with 6 per cent interest); Okla. Stat. Ann., §18–106; 15 Purd. Pa. Stat. Ann., §2852–707; R. I. Gen. Laws (1938), c. 116, §41; S. D. Code (1939), §11.0706; Va. Code (1936), §3840; Vt. Pub. Laws (1933), §5850; Wash. Rev. Stat. Ann. (Rem.), §3803–25. For source of these provisions see §§21, 22, *supra.*

[74] *Hutchinson v. Curtiss,* 45 Misc. 484, 92 N. Y. S. 70 (1904); *Southern California Home Builders v. Young,* 45 Cal. App. 679, 188 Pac. 586 (1920).

[75] 32 Ill. Ann. Stat. (Smith-Hurd 1935), §157.42.

[76] Mass. Rev. Stat. 1836, c. 38, §23. See §8, n. 71, *supra.*

Massachusetts provision as the basis for its Manufacturing Act of 1848, it continued the liability for all corporate debts but dropped the limiting proviso.[77] As a result, directors became in effect penally liable,[78] not for loss to creditors, but merely because an illegal dividend had been declared. This result is unfortunately perpetuated in states which copied the dividend provisions of the New York Act of 1848.[79]

Under the present Massachusetts provision, directors are liable for the debts and contracts of the corporation to the extent of the dividend only.[80] This is likewise still the rule in New Hampshire.[81]

81.3. Amount of Loss

Prior to 1901, the New York Stock Corporation Law had provided that directors should be liable to the corporation and its creditors "to the full amount of the capital, so divided, withdrawn, paid out or reduced." [82] This provision was amended in 1901 to its present form making directors liable "to the full amount of any loss sustained by such corporation or its creditors respectively by reason of such withdrawal, division or reduction." [83] Arkansas,[84] New Jersey,[85] Nevada,[86] and Tennessee [87] likewise have statutes containing provisions for recovery from directors of "any loss" sustained by reason of the withdrawal.

[77] N. Y. Laws 1848, c. 40, §13.
[78] *Rorke v. Thomas,* 56 N. Y. 559 (1874).
[79] Colo. Stat. Ann. (1935), c. 41, §34; Ky. Stat. Ann. (Carroll 1936), §548; Md. Ann. Code (1935 Supp.), c. 23, §87 (as amended, Md. Laws 1931, c. 480 to limit such liability to debts existing at the time of declaration and payment); Mo. Stat. Ann., §4942 (but compare the provision in §4569 which was originally copied from Mass. Rev. Stat. of 1836 and limits liability for debts to an amount not in excess of the dividend); Wyo. Rev. Stat. (1931), §28–131. For source of these provisions see §§19, 23, *supra.* For a case under this type of provision see *Cunningham v. Shellman,* 164 Ky. 584, 175 S. W. 1045 (1915). Cf. Ore. Code Ann. (1930), §25–219 (for debts existing or incurred while directors remain in office to extent of dividend); W. Va. Code (1937), §3090 (liable both for amount of dividend and all existing corporate debts); Wis. Stat. (1937), §182.19 (amount of creditors' claims).
[80] Mass. Laws Ann., c. 156, §37.
[81] N. H. Pub. Laws (1926), c. 225, §80. *Source:* N. H. Laws, June Sess. 1837, c. 322, §21 (taken from Mass. Rev. Stat. (1836), c. 38, §23); N. H. Laws, June Sess. 1846, c. 321, §2(4).
[82] N. Y. Laws 1892, c. 688, §21.
[83] N. Y. Laws 1901, c. 354, §23.
[84] Ark. Stat. (1937), §2184 (full amount of dividend or loss sustained thereby).
[85] N. J. Rev. Stat. (1937), §14:8–19 (to stockholders severally and respectively for full amount of any loss sustained by them or in case of insolvency, to the corporation or its receiver to the full amount of any loss sustained by the corporation).
[86] Nev. Comp. L. (Hillyer 1929), §1674 (by amendment, Nev. Stat. 1925, c. 177, §75; to the full amount of the dividend or any loss sustained thereby).
[87] Tenn. Code Ann. (1934), §3759 (similar provision).

Do these provisions extend possible liability beyond the amount of the dividend, or do they have a limiting effect only, so as to restrict recovery to an amount less than the dividend if the loss suffered is in fact not as great as the dividend? The cases dealing with this question treat loss clauses as restricting rather than extending liability. In *Cox v. Leahy,* for example, the court held that the loss sustained was "the amount that the dividend paid exceeded the surplus profits of the corporation at the time" and not the amount of the dividend.[88] Following the implication of these decisions, it probably does not include consequential loss such as insolvency resulting from a dividend which impairs capital.[89] The possibility otherwise of personal liability in huge sums, where directors may have only declared a relatively small dividend, should favor such construction. In the absence of more explicit language to indicate that loss is intended to extend beyond the dividend itself, construction may well limit maximum recovery to the amount of the dividend.[90] But where the action is brought in New York under Section 58, it is not a complete defense that the dividend leaves sufficient assets to pay creditors; the corporation itself suffers damage by the impairment of capital and has an independent cause of action.[91]

82. Criminal Liability

In quite a number of jurisdictions, directors who participate in the declaration of illegal dividends are made criminally liable. The

[88] 209 App. Div. 313, 204 N. Y. S. 741 (3d Dept. 1924). *Accord: Irving Trust Co. v. Gunder,* 152 Misc. 83, 102, 271 N. Y. S. 795 (1934); *Shaw v. Ansaldi Co.,* 178 App. Div. 589, 165 N. Y. S. 872 (1st Dept. 1917); see *Stratton v. Bertles,* 238 App. Div. 87, 89–90, 263 N. Y. S. 466 (1st Dept. 1933) (§58 makes directors liable "for illegally declared dividends only to the extent that the corporation can show a loss"); *Dykman v. Keeney,* 10 A. D. 610, 42 N. Y. S. 488 (2d Dept. 1896); second trial 16 App. Div. 131, 45 N. Y. S. 137, aff'd on opinion below 160 N. Y. 677, 54 N. E. 1090 (1899) (where the statute contains no provision making directors responsible for illegal dividends, they are not liable to the extent of the dividend but only for the ultimate loss resulting from the distribution).

[89] See *Greene v. Boardman,* 143 Misc. 201, 203–204 (1932). In *Hofkin v. U. S. Smelting Co.,* 266 Fed. 679 (C. C. A. 3d, 1920), decided under a statute of the early Massachusetts type making directors liable for dividends when insolvent or which would render the corporation insolvent, the court used two tests in holding directors were not liable: (1) Did the dividend after payment leave the corporation insolvent? (2) Assuming it did not, was the ultimate insolvency caused by loss of assets used to pay the dividend or by other supervening factors?

[90] In *Cox v. Leahy,* 209 App. Div. 313, 204 N. Y. S. 741 (3d Dept. 1924), it was held that interest on the amount of impaired capital was properly recoverable as an item of loss.

[91] *Irving Trust Co. v. Gunder,* 234 App. Div. 252, 254 N. Y. S. 630 (1st Dept. 1932) (action by trustee in bankruptcy of Delaware corporation). Generally on the right of a solvent corporation to recover, see §83, *supra.*

New York Penal Law makes directors guilty of a misdemeanor who concur in any vote or act by which a dividend other than from surplus, or which reduces capital, is paid. A director present at the meeting is deemed to concur therein unless he dissents; if absent, he is deemed to concur if the facts appear on the minutes of the board and he remains a director for six months without causing his dissent to be entered on the minutes.[92] Amendment of these provisions has not kept pace with amendments to the civil liability provisions of Stock Corporation Law Section 58, with the result that directors cannot safely take advantage of the 1939 amendment which relieves from civil liability where directors have reasonable ground to believe, and do believe, that the dividend does not impair capital.[93] Criminal liability still attaches to any concurrence in an illegal dividend.

In other states directors who vote for, concur in, or assent to, illegal dividends are made criminally liable.[94] The Illinois provision makes directors voting for, or assenting to, the declaration of illegal dividends guilty of a conspiracy.[95] The clause which gives exoneration for acting in good faith on accounting statements and asset valuations is not made specifically applicable to criminal proceedings. This omission may be due to insertion of the criminal clause by the legislature itself rather than the committee which drafted the act.[96]

B. Parties Entitled to Enforce Liability

83. The Corporation: Effect of Solvency or Insolvency

The right of a solvent corporation to recover from directors dividends illegally paid may be asserted on two grounds. Irrespective of

[92] N. Y. Penal Law, §§664, 667, as amended N. Y. Laws 1939, c. 185, §13. Section 667 provides it is no defense that the corporation is a foreign corporation if it carries on business and keeps an office in the state. Utah has a provision similar to §664. Utah Rev. Stat. (1933), §103-12-4.

[93] N. Y. Laws 1939, c. 364, §76.1, n. 27, supra.

[94] Ariz. Rev. Code (1928), §4804 (misdemeanor); Conn. Gen. Stat. (1930), §3386 (fine of $500); Iowa Code (1939), §§8377, 8378; Me. Rev. Stat. (1930), c. 56, §37 (fine not exceeding $2,000 and imprisonment not exceeding one year); Minn. Stat. (Mason 1927), §7489 (declaring, when profits are insufficient to pay the same, a felony, subject to fine not exceeding $5,000 and imprisonment not exceeding three years); S. C. Code 1932, §1353 (criminal code) (fine and imprisonment); Tex. Stat. (Vern. 1936) Penal Code, §1083a (fine not exceeding $1,000 and imprisonment not exceeding two years); Vt. Pub. Laws (1933), §5850 (fine and imprisonment for knowing violation; source: Vt. Laws 1910, No. 143, §8; see recommendation for amendment, Report of Commission to Investigate Certain Corporation Laws, Oct. 5, 1910, pp. 23, 38).

[95] 32 Ill. Ann. Stat. (Smith-Hurd 1935), §157.42(h). The provision purports to impose liability irrespective of good faith and diligence. See Reviser's comment in Chicago Bar Assoc., Illinois Business Corporation Act Ann. (1934) 168.

[96] 1 Dodd and Baker, Cases on Business Associations (1940), 1168, n. 4.

present sufficiency of assets to meet creditors' claims, it may be said the corporation itself is injured by depletion of its capital. To speak of the corporation in the absence of creditors' claims is, however, to speak of the interests of stockholders. And to permit recovery from directors for the benefit of stockholders already paid once, though in violation of statute, does not at first appeal to the sense of justice. But the stockholder may have good cause to be paid, so to speak, twice where the directors have knowingly violated the statute and stockholders have been ignorant of the violation. The theory of a normal dividend is that it is to be paid out of profit. If the director in good faith thinks the disbursement is from profit, and the stockholder likewise, it cannot well be said that the innocent director should reimburse the corporation (and its stockholders) merely because the stockholders spend the dividends thinking they are profits when in fact they are capital. Both directors and stockholders are innocent, but the stockholders have in fact received the money. Where, on the other hand, the declaration by directors is in bad faith, innocent stockholders should be entitled to have the corporate capital maintained intact, as they presumed a dividend from profits had been paid.

From the standpoint of permitting the corporation a cause of action in the right of stockholders, another argument may be made. Normally, stock will be changing hands. Dividends, having been paid presumably from profits, will enhance its market value. New buyers will be making purchases on the theory that the corporation is prospering when in fact the dividends have actually depleted capital. A cause of action by the corporation for the benefit of these new stockholders who did not receive the illegal dividends cannot be called unjust.

The second theory for allowing recovery to the solvent corporation is in the right of creditors. The argument is that, even though the depleted capital is not presently necessary to pay creditors, the purpose of statutes against capital impairment is to preserve continuously for protection of creditors a capital fund of fixed amount, and when by violation of the statute that fund is reduced, directors should be compelled to restore it to the extent of the depletion. If it is necessary to wait until insolvency, general business conditions may be so bad as to render directors likewise insolvent and the right to recover at that date valueless.

In the absence of statutory provisions giving a cause of action to the corporation, there is a tendency to refuse relief to a going solvent corporation in actions against directors for dividends illegally paid.

Thus, in *Spiegel v. Beacon Participations, Inc.*, a minority stockholder's suit to hold directors liable for dividends paid from capital on common law grounds, the court refused recovery upon a showing that the corporation was not insolvent and the money sought to be recovered was not needed to pay creditors.[97] To allow recovery, the court pointed out, would be in effect paying shareholders twice. On the other hand, in *Loan Society v. Eavenson,* a solvent Delaware corporation was allowed to recover dividends negligently paid, without any reference to the Delaware law, the court stating that the corporation represented the interests of creditors and subsequent shareholders, "and it may become necessary in the future if not at present to use the capital for payment of present debts."[98] It also emphasized that the corporation was a going corporation and proposed to use the reinstated capital "to continue business." This is important. If the corporation is in actual liquidation and has sufficient assets to meet creditors' claims, then permitting recovery from directors would be for no other purpose than double payment to stockholders. In this type of situation, actions on behalf of the company are dismissed.[99]

The question whether a solvent corporation may recover illegal dividends depends for the most part on construction of statutory provisions for director liability. The vesting of a right of action in the corporation goes back, like many modern statutory dividend provisions, to the New York Act of 1825. That act gave the right of recovery "to the said corporation, and to the creditors thereof, in

---

[97] 8 N. E. (2d) 895 (Mass. 1937). *Accord: Excelsior Petroleum Co. v. Lacey,* 63 N. Y. 422 (1875) (no corporate cause of action under N. Y. Laws 1848, c. 40, §13, making directors liable for "debts"; none at common law where showing directors acted in good faith); see *Collins v. Penn-Wyoming Copper Co.,* 203 Fed. 726, 730 (D. Wyo. 1912) (stockholders' bill under similar statute).

[98] 248 Pa. 407, 94 Atl. 121 (1915); see Brett, L. J. in *Flitcroft's Case,* L. R. 21 Ch. Div. 519, 535 (Ct. of App. 1882).

[99] *Turquand v. Marshall,* L. R. 4 Ch. App. 376 (1869); *Scott's Executors v. Young,* 231 Ky. 577, 21 S. W. (2d) 994 (1929) (statute only imposed liability for corporate debts); see *Emerson v. Gaither,* 103 Md. 564, 581, 64 Atl. 26 (1906); *Hutchinson v. Stadler,* 85 App. Div. 424, 430–431, 83 N. Y. S. 509 (1st Dept. 1903); *Wallace v. Lincoln Savings Bank,* 89 Tenn. 630, 641, 15 S. W. 448 (1890); cf. *Hochman v. Mortgage Finance Co.,* 289 Pa. 260, 266–267, 137 Atl. 252 (1927); *Minnesota Thresher Mfg. Co. v. Langdon,* 44 Minn. 37, 46 N. W. 310 (1890) (sale of corporate assets by receiver did not include right of action against directors where statute vested such right in creditors). However, in *Cornell v. Seddinger,* 237 Pa. 389, 85 Atl. 446 (1912), a receiver was allowed to recover on common law grounds for dividends negligently paid from capital, although the bill was not filed to secure payment of corporate debts, and the receiver's repor⸱ disclosed that when the company passed into his hands the assets exceeded the liabilities exclusive of capital.

the event of its dissolution." [100] New Jersey, when it copied this provision in 1846, added at the end thereof "or insolvency," the last clause thereby reading "in the event of its dissolution or insolvency." [101] The New York form survives in many states; [102] the New Jersey form in others. [103] The original provision in the New York Act has been amended to give a cause of action to the corporation and to creditors to the full extent of any loss sustained by each. [104]

Do the original New York and New Jersey type provisions vesting a cause of action in the corporation, and creditors thereof, in the event of dissolution or insolvency, entitle a solvent corporation to recover? Creditors are permitted to recover in the event of dissolution or insolvency. Does this limitation also modify "corporation" so as to similarly restrict recovery? In the leading case of *Appleton v. American Malting Company*, [105] it was held not to modify corporation, [106] with the result that a solvent corporation (in a stockholders' derivative suit) was permitted to recover from directors, even though the court recognized the recovery would be the equivalent of double payment to shareholders. The court justified such construction on principle by the contention that, as to present stockholders, the recovery merely restored their interest in the corporation to normal

[100] N. Y. Laws 1825, c. 325, §2. See §7, n. 62, *supra*. Earlier special charters in Pennsylvania had given the cause of action exclusively to the corporation, §6, n. 51, 55, *supra*. With the exception of a few New York charters such as that of the New York Drydock Company, N. Y. Laws 1825, c. 114, §11, which were being approved contemporaneously with the General Act of 1825, no earlier special charters had made provision for liability both to the corporation and creditors.

[101] N. J. Acts 1846, p. 16, §7.

[102] Mont. Rev. Code (1935), §5939; N. D. Comp. L. 1913 (Supp. 1913–25), §4544; Okla. Stat. Ann., §18–106; S. D. Code (1939), §11.0706. For source of these provisions see §22, *supra*.

[103] Del. Rev. Code (1935), c. 65, §35; Kans. Laws 1939, c. 152, §85 ("to the corporation, and to its creditors, or any of them, in the event of its dissolution or insolvency"); N. C. Code (1939), §1179; N. Mex. Stat. (1929), §32–135. For source of these provisions see §§21, 22, *supra*.

[104] N. Y. Stock Corporation Law, §58. *Source:* N. Y. Laws 1892, c. 688, §23; N. Y. Laws 1901, c. 354; N. Y. Laws 1923, c. 787, §58; N. Y. Laws 1939, c. 364. Section 60 of the New York General Corporation Law makes directors liable to account for their official conduct, including neglect in management and disposition of corporate assets, §75, n. 17, *supra*. Section 61 vests such causes of action in the corporation, among others. For source of the latter section, see N. Y. Rev. Stat. (1828), Pt. 3, c. 8, Title 4, Art. 2, §35; Code of Civ. Prov., §1782; N. Y. Consol. Laws (1909), c. 28, §91; N. Y. Laws 1913, c. 633; N. Y. Laws 1929, c. 650, §1(61). That Stock Corporation Law, §58, and General Corporation Law, §§60, 61, are construed together to determine plaintiff's right to sue, see *Shaw v. Ansaldi Co., Inc.*, 178 App. Div. 589, 591, 599, 165 N. Y. S. 872 (1st Dept. 1917).

[105] 65 N. J. Eq. 375, 54 Atl. 454 (Ct. Err. & App. 1903).

[106] See *Morris v. Sampsell*, 224 Wis. 560, 564, 272 N. W. 53 (1937); but see *Stevirmac Oil & Gas Co. v. Smith*, 259 Fed. 650, 654 (E. D. Okla. 1919).

value and that, as to subsequent stockholders, it was only fair to establish the apparent value which dividends had indicated existed. The holding of the *Appleton* case is generally accepted in construing statutes of this type, and the solvent corporation recognized as entitled to recover.[107] The *Appleton* case, however, is no longer controlling in New Jersey. The director liability provisions of the New Jersey statute were amended in 1904 to make directors liable to stockholders severally and respectively to the amount of loss sustained by them, or, in case of insolvency, to the corporation for the loss sustained by it.[108] This is the present New Jersey provision.[109] It prevents a solvent corporation from recovering from directors dividends paid out of capital.[110]

Some statutes vest the cause of action solely and without qualification in the corporation.[111] Under such provisions it would seem the solvent corporation, under the doctrine of the *Appleton* case, is in even stronger position to recover. In Arkansas,[112] Nevada,[113] and Tennessee,[114] transposition of the clause "in the event of its dissolution or insolvency" so as to follow "corporation" rather than both "corporation" and "creditors" removes the statutory doubt as to in-

---

[107] *Siegman v. Electric Vehicle Co.,* 72 N. J. Eq. 403, 65 Atl. 910 (Ct. Err. & App. 1907) (stockholder suit); *Southern California Home Builders v. Young,* 45 Cal. App. 679, 188 Pac. 586 (1920) (under former Cal. Civ. Code, §309, amended so as to remove the original concluding clause "in the event of dissolution," making possible the argument, not mentioned by the court, that recovery by a going corporation was intended); *Hutchinson v. Stadler,* 85 App. Div. 424, 83 N. Y. S. 509 (1st Dept. 1093) (common stockholder suit to compel restoration of dividends paid preferred); *German American Coffee Co. v. Diehl,* 216 N. Y. 57, 109 N. E. 875 (1915) (New York statute giving cause of action to corporation applied to New Jersey corporation doing business in New York); *Hutchinson v. Curtiss,* 45 Misc. 484, 92 N. Y. S. 70 (1904) (similar case); *Irving Trust Co. v. Gunder,* 234 App. Div. 252, 254 N. Y. S. 630 (1st Dept. 1932); *Union Discount Co. v. MacRobert,* 134 Misc. 107, 234 N. Y. S. 529 (1929) (point not discussed); see *Roeblings Sons Co. v. Mode,* 1 Pen. 515, 520, 523, 43 Atl. 480 (Del. 1899).

[108] N. J. Laws 1904, c. 143.

[109] N. J. Stat. (1937), §14:8–19.

[110] *Fleisher v. West Jersey Securities Co.,* 84 N. J. Eq. 55, 92 Atl. 575 (1914) (stockholder suit); see *De Raismes v. U. S. Lithograph Co.,* 161 App. Div. 781, 784, 146 N. Y. S. 813 (1st Dept. 1914).

[111] Cal. Civ. Code (1937), §363 (corporation for benefit of creditors or any of them and shareholders, but only to the extent of the interest of shareholders other than those to whom dividend was paid); Idaho Code Ann., §29–130; 32 Ill. Ann. Stat. (Smith-Hurd 1935), §157.42; Mich. Stat. Ann. (Henderson 1937), §21.48; Minn. Stat. (Mason 1938 Supp.), §7492–22; Ohio Code Ann. (Baldwin 1938), §8623–123b; 15 Purd. Pa. Stat., §2852–707; Wash. Rev. Stat. Ann. (Rem.), §3803–25.

[112] Ark. Laws (1937), §2184.

[113] Nev. Comp. L. (Hillyer 1929), §1674.

[114] Tenn. Code Ann. (1934), §3759.

tention to permit recovery by a solvent corporation. In these jurisdictions, the cause of action is given "to the corporation, or in the event of its dissolution or insolvency, to its creditors."

84. Creditors

Statutory protection for creditors in dividend matters came late. The creditor is not mentioned in English special charters before the end of the seventeenth century. The American origin of the creditor's right to attack a dividend, like that of a director's liability for paying dividends, is to be traced to the Hamilton-drafted charter of the Bank of United States, and in turn to the 1694 charter of the Bank of England from which he copied. In both charters directors were made directly liable to creditors, and only to creditors, for incurring debts in excess of the corporate capital.[115] Subsequent American special charters,[116] and finally the New York Act of 1825, extended to creditors the same right against directors responsible for the declaration of illegal dividends.[117] The Act of 1825 did not give the right of action exclusively to creditors, nor did it do so without qualification. It provided directors should be liable "to the said corporation, and to the creditors thereof, in the event of its dissolution." In this form, or with the addition of insolvency as an alternative to dissolution, this provision exists in many present-day dividend statutes.[118] Under these statutes the creditor of the solvent corporation cannot recover, his right to relief being conditioned on dissolution or insolvency.[119]

In some states the right to recover against directors is conditioned

[115] I Stat. 191, §7, subs. IX (1791); 5 and 6 William and Mary, c. 20, §26 (1694).

[116] See e.g. Newark Banking & Insurance Co., N. J. Acts 1803, c. 109, §14-3; N. Y. Drydock Co., N. Y. Laws 1825, c. 114, §11.

[117] N. Y. Laws 1825, c. 325, §2.

[118] See §83, n. 102, 103, *supra*.

[119] See *Appleton v. American Malting Co.*, 65 N. J. Eq. 375, 380, 54 Atl. 454 (1903); *Roeblings Sons Co. v. Mode*, 1 Pen. 515, 523, 43 Atl. 480 (1899); *Topeka Paper Co. v. Oklahoma Publishing Co.*, 7 Okla. 220, 224, 54 Pac. 455 (1898); *Stoltz v. Scott*, 23 Idaho 104, 129 Pac. 340 (1912) (where statute conditioned recovery on "dissolution" only, held insolvency would effect dissolution giving cause of action to receiver). For a possible common law right of creditors of an insolvent corporation to recover from directors dividends paid in violation of statute or common law doctrines, see *Boyd v. Schneider*, 131 Fed. 223 (C. C. A. 7th, 1904) (directors of a national bank knowingly paying dividends out of capital are liable to depositors as a class for loss sustained; it is no defense that the receiver or comptroller may assert a right to recover); *Spiegel v. Beacon Participations, Inc.*, 8 N. E. (2d) 895, 912 (Mass. 1937) (corporation in a minority stockholder's suit could not recover for benefit of creditors when corporation was solvent and not in need of money to pay creditors); *Lexington & Ohio R. R. Co. v. Bridges*, 7 B. Mon. 556, 559 (1847).

on a prior judgment against the corporation and a return of execution unsatisfied.[120] By amendment to the New York statute, the restriction to recovery by creditors when the corporation is insolvent was removed, making possible suit by a creditor of a solvent corporation if he can sustain the burden of showing loss.[121] In many states the only provision of liability is for debts,[122] following the old liability clause of the Massachusetts Revised Statutes of 1836,[123] or to creditors.[124] Under these provisions creditors are allowed to recover,[125] and there is some authority that the right is personal to them and cannot be asserted by receivers and trustees in bankruptcy.[126] Under the provisions of the Uniform Business Corporation Act, although the cause of action is given exclusively to the corporation, the draftsmen have suggested that it may be reached as an equitable asset by a creditor with judgment and execution returned unsatisfied.[127]

84.1. Individual or Representative Suits

May the cause of action given to creditors against directors be asserted individually, or must it be by representative suit for the benefit of the group? The problem is essentially the race of diligence question. In the absence of controlling statutory provisions, creditors

[120] Ark. Stat. (1937), §2184; Cal. Civ. Code (1937), §363 (judgment creditors may recover if claims arose prior to violation); Conn. Gen. Stat. (1930), §3386 (cause of action given exclusively to creditors existing at the time of declaration who have judgments); Del. Rev. Code (1935), c. 65, §51; N. J. Stat. (1937), §14:7–9 (no sale or satisfaction against any director until judgment against corporation and execution unsatisfied); Tenn. Code Ann. (1934), §3759.

[121] See §83, n. 104, supra. See also General Corporation Law, §61.

[122] Ky. Stat. Ann. (Carroll 1936), §548 (debts then existing and all that shall be thereafter incurred while they or a majority of them continue in office); Mass. Laws Ann., c. 156, §37 (debts and contracts); Md. Ann. Code (1935 Supp.), c. 23, §87 (debts then existing); N. H. Pub. Laws (1926), c. 225, §80 (debts and contracts then existing or contracted while they remain in office); Wyo. Rev. Stat. (1931), §28–131 (similar to Kentucky provision).

[123] Mass. Rev. Stat. (1836), c. 38, §23. See §8, n. 71, supra.

[124] Conn. Gen. Stat. (1930), §3386, see n. 120, supra; La. Gen. Stat. (Dart. 1939), §1107; Va. Code (1936), §3840; W. Va. Code (1937), §3090 (debts then existing).

[125] Calkins v. Wire Hardware Co., 267 Mass. 52, 165 N. E. 889 (1929); Pennsylvania Iron Works v. Mackenzie, 190 Mass. 61, 76 N. E. 228 (1906); Franklin v. Caldwell, 123 Ky. 528, 96 S. W. 605 (1906) (bank depositor allowed to recover without discussion of point); Rorke v. Thomas, 56 N. Y. 559 (1874) (point not discussed). See Seegmiller v. Day, 249 Fed. 177, 180–181 (C. C. A. 7th, 1918); Childs v. Adams, 43 Pa. Super. 239 (1910); Smalley v. Bernstein, 165 La. 1, 17–18, 115 So. 347 (1928).

[126] See §§85, 86, infra.

[127] See Draft of Uniform Business Corporation Act with Explanatory Notes (July 1928), 53.

who file suit first should not be allowed to recover payment in full at the expense of the rest of the group; particularly is this true where the cause of action is only recognized on the corporation's insolvency. Cases under the Massachusetts type statute seem to allow recovery by the individual creditor without discussion of the point.[128] Under the New York type statute,[129] an individual creditor has been held not to have a cause of action, a representative suit by creditor's bill being necessary.[130]

To understand the right of creditors as such to hold directors of a Delaware corporation liable for payment of improper dividends, it is necessary to consider the statutory history in Delaware. The basic dividend provisions of the present Delaware law derive from the Act of 1883 which provided that directors should be liable for the declaration of illegal dividends to the corporation and to the creditors thereof in the event of its dissolution or insolvency.[131] In *John A. Roebling's Sons Company v. Mode,* it was held that an individual creditor could not maintain an action on the case against directors for a violation of this provision.[132] The court stated that the remedy, where the corporation was insolvent, was by a bill in equity where all persons interested might be made parties; and added by dictum that if the corporation was solvent, a cause of action could only be maintained by the corporation itself. A month after this decision, the Delaware legislature amended its dividend law so as to make directors liable in an action on the case "to the corporation and to its creditors or any of them" in the event of dissolution or insolvency.[133] The amendment obviously gave individual creditors a right to proceed against directors upon failure of the corporation.[134] This provision in the Delaware law remained substantially the same until the Act of April 13, 1937, when Section 35 was amended to strike out the

---

[128] See n. 125, *supra.*

[129] See §84, n. 117, *supra.*

[130] *Roebling's Sons Co. v. Mode,* 1 Pen. 515, 43 Atl. 480 (Del. 1899); *Johnson v. Nevins,* 87 Misc. 430, 150 N. Y. S. 828 (1914) (receiver appointed on supplementary proceedings for a single creditor not entitled to recover); but see *Shaw v. Ansaldi, Inc.,* 178 App. Div. 589, 601, 165 N. Y. S. 872 (1st Dept. 1917) ("since there is no other judgment creditor and no objection was taken that the rights of other creditors were involved, a direct recovery in favor of the plaintiff might be sustained").

[131] 17 Del. Laws. c. 147, §7 (1883).

[132] 1 Pen. 515, 43 Atl. 480 (Del. 1899).

[133] 21 Del. Laws, c. 273, §18. In several states statutes still give the right to creditors "or any of them." Ark. Laws (1937), §2184; Kans. Laws 1939, c. 152, §85; Nev. Comp. L. (Hillyer 1929), §1674; Tenn. Code (1934), §3759.

[134] See *Morris v. Sampsell,* 224 Wis. 560, 562, 272 N. W. 53 (1937); *Rockwood v. Foshay,* 66 F. (2d) 625, 628 (C. C. A. 8th, 1933).

clause giving "an action on the case" and the words "or any of them" following creditors.[135] Thus the present law is in practically the identical form of the Act of 1883 under which the *Roebling* case was decided, and it is to be assumed that this decision of the Superior Court is now applicable, vesting the cause of action in the corporation if solvent, in the creditors generally for collection under appropriate proceedings if the corporation is insolvent or in dissolution.[136]

84.2. Prior and Subsequent Creditors

In the absence of proof that subsequent creditors had knowledge of illegal dividend declarations, no distinction should be drawn as to whether the creditor became such before or after the dividend was declared. As to existing creditors who had a right to assume whatever capital the corporation had would not be dissipated in dividends, the injury is very clear. Subsequent creditors have the same right to assume integrity of the corporation's capital, and where dividends have been previously declared, which without their knowledge impair capital, they are allowed recovery.[137] However, if the subsequent creditor has notice of the impairment at the time his credit is advanced, he is in no position to claim injury.[138]

Statutes in some instances cover the prior and subsequent creditor problem. The Massachusetts Revised Statutes of 1836 provided that

[135] 41 Del. Laws, c. 130.

[136] In Virginia the statutory remedy is by bill in equity. Va. Code (1936), §3840.

[137] *Cottrell v. Albany Card & Paper Mfg. Co.,* 142 A. D. 148, 126 N. Y. S. 1070 (3d Dept. 1911); *Quintal v. Greenstein,* 142 Misc. 854, 256 N. Y. S. 462 (1932), aff'd 236 App. Div. 719, 257 N. Y. S. 1034 (1st Dept. 1932); *Christianssand v. Federal Steamship Corp.,* 121 Misc. 627, 201 N. Y. S. 504 (1923); *Calkins v. Wire Hardware Co.,* 267 Mass. 52, 165 N. E. 889 (1929); *Gratz v. Redd,* 4 B. Mon. 178 (1843); *Stoltz v. Scott,* 23 Idaho 104, 129 Pac. 340 (1912); cf. *Jones v. Walker,* 103 U. S. 444 (1880) (legatees not liable to assignee in bankruptcy for partnership dividends where creditors' claims arose after the dividend); but see Ballantine and Lattin, *Cases and Materials on the Law of Corporations* (1939) 495, n. 86. Similarly, subsequent creditors are entitled to participate in recovery against stockholders in jurisdictions allowing recovery against the latter. *Powers v. Heggie,* 268 Mass. 233, 167 N. E. 314 (1929) (creditors whose claims accrued subsequently entitled to share in trustee in bankruptcy's recovery); *Mackall v. Pocock,* 136 Minn. 8, 161 N. W. 228 (1917) (also by trustee); cf. *Coleman v. Booth,* 268 Mo. 64, 186 S. W. 1021 (1916) (trustee in bankruptcy has right to recover for subsequent creditors against transferee of stockholder with notice); *In re Bay Ridge Inn,* 98 F. (2d) 85 (C. C. A. 2d, 1938).

[138] See *First Trust Co. v. Illinois Central R. Co.,* 256 Fed. 830, 831–832 (C. C. A. 8th, 1919). An illegal dividend out of capital creates no liability if capital is then reduced so as to produce a reduction surplus and all creditors become such with full knowledge of the illegal dividend and after the reduction surplus has been created. *Greene v. Boardman,* 143 Misc. 201, 256 N. Y. S. 340 (1932).

directors declaring illegal dividends should be liable "for all the debts of the company then existing, and for all that shall thereafter be contracted, so long as they shall respectively continue in office." [189] This provision was copied into the New York Manufacturing Act of 1848.[140] States deriving their dividend statutes from these earlier provisions still have this rule.[141] Other states specifically limit recovery to creditors existing at the time the dividend was paid.[142]

There is one situation in which recovery should be denied to a prior creditor. A creditor who becomes such before an increase in capital, cannot object to a dividend which merely impairs the increased capital, but not the capital existing at the time his claim arose.[143] The capital upon which he relied, or presumably relied, is still unimpaired.

85. Trustee in Bankruptcy

In some statutes the trustee in bankruptcy is specifically included among those entitled to recover illegal dividends from directors.[144] In the absence of such express provision in the state statute, the claim of the trustee may be asserted under the Bankruptcy Act either in the right of the corporation or in the right of creditors.[145]

(a) If the corporation at the time of bankruptcy has an unqualified cause of action against directors,[146] the trustee will succeed to that right of action under Section 70(a)(5) of the Bankruptcy

[189] Mass. Rev. Stat. (1836), c. 38, §23.

[140] N. Y. Laws 1848, c. 40, §13.

[141] Ky. Stat. Ann. (Carroll 1936), §548 (Kentucky first copied Mass. Rev. Stat. of 1836, Ky. Acts 1840, p. 49, §17, and then the New York Act of 1848, 1 Ky. Acts 1853–54, p. 179, §16; amended to present form Ky. Laws 1891–93, c. 171, §11); Mo. Stat. Ann., §§4569, 4942 (copying both Mass. Rev. Stat. and the New York Act of 1848); N. H. Pub. Laws (1926), c. 225, §80; Ore. Code Ann. (1930), §25–219; Wyo. Rev. Stat. (1931), §28–131. For source of these provisions, see §§19, 23, *supra*.

[142] Cal. Civ. Code (Deering 1937), §363; Conn. Gen. Stat. (1930), §3386; Md. Ann. Code (1935 Supp.), c. 23, §87 (Maryland had originally adopted the provision in the New York Manufacturing Act of 1848 creating liability to both prior and subsequent creditors, Md. Laws 1852, c. 338, §11; amendment was made to the present form in 1931, Md. Laws 1931, c. 480); Miss. Code Ann. (1930), §4149; W. Va. Code (1937), §3090; Wis. Stat. (1937), §182.19.

[143] See *Mackall v. Pocock,* 136 Minn. 8, 11–12, 161 N. W. 228 (1917) (against stockholder).

[144] Cal. Civ. Code (1937), §363; Mich. Stat. Ann. (Henderson 1937), §21.47; R. I. Gen. Laws (1938), c. 116, §41. Cf. N. Y. Gen. Corp. Law, §§60, 61, *supra*, §83, n. 104.

[145] Sometimes a trustee is allowed to recover without discussion of his capacity to sue. *Penzel v. Townsend,* 128 Ark. 620, 195 S. W. 25 (1917); *Branch v. Kaiser,* 291 Pa. 543, 140 Atl. 498 (1928). Or the basis of the remedy is not indicated. *Fell v. Pitts,* 263 Pa. 314, 106 Atl. 574 (1919).

[146] See statutes in §83, n. 111, *supra*.

Act,[147] and possibly under Section 70(a)(6).[148] The difficult question occurs under numerous statutes such as that in Delaware at the present time giving the right of recovery to "the corporation and to its creditors, in the event of its dissolution or insolvency."[149] Under provisions of this character, it is held that the solvent corporation has a cause of action,[150] but does insolvency operate as a defeasance so as to vest the right thereafter exclusively in creditors? In *Morris v. Sampsell,* the Wisconsin Supreme Court, construing this provision in Section 35 of the Delaware Act, held the trustee could not sue in the right of the corporation, since after insolvency the remedy passed to creditors.[151]

(b) Assuming recovery cannot be had in behalf of the corporation, is the trustee entitled to sue in the right of creditors? Unless the creditors' right of recovery belongs to each creditor individually, Section 70(c) of the Bankruptcy Act, vesting the trustee with all the rights, remedies, and powers as of the date of bankruptcy of a judgment creditor holding an execution returned unsatisfied, furnishes a basis for enabling the trustee to sue.[152] The authorities which treat the cause of action as a representative one, rather than the separate property of an individual creditor, support recovery by the trustee.[153]

[147] II U. S. C. A., §110a(5), as amended 52 Stat. 880 (1938). This provision vests the trustee by operation of law with the title of the bankrupt to all "property, including rights of action, which prior to the filing of the petition he could by any means have transferred or which might have been levied upon and sold under judicial process against him."

[148] II U. S. C. A., §110a(6), as amended 52 Stat. 880 (1938). It vests the trustee with the bankrupt's "rights of action arising upon . . . the unlawful taking or detention of or injury to his property." This provision was relied upon to sustain an action by the trustee in *Irving Trust Co. v. Gunder,* 234 App. Div. 252, 254 N. Y. S. 630 (1st Dept. 1932) (irrespective of any injury to creditors). In *Cox v. Leahy,* 209 App. Div. 313, 204 N. Y. S. 741 (3d Dept. 1924) a trustee was held entitled to recover under former §28 of the Stock Corporation Law allowing an action, similar to present §58, by "the corporation or its creditors." The court did not state under what provisions of the bankruptcy act the action could be maintained. In *Walker v. Man,* 142 Misc. 277, 253 N. Y. S. 458 (1931), recovery was permitted under §58, the court stating the trustee represented the corporation.

[149] See §83, n. 101–103, *supra.*

[150] See §83, n. 105–107, *supra.*

[151] 224 Wis. 560, 272 N. W. 53 (1937). Compare the dictum in *Roebling's Sons Co. v. Mode,* 1 Pen. 515, 523, 43 Atl. 480 (Del. 1899). But in *Ulness v. Dunnell,* 61 N. D. 95, 237 N. W. 208 (1931), under the North Dakota statute of this type, the trustee was held to have capacity to maintain the action. Compare the right of a receiver to maintain the action, §86, *infra,* and of a trustee in bankruptcy to recover against shareholders receiving illegal dividends, §97, *infra.*

[152] II U. S. C. A., §110(c), as amended 52 Stat. 881 (1938). The provision was formerly §47a(2) [II U. S. C. A., §75a(2)].

[153] See §84.1, *supra.*

When, prior to the 1937 amendment, the Delaware statute gave the cause of action to creditors, "or any of them," it was held that the claim of creditors was personal, barring recovery by a trustee in bankruptcy.[154] As a result, a trustee, barred also from any remedy in the right of the corporation because it was no longer solvent, was completely without right to recover against directors for illegal dividends. This highly unsatisfactory condition fortunately does not prevail since the 1937 amendment in Delaware.[155] The effect of the amendment striking out the clause "or any of them" is to restore the Delaware law to the position referred to in the dictum of the *Roebling* case, under which upon insolvency the cause of action vests in creditors generally,[156] and consequently in the trustee under Section 70(c). Under statutes containing only a provision that directors shall be liable for "debts" or to "creditors," cases holding that the trustee cannot recover [157] seem to be incorrectly decided in view of the explicit provision of Section 70(c). The Maryland law, by providing that in the event of insolvency the liability of directors shall be collectible by the receiver or other liquidation officers as an asset of the corporation, when considered in conjunction with the prior provision that directors shall be liable for corporate debts, seems to indicate that on insolvency whatever right the individual creditors may have had is divested and given to the proper liquidating officers.[158]

86. Receiver

As in respect to the trustee in bankruptcy, statutes in some states specifically vest a receiver with the right to sue.[159] Again, in the absence of such express authority, the receiver may seek to assert a claim either on behalf of the corporation or in the right of creditors.

(a) It is generally recognized that a receiver succeeds to causes

---

[154] *Morris v. Sampsell,* 224 Wis. 560, 272 N. W. 53 (1937). In *Stratton v. Bertles,* 238 App. Div. 87, 263 N. Y. S. 466 (1933), the trustee of a Delaware corporation was allowed to recover in the right of creditors under Bankruptcy Act, §70, before amendment.

[155] 41 Del. L., c. 140.

[156] See §84.1, *supra.*

[157] *Smalley v. Bernstein,* 165 La. 1, 115 So. 347 (1928) (Huey Long was of winning counsel for appellants); *Seegmiller v. Day,* 249 Fed. 177 (C. C. A. 7th, 1918). The contrary result was reached in *Howard v. Insull,* 294 Ill. App. 20, 13 N. E. (2d) 506 (1938) ("debts or contracts").

[158] Md. Ann. Code (1935 Supp.), c. 23, §87.

[159] Cal. Civ. Code, §363; Mich. Stat. Ann. (Henderson 1937), §21.47; Minn. Stat. (Mason 1938 Supp.), §§7492–51; N. J. Stat. (1937), §14:8–19; R. I. Laws (1938), c. 116, §41; cf. N. Y. Gen. Corp. Law, §§60, 61, *supra* §83, n. 104; 15 Purd. Pa. Stat., §§2852–707, 1108B.

of action which the corporation might have enforced. If the statute gives a right of recovery unequivocally to the corporation, as many statutes do,[160] the receiver should be entitled to sue in succession. If the applicable statute is the type of the New York Act of 1825 giving the right of action to the corporation, and to the creditors thereof, in the event of dissolution,[161] insolvency terminates the corporate cause of action,[162] and the receiver's claim, if maintainable at all, must be in the right of creditors.

(b) Unless causes of action on behalf of creditors are to be deemed personal and individual rights, with the resultant inequality of distribution which that theory produces,[163] the receiver is entitled to collect causes of action vested in creditors for ratable distribution among all claimants.[164] Under the former Delaware provision in Section 35 giving the right of action to the corporation's "creditors or any of them," the cause of action is personal to individual creditors and may not be enforced by a receiver.[165] This type of statute still prevails in several jurisdictions.[166] Since the amendment of 1937 in Delaware striking out the clause "or any of them," the action becomes, under the dictum in *Roebling's* case, one vested in

---

[160] See §83, n. 111, *supra.*

[161] See §83, n. 101–103, *supra.*

[162] *Rockwood v. Foshay,* 66 F. (2d) 625 (C. C. A. 8th, 1933), *cert. den.* 291 U. S. 666 (1934) (former Delaware, §35). But in *Stoltz v. Scott,* 23 Idaho 104, 129 Pac. 340 (1912), where the statute was the type of the New York Act of 1825, it was held a receiver of an insolvent corporation might recover in behalf of the corporation without a dissolution and in any event in the right of creditors. Cf. *Gunkle's Appeal,* 48 Pa. 13 (1864) (assignee for creditors has duty to collect claims against directors for paying illegal dividends where statute gives cause of action to the corporation).

[163] See §84.1, *supra.*

[164] In *Hodde v. Nobbe,* 204 Mo. App. 109, 221 S. W. 130 (1920), without relying on any statutory provision, the court held a receiver might sue even though the corporation or stockholders could not, since he represented creditors. Cf. *Roberts v. Hargis,* 265 Ky. 282, 96 S. W. (2d) 691, 692 (1936) (dictum under statute creating liability for "debts" that bank commissioner might recover) ; *McTamany v. Day,* 23 Idaho 95, 128 Pac. 563 (1912) (individual bank depositor's suit after appointment of receiver dismissed; receiver had duty of collection); *Frederick v. McRae,* 157 Minn. 366, 196 N. W. 270 (1923) (similar facts). In *Belmont v. Gentry,* 62 S. D. 118, 252 N. W. 1 (1933), trustees in liquidation were held not entitled to enforce the claim under a statute making directors liable to "creditors." For the theories upon which a receiver is generally allowed to assert causes of action vested solely in creditors, see Note, 46 Yale L. J. 1229 (1937).

[165] *Rockwood v. Foshay,* 66 F. (2d) 625 (C. C. A. 8th, 1933), *cert. den.* 291 U. S. 666 (1934). In *Cochran v. Shetler,* 286 Pa. 226, 133 Atl. 232 (1926), a receiver of a Delaware corporation was permitted to sue where the statute in Delaware was not before the court.

[166] Ark. Laws (1937), §2184; Kans. Laws 1939, c. 152, §85; Nev. Comp. L. (Hillyer 1929), §1674; Tenn. Code Ann. (1934), §3759.

creditors generally,[167] and should be enforceable by the receiver. If assets are not needed to pay creditors, the receiver is not entitled to recover.[168]

87. The Individual Stockholder

In the usual case where a stockholder complains of the illegal declaration of a dividend, he seeks relief from directors in the normal derivative suit brought on behalf of the corporation.[169] There is very little authority on the right of a stockholder suing in his individual capacity to maintain an action. To meet the decision in *Appleton v. American Malting Company*,[170] the Delaware statute was amended to give stockholders severally and respectively a cause of action for the amount of any loss sustained.[171] Although this amendment was adopted in 1904, to date no recovery has been obtained by a New Jersey stockholder under its provisions. The fact that individual stockholder actions are very rarely brought confirms the attitude of the profession that, in the absence of statute, the stockholder's redress is through the corporation.[172]

[167] *Roebling's Sons Co. v. Mode,* 1 Pen. 515, 523, 43 Atl. 480 (1899). See §84.1, *supra.*

[168] See §83, *supra.*

[169] See §83, *supra.*

[170] 65 N. J. Eq. 375, 54 Atl. 454 (Ct. Err. & App. 1903).

[171] N. J. Laws 1904, c. 143.

[172] Scattered dicta supporting individual recovery do exist in older cases. In *Gaffney v. Colvill,* 6 Hill 567, 574–575 (1844), the court said a stockholder might have a cause of action *qua* stockholder for the amount his stock had depreciated as the result of an illegal dividend. In *Flitcroft's Case,* L. R. 21 Ch. Div. 519, 534 (Ct. App. 1882), Jessel, M. R. said that reduction of the capital might bring ruin to the corporation "in which case the shareholders as such may have a right to complain of what has been done."

CHAPTER 8

REMEDIES AGAINST STOCKHOLDERS WHO RECEIVE ILLEGAL DIVIDENDS

A. Scope of Stockholder Liability

88. Responsibility of the Stockholder

As an original question, it would seem that if a corporation pays an illegal dividend there could be no doubt of the right of injured creditors to recover the wrongful distribution, directly or indirectly, from stockholders, the recipients thereof. In the earliest English charter provisions, liability did fall on stockholders.[1] However, by a curious circumstance of history, American dividend legislation has from its inception shifted the specifically stated statutory liability from stockholders to the directors who declare the dividend.[2] The first American special charters and the basic New York Act of 1825, following a section as to director liability for creating excess indebtedness contained in the first charter of the Bank of United States, made provision for imposing personal liability for illegal dividends on directors, not in any way mentioning stockholders.[3] This fact, perhaps more than any other, accounts for limitations, otherwise strange in principle, which have come to circumscribe the assertion of liability against stockholders.[4]

---

[1] Amendment to Charter of Bank of England, 8 and 9 Will. III, c. 20, §49 (1697); Act authorizing charter of English Linen Company, 4 Geo. III, c. 37 (1764).

[2] See §74, *supra.*

[3] See §§6, 7, *supra.*

[4] Generally on the modern law, see Briggs, *Stockholders' Liability for Unlawful Dividends,* 8 Temple L. Q. 145 (1934); Note, *Actions Against Stockholders to Recover Illegal Dividends,* 33 Col. L. Rev. 481 (1933); Note, *Recovery of Illegally Paid Dividends,* 18 Iowa L. Rev. 516 (1933); Note, *Obligation to Refund Dividends Paid Out of Capital,* 30 Mich. L. Rev. 1070 (1932); Note, *Shareholders' Responsibility for Improper Dividends,* 81 U. of Pa. L. Rev. 314 (1933); Note, *Rights of Various Types of Creditors in Property Unavailable to the Debtor,* 47 Yale L. J. 1164, 1173 (1938); Note, 49 Yale L. J. 492, 498 n. 22 (1940); Annotation, "Liability of stockholders who received dividends paid out of capital," L. R. A. 1917C, 397; Annotations, "Right or duty of corporation to pay dividends; and liability for wrongful payment," 55 A. L. R. 8, 98; 76 A. L. R. 885, 893; 109 A. L. R. 1381, 1393.

89. Insolvency Dividends

Even in the absence of an express provision in dividend statutes prohibiting declaration when insolvent, a corporation, like any other debtor, cannot when insolvent transfer its property in fraud of creditors.[5] A transferee of an insolvent debtor, not a creditor, who pays no value—a stockholder, of course, gives nothing to the corporation for his dividend—is under liability to account for the property received in so far as the needs of creditors require. Under this ordinary principle of fraudulent conveyance law, a stockholder who receives a dividend when the corporation is insolvent, or which renders it insolvent, is under liability in a suit by proper parties to refund the same.[6]

When the dividend is illegal only because paid from capital, and the corporation is not thereby rendered insolvent, a distinction is often made as to stockholders receiving the dividend in good faith.[7] No such distinction obtains where the corporation is insolvent or rendered insolvent. Stockholders are mere donees, and are liable like other recipients of transfers from an insolvent debtor who pay no value irrespective of their good faith in receiving the distribution.[8]

In several states shareholders are made liable by statute for dividends when the corporation is insolvent.[9]

[5] See §19, *supra*.

[6] *Powers v. Heggie,* 268 Mass. 233, 167 N. E. 314 (1929) (comment, 28 Mich. L. Rev. 337), §19, n. 68, *supra; Bartlett v. Smith,* 162 Md. 478, 160 Atl. 440 (1932) (comment, 16 Minn. L. Rev. 706); *Ulness v. Dunnell,* 61 N. D. 95, 237 N. W. 208 (1931); *Osgood v. Layton,* 3 Keyes 521 (N. Y. 1867) (statute prohibited payment out of capital); *Fricke v. Angemeier,* 53 Ind. App. 140, 101 N. E. 329 (1913); *Edwards v. Schillinger,* 245 Ill. 231, 91 N. E. 1048 (1910); *Grant v. Ross,* 100 Ky. 44, 37 S. W. 263 (1896); *Hayden v. Thompson,* 71 Fed. 60 (C. C. A. 8th, 1895); see *Wood v. National City Bank,* 24 F. (2d) 661 (C. C. A. 2d, 1928) (comment, 38 Yale L. J. 542) (common law liability exists for receiving dividends when insolvent in bankruptcy sense; but receiver's bill dismissed where no allegation that any of creditors in existence when the receiver was appointed were creditors when the dividends were paid); *Gilleylen v. Schoolfield,* 183 Ark. 143, 35 S. W. (2d) 356 (1931) (no recovery because corporation was in fact solvent); *Comment of Draftsmen of Uniform Business Corporation Act* (July 1928) 52. In *Wood v. Dummer,* 3 Mason 308, Fed. Cas. No. 17,944 (C. C. Me. 1824), the liquidation dividend, which amounted to 75 per cent of the corporation's capital, also rendered it insolvent. Recovery was allowed on the theory of a trust fund. When the dividend is a liquidation dividend rendering the corporation insolvent, stockholders are clearly liable. See also *South Bend Toy Mfg. Co. v. Pierre Fire & Marine Ins. Co.,* 4 S. D. 173, 56 N. W. 98 (1893).

[7] See §90, *infra.*

[8] *Powers v. Heggie,* 268 Mass. 233, 167 N. E. 314 (1929); *Bartlett v. Smith,* 162 Md. 478, 160 Atl. 440 (1932); *Grant v. Ross,* 100 Ky. 44, 37 S. W. 263 (1896); see *McDonald v. Williams,* 174 U. S. 397, 403-404 (1899); *Comment of Draftsmen of Uniform Business Corporation Act* (July 1928) 52.

[9] Cal. Civ. Code (1937), §§346, 364; Iowa Code (1939), §8378; Minn. Stat.

Whether the equity test of ability to meet obligations as they mature, or the bankruptcy test of excess of assets over liabilities exclusive of capital, is to be used in determining the question of solvency is far from clear in most cases.[10] In *Wood v. National City Bank,* the bankruptcy rule was adopted in the complete absence of statutory provisions.[11] And this is the test used in most cases where it is possible to determine at all which of the two rules is being applied.[12] Frequently statutory provisions, particularly the Uniform Fraudulent Conveyance Act, may be applicable and should determine the test to be applied.[13]

90. Dividends from Capital When Corporation Is Solvent

A dividend illegal because paid from capital may not render the corporation insolvent in either the bankruptcy or equity sense.[14] In such case the illegality is predicated solely on a common law or statutory rule, peculiar to corporate law, which prohibits the distribution of corporate capital.[15] If the dividend is illegal, even though it be under a rule peculiar to corporate law, one might expect the recipients would be forbidden to retain it. But a number of courts do not permit the recovery of dividends paid stockholders from capital so long as the corporation is left solvent and the stockholder receives the payment without knowledge of its illegality.[16] The lead-

(Mason 1938 Supp.), §§7492-21(IIc), 22 (dividends out of net earnings when insolvent); N. H. Pub. Laws (1926), c. 225, §82 ("knowingly" accepting or receiving); Ohio Code Ann. (Baldwin 1938), §§8623-38(c), 123b ("knowingly" accepting or receiving).

[10] See §20, *supra.*

[11] 24 F. (2d) 661 (C. C. A. 2d, 1928). This is in general accord with the federal cases. *McDonald v. Williams,* 174 U. S. 397 (1899); *Ratcliff v. Clendenin,* 232 Fed. 61 (C. C. A. 8th, 1916); cf. *New Hampshire Savings Bank v. Richey,* 121 Fed. 956, 960 (C. C. A. 8th, 1903).

[12] *Bartlett v. Smith,* 162ᵃMd. 478, 160 Atl. 440 (1932); *Miller v. Bradish,* 69 Iowa 278, 28 N. W. 594 (1886); *Gilleylen v. Schoolfield,* 183 Ark. 143, 35 S. W. (2d) 356 (1931).

[13] See §20, *supra.*

[14] See §§16, 20, 21, *supra.*

[15] See §§15, 16, 21-24, *supra.*

[16] *Bartlett v. Smith,* 162 Md. 478, 160 Atl. 440 (1932); *Carlisle v. Ottley,* 143 Ga. 797, 85 S. E. 1010 (1915); *Bates v. Brooks,* 222 Iowa 1128, 270 N. W. 867 (1937) (statute made stockholders liable for "dividends which leaves [sic] insufficient funds to meet the liabilities"); *Quintal v. Adler,* 146 Misc. 300, 262 N. Y. S. 126 (1933), aff'd without opinion 239 App. Div. 775, 263 N. Y. S. 943 (1933), aff'd without opinion 264 N. Y. 452, 191 N. E. 509 (1934); see 1 Dodd and Baker, *Cases on Business Associations* (1940), Note on *Liability of Innocent Shareholders,* 1185. But in the following cases good faith was held not to be a defense to payments from capital, *Mackall v. Pocock,* 136 Minn. 8, 161 N. W. 228 (1917); *Mills v. Hendershot,* 70 N. J. Eq. 258, 62 Atl. 542 (1905); *Detroit Trust Co. v. Goodrich,* 175 Mich. 168, 141 N. W. 882 (1913) (but recovery was barred by the statute of

ing case is *McDonald v. Williams.*[17] When dividends were declared in that case, there were no net profits and capital was already impaired. The dividends were paid from capital but did not render the corporation insolvent. The defendant stockholders, none of whom were officers or directors, received the dividends in good faith believing they were from profits. The defendants were held not to be liable in spite of the National Banking Act provision, in Section 5204 of the Revised Statutes, that "No association, or any member thereof, . . . shall . . . withdraw, or permit to be withdrawn, either in the form of dividends or otherwise any portion of its capital." [18] The court discussed the provision prohibiting any "member" from withdrawing or permitting withdrawal of capital, stating this made necessary positive action by the shareholders. The clause prohibiting the association from withdrawing capital, which rendered the dividend illegal irrespective of the participation of stockholders, was disregarded. Apart from these considerations of the statute, the trust fund doctrine as expounded in *Wood v. Dummer* was held inapplicable to assets of a solvent corporation.

The holding in *McDonald v. Williams* is a singular exception to the normal rule that recovery may be had against good faith recipients of property tortiously transferred for which no value has been paid.[19] Since, unlike most dividend questions, the liability of stockholders who receive dividends from capital is not covered in many corporate statutes, it is extremely important to determine the justification for this common law rule. Legal sanction for permitting recovery might be based on any of several available theories. It is by no means necessary to resort to the trust fund doctrine, rejected in *McDonald v. Williams,* although this has sometimes been the basis for predicating stockholder liability.[20] If corporate capital is

---

limitations); *Roney v. Crawford,* 135 Ga. 1, 68 S. E. 701 (1910); *Mente v. Groff,* 10 Oh. N. P. (N. S.) 148 (1910) (statute provided dividends to be only "from the surplus profits arising from the business"); *Grant v. Southern Contract Co.,* 104 Ky. 781, 47 S. W. 1091 (1898) (no statement as to solvency or insolvency; court said whether solvent or insolvent corporation could not distribute capital to detriment of creditors). In some cases dividends from capital are held illegal as to stockholders without mention of the existence or absence of good faith. *American Steel & Wire Co. v. Eddy,* 130 Mich. 266, 89 N. W. 952 (1902) (statute made stockholders liable if capital was "withdrawn and refunded"); *In re Bay Ridge Inn,* 98 F. (2d) 85 (C. C. A. 2d, 1938) (mortgage to stockholders constituting a secret dividend out of capital under New York Stock Corporation Law, §58, not enforceable).

[17] 174 U. S. 397 (1899).

[18] This provision continues applicable to national banks. 12 U. S. C. A., §56.

[19] Cf. American Law Institute, *Restatement of Restitution* (1937), §123.

[20] *Williams v. Boice,* 38 N. J. Eq. 364 (Ct. Ch. 1884); *Davenport v. Lines,* 72

considered a trust fund, then as in any other situation where it is sought to cut off the interest of the equitable owner, the transferee must not only act in good faith but must be a purchaser for value. The most readily available ground for recovery is simply that the statute prohibiting the declaration of dividends from capital has been violated. Recovery could follow without further discussion —either of good faith of those receiving the illegal funds, or otherwise.[21] Or suit might be allowed on the theory that the corporation represents itself to creditors as having capital of a certain amount, and that it is a constructive fraud on creditors presumed to rely on this capital to pay it out in dividends. Recovery would be allowed on much the same theory used in permitting a creditor to set aside fraudulent conveyances when the corporation is actually insolvent.[22] Also, a dividend predicated on the supposition of profits when it is subsequently shown there were no profits, could be recoverable in some jurisdictions on the theory of payment under mistake.[23]

Ample methods for sustaining a judgment against the innocent stockholder are, therefore, available. Why, then, do many courts refuse to do so? The refusal may be due in some part to the recent tendency to de-emphasize protection to creditors.[24] In many ways the differences between creditors and stockholders of a large corporation have tended to decrease. As the Maryland Court expressed this viewpoint in *Bartlett v. Smith,* "practically they (the stockholders) are in no better position than creditors to know the condition of the company, and it would be an unfair and unreasonable burden to require them to pay back, years after they have been spent, dividends received in good faith from a solvent corporation in regular course of business."[25] Stockholders and creditors alike must

---

Conn. 118, 129, 44 Atl. 17 (director-stockholder liability sustained under statute and at common law).

[21] Cf. *Mente v. Groff,* 10 Oh. N. P. (N. S.) 148 (1910); *In re Bay Ridge Inn,* 98 F. (2d) 85 (C. C. A. 2d, 1938). In *Quintal v. Adler,* 146 Misc. 300, 262 N. Y. S. 126 (1933), aff'd 239 App. Div. 775, 263 N. Y. S. 943 (1933), aff'd 264 N. Y. 452, 191 N. E. 509 (1934), the court said the provision in New York Stock Corporation Law, §58, making directors liable was an indication that shareholders should not be liable.

[22] This was the ground for holding innocent stockholders liable in *Mackall v. Pocock,* 136 Minn. 8, 161 N. W. 228 (1917). Cf. *Hospes v. Northwestern Manufacturing & Car Co.,* 48 Minn. 174, 50 N. W. 1117 (1892). Where the payment is merely from capital it is, of course, not a fraudulent conveyance at common law. *Quintal v. Adler,* n. 21, *supra.*

[23] *Grant v. Ross,* 100 Ky. 44, 37 S. W. 263 (1896); *Gratz v. Redd,* 4 B. Mon. 178 (Ky. 1843) (director-stockholder); *Lexington L. F. & M. Insurance Co. v. Page,* 17 B. Mon. 412 (Ky. 1856).

[24] See §9.1, *supra.*

[25] 162 Md. 478, 160 Atl. 440 (1932). For similar statements of the rule, see

rely on the judgment of the directors in the matter of dividend declaration. If the dividend is actually from profit, the stockholder is entitled to it. Is he as against creditors any the less equitably entitled to a distribution he honestly supposes to be from profits, but which turns out in fact to be from capital? It must be conceded that his retention of such a distribution can only be justified on the admission that the old doctrine of capital to protect creditors has lost much of its vigor, and that as between themselves creditors and innocent shareholders are placed much on a plane of parity with respect to capital assets.

Where the stockholder has notice that the dividend is from capital, quite different considerations govern, and he is forced to refund it.[26] Then there exist no reasons of policy why he should be permitted to reap the benefits of statutory violation. The relationship of the stockholder to the corporation may be such as to charge him with knowledge of its corporate affairs.[27] Common directorates of parent and subsidiary have been held sufficient to charge the parent with knowledge of the illegality of a dividend from the subsidiary.[28] Likewise, when the dividend is a liquidating dividend from capital, stockholders must restore the same if necessary to pay corporate debts.[29]

Quintal v. Adler, n. 21, *supra; Gaunce v. Schoder,* 145 Wash. 604, 261 Pac. 393 (1927).

[26] *Cottrell v. Albany Card & Paper Mfg. Co.,* 142 App. Div. 148, 126 N. Y. S. 1070 (3d Dept. 1911) (comment, 11 Col. L. Rev. 47); *Williams v. Boice,* 38 N. J. Eq. 364 (Ct. Ch. 1884); *Rheinstrom v. Seasongood,* 19 Oh. N. P. (N. S.) 393 (1917); see *Wood v. National City Bank,* 24 F. (2d) 661, 662 (C. C. A. 2d, 1928). Fraud by a stockholder in misrepresenting the position of the corporation, which results in a division of capital, makes the stockholder liable for the dividends received. *Salina Mercantile Co. v. Stiefel,* 82 Kans. 7, 107 Pac. 774 (1910).

[27] Where the recipient is president of a bank, and signs reports of the financial condition submitted to the comptroller, he either knows or is presumed to know actual condition of the bank. *Main v. Mills,* 6 Biss. 98, Fed. Cas. No. 8,974 (C. C. Wis. 1874). In *Rheinstrom v. Seasongood,* 19 Oh. N. P. (N. S.) 393 (1917), the knowledge of a son who was an officer and record holder of stock for the benefit of his father was imputed to the father. Cf. *E. L. Moore & Co. v. Murchison,* 226 Fed. 679 (C. C. A. 4th, 1915) (defendant having transferred stock to another to manage as his agent chargeable with knowledge of the agent). But the normal presumption is that the dividend is legal and a distribution from profits. *McDonald v. Williams,* 174 U. S. 397 (1899); *Blythe v. Enslen,* 219 Ala. 638, 123 So. 71 (1929).

[28] *Grand Rapids Trust Co. v. Grand Rapids G. H. & M. Ry. Co.,* 7 F. Supp. 511 (W. D. Mich. 1931), §22.1, n. 127, *supra;* (statute made stockholders who "knowingly accept or receive" an illegal dividend liable); see *Cottrell v. Albany Card & Paper Co.,* 142 App. Div. 148, 153, 126 N. Y. S. 1070 (3d Dept. 1911).

[29] *Kimbrough v. Davies,* 104 Miss. 722, 61 So. 697 (1913); *First Nat. Bank v. Heller Sawdust Co.,* 240 Mich. 688, 216 N. W. 464 (1927) (under statute making stockholders liable for capital withdrawn before payment of all corporate debts).

Only in a relatively few jurisdictions are there statutes which make stockholders liable for dividends from capital. The decision in *Wood v. Dummer* held that stockholders who received liquidating dividends out of capital were liable to refund the same for the benefit of creditors. In 1828 this rule was expressly incorporated in a Maine statute [30] and continues to be the present law in that state.[31] In California the stockholder must have knowledge of the dividend's illegality, and he is only liable in the event that the corporation is adjudged bankrupt or insolvent within a year following receipt of the dividend.[32] However, in most statutes making stockholders liable for illegal dividends from capital, the question of knowledge is not dealt with, the liability merely being imposed for receipt of the dividend.[33] In states adopting provisions of the Uniform Business Corporation Act, stockholders are liable if directors are not, or if judgments against directors are uncollectible.[34] The chief instance when directors would not be liable will occur when they have acted prudently and without knowledge the dividend is illegal. Since the Iowa statute only makes stockholders liable for dividends which leave insufficient assets to meet liabilities,[35] they are under no duty to pay back dividends merely out of capital.[36]

Some states have statutes providing, apart from dividend provisions, that stockholders shall be liable for reductions of capital not in accordance with the method prescribed.[37] Effort has not often been made to hold stockholders liable for dividends under provisions of

[30] Me. Acts 1828, c. 385, §3, incorporated with modifications in Me. Rev. Stat. (1840), c. 78, §§15, 16.

[31] Me. Rev. Stat. (1930), c. 56, §37, as amended Me. Laws 1933, c. 53.

[32] Cal. Civ. Code (1937), §364.

[33] Mich. Stat. Ann. (Henderson 1937), §21.48 (the same section provides that only directors who wilfully or negligently declare dividends are liable); Minn. Stat. (Mason 1938 Supp.), §7492–22 (similar provisions); Miss. Code Ann. (1930), §4149; R. I. Gen. Laws (1938), c. 116, §38; Vt. Pub. Laws (1933), §5851; Va. Code (1936), §3840 (same section requires knowledge of illegality to make directors liable); Wis. Stat. (1937), §182.19 (directors only liable if they had no reason to believe there were sufficient profits). For a decision under the Wisconsin provision, see *Goetz v. Williams,* 206 Wis. 561, 240 N. W. 181 (1932). In Ohio the stockholder must knowingly accept or receive an unauthorized distribution. Ohio Code Ann. (Baldwin 1938), §8623–123b.

[34] Idaho Code Ann., §29–130; La. Gen. Stat. (Dart. 1939), §1107; Wash. Rev. Stat. Ann. (Rem.), §3803–25.

[35] Iowa Code (1939), §8378.

[36] *Bates v. Brooks,* 222 Iowa 1128, 270 N. W. 867 (1937); *Miller v. Bradish,* 69 Iowa 278, 28 N. W. 594 (1886).

[37] The Massachusetts Manufacturing Corporation Regulation Act of 1830 contained the basic provision of this character. Mass. Laws, Jan. Sess. 1830, c. 53, §10. It was codified in Mass. Rev. Stat. (1836), c. 38, §21. The present Massachusetts provision is Mass. Ann. Laws, c. 156, §35.

this character. In *Penzel v. Townsend,* a trustee in bankruptcy was permitted to recover from stockholders under a statute of this type making the latter liable to any creditor "if the capital stock of any such corporation shall be withdrawn and refunded to the stockholders before the payment of all the debts of the corporation." [38]

91. Liability of Persons Other Than Stockholders

An interesting question, and one on which there is almost no authority, is the liability of a transferee who receives an illegal dividend from a stockholder. In *State v. Bank of Ogalalla,* an illegal dividend was issued from a reduction surplus which did not actually exist.[39] At the time of the dividend, a creditor held the stockholder's stock in pledge as security for an antecedent debt, and, with knowledge as to the fact of reduction, received the dividend in question. The court held that unless the creditor could show it was an innocent holder for value, which could not be shown because of the notice and antecedent character of the indebtedness, the dividend was subject to the same infirmities in its hands as it would be in the hands of the stockholder.[40] Under the trust fund doctrine, there can be no doubt that a bona fide transferee, and only a bona fide transferee, could cut off the equity. The same result should follow under any other theory that is adopted, when the transferee has notice the dividend is illegal.

The important question occurs where the transferee has no notice of the illegality. If in addition to having no notice, he is also a transferee for value, no liability would exist even under the trust fund doctrine. If, however, he is innocent but has not given value, the question whether or not the trust fund doctrine is applicable becomes very material. Strict adherence to it would require holding the transferee liable. In most jurisdictions the trust fund doctrine will not be applicable, and in the majority of jurisdictions even a stockholder similarly without knowledge of the illegality would not be liable.[41] However, even in those jurisdictions such as Minnesota which hold the innocent stockholder liable,[42] the innocent transferee of a stockholder should not be liable. The question is one of the measure of statutory protection to be given a creditor with respect

---

[38] 128 Ark. 620, 195 S. W. 25 (1917).

[39] 65 Neb. 20, 90 N. W. 961 (1902).

[40] A similar result was reached in *Coleman v. Booth,* 268 Mo. 64, 186 S. W. 1021 (1916), where the defendant collected illegal dividend notes issued as collateral to an obligation of a stockholder.

[41] See §90, *supra.*

[42] See §90, n. 16, *supra.*

to corporate capital. It would be carrying this protection to extreme lengths to hold that a creditor, who has voluntarily dealt with a corporation, has a prior claim on its assets over an innocent third party receiving from a stockholder a dividend from capital.

92. Stockholders Liable Even Though Directors Also Liable

It is no defense in jurisdictions recognizing a right of recovery against stockholders that directors may also be liable.[43] Some statutes provide that directors held liable for declaring improper dividends have a right to contribution or reimbursement from shareholders who have knowledge of the illegality when the dividends are received.[44]

93. Measure of Damages

In the absence of statute, stockholders are not liable beyond the amount of illegal dividends respectively received.[45] Where the corporation is still a going concern, recovery may be had for the full amount of the dividend.[46] But where it is in liquidation, stockholders are liable only for the amount required to pay creditors' claims.[47] This prevents circuity of action. Dividends recovered from stockholders beyond the needs of creditors would otherwise only have to be refunded to the paying stockholders.[48] However, if the situation

[43] *Bartlett v. Smith,* 162 Md. 478, 160 Atl. 440 (1932) ; *Powers v. Heggie,* 268 Mass. 233, 167 N. E. 314 (1929) ; *Williams v. Boice,* 38 N. J. Eq. 364 (Ct. Ch. 1884) [but dictum (p. 369) that a recovery against directors would exonerate stockholders]. However, in some cases it has been held the statutory liability of directors indicates that stockholders are not to be held liable. *Quintal v. Adler,* §90, n. 21, *supra; Gaunce v. Schoder,* 145 Wash. 604, 261 Pac. 393 (1927).

[44] Cal. Civ. Code (1937), §363; 32 Ill. Ann. Stat. (Smith-Hurd 1935), §157.42; Mich. Stat. Ann. (Henderson 1937), §21.48 (directors repaying corporation subrogated to right of corporation to recover dividends from stockholders; knowledge not mentioned as prerequisite of corporate cause of action against stockholders) ; Ohio Code Ann. (Baldwin 1938), §8623–123b.

[45] *Mills v. Hendershot,* 70 N. J. Eq. 258, 62 Atl. 542 (1905) ; *Wood v. Dummer,* 3 Mason 308, Fed. Cas. No. 17,944 (C. C. Me. 1824).

[46] See *Gaunce v. Schoder,* 145 Wash. 604, 610, 261 Pac. 393 (1927).

[47] *Gaunce v. Schoder,* 145 Wash. 604, 261 Pac. 393 (1927) ; see *Osgood v. Laytin,* 3 Keyes 521, 524 (N. Y. 1867) (under statute making stockholders liable for payments out of capital). In *Mills v. Hendershot,* 70 N. J. Eq. 258, 62 Atl. 542 (1905), the court said: "As stockholders they are not liable beyond the amounts respectively received, but the liability is not merely for a proportionate share of the indebtedness, and therefore the solvent stockholders must make up, so far as they are chargeable with dividends, the deficiency of the insolvent estate of Stephens to pay its share of the debts." But in *Williams v. Boice,* 38 N. J. Eq. 364 (Ct. Ch. 1884), it was held a receiver did not have to allege there were enough assets to pay debts which had been proved.

[48] Compare the problem of damages where the action is against directors, §§81–81.3, *supra.*

were such that dividends had been paid to one class which ought to have been paid to another, recovery should be allowed for the benefit of those entitled thereto even when the corporation is in liquidation.

The statutory rule of damages like the common law rule is normally the amount of the illegal dividend received.[49]

94. Distributions Not Purporting to be Dividends

Sometimes in small corporations private obligations of stock-holders are paid out of corporate funds without any formal declaration of dividends. When the corporation is solvent at the time of payment, recovery is denied without reference to whether the capital is impaired or not. In *Little v. Garabrant,* a husband and wife who owned beneficially all the corporation's stock consented to payment of insurance premiums on a policy on the life of the husband without any dividend declaration at a time when the corporation was solvent.[50] It was held a receiver was not entitled to the policy, on the ground that in the absence of insolvency stockholders might unanimously agree to dispose of corporate funds as they saw fit.[51] In *Sweet v. Lang,* the corporation's president and other stockholders of a closely held corporation, pursuant to consent of all, paid their personal obligations with corporate checks.[52] The corporation being solvent at the time of payment, it was held a receiver could not recover from the president's creditors the amounts so paid.[53]

[49] Idaho Code Ann., §29–130; La. Gen. Stat. (Dart. 1939), §1107; Mich. Stat. Ann. (Henderson 1937), §21.48; Minn. Stat. (Mason 1938 Supp.), §7492–22; Miss. Code Ann. (1930), §4190 (liability to creditors for debts existing to the extent of the dividend and interest); N. H. Pub. Laws (1926), c. 225, §82 (liable to the extent of the amount received for debts of the corporation then existing or thereafter contracted); Ohio Code Ann. (Baldwin 1938), §8623–123b (with 6 per cent interest); R. I. Gen. Laws (1938), c. 116, §38 (for debts and obligations to the extent of the amount received with interest); Vt. Pub. Laws (1933), §5851; Va. Code (1936), §3840; Wash. Rev. Stat. Ann. (Rem.), §3803–25; Wis. Stat. (1937), §182.19. The 1697 Act amending the charter of the Bank of England made stockholders liable for dividends from capital "so far as the respective shares so by them received upon such dividend will extend." 8 and 9 Will. III, c. 20, §49. The act authorizing a charter to be granted to the English Linen Company in 1764 made stockholders liable for dividends from capital "so far as their respective shares so by them respectively received upon such Dividend or Dividends shall extend, to pay and satisfy the Debts which shall remain due and unpaid by the said company or corporation." 4 Geo. III, c. 37.

[50] *Little v. Garabrant,* 90 Hun 404, 35 N. Y. S. 689 (1895), aff'd on opinion below 153 N. Y. 661, 48 N. E. 1105 (1897).

[51] *Accord:Oliver v. Northwestern Mutual Life Insurance Co.,* 2 F. Supp. 266 (W. D. Pa. 1932) (action against insurance company to recover premiums); *Sweet v. Lang,* 14 F. (2d) 762 (C. C. A. 8th, 1926).

[52] *Sweet v. Lang,* 14 F. (2d) 762 (C. C. A. 8th, 1926).

[53] Compare generally the right of stockholders to declare dividends through informal agreement, §53, n. 8, 9, *supra.*

B. Parties Entitled to Enforce Liability

95. The Corporation

If the right to recover from stockholders is recognized either by statute or as a matter of common law, there is presented the question, as in actions against directors,[54] whether a solvent corporation may recover. In *Salina Mercantile Company v. Stiefel,* the defendant stockholders misrepresented the financial position of the corporation and on that basis succeeded in getting a dividend declared.[55] Recovery was allowed to the corporation, which was solvent, although the dividend only impaired capital and although there was no showing that creditors had been injured. Apart from the question of fraud, the court said the corporation was entitled to a restoration of capital. "It does not follow that if a part of it is returned to the subscribers the general loss to all by the impaired efficiency of the company is fully compensated by the share each individually receives in the distribution." [56]

The principal objection against permitting a solvent corporation to recover from directors—that stockholders are in effect thereby paid a second time—is, of course, absent when stockholders themselves are the defendants. And a good argument can be made that stockholders suffer little real damage as a result of such recovery. Presumably, once it is known capital has been impaired by a dividend, a decline in market value of the stock at least as great as the amount of the impairment will take place. Conversely, if the corporation should now recover from stockholders the capital illegally distributed, the market value will probably rise in an amount close to the dividend per share recovered. Stockholders paying back to the corporation $10 a share in dividends illegally paid from capital might expect to find the market quotation on their stock advance close to 10 points. The effect of the recovery from the standpoint of the stockholder is at the time much like a transfer from one pocket to the other, although admittedly the second pocket is not as liquid. ·From the standpoint of the future, the effect may be much different. The capital is now again a part of the corporation's funds and liable to be impaired by losses or declines in the market level. It was this risk, however, which the stockholder originally contemplated in making a capital stock investment. It would seem that

---

[54] See §83, *supra.*

[55] 82 Kans. 7, 107 Pac. 774 (1910).

[56] Cf. *Gager v. Paul,* 111 Wis. 638, 87 N. W. 875 (1901); see *Lexington L. F. & M. Insurance Co. v. Page,* 17 B. Mon. 412, 442–443 (Ky. 1856).

as against stockholders who receive capital, the claim of the solvent corporation to assert a cause of action in behalf of creditors in order to compel restoration for just these contingencies is strong. Certainly it is stronger than the corporation's claim against directors.[57]

In some statutes the right of recovery against stockholders is vested solely in the corporation.[58] In others the corporation is among those authorized to sue.[59]

The promoter problems presented in the *Old Dominion Copper Company* suits [60] have an interesting corollary in dividend law. If stock dividends are illegally paid to all of a corporation's stockholders at a time when it is intended thereafter to distribute further stock for cash to the public, a situation is created very similar to that where promoters and incorporators fraudulently take stock for their services at a time when there are no other stockholders, but with the intention of distributing that stock to the public or having the corporation distribute further stock to the public. In the latter type of case, the Supreme Court in the *Lewisohn* case held that the corporation had no cause of action, since as of the time of issuance all of the stockholders were parties to the transaction and had consented; in the *Bigelow* case, on the other hand, the Massachusetts court reached the opposite conclusion. In the comparable stock dividend case, where a stock dividend was fraudulently issued to all common stockholders with the intention of selling more stock to the public for cash, it was held in *Pontiac Packing Co. v. Hancock,* on the ground that the *Bigelow* case was law in Michigan, that the corporation might have the stock dividend canceled.[61] The corporation was denied recovery, however, because the statute of limitations had run.

96. Creditors

The early English charters imposing personal liability on stockholders did so for the benefit of creditors. The Act of Parliament authorizing a charter to be granted to the English Linen Company in 1764 provided stockholders receiving dividends from capital should be liable for corporate debts to the extent of the dividend

[57] Compare §83, *supra.*

[58] Idaho Code Ann., §29–130; La. Gen. Stat. (Dart. 1939), §1107; Mich. Stat. Ann. (Henderson 1937), §21.48; Minn. Stat. (Mason 1938 Supp.), §7492–22; Ohio Code Ann. (Baldwin 1938), §8623–123b; Wash. Rev. Stat. Ann. (Rem.), §3803–25.

[59] Cal. Civ. Code (1937), §364 (provided corporation is adjudged insolvent or bankrupt within one year after receipt of the dividend); Vt. Pub. Laws (1933), §5851.

[60] *Old Dominion Copper Co. v. Lewisohn,* 210 U. S. 206 (1908); *Old Dominion Copper Co. v. Bigelow,* 203 Mass. 159, 89 N. E. 193 (1909).

[61] 257 Mich. 45, 241 N. W. 268 (1932) (the dividend was issued on revaluation and write-up of a lease from $14,000 to $86,000).

received, "and the Person or Persons . . . to whom such Debts shall be due and owing, shall and may sue for and recover the same." [62] Some modern statutes likewise give a cause of action to creditors.[63]

Whether the cause of action is individual to creditors or a group cause of action, and whether subsequent as well as existing creditors may recover, are problems analogous to those involved in actions by creditors against directors.[64] In *Osgood v. Laytin,* where the statute made stockholders receiving an illegal dividend liable "to the creditors of said company," it was held that the cause of action was vested in creditors jointly rather than individually, so that a receiver was entitled to bring an action in behalf of all.[65] The statutes in Maine and Rhode Island, however, give the cause of action to "any creditor." [66]

As in the case of actions against directors, subsequent creditors not having notice of the illegality of the dividend should be allowed to recover.[67] New Hampshire by statute makes stockholders liable for debts existing or afterward contracted,[68] while Mississippi limits recovery to existing creditors.[69]

---

[62] 4 Geo. III, c. 37. The earlier provision with respect to the Bank of England made stockholders liable for dividends from capital "so far as the respective shares so by them received upon such dividend will extend . . . to any other persons . . . who by virtue of this act shall and may sue for and recover the same (besides treble costs of suit) by action of debt." 8 and 9 Will. III, c. 20, §49 (1697).

[63] Me. Rev. Stat. (1930), c. 56, §37, as amended Me. Laws 1933, c. 53 (in action on case); Miss. Code Ann. (1930), §4190; N. H. Laws (1926), c. 225, §82; R. I. Gen. Laws (1938), c. 116, §38 (by action on the case or bill in equity after judgment against corporation and execution returned unsatisfied); Va. Code (1936), §3840. In *American Steel & Wire Co. v. Eddy,* 130 Mich. 266, 89 N. W. 952 (1902), a judgment creditor was allowed to recover a dividend paid to a preferred stockholder out of capital where the statute made stockholders liable "to any creditor of such corporation" [Mich. Comp. Laws (1897), §7057].

[64] See §§84.1, 84.2, *supra.*

[65] 3 Keyes 521 (N. Y. 1867). Where there has been an assignment for the benefit of creditors, the cause of action vests in the trustee, barring creditors individually. *Lexington L. F. & M. Ins. Co. v. Page,* 17 B. Mon. 412 (Ky. 1856).

[66] Me. Rev. Stat. (1930), c. 56, §37, as amended Me. Laws 1933, c. 53; R. I. Gen. Laws (1938), c. 116, §38.

[67] *Williams v. Boice,* 38 N. J. Eq. 364 (Ct. Ch. 1884) (receiver allowed to recover for subsequent creditors); *Cottrell v. Albany Card & Paper Co.,* 142 App. Div. 148, 126 N. Y. S. 1070 (3d Dept. 1911) (same as to trustee); Frey, *Cases and Statutes on Business Associations* (1935), Note, 752; but see *Wood v. National City Bank,* 24 F. (2d) 661 (C. C. A. 2d, 1928) (where basis of recovery is that corporation was insolvent in bankruptcy sense, it must be alleged that creditors existing at time of dividend are still creditors); *Ratcliff v. Clendenin,* 232 Fed. 61, 64–5 (C. C. A. 8th, 1916); *Gilleylen v. Schoolfield,* 183 Ark. 143, 147, 35 S. W. (2d) 356 (1931) (suggestion that actual intent to defraud future creditors was necessary).

[68] N. H. Pub. Laws (1926), c. 225, §82.

[69] Miss. Code Ann. (1930), §4149.

In *Wood v. Dummer,* it was held a creditor might recover from stockholders that proportion of his claim that the individual stockholder's stock bore to the total stock of the corporation, but not in excess of the dividends received.[70]

97. Trustee in Bankruptcy

As in the case of directors, statutes sometimes expressly make stockholders receiving illegal dividends liable to trustees in bankruptcy.[71] In the absence of provisions in the state statute, the trustee's right of recovery under the Bankruptcy Act may be predicated on either the claim of the bankrupt corporation or its creditors.

(*a*) Under Section 70a(4) of the Bankruptcy Act, the trustee is vested by operation of law with the title of the bankrupt to all "property transferred by him in fraud of his creditors."[72] Under this section the trustee has authority to recover dividends illegally paid to stockholders when the corporation is insolvent.[73] It is doubtful, however, that, in the absence of authority in the state law for assertion of a cause of action by the corporation, the trustee could set aside, in the right of the corporation, a payment illegal only because made from capital. In such cases, resort must be had to the claim of the trustee in behalf of creditors.

(*b*) Several provisions of the Bankruptcy Act enable the trustee to recover in the right of creditors. Dividends paid previous to the one-year period preceding bankruptcy may be recovered where under state law any creditor having a provable claim might have avoided the same,[74] or on the theory that under Section 70(c) the trustee has all the rights, remedies, and powers as of the date of the bankruptcy of a judgment creditor holding an execution returned unsatisfied.[75]

[70] 3 Mason 308, Fed. Cas. No. 17,944 (C. C. Me. 1824); see *Osgood v. Laytin,* 3 Keyes 521, 524 (N. Y. 1867).

[71] Cal. Civ. Code (1937), §364; Me. Rev. Stat. (1930), §§37, 102, as amended Me. Laws 1933, c. 53; Minn. Stat. (Mason 1938 Supp.), §§7492–22, 51; R. I. Gen. Laws (1938), c. 116, §38; Vt. Pub. Laws (1933), §5851 ("any successor or assignee"). As in suits against directors, trustees in bankruptcy are sometimes allowed to recover from stockholders without discussion of their capacity to sue. See e.g. *Roney v. Crawford,* 135 Ga. 1, 68 S. E. 701 (1910); *Mackall v. Pocock,* 136 Minn. 8, 161 N. W. 228 (1917); *Goetz v. Williams,* 206 Wis. 561, 240 N. W. 181 (1932).

[72] 11 U. S. C. A., §110(a)(4), as amended 52 Stat. 880 (1938).

[73] *Powers v. Heggie,* 268 Mass. 233, 167 N. E. 314 (1929); *Ulness v. Dunnell,* 61 N. D. 95, 237 N. W. 208 (1931).

[74] Bankruptcy Act, §70(e) [11 U. S. C. A., §110(e), as amended 52 Stat. 882 (1938)]; *Cottrell v. Albany Card & Paper Co.,* 142 App. Div. 148, 126 N. Y. S. 1070 (3d Dept. 1911) (for benefit of subsequent creditors).

[75] 11 U. S. C. A., §110(c), as amended 52 Stat. 881 (1938) [formerly §47a(2), 11 U. S. C. A., §75a(2)]; *Ulness v. Dunnell,* 61 N. D. 95, 237 N. W. 208 (1931)

Under Section 67(d)(2), the right of recovery when the dividend is paid during the one-year period prior to bankruptcy is very broad.[76] The dividend is fraudulent (1) as to creditors existing at the time if the corporation is rendered insolvent, without regard to actual intent, (2) as to existing and subsequent creditors. if the capital remaining is unreasonably small for engaging in its business, (3) as to all creditors if the corporation believes it will incur debts beyond its ability to pay as they mature, and (4) as to all creditors if actually fraudulent.

After bankruptcy the claim against stockholders is enforceable only by the trustee and no longer by creditors.[77]

98. Receiver

Some statutes expressly vest the right to recover from stockholders in the receiver.[78] In the absence of express statutory authority, the right of the receiver to recover from stockholders for the general benefit of creditors should be sustained, in the same manner that the receiver's claim is sustained in actions against directors.[79] And receivers frequently are permitted to recover, often without reference to the question of capacity.[80]

[former §47(a)] ; *Coleman v. Booth,* 268 Mo. 64, 186 S. W. 1021 (1916) [against third person taking dividend through stockholder with notice; under former §47(a) it was immaterial that none of the debts allowed against the bankrupt existed at the time the dividend was declared] ; cf. *Ratcliff v. Clendenin,* 232 Fed. 61 (C. C. A. 8th, 1916) (statute not relied upon).

[76] 11 U. S. C. A., §107(d)(2), as amended 52 Stat. 877 (1938).

[77] *Powers v. Heggie,* 268 Mass. 233, 167 N. E. 314 (1929).

[78] Cal. Civ. Code (1937), §364 (if corporation is adjudged insolvent in proceeding begun within one year of receipt of the dividend) ; Me. Rev. Stat. (1930), c. 56, §§37, 102, as amended Me. Laws 1933, c. 53; Minn. Stat. (Mason 1938 Supp.), §§7492-22, 51 ; R. I. Gen. Laws (1938), c. 116, §38; Vt. Pub. Laws (1933), §§5851.

[79] See §86, *supra.*

[80] *Osgood v. Laytin,* 3 Keyes 521 (N. Y. 1867) ; *Kretschmar v. Stone,* 90 Miss. 375, 43 So. 177 (1907) ; *Detroit Trust Co. v. Goodrich,* 175 Mich. 168, 141 N. W. 882 (1913) (statute vested generally all property in receiver for benefit of stockholders and creditors; court said receiver could recover in absence of statute, although he represented no judgment creditors who had exhausted their remedy at law against the corporation) ; *Mills v. Hendershot,* 70 N. J. Eq. 258, 62 Atl. 542 (1905) ; *Grant v. Ross,* 100 Ky. 44, 37 S. W. 263 (1896) ; *Davenport v. Lines,* 72 Conn. 118, 44 Atl. 17 (1899) ; *Bartlett v. Smith,* 162 Md. 478, 160 Atl. 440 (1932).

CHAPTER 9

RIGHT OF SURVIVING CORPORATION TO PAY DIVIDENDS AFTER SALE OF ASSETS, MERGER OR CONSOLIDATION

A. Cash Acquisitions

99. Combination Method: Sale of Assets, Merger or Consolidation

Industrial combinations by sale of assets, merger and consolidation raise questions as to the available fund from which dividends may be paid by the surviving corporation. The problem specifically concerns allocation in the new corporation of proper amounts to (*a*) capital, (*b*) paid-in surplus, and (*c*) earned surplus. Assume that the A and B corporations are to be combined, the pre-combination balance sheets showing:

A

ASSETS		LIABILITIES	
Fixed assets, etc.	$150,000	Capital (par)	$100,000
		Earned surplus	50,000
	$150,000		$150,000

B

Fixed assets, etc.	$300,000	Capital (par)	$200,000
		Earned surplus	100,000
	$300,000		$300,000

The shares in each corporation have a book value of $150. The A corporation or its shareholders might be paid cash $150,000 for a transfer of all assets to the surviving B corporation, or a combination might take place by which the shareholders of the A and B corporations would each have one share in a surviving corporation for each share held in the constituent corporations. In both cases the question arises as to what happens to the earned surpluses of the A and B corporations. If both earned surpluses become capital, they are available for dividends in no jurisdiction.[1] If the earned sur-

---

[1] See §15, *supra*.

plus of either or both is transmuted to paid-in surplus of the new corporation, dividends cannot be paid in many jurisdictions except upon preferred shares.[2] On the other hand, if the earned surplus of each corporation survives, it will be normally available for dividends in all jurisdictions.[3] Thus, it is important in all industrial or utility combines to determine whether prior earned surpluses survive at all as some kind of surplus, and in jurisdictions where there are restrictions as to use of paid-in surplus for dividends, it becomes important to determine the further question whether the surplus is to be treated as earned or paid-in.

The legal method used for effecting the combination may conceivably bear upon answers to these questions. Thus, if in the example put, the B corporation should acquire the assets of A under a sale of assets statute, the consideration would be paid to the A corporation, or with certain risks a short-cut payment directly to A stockholders might be made. In any event, the A corporation would not, in the absence of express statutory provisions, technically become a part of the B corporation, although for practical purposes all of its assets and possessions of worth would have passed to the latter. It might, therefore, be contended that since the A corporation still survives, and since it is not part of the B corporation, its earned surplus cannot be a surplus of the B corporation. Where under the theory of merger the A corporation becomes a part of the B corporation, it may be urged that the surplus of A can become surplus of B, since the entire A corporation is absorbed. If, on the other hand, consolidation is the method employed, the argument may be made that an entirely new corporation is formed and that the assets received from both A and B in their entirety constitute capital of the new corporation.

To permit the particular legal method chosen for combining corporations to govern the future authority of the surviving corporation to declare dividends would put a high premium on the method of unification selected. In some jurisdictions statutes of one type rather than another are alone available, while in other cases tax or business considerations having nothing to do with dividend policy may dictate adoption of one method or the other.[4]

---

[2] See §29, n. 226–230.

[3] See Chapter 2, *supra*.

[4] Graham and Katz draw a distinction between merger and consolidation effected by issuance of stock. On a consolidation they absorb into capital surpluses of all companies. On a merger they preserve the surplus of the continuing corporation. Graham and Katz, *Accounting in Law Practice* (2d Ed. 1938) 380–381, 382–383. See also Montgomery, *Auditing Theory and Practice* (5th Ed. 1934) 416–417.

100. Financing Method Employed

A second factor which may bear upon the survival of surplus in an industrial combination is the method of financing employed. Usually such a unification is effected through the issuance of securities in exchange for securities of some or all of the corporations involved. Bonds may be issued to take care of underlying indebtedness, preferred stocks for assets of stronger corporations, and common stock generally, plus perhaps a certain amount of cash, to liquidate current obligations. But one of the corporations or its stockholders may be paid completely in cash, particularly if the corporation is small and it is a question of elimination. Suppose that in the example put in the preceding section the B corporation buys all of the assets of the A corporation for $150,000 in cash. What will the effect be on the balance sheet of the B company? The journal would show:

```
Assets of A acquired by
  purchase  ...........................  $150,000
      Cash  ..............................           $150,000
```

The resulting balance sheet of B would remain for dividend purposes exactly what it was before the purchase:

ASSETS		LIABILITIES	
Fixed assets, etc.	$150,000	Capital	$200,000
Assets of A acquired by		Surplus	100,000
purchase	150,000		
	$300,000		$300,000

The $50,000 surplus of A is not added to the $100,000 surplus of B to make a new surplus of $150,000.[5] The result of the outright purchase from A for cash is no different than if the B corporation had purchased the same quantity of assets from an individual, or from a partnership whose books showed a profit of $50,000 over an original capital investment of $100,000. The fact that on the books of the A corporation there is a surplus of $50,000 can make no difference to the B corporation or its stockholders. The $50,000 surplus will be divided among the A stockholders or retained by them as a surplus in their own corporation. The B corporation by making a cash purchase cannot thereby create a surplus from which to pay dividends. While the physical asset interests of the A corporation may continue in the B corporation, the interest of A stockholders

[5] York, *Nature of Acquired Surplus*, 69 J. of Accountancy 363, 364 (1940).

does not continue, and it is the latter, if anything, which gives rise to the need of preserving surplus of the A corporation. This need arises when stock rather than cash is delivered to the A stockholders.

In handling this problem, there are, however, statutes in a few jurisdictions which must be considered. Several of these are so worded that, upon a cash merger or consolidation of the type discussed, the surplus of $50,000, appearing on the books of the A corporation, might be entered as earned surplus on the books of B corporation and as such be available for dividends.[6]

Seldom will a cash purchase of assets be exactly at the corporation's book value. If the B corporation had paid $200,000 for assets of the A corporation carried on the A books at $150,000, it would mean either that the assets were undervalued on the books, and that their reproduction value less depreciation was $200,000, or that the B corporation was paying an additional $50,000 purely for goodwill, perhaps represented by earning power of the A corporation. In the latter case accountants may carry the excess $50,000 on the asset side of B's balance sheet as goodwill.[7] This would produce a balance sheet for B as follows:

ASSETS		LIABILITIES	
Fixed assets, etc.	$100,000	Capital	$200,000
Acquisition of assets of A:		Surplus	100,000
Fixed assets, etc.	150,000		
Goodwill	50,000		
	$300,000		$300,000

There is obviously a question mark as to the availability of $50,000 of this surplus for dividends, depending upon whether the $50,000 item of goodwill included in assets actually represents sound value either in added value of the fixed assets of A or goodwill earning power. Where there is any doubt, the goodwill should be charged off against surplus of B.[8]

On the other hand, the B corporation might pay only $100,000 for assets valued at $150,000 on A's books. This would indicate

[6] Cal. Civ. Code (1937), §361(1)(6); 32 Ill. Ann. Stat. (Smith-Hurd 1935), §157.69g (§§61, 62 seem to contemplate more particularly security mergers and consolidations); Mich. Stat. Ann. (Henderson), §21.53; Minn. Stat. (Mason 1938 Supp.), §7492-20 (IX); Ohio Code Ann. (Baldwin 1938), §§8623-38(e), 67(6); 15 Purd. Pa. Stat. Ann., §2852-907.

[7] Graham and Katz, *Accounting in Law Practice* (2d Ed. 1938) 381, 391; Paton and Littleton, *An Introduction to Corporate Accounting Standards* (1940) 92; Sunley and Pinkerton, *Corporation Accounting* (1931) 493.

[8] Cf. Porter and Fiske, *Accounting* (1935) 304-305, and §41, *supra*.

that the assets either were not worth any more than $100,000 or that the corporation was receiving a bargain. The presumption against an accounting entry which would show a surplus out of the very act of purchase, favors carrying the assets at the price paid for them, or sometimes, if carried at their book value with A, a reserve for the difference is set up until the real worth of the assets is determined.[9] From the standpoint of dividends there is real danger only if the assets are sought to be carried at book value to A without any reserve.

B. Par Value Stock Plans

101. Re-domestication

When the financing of a sale of assets, a merger, or a consolidation takes place principally through securities, with par value stock used to pay for the stockholder equity of all shareholders in the constituent corporations, there is a genuine continuity of shareholder interest in the new organization which is absent in outright cash purchases. The shareholders in the constituent corporations, turning over their assets to the combine, should continue to have a proportionate interest in the capital and surplus of the latter resembling that previously existing in the original corporations. The simplest illustration of this type situation is the organization of a new corporation in a new state, which turns over all of its stock to the stockholders of a corporation organized under the laws of another state, in return for a transfer of all the stock and assets of the latter. The A corporation, organized under the laws of Delaware, has par value capital of $100,000 and earned surplus of $50,000. The B corporation, organized under the laws of New York for the purpose of acquiring the assets of the A corporation, issues its par value stock in the amount of $100,000 share-for-share to the stockholders of A, in exchange for a surrender of the stock of the latter and transfer of its assets to B. There can be no doubt that from the accounting standpoint this mere shift in domicil should not capitalize the $50,000 in earned surplus of the A corporation. The books of the B corporation should show capital $100,000 and earned surplus $50,000.[10]

[9] Sunley and Pinkerton, *Corporation Accounting* (1931) 409, 493. Cf. Graham and Katz, *Accounting in Law Practice* (2d Ed. 1938) 391; Paton and Littleton, *An Introduction to Corporate Accounting* (1940) 29; Porter and Fiske, *Accounting* (1935) 304; S. E. C. Accounting Series Release No. 8 (1938).

[10] If a recapitalization program does not bring about a vital change in the corporate entity, there is no objection to carrying forward earned surplus. Paton, *Essentials of Accounting* (1938) 687; Paton and Littleton, *An Introduction to Corporate Accounting Standards* (1940) 107.

102. Surplus Per Share of Constituent Corporations Equal

Another situation in which it should be quite clear that the surplus of the participating corporations should continue available for dividends after the plan of combination is consummated, is that in which the book value of the shares is equal in all corporations. Assume again A and B corporations with the following balance sheets:

A

ASSETS		LIABILITIES	
Fixed assets, etc.	$150,000	Capital (par)	$100,000
		Earned surplus	50,000
	$150,000		$150,000

B

Fixed assets, etc.	$300,000	Capital (par)	$200,000
		Earned surplus	100,000
	$300,000		$300,000

If the A corporation, having 1,000 shares of the net value of $150, is merged into the B corporation which issues 1,000 of its par value $100 shares, also of the net value of $150, in exchange for the shares of A, the new balance sheet of B should show available for dividends $150,000 in a surplus account. The new balance sheet of B might present the effect of the acquisition as follows:

Fixed assets, etc.	$450,000	Capital (par)		$300,000
		Surplus:		
		Earned	$100,000	
		Amount to equalize earned surplus arising upon acquisition of A	50,000	150,000
	$450,000			$450,000

Stockholders having the same *pro rata* interests in different corporations have pooled them, and the result should produce similar *pro rata* interests in surplus and capital of the recapitalized corporation.[11] It is clear, in the case of a merger, that at least the surplus

---

[11] Montgomery, *Auditing Theory and Practice* (5th Ed. 1934) 416–417; Berle, *Corporate Devices for Diluting Stock Participations*, 31 Col. L. Rev. 1238, 1248 (1931); Note, *Declaration of Dividends from Paid-in Surplus*, 31 Col. L. Rev. 844,

of the surviving corporation will remain intact and available for dividends. Nothing has happened to capitalize it. If the B corporation were to issue its stock to an individual for assets of like amount, it could not be contended that any part of the surplus of B should be disturbed by the transaction. From the standpoint of B, the situation is no different if it acquires the assets from another corporation.[12]

In the example under discussion, the surplus of A must also be preserved as equalizing earned surplus on B's new balance sheet wholly apart from doctrines peculiar to merger or consolidation. Under the theory of *Equitable Life Assurance Society v. Union Pacific Railroad Company,* the stockholders of B, having a dividend equity surplus of $50 per share, are entitled to have surplus sufficiently equalized out of assets received upon the issuance of new stock to give all stockholders of the newly capitalized corporation a like dividend surplus equivalent to $50 per share.[13] If the $50,000 surplus of the A corporation is capitalized, it will mean that 3,000 instead of 2,000 shareholders will now have a claim on the original $100,000 of surplus of the B corporation, reducing the dividend equity of the original B shareholders from $50 to $33 per share.[14]

What has been said with respect to the B corporation issuing its stock on a merger or purchase of assets, should apply equally where

---

850–851 (1931); but cf. *Pardee v. Harwood Electric Co.,* 262 Pa. 68, 105 Atl. 48 (1918) (par value preferred under its contract had a right to dividends from "undivided net earnings"; the corporation surviving merger had no net earnings unless the surplus of the constituent companies existing at the date of merger were treated as having survived; the court denied a claim of the preferred to compulsory payment of dividends: "This surplus, which had existed from the time of the merger, could not be regarded as net earnings, nor considered as such on the question of dividends to the holders of preferred stock"). Many accountants take the position that the prior earned surplus becomes paid-in surplus. York, *Nature of Acquired Surplus,* 69 J. of Acc. 363, 364 (1940); Dewing, *Financial Policy of Corporations* (3d Rev. Ed. 1934) 602; Paton and Littleton, *An Introduction to Corporate Accounting Standards* (1940) 106–107; Paton, *Essentials of Accounting* (1938) 687; Sunley and Pinkerton, *Corporation Accounting* (1931) 386, 392 (treating without discussion the result of a merger as freezing earned surplus into paid-in surplus).

[12] Even where the position is taken that all surplus is frozen on consolidation, it is conceded that surplus of the surviving corporation on a merger is not frozen. Cf. Graham and Katz, *Accounting in Law Practice* (2d Ed. 1938) 380–381, 382–383.

[13] 212 N. Y. 360, 106 N. E. 92 (1914), §45.2, n. 169, *supra.*

[14] In order to protect the equity interest of shareholders of the merging corporation in that corporation's surplus, stock might be issued to its stockholders capitalizing this surplus. Cf. *Williams v. Union Telegraph Co.,* 93 N. Y. 162 (1883), and see §45.2, n. 173, §56, n. 77, *supra.* But this would disrupt the relative combination value of shares of the constituent corporations and would ordinarily be impractical for that reason.

an entirely new corporation on consolidation distributes 1,000 shares to the shareholders of A and 2,000 shares to shareholders of B, even though in that situation there is no base surplus of the new corporation such as that of the B corporation against which to make equalizations.[15] The stockholders of the B corporation are as much entitled to have the earned surpluses preserved upon a consolidation as upon a merger. The creation of an entirely new corporation rather than the continuation of B should not prevent this result.

Statutes in a few jurisdictions expressly permit the surpluses of corporations organized on par value mergers or consolidations to be retained to the extent not capitalized.[16] In many states provisions in merger and consolidation statutes for transferring to the surviving corporation all the rights, privileges, and powers of the absorbed corporations [17] might be construed as broad enough to permit exercise of the right to declare dividends out of funds which were available for such purposes prior to the reorganization.

103. Surplus Per Share of Constituent Corporations Unequal

In the usual case, the surplus allocable to shares of the respective constituent companies will not be equal.

(a) One corporation may have a deficit:

A

Fixed assets, etc.	$ 75,000	Capital	$100,000
Deficit	(25,000)		
	$100,000		$100,000

B

Fixed assets	$300,000	Capital	$200,000
		Earned surplus	100,000
	$300,000		$300,000

[15] But cf. Graham and Katz, *Accounting in Law Practice* (2d Ed. 1938) 380–381, 382–383; Montgomery, *Auditing Theory and Practice* (5th Ed. 1934) 416–417.

[16] Cal. Civ. Code (1937), §361(6); 32 Ill. Ann. Stat. (Smith-Hurd 1935), §157.69g; Mich. Stat. Ann. (Henderson 1937), §§21.43, 21.53; Minn. Stat. (Mason 1938 Supp.), §§7492–20 (VIII, IX), 44 (II); N. Y. Stock Corp. Law, §86 ("Any excess in the amount of the assets of the consolidated corporation over the amount of its liabilities, including capital, at the date of consolidation, may be deemed to be surplus of the consolidated corporation"; the "capital" of a New York corporation having par value shares is the amount equal to par, N. Y. Stock Corp. Law, §§12, 13); Ohio Code Ann. (Baldwin 1938), §§8623–38(e), 67(6); 15 Purd. Pa. Stat. Ann., §2852–907.

[17] See e.g. Conn. Gen. Stat. (1930), §3465; Del. Rev. Code (1935), c. 65, §60; N. J. Stat. (1937), §14:12–5; N. Y. Stock Corp. Law, §§85, 88.

If the B corporation now issues to stockholders of A 1,000 of its $100 par value shares for the $75,000 in assets of A, it will be necessary to reduce the surplus of the B corporation $25,000 in order to supply the capital difference necessary to issue the shares,[18] since statutes in most states require that the capitalization for par value shares must be par.[19] The resulting balance sheet will be:

B

Fixed assets, etc.	$300,000	Capital	$300,000
Assets acquired from A ..	75,000	Earned surplus	75,000
	$375,000		$375,000

(b) While the A corporation may not have a deficit, its surplus per share may be less than that of B:

A

Fixed assets, etc.	$125,000	Capital	$100,000
		Earned surplus	25,000
	$125,000		$125,000

B

Fixed assets, etc.	$300,000	Capital	$200,000
		Earned surplus	100,000
	$300,000		$300,000

The shares of A have a net dividend surplus of $25, the shares of B of $50. If A corporation is acquired by B on a share for share exchange of the shares of B, it is clear that the $25 dividend surplus per share of old A stock survives to equalize *pro tanto* the dividend surplus of $50 per share of B stock.[20] This would give the resulting corporation capital of $300,000 and surplus of $125,000, or dividend surplus per share of around $42, a loss in surplus to original B shareholders of about $8. But this loss is the result of insufficient assets received from A to equalize the B surplus.

[18] See 1 Dodd and Baker, *Cases on Business Associations* (1940) 1146, n. 7.

[19] See §45, n. 158, *supra*. But compare the theory of *Goodnow v. American Writing Paper Co.*, §22.1, n. 124, *supra*, in cases where the statute does not expressly provide that the capital of par value stock shall be par. There is some doubt whether the *Goodnow* case would be extended to permit treating as capital only the value of assets received from the A corporation where the B corporation has a surplus which could absorb the difference between the value of A's assets and the par value of the stock issued in payment.

[20] See §102, *supra*.

(c) The surplus per share in the A corporation may be greater than in the B corporation:

A

Fixed assets, etc	$200,000	Capital	$100,000
		Earned surplus	100,000
	$200,000		$200,000

B

Fixed assets, etc	$300,000	Capital	$200,000
		Earned surplus	100,000
	$300,000		$300,000

The A shares have a dividend surplus of $100, the B shares of only $50. If the B corporation issues 1,000 of its shares to A stockholders, and the entire A surplus is carried over as such on the books of the surviving corporation, there will be capital of $300,000 and earned surplus of $200,000, or dividend surplus per share of around $67, a loss in original surplus to A stockholders of around $33, and correspondingly a dividend surplus gift to old B stockholders of $17 per share. In order to remedy this, as on the ordinary sale of stock at a premium in excess of book value, only sufficient earned surplus of A to equalize prior earned surplus of B might be set up on the books of the new corporation, setting apart the balance of A's surplus as a special surplus not available for dividends to old B shareholders.[21] The new B balance sheet might read:

Fixed assets, etc.	$500;000	Capital		$300,000
		Surplus:		
		Earned	$100,000	
		Amount to equalize earned surplus arising on acquisition of A..	50,000	
		Special surplus arising on acquisition of A	50,000	200,000
	$500,000			$500,000

[21] See §45.2, *supra*.

104. Effect of Financing at Other Than Book Value

Thus far problems of preserving dividend surplus have been discussed on the assumption that values on the books of the constituent corporations are adhered to in the plan of combination. This will seldom be the case. The fixed assets are usually entirely revalued,[22] frequently on the basis of reproduction cost less depreciation.[23] And often the factor of difference in earning power of the respective corporations will be capitalized, creating an intangible item of goodwill. The effect of these features of the plan may be illustrated:

A

	Book Values	Under Plan		Book Values
Fixed assets, etc	$150,000	$200,000	Capital	$100,000
Goodwill		50,000	Earned surplus	50,000
	$150,000	$250,000		$150,000

B

	Book Values	Under Plan		Book Values
Fixed assets, etc.	$300,000	$400,000	Capital	$200,000
Goodwill		100,000	Earned surplus	100,000
	$300,000	$500,000		$300,000

If the plan contemplates the consolidation of A and B into the C corporation which is to issue 1,000 shares of $100 par value to A stockholders, and 2,000 shares to B, what is to be the new surplus allocation on the books of C? The combined assets under the plan will total $750,000. With capital of $300,000, there is a surplus of $450,000 to be distributed. Only $150,000 of this amount may be treated as earned surplus, since that is the gross amount of the earned surplus of the constituents. The other $300,000 of surplus must constitute a special or paid-in surplus arising from revaluation and amounts attributed to intangibles. Any other rule would permit corporations by merger and consolidation to evade the rule against declaration of cash dividends from unrealized appreciation.[24]

[22] Graham and Katz, *Accounting in Law Practice* (2d Ed. 1938) 379; Sunley and Pinkerton, *Corporation Accounting* (1931) 385–386.

[23] Couchman, *Accounting for Mergers*, 46 J. of Accountancy 8, 14 (1928).

[24] See Sparger, *Profits, Surplus and the Payment of Dividends*, 8 N. Car. L. Rev. 14, 27–29 (1929), and see §36.5, supra.

105. Reduction of New Capital Below Original Capital of Constituent Corporations

Another possible method for creating dividend surplus by a plan of combination is to reduce the capital of the resulting corporation below that of the constituents. If the original balance sheets show the A corporation with capital of $100,000, earned surplus of $50,-000 and the B corporation with capital of $200,000 and earned surplus of $100,000, a plan of consolidation may be adopted by which one par value $100 share of the new C corporation is exchanged for each two shares of the A and B corporations. The C corporation will have assets of $450,000, capital of $150,000, and surplus of one kind or another of $300,000. Of the latter $150,000 is earned surplus and may continue as such on the books of C, but the other $150,-000 is quite clearly a reduction or paid-in surplus, and, where such surplus is restricted as to use for dividend purposes, should be similarly treated.[25] The C balance sheet would read:

Fixed assets, etc. $450,000	Capital	$150,000
	Earned surplus	150,000
	Surplus arising upon reduction of capital on consolidation of A and B	150,000
$450,000		$450,000

An express statutory provision in Minnesota specifies that upon a consolidation or merger, if the capital of the consolidated or surviving corporation is less than the capital of the constituent corporations, the amount of such difference is to be paid-in surplus.[26]

If there are restrictions as to the amount which capital may be reduced by a corporation, care must be observed so as not to reduce the capital of a surviving corporation below an amount to which

[25] Cf. Dewing, *Financial Policy of Corporations* (3d Rev. Ed. 1934) 602–603. For restrictions upon the use of reduction and paid-in surpluses for dividends, see §§29, 30, *supra*.

[26] Minn. Stat. (Mason 1938 Supp.), §7492-20(V). Ohio provides that upon consolidation the plan may provide that the excess of assets of the consolidated corporation over liabilities plus stated capital "may be declared to be and treated as paid-in surplus of the consolidated corporation, and the earned surplus of the constituent corporations or any part thereof may be declared to be and treated as earned surplus of the consolidated corporation." Ohio Code Ann., §8623-67(6). The California Act provides that the surplus "appearing on the books of the constituent corporations, to the extent to which it is not capitalized by the issue of shares or otherwise, may be entered as earned or paid-in surplus, as the case may be, on the books of the consolidated or surviving corporation, and may thereafter be dealt with as such." Cal. Civ. Code (1937), §364.

it would be legal to reduce the capital of constituent corporations individually. In *Small v. Sullivan,* statutory provisions were such as to make it impossible for the principal constituent corporation individually to reduce its capital to a point where it would have an available dividend surplus.[27] There were no statutory provisions restricting reduction upon consolidation. Yet when capital was reduced under the consolidation plan, and dividends paid by the consolidated corporation, which the principal constituent corporation could not itself have paid from a reduction surplus, directors were held liable to creditors of the principal constituent corporation. The court took the position that although the consolidation statute contained no restrictive provisions as to reduction, the ordinary reduction statute did restrict the constituent and that this prohibition could not be evaded indirectly by a plan of consolidation. In many jurisdictions the only restriction against payment of dividends from reduction surplus is the requirement that the payment should not impair the capital as reduced,[28] and in such jurisdictions *Small v. Sullivan* is not important, since it is to be expected that the consolidated corporation will at least be prohibited from paying dividends from its reduced capital. But in other jurisdictions there are added provisions that the reduction shall not be below a certain amount,[29] and in such cases directors of a consolidated corporation who declare dividends from a surplus created by a reduction of capital below the minimum run grave danger of personal liability under the *Small v. Sullivan* holding. Many statutes provide that rights and remedies of creditors of the constituent corporations shall not be lessened or impaired by the sale or transfer of its assets.[30]

C. No-Par Stock Plans

106. Distinctions Between No-Par and Par Stock Financing

Under modern no-par stock statutes, almost all stock issued will have a stated capital which for most purposes takes the place of par

---

[27] 245 N. Y. 343, 157 N. E. 261 (1927) (comment, Douglas and Shanks, *Cases and Materials on Business Units—Losses, Liabilities and Assets* (1932) 186–188; 13 Corn. L. Q. 276).

[28] See §30, n. 237, *supra.*

[29] See §30, n. 238–249, *supra.*

[30] See e.g. Cal. Civ. Code (1937), §361(7); Del. Rev. Code (1935), c. 65, §63; 32 Ill. Ann. Stat. (Smith-Hurd 1935), §157.69(e); Mich. Stat. Ann. (Henderson 1937), §21.53; Minn. Stat. (Mason 1938 Supp.), §7492-44(I); N. J. Stat. (1937), §14:12-5; N. Y. Stock Corp. Law, §90; Ohio Code Ann., §8623-68; 15 Purd. Pa. Stat. Ann., §2852-907.

capital as to par value stock. To this extent there are involved the same problems arising on unification by par value stocks already discussed. There are two principal differences in the case where no-par stocks are issued. If the constituent corporations are already capitalized with no-par stocks, they will usually have, in addition to the capital and earned surplus ordinarily present in par stock corporations, a paid-in surplus. The allocation on the books of the surviving corporation should, therefore, give effect not only to the prior earned surpluses, but also to paid-in surpluses. In the second place, no-par statutes will be of assistance in preserving at least the prior paid-in surplus. Most no-par statutes authorize an allocation of the consideration received between capital and surplus.[31] The surplus referred to, however, is paid-in surplus—the statute sometimes specifically so stating. While the ordinary no-par statutes thus provide means for the merging or consolidated corporation to preserve the prior paid-in surplus of constituents, they leave the question of preserving prior earned surplus of constituents to the general doctrine of continuity of *pro rata* shareholder interest implicit in mergers and consolidations, and to whatever added support is to be obtained from the surplus equalization theory of *Equitable Life Assurance Society v. Union Pacific Railroad Company*.[32] Opinion generally favors preservation of earned surpluses of constituent corporations on the books of the surviving corporation.[33]

107. Modern Statutes

Statutes which expressly authorize the preservation of earned surpluses of constituent corporations frequently do so without differentiation as to whether the financing is by par or no-par stock.[34] Several statutes, however, deal separately or specifically with unification plans using no-par stock. The only provision in Wisconsin for preserving surplus deals with no-par stock.[35] It provides that upon issuance of no-par shares in exchange for shares of an exist-

---

[31] See §45.1.

[32] See §§101–102, 45.2, *supra*.

[33] Montgomery, *Auditing Theory and Practice* (6th Ed. 1940) 367 (distinguishing as to consolidations); Wildman and Powell, *Capital Stock Without Par Value* (1928) 224; 1 Dodd and Baker, *Cases on Business Associations* (1940) 1146; Note, *Declaration of Dividends from Paid-in Surplus*, 31 Col. L. Rev. 844, 850–851 (1931); cf. Berle, *Corporate Devices for Diluting Stock Participations*, 31 Col. L. Rev. 1238, 1248 (1931) (example given being surplus on par stock financing); but cf. Paton, *Essentials of Accounting* (1938) 687; Sparger, *Profits, Surplus, and the Payment of Dividends*, 8 N. Car. L. Rev. 14, 28 (1929) (taking the position that only the surplus of the merging corporation should survive).

[34] See §100, n. 6; §102, n. 16, *supra*.

[35] Wis. Stat. (1937), §182.14.

ing business then having a surplus, such surplus may be retained as a surplus available for the payment of dividends.

Section 86 of the New York Stock Corporation Law contains an important provision for preserving surplus upon consolidation. Section 58 prohibits the payment of dividends from capital,[36] and in Section 12 two alternatives are provided for determining capital as to no-par stock.[37] If the certificate of incorporation adopts alternative A, the capital is the amount fixed therein but not less than $1 per no-par share. Under this provision, prior paid-in surplus and earned surplus can both be preserved as surplus on merger or consolidation. It is immaterial for dividend purposes in New York whether the surplus be paid-in or earned. But if the certificate contains plan B of Section 12, the capital as to no-par shares is the aggregate amount of consideration received. In the absence of Section 86, a consolidation by a corporation using plan B would freeze into capital all prior surpluses, earned or paid-in. Section 86, however, provides that, as to consolidations effective under plan B, the amount of consideration received by the surviving corporation for its no-par shares shall be deemed to be (a) par value as to par value shares of constituent corporations, or (b) if the actual value of the shares is less than par, then the actual value, or (c) if issued for no-par shares of the constituents, then the amount of capital represented by the shares of the constituents, or (d) if the actual value of the no-par shares of constituents is less than their capital value, then the actual value. This provision enables the preservation of both earned and paid-in surplus as a general surplus available for dividends. No similar provision is made with respect to mergers.

In Ohio the general dividend test is a balance sheet surplus, based on excess of assets over liabilities including stated capital.[38] Where shares without par value are issued in a consolidation, the stated capital is the amount set forth in the agreement of consolidation, but not less than $500.[39] The earned surplus of the constituent corporations may be carried over as earned surplus of the consolidated corporation, and any excess surplus is paid-in surplus.

Minnesota provides that earned surplus of an acquired corporation may be preserved to the extent that the stated capital, paid-in surplus, and earned surplus of the acquired corporation, in other

---

[36] See §21, n. 94, *supra*.
[37] See §45.1, n. 162, *supra*.
[38] Ohio Code Ann. (Baldwin), §8623–38. See §21, n. 95, *supra*.
[39] §§8623–37(6); 8623–67(6).

words its assets, exceed the consideration given by the acquiring corporation including par value of par shares and "stated capital" of no-par shares.[40] The stated capital of the acquiring corporation as to no-par shares is the amount designated by the agreement of consolidation.[41]

[40] Minn. Stat. (Mason 1938 Supp.), §7492–20 (VIII).

[41] §7492–44 (II) (but if no-par shares are entitled to preference on liquidation, then stated capital not to be less than such amount).

CHAPTER 10

CHOICE OF LAW IN DETERMINING VALIDITY OF DIVIDENDS

A. Where Only Statute Purporting to Regulate Corporation's Dividends Is That of the Domicil

108. The Choice of Law Problem

Many corporations do business in more than one state. Many others, while confining their business activities to a single jurisdiction, are incorporated under the laws of another state. Does the law of the state of incorporation or that of some one or more other states in which the corporation does business determine what dividends may be paid and what, if any, liability falls upon directors and stockholders if illegal dividends are distributed? In many cases the only statutes purporting to control a corporation's dividend declarations will be those of the state of incorporation. Often, however, statutes subject foreign corporations doing business in the state to the same duties and liabilities as domestic corporations, or require specifically that dividends declared by foreign corporations be in compliance with local statutes.

A corporation incorporated under the laws of New York does business in 20 states of the Union, some having dividend statutes similar to that of New York, some materially different, while still others may contain requirements in direct conflict with the New York statute. Why, it may be asked, should the directors not comply with the statutes of all states in which the corporation does business? A board of directors considering the declaration of dividends, which if illegal will subject members to personal liability, should be able to make its determination on the theory that the law of some one state is controlling. Compliance with the dividend laws of states in which requirements are directly in conflict will in some cases be impossible. It is desirable as a matter of conflict of laws that a person about to perform a voluntary act should be able to test the legality of his conduct by one law in order that he may know its prohibitions and avoid their violation.

To illustrate the difficulties involved, under the statutes in some jurisdictions directors are under an obligation to distribute all profits over and above a certain amount reserved as working capital.[1] These provisions are in conflict with the statutory rule in a few states,[2] and the common law rule in almost all states,[3] that directors have discretion as to whether or not dividends shall be declared.[4] Directors cannot apply both rules.

Under neither the law of New York nor Delaware can dividends be paid directly from capital.[5] But under the law of New York, dividends cannot be paid when capital is impaired, whereas under the law of Delaware dividends may be paid from current net profits even though capital is impaired.[6] Similar conflicts may arise with respect to director liability. Under the law of New York, directors who paid dividends from capital prior to 1939 are liable irrespective of their good faith or due care, and a similar liability may still prevail in some states; under the law of Delaware, directors relying in good faith upon financial statements presented by corporate officers are under no liability.[7] While the standards of the respective states differ in the last two situations, it is possible to comply with the law of one state, that having the stricter provisions, and thereby comply with the law of the other state. By refraining from declaring dividends which would impair capital or when capital

---

[1] See §54, n. 30, 31, and 33, *supra*.

[2] See §54, n. 29, *supra*.

[3] See §§54–54.3, *supra*.

[4] The effect of this conflict may sometimes be avoided under cases holding that non-domiciliary states will generally refuse to take jurisdiction of suits to compel payment of dividends by foreign corporations. *Cohn v. Mishkoff Costello Co.*, 256 N. Y. 102, 175 N. E. 529 (1931) (jurisdiction of action in New York courts against Indiana corporation to compel redemption of shares or in alternative declaration of an equitable dividend refused) ; *Hogue v. American Steel Foundries*, 247 Pa. 12, 92 Atl. 1073 (1915) (jurisdiction by Pennsylvania courts over suit to compel payment of dividends to preferred shareholders not assenting to reorganization plan of New Jersey corporation refused) ; *In re Fryeburg Water Co.*, 79 N. H. 123, 106 Atl. 225 (1919) (petition for approval by New Hampshire public service commission of a stock dividend issued by a Maine public utility doing part of its business in New Hampshire dismissed, on ground New Hampshire commission had no power to approve or disapprove the dividend) ; *Berford v. New York Iron Mine*, 24 Jones & S. 236, 4 N. Y. S. 836 (1888) ; Restatement of Conflict of Laws (1935), §198; but cf. *Prouty v. Michigan, Southern & Northern Indiana Railroad Co.*, 1 Hun 655 (1st Dept. 1874) (New York court had jurisdiction in preferred stockholder's action to compel payment of dividends by a foreign corporation under statute providing that suits could be maintained by local residents against foreign corporations for any cause of action) ; see *Edwards v. Schillinger*, 245 Ill. 231, 241, 91 N. E. 1048 (1910) ; *Guilford v. Western Union Telegraph Co.*, 59 Minn. 332, 340, 61 N. W. 324 (1894). The practical effect of these cases will be to resolve the conflict in favor of the single law of the domicil.

[5] See §21, n. 94, 102, *supra*.

[6] See §§21, 27, *supra*.

[7] See §§76.1, n. 24, 76.3, n. 49, *supra*.

is impaired under New York law, the Delaware requirement is automatically complied with in the first of these cases. In the second, since it is immaterial under New York law whether good faith or due care is used, there can be no violation of the less stringent standards of Delaware if the New York rule is followed. Conceivably a corporation doing business in 20 states might find some one law stricter than that of all other states and which, if complied with, would meet all restrictions in the laws of the other 19 states. Assuming such rather improbable situation, the question would still remain why the law of that particular state, merely because it was most restrictive, should be held to regulate the dividend declarations of a corporation doing business in 19 other states. Novel and onerous restrictions might be imposed by the law of this strictest state, so stringent as to make the declaration of any dividends very difficult or even impossible.

109. Dividend Legality Normally Determined by Law of the Corporation's Domicil

In selecting a single law to regulate internal management matters of general concern to creditors,[8] stockholders,[9] and directors [10] of corporations, the conflict of laws practice has generally been to adopt the law of the state of incorporation. A well-known statement by Justice Holmes in *Modern Woodmen v. Mixer* [11] as to the rights of beneficiaries of a life insurance policy has often been cited in connection with internal management of corporate affairs: [12] "The indivisible unity between the members of a corporation of this kind in respect of the fund from which their rights are to be enforced and

---

[8] *Martyne v. American Union Fire Insurance Co.*, 216 N. Y. 183, 110 N. E. 502 (1915); *Canada Southern Railway v. Gebhard*, 109 U. S. 527, 536–538 (1883) (bondholders); *Harrigan v. Bergdoll*, 270 U. S. 560 (1925) (trustee in bankruptcy).

[9] *Nashua Savings Bank v. Anglo-American Land Mortgage & Agency Co.*, 189 U. S. 221 (1903) (liable for stockholder assessments in accordance with law of domicil); *Broderick v. Rosner*, 294 U. S. 629 (1935) (liability for double assessment); *Rogers v. Guaranty Trust Co.*, 288 U. S. 123 (1933) (as to validity of stock profit-sharing plan); *Southworth v. Morgan*, 205 N. Y. 293, 98 N. E. 490 (1912) (but where law of the foreign state is not proved it is presumed to be the same as the common law of forum); see *Pinney v. Nelson*, 183 U. S. 144, 147–148 (1901).

[10] Restatement of Conflict of Laws (1934), §187; cf. 2 Beale, *Conflict of Laws* (1935) 866. Generally see Murfree, *Law of Foreign Corporations* (1893) 306.

[11] 267 U. S. 544, 551 (1925).

[12] See e.g. *Broderick v. Rosner*, 294 U. S. 629, 643–644 (1935); *Union & New Haven Trust Co. v. Watrous*, 109 Conn. 268, 277–278, 146 Atl. 727 (1928) (vesting of right to a corporate dividend as between life tenant and remainderman under a trust).

the consequence that their rights must be determined by a single law, is elaborated in *Supreme Council of the Royal Arcanum v. Green.* . . . The act of becoming a member is something more than a contract, it is entering into a complex and abiding relation, and as marriage looks to domicil, membership looks to and must be governed by the law of the State granting the incorporation."

In the absence of statutes outside the state of incorporation purporting to regulate the dividend declarations of foreign corporations doing business within the state, the general conflict of laws rule as to internal affairs is followed, and questions "in respect of the fund" from which dividends may be paid are determined by the law of the corporation's domicil.[13] Specific application of this principle means a dividend illegal under the law of the domicil is illegal in suits against stockholders and directors elsewhere,[14] and

---

[13] *In re Fryeburg Water Co.,* 79 N. H. 123, 106 Atl. 225 (1919) (stock dividend of a public utility corporation "exclusively subject" to the law of the state of incorporation, even though corporation does a portion of its business in a second state where approval of the dividend by the local public service commission is sought) ; *Harr v. Pioneer Mechanical Corp.,* 65 F. (2d) 332 (C. C. A. 2d, 1933), *cert. den.* 290 U. S. 673 (1933) (right to enjoin a plan cancelling accumulated preferred dividends of a Delaware corporation depends on the law of Delaware) ; *National Lock Co. v. Hogland,* 101 F. (2d) 576 (C. C. A. 7th, 1938) ; *Union & New Haven Trust Co. v. Watrous,* 109 Conn. 268, 146 Atl. 727 (1928) (time dividend becomes a debt as between life tenant and remainderman determined by law of domicil) ; see *German-American Coffee Co. v. Diehl,* 216 N. Y. 57, 61, 109 N. E. 875 (1915). In the following New York cases, actions have been sustained to enforce liabilities against directors of foreign corporations for violating dividend statutes of the state of incorporation: *Stratton v. Bertles,* 238 App. Div. 87, 263 N. Y. S. 466 (1st Dept. 1933) (Delaware corporation) ; *Hutchinson v. Stadler,* 85 App. Div. 424, 83 N. Y. S. 509 (1st Dept. 1903) (dividend of a New Jersey corporation violated both law of New Jersey and New York prohibiting dividend from capital, but court stated question of substantive illegality was determined by law of New Jersey) ; *Hutchinson v. Curtiss,* 45 Misc. 484, 92 N. Y. S. 70 (1904) (New Jersey law applied to determine fund available for dividends of a New Jersey corporation, but New York Stock Corp. Law, §114 (then §60), as to defenses; as to problems under §114, see §§112–112.3, *infra*) ; see 1 Dodd and Baker, *Cases on Business Associations* (1940), Note on Liability of Directors of Foreign Corporations, 1179. But a corporation paying dividends in a manner to violate the law of the state in which it is doing business, and in the absence of any showing to the contrary, presumably also of the law of its domicil, may be ousted from doing business in the foreign state. *State v. Brictson Mfg. Co.,* 113 Neb. 781, 205 N. W. 246 (1925).

[14] Restatement of Conflict of Laws (1935), §189; see §80, *supra;* cf. Goodrich, *Conflict of Laws* (2d Ed. 1938) 268; 1 Beale, *Cases on Conflict of Laws* (2d Ed. 1927) 772–773n.; Lorenzen, *Cases on Conflict of Laws* (4th Ed. 1937) 675n. California provides that directors of foreign corporations shall be liable to the corporation, shareholders, creditors, and liquidating officers for unauthorized dividends according to the laws of the state of incorporation, whether declared in California or elsewhere. Cal. Civ. Code (1937), §412. See Ballantine and Sterling, *California Corporation Laws* (1938 Ed.), §341 for comment on this provision.

conversely, when the dividend is legal by the law of domicil, it is legal elsewhere.[15]

When in actions in foreign jurisdictions no proof of the domiciliary law is made, it becomes necessary to resort to common law doctrines.[16] In cases of this character it is frequently impossible to tell whether the common law of the forum or that of the state of incorporation is applied. Generally the law of the forum is applied under the presumption that the common law of the foreign state is like that of the forum.

110. Obligation of Non-domiciliary States to Enforce Dividend Law of the Domicil

The full faith and credit clause provides that "Full Faith and Credit shall be given in each State to public Acts . . . of every other State." [17] If a statute or judgment of a foreign state is penal, a state is not required to give it full faith and credit. Although earlier decisions were to the contrary, it has been quite generally conceded, since the decision in *Huntington v. Attrill,* that statutes of the domicil imposing liability upon directors for acts in the management of corporate property are not penal within the meaning of the full faith and credit clause.[18] The early doubt likewise existing, as to whether the full faith and credit clause merely required extra-state recognition of judgments obtained against corporate stockholders at the domicil or also direct recognition of the domiciliary statute,[19]

---

[15] In the absence of statutory provisions making local laws applicable to foreign corporations they are construed as applying only to domestic corporations. *Vanderpoel v. Gorman,* 140 N. Y. 563, 35 N. E. 932 (1894) (assignment for benefit of creditors by New Jersey corporation in New York was valid under law of New Jersey and at common law, but invalid by statute in New York; held, the New York statute relates only to local corporations and recognition of the assignment does not violate the public policy of New York); see *Bogardus v. Fitzpatrick,* 139 Misc. 533, 535, 247 N. Y. S. 692 (1931); see also 2 Beale, *Conflict of Laws* (1935) 782.

[16] See §14, n. 25, *supra.*

[17] U. S. Constitution, Art. IV, §1.

[18] 146 U. S. 657 (1892) (a creditor of a New York corporation obtaining a judgment in New York against a director under a statute making the latter liable for filing a false certificate that capital stock had been paid-in was held entitled to collect the same under the full faith and credit clause in Maryland). The same statute was also held not penal under principles of general international law in *Huntington v. Attrill* (1893), A. C. 150. Specifically as to dividends, see §80, n. 69. See also Restatement of Conflict of Laws (1935), §189; Annotation, 25 A. L. R. 1428.

[19] Cf. *Converse v. Hamilton,* 224 U. S. 243 (1912); Langmaid, *The Full Faith and Credit Required for Public Acts,* 24 Ill. L. Rev. 383, 393 (1929); Ross, *Has the Conflict of Laws Become a Branch of Constitutional Law?* 15 Minn. L. Rev. 161, 175–177 (1931).

was resolved in favor of the latter view by *Broderick v. Rosner.*[20] In the latter case it was held that New Jersey was required to give full faith and credit to a double liability assessment based solely on the statute of New York, the domicil of the corporation, even though New Jersey had a statute [21] which specifically forbad the maintenance of such an action against local stockholders except under conditions with which it was impossible for the statutory liquidator to comply. New Jersey was required to permit enforcement of the New York assessment, since New York was the domicil and "the subject matter is not one as to which the alleged public policy of New Jersey could be controlling." [22]

By parity of reasoning liability imposed by the domicil upon stockholders receiving illegal dividends must be given full faith and credit in other states, since the obligation created has much more foundation than an extra assessment imposed upon stockholders who have received no distribution of corporate property.[23] There is no reason to suppose that any different rule would be applied to the obligations of directors under the law of the state of incorporation.[24]

In the *Converse* and *Broderick* cases, the non-domiciliary states were required to give full faith and credit to liabilities imposed by the law of the domicil. In the absence of a statute in the non-domiciliary state purporting to require application of its laws to the declaration of dividends by foreign corporations, it would seem that, if in the converse situation there was no liability for declaring or receiving the dividend under the law of the domicil, the full faith and credit clause would likewise require that there be no liability in the non-domiciliary state. Justice Brandeis stated in the *Broderick* case, with respect to "an incident of the incorporation

---

[20] 294 U. S. 629 (1935). See Ross, *Full Faith and Credit in a Federal System,* 20 Minn. L. Rev. 140, 176 (1936) ; Smith, *The Constitution and the Conflict of Laws,* 27 Geo. L. J. 536, 568 (1939).

[21] N. J. Stat. (1937), §14:7–11.

[22] In *Converse v. Hamilton,* 224 U. S. 243 (1912), a general local public policy of Wisconsin against double liability not based on any statute prohibiting recovery was similarly held to be no bar.

[23] In *Sovereign Camp of Woodmen v. Bolin,* 305 U. S. 66 (1938) (comment, 33 Ill. L. Rev. 714), it was held that an insurance society contract *ultra vires* under the law of Nebraska, its domicil, must be treated as such in an action in Missouri: "the court below failed to give full faith and credit to the petitioner's charter embodied in the statutes of Nebraska as interpreted by its highest court."

[24] It has been pointed out that if the full faith and credit clause imposes an obligation to recognize the validity of a state statute, then to say that the statute may be valid, but is not operative as law except for the courts of the state in which it is enacted, is to make the clause practically meaningless. Dodd, *Power of the Supreme Court to Review State Decisions in the Field of Conflict of Laws,* 39 Harv. 533, 544 (1926).

. . . the subject matter is peculiarly within the regulatory power of New York, as the State of incorporation. 'So much so,' as was said in *Converse v. Hamilton,* 'that no other State properly can be said to have any public policy thereon.' " [25]

States have somewhat more latitude in declining to follow the dividend law of foreign countries under which corporations may be incorporated, since the full faith and credit clause is not applicable.[26]

B. Where Statute in State in Which Foreign Corporation Does Business Purports to Regulate Dividends

111. General Statutory Provision of Non-domiciliary States Subjecting Foreign Corporations Doing Business in the State to the Same Duties and Liabilities as Domestic Corporations

In some corporate statutes, particularly those more recently enacted, it is expressly provided that nothing contained in the domestic law shall be construed as applying to the internal affairs of foreign corporations.[27] Other states, however, have statutes which either specifically, or, might by construction, apply to the declaration of dividends by foreign corporations transacting business within the state. The most common type of statute provides in broad general terms that foreign corporations doing business in the state shall be subject to the same duties and liabilities as domestic corporations.[28] Statutes in general terms such as these are construed as applying only to general corporate activities of foreign

[25] 294 U. S. 629, 643 (1935).

[26] Compare the result in *Pope v. Heckscher,* 266 N. Y. 114, 194 N. E. 53 (1934) (the New York court refused to enforce a judgment for the unpaid balance on a stock subscription obtained in a Canadian province by mailing notice to a New York stockholder in accordance with the law of Canada, the corporation's domicil).

[27] 32 Ill. Ann. Stat. (Smith-Hurd 1935), §157.102; La. Gen. Stat. (Dart. 1939), §1154 (provisions generally inapplicable to foreign corporations); 15 Purd. Pa. Stat. Ann., §2852–1001. The penalties imposed for declaring illegal dividends in Delaware and Kansas apply only to domestic corporations. Del. Rev. Code (1935), c. 65, §35; Kans. Laws 1939, c. 152, §85.

[28] Arizona Rev. Code (1928), §4809; Iowa Code (1939), §8432; Minn. Stat. (Mason 1938 Supp.), §7495–8; Miss. Code Ann. (1930), §4177; Mont. Rev. Code (1935), §6659; Ore. Code Ann., §25–1117; S. C. Code (1932), §7776; S. Dak. Code (1939), §11.2101 (foreign corporations and their officers subject to liabilities and restrictions imposed on local corporations); Tenn. Code Ann. (1934), §4127; Vt. Pub. Laws (1933), §5986 (foreign corporation not to have authority to do any acts in state except such as domestic corporation might do); Va. Code (1936), §3844 (foreign corporation to be deemed and treated as local corporation); W. Va. Code (1937), §3091.

corporations and not as regulating their internal affairs.[29] A statute specifically applying local laws concerning such internal affairs as dividends is necessary to displace the ordinary conflict of laws rule that the law of the domicil is controlling.

112. New York Stock Corporation Law Section 114

New York specifically requires foreign corporations doing business in the state to comply with local dividend requirements. Section 114 of the New York Stock Corporation Law provides that the directors and stockholders of foreign corporations transacting business in the state, except moneyed or railroad corporations, shall be liable under its provisions for the making of unauthorized dividends in the same manner and to the same extent as the directors and stockholders of a domestic corporation.[30]

To understand the scope of this provision, a consideration of its statutory history is necessary. The section was added by amendment to the Stock Corporation Law in 1897.[31] It culminated a series of legislative investigations of trusts and foreign corporations.[32]

[29] *In re Fryeburg Water Co.,* 79 N. H. 123, 106 Atl. 225 (1919) (statute conferring authority on public service commission to control issuance of stock by a corporation doing business in state, not applicable to stock dividend of foreign corporation) ; *Hamilton v. United Laundries Corporation,* 111 N. J. Eq. 78, 161 Atl. 347 (1932) (New Jersey statute providing that "foreign corporations doing business in this state shall be subject to the provisions of this act, so far as the same can be applied to foreign corporations" did not make the New Jersey dividend section applicable to the declaration of dividends by a Delaware corporation) ; *Sidway v. Missouri Land & Livestock Co. Ltd.,* 101 Fed. 481 (S. D. Mo. 1900) ; *North State Copper & Gold Mining Co. v. Field,* 64 Md. 151, 20 Atl. 1039; see *Bogardus v. Fitzpatrick,* 139 Misc. 533, 535, 247 N. Y. S. 692 (1931) ; Note, *Internal Regulation of Foreign Corporations,* 29 Col. L. Rev. 968, 969 (1929).

These cases are in accord with the presumption that legislation is not intended to alter principles of conflict of laws. Note, *Preserving the Inviolability of Rules of Conflict of Laws by Statutory Construction,* 49 Harv. L. Rev. 319 (1935).

[30] Under §667 of the N. Y. Penal Law, directors of foreign corporations carrying on business or keeping an office in New York are guilty of a misdemeanor if, in violation of §664, they declare a dividend other than from surplus or which reduces capital. Similar provisions appear in the Utah law. Utah Rev. Stat. (1933), §§103–12–4, 11. New York General Corp. Law, §222, makes certain New York receivership and injunction provisions applicable to foreign corporations, their directors and officers, when the corporation does business within the state or maintains a fiscal or stock transfer agency therein.

[31] N. Y. Laws 1897, c. 384, §4. See Mann, *Law of Foreign Business Corporations Doing Business in New York* (1906) 205; *Juridical Status of Foreign Corporations in the American Republics* (U. S. Govt. Printing Office 1928) 71. For subsequent history of the section see N. Y. Consol. Laws (1909), c. 61, §70; N. Y. Laws 1923, c. 787.

[32] See Report on Investigation Relative to Trusts, N. Y. Sen. Doc. No. 50 (1888) ; Report Relative to "Trusts" and "Sugar Trusts," N. Y. Sen. Doc. No. 79 (1891) ; Lexow Committee Report on Investigation of Trusts, N. Y. Sen. Doc. No. 40 (1897).

In 1890 the New York Court of Appeals had sustained an order dissolving the "Sugar Trust,"[33] whereupon a new corporation was immediately organized with the same directors under the laws of New Jersey and continued to do business in New York as before.[34] The Senate investigating committee found the purpose of New Jersey incorporation was to avoid New York tax provisions and corporate regulations. Other corporations conducting their business in New York were likewise found to be incorporating in New Jersey.

By 1897 conditions had become so bad that the Lexow Committee was appointed with instructions to draft such legislation as might be found necessary to regulate trusts.[35] Wholesale migration to other states, particularly New Jersey, was found to be taking place.[36] The committee deemed a change in New York legislative policy to permit it to "traffick" in "colorable charters" as a means of meeting competition of other states inadvisable. Instead, it adopted the policy of recommending legislation to discourage resort to other states for incorporation. "All requirements of the local law especially designed for the protection of creditors and shareholders should be imposed upon foreign corporations operating here. In this way the main incentive for foreign organization of domestic interests will be removed. . . . A bill is in preparation to accomplish this recommendation and will be submitted."[37] The bill included the provisions presently contained in Section 114 and became effective in May of 1897 as Section 60 of the Stock Corporation Law.[38]

---

[33] *People v. North River Sugar Refining Co.*, 121 N. Y. 582, 24 N. E. 834 (1890).

[34] Report on "Trusts" and "Sugar Trusts," N. Y. Sen. Doc. No. 79 (1891), pp. 10–14.

[35] Report on Investigation of Trusts, N. Y. Sen. Doc. No. 40 (1897).

[36] Under the heading "Foreign Incorporation" the Committee referred to instances of incorporation in New Jersey when the corporation did no semblance of business there and continued to "carry on its business in this State, free from compliance with the beneficial restrictions of our laws." In many cases the purpose of foreign incorporation was "to relieve the corporation so formed of some duty or obligation which would have rested upon it had it been organized under the laws of this State." "Hence, although for all practical purposes a corporation of this State, operating here, receiving the protection of our laws, and the opportunities of our markets, it is permitted by a mere fiction to escape duties and obligations imposed on corporations similarly situated but created in our own State." *Id.*, pp. 21, 22.

[37] Report on Investigation of Trusts, N. Y. Senate Doc. No. 40 (1897), p. 36.

[38] See n. 31, *supra*.

112.1. Corporations Doing All or the Largest Part of Their Business in New York

As demonstrated by the report of the committee which drafted the original provisions of Section 114, it was enacted to meet a specific and special situation—in order to remove "the main incentive for foreign organization of domestic interests." Assuming that in the absence of Section 114 the law of the state of incorporation would govern the legality of dividend declarations of foreign corporations, may New York under this section require corporations incorporated elsewhere for the purpose of doing all or the major portion of their business in New York to comply with dividend statutes applicable had the corporation been domestically incorporated?

The leading case holding that in this situation the law of New York and not that of the state of incorporation applies to determine the liability of directors for participating in declaration of dividends, is *German-American Coffee Company v. Diehl.*[39]   In that case the Court of Appeals, in an opinion by Judge Cardozo, overruled a demurrer to the complaint of a solvent New Jersey corporation based on Section 114 (then Section 70) alleging that the plaintiff was duly authorized by certificate to do business in New York; that for a period of over ten years it had maintained its main business office there; that it had "generally . . . managed, directed and conducted its business" in New York; and that during successive years the directors, including the defendant, as part of their administration of business in New York had declared dividends out of capital.

Under both the law of New Jersey, which was pleaded, and the law of New York dividends from capital were illegal, but under the law of New Jersey a solvent corporation had no cause of action, only stockholders individually being entitled to recover for their respective loss, whereas under the New York statute a cause of action was given to the corporation. It was argued that Section 114 merely permitted the enforcement of such liabilities as were created under the law of the domicil by parties entitled to sue under that law.[40]   The court stated in broad *dicta* which might apply to any

[39] 216 N. Y. 57, 109 N. E. 875 (1915).

[40] It had been held in earlier New York cases construing §114 that the purpose of the latter was simply to remove all doubt as to the right to enforce in New York courts causes of action created by the domicil. *Hutchinson v. Stadler,* 85 App. Div. 424, 83 N. Y. S. 509 (1st Dept. 1903) (then §60); *Hutchinson v. Curtiss,* 45 Misc. 484, 92 N. Y. S. 70 (1904) (the New Jersey corporation involved had no plant or property in New Jersey; held a stockholder suit might be maintained under §60 to enforce director liability for paying dividends illegal under the law of New

corporation transacting business in New York that the intent of
the statute was to create a substantive right under the law of New
York, irrespective of the law of the domicil, and that as so construed New York had power to condition the general doing of
business by foreign corporations upon a compliance with New York
dividend law. The court finally concluded, however, by stating
that as a matter of substantive law the dividend was illegal in both
states and that permitting recovery to the solvent corporation, as
allowed by New York but not permitted by New Jersey, was merely
a shift in the remedy from stockholders to the corporation.[41]

This construction will hardly bear analysis. The effect of
the decision was to permit a substantive recovery which could
not have been had under the law of New Jersey. It was not merely
a question of what party should be able to subject the directors
to a fixed liability. It was the extent of liability itself which
was at issue. Had New Jersey law been applied, although the dividend was illegal, it was only illegal as to individual stockholders.
What, if any, damages most stockholders as recipients of such illegal dividends would have recovered is highly conjectural. Although the statute has been in force since 1904, no case has as yet
arisen granting recovery to a stockholder under it. Whatever
liability exists would be limited to the interest of the particular stockholder. Under the law of New York, on the other hand, directors
were subjected to the complete loss of the corporation, which would
permit recovery probably many times larger than that which would
be allowed any stockholder.

Disregarding the broad statements concerning the general power
over corporations doing business in New York, it seems reasonably
clear that a correct result was reached upon the facts in the *Diehl*
case. Here was a corporation doing most, if not all, of its business
in New York, stepping across the boundary to New Jersey for in-

---

Jersey) ; *De Raismes v. U. S. Lithograph Co.,* 161 App. Div. 781, 146 N. Y. S. 813
(1st Dept. 1914) ; *Siegman v. Rice,* N. Y. Law J., Oct. 11, 1905, p. 119.

[41] Cf. *Harrigan v. Bergdoll,* 270 U. S. 560, 564 (1925) (holding that the law of
the domicil governed the statute of limitations in an action by a trustee in bankruptcy
to recover a stockholder assessment: "The nature, the extent, and the conditions of
the liability of a stockholder on account of stock not full-paid depend primarily upon
the law of the State or country by which the corporation was created. . . . That
law determines whether the liability is to the corporation or is to creditors") ;
Russian Reinsurance Co. v. Stoddard, 240 N. Y. 149, 154, 147 N. E. 703 (1925)
("If the existence of the corporation, its capacity to sue, or the authority of its
directors to represent it or to bring the action is challenged, we look to the charter
and the law of its corporate domicile for the data upon which we may rest our determination of such questions").

corporation under statutory provisions thought to be more favorable. It was to remedy precisely this situation that the statute was passed. It was, therefore, properly construed as applicable and there remains solely the question of power to effectuate this result.

In a large number of cases it has been either held or stated that action of foreign corporations doing business in New York is governed by New York law in virtue of Section 114.[42] In many of these cases it is not clear that all or even substantially all of the foreign corporation's business was being transacted in New York. However, in the situation in the *Diehl* case where New York is the "business situs" of the corporation, it is very difficult to contend that New York has insufficient interest in the subject matter to compel application of its dividend law rather than that of the state of incorporation. For all practical purposes a corporation which has its business situs in New York is a New York corporation, without regard to where

[42] *Irving Trust Co. v. Gunder,* 234 App. Div. 252, 254 N. Y. S. 630 (1st Dept. 1932) (defenses to a complaint against directors of a Delaware corporation for declaring dividends from capital in violation of New York Stock Corp. Law, §58, stricken; no reference to Delaware law); *Irving Trust Co. v. Allen,* 244 App. Div. 788, 280 N. Y. S. 965 (1st Dept. 1935) (affirming without opinion an order of the lower court striking defenses under Delaware law pleaded by directors of a Delaware corporation sued by the corporation's trustee in bankruptcy for payment of dividends illegal under §58); *Irving Trust Co. v. Maryland Casualty Co.,* 83 F. (2d) 168 (C. C. A. 2d, 1936), *cert. den.* 299 U. S. 571 (1936) [transfers by an insolvent Delaware corporation held illegal under §114 (4)]; see *In re Burnet-Clark,* 56 F. (2d) 744 (C. C. A. 2d, 1932) (dictum that on a new trial directors of a Maryland corporation licensed to do business in New York and having a place of business there would be liable under New York Stock Corp. Law, §58, and New York Penal Law, §§664 and 667, for purchasing stock out of capital; no reference to law of Maryland); *Stratton v. Bertles,* 238 App. Div. 87, 90, 263 N. Y. S. 466 (1st Dept. 1933); *Christianssand v. Federal Steamship Corp.,* 121 Misc. 627, 629, 201 N. Y. S. 504 (1923); *Bogardus v. Fitzpatrick,* 139 Misc. 533, 534, 247 N. Y. S. 692 (1931); Lorenzen, *Cases on Conflict of Laws* (4th Ed. 1937) 676; cf. *Hamilton v. Offutt,* 78 F.(2d) 735, 738 (Ct. App. D. of C. 1935), *cert. den.* 296 U. S. 592 (1935) (dictum Congress has power to impose double liability on banks incorporated in states outside the District of Columbia, but doing business in the District). Compare the following dictum of Judge Learned Hand in *Borg v. International Silver Co.,* 11 F. (2d) 147, 151 (C. C. A. 2d, 1925): "It is not unlawful in New Jersey to pay dividends out of profits though the capital be in fact impaired. . . . The plaintiffs apparently recognizing this, and that there is no evidence that any dividends were illegally paid under New Jersey law, resort to the curiously fanciful argument that nevertheless the payments were unlawful under the law of New York, where the defendant did part of its business. (*German-American Coffee Company v. Diehl.*) That case does not decide that a dividend paid by a New Jersey corporation lawfully under the laws of New Jersey may be unlawful in New York, because the corporation does business there under a New York license. The payment there at bar was unlawful in New Jersey, as well as in New York, and the court merely held that the New York directors were liable for the repayment under New York law. We hardly suppose that one rule applies to a New Jersey corporation in New Jersey and another in New York; but, if so, at least it has never been so held. . . ."

it may have been formally incorporated. There is considerable to be said for a general conflict of laws rule that even in the absence of statute a corporation is governed by the law of the state in which it has its business situs rather than the law of the state of incorporation. As Judge Cardozo stated in the *Diehl* case, "In these days, when countless corporations, organized on paper in neighboring states, live and move, and have their being in New York, a sound public policy demands that our Legislature be invested with this measure of control."

Cases dealing with stockholder liability tend to support the legislative jurisdiction of New York in this type situation. Where the articles of incorporation specifically provide that a corporation organized in one state shall do its principal out of state business in a second state,[43] or such state is otherwise consented to as a place of business by stockholders,[44] the latter are liable under a statute of the second state imposing double liability on stockholders of foreign corporations engaged in business in the state, irrespective of the fact that under the law of the state of incorporation no such liability exists. It would hardly seem necessary that stockholders should give their express consent to the doing of business in the non-domiciliary state. Directors act in their behalf and, if any consent is necessary to make the non-domiciliary laws applicable, it may normally be implied from the action of directors in bringing the corporation into the state for business.[45] As to directors, they are in no event in a position to plead non-assent to the corporation's transaction of business in the state.

Where the corporation conducts substantially all of its business activities in New York, is it material that the meeting at which directors declare a dividend illegal under New York law is held in Delaware, the state of incorporation, under which the distribution is

[43] *Pinney v. Nelson*, 183 U. S. 144 (1901); see Note, *Foreign Enforcement of Stockholder Liability*, 36 Col. L. Rev. 1108 (1936).

[44] *Thomas v. Matthiessen*, 232 U. S. 221 (1914) (no express discussion of constitutional questions but *Pinney v. Nelson* cited as applicable); *Thomas v. Wentworth*, 158 Cal. 275, 110 Pac. 942 (1910); but cf. *Leyner Engineering Works v. Kempner*, 163 Fed. 605 (S. D. Texas 1908) (stockholder of Texas corporation not liable to Colorado creditor under Colorado statute making stockholders of foreign corporations failing to file certificate of doing business liable to local creditors).

[45] *Provident Gold Mining Co. v. Haynes*, 173 Cal. 44, 159 Pac. 155 (1916) (double liability sustained against stockholders of an Arizona corporation under California statute applicable to stockholders of foreign corporations; the Arizona articles provided stockholders should not be subject to liability for corporate debts and authorized the corporation to carry on business "in any other state or territory as the board of directors may from time to time deem necessary"); *contra: Risdon*

valid?[46] Section 114 imposes liability upon directors of foreign corporations "transacting business in this state," and that is its only requirement. If mere withdrawal from the state at the time of dividend declaration renders the provision inoperative, an extremely facile method of defeating the legislative purpose is at hand. At least if the action is brought in New York to hold directors liable, it is not probable that this simple method of evasion would be sustained. It was said in the *Diehl* case, "Even if the prohibited act is done in the home state it may be so bound up in its results with the business in this state that we cannot view it with indifference."

On the other hand, no matter where a dividend is declared, if it is valid according to the law of the state of incorporation and its payment is attacked in the state of incorporation, it could not well be contended that the state which gave birth to the corporation must disregard its own law and enforce a liability created by New York law under Section 114.

What of the case where the action is brought in neither the state of incorporation nor New York? In these circumstances, since New York is the real home of the corporation, the third state might well look to it for validity of the dividend.[47]

112.2. Corporations Doing Only a Small or Minor Amount of Their Business in New York

Where the business activities of the corporation in New York are incidental rather than substantial, a reasonably clear case is presented against application of the New York dividend law, at least not beyond the extent necessary to protect local creditors and stockholders. Literal construction of the jurisdictional condition of Section 114, that a foreign corporation be "transacting business in this state," would make Section 58 applicable whenever any business was done in the state. However, the phrase "transacting business" is of extremely vague and uncertain content,[48] and should

---

Iron and Locomotive Works v. Furness (1906) 1 K. B. 49 (Ct. of App.); cf. 1 Beale, *Conflict of Laws* (1935) p. 320. The *Risdon* case early received the criticism of Hohfeld, *Nature of Stockholder's Individual Liability for Corporation Debts*, 9 Col. L. Rev. 284, 493 (1909); 10 Col. L. Rev. 283, 520 (1910).

[46] The Restatement of Conflict of Laws, §188, adopts the rule that directors of foreign corporations doing business in a state are liable for acts done within the state.

[47] Cf. *Thomas v. Matthiessen*, 232 U. S. 221 (1914) (New York federal court applied California statute imposing liability on stockholders of Arizona corporation doing business in California).

[48] Haring, *Doing Business in Other States* (1927) 52; Stevens, *Corporations* (1936) 837. In the Uniform Foreign Corporation Act "doing business" is defined

be construed with reference to the purpose of the particular statute. Fortunately, in this case it appears that the draftsmen of Section 114 had reference to the transacting of business by corporations which did all or substantially all of their business in New York.[49] Apart from this legislative history, two familiar canons of statutory construction favor non-application of the section to corporations transacting a minor part of their business in New York. First, the presumption that legislation is not intended to alter ordinary principles of conflict of laws,[50] under which in this situation the law of the state of incorporation would be controlling. Second, the rule that a statute will be construed where possible to avoid serious questions as to constitutionality.[51]

Assuming that New York courts were to construe Section 114 otherwise, so as to subject a foreign corporation doing a small part of its business in the state to regulation of its dividends according to New York law, should this assertion of authority be sustained? Since it is assumed a specific statute is now construed to have this effect, the question is no longer one simply of conflict of laws. Unless the statute is unconstitutional for want of legislative power by New York, foreign corporations are subject to its regulation. It is difficult to see how the legislative interest of New York reaches

---

as transaction of "some part of its business substantial and continuous in character and not merely casual or occasional." *Handbook of Commissioners on Uniform State Laws* (1934) 287.

[49] See §112, n. 37, *supra*.

[50] See Note, *Preserving the Inviolability of Rules of Conflict of Laws by Statutory Construction,* 49 Harv. L. Rev. 319 (1935). The Uniform Foreign Corporation Act makes no attempt to regulate the dividend declarations of foreign corporations, and by a provision that acts of management or control of internal affairs of the corporation in the non-domiciliary state shall not constitute doing business in the state in effect negatives any such application of local laws. *Handbook of Commissioners on Uniform State Laws* (1934) 288.

[51] Where the question is one of qualifying to do business in the state and regulation thereof, a higher degree of corporate activity within the state is usually required than where the question is merely "doing business" within service of process or tax statutes. Isaacs, *An Analysis of Doing Business,* 25 Col. L. Rev. 1018, 1024 (1925). It is quite clear that isolated and single transactions do not satisfy even the requirements of ordinary statutes as to doing business. Haring, *Corporations Doing Business in Other States* (1927) 53; Mann, *Laws of Foreign Business Corporations Doing Business in New York* (1906) 205; *Handbook of Commissioners on Uniform State Laws* (1934) 287. The Massachusetts provisions subjecting the regulation of dividends by foreign corporations to local law have been drawn with particular reference to certain corporations doing a local business within the state. Officers and directors of foreign corporations engaged principally in banking or public utility business and having a usual place of business in the state are subject to Massachusetts dividend regulations applicable to that type corporation. Mass. Laws Ann., c. 181, §§14.7; c. 158, §44.

beyond application of New York dividend law to the extent necessary to protect local creditors and stockholders. The authorities tend to support application in so far as it is necessary to protect local creditors.[52]

The effect of giving broader application to the statute may be illustrated by reference to a specific situation. Assume a mining corporation incorporated in Delaware owns mines and does its principal business in California, Colorado, and Montana, but maintains an office in New York and a warehouse at which it regularly purchases and stores supplies for shipment to its mines. No other business is done in New York. Of the five states which might lay claim to the right to regulate the corporation's dividends, that of New York is in some respects the weakest—certainly it is weaker than that of California, Colorado, or Montana. Of the five states, the dividend law of New York is probably the most stringent.[53] Should the circumstance of New York's strategic commercial position, by which it becomes necessary for a large part of the nation's corporations to do at least some part of their business there, enable it to run the dividend policy and other affairs of foreign corporations specified in Section 114? It is fortunate again that the Lexow Committee, in drafting monopoly legislation which accompanied Section 114, recognized that "no state law will operate extra-territorially, nor may we bring within the scope of our punitive power any acts committed in other jurisdictions." [54] A similar limitation must have been recognized as inhering in the power of the state under Section 114. In the absence of a substantial part of the corporation's business being transacted in New York to give basis to a local public policy, there is much language in *Broderick v. Rosner* to support a rule compelling New York, in the example suggested, to recognize the Delaware dividend law under the full faith and credit clause. The court stated that when the full faith and credit clause is involved, "the room left for the play of conflicting policies is a narrow one," and even went so far as to say that as to "an incident

---

[52] In *German-American Coffee Co. v. Diehl,* 216 N. Y. 57, 66, 109 N. E. 875 (1915) Judge Cardozo, speaking of the right of recovery under §114, said, "We have no doubt that it may be given to creditors who have dealt with the corporation here. *Thomas v. Matthiessen.*" In the latter case recovery under the California double liability statute was allowed to local creditors, whose claims arose in California, against a New York stockholder of an Arizona corporation. See also *Pinney v. Nelson,* 183 U. S. 144 (1901) ; *Thomas v. Wentworth,* 158 Cal. 275, 110 Pac. 942 (1910).

[53] Cf. §21, n. 94; §22, n. 114; §23, n. 155; §27, n. 206; §28, n. 209, *supra.*

[54] N. Y. Sen. Doc. No. 40 (1897), p. 28.

of the incorporation"—and a dividend would seem to be that—"no other state properly can be said to have any public policy thereon." [55]

However, in the *Diehl* case the court held that Section 114 was not limited to the protection of local creditors, but conferred a complete cause of action in favor of the corporation where the corporation did its general business in New York. To extend the broad language of the opinion to permit similar application of New York law to corporations only doing a minor part of their business in New York, would make New York the corporate legislator for perhaps a majority of corporations in this country, in so far as their activities fall within the scope of Section 114.

It has been suggested that if a corporation does all of its business in New York, it should be immaterial that it goes to the state of domicil to declare its dividends, that New York law ought, nevertheless, to govern in suits elsewhere than at the domicil. If the corporation does only a minor part of its business in New York, it is, on the other hand, certainly advisable to observe all formalities possible to avoid application of New York law. The dividend should not be declared in New York state and a case against application of New York law would be aided by a declaration at the domicil. If the dividend is declared in New York, analogy to the conflicts rule that the place of tort determines the choice of law is strong.

112.3. Corporations Doing a Substantial But Not the Major Part of Their Business in New York

The most difficult case under Section 114 is that in which a foreign corporation, which transacts large parts of its business in a number of states, also does a substantial business in New York. The same problems discussed in the preceding subsection are involved, but the answers are more difficult. Principal help comes again on the question of construction. The purpose of the drafting committee was to prevent migration of essentially New York enterprises to other states for incorporation and to protect local creditors and stockholders.[56] At least to the latter extent, New York law can probably be invoked.[57] The cases decided under Section 114 pay no particular attention to the amount of business necessary in New York before the section can be considered applicable.[58]

[55] 294 U. S. 629, 642–643 (1935).
[56] N. Y. Sen. Doc. No. 40 (1897), pp. 21–22, 36.
[57] See §112.2, *supra*.
[58] See §112.1, n. 42, *supra*.

113. Dividends Violating Prohibitions in State of Declaration Against Transfers When Insolvent

In view of the fact that directors' meetings at which dividends are declared are frequently held outside the state of incorporation, it may sometimes be important to determine the applicability of local statutes prohibiting fraudulent conveyances. The question is perhaps not quite as important as that concerning application of local dividend statutes, since normally a dividend which renders the corporation insolvent will be illegal no matter what law is applicable.[59] On the question whether the bankruptcy or equity test is applicable, it may still make a difference, however, as to which law is controlling.[60] The conflicts rule that the place of tort governs the law applicable may furnish ground for applying insolvency statutes of the state in which the dividend is declared, and this seems to be the basis of the rule promulgated in the Restatement of Conflict of Laws that, so far as directors are participants in acts within the state in which the corporation does business, they may be subjected to liability.[61] New York Stock Corporation Law Section 114 has been held to make Section 15 applicable to local transfers of insolvent foreign corporations.[62]

114. Multiple Incorporation

The choice of law difficulties inherent in all cases of multiple incorporation are accentuated with respect to internal management problems such as the declaration of dividends. In the absence of any dividend decisions, some of the considerations involved may be suggested. Where a corporation is chartered by more than one state, the cases are divided as to whether with respect to questions of internal management the laws of all the charter states must be complied with or whether compliance with the laws of any one state will suffice.[63] The desirability of selecting one law rather than several as

[59] See §19, *supra.*
[60] See §20, *supra.*
[61] Restatement of Conflict of Laws (1934), §188.
[62] *Irving Trust Co. v. Maryland Casualty Co.,* 83 F. (2d) 168 (C. C. A. 2d, 1936), *cert. den.* 299 U. S. 571 (1936) (comment, 50 Harv. L. Rev. 129); cf. *Upright v. Brown,* 98 F. (2d) 802, 804 (C. C. A. 2d, 1938).
[63] Holding compliance with laws of one state sufficient: *Brown v. Boston & Maine Railroad,* 233 Mass. 502, 124 N. E. 322 (1919) (shareholders' meeting valid under proxy statute of Massachusetts sustained even though under law of New Hampshire where corporation was also incorporated such meeting might have been invalid) ; *Bachman v. Supreme Lodge,* 44 Ill. App. 188 (1892) (an insurance benefit certificate valid under the laws of one of the states in which the lodge was incorporated was binding irrespective of the law in a second state of incorporation) ; cf. *Graham v. Boston, Hartford & Erie Railroad Co.,* 118 U. S. 161 (1886)

controlling points to two situations at least in which that may be done. If the corporation is chartered in several states but does the major part of its business in one state, the law of that one state could well be selected. If the corporation does the principal part of its business in a state other than one of the incorporating states, it is possible that the law of that state should be adopted as the choice between a single law and a set of conflicting laws supplied by the domicils. If the corporation does substantially the same amount of business in each of the incorporating states, it seems not unreasonable to require that since it has sought incorporation in these states it must comply with the dividend laws of all, unless the situation is such that compliance with the law of the strictest state would violate the law of some other state. In the latter situation, the dividend should be deemed valid in all states if valid in a state of incorporation in which the directors' meeting declaring the dividend is held.

(mortgage authorized by stockholders at a New York meeting and valid under New York law was binding elsewhere) ; 2 Beale, *Conflict of Laws* (1935) p. 910. Holding action must be valid under law of all incorporating states: *Pollitz v. Wabash R. Co.*, 150 App. Div. 709, 135 N. Y. S. 785 (1st Dept. 1912) (approval of plan for exchange of stock and bonds for outstanding debenture bonds) ; *Fisk v. Chicago, Rock Island, & Pacific Railroad Co.*, 53 Barb. 513 (N. Y. 1868) (stock issued by corporation incorporated in Iowa and Illinois could not be ratified solely by Iowa legislature, the action of both states being necessary) ; see Foley, *Incorporation, Multiple Incorporation, and the Conflict of Laws,* 42 Harv. L. Rev. 516, 540–541 (1929).

CHAPTER 11

THE FEDERAL INCOME TAX ON DIVIDENDS

A. Cash and Property Dividends

115. Interest of Corporation in Dividend Tax Liability of Stockholders

The taxation of corporate dividends is primarily the concern of the stockholder, since the federal taxing system imposes its levy with respect to dividends upon stockholders rather than the corporation. However, questions of taxability also bear directly upon the action of the corporation in its declaration of dividends. Whether a corporate distribution in the particular form made will or will not constitute taxable income to the stockholder recipient is a major factor to be considered by the board of directors in voting its approval.[1] Furthermore, should the undistributed profits tax, enacted in 1936 and repealed in 1939,[2] be re-enacted in the future, the taxability of dividend distributions will become extremely important in the determination of the corporation's own tax liability, since the dividends paid credit, which measures the amount by which the corporation's undistributed profits tax shall be reduced, is only allowed as to dividends taxable to the stockholder receiving the same.[3]

[1] Only taxability of dividends paid in the ordinary course of business is considered. Special problems arise with respect to the payment of dividends in partial or complete liquidation [I. R. C., §115(c)] and distributions falling in the category of reorganizations [I. R. C., §§112, 113].

[2] §14(b) of the Revenue Act of 1936 imposed a tax varying in amount from 7 to 27 per cent on the corporation's undistributed income, 49 Stat. 1656. The tax was reduced to a maximum of 2½ per cent by the Revenue Act of 1938 (52 Stat. 455) and completely repealed, effective December 31, 1939, by the Revenue Act of 1939 (Pub. No. 155, 76th Cong. 1st Sess., §201; H. Rept. No. 855, 76th Cong. 1st Sess., pp. 3-4). Proposals for an undistributed profits tax had been made as early as 1918 and in 1924 such a tax was adopted by the Senate but eliminated in Conference. Blakey, *The Federal Income Tax* (1940) 243-244.

[3] §§27(e),(h), Revenue Act of 1936, 49 Stat. 1665. Undistributed profits tax problems arising under these provisions are treated in the following discussions: Hendricks, *The Surtax on Undistributed Profits of Corporations,* 46 Yale L. J. 19 (1936); Martin, *Taxation of Undistributed Corporate Profits,* 35 Mich. L. Rev. 44 (1936); Peper, *Corporate Policy Under the Surtax on Undistributed Profits,* 22 Wash. L. Q. 1 (1936); Paul, *The Federal Corporate Surplus Tax,* 23 Corn. L. Q. 72 (1937); Note, *Use of Stock Dividends to Avoid Undistributed Earnings Tax,* 4 U. of Chic. L. Rev. 311 (1937); Note, *The Corporate Undistributed Profits Tax,* 36 Col. L. Rev. 1321; Note, 25 Geo. L. J. 423 (1937); Note, 50 Harv. L. Rev. 332 (1936); Note, 85 U. of Pa. L. Rev. 83, 100 (1936).

116. Internal Revenue Code Sections 22(a) and 115

From the first federal income tax act of 1861 [4] down through the present Internal Revenue Code, a tax has been specifically levied on "dividends." In 1862 there was levied on all residents a tax of 5 per cent on "gains, profits or income . . . derived from . . . dividends." [5] This provision has its current survival in Internal Revenue Code Section 22(a) which, in the section supplying the general definition for gross income, provides " 'Gross income' includes gains, profits and income derived from . . . dividends." [6]

The mere fact a corporation has declared what constitutes under the law of the state of incorporation a dividend, even though it be a cash dividend, does not mean that stockholders are liable for a federal income tax thereon. Under Section 115(a) of the Internal Revenue Code, the term "dividend" is defined as any distribution to stockholders, whether in money or other property "(1) out of its earnings or profits accumulated after February 28, 1913, or (2) out of the earnings or profits of the taxable year (computed as of the close of the taxable year without diminution by reason of any distributions made during the taxable year), without regard to the amount of the earnings and profits at the time the distribution was made." Since the Revenue Act of 1936, corporate dividends of a class subject to taxation are subject to both the normal tax and the surtax.

117. A "Distribution . . . in Money or in Other Property"

The keystone of taxability is the realization by the stockholder of corporate profit through a distribution to him. That it is the distribution to the stockholder, and not the earning by the corporation, which constitutes the test is provided by the statute and demonstrated by *Lynch v. Hornby*.[7] In that case a cash divi-

[4] The Act of 1861 levied a tax of 5 per cent on dividends accruing on securities or stocks owned in the United States by any citizen of the United States residing abroad. 12 Stat. 309, §49.

[5] 12 Stat. 473, §90. For regulations affecting dividends under the early income tax acts, see Estee, *The Excise Tax Law* (1863), 298; Reg. 4, Instruction 39 (1866); Reg. 21, p. 20 (under Act of 1894).

[6] The first Revenue Act under the Sixteenth Amendment contained a similar provision. Act of Oct. 3, 1913, 38 Stat. 167, §II, B. The regulations promulgated under this act also covered dividends. Reg. 33, Art. 4 (Jan. 5, 1914).

[7] 247 U. S. 339 (1918). Cf. *U. S. v. Phellis*, 257 U. S. 156 (1921); *Rockefeller v. U. S.*, 257 U. S. 176 (1921); *Cullinan v. Walker*, 262 U. S. 134 (1923); *Weiss v. Stearn*, 265 U. S. 242 (1924); *Marr v. U. S.*, 268 U. S. 536 (1925). In *Eisner v. Macomber*, 252 U. S. 189, 218 (1920), the Supreme Court disapproved an earlier statement in *Collector v. Hubbard*, 12 Wall. 1 (1870), that Congress had the power to tax accumulated corporate profits to stockholders prior to their distribution in

dend earned prior to the effective date of the Sixteenth Amendment, but distributed out of the prior surplus after March 1, 1913, was held subject to the tax. It was the severance and payment to the stockholder upon which the court held the incidence of the tax constitutionally fell: ". . . just as we deem the legislative intent manifest to tax the stockholder with respect to such accumulations only if and when, and to the extent that, his interest in them comes to fruition, as income, that is, in dividends declared, so we can perceive no constitutional obstacle that stands in the way of carrying out this intent when dividends are declared out of a pre-existing surplus." [8]

The provision in Section 115(a) taxing "any distribution . . . in money or in other property" is comprehensive. Under the regulations, a dividend comprises any distribution in the ordinary course of business though extraordinary in amount.[9] Section 115(a) is further restricted and also further amplified by subsequent subdivisions.

Cash dividends and ordinary property dividends create no problems as to the power of Congress to impose an income tax thereon. However, since the decisions in *Towne v. Eisner* [10] and *Eisner v. Macomber*,[11] early in the history of the income tax, it has been recognized that dividends in the stock of the declaring corporation are not necessarily subject to the same rule of taxation as other corporate distributions. Distributions of this type have again been brought to the fore by the recent decisions in *Koshland v. Helvering* [12] and *Helvering v. Gowran*,[13] with the result that stock dividends must continue to be accorded separate treatment. Under Section 115(f), stock dividends and distributions of stock rights are not treated as dividends to the extent that they do not constitute income to the shareholder within the meaning of the Sixteenth Amendment.[14] It is well settled, however, that dividends in the

---

dividends. In this regard an interesting question is raised by I. R. C., §337(a), which taxes stockholders of foreign personal holding companies on the undistributed net income of the latter. Should this tax be sustained in a situation where the sympathies are strongly in favor of the tax, it would constitute a precedent, difficult to distinguish, for taxing stockholders of all corporations on undistributed income.

[8] By statute, earnings and profits accumulated prior to Mar. 1, 1913 may now be distributed exempt from the tax. I. R. C., §115(b) ; see §119, *infra*.

[9] Reg. 103, §19.115–1.

[10] 245 U. S. 418 (1918).

[11] 252 U. S. 189 (1920).

[12] 298 U. S. 441 (1936).

[13] 302 U. S. 238 (1937).

[14] §§122–127, *infra*, discuss stock dividends.

stock of a corporation other than the declarant constitute property dividends, and as such have always been held subject to the tax.[15] Under Section 115(j), property dividends, including distributions in stock of other corporations, are taxed to the stockholder not on the basis of cost to the corporation, but at their fair value at the time distribution is made.[16] The stockholder thus pays a tax on the appreciation which is unrealized to the corporation. It is significant, also, to note that a dividend of specified amount, declared to be payable in stock of another corporation at the appreciated value of the latter, does not constitute taxable gain to the corporation for the difference between cost and fair market value at the time of the declaration.[17] Such a transaction does not amount first to the creation of an obligation and then its discharge by delivery of property costing less than the amount of the obligation; it is simply the distribution of a property dividend, there never having been any obligation to pay a separate amount in cash. On the other hand, if a dividend of fixed amount is declared, and the corporation thereafter satisfies the obligation by a payment in property, it is accountable for gain on the difference between cost of the property and the amount of the dividend.[18] The principle of *United States v. Kirby Lumber Company*,[19] that the discharge of an obligation at less than its face value, effected in this case by using property carried on the corporate books at a cost less than the face amount of the dividend, applies to render the difference taxable income.

117.1. Redemption or Cancellation Having the Effect of a Dividend

If corporations could declare tax-free stock dividends, and then by cancellation or redemption of the shares issued, distribute the amount capitalized in cash, a ready means for avoiding an income

---

[15] *Peabody v. Eisner,* 247 U. S. 347 (1918) ; *Commissioner v. Scatena,* 85 F. (2d) 729 (C. C. A. 9th, 1936) ; *Charles Owen,* 3 B. T. A. 905 (1926) ; *Sam F. Ziliox,* 19 B. T. A. 679 (1930) ; Annotation, "Distribution by corporation to its stockholders of stock of other corporation," 61 A. L. R. 360 ; see also Paul, *Ascertainment of "Earnings or Profits" for the Purpose of Determining Taxability of Corporate Distributions,* 51 Harv. L. Rev. 40 (1937) ; Note, 47 Yale L. J. 139, 140 (1937). The first comprehensive income tax regulations provided that "A dividend paid in stock of another corporation is not a stock dividend." Reg. 45, Art. 1543 (Revenue Act of 1918).

[16] *Binzel v. Commissioner,* 75 F. (2d) 989 (C. C. A. 2d, 1935), *cert. den.* 296 U. S. 579 (1935) ; *Susan T. Freshman,* 33 B. T. A. 394 (1935).

[17] *General Utilities Co. v. Helvering,* 296 U. S. 200 (1935) ; *Commissioner v. Columbia Pacific Shipping Co.,* 77 F. (2d) 759 (C. C. A. 9th, 1935).

[18] *Bacon-McMillan Veneer Co.,* 20 B. T. A. 556 (1930) ; cf. *Callanan Road Improvement Co.,* 12 B. T. A. 1109 (1928) (payment of a cash dividend in property at market value below cost results in a deductible corporate loss).

[19] 284 U. S. 1 (1931).

tax in whole or in part would be at hand.[20] This loophole is closed by Section 115(g) which provides that if a corporation cancels or redeems a stock dividend at such time and in such manner as to make the cancellation or redemption in whole or in part essentially equivalent to the distribution of a taxable dividend, the distributee is liable for an income tax to the extent that the distribution represents earnings or profits accumulated after February 28, 1913.[21] The problem as indicated by the cases under Section 115(g) is one of fact. If the stock dividend is part of a plan which amounts merely to a delayed cash dividend, then the cancellation or redemption is taxable as if it were a cash dividend, and not merely as though it were a sale of stock to the corporation.[22] Redemption or retirement within a short interim after the purported stock dividend is issued should be treated as indicating the dividend was originally intended as a cash distribution.

117.2. Bargain Purchases by Stockholders

As noted in discussing the methods by which a dividend may be paid, it is not necessary that the distribution be made to stockholders without cost to them. It is possible to distribute property to stockholders upon their payment to the corporation of an amount less than the fair value thereof, the difference between the amount paid and the fair market value constituting a dividend.[23] For example, it would not be uncommon for a corporation owning stock in a subsidiary worth $200 a share on the market to "sell" the same to its stockholders at $100 a share. The $100 difference between market value and purchase price would constitute a dividend. This type of problem arises quite frequently in tax cases. The regulations provide that if property is transferred by a corporation to a shareholder for an amount substantially less than its fair market value, regardless of

[20] This avoidance device was much more susceptible of use before the decision in *Helvering v. Gowran,* 302 U. S. 238 (1937), holding a preferred dividend on common stock, both classes already outstanding, to be taxable. The corporation would declare a dividend of preferred stock on its common, which was under the statute tax-free, and then shortly redeem or retire it. For example, this was the procedure in the *Gowran* case.

[21] ". . . the obvious device, by a close corporation having a surplus, consisting of an expansion of capitalization, a stock issue and stock redemption, all within a short time pursuant to a unified plan, is plainly within the statute." *Pearl B. Brown,* 26 B. T. A. 901, 906 (1932), aff'd on other grounds 69 F. (2d) 602 (C. C. A. 7th, 1934), cert. den. 293 U. S. 570 (1934) ; see also VIII–2 Cum. Bull., 133 (1929).

[22] Cases under varying factual situations are collected in Note, *Stock Redemption or Cancellation Taxable as Dividends,* 49 Harv. L. Rev. 1344 (1936) ; Annotation, 105 A. L. R. 761, 774.

[23] See §55, *supra.*

whether the transfer is in the guise of a sale or exchange, the shareholders shall include in gross income the difference to the extent that such difference is in the nature of a distribution of earnings or profits taxable as a dividend.[24] The test adopted by the Supreme Court in *Palmer v. Commissioner* is whether the transaction between corporation and stockholder is a *bona fide* sale or, as stated in the regulations, merely a dividend in the guise of a sale: ". . . the bare fact that a transaction on its face a sale, has resulted in a distribution of some of the corporate assets to stockholders, gives rise to no inference that the distribution is a dividend within the meaning of §115. To transfer it from the one category to the other, it is at least necessary to make some showing that the transaction is in purpose or effect used as an implement for the distribution of corporate earnings to stockholders." [25] Thus, rights to subscribe to stock of another corporation owned by the distributing corporation are taxable to stockholders at their market value.[26] If a direct distribution of the other corporation's stock were made, it would clearly be taxable under *Peabody v. Eisner*.[27] Certainly, if part consideration is paid upon exercise of a right, the balance, still constituting a dividend, remains equally taxable. Otherwise distributions in the stock of another corporation, taxable if unqualifiedly paid out in dividends, may be made tax free simply by requiring stockholders to make a payment less than the value of the stock to the corporation.[28] The position of the Treasury Department, that a sale of corporate property *pro rata* to stockholders at a price less than market value constitutes a dividend as to the difference between fair market value and the price paid, should be sustained.[29] Where the sale to stockholders is not in proportion to their stockholdings, it has been held, however, that the bargain differential does not constitute a dividend, since a dividend is a ratable distribution among stockholders.[30] In

---

[24] Reg. 103, §19.22(a)-1.

[25] See *Palmer v. Commissioner,* 302 U. S. 63, 69–70 (1937). Since the court found that the fair market value of the property received was not in excess of the purchase price paid by stockholders, no dividend was in any event distributed or subject to tax under the act, and the court's statement is, therefore, *obiter.*

[26] *Metcalf's Estate v. Commissioner,* 32 F. (2d) 192 (C. C. A. 2d, 1929) ; cf. *Moran v. Lucas,* 36 F. (2d) 546 (Ct. App. D. of C. 1929).

[27] 247 U. S. 347 (1918), §117, n. 15, *supra.*

[28] Cf. *Palmer v. Commissioner,* 302 U. S. 63, 69–70 (1937).

[29] See A. R. R. 6940, III–1 Cum. Bull. 32 (1924) ; Note, *Avoidance of Income Tax Through Purchase,* 50 Harv. L. Rev. 500, 509 (1937). Cf. *Rubay Co.,* 9 B. T. A. 133 (1927) (sale of assets to stockholder at a bargain did not constitute basis for claiming a loss by corporation because transaction was in effect a liquidating distribution) ; *M. I. Stewart & Co.,* 2 B. T. A. 737 (1925) (same).

[30] *Taplin v. Commissioner,* 41 F. (2d) 454 (C. C. A. 6th, 1930).

Commissioner v. Van Vorst, the taxpayer, owning over 46,000 out of 50,000 shares of the corporation's stock, bought from the latter parcels of property having a fair market value of $154,000 for $54,-000. The transaction was held to constitute a sale rather than a taxable dividend without any direct reference to the fact that the distribution to stockholders was not *pro rata.*[31] The court proceeded on the broader ground that the purchase of property could not constitute a gain or profit. The more recent opinion of the Supreme Court in the *Palmer* case indicates that under proper circumstances a bargain purchase may constitute gain[32] and must be deemed a limitation of the Van Vorst *rationale.* On its facts, the result in the latter case is also doubtful. A bargain sale to a single stockholder who owns the vast majority of the stock should be treated as a *pro tanto* dividend, even though the minority stockholders are not accorded a right to participate in the purchase.

118. "Earnings or Profits"

A dividend is taxable income under Section 115 only if it is paid from "earnings or profits accumulated after February 28, 1913" or "out of earnings or profits of the taxable year."[33] A provision limiting taxation of dividends to distributions out of earnings or profits first appeared in the Revenue Act of 1916,[34] but there is no indication in the committee reports of that year as to what Congress intended the phrase to mean. In spite of the relatively long period during which dividends have been taxed under this classification, the meaning of earnings or profits under decided cases is still vague. One thing seems clear, that taxable corporate net income and earnings or profits are not coterminous. Items which do not constitute income to the corporation may constitute a part of earnings or profits taxable as dividends to stockholders. Thus, constitutionally immune or statutorily exempt income of the corporation is included in determining earnings and profits.[35] On the other hand, some

---

[31] 59 F. (2d) 677 (C. C. A. 9th, 1932) [cited in *Blatt Co. v. U. S.,* 305 U. S. 267, 279 (1938)]; but cf. *H. K. L. Castle,* 9 B. T. A. 931 (1927).

[32] 302 U. S. 63, 69 (1937), n. 25, *supra.*

[33] See also Reg. 103, §19.115.1. Generally, see Paul, *Ascertainment of "Earnings or Profits" for the Purpose of Determining Taxability of Corporate Distributions,* 51 Harv. L. Rev. 40 (1937).

[34] 39 Stat. 757, §2a.

[35] Reg. 103, §19.115–3; *Commissioner v. F. J. Young Corp.,* 103 F. (2d) 137 (C. C. A. 3d, 1939) (gain on tax-free exchanges not included in computing corporate income is a part of earnings or profits); *John T. Wilson,* 31 B. T. A. 1022 (1935), *app. dism.* 82 F. (2d) 1023 (C. C. A. 4th, 1936) (interest paid corporation on United States Government obligations included); *R. M. Weyerhaeuser,* 33 B. T. A. 594, 597 (1935) (dictum to same effect); see *Charles F. Ayer,* 12

extraordinary expenses, charitable contributions of various amounts, taxes paid the federal government, and local benefit taxes, not deductible in computing corporate net income, may be deducted in determining earnings and profits.[36]

If earnings or profits are not the equivalent of taxable corporate net income, do the terms comprehend any distribution which is a legal dividend under the laws of the state of incorporation? While there is no direct authority on the question, in many cases it will probably be true that a distribution legally made under the law of the domicil is a distribution from earnings or profits within the purview of the federal income tax.[37] However, it does not follow that a distribution, illegal under some peculiar dividend law of the state incorporation, will not be a taxable dividend. The federal taxing system has its own statutory definition of a taxable dividend. If that is met, and there are no constitutional infirmities, the stockholder is liable for the tax, irrespective of the state provisions.[38]

Analysis of the phrase "earnings or profits" in Section 115(a) presents fundamental accounting issues similar to those involved in the determination of what constitutes profit under state dividend statutes.[39] Does it mean profit and loss statement income for the particular year or years, or does it mean a balance sheet earned surplus? The statute until 1936 only taxed dividends from earnings and profits accumulated after February 28, 1913, but in that year Section 115a(2) was added,[40] so that now a tax is imposed if the corporation

---

B. T. A. 284, 287 (1928) (interest on obligations of states and municipalities). The first of the comprehensive income tax regulations affecting dividends provided that income not taxable to the corporation should be included in ascertaining profits subject to dividend distribution. Reg. 45, Art. 1541 (Revenue Act of 1918).

[36] See Paul, *Ascertainment of "Earnings or Profits" for the Purpose of Determining Taxability of Corporate Distributions,* 51 Harv. L. Rev. 40, 45 (1937); *R. M. Weyerhaeuser,* 33 B. T. A. 594, 597 (1935).

[37] Montgomery takes the view that earnings or profits means corporate net income computed in accordance with state laws and good accounting practice. Montgomery, *Fed. Income Tax Handbook 1938–39,* 239. In *R. M. Weyerhaeuser,* 33 B. T. A. 594, 597 (1935), the Board stated: "Earnings and profits . . . are not defined by the act; but they have a settled and well-defined meaning in accounting. Generally speaking, they are computed by deducting from gross receipts the expense of producing them."

[38] Cf. *Helvering v. Northwest Steel Rolling Mills, Inc.,* 61 Sup. Ct. 109 (1940) (corporation having a deficit, so that it was illegal under the law of the state of incorporation to distribute current earnings, held nevertheless subject to the undistributed profits tax under the Revenue Act of 1936 for not distributing the same in dividends); *Crane-Johnson Co. v. Commissioner,* 105 F. (2d) 740 (C. C. A. 8th, 1939), aff'd 61 Sup. Ct. 114 (1940); *Bastian Bros. v. McGowan,* P. H. 1940 Fed. Tax Serv., §62, 488 (D. N. Y. 1940); I. T. 3016, XV–2 Cum. Bull. 73 (1936).

[39] See Chapters 2, 3, and 4, and particularly §§16–18, *supra.*

[40] 49 Stat. 1688.

has such earnings or profits, or if there are earnings or profits of the current taxable year. The federal income tax now resembles somewhat the dual dividend classification under state corporation acts of the Delaware type. The tax is imposed substantially on: (1) surplus (but only to the extent of earnings), or (2) current profits.[41]

118.1. "Earnings or Profits Accumulated After February 28, 1913"

Pursuant to Section 115a(1), dividends from profits accumulated after February 28, 1913, the effective date of the Sixteenth Amendment, are taxable. Section 115(b) further provides that earnings or profits accumulated prior to March 1, 1913, may be distributed exempt from tax, after earnings and profits accumulated subsequent to February 28, 1913 have been distributed. Under *Lynch v. Hornby,* there is no constitutional objection to taxing dividends paid after February 28, 1913 out of earnings previously accumulated.[42] The provision limiting the incidence of the tax to distributions out of subsequent earnings is one of statutory grace. But efforts in Congress to subject earnings prior to March 1, 1913 to the tax have failed.[43]

A literal application of the language in Section 115a(1) would result in imposition of a tax if the total of earnings and profits for the years after February 28, 1913 exceeded the total of losses for those years and the distribution were made from such excess of profits. With two important exceptions, this interpretation is used. While distributable earnings accruing after February 28, 1913 are reduced for tax purposes by losses in years subsequent to the earnings,[44] losses after February 28, 1913 do not reduce earnings of subsequent years if there is a surplus prior to March 1, 1913. In other words, distributions from earnings most recently accumulated are taxable under Section 115a(1), even though there is a deficit in total earnings for the period after February 28, 1913, provided that the balance sheet of the corporation (by virtue of surplus prior to March 1, 1913) shows a surplus. This rule was established by

---

[41] Cf. §27, *supra.*

[42] 247 U. S. 339 (1918) ; see *Helvering v. Canfield,* 291 U. S. 163, 167 (1934).

[43] H. Rept. No. 704, 73d Cong., 2d Sess., p. 15; S. Rept. No. 558, 73d Cong. 2d Sess., p. 36; Conf. Report, H. Rept. No. 1385, 73d Cong., 2d Sess., p. 22; see also S. Rept. No. 665, 72d Cong., 1st Sess., p. 30; H. Rept. No. 2, 70th Cong., 1st Sess., p. 20; Conf. Report, H. Rept. No. 1882, 70th Cong., 1st Sess., p. 14.

[44] A. R. M. 82, 3 Cum. Bull. 36 (1920) adhered to in G. C. M. 3532, VII–1 Cum. Bull., 190 (1928) ; *Helvering v. Canfield,* 291 U. S. 163 (1934) ; *Hoffman v. U. S.,* 53 F. (2d) 282 (Ct. Cl. 1931).

Helvering v. Canfield[45] which furnishes a good illustration of its operation. In that case the corporation had a surplus of $4,000,000 on March 1, 1913. For the year 1914 it had a profit of $4,000; for 1915, a loss of $190,000; for 1916, a loss of $210,000; and from 1917 to 1923, profits of $2,450,000. In 1923 the corporation paid a dividend of $5,100,000. The Revenue Act of 1921 imposed a tax on distributions from earnings or profits accumulated since February 28, 1913 and provided that all distributions were from the most recently accumulated profits, provisions, therefore, similar to those in present Section 115. The stockholder contended that in computing what portion of the distribution was from earnings subsequent to February 28, 1913, the losses for 1915 and 1916 should be deducted from the total profits for the years 1917 to 1923 and 1914. This left, after deducting prior dividends, $760,000 as having been paid out of earnings subsequent to February 28, 1913. The Commissioner contended, on the other hand, that the 1915 and 1916 losses wiped out the small profit of 1914 and then reduced the surplus of March 1, 1913, with the result that on January 1, 1917 the losses had been completely handled, leaving the earnings of 1917 to 1923 as earnings accumulated after February 28, 1913. Under this theory $1,160,000 was taxable. The position of the Commissioner was sustained by the court.[46] It is to be noted, therefore, that earnings and profits accumulated since February 28, 1913 are not the equivalent of net earned surplus since that date.[47] In the *Canfield* case, earnings and profits were construed to include an amount substantially in excess of annual profits over annual losses subsequent to February 28, 1913. The regulations incorporate the rule in the following form: "A loss sustained for a year prior to the taxable year does not affect the earnings or profits of the taxable year."[48] However, cases decided before the amendment of 1936, taxing also

[45] 291 U. S. 163 (1934).
[46] *Accord: Blair v. U. S.*, 63 Ct. Cl. 193 (1927), *cert. den.* 275 U. S. 546 (1927); *Robert S. Farrell*, 30 B. T. A. 627 (1934); *R. M. Weyerhaeuser*, 33 B. T. A. 594 (1935). Prior to the *Canfield* case, it had been held, in the absence of a showing of existence or non-existence of Mar. 1, 1913 surplus, that operating deficits sustained after Feb. 28, 1913, but prior to the taxable year, did not reduce distributable income of the taxable year. *Hoffman v. U. S.*, 53 F. (2d) 282 (Ct. Cl. 1931).
[47] The statement in *Foley Securities Co. v. Commissioner*, 106 F. (2d) 731, 732 (C. C. A. 8th, 1939), made in discussing the credit under the personal holding company undistributed profits tax of the Revenue Act of 1934, that §115(a) has been uniformly construed "to mean a distribution out of earned surplus accumulated since February 28, 1913" is inconsistent with the holding in the *Canfield* case. Compare a similar statement in *Hadden v. Commissioner*, 49 F. (2d) 709, 711 (C. C. A. 2d, 1931).
[48] Reg. 103, §19.115-3. See also A. R. M. 82, 3 Cum. Bull. 36 (1920).

earnings or profits of the taxable year without regard to the amount of earnings or profits when the distribution was made, indicate that this statement is too broad. These cases hold that a loss sustained in a prior year if it impairs capital [49] or even paid-in surplus [50] must be made good out of earnings or profits of subsequent years before there can be any taxable dividend distribution. Cases have even gone so far as to hold that operating deficits written off by revaluation of assets [51] or donations back of stock [52] must still be considered as reducing subsequent current earnings. [53]

If a corporation in a balance sheet surplus jurisdiction should declare a dividend out of capital in one year and the succeeding year should have earnings less than the capital deficit but equivalent to dividends paid in the succeeding year, the latter distributions would, nevertheless, be considered payments from capital under the law of the state of incorporation. It is important to note, however, that for income tax purposes the earnings in the succeeding years cannot be considered as a restoration of the deficiency and, therefore, when paid out as being dividends of capital. Such distributions are taxable as dividends from profits. [54] The reason for different treatment in tax cases is clear. A corporation might otherwise, by taking proper corporate steps, make a voluntary dis-

[49] *Hadden v. Commissioner,* 49 F. (2d) 709 (C. C. A. 2d, 1931) (limiting restoration to losses subsequent to March 1, 1913); *Arthur C. Stifel,* 29 B. T. A. 1145 (1934) (as to capital of a corporation incorporated subsequent to March 1, 1913); *Louise Glassell Shorb,* 22 B. T. A. 644 (1931); see *Roy J. Kinnear,* 36 B. T. A. 153, 155 (1937), *app. dism.* by consent on motion of petitioner, 95 F. (2d) 997 (C. C. A. 9th, 1938); *Loren D. Sale,* 35 B. T. A. 938 (1937). The ruling in G. C. M. 1552, VI–1 Cum. Bull. 10 (1927) states: "Although it is provided in Section 201(b) that for the purposes of the Act every distribution is made out of earnings or profits to the extent thereof, and from the most recently accumulated earnings or profits, there can be no accumulation of earnings until an operating deficit is made good. As there was no surplus from which a dividend could have been paid, it necessarily follows that the distribution must have been out of capital." See also I. T. 2016, III–1 Cum. Bull. 29 (1924).

[50] *Roy J. Kinnear,* 36 B. T. A. 153 (1937), *app. dism.* by consent on motion of petitioner, 95 F. (2d) 997 (C. C. A. 9th, 1938) (impairment of March 1, 1913 paid-in surplus by operating losses thereafter must be made good out of current earnings); *Arthur C. Stifel,* 29 B. T. A. 1145 (1934).

[51] *Chapman v. Anderson,* 11 F. Supp. 913 (S. D. N. Y. 1935).

[52] *Henry Hadley Plant,* 30 B. T. A. 133 (1934), aff'd on other grounds 76 F. (2d) 8 (C. C. A. 2d, 1935).

[53] Montgomery takes the position that losses should be applied backward in reduction or exhaustion of earnings and profits of prior years until such earnings are exhausted, and that any unsatisfied deficit should reduce earnings of subsequent years. Montgomery, *Federal Income Tax Handbook 1938–39,* 243.

[54] *F. W. Henninger,* 21 B. T. A. 1235 (1931); cf. *Stanley M. Bolster,* 23 B. T. A. 347 (1931) (reduction in paid-in surplus caused by payment of dividends in prior years not restorable out of current earnings).

tribution from capital in one year which would be "restored" out of earnings of the following year. The corporation could then continue making distributions from "capital" to the extent of current earnings—distributions which would, however, in effect be distributions from current profits. In order to be able to use profits to wipe out a deficit in capital, that deficit must have arisen from causes other than a voluntary previous distribution of capital to stockholders. Such causes would include deficits arising from operations, destruction of assets through casualty losses and possibly impairments resulting from declines in market value. Even to this last statement there is a qualification. To the extent that dividends do not exceed earnings or profits of the taxable year, they are taxed under Section 115(a)(2) without regard to an existing capital deficit.

118.2. "Earnings or Profits of the Taxable Year"

Until 1936 only dividends out of earnings or profits accumulated after February 28, 1913 were taxed. The Revenue Act of 1936 amended Section 115(a) to tax, in addition to distributions from accumulations after February 28, 1913, distributions from earnings or profits of the taxable year without regard to the amount of earnings or profits at the time the distribution is made.[55] This provision was added to avoid an undistributed profits tax on corporations having a capital impairment but paying out all of their current earnings.[56]

This new provision is very important with respect to taxation of dividends paid by corporations from annual profits when capital is impaired under statutes of the Delaware type. It raises interesting questions. The first is a question of construction. The section provides for a tax on distributions from earnings of "the taxable year" irrespective of prior deficits. Does this mean from earnings of the current year in which the dividend was declared or does it mean from earnings in any taxable year after a deficit has been sus-

---

[55] 49 Stat. 1688, §115(a)(2).

[56] S. Rept. No. 2156, 74th Cong. 2d Sess., p. 18. The dividend paid credit used in computing the undistributed profits tax was only allowed if the corporation paid a dividend which was taxable. Revenue Act of 1936, §27(e)(h). Under decisions construing §115(a) before the amendment, a distribution out of current earnings at a time when the corporation had a capital deficit would not be a taxable dividend (§118.1, n. 49, *supra*) and the corporation would still be subject to the undistributed profits tax. *Foley Securities Corp. v. Commissioner*, 106 F. (2d) 731 (C. C. A. 8th, 1939) (decided under the personal holding company undistributed profits tax in the Revenue Act of 1934 which contained no provision giving credit for dividends from current earnings).

tained? The question is material in determining to what extent the statute purports to supersede decisions holding that an impairment of capital or paid-in surplus of prior years must be made up through restoration of current earnings.[57] Suppose that on January 1, 1937 a corporation has an operating deficit of $1,000,000 and earnings for the years 1937, 1938, and 1939 of $250,000 a year. If the corporation during 1939 declares a dividend of $750,000, is it taxable in entirety or only to the extent of $250,000, the current earnings for the year 1939, the balance going to satisfy the deficit, and being when paid out a distribution of capital? The Senate Finance Committee Report accompanying the Revenue Act of 1936 indicates that the statute purports only to tax the current 1939 distribution.[58]

The second question is whether a tax on current earnings at a time when the corporate balance sheet shows a deficit, and when the distribution of current earnings still leaves a deficit, is a tax on income or a tax on capital under the Sixteenth Amendment. To illustrate, suppose a stockholder purchases a share of the corporation's stock on organization, January 1, 1937, for $100; that during the years 1937 and 1938 the corporation sustains operating losses creating a deficit of $50 a share; and that in 1939 it has earnings of $10 per share which under a statute of the Delaware type it pays out to stockholders in dividends. Is the dividend of $10 income or a return of depleted capital? If the corporation instead of distributing the $10 in earnings, had dissolved in 1939, paying back to stockholders the $60 per share in assets which it held, it would be clear that the stockholder would not be taxable for any income, but on the contrary would have sustained a loss of $40. Is income realized where only $10 is returned to the stockholder, or is the transaction merely a diminution in a capital loss?[59] There is as yet no decision on this question.[60] However, it has been held that a corporation must

---

[57] See §118.1, n. 49–52, *supra*.

[58] The Committee heads its discussion of the amendment, "Section 115(a). Dividends Out of Current Earnings." The report states, "In order to enable corporations without regard to deficits existing at the beginning of the taxable year to obtain the benefit of the dividends paid credit for the purposes of the undistributed profits surtax, section 115(a) changes the definition of a dividend so as to include distributions out of the earnings or profits of the current year." S. Rept. No. 2156, 74th Cong. 2d Sess., p. 18.

[59] Cf. *Bowers v. Kerbaugh Empire Co.*, 271 U. S. 170 (1926); but cf. *Burnet v. Sanford & Brooks Co.*, 282 U. S. 359 (1930).

[60] The Treasury at an early date took the position that a dividend is deemed to be paid out of current earnings to the extent possible, and taxable to the recipient accordingly, notwithstanding an actual impairment of capital. 1 Cum. Bull. 28 (1919).

pay an undistributed profits tax on undistributed current earnings even though it has a capital deficit at the time.[61]

118.3. "Every Distribution Is Made . . . from the Most Recently Accumulated Earnings or Profits"

Section 115(b) provides that for purposes of the income tax "every distribution is made out of earnings or profits to the extent thereof, and from the most recently accumulated earnings or profits." [62] The statute creates a rule of law that all distributions are from the most recent earnings if earnings are available, irrespective of the fact the corporation may purport to distribute dividends out of paid-in surplus, capital, or some other source not taxable.[63] The statute does not thereby tax distributions which are not income. It simply requires that if there are earnings or profits, they must be distributed before other sources are resorted to.

Under the regulations, distributions are treated as made from the

[61] Helvering v. Northwest Steel Rolling Mills, Inc., 61 Sup. Ct. 109 (1940); Crane Johnson Co. v. Commissioner, 105 F. (2d) 740 (C. C. A. 8th, 1939), aff'd 61 Sup. Ct. 114 (1940) (No showing whether deficit occurred from operating losses or prior capital distributions in excess of earnings); Bastian Bros. Co. v. McGowan, P. H. 1940 Fed. Tax Serv., §62, 488; Foley Securities Corp. v. Commissioner, 106 F. (2d) 731 (C. C. A. 8th, 1939) (personal holding company undistributed profits tax). In Helvering v. Canfield, 291 U. S. 163 (1934), the court held it was not necessary to restore a reduction of pre-Mar. 1, 1913 surplus depleted by losses, but it distinguished the situation where the impairment was one of capital or paid-in surplus, saying, "The argument that the surplus of March 1, 1913, constituted capital is unavailing. We are not here concerned with capital in the sense of fixed or paid-in capital, which is not to be impaired, or with the restoration of such capital where there has been impairment. No case of impairment of capital is presented" (p. 167). In the Canfield case, as in cases thus far decided holding capital deficits must be made up, it was a question of construing the meaning of "earnings and profits accumulated since February 28, 1913," there being no express statutory provision as in the present law that, irrespective of deficits, current earnings should be taxable. In Willcuts v. Milton Dairy Co., 275 U. S. 215 (1927), it was held that for purposes of computing the statutory excess profits credit allowed as to "earned surplus and undivided profits" current profits less than an existing capital deficit must be used to reduce the latter: ". . . it is a prerequisite to the existence of 'undivided profits' as well as 'surplus' that the net assets of the corporation exceed capital" (p. 218).

[62] Section 201 of the Revenue Act of 1918 provided that every distribution "shall be deemed to have been" from earnings or profits. 40 Stat. 1059, §201(b). In the 1921 Act the word "is" was substituted for the words "shall be deemed to have been" with the purpose of creating a conclusive presumption. 42 Stat. 228, §201(b); Sen. Rept. No. 275, 67th Cong. 1st Sess., p. 10.

[63] Edwards v. Douglas, 269 U. S. 204 (1925) (if there are sufficient current earnings the distribution is made from current earnings); Leland v. Commissioner, 50 F. (2d) 523 (C. C. A. 1st, 1931), cert. den. 284 U. S. 656 (1931); Nolde v. U. S., 64 Ct. Cl. 204 (1927), cert. den. 276 U. S. 634 (1928); see Faris v. Helvering, 71 F. (2d) 610, 611 (C. C. A. 9th, 1934), cert. den. 293 U. S. 584 (1934); cf. Mason v. Routzahn, 275 U. S. 175 (1927).

following sources in the order named: (1) earnings or profits of the taxable year; (2) earnings or profits accumulated after February 28, 1913; (3) earnings or profits accumulated prior to March 1, 1913; and (4) sources other than earnings or profits.[64] If there are earnings and profits of the current year at least equal to distributions made, the dividend is taxable and no further consideration need be given the corporation's financial position.[65] Whether or not there are current earnings for the year is determined, as of the close of the year, without deduction of dividends paid during the year.[66]

119. Exemption of Dividends Out of Earnings and Profits Prior to March 1, 1913

Although distributions from earnings accumulated prior to March 1, 1913 are constitutionally taxable, Revenue Acts since 1916 have only taxed dividends out of earnings or profits accumulated after February 28, 1913.[67] However, before a distribution can be made from such prior earnings for tax purposes, it is necessary that the corporation establish that it has no earnings subsequent to February 28, 1913 which could be distributed.[68]

120. Dividends from Paid-In or Reduction Surplus

A dividend from capital is not income and therefore not taxable under the Sixteenth Amendment. A tax on such a distribution would have to meet the constitutional requirements of apportionment among the several states according to population.[69] The tax under Section 115, by its application only to distributions from "earnings or profits," is not sought to be imposed on capital distributions. It is held, therefore, that dividends from paid-in surplus [70] and reduction

---

[64] Reg. 103, §19.115–2.

[65] I. R. C., §115(a) (2); Reg. 103, §19.115–2.

[66] *Ibid.* Cf. *Dorothy Whitney Elmhurst*, 41 B. T. A. 348 (1940), decided under the Revenue Act of 1932, which did not contain the present provision in §115a(2). It was held that earnings and profits should be computed as of the date of distribution, and that the stockholder, having the burden to show there are no earnings at that date, fails if he merely shows a deficit at the end of the annual period, and not the existence of a deficit when the distribution was made.

[67] I. R. C., 115(b); Reg. 103, §19.115–2; see also §118.1, *supra.*

[68] *Ibid.; Tate v. Commissioner*, 97 F. (2d) 658 (C. C. A. 8th, 1938), cert. den. 305 U. S. 639 (1938); see also §118.3, *supra.*

[69] Art. 1, Sec. 2, Cl. 3; Art. 1, Sec. 9, Cl. 4.

[70] *Weaver v. Commissioner*, 58 F. (2d) 755 (C. C. A. 9th, 1932); *Henry Bradley Plant*, 30 B. T. A. 133 (1934), aff'd on other grounds 76 F. (2d) 8 C. C. A. 2d, 1935) (paid-in surplus contributed after Mar. 1, 1913); *Arthur C. Stifel*, 29 B. T. A. 1145 (1934) (same); see *Leland v. Commissioner*, 50 F. (2d) 523 (C. C. A. 1st, 1931), cert. den. 284 U. S. 656 (1931).

surplus,[71] whether created before or after March 1, 1913, are not taxable, being in their nature essentially capital distributions. It should be observed, however, that the premium paid on newly issued stock may sometimes be credited to a paid-in surplus account when the amount thereof is actually an equalization of prior earned surplus.[72] Whether dividends from this type of paid-in surplus should be taxable is at least doubtful. From the standpoint of the corporation and older stockholders, dividends from this paid-in surplus are like dividends from earned surplus to the extent the premium equalized original earned surplus. But from the standpoint of the new stockholder, the return is a capital return as much as any other paid-in surplus dividend would be.

Tax-free distributions from paid-in or reduction surplus can only be made after the corporation has exhausted available earnings accumulated both before and after March 1, 1913.[73]

121. Dividends from Unrealized Appreciation

Under many incorporation acts and by decision in some jurisdictions, cash dividends cannot be paid from unrealized appreciation, whereas in some states stock dividends based on such unrealized increment are permitted.[74] It would not necessarily be true, however, that a distribution constituting an illegal dividend under state law would not be a taxable distribution within the federal income tax.[75] But with respect to distributions out of increase in value of property accrued prior to March 1, 1913, a specific exemption is granted by Section 115(b).[76] Under the regulations, distributions from such appreciation are tax-free whether realized before or after March 1, 1913.[77]

[71] See *Elizabeth Berthold,* 12 B. T. A. 1306 (1928) (distribution from reduction surplus cannot be made for tax purposes until all post-Feb. 28, 1913 earnings are distributed); Montgomery, *Federal Income Tax Handbook,* 1938–39, 261–262.

[72] See §45.2, *supra.*

[73] Reg. 103, §19.115–2; *Leland v. Commissioner,* 50 F. (2d) 523 (C. C. A. 1st, 1931), *cert. den.* 284 U. S. 656 (1931); *Elizabeth Berthold,* 12 B. T. A. 1306 (1928); *Stanley M. Bolster,* 23 B. T. A. 347 (1931); G. C. M. 1232, VI–1 Cum. Bull. 9 (1927).

[74] See §36.5, *supra.*

[75] Cf. *Faris v. Helvering,* 71 F. (2d) 610, 611 (C. C. A. 9th, 1934), *cert. den.* 293 U. S. 584 (1934); *Burdick v. Commissioner,* 76 F. (2d) 672, 673 (C. C. A. 3d, 1935).

[76] See also Reg. 103, §19.115–2.

[77] Reg. 103, §19.115–2; *Hoffman v. U. S.,* 53 F. (2d) 282 (Ct. Cl. 1931). The Revenue Act of 1918 which exempted only "earnings or profits accumulated since February 28, 1913" [40 Stat. 1058, §201(b)] was construed not to include dividends paid from unrealized appreciation accrued prior to March 1, 1913 but realized thereafter by the corporation's sale of property. L. O. 1073, 5 Cum. Bull. 26 (1921). The Revenue Act of 1921 thereupon amended the provision to the present form to

No express provision is made in the statute with respect to dividends out of unrealized appreciation accrued after February 28, 1913. However, it is doubtful that unrealized appreciation constitutes "earnings or profits" within the general provisions of Section 115(a) taxing dividend payments.[78] Section 115(d) raises an important question where stock dividends are paid from unrealized appreciation accruing after February 28, 1913. Assuming that such a dividend is not a distribution of "earnings or profits" so as to constitute a dividend under Section 115(a), then Section 115(d) provides that the distribution shall, nevertheless, be taxable as a capital gain to the extent that the distribution exceeds the adjusted basis of the stock on which the dividend is declared. This raises the question whether a stock dividend based not on earnings or profits, but merely upon an unrealized write-up in corporate assets, can ever constitute income within the meaning of the Sixteenth Amendment.[79]

B. Stock Dividends

122. Test of Taxability as to Stock Dividends

It was thought that the decision of *Eisner v. Macomber*[80] in 1920 established a general rule that stock dividends without exception were not taxable upon declaration; that such distributions merely constituted a division of capital between the old and new shares; and that income was not earned until a subsequent sale of either.[81] For

---

exempt "any earnings or profits accumulated or increase in value of property accrued prior to March 1, 1913." 42 Stat. 228, §201(b).

[78] See Paul, *Ascertainment of "Earnings or Profits" for Purpose of Determining Taxability of Corporate Distributions,* 51 Harv. L. Rev. 40, 52–61 (1937).

[79] This problem was directly involved in *Chapman v. Anderson,* 11 F. Supp. 913 (S. D. N. Y. 1935). A corporation having an operating deficit which would have been eliminated by taking into account a writing up of its assets to reflect Mar. 1, 1913 value declared a stock dividend. It was held that the unrealized appreciation did not eliminate the deficit since it did not constitute earnings or profits, and that consequently the stock distribution, made while a deficit existed, was not taxable.

[80] 252 U. S. 189 (1920).

[81] Generally see Clark, *Eisner v. Macomber and Some Income Tax Problems,* 29 Yale L. J. 735 (1920); Hall, *Federal Taxation Note,* 20 Ill. L. Rev. 601 (1926); Hills, *Federal Taxation v. Corporation Law,* 12 Wis. L. Rev. 280, 286 (1937); James, *The Present Status of Stock Dividends under the Sixteenth Amendment,* 6 Univ. of Chic. L. Rev. 215 (1939); Magill, *Taxable Income* (1936), Ch. 2; Powell, *Stock Dividends, Direct Taxes, and the Sixteenth Amendment,* 20 Col. L. Rev. 536 (1920) [reprinted in 1 Select Essays on Constitutional Law (1938) 750]; Powell, *Income from Corporate Dividends,* 35 Harv. L. Rev. 363 (1922); Rottschaefer, *The Concept of Income in Federal Taxation,* 13 Minn. L. Rev. 637 (1929); Seligman, *Implications of the Stock Dividend Decision,* 21 Col. L. Rev. 313 (1921); Smith, *Federal Taxation of Stock Dividends When Received and*

fifteen years such continued to be the law. The Treasury Department promulgated rules to that effect [82] and Congress amended the statute to provide that "A stock dividend shall not be subject to tax. . . ." [83] The statute remained in this form until the decision in *Koshland v. Helvering* in 1936 made it clear that some types of stock dividends are constitutionally taxable.[84] In the Revenue Act of 1936, the provision with respect to stock dividends was amended to the form as it presently appears in Section 115(f) : "A distribution . . . in . . . stock or in rights to acquire . . . stock shall not be treated as a dividend to the extent that it does not constitute income to the shareholder within the meaning of the Sixteenth Amendment to the Constitution." [85]

In the case of a stock dividend, the corporation makes no distribution of corporate assets. It retains the same amount of assets after the dividend is paid that it had before. The essential change from the corporate standpoint is capitalization of surplus upon the books of the corporation. This may be illustrated in the declaration of a share-for-share common stock dividend by a corporation having outstanding 1,000 common shares of the par value of $100 and surplus of $100,000.

BEFORE DECLARATION

ASSETS		LIABILITIES	
Cash, etc.	$200,000	Capital (1,000 shares) ..	$100,000
		Surplus	100,000
	$200,000		$200,000

Their Cost Basis When Sold, 15 Tax Mag. 593 (1937) ; Traylor, *A Critique of Koshland v. Helvering,* 16 Tax Mag. 453 (1938) ; Warren, *Taxability of Stock Dividends as Income,* 33 Harv. L. Rev. 885 (1920) ; Note, 38 Col. L. Rev. 363 (1938) ; Note, 45 Yale L. J. 1122 (1936) ; Annotation, "Income tax in relation to stock dividends," 105 A. L. R. 761.

[82] T. D. 3052, 3 Cum. Bull. 38 (1920) ; T. D. 3059, 3 Cum. Bull. 38 (1920) ; O. D. 732, 3 Cum. Bull. 39 (1920) ; O. D. 801, 4 Cum. Bull. 24 (1921) (providing that "A stock dividend paid in true preferred stock is exempt from tax the same as though the dividend were paid in common stock").

[83] Revenue Act of 1921, 42 Stat. 228, §201(d).

[84] 298 U. S. 441 (1936).

[85] 49 Stat. 1688. In contrast to the statute, taxability is asserted affirmatively in the regulations: "A distribution made by a corporation to its shareholders in its stock or in rights to acquire its stock shall be treated as a dividend to the full extent that it constitutes income to shareholders within the meaning of the Sixteenth Amendment to the Constitution." Reg. 103, §19.115-7. The original House Ways and Means Committee Draft of the Bill had also provided affirmatively that a stock distribution should be treated as taxable to the extent that such distribution constituted income within the meaning of the Sixteenth Amendment. H. R. 12395, p. 110; H. Rept. 2475, 74th Cong. 2d Sess., p. 10.

AFTER DECLARATION

ASSETS		LIABILITIES	
Cash, etc.	$200,000	Capital (2,000 shares)	$200,000

A stockholder having shares prior to the dividend worth $200 each, now has twice as many shares worth $100 each (or perhaps slightly more due to wider marketability of shares having a lower sale price). The constitutional question raised for the first time in *Eisner v. Macomber* [86] was whether a tax on such a distribution, where the dividend to the stockholder merely divided the interest he already had, was a tax on income or a direct tax on capital and invalid unless apportioned. Under the requirement that income must be realized to be taxable,[87] it was necessary to find the receipt by the stockholder of property he did not already possess. In the case supposed, the stockholder receives an extra certificate of stock for each share held, which he may sell while retaining his old certificate, reducing thereby, however, his proportionate interest in corporate assets. But this additional certificate of stock was held insufficient as a constitutional basis of taxation. The *rationale* of *Eisner v. Macomber* is important, as it constitutes the foundation for all stock dividend tax cases. Although the opinion is long, the reasons relied upon are perhaps best indicated by that part, quoted from the earlier case of *Towne v. Eisner*,[88] where a stock dividend was held non-taxable on a question of construction under the 1913 Act: " . . . we cannot doubt that the dividend was capital. . . . A stock dividend really takes nothing from the property of the corporation, and adds nothing to the interests of the shareholders. Its property is not diminished, and their interests are not increased. . . . The proportionate interest of each shareholder remains the same. The only change is in the evidence which represents that interest, the new shares and the original shares together representing the same proportional interest that the original shares represented before the issue of the new ones." Three possible tests of taxability are suggested: (1) loss by the corporation through the dividend of physical assets; (2) addition to the interest of the shareholder; or (3) change in the proportionate interest of the shareholder in the assets of the corporation.

We have since learned that the first test is unreliable, because in spite of the fact that no stock dividend ever distributes physical assets of the corporation, nevertheless some stock distributions are

[86] 252 U. S. 189 (1920).
[87] See §117, n. 7, *supra*.
[88] 245 U. S. 418 (1918) (comment, 31 Harv. L. Rev. 787).

held taxable. Thus, a common stock dividend on preferred [89] or a preferred stock dividend on common,[90] when both classes are at the time outstanding, have both been treated by the Supreme Court as taxable. In any event, loss of assets by the corporation seems irrelevant as a test; since the stockholder is the taxpayer, the criteria of taxability should relate to whether or not he has received income.

The adequacy of the second test—that there be some addition to the interest of the shareholder—is more difficult of appraisal. If in the example supposed a cash dividend of $100,000 had been paid to stockholders, there would be no dispute as to taxability. Each stockholder would receive $100 cash for each share of stock held. But if the dividend is in stock, he receives a share of stock also worth $100 which ordinarily can be forthwith converted into the cash equivalent. In both cases his economic interest is $200. In neither case does he receive any addition to his total economic interest. Yet the stock dividend under *Eisner v. Macomber* is treated differently and is not taxable. In both cases the value of the original share of stock is reduced by the respective dividends to $100. The only difference is that in the case of the stock dividend, the stockholder, in order to retain his right to *future* proportionate earnings of the corporation, must retain the dividend share.[91] Whereas in the case of the cash dividend, the $100 may be spent, but the right to proportionate participation in future earnings remains intact.

The crucial test which survives from *Eisner v. Macomber* seems, therefore, to have nothing to do with whether the corporation distributes assets or the stockholder receives something he did not have before. It is rather a question whether the stockholder has received a distribution which varies his proportionate interest in the assets of the corporation. Whether such variance in proportionate interest remains the test since *Koshland v. Helvering* [92] is the question. In that case it was held a common dividend declared on preferred stock constituted income and not a division of capital, so that upon a subsequent redemption of the preferred stock, its base was not subject to reduction by allocation of the original cost between the old preferred and the new common stock. The present confusion as to taxability of stock dividends arises from language used by the court suggesting the possibility of two tests: (1) change in proportionate interest as

[89] *Koshland v. Helvering,* 298 U. S. 441 (1936).
[90] *Helvering v. Gowran,* 302 U. S. 238 (1937).
[91] See *Eisner v. Macomber,* 252 U. S. 189, 212 (1920).
[92] 298 U. S. 441 (1936).

indicated by *Eisner v. Macomber*, or (2) creation of "different rights or interests" than those possessed by the old stock.[93] Whether we now have these two tests or only the proportionate interest test is important. If all that is required is a stock interest different from the old stock, then any change in provisions of the new stock, or any change of class, makes it income, and the question of taxability of stock dividends is greatly simplified. Only a dividend falling within the precise facts of *Eisner v. Macomber* would be immune from the tax. On the other hand, if the *Koshland* case by referring to creation of different interests was merely restating the rule that a change in the ratable interest of stockholders in assets is necessary, questions of considerable nicety remain. The answer to this problem is vital, since Congress in the Revenue Act of 1936 limited taxation of stock dividends solely by the touchstone of constitutional power, although it is apparent from the discussion in the House that the Ways and Means Committee understood the test of taxability to be change in proportionate interest.[94] Moreover, the definition of a taxable dividend set forth in the *Koshland* case has been incorporated almost

[93] That change in proportionate interest might constitute a basis for taxing stock dividends should not have come entirely as a surprise. It had been foreshadowed in language of the reorganization cases such as *Marr v. U. S.*, 268 U. S. 536 (1925). Referring to the reorganization cases decided shortly after *Eisner v. Macomber* (§117, n. 7, *supra*), the court stated in the *Koshland* case: "Soon after the passage of that Act [exempting stock dividends], this court pointed out the distinction between a stock dividend which worked no change in the corporate entity, the same interest in the same corporation being represented after the distribution by more shares of precisely the same character, and such a dividend where there had either been changes of corporate identity or a change in the nature of the shares issued as dividends whereby the proportional interest of the stockholder after the distribution was essentially different from his former interest." The reference to change in corporate identity concerns issuance of shares of a new corporation of the type involved in the reorganization cases. This portion of the opinion adheres, therefore, to the change in proportional interest test. The court went on, however, to say: "Under our decisions the payment of a dividend of new common shares, conferring no different rights or interests than did the old,—the new certificates, plus the old, representing the same proportionate interest in the assets of the corporation as did the old—does not constitute the receipt of income by the stockholder. On the other hand, where a stock dividend gives the stockholder an interest different from that which his former stockholdings represented he receives income." Here, apparently is a second and alternative test—that of interest different from that which his former stockholdings represented.

[94] "As we see it, a stock dividend that is not taxable is one in which the relative interest of each shareholder of a corporation is unchanged in his stock ownership." "The proposed plan does not change the law and does not in the slightest degree strike at the decision of the Supreme Court in the case of *Eisner v. Macomber* in respect of a stock dividend where there is no change in the proportion of ownership by the shareholder." 80 Cong. Rec. 6215, 6309.

verbatim in the regulations.[95] The recent decisions of the Board of Tax Appeals, in holding stock dividends taxable, have placed increasing emphasis on the fact of change in interest rather than change in proportionate ownership. Thus, in *Frank J. Kelly Trust,* the Board held a preferred dividend on common stock when the latter was the only class outstanding to be taxable because (1) the stock-

[95] Reg. 103, §19.115-7. Even though a stock dividend is constitutionally immune from taxation, income may be realized by its resale. In such case, or in the event of a resale of the stock upon which the dividend is declared, questions as to base in determining gain on the stock sold are presented. In *Koshland v. Helvering,* 298 U. S. 441 (1936), n. 92, *supra,* the court held that a common dividend on preferred was income, and that since it was income, regulations requiring an apportionment of the base of the original preferred between the dividend stock and the old stock were unauthorized by the statute then in force, which prescribed cost as the general basis for determination of gain on sales. In *Helvering v. Gowran,* 302 U. S. 238 (1937), a dividend of preferred stock on common was likewise held to be income, but since Congress had granted a statutory exemption to all stock dividends, the base on a redemption of the preferred stock was held to be zero, it having cost the stockholder nothing in the tax sense. Thereupon Congress in the Revenue Act of 1939 amended the statute to authorize the Commissioner to require, with certain exceptions, an allocation of base between old stock and dividend stock (1) on *all* stock dividends declared prior to Jan. 1, 1936 (the effective date of the amendment taxing all future dividends constitutionally taxable) and (2) on dividends subsequent to Dec. 31, 1935 which are not constitutionally taxable. I. R. C., §113(a)(19), as amended Revenue Act of 1939, §214. The purpose of the amendment was to validate regulations of the type declared to be unauthorized by statute in the *Koshland* case. Report of Committee on Ways and Means, H. Rept. No. 855, 76th Cong. 1st Sess., pp. 5-6. In so far as dividends prior to 1936 were non-taxable under the Sixteenth Amendment they are, under *Eisner v. Macomber,* returns of capital, and an allocation of original base between old and new stock is properly required. It is at least arguable that as to dividends both before and after Jan. 1, 1936 which are not constitutionally taxable, the statute and regulations thereunder requiring reduction of the cost base of the original stock are unconstitutional, because to the extent of the reduction they tax capital and not income on a resale of that stock. Assume that a shareholder owning a share of preferred stock for which he has paid $100 receives a taxable dividend in common stock in 1934, and that pursuant to the regulations he is now required to allocate $25 of his base to the common stock. If he sells his preferred stock in 1940 for $100, the amount he paid for it, is he taxable for income of $25, the difference between the sale price and the statutory $75 base? Or since the common dividend was income, even though it was not taxed by the Revenue Act of 1934, is his base still $100 on the preferred stock and the attempted levy one on capital and invalid? In response to the stockholder's contention in the *Koshland* case that even though exempt the stock dividends there involved "were none the less income and cannot be treated as returns of capital in computing gain," the court stated, "We hold that the dividends were income and may not be treated as capital." (298 U. S. 441, 443.) It is true that the court thereafter stated that the statute did not authorize the regulations in question requiring allocation, and it is presumably this language upon which the Treasury relied in obtaining the 1939 amendment. But the constitutionality of the new provisions will certainly be contested on authority of the *Koshland* case. Generally on the 1939 amendments as to allocation see Alvord and Biegel, *Basis Provisions for Stock Dividends under the 1939 Revenue Act,* 49 Yale L. J. 841 (1940); Eichholz, *The Revenue Act of 1939 and the Basis of Stock Dividends and Rights,* 40 Col. L. Rev. 404 (1940).

holder received a greater right to compel dividends on the new stock
and (2) his interest was now transferable in parts.[96] The dividend
was held taxable in spite of the fact that there was no change in the
proportionate interest in corporate assets. Stockholders entitled to
the entire equity of the corporation in virtue of their common stock
were now entitled to that same equity through ownership of two
classes of stock rather than one.

Whether the proportionate interest test will survive comes down
to the soundness of *Eisner v. Macomber*. At present that decision is
accepted as law in the regulations, so that a common dividend on
common stock when that is the only class outstanding is not taxable,[97]
but the question remains whether such a dividend should be free
from taxation while other types of stock dividends are taxed. Why
a stockholder should be protected from taxation on dividends which
do not vary his proportionate interest, is not entirely clear. There
seems implicit a feeling that to tax common stock dividends might
compel stockholders involuntarily to sell the dividend shares to pay
the tax, thus losing their equitable *pro rata* interests in corporate
assets, present and future.[98] But there is an adequate basis for the tax.
The stockholder does receive something he did not have before in the
additional stock which is issued as a dividend. He receives a new
share which could be treated as income since it is issued upon a
capitalization of income. The fact that there is no increase in his
total net worth is immaterial.[99] If a shareholder owns a share of

[96] 38 B. T. A. 1014 (1938), remanded for further proceedings on stipulation of
parties 106 F. (2d) 1002 (C. C. A. 8th, 1939). In *Albert E. Smith*, 39 B. T. A. 80
(1939), remanded on other grounds 107 F. (2d) 1020 (C. C. A. 6th, 1939), a
dividend of junior preferred stock on common stock, common and preferred being
at the time outstanding, was held taxable: "In our opinion there is no question but
that the stock received possessed substantially different attributes from the common"
(p. 85); see *Commissioner v. Tillotson Mfg. Co.*, 76 F. (2d) 189, 190–191 (C. C. A.
6th, 1935) (mentioning change in voting rights as a factor); *John M. Keister*,
42 B. T. A. 488 (1940); Note, 51 Harv. L. Rev. 702, 705 (1938). In some of the
reorganization cases there is language indicating a change in "rights and powers"
conferred by the new stock may be sufficient to sustain a tax. See *Marr v. U. S.*, 268
U. S. 536, 541 (1925).

[97] Reg. 103, §19.115–7, ex. 2.

[98] *Eisner v. Macomber*, 252 U. S. 189, 212 (1920).

[99] In *U. S. v. Phellis*, 257 U. S. 156 (1921), shares received upon a reorganization were held taxable. The court said: "That a comparison of the market value of
claimant's shares in the New Jersey corporation immediately before, with the
aggregate market value of those shares plus the dividend shares immediately after
the dividend showed no change in the aggregate—a fact relied upon by the Court
of Claims as demonstrating that claimant neither gained nor lost pecuniarily in the
transaction—seems to us a circumstance of no particular importance in the present
inquiry. Assuming the market values were a precise reflex of intrinsic values, they
would show merely that claimant acquired no increase in aggregate wealth through

stock worth $200, of which $100 represents capital and the other $100 surplus, a cash distribution of $100 will leave him no richer than he was before. His stock will now be worth $100 and he will have $100 in cash. Yet in spite of the absence of increase in the stockholder's net worth, he is taxable upon the $100 received as a dividend.

Nor can it be important that the stockholder may have to sell one of his shares of stock in order to be able to pay the tax. If the corporation were to pay a dividend in property, the same necessity of selling the property, and thereby reducing the stockholder's ownership of assets might arise, and yet the stockholder does not escape taxation for this reason. But it is argued that the sale of stock of a corporation is different, because thereupon the stockholder loses not merely a present property interest but also his *pro tanto* equity in corporate assets of the future. Granting this fact to be true, it does not demonstrate that what he receives is not income, it merely shows a sale of the dividend stock will reduce his claim to share in future corporate income. Particularly is the argument of loss of proportionate interest in corporate assets weakened when it is considered that other types of stock dividends are taxable, even though a sale of the dividend by one stockholder in order to pay the tax will reduce his future equity in the distribution of corporate assets as against those stockholders who do not sell their stock. Take the situation in the *Koshland* case of a common dividend on preferred stock. Let us suppose that shareholders A and B each own 1,000 shares of preferred stock entitled to 7 per cent cumulative dividends and no more. The corporation now pays a dividend of one share of common on each share of preferred. Shareholder A, having insufficient funds to pay the tax on his common dividend, sells 250 shares of the common stock and pays the tax, while shareholder B retains the 1,000 shares of common stock he received. In subsequent years shareholders A and B will both be entitled to their preferred dividends of 7 per cent, but as to the excess surplus, A will now be entitled to participate only to the extent of 750 shares while B participates to the extent of 1,000 shares. It is not very convincing to tell A that it makes no difference that he has to sell part of his common dividend in order to pay the tax, thereby losing his proportionate interest in

the mere effect of the reorganization and consequent dividend, not that the dividend did not constitute income . . . a comparison of aggregate values immediately before with those immediately after the dividend is not a proper test for determining whether individual income, taxable against the stockholder, has been received by means of the dividend" (170–171).

future assets, but that a shareholder receiving a common dividend on common stock, no other stock outstanding, is not taxable because to tax him might compel him to sell his dividend stock, thereby losing his proportionate interest in future assets.

On the merits, there seems no good reason why one stock dividend should be any less immune from tax than another. Should the Treasury in the future change its position and assert that a common dividend on common is constitutionally taxable, there is good reason to argue for an overruling of *Eisner v. Macomber,* with the result that all stock dividends would be taxable. Such a rule would greatly simplify the tax structure, eliminating the troublesome niceties of what constitutes a sufficient change in interest to create a taxable dividend plus the hierarchy of intricacies attendant to determination of tax base on resale of either the original or the dividend stock. However, taxation of all stock dividends, in view of the position taken by the Treasury, is still only a desideratum, and we are left with the problem of applying the existing formulae to varying types of stock dividends.

123. Stock Dividends from February 28, 1913 to January 1, 1936

The problem of taxability of stock dividends paid prior to January 1, 1936 involves consideration of the operative statute at the time the dividend was paid. The question may arise in two ways: first, as to dividends on which the statute of limitations has not run either as to original assessment or refund; second, the taxability of the dividend may become material in determining the base on a resale before or after January 1, 1936.

The time prior to January 1, 1936 is divided into three periods. The period from February 28, 1913 to January 1, 1916 is covered by the Revenue Act of 1913. It contained no provision specifically taxing stock dividends. The 1913 Act only imposed a tax on "dividends," [100] which in *Towne v. Eisner* was held, as a matter of statutory construction, not to cover stock dividends. [101]

For the period from January 1, 1916 to January 1, 1921, the Revenue Acts of 1916 [102] and 1918, [103] then in force, imposed a tax specifically on stock dividends. In the light of *Koshland v. Helvering,* invalidation of the 1916 tax on a common dividend by *Eisner v. Macomber* must not be taken to hold the 1916 Act, and by parity of reasoning, the 1918 Act, invalid as to all stock dividends. Stock

[100] 38 Stat. 167, §IIB.
[101] 245 U. S. 418 (1918).
[102] 39 Stat. 757, §2(a).
[103] 40 Stat. 1059, §201(a).

dividends declared in the period from 1915 to 1921, barring considerations of the statute of limitations, are therefore taxable to the same extent as stock dividends since January 1, 1936.

From 1921 to 1936 the Revenue Acts provided that, "A stock dividend shall not be subject to tax." [104] This type provision exempted all stock dividends from taxation, and not merely dividends immune constitutionally from the tax.[105] Consequently, there is no liability for an income tax on any stock dividends paid between 1921 and 1936.

124. Dividends After January 1, 1936

Effective January 1, 1936, Revenue Acts have provided that distributions in stock or stock rights shall not be treated as a taxable dividend to the extent that they do not constitute income to the shareholder within the meaning of the Sixteenth Amendment,[106] and the regulations provide that to the extent such distributions do constitute income within the meaning of the amendment, they shall be taxable.[107] It is important here to note that even though a stock dividend is of a type recognized to be constitutionally taxable, the distribution is not taxable unless the dividend is from "earnings or profits" as defined in the subdivisions of Section 115(a) or is a taxable distribution under Section 115(d).

124.1. Common Stock Dividend on Common Stock

It was the intention of the Ways and Means Committee in amending the Revenue Act of 1936, to exempt from taxation a common stock dividend on common stock when that is the only class of stock outstanding, as in *Eisner v. Macomber*.[108] This exemption continues to be recognized in the regulations.[109] Variations of the *Eisner v.*

---

[104] 42 Stat. 228, §201(d) (1921); repealed 49 Stat. 1688, §115(f) (1936).

[105] *Helvering v. Gowran*, 302 U. S. 238 (1937); *Helvering v. Pfeiffer*, 302 U. S. 247 (1937). There was ground for contending that the 1921 amendment exempting stock dividends from taxation [42 Stat. 228, §201(d)] was only intended to cover the situation in *Eisner v. Macomber*, and not to make all stock dividends immune. The amendment was added so as to modify "the definition of dividends in existing law by exempting stock dividends from the income tax, as required by the decision of the Supreme Court in *Eisner v. Macomber* (252 U. S. 189)." H. Rept. No. 350, 67th Cong. 1st Sess., p. 8; S. Rept. No. 275, 67th Cong. 1st Sess., p. 9; Conf. Report, H. Rept. 486, 67th Cong. 1st Sess., p. 16.

[106] 49 Stat. 1688, §115(f)(1); I. R. C., §115(f)(1).

[107] Reg. 103, §19.115–7.

[108] See §122, n. 94, *supra*.

[109] Reg. 103, §19.115–7, ex. 2. The view has been expressed that *Eisner v. Macomber* is now limited to situations in which the facts are similar. James, *The Present Status of Stock Dividends under the Sixteenth Amendment*, 6 Univ.

Macomber facts may be supposed, but where the dividend declared is really no different in substance. Thus, new no-par value common shares might be issued on par value old common shares. If the new shares are entitled to the same dividends and to share equally with the old common on liquidation, there is no reason why the dividend should not be tax free. Of course, if the change in rights and interest doctrine rather than the change in proportionate ownership rule is broadly accepted, the dividend would be taxable. The same would apply as to a non-voting common dividend on voting common or a voting common dividend on non-voting common.

Pursuing the theory of *Eisner v. Macomber,* a stock split-up of common shares would not constitute a taxable dividend.[110] In *Michaels v. McLaughlin,* stock of the par value of $100 had only been paid up to the extent of $80. It was held that a transfer of $20 per share from surplus to capital and the issuance of fully paid up shares was the equivalent of an *Eisner v. Macomber* stock dividend.[111]

If both common and preferred are outstanding at the time a common dividend is declared on common, a new factor bearing on change in proportionate interest must be considered. If the preferred is limited both as to dividends and on liquidation, then the old common is entitled to the balance, and to split further that part of the melon among common does not vary their existing *pro rata* interest in assets.[112] However, if the preferred is participating as to dividends, or is entitled to share ratably with common on liquidation, paying a

---

of Chic. L. Rev. 215, 222–223 (1939). In *John M. Keister,* 42 B. T. A. 488 (1940), a dividend of non-voting common stock on voting common was held taxable. At the time of the dividend both voting common and non-voting common were outstanding.

[110] Apparently, even the dissenting justices in *Eisner v. Macomber* would treat such a distribution as non-taxable. See *Towne v. Eisner,* 245 U. S. 418, 426–427 (1918) (Justice Holmes); *Marr v. U. S.,* 268 U. S. 536, 540–541 (1925) (Justice Brandeis). It is somewhat difficult to see how it makes any difference from the tax standpoint whether a corporation with $100 par value shares and $100 per share of surplus declares a stock dividend of one share, or reduces the par value of its old shares to $50 issuing two for one—except that in the latter case, the $100 surplus is still available for cash distribution, whereas in the case of a stock dividend it would be capitalized. Thus it may be argued that since surplus remains intact no distribution of profit even in form can be said to have taken place.

[111] 20 F. (2d) 959 (S. D. Cal. 1927); *Accord: J. F. Carlston,* 22 B. T. A. 217 (1931).

[112] In *Albert E. Smith,* 39 B. T. A. 80 (1939), remanded on other grounds 107 F. (2d) 1020 (C. C. A. 6th, 1939), a junior preferred dividend on common stock, common and preferred being outstanding at the time, was held taxable, principally under the new rights and interests test. The result is open to criticism under the proportionate ownership rule. Since the new preferred was a junior issue, it amounts only to a new division of what the common was already entitled to.

dividend to the common shareholders does materially increase the proportionate interest of the latter in corporate assets,[113] and under the proportionate ownership test would be taxable. The tax would probably also apply under the new rights and interests rule.

124.2. Preferred Stock Dividend on Common Stock

Where both common and preferred stock are outstanding at the time a preferred dividend is declared on the common, the dividend is taxable under the decision in *Helvering v. Gowran*.[114] This result is sound whether the change in proportionate ownership or change in rights and interests rule is applied. There is, to be sure, at least one situation where it might be argued that a preferred dividend on common does not change the proportionate interest. If the corporation is earning much more than sufficient to pay dividends on both the old and new preferred, it may be said the common stock is not getting any dividend rights it does not already have. Under the new arrangement it merely takes the preferred percentage as a preferred dividend and the balance as a common dividend, whereas before the dividend it took the entire balance after paying old preferred as a common dividend. If the corporation should not do so well, however, the common stockholder has acquired a new right in the preferred stock because now whatever earnings there are will have to be divided between all preferred stockholders, new and old, *pro rata*. Likewise, if assets are below the amount required to pay in full all preferred stock on liquidation, the common stockholder will have gained an advantage by a preferred dividend. These possible additional advantages should be sufficient to satisfy the change in proportionate interest requirement.

A more difficult case is that in which a preferred dividend is declared when there is only common stock outstanding. There is certainly no shift in the proportional interest by such a distribution. What the stockholders were previously entitled to as common stockholders, they are now entitled to as preferred and common stock-

---

[113] For equitable limitations upon the declaration of dividends of this character, see §62, *supra*.

[114] 302 U. S. 238 (1937). For comments on the case, see Traynor, *Tax Decisions of the Supreme Court, 1937 Term*, 33 Ill. L. Rev. 371, 382 (1938) and notes, 51 Harv. L. Rev. 702 (1938); 38 Col. L. Rev. 363 (1938); 5 Univ. of Chic. L. Rev. 512 (1938). For cases in accord prior to the *Gowran* decision see *James H. Torrens*, 31 B. T. A. 787 (1934), *dism.* without written opinion P. H. Fed. Tax Citator 1464 (C. C. A. 2d, 1936); *Joseph Paper*, 29 B. T. A. 523 (1933); see also Note, 50 Harv. L. Rev. 332, 335 (1936). Cf. *Albert E. Smith*, 39 B. T. A. 80 (1939), remanded on other grounds 107 F. (2d) 1020 (C. C. A. 6th, 1939) §124.1, n. 112, *supra*.

holders. Reversing itself on the result reached in earlier cases,[115] and following the change in rights and interest doctrine as distinguished from the change in proportionate ownership rule, the Board in *Frank J. Kelly Trust* has held a preferred dividend on a single class of outstanding common stock to be taxable.[116]

124.3. Common Stock Dividend on Preferred Stock

With both classes of stock outstanding, a common dividend on preferred, where the preferred is limited as to dividends and on dissolution, is taxable.[117] By such a dividend the old preferred shareholder acquires a right to participate in dividends on the new common beyond the preference rate of his preferred and the privilege of sharing the liquidation preference of the preferred in assets on liquidation, both new claims against the corporate assets which he did not previously possess. But a very different situation may arise in a case such as *Branch & Company v. Riverside & Dan River Cotton Mills,* where the preferred only had a preference as to dividends but not on liquidation.[118] No tax question was involved, but the court indicated that preferred stockholders were entitled to participate in a proposed common dividend in order that they might, since preferred shared with common on liquidation, preserve their *pro rata* interest in capital. The preservation of ratable interest in capital is the theory upon which the dividend was held non-taxable in *Eisner v. Macomber.* The common dividend on preferred in this last type of situation differs, however, from the *Eisner v. Macomber* dividend. Whereas the preferred stockholder gets nothing but a *pro rata* protection as to capital on liquidation through the common dividend, he acquires also

---

[115] *August Horrmann,* 34 B. T. A. 1178 (1936) (distinguishing the *Koshland* case on the ground that both preferred and common were outstanding when a common dividend on preferred was declared) ; *Pearl B. Brown,* 26 B. T. A. 901 (1932), aff'd without expressing opinion on the point 69 F. (2d) 602 (C. C. A. 7th, 1934), cert. den. 293 U. S. 570 (1934) (before *Koshland* case) ; *Frances Elliott Clark,* 28 B. T. A. 1125 (1933), app. dism. Clark v. Commissioner, 77 F. (2d) 89 (C. C. A. 3d, 1935) (same) ; *Alfred A. Laun,* 26 B. T. A. 764 (1932) (same) ; *Gertrude B. May,* 26 B. T. A. 1413 (1932) (same).

[116] 38 B. T. A. 1014 (1938), remanded by stipulation on other grounds 106 F. (2d) 1002 (C. C. A. 8th, 1939). In *John M. Keister,* 42 B. T. A. 488 (1940), a dividend in non-voting preferred on both voting and non-voting common was held taxable. For the contrary view see Traynor, *A Critique of Koshland v. Helvering,* 16 Tax Mag. 453, 454 (1938) ; Note, 38 Col. L. Rev. 363, 366–367 (1938) ; but see James, *The Present Status of Stock Dividends under the Sixteenth Amendment,* 6 Univ. of Chic. L. Rev. 215, 225–226 (1939).

[117] *Koshland v. Helvering,* 298 U. S. 441 (1935) (comment, 25 Calif. L. Rev. 499; 21 Minn. L. Rev. 225; 14 N. Y. U. L. Rev. 113) ; see also Pearce, *Income Tax Fundamentals* (1937) 429.

[118] 139 Va. 291, 123 S. E. 542 (1924), §62, n. 18, *supra.*

a right to participate in common dividends which he did not possess before, unless the preferred happened to be participating. This new dividend right should be a sufficient change in proportionate interest to render the distribution taxable.

124.4. Preferred Stock Dividend on Preferred Stock

When both common and preferred stock are outstanding, a preferred dividend on preferred is quite clearly taxable.[119] The new preferred will give the old preferred shareholders a further priority claim in either dividends or assets on liquidation, or both—rights acquired at the expense of the ratable interests of existing common stockholders.

124.5. Dividends in Treasury Stock

The taxability of dividends paid in treasury stock should depend upon whether a new issue of stock of that character paid to that class of stockholders would constitute a taxable distribution under considerations already considered. The origin of the dividend stock is immaterial from the standpoint of the stockholder. Thus, a common stock dividend in treasury shares on common stock has been held tax-free.[120]

124.6. Stock Dividends under State Income Tax Statutes

Many states in adopting their income tax statutes followed the federal Revenue Acts prior to the *Koshland* case, with the result that they exempt stock dividends of the declaring corporation.[121] North Dakota provides that taxable dividends shall include stock divi-

[119] *Joseph Paper*, 29 B. T. A. 523 (1933); Magill, *Taxable Income* (1936) 48; Traynor, *Tax Decisions of the Supreme Court, 1937 Term,* 33 Ill. L. Rev. 371, 383 (1938).

[120] *James Kay*, 28 B. T. A. 331 (1933), *app. dism.* by consent on motion of *petitioner* 70 F. (2d) 1017 (C. C. A. 4th, 1934) (decided prior to *Koshland* case); I. T. 2449, VIII–1 Cum. Bull. 101 (1929) (also prior to *Koshland* case).

[121] Ariz. Laws 1933, c. 39, §26(e); Ark. Tax Reg., Art. 336 [but Ark. Stat. (1937), §14031, includes "dividends" in gross income with a provision that dividends are not taxable if the income used to pay the dividend was assessable to the corporation]; Del. Rev. Code (1935), c. 6, §112(a)(6); Idaho Code Ann. (1932), §61–2404(e); Mass. Gen. Laws, c. 62, §1(b) (also Reg. 2518); Miss. Tax. Reg., Art. 90 [statutory provision similar to that of Arkansas, Miss. Code (1938 Supp.), §1610(a)]; N. Y. Tax Law, §359(2)(m), added by N. Y. Laws 1926, c. 543, effective retroactively as of Jan. 1, 1919 [under §350(8) a stock dividend is defined as new stock issued to shareholders in proportion to their previous holdings; see also Reg., Art. 64]; Ohio Code Ann. (Baldwin), §5389, as amended 1939 (an intangible property tax measured by income, excludes from income stock dividends); Wis. Stat. (1937), §71.02(b)(5).

dends.[122] Following the decision in the *Koshland* case, California [123] and Minnesota [124] amended their statutes to conform to the federal law. Other states now broadly exempting stock dividends may follow this lead, or even reverse their policy entirely, taxing all stock dividends.

125. Taxability of Stock Rights

If a stock dividend would not be taxable, a distribution of rights [125] entitling the stockholder upon further payment of capital to acquire similar stock is not taxable. For example, if a corporation having a surplus of $100 a common share, instead of declaring outright a stock dividend share-for-share, issues rights to subscribe to one new share at $50, the added interest in corporate assets which the shareholder acquires beyond his outlay of $50 is the equivalent of a nontaxable stock dividend. The value of the dividend diminishes to the extent that required contribution to capital is increased. But pursuing the doctrine of *Eisner v. Macomber,* the receipt of common stock rights, where common stock is the only stock outstanding, will not be taxable any more than would a full stock dividend.[126] Conversely, if the right is to subscribe to stock which, if issued as a straight dividend, would be taxable, the right if exercised should also be income to the extent of its fair market value. In *Palmer v. Commissioner,* Justice Stone stated that the mere issuance of a right is not a taxable dividend.[127] The right must be sold or exercised. Nor is the exercise taxable if at the time the plan is proposed the price at which the stockholder is permitted to buy the stock is not less than its

[122] N. D. Comp. L. Ann. (1925 Supp.), §2346a-1 (12).

[123] Cal. Stat. 1937, c. 668, p. 1837 (enacting substantially the provision in the Federal Revenue Act of 1936, §115(f), that a stock dividend shall not be taxable to the extent that it does not constitute income within the meaning of the Sixteenth Amendment of the federal Constitution).

[124] Mason Minn. Stat. (1938 Supp.), §2394-21c (stock dividends are exempt, but a distribution is only a stock dividend if made in stock of the same kind or class as that with respect to which it is distributed).

[125] On the taxation of stock rights generally see notes, 37 Col. L. Rev. 664 (1937); 51 Harv. L. Rev. 515 (1938); 47 Yale L. J. 139 (1937).

[126] See *Miles v. Safe Deposit & Trust Company,* 259 U. S. 247, 251-252 (1922); *U. S. v. Mellon,* 281 Fed. 645 (C. C. A. 3d, 1922). In *T. I. Hare Powel,* 27 B. T. A. 55 (1932), it was held that an issuance of rights to buy bonds convertible into stock of the corporation was not taxable, even though the stockholder exercised the rights and ultimately exchanged the bonds for stock. After nonacquiescence, the holding was finally approved in G. C. M. 13275, XIII-2 Cum. Bull. 121 (1934). The same result would probably not be reached since the *Koshland* and *Gowran* cases. The bond gives added interests in corporate assets which a plain stock right would not, and should be held taxable under those cases.

[127] See 302 U. S. 63, 71 (1937); *Board v. Commissioner,* 51 F. (2d) 73 (C. C. A. 6th, 1931), *cert. den.* 284 U. S. 658 (1931).

fair market value. But if there is a difference, the difference represents taxable income.[128] If, as in the *Koshland* case, a dividend of common stock on preferred stock is taxable, a distribution to preferred stockholders of a right to purchase a share of common stock at a price below its value must, when exercised, be a dividend to the extent of the difference between the value of the common stock and the amount payable on exercise of the right. Otherwise, a simple device for rendering all stock distributions non-taxable would be at hand. By requiring a part payment from the stockholder on exercise of the right, a tax on the balance of the distribution could be avoided.

126. Option Dividends in Stock, Cash or Property

Section 115(f)(2) provides that if any stockholders have an election to have the dividend paid in stock which would not be a taxable distribution under the Sixteenth Amendment, or in money or property or stock taxable under the Sixteenth Amendment, the distribution shall constitute a taxable dividend, irrespective of which election is ultimately made. In other words, if a stockholder having such an election chooses to take what would otherwise be a non-taxable stock dividend, he is, nevertheless, subjected to a tax under the section.[129] Thus, election to take a non-taxable dividend makes that dividend taxable because the stockholder waived the right to take a dividend which was taxable.

Three possible situations may arise. What amounts to a cash or property dividend may be declared. If it is from earnings or profits accumulated since March 1, 1913, it is taxable. Second, a stock dividend may be distributed which may or may not be taxable. And finally, a dividend may be payable at the option of shareholders either in stock or cash. If the type of stock dividend with respect to which the option is extended falls in the category of taxable dividends within the meaning of the *Koshland* and *Gowran* cases, no substantial problem is presented, as the distribution is clearly taxable. On the other hand, if the stock dividend is not of the type constitutionally taxable, a question as to taxability does arise if stockholders elect to take the stock dividend. There can be no doubt of the power of Congress to tax such distributions as provided in Section 115(f)(2).[130] But there must be a real election by the stockholder. Under the statute

---

[128] See Note, 50 Harv. L. Rev. 332, 335 (1936).

[129] See also Reg. 103, §19.115–8. Immediately following *Eisner v. Macomber* the Treasury Department ruled that a stockholder was taxable if given "a real option" either to keep money under a cash dividend or reinvest it in stock. T. D. 3052, 3 Cum. Bull. 38 (1920).

[130] See *Eisner v. Macomber*, 252 U. S. 189, 217, and Dissent 225 (1920).

the dividend is taxable whether the stockholder exercises his election before or after the declaration. Older cases holding that when stockholders made an agreement prior to the dividend to use the proceeds for purchase of stock the dividend was not taxable,[181] are superseded. But a real stock dividend remains such in spite of the fact that it is carried out by first issuing checks to stockholders which are endorsed back to the corporation in return for the stock.[182]

127. Effect of Non-taxable Stock Dividends on Subsequent Distributions

Section 115(h) provides that a distribution of stock shall not constitute a distribution of earnings or profits under the act if the distribution is a non-taxable stock dividend. While a stock dividend under most state corporation acts will capitalize surplus to the extent thereof,[133] it is important to note that so far as the federal income tax is concerned this capitalization of surplus is disregarded. If a stock dividend is non-taxable, the dividend has no effect for tax purposes on earnings or profits available for subsequent cash dividends. Therefore, it was held, even before incorporation in the Revenue Acts of any provision similar to Section 115(h), that irrespective of prior stock dividends a cash dividend was taxable if the corporation had earnings or profits accrued subsequent to February 28, 1913.[134] These cases hold that after a stock dividend large enough to capitalize earnings since February 28, 1913 is paid, a subsequent cash dividend less than earnings since February 28, 1913 is taxable as post-February 28, 1913 income. The net result is that a corporation cannot distribute pre-March 1, 1913 surplus tax-free, unless it first distributes its post-February 28, 1913 surplus in cash or property.

181 *Jackson v. Commissioner,* 51 F. (2d) 650 (C. C. A. 3d, 1931); *Irving v. U. S.,* 71 Ct. Cl. 62, 44 F. (2d) 246 (1930). Compare the Board cases prior to §115(f) (2) holding that where a formal cash distribution was by prior agreement used to buy stock, the dividend was nevertheless taxable as a cash distribution, *W. J. Hunt,* 5 B. T. A. 356 (1926); *Margaret B. Payne,* 19 B. T. A. 1305 (1928); *L. Elmer Wood,* 29 B. T. A. 735 (1934).

182 *Deitz v. U. S.,* 6 F. Supp. 944 (D. W. Va. 1933); *B. R. Norvell,* 6 B. T. A. 56 (1927); *H. C. Wiess,* 7 B. T. A. 467 (1927). In *George T. Smith,* 21 B. T. A. 782 (1930), where a 90 per cent agreement to subscribe to stock out of a cash dividend was required before it should be effective, the dividend was held to be a stock distribution.

133 See §§56, 56.1, *supra.*

134 *Walker v. Hopkins,* 12 F. (2d) 262 (C. C. A. 5th, 1926), *cert. den.* 271 U. S. 687 (1926); *Nolde v. U. S.,* 64 Ct. Cl. 204 (1927), *cert. den.* 276 U. S. 634 (1928); *Hugh R. Wilson,* 3 B. T. A. 957 (1926); *J. W. McCulloch,* 29 B. T. A. 67 (1933); *Marion H. Kennish,* 4 B. T. A. 303 (1926); *August Horrmann,* 34 B. T. A. 1178 (1936).

APPENDIX

Note A

New Haven Insurance Co. (1797), 1 Conn. Priv. Laws (1837 Ed.), p. 680, §6.
Arnold Manufacturing Co. (1814), 1 Conn. Priv. Laws, *supra,* at pp. 724, 725.
Farmers Bank of Delaware (1807), 4 Del. Laws, c. 39, §12–13th.
Savannah Navigation Co. (1799), Marbury & Crawford's Ga. Dig. (1802), p. 371, §8–9th.
Bank of Maryland, Md. Laws 1790, c. 5, §8.
Newbury Port Woolen Manufactury (1794), Mass. Laws and Resolves 1792–93 (1895 Repr.), 1793–c. 27, pp. 427, 431.
Society for Establishing Useful Manufactures, N. J. Acts, Oct. Sess. 1791, c. 346, p. 730, §8 (most expertly drafted manufacturing corporation charter prior to 1800; generally credited to Hamilton, 1 Davis, n. 15, p. 5, *supra,* at 378; the Society was the most important of nineteenth-century American industrial corporations; *id.* at 349).
Bank of New York, N. Y. Laws 1791, c. 37, p. 25.
Bank of Albany, N. Y. Laws 1792 (15th Sess.), c. 61, pp. 64, 65.
Bank of Pennsylvania (1793), 3 Dallas Laws of Pa. 1790–95, p. 323, §14.
Insurance Company of Pa. (1794), 3 Dallas, *supra,* at p. 512, §9–7th.
Providence Bank, R. I. Laws, Oct. Sess. 1791, pp. 11, 13–14.
Newport Insurance Company, R. I. Laws, Feb. Sess. 1798, pp. 13, 16.
Greenwich Turnpike, R. I. Laws, Feb. Sess. 1803, pp. 20, 23–24.
State Bank, S. C. Laws 1802, p. 44, Rule 19th.
Mattapony Trustees, Va. Laws, Oct. Sess. 1788, c. 43, §5 (corporation for improving river navigation).
Bank of Alexandria, Va. Laws, Oct. Sess. 1792, c. 76, p. 104, §9.
The dividend section of the charter to the Second Bank of United States (1816) followed the form in the earlier act. 3 Stat. 266, §11–13th.

Note B

Tombeckbe Bank, Ala. Terr. Acts, 1st Sess. 1st Assembly, 1812, p. 62, §12.
Bank of Florida, Fla. Terr. Acts 1828, p. 265, §8–12th.
Bank of Pensacola, Fla. Terr. Acts 1831, p. 47, §6–10.
Dubuque Insurance Co., Iowa Terr. Laws, Dec. Sess. 1841, c. 119, §8.
Bank of Illinois, Ill. Terr. Laws 1816, p. 9, §7–12.
Bank of Michigan (1817), Mich. Terr. Laws 1827, p. 505, §13.
Bank of Mississippi, Miss. Terr. Acts, Feb.–Dec. 1809, p. 130, §2d–11th.
Planters & Mechanics Bank of Huntsville, Miss. Terr. Acts 1817, p. 42, §8–12th.

Columbia Transporting Co., Ore. Terr. Laws 1845, p. 25, §7 (no dividend in any one year to exceed two dollars).

Louisiana Bank (1804), Orleans (La.) Terr. Laws and Ordinances (Compilation of 1806), pp. 140, 146 (probably the only example in United States law of a charter granted by the executive without specific legislative authorization).

Planters Bank, Orleans Terr. Acts 1811, c. 22, §7.

Miners' Bank of Dubuque, Wis. Terr. Acts, First Terr. Sess., 1836, p. 18, §13.

The charter granted by the Republic of Texas in 1837 to the Brazoria Insurance Company authorized the president and directors to pay dividends out of "so much of the profits of the business of the said corporation as in their discretion they shall deem safe and proper." 2 Law Rep. of Texas, p. 80, §7.

Note C

Patowmack Company, Md. Laws 1784, c. 33, §8. (An identical provision was contained in its Virginia charter, Va. Acts, Oct. Sess. 1784, p. 24, §8.)

Coosa Navigation Co., Ala. Acts 1823, p. 62, §15 (net proceeds).

Chesapeake & Delaware Canal Co. (1801), 3 Del. Laws, c. 78, §7.

Kentucky River Co., Ky. Laws 1801, c. 8, §5.

Roanoke Navigation Company, N. C. Laws, Nov. Sess. 1796 (Iredell), c. 13, Appendix p. 10, §7.

Appomattox River Navigation Co., Va. Laws, Oct. Sess. 1788, c. 82, §5.

Illinois Navigation Co. (1818), Ill. Terr. Laws 1817–18, p. 57, §5.

Detroit and St. Joseph Railroad Co., Mich. Terr. Acts 1832, p. 68, §17.

Compare English charters of Company for Navigation of River Dee, *supra*, p. 4, n. 7, and New River Company, *supra*, p. 4, n. 6.

Note D

Western Turnpike Co. (1838), Ark. Acts 1837, pp. 104, 113.

Gap & Newport Turnpike Co. (1808), 4 Del. Laws, c. 59, §16.

Wilmington & Kennet Turnpike Co. (1811), 4 Del. Laws, c. 135, §16.

Troy & Schenectady Turnpike, N. Y. Laws 1802, c. 95, §13 (expenses of "repairing, altering, and management").

Montgomery Bridge Co., N. Y. Laws 1803, c. 91, pp. 287, 292 (deduction for amount in "making, repairing and rebuilding the said bridges").

Note E

Wabash Navigation Co. (1825), Ill. Laws 1824, p. 96, §7.

Indianapolis & White Water Turnpike Co. (1828), Ind. Laws 1828, c. 36, p. 47, §21.

Washington Turnpike Road, Md. Laws 1796, c. 69, §18 (first of that number).

Rancocus Creek Navigation Co. (1795), N. J. Acts, Oct. Sess. 1794, c. 544, §14.

Western Turnpike Road, N. Y. Laws 1798, c. 88, pp. 476, 482 (in the early 1800's this was the standard clause for innumerable New York turnpike charters).

Schuylkill & Susquehanna Navigation Co., 3 Dallas Laws of Pa. 1790–95, p. 133, §15.

Delaware & Schuylkill Canal Navigation Co. (1792), 3 Dallas, *supra,* at p. 273, §18.

Fairfax & Loudon Turnpike Co., Va. Acts 1795, c. 31, p. 25, §17.

Note F

Middleton Insurance Co. (1803), 1 Conn. Priv. Laws (1837), p. 674, §7.

Baltimore Insurance Company, Md. Laws, Nov. Sess. 1795, c. 59, §8.

Maryland Insurance Co., Md. Laws, Nov. Sess. 1795, c. 60, §11.

Massachusetts Fire Insurance Co. (1795), Mass. Laws and Resolves 1794–95 (1896 Repr.), 1795–c. 22, pp. 362, 364.

Boston Marine Insurance Co. (1799), Mass. Laws and Resolves 1798–99 (1897 Repr.), 1798–c. 50, pp. 62, 65.

New Hampshire Insurance Co. (1799), 6 Laws of N. H. 1792–1801 (1917 Repr.), p. 570, §7.

United Insurance Co., N. Y. Laws 1798, c. 41, pp. 336, 341.

Columbian Insurance Co., N. Y. Laws 1801, c. 27, pp. 53, 59.

Providence Insurance Co., R. I. Laws, Feb. Sess. 1799, pp. 3, 6.

Warren Insurance Co., R. I. Laws, Feb. Sess. 1800, pp. 12, 15–16.

Marine Ins. Co. of Alexandria, Va. Laws, Dec. Sess. 1797, c. 20, §10.

New Orleans Ins. Co., Orleans Terr. Acts, First Sess. 1804, c. 20, §9.

Subsequent Pennsylvania insurance charters included an equivalent section. Union Insurance Co., Pa. Acts 1804, c. 20, §7–2d.

For the unusual application of this type provision to an industrial charter, see American Fur Company, N. Y. Priv. Laws 1808, c. 140, pp. 160, 167–168 (expertly drawn charter for John Jacob Astor's Company).

Note G

Bank of Augusta, Ga. Acts 1810, p. 9, §6, Rules 16, 17.

Planters Bank, Ga. Acts 1810, p. 78, §7–12 (no provision for director liability).

Amite Navigation Co. (1813), La. Acts 1812–13, p. 88, §8–9th.

Mechanics Bank of Baltimore, Md. Laws 1806, c. 19, §11–18th, 19th.

Franklin Bank of Baltimore, Md. Laws 1810, c. 67, §11–17, 19.

New York Sugar Refining Co., N. Y. Laws 1811, c. 62, §7 (Pennsylvania rule without directors' liability).

Farmers & Mechanics Bank (1813), 11 Ohio Laws 1812–13, c. 33, §§13 and 14.

Group of Ohio Banks (1816), 2 Ohio Stat. (Chase 1834), p. 913, §§27 and 28.

Note H

New Prospect Cotton & Woolen Factory, Ark. Acts 1850, p. 254, §3 (no part of capital to be withdrawn or refunded until liabilities paid).

Wilmington & Susquehanna Railroad Co. (1832), 8 Del. Laws, c. 110, p. 107, §10.

Bank of Kentucky, Ky. Acts 1834, p. 618, §14 (surplus reserve also to be created; liability to stockholders or any creditor).

New Orleans & Ohio Telegraph Co., Miss. Laws 1848, p. 76, §13 (no director liability).

Note I

Bank of Tallahassee, Fla. Terr. Acts 1832, p. 114, §8, Rule 12 (no director liability).

Southern Life Insurance & Trust Co., Fla. Terr. Acts 1835, c. 826, p. 265, §23.

Farmers and Mechanics Bank (1814), Ind. Terr. Laws 1809–16 (1934 Repr.), p. 747, §7 (no director liability).

Bloomington Insurance Co., Iowa Terr. Laws, Nov. Sess. 1839, c. 41, §9 (no director liability).

Bank of River Raisin, Mich. Terr. Acts 1832, p. 76, §13 (no director liability).

Bank of St. Louis, Mo. Terr. Acts, July–Aug. 1813, p. 65, §14.

Bank of Missouri (1817), Mo. Terr. Laws 1816–17, p. 96, §11, 13.

Belmont and DuBuque Railroad Co., Wis. Terr. Acts, 1st Terr. Sess., 1836, p. 54, §15.

INDEX

Absence,
  statutory exoneration for directors declaring illegal dividends, 239
Absolute priorities, rule of,
  effect on reorganization of preferred stock, 216
Abuse of discretion,
  basis for compelling declaration, 162
Accounting,
  favoring profits as dividend test, 58 n
  for capital, 28
  importance in dividend determinations, 83
  interrelation of law and, 25
  regulations of S. E. C., 81
  under balance sheet surplus test, generally, 83–146
  under net profits test, generally, 147–153
Accounts receivable,
  as current asset, 104
  effect of contract commitment on, 112
  valuation, 105
  when account accrues for dividend purposes, 104
Accrued interest,
  availability as asset, 107
Accrued liabilities,
  accounting for, 121
Amendment of charter,
  to modify preferred dividend rights, 201
Amount of dividend,
  change in, as to preferred stock, 205
  requirement against discrimination among stockholders, 169

Bad debts,
  necessity for charging off, 105
  statutes, 106
Balance sheet,
  accounting, generally, 83–146
  use in surplus jurisdictions, 83
Bank deposits,
  as current asset, 104
  foreign,
    valuation of, 104
Bank of United States,
  dividend section, 6

Bargain purchase as form of dividend, 171
Bond discount,
  accounting for,
    on issuance, 120
    on redemption, 120
    as deferred asset, 115
Bonds,
  accounting for, where purchased at discount, 140
  as form of dividend, 173
Book value,
  effect of mergers and consolidations on basis other than, 294
Books,
  reliance of directors in declaring dividends, 244
Borrowing to pay dividends, 170
Burden of proof,
  on discretion of directors in declaration, 169
By-laws,
  effect of restrictions in, on fund available for dividends, 81

California,
  statutory dividend test, 66
Cancellation of past accrued preferred dividends,
  constitutional question, 210
  earned, 211, 213
  merger method, 211
  unearned, 211, 214
Capital,
  accounting for,
    methods of, 28
    no-par stock, 131
    par value stock, 130
    statutes, 131, 132
  determining amount,
    consideration for stock less than par, 46
    consideration more than par, 48
    effect of impairment at opening of accounting period, 49
  directors' liability for dividends from, 236
  early English law, 3
  first restriction against impairment, 4

357

Capital (*continued*)
liability of stockholders for dividends from,
received in good faith, 271
with knowledge, 274
liability of third persons for dividends from, 276
meanings of, 24
no-par stock,
accounting, 54
as reducing creditor protection, 17
revocation of dividend impairing, 185
rule against impairment,
effect of *Wood v. Dummer,* 15, 23
historical development, 8, 15
New York Act of 1825, 11, 15
trust fund doctrine, 15, 23
statutes prohibiting impairment,
division of capital type, 44
excess of assets over liabilities, 41
restrictions against diminishing capital, 52
stock dividends,
no-par, 176
par, 176
Cash,
as current asset, 103
defined, 104
Cash dividends,
borrowing to pay, 170
creating a debt, 180
federal income tax on, 319
normal form, 170
payments partly in, and partly in property, 169
revocation of, 184
statutes, 172
Chandler Act,
modification of preferred dividend rights under, 216
Charter of Bank of England,
effect on American law, 5
Charters,
effect of restrictions in, on fund, 81
Choice of law,
dividends violating insolvency prohibitions in state of declaration, 317
domicil having only statute,
domiciliary law normally applicable, 302
obligation of non-domiciliary states to enforce, 304
effect of general statute in state of doing business, 306
multiple incorporation, 317

Choice of law (*continued*)
New York Stock Corporation Law (§114),
background of enactment, 307
corporation doing most of its business in New York, 309
corporation doing small amount of business in New York, 313
corporation doing substantial business in New York, 316
problem of, in dividend declarations, 300
where law of domicil not pleaded, 304
Commodities as form of dividend, 171
Common law restrictions,
against payment from capital, 23
limiting to payment from profits, 21
when applicable,
interpretation of statutes, 21
where law of domicil not in evidence, 22
Common stockholders, (See "Preferred and common stockholders")
Conflict of laws, (See "Choice of law")
Consolidated balance sheets,
problems presented by, 145
unrealized gains and losses, 145
Consolidations,
(See "Mergers and consolidations")
to modify preferred dividend rights, 204
Constitutionality of,
cancellation of past preferred dividends,
earned, 211
unearned, 211, 214
modification in preferred dividend rights, generally, 206
Construction,
dividends during period of, 170
Contingent claims,
reserves for, 129
Corporation,
party,
against directors, 255
against stockholders, 279
recovery by, against directors,
historical development, 11
Cost of goods sold,
determination of, 148
Creditors,
actions against directors,
historical background, 11, 260
individual or representative suits, 261
prior and subsequent creditors, 263
receiver, on behalf of, 267

Creditors (*continued*)
actions against directors (*continued*)
statutes, 260
trustee in bankruptcy, on behalf of,
265
actions against stockholders, 280
breakdown of distinction between, and
stockholders, 19
dividend regulations protecting, 14
effect of stock dividend,
prior, 175
subsequent, 176
Criminal liability of directors,
for illegal dividends, 254
Cumulative preferred dividends,
(See "Preferred dividends")
express provision for, 188
participation beyond preference rate,
190
Current assets,
cash, 103
inventory, 108
securities, 106
unrealized appreciation, 112
Current liabilities,
accounting for, 121
Current profits,
as basis for stock dividends, 178
test for federal income tax, 330

Debt,
dividend as creating, 180
effect of placing dividend with de-
pository, 182
time dividend obligation accrues, 180
Declaration,
as creating a debt,
effect of placing with depositary,
182
when, 180
by stockholders,
through unanimous agreement, 170
choice of law governing, 300
discretion of directors,
affected by size of surplus, 163
burden of proof, 169
cash and stock, 157
claim of common to excess earnings
over preferred requirements, 167
discrimination in same class, 169
effect of charter provisions, 157
effect of, on common stockholder,
159
equitable interference to protect
minority, 163
factors influencing, 162

Declaration (*continued*)
discretion of directors (*continued*)
form, 180
historical development, 156
in absence of fraud or bad faith,
157
injunctions against payment, 157
judicial non-interference, 158, 160
non-cumulative preferred, 167
preferred stock generally, 164
reasons for sustaining, 158
reduction surplus, 164
resolution provisions, 155
statutes, 159
necessity for, by directors, 154
power of directors,
historical development, 154
informal declaration, 155
statutes, 154
power of equity to compel,
common, 160
preferred, 164
real estate corporations, 161 n
power of stockholders, 156
Deferred charges,
availability as assets, 113
bond discount, 115
writing off, 114
Deficit,
effect of, on part of one constituent in
merger or consolidation, 291
Definition of
cash, 104
earnings or profits for federal income tax, 325
fixed assets, 85
funds available, 14
preferred dividends, 187
profits, 55
wasting asset corporations, 125
Delaware, statutory test, 43, 64
Depletion,
wasting asset doctrine,
as to creditors, 125
as to preferred stockholders, 225
Depositary for dividends,
effect of insolvency of, 182
Depreciation,
base, 124
computation of amount, 124
reserves for, 123
statutes, 123
Development expenses as deferred asset, 114
Diminution of capital,
statutes prohibiting, 52

Directors,
   declaration by, generally, 154–170
   liability for illegal dividends,
      at common law, 236
      basis for, 235
      criminal, 254
      effect of no recourse provisions,
         248
      effect of recoupment of assets, 250
      exoneration for absence or dissent
         under statutes, 239
      good faith, 247
      historical background, 9, 11, 235
      measure of damages, 251
      negligent violations, 243
      parties entitled to sue, 255
      ratification by stockholders, 248
      recovery in states other than cor-
         poration's domicil, 251
      time illegality is determined, 248
      voting for or assenting to, 242
      wilful violations, 243
Disclosure,
   necessity of, in plans for reorganiza-
      tion of preferred interests, 223
Discount on bonds,
   accounting for,
      on issuance, 120
      on redemption, 120
Discrimination between shareholders of
      same class, 169
Dissent as statutory exoneration for
      directors declaring illegal dividend,
      239
Dissolution distributions on preferred
      stock, 195
Double entry bookkeeping,
   effect on dividends, 28
Doubtful debts,
   reserves for, under balance sheet test,
      105, 122
   reserves for, under net profits test,
      150
Due care as defense to director liability,
      236

English law,
   early,
      absence of restrictions against pay-
         ment from capital, 3
      profit restrictions, 4
   rule against capital impairment, 51 n
Equalization of earned surplus,
   stock issued at a premium,
      at book value, 133
      at market value, 135

Equity compelling declaration,
   common, 160
   examples, 162
   preferred, 164
Excess of assets over liabilities,
   as statutory test, 41

Federal income tax,
   (See "Income tax")
First-in first-out rule for valuing in-
      ventory, 109
Fixed assets,
   accounting for, 85
   definition of, 85
   realized gains, 98
   realized losses, 90
   unrealized gains, 99
   unrealized losses, 91
   valuation,
      as including expense of moving and
         placement, 87
      fairness of transaction, 86
      original cost, 85
      overvaluation of property, 88
      property sold for securities, 87
      sales between parent and subsidi-
         ary, 86
Fixed charges,
   allowance for, under net profits test,
      150
   amortization of fixed obligations
      under net profits test, 150
Fixed liabilities,
   accounting for,
      issued at discount, 120
      issued at par, 120
      redeemed at discount, 120
   amortizing of, under net profits test,
      150
Foreign corporations,
   choice of law in declaring dividends,
      general statutory provisions in state
         of doing business, 306
      New York Stock Corporation Law
         (§114), 307
      normally determined by law of
         domicil, 302
Form of dividend,
   bargain purchases, 171
   bonds, 173
   cash, 170
   property, 171
   scrip, 172
   stock,
      at common law, 174
      consideration for, 175, 176

Form of dividend (*continued*)
stock (*continued*)
of other companies, 174
of subsidiaries, 174
purpose, 173
statutes, 174
Fraud,
basis for compelling declaration, 162
liability of directors for declaring
dividends, 237
Fraudulent conveyances,
effect of statutes prohibiting, on dividends, 36
Full faith and credit,
to law of corporation's domicil, 304
Fund available, 14
at common law, 21
under statutory regulations, 25

Gains,
capital, under net profits test, 151
realized from sale of fixed assets, 98
unrealized,
accruing from growth or productivity, 100
availability for stock dividends, 101
nonavailability for cash dividends, 100
statutes, 102
Good faith as defense to director liability,
at common law, 236
statutes, 247
Goodwill,
availability as asset,
non-purchased, 117
purchased, 116
concealment of, 117
separate entry for, 88
valuation, 116
Gross sales, computation of, 148

Hidden reserves,
availability as assets, 119
created by overdepreciation, 118
Historical background,
American special charters,
banks, 5
capital impairment limitations, 8
profit limitations, 7
charter of Bank of England, 4
creditors as parties plaintiff in actions against directors, 260
directors' liability for illegal declaration, 235
dividend law of modern origin, 3

Historical background (*continued*)
early English law,
absence of restrictions against payment from capital, 3
profit restrictions, 4
early joint-stock company dividends, 3
federal income tax on dividends, 320
Massachusetts insolvency regulation of 1830, 13
modification of preferred dividends,
amendment statutes, 201
merger and consolidation statutes, 204
New York Act of 1825, 11
preferred dividends, 187
stockholder liability, 269

Improvements,
accounting for, under net profits test, 149
Income tax,
cash and property dividends,
bargain purchases as, 323
basis on property, 322
definition of from "earnings or profits," 325
distribution the test, 320
earnings accumulated after Feb. 28, 1913, 327
earnings or profits of the taxable year, 330
effect of losses, 327
exemption of earnings prior to Mar. 1, 1913, 333
from paid-in surplus, 333
from reduction surplus, 333
historical background, 320
interest of corporation in taxability of, 319
on current earnings when capital is impaired, 330
presumption of distribution from most recent earnings, 332
redemption or cancellation of stock dividends as, 322
stock of other corporations as constituting, 321
unrealized appreciation, 334
option dividends in stock, cash or property, 350
stock dividends,
addition to interest of shareholder as test, 338
change of proportionate interest of shareholder as test, 338

Income tax (*continued*)
  stock dividends (*continued*)
    common on common, 344
    common on preferred, 347
    effect of non-taxable, on subsequent
      distributions, 351
    loss of assets by corporation as
      test, 337
    nature of distribution, 336
    paid from 1913 to 1936, 343
    paid after 1936, 344
    preferred on common, 346
    preferred on preferred, 348
    should always be taxable, 341
    state statutes taxing, 348
    stock rights, 349
    stock split-up, 345
    test of taxability, 335
    treasury stock, 348
Insolvency,
  bankruptcy and equity tests, 27, 37
  choice of law, when dividend violates
    local provisions, 317
  directors' liability for dividends dur-
    ing, 236
  dividend test,
    application in addition to other re-
      strictions, 41
    at common law, 36
    effect on other restrictions, 41
    historical development, 13, 33
    in Massachusetts, 26
    no-par stock, 41
    states in which applicable, 33
    under Uniform Fraudulent Con-
      veyance Act, 35
  effect on declared dividend,
    corporation insolvent, 182
    depositary insolvent, 182
  liability of stockholders for dividends,
    270
Installment sales,
  accounting for, 108
  statutes, 108
Intangibles,
  separate accounting for, 88
Interest-dividends,
  payable during period of construction,
    170
Inventory,
  statutes, 112
  valuation, 108

Laches,
  effect of, where preferred dividend
    arrearages are canceled, 211 n

Liabilities,
  accounting for, generally, 120–145
  capital stock, 130
Limited liability,
  as requiring maintenance of capital,
    14
  historical development, 14
Liquidating corporations,
  dividends by, from capital, 51 n
Liquidating dividends,
  distinguished, 23
  effect of prior voluntary reorganiza-
    tions on preferred rights, 209
Liquidation preferences,
  effect on capital for no-par stock, 176
  preferred stock provisions protect-
    ing, 232
  protection under Public Utility Hold-
    ing Company Act, 79
  wasting asset doctrine, 225
Losses,
  capital, under net profits test, 151
  effect on computing capital, 51
  realized,
    necessity for taking, 90
    statutes, 90
  treating as deferred assets, 115
  unrealized,
    determination of new value, 95
    effect on stockholders, 92
    handling by write-off or reserve, 95
    normal market declines, 93
    problem of declines in price level,
      91
    pronounced changes in price level,
      93
    statutes, 93
    two theories of change in capital
      valuation, 91
    unrealized appreciation as offset to,
      95
    write-off through earned or paid-in
      surplus, 97

Massachusetts,
  statutory dividend test, 33
Measure of damages,
  actions against directors,
    amount of dividend, 252
    corporate debts and liabilities, 252
    historical development, 11, 13
    loss, 253
  actions against stockholders, 277
Merger,
  as method for cancellation of accrued
    preferred dividends, 211

Merger (*continued*)
 to modify preferred dividend rights,
  204
Mergers and consolidations,
 cash plans,
  acquisitions at discount, 287
  acquisitions at premium, 287
  statutes, 287
  where book value of constituents
   equal, 286
 combination method, 284
 financing method, 286
 no-par stock plans,
  distinguished from par stock plans,
   296
  statutes, 297
 par stock plans,
  effect of financing at other than
   book value, 294
  one corporation having deficit, 291
  re-domestication, 288
  reduction of capital by, 295
  surplus of constituents equal, 289
  surplus of one constituent larger,
   293
  surplus of one constituent smaller,
   292
Modification of preferred dividend
  rights, 200–225
 adequate disclosure of reorganization
  plan, 223
 basis for objection to, 205
 cancellation of past accruals, 210
 change in amount of future dividends,
  205
 change in priority of claims, 207
 earned arrearages, 209, 213
 methods,
  amendment of charter, 201
  merger, 201, 204
  under Chandler Act, 216
  under Public Utility Holding Company Act, 218
 when needed, 200
Multiple incorporation,
 choice of law in declaring dividends,
  317

Negligence,
 liability of directors for dividends,
  237, 243
Net profits or surplus,
 as test for fund, 59
 meaning of net profits, 61
 net profits or earned surplus as test,
  66

Net profits test,
 accounting under, generally, 147–153
 allocation of market decline in inventory to current accounting period,
  148
 comparison of, with surplus as test,
  32
 growth of, 31
 historical background, 6, 7, 55
 in Delaware and New Jersey, 30.
 meaning of, 30
 statutory definitions of,
  current net profits or surplus, 64
  net profits or earned surplus, 66
  net profits or surplus, 59
  profits, 55
  surplus profits, 55
New Jersey,
 statutory dividend test, 59
New York,
 statutory dividend test, 42
No-par stock,
 merger and consolidation plans, 296
 stated capital required for, 54
 stock dividends,
  allocation of consideration to
   paid-in and earned surplus, 178
  capital for, 176
  not out of paid-in surplus, 178
 watering of, 177
No-recourse provisions,
 effect on liability of directors, 248
Non-cumulative preferred dividends,
  (See "Preferred and common
   stockholders")
 earned, 196
 unearned, 196

Obsolescence,
 reserves for, 125
Organization expenses as deferred assets, 114
Overvaluation,
 effect on determining fund, 87
 necessity for correction through subsequent earnings, 89

Paid-in surplus,
 allocation to, on no-par stock dividends, 178
 availability for dividends, 68
  common, 71
  in balance sheet surplus jurisdictions, 54
  preferred, 70

Paid-in surplus (*continued*)
  determination of amount, 54
  effect of merger or consolidation on
    prior, 284
  effect of Public Utility Holding Com-
    pany Act, 79
  equitable limitations where both pre-
    ferred and common stock out-
    standing, 70
  exemption of dividends from federal
    income tax, 333
  use of, to eliminate unrealized losses,
    96
Par stock,
  capital for,
    accounting, 130
    stock dividends, 176
  effect of, on survival of dividend sur-
    plus in mergers and consolida-
    tions, 288
Parent and subsidiary,
  dividends from unrealized gain, 102
  valuation of,
    sales between, 86
    stock of parent in subsidiary, 87
Participating preferred,
  effect of provision for participation on
    liquidation
    with, 191
    without, 192
  statutes, 193
Parties,
  actions against directors,
    corporation, 255
    creditors, 260
    individual stockholder, 268
    receivers, 266
    trustee in bankruptcy, 265
  actions against stockholders,
    corporation, 279
    creditors, 280
    receiver, 283
    trustee in bankruptcy, 282
Payment of dividends,
  cash, 180
  revocation, 184
  stock, 184
Power to pay,
  implied at common law, 21
Preferences,
  (See "Preferred and common
    stockholders")
  modification of,
    amendment of charter, 203
    merger and consolidation statutes,
      204

Preferred and common stockholders,
  conflicting interests where capital is
    impaired, 188
  discretion of directors in declaring
    dividends,
    claim of common to excess earnings
      over preferred requirements, 167
  effect of overvaluation of assets on
    fund available for dividends, 89
  equitable restrictions on,
    paid-in surplus, 70
    reduction surplus, 76
  modification of preferred dividend
    rights, 200–225
    adequate disclosure of plan, 223
    basis for objection to, 205
    cancellation of past accruals, 210
    change in amount of future divi-
      dends, 205
    change in priority of claims, 207
    earned arrearages, 209, 213
    under Chandler Act, 216
    under Public Utility Holding Com-
      pany Act, 218
  protection of liquidation preferences,
    generally, 225
    provisions for, 232
  relative rights of, generally, 187–234
  shift of voting control on dividend de-
    fault, 194
Preferred dividends,
  as requiring cash payment, 157 n
  cumulative, 187–196
    effect of whether or not earned,
      189
    express provisions for, 188
    not impairing capital, 188
    participation beyond preference
      rate, 190
    provision for preferred dividends,
      as implying, 189
  discretion of directors,
    burden of proof, 168
    non-cumulative, 167
  dissolution distributions, 195
  historical background, 187
  meaning of net earnings, 58 n
  non-cumulative, 196–199
    earned, but not paid, 196
    unearned, 196
  power of equity to compel,
    cumulative stock, 165
    effect of dissolution preference
      right, 166
    guaranteed stock, 165
    non-cumulative stock, 165, 167

Preferred dividends (*continued*)
  wasting asset doctrine, 225
Premium on stock,
  accounting for,
    issued on organization, 133
    issued after organization, 133
  statutes, 137
Prepaid expenses,
  availability as assets, 112
Prior preferred,
  creation of,
    authority for, 208
    effect on existing issues, 207
Priority of claims,
  change in, as to preferred dividends,
    207
Profit and loss statement,
  accounting requirements, 147
Profits as test, 55
  English law, 57
  historical background, 55
  necessity for earnings, 56
Property,
  as form of dividend, 171
Property account,
  valuation, 87
Property dividends,
  federal income tax on, 319
  statutes, 172
Public Utility Holding Company Act,
  modification of preferred dividend
    rights under, 218
  regulations under §12(c), 76
  simplifications, 218
Purpose of dividend regulation,
  adequate accounting disclosure, 20
  protection for creditors, 14
    modern tendency to minimize, 17
  protection of public interest, 20
  protection of stockholders, 18

Quasi-reorganizations,
  elimination of unrealized losses, 96
  use of paid-in surplus, 97

Ratification by stockholders,
  of illegal dividends, 248
Receivers,
  actions against directors,
    on behalf of corporation, 266
    on behalf of creditors, 267
  actions against stockholders, 283
Reduction of capital,
  effect on creditors, 17
  effected through merger and consoli-
    dation, 295

Reduction surplus,
  availability for dividends,
    in absence of statute, 73
    statutes, 74
  exemption of dividends from federal
    income tax, 333
Reorganizations,
  modification of preferred dividend
    rights, 200–225
    cancellation of past accruals, 210
    earned arrearages, 209, 213
    methods, 205
    under Chandler Act, 216
    under Public Utility Holding Com-
      pany Act, 218
  of capital structure, to eliminate
    losses, 96
Repairs and maintenance,
  effect of provision for, on deprecia-
    tion allowance, 124
  under net profits test, 149
Reserves,
  accounts receivable, 105
  allowance for, under net profits test,
    149
  an accounting matter, 121
  contingent claims, 129
  depletion,
    as protection to creditors, 125
    wasting asset doctrine, 125
  depreciation, 123
  doubtful debts, 122
  entry on asset or liability side, 122
  obsolescence, 125
Revocation of dividends,
  cash, 184
  stock, 185
  when impairing capital, 185

Salary as constituting a dividend, 155 n
Sale of assets,
  (See "Mergers and consolida-
    tions")
Scrip dividends,
  as form for payment, 172
  necessity for available funds, 172
S.E.C.,
  accounting regulations, 81
  modification of preferred dividend
    rights,
    requirements for disclosure, 223
    under Public Utility Holding Com-
      pany Act, 218
  regulations under Public Utility Hold-
    ing Company Act, 76

Securities,
  valuation, 106
Simplification under Public Utility
  Holding Company Act, 218
Special charter limitations,
  American banks, 5
  American capital impairment limita-
    tions, 8
  American profit limitations, 7
  Bank of England, 4
  English profit limitations, 4
Statutory restrictions,
  balance sheet surplus, 27
  insolvency test, 26
  National Banking Act, 45
  net profits test, 30
Stock dividends,
  actions to compel payment, 184
  at common law, 174
  capitalization of surplus, statutes, 176
  consideration for, 175, 176
  distinguished from stock split-up, 179
  effect on creditors,
    prior, 175
    subsequent, 176
  federal income tax on, 335
  from current earnings, 178
  of other companies, 174
  of subsidiaries, 174
  purpose, 173
  revocation of, 185
  state income taxes on, 348
  statutes, 174
  treasury shares as, 179
Stock split-up,
  distinguished from stock dividend, 179
Stockholder reorganizations, 200–225
  methods,
    amendment of charter, 201
    merger, 201, 204
  when needed, 200
Stockholders,
  actions by, against directors for il-
    legal dividends, 268
  breakdown of distinction between, and
    creditors, 19
  power to declare dividends, 156
Stockholders' liability, 269–283
  dividends from capital when corpora-
    tion is solvent,
    received in good faith, 271
    with knowledge, 274
  effect on, of directors' liability, 277
  for distributions not purporting to be
    dividends, 278
  historical background, 269

Stockholders' liability (continued)
  insolvency dividends, 270
  measure of damages, 277
  parties,
    corporation, 279
    creditors, 280
    receiver, 283
    trustee in bankruptcy, 282
Subordination of preferred stock, 207
Subsidiaries,
  declaration to parent, 155
  dividends to parent, in stock of, 174
  use of, to pay dividends from un-
    realized gains, 102
Surplus,
  balance sheet entry for, 144
  capitalization for stock dividend, 176
  comparison of, with net profits as test,
    32
  meaning of, 27
  survival on merger or consolidation,
    284
Surplus profits test,
  accumulated earned surplus or cur-
    rent net profits, 58
Surplus test, 41–55
  alternative to net profits, 43
  methods of computing, 28
  New York, 27
  statutory definitions of
    excess of assets over liabilities, 41
    restrictions against diminishing
      capital, 52
    restrictions against division of
      capital, 44

Third persons,
  liability for illegal dividends, 276
Time of payment,
  requirement of uniformity, 169
Transferee,
  liability for receipt of illegal divi-
    dends, 276
Treasury stock,
  accounting for,
    on purchase, 137
    on resale, 141
  basis for stock dividends, 179
Trust,
  dividend not a, 182
Trust fund doctrine,
  effect of *Wood v. Dummer*, 15, 23
  protection for creditors, 15
Trust indentures,
  effect of restrictions in, on fund, 82
  wasting asset provisions, 129

Trustee in bankruptcy,
actions against directors,
on behalf of corporation, 264
on behalf of creditors, 265
actions against stockholders,
on behalf of corporation, 282
on behalf of creditors, 282

Unaccrued liabilities,
omission from balance sheet, 121
Unearned surplus,
dividends from, by public utility holding companies, 77
Uniform Fraudulent Conveyance Act,
applicability to dividends, 35
Unrealized appreciation,
taxability of dividends from, 334
use to write off deficit, 51

Valuation,
accounts receivable, 105
inventory, 108
securities,
unrealized gains, 106
unrealized losses, 106
work in progress, 112

Vested rights,
claim of preferred against modification, 205
Voting control,
shift of, to preferred on dividend default, 194

Wages as constituting dividends, 169
War,
effect on duty of directors declaring
dividends, 249
Wasting asset doctrine,
American cases, 127
as to creditors, 125
as to preferred stockholders,
at common law, 225
common capital impaired, 227
impairment of preferred capital,
226
corporations to which applicable, 125
Delaware, 128
England, 126
statutes, 127, 229
Watered stock,
no-par, 177
Work in progress,
valuation, 112

The History of Accounting

An Arno Press Collection

Bennet[t], James [Arlington]. **The American System of Practical Book-Keeping** and Foster, B[enjamin] F[ranklin], **The Origin and Progress of Book-Keeping.** 1842/1852. Two vols. in one

Brief, Richard P., editor. **The Late Nineteenth Century Debate Over Depreciation, Capital and Income.** 1976

Brief, Richard P. **Nineteenth Century Capital Accounting and Business Investment.** 1976

Bruchey, Stuart W[eems]. **Robert Oliver and Mercantile Bookkeeping in the Early Nineteenth Century.** 1976

Church, A[lexander] Hamilton. **Production Factors in Cost Accounting and Works Management.** 1910

Cole, William Morse. **Accounts:** Their Construction and Interpretation for Business Men and Students of Affairs. 1908

Dicksee, Lawrence R[obert]. **Advanced Accounting.** 1903

Dicksee, Lawrence R[obert]. **Auditing:** A Practical Manual for Auditors. 1892

Dicksee, Lawrence R[obert]. **Auditing:** A Practical Manual for Auditors. Authorized American Edition, Edited by Robert H. Montgomery. 1905

Dicksee, Lawrence R[obert]. **Depreciation, Reserves, and Reserve Funds.** 1903

Dicksee, Lawrence R[obert] and Frank Tillyard. **Goodwill and Its Treatment in Accounts.** 1906

Folsom, E[zekiel] G[ilman]. **Folsom's Logical Bookkeeping:** The Logic of Accounts. 1873

Garcke, Emile and J[ohn] M[anger] Fells. **Factory Accounts, Their Principles and Practice.** 1893

Hatfield, Henry Rand. **Modern Accounting:** Its Principles and Some of its Problems. 1916

Kehl, Donald. **Corporate Dividends:** Legal and Accounting Problems Pertaining to Corporate Distributions. 1941

Leake, P[ercy] D[ewe]. **Depreciation and Wasting Assets and Their Treatment in Assessing Annual Profit and Loss.** 1912

Lisle, George. **Accounting in Theory and Practice.** 1900

Matheson, Ewing. **The Depreciation of Factories, Mines and Industrial Undertakings and Their Valuation.** 1893

Montgomery, Robert H. **Auditing Theory and Practice.** 1912

Norton, George Pepler. **Textile Manufacturers' Book-Keeping for the Counting House, Mill and Warehouse.** 1894

Paton, William A[ndrew] and Russell A[lger] Stevenson. **Principles of Accounting.** 1916

Pixley, Francis W[illiam]. **Auditors:** Their Duties and Responsibilities Under the Joint-Stock Companies Acts and the Friendly Societies and Industrial and Provident Societies Acts. 1881

Reiter, Prosper, Jr. **Profits, Dividends and the Law.** 1926

Scott, DR. **Theory of Accounts.** 1925

Scovell, Clinton H. **Interest as a Cost.** 1924

Sells, Elijah Watt. **The Natural Business Year and Thirteen Other Themes.** 1924

Soulé, Geo[rge]. **Soulé's New Science and Practice of Accounts.** 1903

Sprouse, Robert T[homas]. **The Effect of the Concept of the Corporation on Accounting.** 1976

Zeff, Stephen A., editor. **Asset Appreciation, Business Income and Price-Level Accounting: 1918-1935.** 1976

Date Due